SOCIAL ENVIRONMENT AND BEHAVIOR

SOCIAL ENVIRONMENT AND BEHAVIOR

Edited by

HAROLD GREENBERG

SCHENKMAN PUBLISHING COMPANY, INC.
3 Revere Street, Cambridge, Mass.

Schenkman books are distributed by
GENERAL LEARNING PRESS
250 JAMES STREET
MORRISTOWN, NEW JERSEY

TABLE OF CONTENTS

SECTION I

Social Environment and Behavior

INTRODUCTION

Before approaching the question of the social environment and how it relates to behavior, we need to have some understanding of the intended scope of this volume. For practicing social workers as well as for students, this work aims at bringing together key concepts, concerns and ways of looking at those social phenomena pertinent to social work at the beginning of the 1970's.

As part of their professional preparation, social work students generally take course work in Human Behavior, Development and Social Environment. Under whatever title, the aim of this part of their education is to bring to them a body of knowledge drawn from the behavioral sciences. There would appear to be a distinct lack of an up-to-date text focusing upon sociology and its contribution. It is to this aspect of professional knowledge that this present work is especially addressed. Other components of the curriculum of the School of Social Work such as Social Policy, also draw on socio-cultural information, and it is not intended that this text meet all such needs. Furthermore, most students have an opportunity to examine particular aspects of social pathology and deviance in subsequent courses. Thus problems and dysfunction will be touched upon but are not the central focus. We will look at some of the sociological factors and forces which serve as a backdrop for the social work profession, on the assumption that understanding these will facilitate the functioning of the social worker.

We begin with an attempt to understand the relationship between sociology as a producer of information and social work as a potential consumer. We go on to look at basic tool concepts such as the nature of culture, proceed to discussion of two fundamental social institutions and two key elements in social interaction (class and ethnic groups) and finally seek to identify major trends in our changing social environment. In all of this, an effort is made to develop a conceptual frame of reference with only secondary attention paid to terminology. Because of the students' load, articulated readings will no doubt be a welcome alternative to the usual time-consuming struggle to locate professional articles at university libraries.

3

AN UNRESOLVED RELATIONSHIP

The exact nature of the relationship between sociology and social work is not settled, just as the nature of the relationship between social work and all of the behavioral sciences is not yet resolved to any degree of general satisfaction. With regard to sociology, the nature of the relationship is all the more unclear because social work has historically drawn primarily on a different field for its basic conceptual frame of reference. That is, it has primarily drawn on a psychoanalytical perspective. This is somewhat of an enigma since the name itself, social work, erroneously suggests a very close relationship to sociology.

The connection is not entirely a comfortable one, and sociologists too have been uncomfortable with the popular assumption of a tie between their science and social work. One interesting comment is found in *An Invitation to Sociology* by Peter Berger. In it, he is quite critical of the idea that sociology is sometimes understood by the layman as social work. It would seem that the field of sociology has its own identity problems to resolve. Thus, in explaining what sociology is, he first rejects the idea that sociology is a kind of social work, trying to ameliorate or trying to help "adjust" the individual to society. He goes on even to refute the assumption that it is a significant foundation or intellectual underpinning for the field of social work. In any case, American social work would appear to have been far more influenced by psychology and psychoanalysis than by sociology in development of its theoretical base.[1] Probably, this fact is not unrelated to the relative status of sociology and psychology in the popular imagination. Social work, whatever its theoretical rationale, is a practice within society. Sociology is not a practice, but an attempt to understand. Even if social work was rooted in sociology, they would still differ, social work being an applied practice profession, while sociology is primarily concerned with unearthing facts about society.

QUEST FOR A THEORETICAL BASE

Currently, social work seems to be undergoing considerable change in relation to the various behavioral sciences. It is drawing much closer to the social and behavioral sciences generally, psychology as well as anthropology, economics and to the research enterprise. It seeks, now more than ever before in its history, to draw upon empirical data and a theoretical base rather than on its intuitive practice knowledge. As social work becomes a major, more expensive social and political concern, its sources of revenue increasingly entail financing by government and foundations. We can anticipate accompanying pressure for the development of the kinds of objective, empirical measures of its effectiveness now demanded of the applied physical sciences and industrial undertakings.

Social work also seems to be undergoing a major reorientation with regard to its psychoanalytic and psychological stance. While through much of its history as a profession, social work has drawn very heavily on the psychotherapeutic model, recent experience suggests that there are problems that individuals may experience which don't necessarily fit that model. Furthermore, they don't particularly respond to the kind of verbal psychotherapeutic approach that has come to typify the profession. It is conceivable for the "multi-problem" family to be disrupted by the absence of a father, early school-leaving, delinquency of children, poor health, and so on, and for this family nevertheless to be making a realistic adjustment to the conditions of the social environment in which it must function. Many poor people in urban slums, for example, display remarkable "cope-ability" in the face of problems which might overwhelm and immobilize those of the middle class. They may not result in living the way we would, they may not be living according to standards that would please us or perhaps even themselves. Nevertheless, a case can be made for the possibility that these people are well adjusted, within their dreadful living conditions, and that the need in these cases is not to help these people readjust psychologically.

THE HISTORICAL CYCLE

Now, as social workers increasingly confront this order of problem, they have to draw more on a broader spectrum of the social sciences for concepts that would be helpful in dealing with clients whose backgrounds are quite different from their own. This is not really a new phenomenon to social work. We know that in its early, perhaps pre-professional, origins, the social worker was of a different socio-economic class from his clients. In these "good old days" when social work represented good Christian charity, it was clear that those being served were an under-class, sinful to boot, while those providing the service were good, kind, helpful representatives of the upstanding elements of society. As social work, before World War I, was secularized, the difference in class, in cultural and social background of professional and client, was de-emphasized. This was the period of the settlement house and the muck-raking tradition. Social work was just beginning its own professionalization. This coincided with post-World War I enchantment with psychoanalysis. The relationship which increasingly served as a model for the profession was that of psychotherapist and client or at least physician and patient. The relationship was not so much a social one as a professional one, stressing specialized information or knowledge regarding treatment.

CHANGE OF FUNCTION AND UNCERTAINTY

In recent years, however, many circumstances have forced social work to reconsider the possibility that many of its concerns are unrelated to the professional mental health worker image, but really have to do with broader social problems, forces that operate which go beyond the maladjustment of some individual or of a family constellation. In a sense, the social worker may really be a "change agent." This has made many social workers uncomfortable about their work, and the profession seems to be undergoing much soul searching. It certainly has been exposed to considerable criticism. Once you start thinking along these lines, there are questions raised as to what the function of the social worker now is or should be. Is he supposed to help individuals adjust to a bad situation? Is he supposed to help an individual change the system? Does he bring to his professional service the orientation, the perspective of his own class and perhaps ethnic background? These are problems that social work and social workers have increasingly had to look at in response to both external and self-criticism currently so widespread.

THE CURRENT STATE OF SOCIOLOGY

Since sociology contributes so much to our analysis of these factors, we need to take at least a brief look at what sociology is currently about. As we have already seen, sociology is also faced with a considerable problem of interpreting itself professionally internally as well as to the non-professional world. As one of the new sciences represented by behavioral science, sociology is perhaps the newest. It works in areas that make the development of hard and fast rules and conclusions extremely difficult, and its subject matter tends to be familiar to anyone who lives in human society. When one physicist talks to another professionally, the subject matter of their conversation tends to be rather esoteric. You wouldn't find people on a bus "conversing in physics." But if a sociologist stops to talk with a colleague about any subject of interest to sociologists, lo and behold, they are talking about family, generation gap, marriage, divorce, the growth of higher education, race relations, items that make the news, and public issues, topics that are rather everyday to laymen. As a result, the sociologist is faced with a problem of carving out for himself a domain that is his professional province. To do this, some sociologists have fallen into a common practice of using highly specialized jargon for their everyday topics. Even if we avoid that trap, it is necessary to look at what it is that the sociologist is after.

Sociology basically represents an attempt to scientifically study society, group behavior, relationships among men, and the factors that are involved in the development of those relationships. In that effort the sociologist makes use of what might be called "the scientific method" adapted to his own peculiar problems and difficulties of procedure. Many of his hypotheses are suggested by "common sense" — thus the identity problem. What we take to be common sense is not necessarily common, and certainly, while it seems on the surface to be sensible, is often quite the opposite from the actual fact. The sociologist, by applying exact measurement techniques, seeks to confirm or deny popular assumptions about the nature of human relationships in society. The fact is that common sense is rather imprecise, sometimes containing a grain of truth, often containing a generalization from someone's or some group's peculiar experience that needs to be examined. The sociologist is highly concerned with what we take to be common sense, because his subject matter is open and available to anyone and everyone. His area of expertise lies in the fact or in the assumption that if scientific procedures are applied to the nature of society as they are applied to the physical sciences, we can come up with much more precise and therefore much more useful information about the social forces of the groups in which we lead our lives.

Originally, sociology in its orientation was a form of social philosophy and as such its theories were reasonable ideas formulated by some social philosophers who thought that these really matched their pictures of society. An example of such a global theory might be one's conception of the nature of social change: Do societies improve until they reach some kind of peak or zenith and then decline? Is there really unending progress or is a cyclical model most accurate? Early theories, though fruitful in stimulating thought about society, were neither tested nor did they lend themselves to testing by empirical rules of evidence. Leaving such global philosophies, sociology gradually aligned itself with the sciences rather than the humanities where its inception lay. But the change went so far as to push some sociologists into the corner of being ready to make a statement only on empirically proven hypotheses of the kind based on research techniques that are reasonable for physical sciences. Thus sociologists very rapidly left larger social theories and reduced their scope until they seemed to have fallen into the trap of constantly testing the trivia of human behavior in order to have verifiable material. This trend can still be seen in some kinds of material found in sociological journals. Today we have a kind of middle which seems to be popular or most accepted among sociologists.

Recently, a Yugoslav sociologist sampled thirty prominent American sociologists, reaching the following conclusions: There is no general theory which dominates or is overall accepted by American sociologists. However, one or two points of view are more acceptable (at least in this sample of thirty prominent sociologists) than any other. These you might call Merton's concept of the middle range, and structural-functionalism, broadly implying a central concern with the interrelatedness of components of society.[2] Merton was also concerned with the sociologist's shift of attention from global theory to minutiae. He proposed that what we needed was a middle range, putting it as follows: "Like so many words which are bandied about, the word 'theory' threatens to become emptied of meaning. The very diversity of items to which the word is applied leads to the result that it often obscures rather than creates understanding." As he uses social theory, it refers to:

> logically interconnected conceptions which are limited and modest in scope rather than all-embracing and grandiose. Throughout I attempt to focus attention on what might be called theories of the middle range,

theories intermediate to the minor working hypotheses evolved in abundance during the day-by-day routines of research and the all-inclusive speculation of a master conceptual scheme from which it is hoped to derive a very large number of empirically observed uniformities in social behavior.[3]

This idea of theories of a middle range, broader than the very small working hypotheses and yet not global, seems to be most widely accepted and acceptable in contemporary sociology. Yet sociology has difficulty in presenting ideas which are at one time useful in general and specific enough to be tested and verified with scientific methods. In trying to do this, we have often to rely on "what we really know, what we nearly know, what we think we know, and what we claim to know."[4] Someplace in that set of four there are areas which sociologists know a great deal about human beings in groups.

It should be noted that in certain areas not only do we know a great deal, but we have even had enough information to feed it directly into the process of formation of social policy in our society. All behavioral sciences shared in this kind of contribution recently. In 1954, a decade of research on intergroup behavior, and what it means to be a member of a minority or a majority, provided us with a backlog of fact that was introduced into our courts. For the first time, the Supreme Court cited behavioral science research as evidence with regard to the famous court decision on separate but equal being inherently disequal. The remarkable thing is that from 1954 to the present, we have experienced an amazing turnabout where society has refused to take the next step, that is, to apply information that the behavioral sciences were giving it with regard to race and ethnic relations. For one brief moment in our history this information did have a real, concrete effect on social policy. Yet, one suspects that the problem lies in part in the fact that sociology is a weak science about which society is still unsure.

Like most scientists whose work touches the lives of mankind, sociologists have been experiencing second thoughts about their historically amoral, neutral position on the implications of their research and their findings. Nevertheless, most appear to retain substantially just this view of their role as professionals, regardless of their private commitments. The view of the sociologist as a detached, controlling manipulator of society not only makes the sociologist uncomfortable, but seems unreal only because of the imperfection of the field and failure of policy-makers to accept and act upon sociological proposals. Barring this, sociologists might indeed be as interested in modifying behavior as are social workers.

OVERLAPPING DISCIPLINES

At one time it was perhaps possible to divide the behaviorial sciences neatly into packages and to identify the domain of the sociologist, the anthropologist, the psychologist or perhaps the social psychologist. We had what Kluckhohn called neat little "gardens of knowledge" which each profession or each science tended in its own corner.[5] This is no longer the case. This is true not only in the behavioral sciences, but in the physical sciences as well. There is tremendous overlapping of investigation and interest as well as cross-seminal ideas which have an impact on all fields of human knowledge in the broadest sense. In the behavioral sciences, one could say in earlier times that the sociologist was mainly interested in the study of Western industrial society as analyzed through the use of quantitative data. By contrast, one could identify the anthropologist's main interest as pre-industrial, non-Western societies, small human groupings, which lent themselves to such non-quantified techniques as participant observation, and anecdotal reporting of observations. Today, both sociology and anthropology are crossing subject matter boundaries so that you find sociologists investigating the nature of pre-industrial societies and sociologist using the non-quantitative techniques of the anthropologist to study urban neighborhoods. By way of illustration, one fine sociological investigation was Herbert Gans's *The Urban Villagers,* which hardly contains a statistic in the body of the investigation.[6] By contrast, you find anthropologists borrowing quantitative measures not only from sociologists, but from psychologists as well.

Where does social work research fit into this picture? The sociologist is interested in disclosing the broad general principles that operate in a society or in a particular group context within society. Social work research is more applied research, and is more directed to the specific kinds of questions that social workers need to have resolved. That in itself is not a complete answer because we know very well that there is a constant feedback from applied to certain basic research areas, and the other way around. Whether a particular question should be studied by a social work researcher or by a sociologist or a social anthropologist or a social psychologist, is a moot question. For this reason alone it would no longer be practical to draw hard and fast lines. What is now increasingly happening is that major research has gone beyond the point where one researcher can undertake a project. Instead larger teams of scientists must undertake work on any given piece of research. Often the sponsorship of the research more than the subject area, determines which discipline will provide its leading thrust. Increasingly, the members of the research team are drawn on a cross-disciplinary basis. This is true of both the behavioral and the physical sciences.

DIFFERING PERSPECTIVES

It should be pointed out that a sociologist would have a different perspective on the nature of human behavior than would the social worker. Bear in mind that essentially the social worker is clinically oriented, thus he is interested in the first instance in abnormality, in the unusual behavior he is bound to face in his practice. The sociologist is interested in the norm and the degree of variation from this norm. The sociologist would see the abnormal as a percentage of what one might expect within the range of possibility in the way people behave. One does well to anticipate that social workers would be impatient with the scientist for not having ready tools to assist them and that sociologists would tend to belittle the unscholarly impatience of the practioner. However, the reality is that social workers are often called upon to render service in areas where adequate analysis, let alone remedies, are not yet available to anyone. Furthermore, with a troubled client before him, he cannot indulge in the luxury of waiting until he knows more.

REFERENCES

1. Peter Berger, *An Invitation to Sociology.* New York: Anchor Books, 1963, pp. 1-5.
2. Mihailo Popovich, "What American Sociologists Think About Their Science and Its Problems," *American Sociologist.* May 1966, vol. 1, No. 3, p. 133.

3. Robert Merton, *Social Theory and Social Structure*. New York: Free Press of Glencoe, 1957, pp. 5-6.

4. Bernard Berelson and Gary Steiner, *Human Behavior*. New York: Harcourt, Brace and Co., p. 3.

5. Clyde Kluckhohn, *Mirror For Man*. New York: Premier Books, 1954, pp. 221-229.

6. Herbert Gans, *The Urban Villagers*. New York: Free Press of Glencoe, 1962.

SOCIOLOGY, SOCIAL WORK, AND SOCIAL PROBLEMS

DAVID J. KALLEN
DOROTHY MILLER
ARLENE DANIELS

Both sociology and social work have contributions to make to the solution of social problems. It seems probable that as social science becomes less academic and more involved in the real world, and as social work becomes less psychiatrically oriented, there will be an increasing need for the two fields to cooperate in the solution of social problems. It, therefore, seems appropriate to discuss the present stance of each discipline with respect to social problems. In order to do this, we must first define social problems (Lee and Lee, 1949; Frank, 1949; Rose, 1964) and define various ways in which they can be solved.[1]

For present purposes, we define a social problem as a dislocation or dysfunction in the social system which is regarded by the society as requiring intervention by its designated agents. In this view, there are three requirements for a given social condition to be regarded as a social problem:

1. It must be social in origin.
2. It must be regarded by the society as a problem.
3. It must require some form of social intervention.

Currently, social problems are seen in such conditions as: socially created inequalities in the distribution of income, rights, or education, and in the growing chaos of our major cities. Crime, juvenile delinquency, care of the mentally ill, sexual deviance and other related consequences of these conditions are also defined as social problems. But if events are not defined as problems by the society, no social problem exists. For example, changing standards of individual sexual behavior among middle class persons are not really a social

Reprinted from the *American Sociologist* (August, 1968) pp. 235-239, by permission of the American Sociological Association and the authors.

13

problem. Although public concern is expressed about such matters, no effort is made by the society to sanction and regulate sexual activity in this group. However, the production of illegitimate children among women of low income, where the society must make provision for the support of the infants, is defined as a social problem. And so society enforces negative sanctions on sexual activity by these women. The emergence of the "hippy" culture, and the use of psychedelic drugs, particularly by young people, appears to be emerging as a new social problem. Significant segments of the society, particularly those with formal social control responsibilities are urging and enforcing negative sanctions for use (and possession) of psychedelic drugs. At the same time, there are considerable segments of opinion, particularly young, that support this concern with inner experience as legitimate. Thus, what one part of society defines as a social problem another part does not. In fact, the social problem may be more in the conflicting definitions of legitimacy than in the use of these substances per se.

There are at least four separate ways in which a society can respond to a recognized social problem:

1. Efforts can be made to ameliorate the negative outcomes or symptoms without affecting the underlying causes.

2. Attempts can be made at prevention by modifying the single social institution seen as the source of the problem.

3. Revolutionary restructuring of the society involving major modifications in the structure and relationship of an interdependent system of social institutions may be attempted.

4. Symptom exacerbation may occur when no clear solution is visible; but there is a concerted effort by one or more subgroups in the society to exert pressure. This pressure (Eglinton, 1964:40) is exerted on the theory that any change is preferable to a continuation of the status quo.[2]

Each of these response patterns arise from different structural situations, and each draws social change agents from different subspecialties or subgroups within society. These four patterns can be seen as arising from two different social processes: prevention and amelioration responses arise from social planning within established institutional patterns; revolutionary responses and symptom exacerbations arise from social movements and are patterns of elementary collective behavior (Case, 1964:11).[3] The agents of social change vary correspondingly. In the first type of social process, they may come from within the central structure of the society, being appointed, in effect, by the system, to deal with the problems created by the dysfunctional situation. In the second type of social process, they may be self-selected, coming essentially from outside the established system. Accordingly, amelioration and prevention responses will tend to be the result of actions by the designated agents of the social system. Revolutionary responses and symptom exacerbation will be instituted by agents who "emerge as natural leaders" from social movements.

Thus, for example, our public welfare system is a form of amelioration which is handled essentially by designated agents of the social system. Public assistance programs are seen as one form of social insurance and are written into the broader Social Security Act. Social engineers designed public assistance programs to ameliorate economic distress rather than to attack the inherent flaws within the economic system. As Franklin D. Roosevelt said (Cohen *et al.*, 1948:101) in 1934:

> We are compelled to employ the active interest of the nation as a whole through government in order to encourage a greater security for each individual who composes it.

Such a social plan did not seem to require any basic structural change in either the social or economic system which was in existence in the United States during the depression years. This program could be operated with technicians; e.g., intelligent college graduates who could determine legal eligibility and administer the financial payments. Currently, however, welfare recipients are anything but financially or personally secure. Substandard levels of assistance are provided through a system which has actually developed in a manner which perpetuates a negative self-image and stifles individual initiative. Such a system was originally intended to be a solution to the dysfunctions arising from the inequalities in the distribution of income but it has created another kind of social problem. Although the negative consequences of absence of income are somewhat ameliorated, the basic causes of poverty are left unchanged or have even been exacerbated.

While social planning may be devised as an economic or political strategy, it is often administered by persons who work, not only to administer a law but also to change the distressed individual, i.e., to change not the system but the self. Social welfare planning, for example, led to the design of a "law to flatten out the peaks and valleys of deflation and of inflation—in other words, a law that will take care of human needs and at the same time provide for the United

States an economic structure of vastly greater soundness (Roosevelt, 1935)."[4]

But the administration of that law rapidly developed in two divergent paths. One, the social insurance sections of the Social Security Act, was administered by government clerks in the private insurance patterns (efficient, rational, impersonal, and equitable). The other, the public assistance section (Galbraith, 1958:252-253), was administered by professional social workers, who began to seek for the "causes" of economic distress within individuals. These staffing patterns of a twin program designed to ameliorate a social problem have had far-reaching consequences.[5] Chief among these has been the separation of the poor into the "deserving" and the "undeserving." The "deserving" poor have had at least limited success in the labor market, and are, therefore, eligible for earned insurance benefits through Social Security, a system applied universalistically for all who meet the eligibility requirements. The "undeserving" poor are dependent on public charity through Public Welfare systems, which varies in eligibility requirements and size of payment from state to state. It should be noted that the public welfare provisions were originally designed as much to keep females out of the labor force as to provide support, while presently, at least in some states, efforts are made to return persons on welfare to the labor force.

The ameliorative approach to social problems often rests upon the assumption that the individual's psychological responses need to be restructured. In this view (Furie, 1966; Lubove, 1965 (1)), the possibility that social problems arise from the social system is minimized. Hence, attempts at restructuring the individual personality may represent an effort to adjust the individual to a dysfunctional social situation. The ameliorative approach, then may beg the question of the underlying difficulty and avoid consideration of more revolutionary and far reaching solutions to social problems.[6]

Methods for the resolution of social problems through prevention (Fried, 1963:151-171) follow public health models. In the public health model, once a disease has been identified and its carriers specified, massive intervention programs are mounted. Such programs push to vaccinate the population against the disease or to persuade individuals to modify their behaviors so as to eliminate the disease-carriers. However, in the field of social problems, the preventive approach appears to generate as many new problems as it solves. The preventive approach attempts to change only a given institution; it ignores the systematic interrelationships of institutions within the social structure. Thus, one reason for the development of public housing programs, combined with massive slum clearance programs, was to provide sanitary housing and other advantages which would then eliminate crime in the slums. This effort did not take into consideration the dysfunctional effects of the destruction of existing neighborhood social organizations.[7] Nor did it consider the possible deleterious effects of the new social organization (Beyer, 1965; Wilner *et al.*, 1962; Jacobs, 1961), creating a great density of unrelated populations. The difficulty of adequate social controls which characterizes the social and physical conditions of the great, high rise, public housing projects created a whole new complex of social problems which have not been solved.[8]

The revolutionary response to social problem has been defined as a restructuring of interdependent institutions. The successful American labor movement represents one example of this type of response. The success of the labor movement resulted not only in a new relationship between labor and management; but even more important, it created a new form of social mobility. In the past, social mobility had essentially been a movement of an individual through the social system. The labor movement created upward mobility on the part of entire groups as these groups were able to achieve a greater share of the goods and services of the society, and a greater degree of economic security (Hardman, 1962:431-436). This restructuring of the form and means of social mobility (Foster, 1956; Hill, 1957; LaBarre, 1951; Wilensky, 1959; Yinger, 1966), along with other changes in the economic organization of the society, had repercussions for the education system and the structure, organization, and function of the family.

The civil rights movement has many of the characteristics of a revolutionary movement (U. S. Department of Labor, 1965). It appears to be effecting changes in some of the structures of society.[9] However, the civil rights movement also has many characteristics of the exacerbation response. In many ways, it represents an attempt to achieve change for its own sake without a clear program or goal. Thus, events such as the Watts and other riots, tend to exacerbate the racial tensions. These riots can be seen as events which keep things stirred up without creating a clear purpose or program.[10]

In the perspective presented here social problems have their genesis in the structure of the social system. And so a concern with their definitions and solutions may well be the proper concern of sociology. Unfortunately, in recent years, sociology has avoided this concern, preferring to join with the rest of society in delegating this task to legislatures, pressure groups, formal agents of social control, and the profession of social work. For an example of the sociologist's view, Talcott Parsons (1959) reports that sociology is "universally conceived as a scientific discipline which is clearly primarily dedicated to the advancement and transmission of empirical knowledge in its field and secondarily to the communication of such knowledge to non-members and its utilization in practical affairs." Parsons clearly feels that the primary role of sociology is in research and university teaching. Edgar Borgatta (1959) puts the case even more strongly, reporting that, "Not only can the use of graduate school resources for training practitioners be extremely wasteful, it can also lower the standards necessary for training research personnel." Borgatta implies the desirability of setting up first and second class citizens in sociology: first class citizens will obtain their degrees in graduate schools and make careers in university research and teaching; second class citizens will obtain their degrees in professional schools and end up in some applied field.[11]

In one recent publication (Mack, 1964:25), the (ideal) social scientist is described as a "man alienated from his society . . . As citizen, a sociologist may have democratic concepts of justice and deplore the ways in which poverty and racial discrimination cause his society to fall short of its own ideals. But at work . . . the sociologist must invest his work time in analyzing the effectiveness of special interest groups, not in cheerleading. . . . Political leaders, educators, businessmen, church administrators are making policy decisions based upon data gathered by social scientists. The growing acceptance of science as a frame of reference can encourage belief that decision makers may come to feel more at home with science as a frame of mind."

Although science implies prediction and control, few social scientists feel comfortable about making predictions or recommendations for programs designed to create social change. The decision makers often distrust the so called scientific "data" offered by "social scientists" who do not, themselves, seem to see much of genuine scientific worth arising from their work. For example, a quarter of a century of research in race relations has not led to the development of effective corrective or remedial social programs for the American Negro.

He has come to know that whatever gain he will make will arise out of political power, not out of "scientific studies."[12]

Perhaps the reluctance of many sociologists to enter the social planning area can be traced to their sense of impotence in the face of the enormous social problems arising out of our social structure.

There are some positive trends visible in the sociological world, however. Two new sociological readers, *Applied Sociology* (Ross, 1965) [13] and *Social Welfare Institutions* reflect this trend. Zald (1965), states ". . . But just as it seems to some observers that social work in its drive toward professionalization, deserted the poor, so, too, sociology, in its pursuit of scientific status, deserted the value-laden problems of social welfare." Almost in a "reaction formation, social problems and welfare problems become taboo topics for sociology . . . the study was not quite intellectually respectable."[14]

If sociology has avoided a social change responsibility, the profession of social work has done little better. One consequence of the ameliorative approach in social work has been the focus on what can be called the *quality* of life of the client rather than the *conditions* of life affecting the clients. The quality of life refers to internal psychological motivations and to personal characteristics of individuals. The conditions of life refer to the consequences of social structures and institutions which affect the individuals' opportunities (Matza, 1964; Cloward and Ohlin, 1960). While current trends may focus on personality problems, the great, early research of social work was concerned with a description of social conditions. Thus, the work of such pioneers as John Howard (1784) in his investigation of English prison[15] or Charles Booth (1904) in his studies of London poor pitched social reform to the gathering of information about the nature of relevant social institutions, as well as life qualities. This type of work was also an attempt to locate the social causes of the unacceptable individual behavior which created social problems.

But the work of these early pioneers came at a time when private fortunes could support most of the work, and the social system was still simple enough so that the efforts of one individual could beget the possibility of significant social change. For example, Dorothea Dix came close to revolutionizing the care of the mental patients through a combination of persistence, indignation and observation.

These surveys and studies reflected the search for causes and carriers of problems and focused on the preventive approach. The consequences of this approach can be seen in such social reform move-

ments as prohibition. For the supporters of the prohibition movement, the hope was that abolition of alcohol would cure the ills of
the immigrant, i.e., poverty, ignorance and disease. When such attempts proved fruitless—eventually generating more problems than
they solved—the social reform movement fell into disrepute.

The social reformers went on to such issues as the feminist movement. But the system of social reform had already created government and private agency structures which led quickly to the professionalization of the helping function. And these professionals, the
social workers, soon became devotees of the personal approach to the
solution of social problems. One of the best examples of the pattern
that developed is Mary E. Richmond's *Social Diagnosis* (1917) which
provided the rationale for the casework method. The mental hygiene
movement added the psychoanaytical and dynamic mystique to the
individualist social approach to problematic persons. The completed
product was an ideology and a rationale for locating all social problems within the individual (Davis, 1935:55-65).

As the social system became more complex, and as the possibility
of effective individual action lessened, the change in social work from
reform to amelioration became understandable (Eckland, 1967). The
great impetus for this change was twofold: the shift of income maintenance from a private to a public function and the coincident professionalization of the casework function. If social work no longer has
a significant social change function (in part because of the complexities of the social system and the increasing difficulty in instituting
planned social change) then the focus on the quality of life becomes
a legitimate area of concern. The profession no longer has the right
or the responsibility to differentiate between the deserving and the
undeserving poor. This distinction of the deserving poor is now fulfilled by the provision of social insurance through the Social Security
programs. The undeserving poor receive charity through the Public
Welfare program. The distinction between the deserving and undeserving rests on their work history. But different criteria are implicit
in social work. In the development of social work philosophy, the
undeserving poor do not fulfill the expectations that society has on
its members. This inability can be attributed to the quality of poor
people rather than to their conditions.[16] Social work practice thus
becomes a mechanism for the maintenance of the status quo, despite
the generally egalitarian values of the social workers. Attention is
directed away from the idea that life conditions should be changed.

But if the conditions of life cannot be changed, the quality of individual lives can be—at least in theory—to reduce the discontent and to provide more individual satisfactions. If the person is unable to find a job, egalitarian values and the American dream makes it imperative to focus on that individual's failure rather than economic dislocation or poor preparation for the labor market. Hence, the social worker attempts to manipulate the accessible individual rather than to restructure the inaccessible institutional basis of his participation—or lack of it—in the labor market.

Under these conditions, it is not surprising that social workers and their clients do not agree on the problems which the client has, particularly when the client is lower class. Thus, according to Beck (1962), many lower class clients were seen by caseworkers in family service society agencies to have problems different from those presented by the client. Miller (1965) found that on admission to the mental hospital, patients and their families reported quite different problems from those perceived by the social workers. If what the client needs is adjustment to a dysfunctional social system, it is not surprising that he and the worker do not agree on the problem. Mary MacDonald (1960) has claimed that the social worker is "the keeper of the community's conscience." The idea of a social conscience, which the social worker should represent, ignores the significance of different life styles and their relation to place in society and to the values which are held. These styles and the related values result from the division of labor, the existence of a social gratification system and consequent differential opportunities. The values of the social worker and her client are thus radically different. However, the social worker has greater social power than the client (Landy, 1960:127-144). And so her notions of values and how they should be given priorities outweigh those of the client. She can attempt to impose her values on the client. Thus, the social work view of the community consciences, derived from middle class training and experience, upholds the *status quo*. A more pluralistic view of values and a greater understanding of the socially determined nature of behavior might lead to a greater emphasis on revolutionary changes rather than amelioration for the solution of social problems.

It is here that there may be a *rapprochement* between sociology and social work. The sociologist, by training, is concerned with the nature and interrelationships of the social system. But there is current disinterest from sociologists in the practical use of their knowledge and skills for the solution of social problems. In addition, those sociologists who have shown an interest have been disillusioned (Radman and Kolodny, 1965:93-112). Applied sociologists have complained at length about how they are treated when they intervene in social issues. Nevertheless, the knowledge and skill of sociologists might help to create a social accountability system which would in turn help social work to understand and help to change the life conditions of those about whom society is legitimately concerned. If social work has so far been guilty of acting without conceptualizing, sociology has been guilty of conceptualizing without acting.

The solutions to social problems can strengthen a society as it evolves or they can tear it apart. The successful solution of a social problem must be revolutionary in some form; ameliorative and preventive solutions would seem not to work in the long run, and the exacerbation of symptoms is not a solution. It seems to us that there must be a joint effort to translate sociological knowledge into social action. The skills of the sociologist as a social theoretician and a research investigator, and the skills of the social worker as a designated agent of social change in the society can be used for the solution of social problems.

There is some reason to believe that social work is making greater efforts in this direction than is sociology. Some doctoral programs in social work appear to be providing training that integrates the skills of social science and social work. The importance of this integration of skill and understanding cannot be underestimated. It is to be hoped that social science, in general, and sociology in particular, will also develop such integrated programs for the development of new agents of social change.

The increasing attention that decision makers are paying to social science indicates that social scientists will increasingly be called upon to utilize their skills in areas of social relevance. In meeting these social concerns—in seeking ways to solve rather than rearrange social problems there may be a rapprochement between social work and sociology as both disciplines bring their best thinking to bear on these issues.

REFERENCES

Beck, Dorothy Fehs. *Patterns in Use of Family Agency Service.* New York: Family Service Association of America, 1962.

Bendix, R. "Social Science and Social Action in Historical Perspective." *Ethics*, 1945-46, 56:208-218.

Beyer, Glen H. *Housing and Society*. New York: MacMillan Company, 1965.

Booth, Charles. *Life and Labor of the People in London*. London: MacMillan and Company, 1904.

Borgatta, E. "Sociologists and Sociologically Trained 'Practitioners'." *American Sociological Review 24*, October, 1959, 695-697.

Case, C. "A Definition of Social Problems." J. Gould and W. L. Kolb (eds.), *A Dictionary of the Social Sciences*. New York: The Free Press, 1964, p. 11.

Cloward, Richard A., and Lloyd E. Ohlin. *Delinquency and Opportunity: A Theory of Delinquency Gangs*. New York: The Free Press, 1960.

Davis, K. "Mental Hygiene and Class Structure." *Psychiatry 1*, February, 1938, 55-56.

Eckland, R. "Genetics and Sociology. A Reconsideration." *American Sociological Review*, 32, April, 1967, 173-194.

Eglinton, J. Z. *Greek Love*. New York: Oliver Layton Press, 1964.

Foster, R. "Effect of Mobility on the Family." *American J. Public Health 46*, July, 1956, 812-818.

Frank, L. "The Character of Social Problems." Alfred McClung Lee and Elisabeth Briant Lee (eds.), *Social Problems in America*. New York: Henry Holt and Company, 1949, p. 5.

Fried, M. "Grieving for a Lost Home." Leonard J. Duhl (ed.), *The Urban Condition*. New York. Basic Books, 1963, pp. 151-171.

Furie, S. "Birth Control and the Lower Class Unmarried Mother." *Social Work 11*, January, 1966, 42-49.

Galbraith, John. *The Affluent Society*. New York: A Mentor Book, 1958.

Haber, William and Wilbur Cohen (eds.). "Social Security Developments in the United States." *Readings in Social Security*. New York: Prentice-Hall, Inc., 1948, p. 101.

Hardman, J. B. S. "The Power Motivations of the American Labor Movement." S. Nesow and W. H. Forin (eds.), *Man, Work and Society*. New York: Basic Books, 1962, pp. 431-436.

Hill, R. "The Changing American Family." *Social Welfare Forum*, 1957, 84:68-80.

Howard, John. *John Howard*. Warrington: W. Eyres, 1784.

Jacobs, Jane. *Death and Life of Great American Cities*. New York: Random House, 1961.

Kallen, D. J. "Scientific Manpower Resources." *American Sociologist 1*, May, 1966, 149.

LaBarre, W. "Appraising Today's Pressures on Family Living." *Social Casework 32*, February, 1951, 5:1-57.

Landy, D. "Problems of the Person Seeking Help in our Culture." *Social Welfare Forum*, 1946, 127-144.

Lee, Alfred M. and Elizabeth B. Lee. *Social Problems in America.* New York: Henry Holt and Company, 1949.

Lubove, Roy. *The Professional Altruist.* Cambridge: Harvard University Press, 1965.

MacDonald, M. "Social Work Research, A Perspective." Norman A. Polansky (ed.), *Social Work Research.* Chicago: University of Chicago Press, 1960, pp. 1-23.

Mack, R. *Trans-Action.* 1964, 2:25.

Matza, David. *Delinquency and Drift.* New York: Wiley, 1964.

Miller, Dorothy and William Dawson. *Worlds that Fail, Part II: Disbanded Worlds.* Sacramento: California State Department of Mental Hygiene, 1965.

Mills, W. "The Labor Leader." S. Nosow and W. H. Form (eds.), *Man, Work, and Society.* New York: Basic Books, 1962, pp. 391-395.

Parsens, T. "Some Problems Confronting Sociology as a Profession." *American Sociological Review 24*, October, 1959, 695-697.

Radman, R. and R. Kolodny. "Organizational Strains in the Research-Practitioner Relationship." A. W. Gouldmer and S. M. Miller, *Applied Sociology.* New York: The Free Press, 1965, pp. 93-113.

Rainwater, L. and W. L. Yancey. "Black Families and the White House." *Trans-Action 3*, July-August, 1966, 6 ff.

Richmond, Mary E. *Social Diagnosis.* New York: Russell Sage Foundation, 1917.

Rose, A. "What Is a Social Problem." J. Gould and W. L. Kolb (ed.), *A Dictionary of the Social Sciences.* New York: The Free Press, 1964, pp. 662-663.

Ross, R. "Moral Obligations of the Scientist." A. W. Gouldner and S. M. Miller (ed.), *Applied Sociology,* New York: The Free Press, 1965, pp. 429-438.

Rovere, R. "The White House Conference on Civil Rights." *The New Yorker*, 1966.

U. S. Department of Labor. *The Negro Family.* Washington: U. S. Department of Labor Press, 1965.

Wilensky, H. L. "The Impact of Industrialization on Family Life." *Social Welfare Forum*, 1956, 83:202-219.

Wilner, D. M. *et al. The Housing Environment and Family Life.* Baltimore: Johns Hopkins Press, 1962.

Yinger, J. M. "The Changing Family in a Changing Society." *Social Casework 40*, October, 1959, 419-428.

Zald, Mayer N. (ed.). *Social Welfare Institutions.* New York: John Wiley and Sons, 1965.

FOOTNOTES

[1] Frank (1949) defines a social problem as any difficulty or misbehavior of a fairly large number of persons which we wish to remove or correct.

[2] Eglinton (1964) argues that there is perhaps one other way of "solving" a social problem: to legalize actions heretofore labeled "illegal," "deviant," or "sinful." One example of such a solution might be seen in the repeal of the 18th Amendment, another in 'Parliament's move to legalize homosexuality in England. This is a technique of solving social problems by revising the sanction system of a society. The argument that legalizing ancient Greek patterns of homosexual love between a patron and an adolescent boy would solve a social problem by reducing alienations of the adolescent from the adult world, i.e. juvenile delinquency. By legalizing homosexuality, Eglinton argues, one would remove two social problems, homosexuality and juvenile delinquency — an interesting, but hardly respectable idea, at this time.

[3] Case (1964) discusses social problems as results of social processes, themselves part of social change.

[4] Roosevelt (1935) statement upon signing of the Social Security Act, August 14, 1935.

[5] Galbraith (1968) discusses two forms of poverty in the United States, i.e., "case poverty" and "insular poverty." One is located in some defect in the individual, the other is some type of social dislocation. What may ameliorate one type will only confuse the other.

[6] Furie (1966) discusses the adverse reaction to social planning by persons who must undergo the "psychological-motivational" assessments of professional social workers in order to benefit from a social plan. See also Lubove's (1965) discussion of the development of social casework as an alternative to social reform.

[7] Fried (1963) discusses the effects of forced urban relocation.

[8] Beyer (1965), Wilner *et al* (1962), Jacobs (1961) report, for example, a recent study of persons living in new public housing and another group living under slum conditions which does not show large differences between the groups in regard to more adequate or health life styles.

[9] United States Department of Labor (1965) in a recent publication of the Office of Policy Planning and Research, *The Negro Family,* reviewed the crises in race relations and argued that the solution to the social problem created by the emerging Negro movement called for a new approach: "A national effort is required that will give a unity of purpose to the many activities of the Federal government, in this area, directed to a new kind of national goal: *the establishment of a stable Negro family structure"* (emphasis ours). This is an interesting answer to a large minority group's claim to social justice — i.e., full citizenship and social justice can be granted

only to persons with middle class nuclear family backgrounds! While the present power structure of the country may be in the hands of persons who seem to have such family backgrounds (with certain notable exceptions) it does not seem to follow that full participation of Negroes in the economic and political life requires a stable family structure. Some might argue that the present middle class family structure creates as many problems as it is reputed to solve. The divorce rate, the neurosis rate, and the suburban gang, reveal that middle class family life may, in fact, drive its members into sterile, power-laden, conformist actions which constitute a great barrier to the basic tenets of democracy. Thus, while the civil rights movement calls for social justice, the suggested solution in this report calls for personal and family changes not clearly related to the claim for economic and political freedom. Also see, Rovere (1966) for an account of some of the furor such middle class oriented recommendations made among the various spokesmen of the civil rights movement. Also see, Rainwater and Yancey (1966). They point out that the report itself attributes the breakdown of the Negro family to social and economic conditions. However, because of the way the material was released to the public, the demand for the strengthening and restructuring of the Negro family was perceived, and reacted to, as the major message. In this instance, then, the major social response was to the perceived content, and not necessarily the actual content, of the report. However, the insistence that the Negro family emulate the white family in organization, structure, and motivation, is part of the report, and represents an interesting displacement of a social problem from social conditions to individual characteristics of the problem group!

[10]Although, this was true when this was first written during the summer of 1966, it is even more true today, when what are perceived as excesses by civil rights militants exacerbate problems without providing solutions. The actions of groups opposed to military involvement in Vietnam also have many characteristics of exacerbatory responses, particularly since their call for unilateral de-escalation of the conflict or total withdrawal is not seen as a visible alternative by most of the population, not to mention the primary decision-makers. Nor do they appear to have given thoughtful consideration to the consequences of an unilateral decision to withdraw, any more than the proponents of further escalation appear to have considered — at least publically — the consequences of continued escalation. So far, the "peace groups" have been able to do nothing but protest, without, apparently, affecting policy. Hence, symptom exacerbation results. On the other hand, it is certainly not clear that any other action is open to them at this point in time.

[11]Kallen (1966) states that the recent distribution of a questionnaire on Scientific Manpower Resources by the American Sociological Association

tends to perpetuate this distinction; sociologists were given the choice of self-identifications as "applied" or "theoretical."

[12] Supreme Court (1954) recognized that the decision desegregating public schools was based, in part, on social science evidence that separate schools were inherently unequal. But since that time, little use has been made of social science in the solution of a series of racial crises.

[13] Rose (1965) calls upon the scientific associations to "design the means by which social problems which science can help are brought to the attention of scientists, and whatever in science is relevant to these problems is brought to the attention of the appropriate laymen."

[14] Bendix (1945-46) comments on the interesting formulation of the scientist-social actor conflict. He stated: "This ambivalence in the role of the social scientist indicates that in our culture the inherent radicalism of the scientific approach is either neutralized by turning social scientists into professional employees or that it is emasculated by confining them to the academic preserve."

[15] Howard (1784) reported on the state of prisons in England and Wales, with preliminary observations and an account of some foreign prisons and hospitals.

[16] Eckland (1967) feels that recent theorizing suggests that there may be some truth to this assertion, although for reasons different than those suggested by the social workers attribution of personal quality. Eckland, for example, makes a strong case for the differences in the genetic pool of different social classes, with the lower class having less genetic potential.

SOCIOLOGY'S RELEVANCE FOR CASEWORK RESEARCH

JOHN E. MAYER

It has frequently been observed that the development of social work practice is largely dependent on the maturity of the basic sciences on which it rests. Thus Coyle, writing about a decade ago, noted:

> It is obvious that what can be accomplished in any practice depends largely on the stage of development of its basic sciences. Medicine, engineering, education and many other professions give clear evidence that their technical advance comes only as the increased store of scientific knowledge produces theory and data relevant to their functions.[1]

With this in mind, social workers who are impatient with the progress of their discipline are apt to blame the crude and undeveloped nature of the sciences on which it rests.

While one cannot quarrel with these critical assessments, there is another facet of the behavioral science-social work relationship that is frequently overlooked: To what degree does social work actually draw on the social sciences, that is, make use of what is currently available? Since the author will restrict his focus, for the most part, to casework research and sociology, the question is more specifically: To what extent does casework research exploit the perspectives and concepts that sociology has to offer?

It is the author's opinion that casework research has done little to exploit sociology's potential and that this has had an impoverishing effect on the work undertaken. This failure possibly helps to account for some of the critical assessments that have been made of social work research (of which casework research is, of course, a part). For example, various members of the profession have held that it lacks theoretical development, it is noncumulative, studies undertaken bear

Reprinted with permission of the National Association of Social Workers, from *Social Work*, Vol. 14, No. 1 (January 1969) pp. 95-105.

little relation to each other, social work research has produced little in the way of solid, usable knowledge, and so forth.[2]

TYPES OF STUDIES

In what ways is casework research not exploiting sociology? Let us begin by surveying briefly the types of studies undertaken, since this will highlight the points at which sociology has most to offer. The useful summaries of research by Briar, Massarik, Shyne, and others indicate that studies undertaken by casework researchers can be loosely characterized as descriptive, toolmaking, or explanatory (or some combination of these).[3]

Descriptive studies depict aspects of the social landscape that are relevant to social workers and have traditionally occupied a central place in social work research. Most of these studies, Shyne notes, are small scale and describe the clientele or services of a specific agency. While their findings tend to be of local interest only and primarily to administrators, such studies are becoming more comprehensive in scope and systematic in execution; for example, broadly based data are now available on children in foster care, day care facilities in the United States, staff turnover in child welfare and family service agencies, and the like.[4] Factfinding studies of this type are obviously important. Among other things, they enable researchers to identify areas that are troublesome to the profession and hopefully can be rectified in the future.

Understandably, social workers are interested in the social functioning of their clients, especially any changes brought about by their intervention. Unfortunately, however, social functioning—unlike other variables of interest to the profession—is not easy to measure. Accordingly, considerable research energy has gone into the construction of measuring devices, e.g., the movement scale developed at the Community Service Society of New York, the work conducted in connection with the St. Paul studies, and so forth.[5] Despite obvious differences between tool-making and descriptive studies, there is nonetheless an important similarity: both can be construed as essentially fact-finding enterprises, in that the ultimate aim of tool-making research is to be able to describe (and thus classify and differentiate) groups of clients in terms of their social functioning.

In contrast to fact-finding research, *explanatory studies* seek to "understand" certain situations, typically by focusing on certain antecedent conditions and studying their bearing on the phenomenon in question. A review of such studies indicates that researchers have concentrated their attention heavily on the outcome of treatment and, in particular, the bearing that different types of treatment approaches have on outcome. For example, such treatment approaches as the following have been the subjects of study: using trained versus relatively untrained workers, limiting the case load of practitioners, offering "intensive" casework treatment, providing the client with a collaborative service (e.g., a caseworker *and* a public health nurse), providing short- or long-term treatment, and so forth.[6] The procedural aspects of treatment have also been investigated, e.g., the effects on outcome of charging fees, of having a waiting list, and the like.[7]

Significantly, however, many other factors also affect the outcome of treatment—ones that have engaged sociologists in general but have scarcely entered into casework research. The primary contribution of sociology, in the opinion of the author, is located precisely at this point: by bringing to bear certain explanatory variables, sociology can illuminate important problems in casework. In the following discussion, several such variables (or concepts) will be discussed.

Uses of Sociology

In studying the effects of different treatment approaches, casework researchers, by and large, have restricted their attention to the beginning and terminal phases of the casework process. A certain treatment method is used, its effects are assessed, but, significantly, little attention is directed to intervening processes. It is vitally important, however, to identify the specific factors that bring about the observed effects. Unless one has some understanding of them, one has no basis for predicting whether treatment approaches that prove successful with some groups can be usefully extended to others.

Suppose, for example, that a group of middle-class wives with alcoholic husbands were helped more by male than female workers. Would the same thing hold true for working-class wives? Before one can even begin to answer such a question, one must know what it is about a male worker that produced the observed effects. Moreover, in view of the underlying rationale for much casework research, the study of intervening processes becomes even more important. Many of these investigations take the form of "demonstration" projects: new treatment approaches are tried out in the expectation that they will be extended if they prove successful.

CLIENT'S PERSPECTIVE

The client's "definition of the situation" represents a major intervening variable that has been largely ignored by casework researchers. Clearly, whatever treatment techniques produce is not mechanically brought about but is filtered through the client's cognitive and perceptual frameworks. Clients define for themselves what their caseworkers are doing and then, on the basis of their interpretations, respond to the caseworker's efforts, suggestions, and techniques. In sociological terms, it is said that persons who are located in different sectors of the social structure (the working-class client and middle-class social worker provide a good example) will have different perspectives, which in turn will shape the ways they define situations. Thus, unless one is aware of clients' perceptions, one cannot understand the reasons for their responses and, in turn, why they benefit or do not benefit from the treatment approach used.

The point can be illustrated by drawing on a study, carried out by Noel Timms and this author, of working-class clients' reactions to casework treatment. It was found that practitioners who had offered insight therapy to clients who had subsequently dropped out of treatment typically attributed the clients' discontinuance to "resistance"—to the fact that emotionally charged topics had been introduced and had provoked anxiety. Interviews with clients, however, brought to light entirely different factors. Clients did not understand why their workers were not taking a more active part (e.g., giving advice, actively intervening), nor did they understand the intellectual assumptions underlying insight therapy. As they saw it, the worker's passivity was a sign that he was not interested in them, was bewildered by their case and did not know what steps to take, or lacked the authority to take the kind of action the situation called for (e.g., giving advice, actively intervening), nor did they understand the intellectual assumptions underlying insight therapy. As they saw it, the worker's passivity was a sign that he was not interested in them, was bewildered by their case and did not know what steps to take, or lacked the authority to take the kind of action the situation called for (e.g., giving their husbands a "good talking to" or threatening them in some way). Thus treatment was unsuccessful in these instances, not because of resistance (or not *only* because of it), but because the clients unsuspectingly defined the situation in a way that negated the caseworker's efforts.[8] Therefore, if casework researchers are to understand the processes by which certain treatment approaches produce certain effects, they might well follow their own maxim: start where the client is.

WORKER'S AND CLIENT'S ROLE-SET

The worker's efforts and the client's perception of them are not the only factors affecting outcome. During the course of treatment, both worker and client will probably interact with a variety of people, a situation that may well affect their interaction with each other. This concept derives from a basic tenet of sociology: If you want to understand the relationship between two persons, you must take into account the relationships each has with other persons in his role-set.[9]

During the course of treatment, the client will very likely interact with friends, relatives, or other persons who are important to him. These people may have strong feelings about whether it is proper to seek professional help and their outlook may influence the client, possibly determining whether he ever becomes a client at all. Moreover, once treatment is under way, they may have definite views concerning the manner in which his problems are being handled. It should constantly be borne in mind that social workers are not the only persons with whom troubled persons discuss their problems or who have views concerning the management of a client's difficulties. This inevitably raises questions concerning the compatibility of outlook between the client's two sets of helpers and the consequences of this for the social worker's efforts. It may turn out, for example, that members of the client's network heartily approve of the social worker's interpretations, recommendations, or actions and thus in a sense become his "allies." On the other hand, they may intensely disapprove of what the practitioner is saying and doing and their attitude may impede his efforts, intentionally or otherwise. In short, if one is to account for differences in treatment outcomes, it is not enough to learn what the caseworker is doing or even the client's perceptions of what he is doing. One must also take into account the ways in which persons important to the client respond to the treatment situation and the degree to which the client is subject to their influence.[10]

Casework researchers have paid little heed to considerations of this nature, despite the fact that their relevance has been repeatedly demonstrated. For example, studies of prisons, residential treatment centers, mental hospitals, and so forth reveal that inmates of these settings are strongly influenced by their relations with peers and that these relationships, in turn, may advance or, what is more likely, impede professional efforts to rehabilitate them.[11] That these processes take place within institutional settings should not obscure the likelihood that similar ones operate in the outside world, affecting the behavior, for example, of those who voluntarily go to social agencies.

As for the caseworker, he will very likely be interacting with agency administrators, supervisors, other professionals, and colleagues, among others. Any of these relationships may affect the ways in which he deals with clients. Certainly supervisors or other training personnel may explicitly try to influence his interaction with clients by changing or refining his practice techniques in some way. It would be a mistake to assume, however, that less didactic influences will not also affect his interaction with clients.

In this connection, the worker's morale is apt to be an important consideration. If his morale is high, he may put a lot of effort into the case and be able to sustain setbacks of one kind or another. If it is low, however, he may become impatient with clients, easily irritated, and less willing to persevere. The point to note, however, is that morale, for the most part, is not something brought *into* the organization but something produced *by* it.

To some extent, the morale of practitioners will be a by-product of the extent to which conflicting tendencies are present in the organization. In this connection, sociologists have delineated certain strains to which professionals working in bureaucratic settings are typically subject.[12] Evidence suggests that social workers in particular are heirs to these strains.[13] For example, there may be a conflict between the policy of the agency and the worker's professional standards; he may resent having to do certain things he considers "unprofessional."

Also, his relations with his supervisor may be a source of discomfort and frustration, largely as a result of certain structural incompatibilities that are built into the supervisory role. Characteristically, the supervisor is both teacher-friend and an evaluator of the worker's professional performance. Thus, while the worker may wish to express himself openly and may in fact be encouraged to do so, he is at the same time restrained by the harsh reality of the supervisor's authority. Situations of this kind are typically stressful and involve all kinds of painful adjustments. It would be strange indeed if some of the strains experienced by the worker did not seep into the worker-client relationship.

Relationships with colleagues, as well as those with supervisors and administrators, also have bearing for the topic at hand. For example, Blau and Scott have shown that collegial relationships may determine how "procedure" or "service" oriented a social worker is with clients and may, in addition, affect how emotionally detached he is from those he is treating.[14]

In concentrating on different treatment methods and their bearing on outcome, casework researchers have seemingly acted as though the worker's professional skills were all that really mattered.[15] Certainly, effective services cannot be provided by those whose skills are deficient. At the same time, adequate skills do not insure effective professional performances. A worker may not be motivated to bring his skills to bear, at least in full. Moreover, even though he is motivated, other factors such as those previously mentioned may deter him from implementing them. In language that should strike a familiar chord, the worker's performance, like the client's, will depend not only on his "capacity," but also on his "motivation" and "opportunity."

FINDINGS IN OTHER FIELDS

Medical sociology. Not only have relevant explanatory concepts not been exploited (those mentioned constitute merely examples) , but research findings in closely related fields have largely been ignored. One thinks especially of medical sociology, in which much work has been carried out dealing with topics such as the following: the ways in which people define illness, the processes leading them to seek professional help, strains in the doctor-patient relationship, conditions under which medical advice is or is not followed, obstacles in treating persons of different cultural backgrounds. It would be surprising indeed if this material did not have at least *some* bearing on the activities of social workers.[16]

Cultural concepts. This is not to say that sociology has had *no* influence. Certainly it has, as witness the widespread acceptance of cultural concepts.[17] Social workers recognize, for example, that differences between groups in our society (e.g., social classes) may be cultural in origin, that is, due not merely to "personality" or situational factors.[18] Moreover, they are well aware that these differences, in entering into the treatment situation, may be a source of strain between worker and client and as a result may impede the treatment process.

But even here one is struck by the fact that these concepts have not been taken up by casework researchers and seriously pursued. While those ideas have received further documentation of a kind,[19] they have not been brought to bear on critical issues in the field. For example, one might have expected that much research activity would have been devoted to helping practitioners deal more effectively with situations of contact between cultures. Such, however, has not been the case. As things now stand, practitioners are periodically warned that they should be alert to cultural differences and, if cultural differences are discerned, they should proceed cautiously, neither blindly promoting their own values nor docilely subscribing to those of their clients. But such admonitions provide little basis for positive action. What should the social worker do, for example, when confronted with a client whose aspirations and values are entirely different from his own? Assuming that such differences are relevant and require the worker to take a stand, whose cultural outlook should be endorsed and on what basis should the worker reach a decision?

If researchers are to help practitioners cope with such problems, they will have to learn a lot more about treatment situations involving those who are culturally dissimilar. They will have to focus on the types of difficulties that arise in such situations, the ways in which practitioners try to cope with them, the conditions under which they are successful or not successful, and so forth. Once information of this type becomes available, the social work profession will be in a better position to develop guidelines for its workers—working principles that will enable them to deal more effectively with those who are culturally alien.

In response to the criticisms and suggestions raised in this article, the casework researcher might reply: "Yes, I agree the considerations you raise are relevant, but after all, we cannot study everything at once." However, it is precisely because everything cannot be studied at once—because the researcher *must* be selective—that research plans shouid be made in the light of as wide a range of relevant factors as possible. Yet one has the impression that this is simply not the case; research decisions are apparently being made without awareness of or interest in sociological concepts. There is, however, no intrinsic reason why this should be so or, correlatively, why ongoing research need be confined to investigating the effects of different treatment methods. Indeed, to impose arbitrary restrictions of this kind is to subvert the very purpose of such research—to improve the effectiveness of service.

BARRIERS TO SOCIOLOGICAL IDEAS

If one wishes to bring sociology to bear more fully on casework, it is not enough to map out ways in which sociology might be of benefit. One must also attend to factors that have curbed its utilization in the past and that may continue to do so in the future. In addition to its immediate relevance, this specific matter bears on a wider question that Young called attention to some years ago—the conditions that foster or impede utilization of the behavioral sciences by those in the applied professions.[20]

There are several obvious and important reasons why sociology has remained unexploited. Casework researchers are not apt to be trained in sociology, having come to research, one suspects, either by way of traditional social work channels or academic psychology. Moreover, since sociology has advanced rapidly during the last few decades, this has made those casework researchers whose formal education ended some time ago even more out of touch.

Over and above the fact that casework researchers are not apt to be familiar with sociological ideas, few sociologists have been or are involved in casework research. Unfortunately, figures on this point are not available. However, it is suggestive that comparatively few sociologists are involved in the social work field as a whole, at least if one takes as a benchmark the number of sociologists affiliated with different types of professional schools. According to the 1959 membership list of the American Sociological Association, there were 126 sociologists affiliated with professional schools of medicine (including nursing and dentistry), 96 with schools of education, but only 40 with schools of social work.[21]

EFFECTS OF PROFESSIONALIZATION

In the remainder of this paper attention will be focused on a different type of barrier that has effectively blocked the utilization of sociological ideas. While it is common knowledge that social workers have been striving to become professionalized, it is less commonly recognized that the processes of professionalization may have insidious as well as benign effects.[22] One of the undesirable effects is that it has curbed the utilization of sociology by casework researchers.

Presumably all would agree that if social work is to become professionalized and thus achieve the recognition it seeks, it will have to demonstrate that its members have skills that cannot be performed by other persons, lay or professional. If everyone can do what social workers do with little or no specialized training, then it is unlikely that social workers will be accorded any particular esteem. It is thus quite understandable why the social work profession has been actively engaged in clarifying the ways in which its skills and activities differ from those of other professionals and laymen.[23]

The desire for differentiation, however, has been carried over into a sphere in which it is not appropriate. That is, social workers not only state that they perform distinctive activities, but they occasionally proclaim that these activities flow from a unique body of knowledge, one that, at least in part, is unconnected with or distinct from the behavioral sciences. To illustrate, Kahn states:

> Although the social work knowledge core now in use does include a good deal of borrowed psychiatry and psychological concepts, and much less borrowing from sociology, social anthropology and related disciplines, we also base our actions on a body of *original* social work knowledge dealing with individual and group phenomena and with the ways in which people, groups and communities respond to situations and to actions. [Italics added.][24]

Since efforts to identify this special knowledge have thus far been unsuccessful, those who subscribe to such views have had to put their faith in the future. Thus Bartlett, in contrast to "those who regard social work as an applied science," anticipates that social work will have its "own body of professional knowledge" in the future.[25]

She concludes:

> We have arrived at a point of maturity in our profession when
> we should be able to identify a number of knowledge propositions,
> distinctly social work in character, that underlie the practice of all
> social workers.[26]

One suspects that views of this nature are fairly widespread. For example, Briar notes that "a misguided provincialism can be detected
here and there in the literature" and goes on to explain:

> Many believe that because social work has a unique concern with
> certain human problems and has developed its own methods for
> dealing with them, social work needs to formulate its own theory
> and fashion research tools especially suited to its needs.[27]

It is not suggested that the profession's efforts to assemble and
codify social work knowledge as such are in any sense amiss. As
Greenwood has pointed out, the professions not only rest on distinctive skills, but the skills themselves "flow from and are supported by
a fund of knowledge that has been organized into an internally consistent system."[28] Rather, views concerning the *derivation* of social
work knowledge are being questioned, that is, whether such knowledge is or should be, in any important sense, independent of the behavioral sciences. Put slightly differently, the separatist notions expressed do not accord with the relationship, as commonly conceived,
between the basic sciences and the practicing professions, of which
sociology and social work are instances. Practicing professions, such
as medicine and education, do not rest, even in part, on "pristine"
knowledge but on knowledge ultimately derived from the basic
sciences (which admittedly becomes reshaped as it is brought to bear
on the specific concerns of the professions). One might also add that
even if certain professions *did* possess unique (and valid) substantive
propositions, basic scientists would be likely to incorporate them
into their conceptual schemes, thus robbing them of their "unique-
ness."[29]

The uniqueness-of-knowledge views are not merely inaccurate.
What is more important, they impede the flow of sociological ideas
into social work, a process that in turn affects the nature of casework
research. One might suggest that these views block the utilization
of sociology in the following ways:

1. The profession's emphasis on developing its "own" knowledge
has presumably lessened the time, energy, and resources available for

other pursuits, among them the cultivation of sociology. The following prescription, if followed, would undoubtedly have such an effect:

> To some extent, social workers with training in one or another of the social sciences may learn to translate its knowledge into answers to social work questions. But *probably to a far greater degree,* the social work task will be one of formulating and testing knowledge that grows out of social work operations and problems, and of developing that knowledge for general use, within and without the profession. [Italics added.][30]

2. Those who might otherwise pursue sociological ideas are perhaps deterred by an unsympathetic climate of opinion, one that may even go so far as to view the pursuit of such activities as constituting a "betrayal" of the profession. In this connection, French notes:

> There is already a considerable body of opinion which holds that building research activity in social work on the concepts and research methods of the social sciences represents an *abdication* of social work's responsibility for formulating and improving its own principles and practice. [Italics added.][31]

3. The type of separatist thinking discussed curbs the potential contribution of sociologists themselves. To the extent that sociology is looked on as a peripheral activity, sociologists will not be motivated to undertake casework research, at least under the auspices of social work personnel. Moreover, sociologists who are currently employed in social work settings may find they have become converted into "methodological eunuchs"—that is, retained for their technical research skills rather than for any substantive contributions they might make. Processes of this nature—and they are certainly not unfamiliar—effectively curb the infusion of sociological ideas.[32]

In wider perspective, the uniqueness-of-knowledge views discussed appear to be both benign *and* insidious. They are benign in the sense that they foster professional pride—pride that the profession possesses (allegedly) a distinctive body of knowledge, something important that sets its members off from others in the community. However, these views also are insidious in the sense that they block the utilization of sociological ideas and thus impoverish, in the long run, the very knowledge base the profession is endeavoring to develop.[33]

What, if anything, can be done about this situation? Perhaps a fuller realization of the complexities involved in applying the behavioral sciences might help to resolve the dilemma. As things now stand, the task of applying behavioral knowledge tends to be regarded as a mundane and pedestrian activity—a questionable view to say the least. Suppose, for example, that one is treating working-class parents of Italian descent whose son is in trouble with the police. Sociology might supply generalizations about interaction within working-class families, Italian cultural patterns, and the sociocultural sources of delinquent behavior. But it is up to the caseworker to discern which of these generalizations apply to the specific family, whether they shed any light on the family's difficulties, and what bearing, if any, they have on the formulation of treatment plans. In truth, little is known about the actual steps involved in "application."[34] However, if and when these steps become subject to investigation— and they should be—the process of application will very likely turn out to be a good deal more complex than had been suspected. When it becomes realized, in turn, that the task of applying knowledge is a demanding one, social workers should receive the recognition they desire and as a result may experience less need for a "unique body of knowledge."

Conclusion

In conclusion, there are certainly other factors that curb the utilization of sociological ideas by casework researchers. To name only one: Social work agencies are dependent on outside sources for funds and moral support, and their vulnerability may lead them to promote studies that are "safe" and shy away from those that utilize unfamiliar approaches and concepts. Clearly, matters of this nature are in need of study.[35] Put more broadly, if social workers are to increase the utilization of sociology, they must not only give more thought to sociology's precise bearing on social work and casework specifically, but must also learn more about resistance to its utilization.

Footnotes

[1] Grace Longwell Coyle, *Social Science in the Professional Education of Social Workers* (New York: Council on Social Work Education, 1958), p. 55.

[2] *See*, for example, Scott Briar, "Family Services," in Henry S. Maas, ed., *Five Fields of Social Service* (New York: National Association of Social Workers, 1966), p. 50; Coyle, *op. cit.*, p. 9; Ernest Greenwood, "Social Sci-

ence and Social Work: A Theory of Their Relationship," *Social Service Review*, Vol. 29, No. 1 (March 1955), pp. 20-33; Alfred Kadushin, "The Knowledge Base of Social Work," in Alfred J. Kahn, ed., *Issues in American Social Work* (New York: Columbia University Press, 1959), p. 53; Robert D. Vinter, "Small-Group Theory and Research," in Leonard S. Kogan, ed., *Social Science Theory and Social Work Research* (New York: National Association of Social Workers, 1960), p. 123. Also relevant are the results of a recent study indicating that practitioners themselves fail to find research studies helpful. *See* Aaron Rosenblatt, "The Practitioner's Use and Evaluation of Research," *Social Work*, Vol. 13, No. 1 (January 1968), pp. 53-59.

³Briar, *op. cit.*, pp. 9-50; Fred Massarik, "The Survey Method in Social Work: Past, Present, and Potential," in Charles Y. Glock, ed., *Survey Research in the Social Sciences* (New York: Russell Sage Foundation, 1967), pp. 377-422; Ann W. Shyne, "Casework Research: Past and Present," *Social Casework*, Vol. 43, No. 9 (November 1962), pp. 467-473; and Shyne, "Social Work Research—An Overview and Appraisal," *Child Welfare*, Vol. 43, No. 3 (March 1964), pp. 109-116.

⁴Shyne, "Social Work Research—An Overview and Appraisal," pp. 110-111.

⁵References can be found in Briar, *op. cit.*, pp. 16-21.

⁶Summaries of these studies are in David Wallace and Jesse Smith, *The Chemung County Research Demonstration with Dependent Multi-Problem Families* (New York: State Charities Aid Association, 1965); and *Studies in Welfare and Health* (New York: Community Service Society, 1967).

⁷Briar, *op. cit.*, pp. 31-32.

⁸John E. Mayer and Noel Timms, "Clash in Perspective between Worker and Client," *Social Casework*, Vol. 50, (January 1969), pp. 32-40. The research (of which the preceding is an excerpt) was carried out in London and will be published by Routledge and Kegan Paul in 1970 with the title *The Client Speaks: Working-Class Impressions of Casework*.

⁹For a general discussion of role-set *see* Robert K. Merton, *Social Theory and Social Structure* (rev. ed.; New York: Free Press of Glencoe, 1964), pp. 368-384. Its specific utility for social work is discussed in Aaron Rosenblatt, "The Application of Role Concepts to the Intake Process," *Social Casework*, Vol. 43, No. 1 (January 1962), pp. 8-14.

¹⁰For a fuller discussion of this view and an empirical test of one of the ideas flowing from it, *see* John E. Mayer and Aaron Rosenblatt, "The Client's Social Context: Its Effect on Continuance in Treatment," *Social Casework*, Vol. 45, No. 9 (November 1964), pp. 511-518; and Rosenblatt and Mayer, "Client Disengagement and Alternative Treatment Resources," *Social Casework*, Vol. 47, No. 1 (January 1966), pp. 3-12.

¹¹Lloyd E. Ohlin and William C. Lawrence, "Social Interaction Among Clients As a Treatment Problem," *Social Work*, Vol. 4, No. 2 (April 1969), pp. 3-13.

[12] There is considerable literature on this topic, which is conveniently summarized in W. Richard Scott, "Professionals in Bureaucracies—Areas of Conflict," in Howard M. Vollmer and Donald L. Mills, eds., *Professionalization* (Englewood Cliffs, N.J.: Prentice-Hall, 1966), pp. 265-275.

[13] For a summary picture, *see* Robert D. Vinter, "The Social Structure of Service," in Alfred J. Kahn, ed., *Issues in American Social Work* (New York: Columbia University Press, 1959), pp. 242-269. Some of the strains confronting social workers in the field of corrections are forcefully depicted in Lloyd E. Ohlin, Herman Piven, and Donnell M. Pappenfort, "Major Dilemmas of the Social Worker in Probation and Parole," *National Probation and Parole Association Journal*, Vol. 2, No. 3 (July 1956), pp. 211-225; and Piven and Pappenfort, "Strain Between Administrator and Worker: A View from the Field of Corrections," *Social Work*, Vol. 5, No. 4 (October 1960), pp. 37-45.

[14] Peter M. Blau and W. Richard Scott, *Formal Organizations* (San Francisco: Chandler Publishing Co., 1962), pp. 87-115 and 236. *See also* Blau, "Orientation Toward Clients in a Public Welfare Agency," *Administrative Science Quarterly*, Vol. 5, No. 3 (December 1960), pp. 341-361.

[15] Relevant here is Scott Briar's conclusion, based on a review of the literature, of how social workers in child placement believe they choose between institutional and foster family care: ". . . all references reviewed assumed, either explicitly or implicitly, that this decision is made on diagnostic grounds. That is, it is assumed that the social worker looks at the data in each case, makes inferences from these data about the child's needs, and chooses the form of foster care best suited to meet those needs." Briar goes on to point out that this model ignores certain realities in the area of foster care. "Clinical Judgment in Foster Care Placement," *Child Welfare*, Vol. 42, No. 4 (April 1963), p. 162.

[16] Material on or references to the topics mentioned can be found in Samuel W. Bloom, *The Doctor and His Patient* (New York: Russell Sage Foundation, 1963); Howard E. Freeman, Sol Levine, and Leo G. Reader, *Handbook of Medical Sociology* (Englewood Cliffs, N.J.: Prentice-Hall, 1963); E. Gartly Jaco, ed., *Patients, Physicians, and Illness* (New York: Free Press of Glencoe, 1958); Benjamin D. Paul, ed., *Health, Culture, and Community* (New York: Russell Sage Foundation, 1955); *The Sociology of Medicine: A Trend Report and Bibliography*, Vol. 10-11, No. 3 (1961-62) and Edward A. Suchman, "Public Health," in Paul F. Lazarsfeld, William H. Sewell, and Harold L. Wilensky, eds., *The Uses of Sociology* (New York: Basic Books, 1967), pp. 567-611.

[17] Coyle, for example, notes, after studying the curricula of social work schools, that "perhaps the single most used concept, and the first to gain wide acceptance, is that of culture." *Op. cit.*, p. 26.

[18]Cultural concepts, it is interesting to note, were first brought to the full attention of social workers by R. M. MacIver over thirty-five years ago in *The Contribution of Sociology to Social Work* (New York: Columbia University Press, 1931). Since then they have been kept in the forefront of social workers' attention by such works as Herman D. Stein and Richard A. Cloward, eds., *Social Perspectives on Behavior* (New York: Free Press of Glencoe, 1958); Stein, "Social Work and the Behavioral and Social Sciences: Reflections on Developments," *Journal of Jewish Communal Service*, Vol. 41, No. 1 (Fall 1964), pp. 16-28; and Hope Jensen Leichter and William E. Mitchell, *Kinship and Casework* (New York: Russell Sage Foundation, 1967). British social workers have been exposed to these concepts in the works of Peter Leonard, *Sociology in Social Work,* and Noel Timms, *A Sociological Approach to Social Problems* (London, Eng.: Routledge and Kegan Paul, 1966 and 1967 respectively); and Brian J. Heraud, *Sociology and Social Work: Perspectives and Problems* (published by Pergamon Press in 1969).

[19]Data suggest that the greater the dissimilarity between worker and client in the definition of the client's situation, the more likely is the client to discontinue treatment. Briar, "Family Services," p. 25. *See also* Jona Michael Rosenfeld, "Strangeness Between Helper and Client: A Possible Explanation of Non-Use of Available Professional Help," *Social Service Review*, Vol. 38, No. 1 (March 1964), pp. 17-25.

[20]Donald Young, "Sociology and the Practicing Professions," *American Sociological Review*, Vol. 20, No. 6 (December 1955), pp. 641-648.

[21]Matilda W. Riley, "Membership of the American Sociological Association, 1950-59," *American Sociological Review*, Vol. 25, No. 6 (December 1960), pp. 914-926. These figures, of course, say nothing about changes over time in the number of sociologists involved in social work. Evidence suggests that the numbers employed in schools of social work and as researchers in social agencies have definitely increased during the last decade or so. *See* Henry J. Meyer, Eugene Litwak, Edwin J. Thomas, and Robert D. Vinter, "Social Work and Social Welfare," in Lazarsfeld, Sewell, and Wilensky, eds., *op. cit.,* pp. 156-190.

[22]In this connection, Herbert Bisno forcefully reminds us that the processes of professionalization may adversely affect the general welfare of society. "There is the implicit belief that the professional advancement of social work is correlated with the general welfare of society. Again and again in the literature of social work we find this assumption of an 'automatic harmony' between the status aspirations of the profession and the effective performance of a truly 'socialized function' that will take into account ends as well as means. Here we seem to have an 'invisible hand' theory in modern dress. . . ." "How Social Will Social Work Be?" *Social Work*, Vol. 1, No. 2 (April 1956), pp. 17-18. *See also* Alvin W. Gouldner, "The

Secrets of Organizations," *Social Welfare Forum, 1963* (New York: Columbia University Press, 1963), pp. 161-177.

[23] The efforts at self-differentiation, in the author's opinion, explain much else about the field of social work. One has the impression, for example, that social workers rarely pride themselves on providing concrete, practical services to clients (i.e., nondifferentiating services), even though these may be greatly appreciated by recipients. *See,* for example, Barbara N. Rogers and Julia Dixon, *Portrait of Social Work* (New York: Oxford University Press, 1960), pp. 211-212. Consistent with this is the fact that social workers prefer to do casework or, better yet, "insight-oriented" casework. All this gives rise to a perplexing problem: how to instill in social workers the wish to provide services that are important to clients but that may not demand highly specialized skills. In addition, the differentiating efforts of the professions help to explain the social workers' outlook toward using nonprofessional or indigenous workers. If the latter can be brought into the social work Establishment so that they do not blur the distinction between professional social work activities and those undertaken by "ordinary" persons, untrained workers are apt to be accepted and even welcomed. On the other hand, if they muddy this "inside-outside" distinction, they are likely to be viewed as threatening and will be resisted. It would appear that the profession is now well on its way to solving this problem after an initially difficult beginning in which there was uncertainty as to the tasks nonprofessionals could or should perform.

[24] Alfred J. Kahn, "Sociology and Social Work: Challenge and Invitation," *Social Problems,* Vol. 4, No. 3 (January 1957), p. 220.

[25] Harriett Bartlett, "The Place and Use of Knowledge in Social Work Practice," *Social Work,* Vol. 9, No. 3 (July 1964), p. 37.

[26] *Ibid.,* p. 45. For a collection of papers expressing a range of views *see Building Social Work Knowledge* (New York: National Association of Social Workers, 1964).

[27] "Family Services," p. 49.

[28] Ernest Greenwood, "Attributes of a Profession," in Vollmer and Mills, eds., *op. cit.,* p. 11.

[29] It should be noted that a closer liaison between the social sciences and social work has been forcefully advocated by certain members of the social work profession. *See* especially David G. French, *An Approach to Measuring Results in Social Work* (New York: Columbia University Press, 1952).

[30] Alfred J. Kahn, "The Nature of Social Work Knowledge," in Cora Kasius, ed., *New Directions in Social Work* (New York: Harper & Bros., 1954), p. 206.

[31] *Op. cit.,* p. 80.

[32] Leonard S. Cottrell, Jr., and Eleanor B. Sheldon, "Problems of Col-

laboration Between Social Scientists and the Practicing Professions," in Vollmer and Mills, eds., *op. cit.*, pp. 232-236.

[33] The social work profession—at least segments of it—is not alone in eschewing the use of the behavioral sciences. Note, for example, the following course advocated for the nursing profession: "In the present state of the behavioral sciences and nursing, we doubt that the integration of relevant basic sciences into clinical nursing is a visible means of building nursing theory. An alternative that has been overlooked is to begin with practical nursing experience and develop concepts from an analysis of that clinical experience, rather than try to make borrowed concepts fit. . . . In developing its own theories, nursing would become an independent 'discipline' in its own right. In freeing themselves from the burden of looking only for applications of the 'basic' sciences in their practice, nurses would at the same time take on the responsibility of developing their own science." Florence S. Wald and Robert C. Leonard, "Toward Development of Nursing Practice Theory," in Jeannette R. Folta and Edith S. Deck, eds., *A Sociological Framework for Patient Care* (New York: John Wiley & Sons, 1966), p. 317. Views of this nature are possibly characteristic of professions during the early stages of their development.

[34] *See,* however, Coyle's brief, but helpful, observations on this topic. *Op. cit.,* pp. 45-46.

[35] So, too, are factors *fostering* the utilization of sociology, e.g., the growing number of attacks on traditional psychotherapy, which, for its own part, has helped to "open the door" to sociological ideas:

SOME CONSEQUENCES OF SOCIAL WORK PROFESSIONALISM

WILENSKY & LEBEAUX

The development of professionalism has had several effects on the practice of social work. Four will be commented upon here: problems of recruitment, interprofessional relations, role conflict among social workers, and definitions of the field for future growth.

Recruitment and Public Images of the Profession. Recruitment of new practitioners is a particularly critical problem in the drive toward social work professionalization. Figures on the number of professionally trained workers greatly underestimate the true growth of professional consciousness, and public recognition of the profession in recent years. The evidence is that many more people identify themselves as social workers than graduate from schools of social work, and many more positions calling for trained social workers exist than there are trained people to fill them. A situation has arisen in which the public demand built up for social workers cannot be met because too few students are presenting themselves for training. Although this makes for "good pickings" for present workers, and is tending to push salaries up, it also tends to frustrate public expectation, and invites preemption of the jobs by other occupations. Table 11 shows the number of graduates from the two-year social work curriculum in recent years, and gives a ratio of social work graduates to the total number of college graduates two years earlier. It is clear that these numbers, whatever their trend, are not enough to staff a profession of 75- to 100-thousand members.

The reasons for these recruitment difficulties are partly social, partly economic. The social aspect relates in part to the public image of the profession—always an important element in career choices. Too little is known about the current content of popular stereotypes of the social worker. The obvious negative phrases "do-gooder" or "cold snooper" may reflect more the social workers' anxieties about a hostile public than the actual feelings of that public. Research on this matter is needed.

There are, however, three suggestive studies of the relative prestige or social status of social work. A national cross-section of the population was asked in the spring of 1947 to rank prestigewise a list of 90 occupations. Social work was not among the occupations listed but "welfare worker for a city government" ranked forty-sixth in the list

TABLE 11. TRENDS IN GRADUATE SOCIAL WORK EDUCATION

Year	Number of graduates from two-year social work curriculum	Per cent of all college graduates of two years prior
1949-1950	1,804	.67
1950-1951	1,923	.52
1951-1952	1,946	.45
1952-1953	1,844	.48
1953-1954	1,651	.50
1954-1955	1,590	.52

SOURCE: French, David G., "An Estimate of the Number of Persons Who Will Be Graduated from Schools of Social Work in the United States, 1955 to 1965."

of 90—around "electrician," "trained machinist," "undertaker," and "reporter on a daily newspaper." The only other welfare-type occupation was "playground director," which ranked fifty-fourth, around "tenant farmer" and "traveling salesman for a wholesale concern," "policeman," and "railroad conductor." The "welfare worker" noted above had a score of 73, compared to the following for some other occupations:

Professional and semi-professional workers as a whole	80.6
Physician	93
College professor	89
Lawyer	86
Public schoolteacher	78

The only other studies that have come to the writers' attention show similar results. One used as raters 700 high school seniors in two Cleveland suburbs; the other used 72 Wayne University students One suggests that social workers rank higher among lower-class students, lower among middle-class students. All three studies show striking consistency: it is fairly clear that the public does not rank social work as one of the high prestige professions. It is a plausible hypothesis, however, that the image held by the middle-class public will become more favorable as the clientele of social work shifts up-ward (more middle-income families have firsthand exposure), and as the education level of the average social worker rises. But at the mo-ment, in so far as the status of a professional is a factor in occupa-tional choice, we have in the middling prestige of social work one reason for recruitment difficulties.

The different amounts of prestige attached to specialties within the profession also affect recruitment. Psychiatric social work has been, and still largely is, the specialization with the most prestige, a fact which has a definite effect on work opportunities and condi-tions. A psychiatric caseworker is welcome in a family agency, but a family caseworker does not usually qualify for a child guidance clinic job. Often there is a salary premium attached to the psychiatric job classification. It is no accident that students choose the psychiatric sequence in preference to family or child casework, or to social group work.[1]

Low pay is a second block to easy recruitment. Dean Fedele F. Fauri of the University of Michigan has discussed the unfavorable position of social workers as compared to other professions requir-ing a similar amount of training. The public school-teacher, for instance, earns the basic professional education degree in four years of college, and goes into jobs with a pay range like that in social work. The Master's degree in education requires but one year of study, and that can be done during summer vacation periods. The basic professional social work degree, in contrast, requires two years of graduate work beyond the A.B. level—a pattern laid down in the 1920's and 1930's and now standard in the 60-odd Schools of Social Work in the U.S. and Canada. Only rarely can the two years be shortened by summer school classes, because in the vast majority of schools the "integrated curriculum" requires that classroom "methods" courses be taken simultaneously with the "field work" assignment, and field work is tied to the nine months of the normal academic year. Many a career-seeking college junior avoids the path to social work when he learns that social workers train longer to earn about what teachers get.

Proposals to shorten the two years of graduate training, or to per-mit admission to professional school at the end of the college junior year, have so far met with disfavor by professional associations and accrediting bodies.[2] It is felt that any relaxation in training requirements would undermine professional standards and thwart the achievement of solid professional status. The major device used to overcome the economic handicap to recruitment, aside from publicity, is substantial subsidization of students through work-study plans (salary while in training), agency and Community Chest "stipends," training grants offered by units of the Department of Health, Education, and Welfare. A handful of schools have for a long time offered plans which spread the training period over more than two years, so that a student may hold down a nearly full-time job while earning his Master's degree. Such programs, now spreading rapidly to other Schools, do not cut the training period, but do sacrifice the "integrated curriculum" concept.

Recruitment, in the sense of winning the allegiance of already employed groups, has also been affected by the way in which social work competence is defined, and the standard set for membership in professional associations. A pattern has crystallized which tends to disaffect persons in social work positions who do not meet the membership standard set by the newly merged professional association, the National Association of Social Workers. This standard calls for two years of graduate education in an accredited school of social work. In the past many persons have entered social work programs who had obtained their training in other fields, and indeed some of the outstanding leaders in the field of social work are in this group. Several of the larger schools of social work have had as deans social workers who did not hold a social work degree, and the first two nominees for president of the National Association of Social Workers, which proclaimed the two-year degree standard, both lacked social work degrees.

It may be predicted that the new membership standard in the professional association, if sustained, will have the effect of strengthening the place of casework in professional social work at the expense of other types of practice. The schools of social work under the new standard become the sole channel through which persons may enter the professional association. And the schools have for years invested their major resources in developing competence for the field of casework. The best available index of student specialization in schools of social work is the type of field work students take in their second year. The 1956 figures reveal the following:

TABLE 12. TYPE OF FIELD-WORK PLACEMENT OF SECOND-YEAR
STUDENTS IN SCHOOLS OF SOCIAL WORK AS OF
NOVEMBER 1, 1956

Type of field work	Percentage of students
Casework	86
Group work	10
Community organization	2.5
Administration	.8
Research	.3
Total	100

SOURCE: *Statistics on Social Work Education,* 1956. Council on Social Work Education, 1956.

The new doctoral programs being offered in schools of social work seek to give emphasis to broad social welfare programs as well as to casework, but it is safe to assert that the professional image which the schools both reflect and reinforce puts casework, and as a poor second, group work, at the core of professional social work. Administration, community organization, development of social policy, social insurance, research—these are in danger of becoming even more peripheral to the professional image of social work than they were under the more loosely defined professional associations which existed prior to the establishment of the National Association of Social Workers.

Interprofessional Relations. The drive toward professionalization in social work—reflected in raised training standards, crystallization of the area of competence, and restriction of entry to the professional association—leads social work into hard competition with neighboring occupations.

Social work may be classified roughly in the "human relations" area of occupational specialization. As such, it is among the service occupations, based on wealth and division of labor made possible by advanced industrialization.

All occupations in the human relations field have only tenuous claims to exclusive competence. This results not only from their newness, uncertain standards, and the embryonic state of the social and psychological sciences on which they draw, but also from the fact that the types of problems dealt with are part of everyday living. The lay public cannot recognize the need for special competence in an area where everyone is "expert."

The problem is especially evident in "interpreting" social work to the public. Inability to implant in the public mind and the minds of other professions a clear image of social work is a matter of constant concern to the profession. However, this is a problem shared with sister occupations in the human relations field, resulting predictably from the nature of the task and the as yet modest degree of professionalization.

Social workers concerned about the negative stereotypes of social work held by other groups should note a recent study of interprofessional relations. Zander and others interviewed 156 psychiatrists, 165 clinical psychologists, and 159 psychiatric social workers—all working in teams in larger metropolitan areas. They found that "psychiatrists stereotype their own professional group less favorably than do social workers." And, although social workers describe themselves with many pleasant labels, "they also view themselves as more 'mercenary,' 'condescending,' and 'striving' than do the psychiatrists." Clinical psychologists, it was found, are more critical of their own profession ("dogmatic," "mercenary," "condescending," and "striving") than are either social workers or psychiatrists. Social workers in general display a penchant for public self-criticism and a strong concern about acceptance by other groups—though this is less true of those whose status and professional commitment are unusually high. From this study (especially pp. 72-75) one might hypothesize that the more prestige a profession achieves, and the stronger its inner fraternity, the less it will be concerned about negative public images and the opinions of other professionals.

Social work knowledge and skill are such as to create ambiguity in contacts with related professions. Social work's orientation to psychoanalytic theory was stressed above; from it, serious problems of professional jurisdiction have arisen, because several other professions or would-be professions (analytic psychiatry, the counseling branch of clinical psychology, the several brands of "guidance") have evolved which base their practice on much the same body of theory.

Social work claims distinction from the others on grounds of greater attention to the social environment. The stress on the social is counterposed to preoccupation with intrapsychic phenomena, though as we have suggested, this is played down in practice. Social work claims further distinction by incorporating humanitarian sentiments into its body of technical "principles" ("the right of an individual to fullest expression of his capacities," and so on) —in other words, by a general attempt to wed science to ethics.

In practice, however, the types of problems and clients treated by the several groups are often overlapping, theoretical formulations of diagnosis and treatment may be similar or identical, and certain treatment techniques are used in common. The matter has come to a head in recent years in discussions of such questions as: What is psychotherapy? Who has a right to practice psychotherapy? Is casework a form of it?

The growth of professional social work has taken it into a relationship increasingly typical of modern professional practice—the professional "team." The focus of each discipline on its own technical interests has tended to slice up the client and parcel him out. As the worried medical specialists say, "Who sees the patient as a whole?" By gathering complementary specialists into a team, the stereoscopic view destroyed by specialization can be regained. The hospital team of physician, nurse, and medical social worker is one example; the mental hygiene clinic team of psychiatrist, clinical psychologist, and psychiatric social worker is another. The mutual understanding which such arrangements provide may be needed in other areas, too. Lawyers in child welfare work, for example, have complained of difficulty in working with social workers because of ignorance of the law among the latter. Social workers in turn may feel lawyers are blind to child needs.

The problem of jurisdictional conflict in and out of teams is highlighted by the Zander study of interprofessional relations mentioned above. Analysis shows that these three kinds of specialists agree pretty well about one another's proper functions, but "of the social workers 30% see [interviewing] as a unique ability that they possess, while only 12% of the psychiatrists attribute this skill to them" (p. 59). Social workers seem to feel more secure regarding their jurisdiction over case-history writing and community contact work than when doing diagnosis and therapy, but they are strongly attracted to the latter functions and "many wish they were psychiatrists rather than social workers" (pp. 14, 57, 62). In general, however, though they want more responsibility, the social workers accept their subordinate status. One reason for this is the fact that in this case interprofessional relations are also cross-sex relations with the dominant profession also being dominantly male. (Cf. pp. 117-119). The major cleavage in this trio seems to be between dominant male psychiatrists teamed with female social workers, on the one hand, and subordinate male psychologists, on the other. For instance, skills in psychometrics are seen both by social workers and psychiatrists as "almost the *only* contribution of the clinical psychologists," while fewer than half of the psychologists claim this as a major skill—aspiring instead to therapy, diagnosis, and other tasks (p. 139) .[3]

If in what may be the clearest and most stable working relationship in the mental health field we find unsolved vital issues concerning who should do what, how best to collaborate and maintain professional status, then it is easy to see how in other interprofessional contacts among the human relations professions the cleavages might be deep. Ultimate division of function among occupations in areas such as psychotherapy will be determined, of course, not only by the criterion of technical competence, but also by ability to mobilize public and political support, as illustrated by the already considerable success of the medical profession in achieving legal preemption of the "mental healing arts."

Profession, Agency, Social Movement, and Sex: Role Conflict Among Social Workers. The nature of the area of competence, professional norms governing relations with clients and colleagues, and interprofessional rivalry and collaboration are not the only factors shaping the social worker's behavior on the job. For the social worker is more than a professional: he is, among other things, an agency staff member, a humanitarian, and a representative of his sex, male or female. The interplay between these identities presents the social worker with some dilemmas fateful for the development of both the practice and philosophy of social work.

In this section we will first consider two types of "role conflict" evident in all of social life, and then apply this concept to the situation of the social worker. The aim is to bring together our analysis of agency structure and operation, and social work professionalism.

If Johnny, aged ten, comes upon his father while the latter is telling an off-color joke to adult friends, the father will falter in his tale, display mixed emotions, perhaps fall silent. If a male social worker receives an order from a female supervisor of similar age, he may experience vague discomfort. In the first instance, the behavior appropriate for a father is inconsistent with the behavior appropriate to an adult friend in a peer group; in the second, behavior expected of a subordinate is inconsistent with the behavior typically expected of a man.

Or take examples of a different kind: a family physician who has become Mr. Jones' friendly confidant feels uneasy collecting fees from that same Mr. Jones when the latter is short of cash. A case-work-trained probation officer finds himself torn between behavior expected of a permissive counselor aiming at rehabilitation and the authoritative behavior expected of an officer of the court to keep the "con" in line.

"Role conflict" is the label sociologists use to describe this pervasive phenomenon. It refers to cases in which a person playing a role is obligated to behave (that is, act, think, feel) in incompatible ways simultaneously, all of which ways are defined as proper to the role or roles he is playing. Two types of role conflict are illustrated above: conflict involving (1) two roles in two groups which expect, prefer, or allow contradictory behavior—father versus adult friend, social worker versus male; and (2) one role containing conflicting expectations of behavior—the doctor who must be at once friendly confidant and businesslike fee collector, the probation officer who must be at once permissive and authoritative.

The opportunities for role conflict are many in a complex and changing society. Most behavior is structured in roles—we take the parts of parent, worker, supervisor, theater-goer, guest, stranger, and so on, acting out their rights and obligations. Often behavior called for in one role does not "fit" another. Since we play many roles in continual succession and sometimes simultaneously, and since roles are continually being redefined (note Chapter IV on the search for new identity among women), role conflict pervades our experience.

The person caught in the cross-fire of competing claims typically makes some kind of adjustment: he tries to reshape the role or roles to make the demands compatible; he quits the role; he adapts to the role by playing up one set of obligations, playing down another, and so on. Whatever strategy of adjustment he uses, it is easy to see that these resolutions of role conflict exert a strain toward change in both the person and the groups in which he participates. Here lies the significance of role conflict: if we understand the structured strains in the role of social worker we can better understand the transformations that occur in the worker as he moves through his career and experiences these recurrent dilemmas, as well as the pressure the worker in turn exerts for changes in the welfare organizations in which he works.

The main sources of role conflict among social workers are these sometimes conflicting identities: (1) profession versus agency; (2) social movements and reform groups sustaining humanitarian sentiments versus agency and profession; (3) sex versus agency or profession.

Social work, like every skilled occupation, *develops work standards and other norms which may deviate from those enforced by agencies in which workers are employed.* In school and in the professional association the worker is indoctrinated with these standards, which will include notions about the proper sizes of caseload and groupload, the right to professional supervision, access to consultants (for example, a psychiatrist in a family service agency), the amount of time to be spent on an interview, the number of interviews per day or week, the necessity of private offices for interviewing, confidentiality of case material, the rights of clients (for example, permission must be obtained before speaking to relatives), exclusion from the staff of the professionally untrained, and so on. In varying degrees agencies incorporate professional work standards and norms into their own operating standards. Thus, Simon and others note that the practice of consultation is highly developed and approved by administration in agencies staffed by social workers. Often, however, agencies have operational requirements, set by law, tradition, policy, or public pressures, which depart from professional standards. This is particularly true of public agencies operating within a legal framework, a situation which sets the stage for role conflict.[4]

The administration of public assistance, for instance, presents many points of profession-agency disagreement. The crisis in public assistance after World War II—with legislators, newspapers, and public welfare commissions crying "fraud" and "mollycoddling," while social workers responded, "undermining of professional standards"— hinged on such conflicts. Professional social workers who had hung on in line and administrative positions from the depression thirties considered it good professional casework: (1) to disregard for budgeting purposes some kinds of financial resources (paper-route earnings of a boy in the family, the occasional contributions of an estranged father); and (2) to refuse to impose moral standards as a condition of financial eligibility (overlook expenditure of relief grant for cigarettes or liquor, the presence of a "boy friend"). The public assistance agency manual, however, is explicit: all family income must be deducted from the grant, relief funds may not be spent on beverage alcohol, the birth of a second illegitimate child to an unmarried mother on ADC calls for a review of her moral "suitability" to receive a relief check. The worker is caught between conflicting directives of agency and profession.

In the field of corrections the professional social worker is subjected to even sharper contradictions. Social workers, as Ohlin observes, "have approached correctional problems with a well integrated philosophy and clearly defined casework principles and procedures" which are at variance with traditional correctional practices. The social worker as parole or probation officer expects to have neutral, nonjudgmental relations with a client who has selected the agency and comes motivated for treatment, access to skilled casework supervision, the right to treat the client in accordance with the latter's individual needs, agency protection from the pressures of public opinion in the exercise of professional skills. But, in fact, the typical probationer or parolee has not "selected the agency," is not motivated for treatment, does not recognize that he has problems with which the practitioner can help, and usually refuses proffered assistance. The man who has been promoted to supervisor is not the skilled professional caseworker, but a political appointee or a fellow skilled in public relations or high in seniority, who is very often indifferent or hostile to social work precepts. Far from being able to individualize the client, the worker is bound by "rules of client supervision" which arose historically as a defense for the agency against public criticism of coddling the offender. The parolee must observe a curfew, abstain from drink, avoid old pals, get permission to change jobs or living quarters—and the worker is expected to enforce these rules no matter how they clash with his professional views on proper treatment plans for the client. At almost every point the worker is torn between agency and professional norms.

A second source of role conflict is the *clash between humanitarian values and agency and professional norms.* Many, if not most, social workers are "graduates" of liberal, social-reform movements, and carry with them into school, profession, and agency, identification with such movements, expressed in humanitarian sentiments about how people should be treated. In some agencies and programs, however, humanitarianism is not the controlling philosophy. General relief offices up and down the country are still largely wedded to pauper law principles of harshness and deterrence. The practice of correctional institutions likewise reflects their traditional purposes of punishment and deterrence. In such circumstances the worker will often break agency rules in order to treat the client humanely—the probation officer will knowingly permit infractions of curfew, the relief worker will advise recipients to keep beer bottles (and boy friends) out of sight. But any worker who tries to be a good humanitarian and a good agency representative at the same time is in for torment of conscience.

Humanitarian sentiments clash also with professional norms. This shows up most clearly in the student beginning his professional school training. He comes to school, as cursory examination of applications for admission will show, imbued with a desire "to help people"; and from the school he wants training in the techniques of help. To his distress, however, he soon finds out that clinical therapeusis is expressed in ways quite alien from those suggested by the naive impulse to help. The humanitarian in him would bind the client's wound directly; the professional clinician, he is taught, explores the wound with seeming indifference to the client's pain. The humanitarian would meet the need as expressed; the clinician teaches that expressed needs are rarely the real ones. The humanitarian takes people at face value; the clinician is sure that faces are but masks for deeper drives that must be probed. The humanitarian, feeling that all men are brothers, offers friendship to those he succors; the clinician knows he must maintain social distance from those he would help. Some students are simply unable to reconcile the contradictions, and drop out of school. And the ambivalence of the professional social worker toward participating in social action on the local scene suggests that those who do go on into practice seldom resolve the profession vs. humanitarian conflict completely.

A third area of conflict derives from discrepancies between sex role and agency and professional roles. It is mainly the rank-and-file male social worker and the female supervisor who experience this clash— which helps to explain why men do not long remain in direct service positions, and women are not often assigned to top administrative posts.

Social work jobs for women can be seen as extensions of sex roles derived from norms governing the behavior of wife and mother. As woman she is traditionally expected to provide care to children, the aged, the sick: to be nurturant, gentle, kind, receptive; in short, feminine. As caseworker, though professionalism and agency procedures hold this in check somewhat, she functions in a similar way— as does the nurse or the elementary schoolteacher. So far, there is some, but not much discrepancy between occupational and sex roles. It is when she becomes a supervisor with male subordinates that her troubles may begin. There is a norm still prevalent in American culture which says, "Women should not be in authority over men of roughly the same social class and age." Further, the next step up is likely to be blocked for the female supervisor, because of the notion that women are not good risks for top administration. The rationale goes like this: if they marry, they may quit; if they do not quit, they may have difficulty getting along with their husbands, since it is still thought that women should not exceed their husbands in status and authority. In addition, the active, aggressive entrepreneurial behavior needed to develop professional and community contacts and to gain access to men of power—both essential for agency survival—is often deprecated for women.

For the young male social worker, these same definitions of sex role present an even more poignant problem, at the same time that they spur his upward climb. With the present sex ratio in social work, his supervisors will most often be female; and despite the partial shift toward equality of sexes, most men still feel demeaned and threatened, their self-image wounded, by subordination to women at work. The male social worker is surrounded by many other reminders of the conflict between his sex role and occupational role. Popular stereotypes of the social worker—whether as motherly healer, cold snooper, or Lady Bountiful—are almost exclusively female. In popular literature, the model of the social worker is a flat-heeled female; even in the daily press, personal items about social workers will likely appear on the Woman's Page. The major historical figures that leap to mind —Jane Addams, Mary Richmond—are women; the men are more likely to be remembered as reformers—Charles Loring Brace, Harry Hopkins. There is a noticeable trend in current professional social work literature to use "she" rather than the standard English "he" to refer to a worker of indeterminate sex. In hospital settings—medical and psychiatric—a host of female ancillaries (nurses, nurses' aides, social workers, medical technicians, receptionists) swarm in comfortable, acknowledged subservience around the dominant doctor. The male social worker in such settings is classed with the female helpers rather than with the male doctors, and he may thereby feel his masculinity threatened.

These illustrations are sufficient to indicate the implications of role conflict among social workers. The problems of recruitment to the profession, and staffing of agencies with trained workers, are particularly affected. Conflicts among professional, agency, and humanitarian identities drive social workers to avoid or abandon some important social welfare fields, to loosen connections with the profession, to give less than full allegiance to the agency. Students are baffled or repulsed by the inner contradictions of the roles they are asked to learn. Much-needed recruitment of males to the profession is blocked by the difficulties they face in maintaining a self-respecting sex identity, though at the same time this difficulty may act as a pressure to achieve higher administrative position once they get into social work—which could be one explanation of the skyrocketing careers observers note among young men in this field.

Analysis of the sources and kinds of role conflict, the points in the career pattern where the dilemmas are felt most urgently, and the typical strategies of adjustment by which they are resolved could increase our understanding of the behavior of social workers on the job. More important, such analysis could tell us something about the circumstances under which role conflict adds a bit of needed flexibility, change, and novelty to the profession and when it hinders its proper functions and threatens its future. Thus, the Ohlin group, although they also emphasize the need for further research, on the basis of their study of role conflict among social workers in the correctional field, are able to recommend specific revisions in preparation for the field: (1) recognition of the real divergence of interest between agency and social worker that often exists in the corrections field, and training in how to deal with it; (2) the discovery and teaching of treatment skills which are effective in situations where alternatives are circumscribed (as opposed to the exhortation that "the worker must accept the limitations of the agency"); (3) training in how to deal with the client who has limited capacity for change, or is "not motivated for treatment." Recent contributions to the social work literature on training for correctional work, notably those of Elliot Studt, underscore the importance of Ohlin's observations.

Study of role conflict in settings other than corrections and subsequent planning to reduce the elements of strain in the social worker's role would be worth the effort. It is by no means certain, however, that we would want to eliminate all the conflicts described above even if we could. If the humanitarian sentiments sustained by sex role and reform groups were all eliminated wherever they interfered with rigid adherence to professional and agency standards, and no one ever experienced a second thought about them, the welfare world might be a bleak one indeed.

NOTES

1 But in 1956 a study commission of the Council on Social Work Education (the accrediting body for schools of social work) made the drastic recommendation that "there should be no accrediting of any specializations by any definition." If this aim is achieved, the psychiatric tag is likely to lose its value.

2 The National Association of Social Workers has recently declared it "strongly opposes vocationally oriented undergraduate programs" of social work education.

3 This looks very much like one of the classical games of social life — a very big and powerful unit (psychiatrist) and a very small unit (psychiatric social worker) ganging up on a third, medium-sized unit (clinical psychologist) which the established power sees as an aggressor. One can find this phenomenon in jurisdictional conflicts among siblings, unions, nations, and other social units. (Cf. 51.)

4 The discrepancy between professional and agency norms stems from a basic conflict in principles of organization which appears in all bureaucratic systems—in factories (with engineers, accountants, personnel managers), in universities (with faculty, nonacademic administrators, and the like), in hospitals (with doctors, technicians, nurses). In all of these organizations, different professional groups are arranged in a hierarchy. Thus, the *colleague principle* (a group whose members have *similar* technical training and occupational position, common professional norms developed by training and initiation, and who are formally equal) is in conflict with the *hierarchical principle* of the bureaucracy (a group whose members have *dissimilar* training and position, are formally *unequal*, and who in on-the-job training and indoctrination develop common *organizational* norms.) Macmahon and others in a chapter entitled "Rival Claims of Hierarchy and Specialty" in their study of the WPA, give a detailed account of how professional specialists in education, art, and construction engineering fought with the line command of the hierarchy for control of the work relief programs for unemployed professionals.

SECTION II

Culture: Background for Behavior

INTRODUCTION

Although the life cycle of all men is similar, one readily observes great diversity in the way they deal with their problems. To begin with, no other living creature is so widely dispersed over the face of the earth. This dispersal is not based on substantial human anatomical differences, but on adaptations in the way of life of differing groups of men. Lest we jump to the conclusion that human variation is a product of necessity, we should bear in mind that such variation is to be found even in neighboring societies living under identical conditions.

Human food habits can well illustrate many characteristics of culture. All humans must eat to survive, yet the Eskimo's diet was fish and meat while the Mexican Indian still eats cereals and vegetables. Milk is a delicacy in parts of East Africa, but considered poisonous in West Africa. The Eskimo would not eat meat and fish at the same meal, while the Jew would not eat meat and milk together. Recent disclosures of irregularities in a New York meat packing corporation caused revulsion, not because the meat was tainted, but because it was kangaroo and horsemeat instead of beef. One man's meat is literally another man's poison. While dire necessity may often drive men to eat anything, given some option, mankind is very choosy about what is considered food. In addition, we have elaborate and differing procedures for preparing food, actually eating and determining when and with whom we eat. It should be quite clear that these components are not necessary responses to the physical need to ingest food for sustenance.

What is true for eating habits is also obvious with regard to clothing. One is hard pressed to identify human clothing with purely utilitarian functions. The richly ornamented native of the tropics is hardly trying to protect himself from the elements. One must also doubt the extent to which the mini-skirted coed on a freezing winter day has utilitarian thoughts in mind. Similar observation of human sexual behavior makes it clear that a great deal of preference and elaboration occurs which is unrelated to actual physical drives.

The Elements of Culture and Social Control

To understand the richness of human variation we should therefore look more to social learning than response to necessity. Man does learn more of his behavior than does any other animal. Such learning takes place in groups from the very moment of birth and we should not be surprised to find that each society, in teaching its young, imparts modes of behavior peculiar to itself. It is these learned distinctive modes of behavior, shared within one's society, which we refer to as culture. Whether we conceive of man as subject to drives or instincts or not, it is clear that there is a cultural overlay which so insulates the individual from the "natural" environment that it might be seen as all but superseded by a man-made social environment.

The patterns of behavior in each society's culture are not only those to which all members are expected to adhere. Every society has forms of behavior which apply to all members as well as those reserved for particular members in given situations. Thus, if you found a blue-collar worker in your friendly neighborhood tavern enjoying a beer, you would probably think nothing of it. However, if you found your clergyman at the same pursuit, you might wonder.

Any examination of culture must consider both overt aspects known to the participants, as well as covert ones revealed only through careful investigation of "the manifest and latent functions."[1] Further, culture content involves the ideal as well as the actual behavior of the society. In all groups we find some discrepancies between the stated beliefs and principles, and some aspects of day-to-day practices of the members. This means that one cannot fully understand a society either from its laws or its prisons. When a society is experiencing rapid social change, the discrepancy between ideals and actual behavior is greatest. Even in such a society, both of these are important, if only to understand what its members are likely to feel guilty about.

Finally, not all forms of behavior are of equal significance to society. There are some forms of behavior which are usual among "proper" members, yet deviation from these norms is not taken too seriously. Often the original significance has long been obscured. At most, too many such deviations lead others to feel that the individual is not polite, well-mannered, or "cultured" in the sense of refined. Most of the etiquette of our society tends to fall into this category and violations of this order usually mark the outsider who is unfamiliar with the life of the group.

Much more serious are those norms which the society takes to be associated with its morals and perhaps even its well-being as a society. These one violates only at his own risk for the reaction to such threats is bound to be severe. It may take the form of ostracism or "shunning," or physical attack like "tarring and feathering," or even lynching. Sumner referred to norms of the first of these categories as folkways and to the latter as mores.[2]

In more complex societies, certain mores are incorporated into a body of law written or oral, which comes to be formally institutionalized. There are designated officials to whom the society delegates enforcement powers and prescribed punishments for various violations. Unless there is substantial consensus regarding the mores upon which the laws are based, enforcement becomes highly problematic. Such was the case with prohibition in the United States. This may be involved in the difficulties of legislating modifications in race relations as well as racially differing crime rates in cities today. The average American is often faced with the problem of ambivalence in seeking to observe a law which may not reflect his personal values. This occurs either because the law is based on mores which have changed or because our multi-cultured society contains population segments with divergent mores.

In many industrial countries today, our own included, there is considerable resentment toward both law and those who are designated to enforce it. There is widespread belief that law is not legislated on behalf of all nor enforced with equity. Even in democratic societies, bodies of law are thus construed, especially by the young, as a repressive imposition by a small group upon an unwilling society. Anarchy seems never to have been so appealing a philosophy. It is true that one finds a wide range of freedom and constraint as he examines the cultural norms of various societies, some societies being extremely repressive of individual freedom of action. At the same time it is valuable to keep in mind that the traditional folksociety, not industrial society, is most likely to be intolerant of deviation from social norms. Traditional societies were not only too homogeneous to allow for much variation, they were also too small to provide either sheltering mass anonymity or the possibility of finding a minority of kindred maverick spirits. This is one of the features which excites Glazer and Moynihan about New York City life.[3]

At any rate, society ultimately depends upon a certain relinquishing of autonomy by its individual participants, without which it would lack the necessary cohesion to develop a sense of belonging. This is true of any human group regardless of size. Without this we could speak of no social norms, expectations or roles. One would never know how to react to his surroundings or those with whom he shares them. For the benefits derived from participation in society, man has sacrificed, albeit grudgingly, a degree of self-determination. In modern society the sacrifice is perhaps no greater than before and conformity is really promoted by technology more than by force, although the force is potentially present. However, not everyone feels that he is getting a fair return for his sacrifice (obviously, not everyone is). Others react in frustration to the realization that they are conforming for the carrot on the stick, and like it in spite of themselves.

SYMBOLISM

The capacity of man for learning is related to his unique ability to create and manipulate symbols.[4] While the learning and interpretation of signs requires concrete, first-hand experience, symbolism enables man to deal vicariously with abstractions beyond his immediate experience. Spoken and then written language was one of his early and most widespread achievements, but other symbolic forms for communicating ideas such as musical notation, art and the language of mathematics, are well known. Man can take the shapes RED, assign to them a sound and assign to this sound a range of meanings. At different times this symbol stands for a color, an economic system, a member of a political movement, danger, anger, a house of ill repute, all without any inherent meaning to the shape of the markings. Man's propensity for symbols has enabled his imagination to span distance and time. But for this capacity, each generation would expend its effort in rediscovering the wheel instead of building upon the experiences of its predecessors. Therefore, man's unique advantage in being able to experience vicariously enables him to constantly advance his store of experiences. However, it makes him all the more dependent on learned culture, rather than instinct, in leading his life.

TRANSMITTING CULTURE

Human societies are greatly concerned, not only with the production of subsequent replacement generations to continue the species, but also with the transmission of their culture heritages from one generation to the next. The process by which this is achieved is termed socialization. Every society has institutions which serve to educate the young into the ways of the group. In preliterate societies, these arrangements are informal since such societies tend not to have specialized division of labor. The task is vested in the family, as well as others with whom the child is in contact such as peers, neighbors and extended family members. In our society the task of socialization is also shared by other specialized institutions like education, government and religion, and by such innovations as community centers, commercial recreation and the mass media. The degree to which the latter preempts the socializing role of the family and education should not be underestimated. The media have a profound effect directly on the young and indirectly by influencing adult thinking on how the young should be reared.

We should not simply equate socialization with education in the sense of acquiring a body of knowledge, although that is a part of it. Socialization involves the internalization of attitudes and beliefs held in common with other members of the group. So deeply does this run that the individual not only learns to accommodate to living as a member of society, but finds it uncomfortable or unpleasant to do otherwise.

From early childhood, our deepest pleasures or displeasures are those we experience in the company of others. Socialization is made possible through the conditioning of the individual to people and their expectations. These people first involve the parents, then siblings and other individuals in his community to whom he must adjust, such as peers. From the reactions by these "significant others" to him and his actions, the individual learns the role behavior which evokes approval or disapproval from those around him.[5] So intense are these experiences that it has been suggested that the attitudes so learned become an integral part of the individual's personality, shaping his social self and forming the basic pattern upon which he builds all further social roles. From them he learns the expectations others have and those he may have in the society.

Interestingly, although concerned with personality development, Freud's attention to larger social processes has only limited value. Freud tended to emphasize the significance of interpersonal relationships in the nuclear family during infancy and early childhood.[6] This limited view circumscribed the scope of earlier Freudian thinking on socialization. However, many of the "neo-Freudian" psychoanalysts express much more interest in additional relationships which occur in all societies, as well as development of the personality past early childhood.[7] Clearly, socialization is a life-long process. One gets his first insights into how a father relates to his children, as a child on the lap of his own father. However, the child's impression of what it means is only completed when he himself is called upon to actually fulfill the reciprocal position. Then he draws, not only on emotions and memory, but on his judgment, capacity and the example of other fathers — peers among the members of the society. The same is true throughout the various stages of the life cycle.

THE QUESTION OF MODAL PERSONALITY

Everything that has been said thus far regarding group culture and socialization suggests that when an individual is born he has no possibility of making choices or acting in ways which run counter to the values or norms of his society. This line of thinking gave rise to the concept of "National Character" or "Modal Personality." "To what extent do the patterned conditions of life in a particular society give rise to certain distinctive patterns in the personalities of its members? To what extent, that is, does the socio-cultural system produce its distinctive forms of 'social character,' 'basic personality structure' or 'modal personality'?"[8] Many behavioral scientists have found the idea attractive.[9] After all, if the culture provides the rules for reinforcing or extinguishing attitudes and behavior, and the techniques of socializations are so overwhelming, why can't we speak of the Russian personality, the American personality or, in complex societies, even the personality types of various subcultural groups? The obvious problem with this approach is that it is only an intellectual hairsbreadth away from group stereotyping of the most dangerous order. Somewhat more subtle are the implications of this doctrine for individuality and individual differences. One finds a strong trend toward acceptance of the concept of modal personality from the 1930's to the 1950's. There was growing criticism of the approach in the later 1950's and by the '60's many were having second thoughts and backing off.[10]

Inability to resolve the question of the precise relation of socio-cultural factors to personality development reflects the interaction of multiple factors in shaping personality. The individual personality is, after all, a product of genetic, physiological, cultural and idiosyncratic experiences. To isolate one or another factor in a complex interrelated system is generally a futile task, although in specific cases, one can point to the dominance of one influence. Barnouw has criticized earlier anthropologists who have overlooked individual variations in the search for group patterns.[11] Multiple causation more than any other view explains the objective observation that as one gets to know any group, he begins to perceive the members as individuals with their own characteristics and not just die cast duplicates. In the most conformist of societies, one finds these differences.

Failure of individuals to make the cultural values a part of their lives, leads to their own and/or their group's distress. In the extreme, such variation is seen by the society as deviant behavior. Such a breakdown in cultural continuity may stem from failure to adequately inculcate the values acceptable to the society because the parents themselves don't adhere to the values or are inadequate in communicating them. However, it may also be related to some shortcoming in the child or the values themselves, in light of changing societal demands. Behind each of these inadequacies may be any combination of genetic, physiological, socio-cultural or idiosyncratic problem.

CULTURAL RELATIVITY AND TRANSMISSION OF CULTURE

Socialization of the child in all societies has been conducted under the protective atmosphere of ethnocentricism which generally marks human groups. Such ethnocentricism permits the group to transmit its norms as though they were either the only possibilities or at least the best of all known possibilities. This was facilitated by the fact that one knew better and emotionally felt more comfortable with the ways of his own people than anyone else's. Doing things in a different way automatically marked the other group, not only as outsiders or strangers but as savages and barbarous as well. Ethnocentricism has been an element in the promotion of social cohesion in human society although it has its potential shortcomings, discouraging larger unities. Individual allegiance can be readily maintained to a system believed to be plainly superior to all others.

In the West, an awareness of the relative nature of culture is actually a very recent social phenomenon. True, returning travelers to exotic places would amuse their compatriots with tales of the wondrous life and strange customs of people from different groups. However, these tales tended to retain their mythical quality so that their full implications were not likely to be considered. Anthropologists began to explore cross-culturally under the protection of an evolutionary doctrine which allowed them ethnocentrically to assign highest placement to the technologically advanced Western world. Only recently have we realized that the Aborigines' society has been evolving about as long as ours, only theirs took a different turn.

Modern communications and transportation have no doubt made ethnocentricism less tenable for many who are thus left at loose ends. This occurs in developing nations suddenly exposed to Western societies and their advanced technology. It also happens to our own society. Examples of cross-cultural borrowing may be seen in the recent adoption of self-immolation as a form of social protest. To the Buddhist, with his belief in successive reincarnation, the same act has very different significance than it does to a Westerner, yet some have learned it nonetheless. On the other side, the machete, a product of Western technology, was introduced into societies in underdeveloped countries around the world. In each country, the first use it was applied to was simply an improvement of the same kind of tasks already known in the culture. Only later, when forced by innovation brought on by the small change, did the basic tasks begin to reflect a new technology.

These illustrations point up the "structural-functional" interrelatedness of the various elements of society's institutions and its culture. In recent years, quest for these underlying patterns of relatedness has largely replaced the often frustrating speculation about the origins of social institutions on the part of American social scientists. This interrelatedness explains why change in any element of the way of life of the group, through cross-cultural contact or internal innovation, has profound significance for other aspects of culture. Often, exposure to such conditions of change or cross-cultural contact gives rise to a condition of "culture shock."

Implications for Social Work

Our discussion of the nature of culture, its transmission and its relation to the individual personality, is very significant for the social worker. The professional's ability to help depends on a rational, sophisticated insight into his client's condition, self-awareness, and a conscious use of self. Our society is one of involved complexity. The cultural factors provide more than the usual background influences on behavior, they often play a disruptive role in behavior. Individuals are exposed to the conflicting and competing values of many sub-cultures in a society experiencing a technological revolution. Inadequate socialization is at the heart of much family conflict and social deviance. Cross-cultural contact between ethnocentric groups thrown together in our cities is at the heart of much unrest. Culture shock among migrants is still a part of our society, while behind it all, the need to absorb changing technology and related values leaves us all groping without experience.

In such a society, a social worker can do little to help without seeking to assess the socio-cultural elements in his clients' background. Of at least equal importance is his own cultural background. It is quite usual for the worker and the client to bring many divergent views to their encounter. Whether these originate in class, religious or ethnic difference, urban vs. rural orientation, or age differentials, to cite but a few, the worker must be prepared for his own, often unconscious, distortions. Rosenthal and Jacobson's research on the effect of expectations on subject performance is highly pertinent here.[12] This distortion can occur at times in subtle, unexpected ways. A liberal worker might identify with the views of a youngster acting out against authority figures in his home or school. The acculturated worker of any ethnic background might find it difficult to work sympathetically in a strongly identified ethnic neighborhood. The worker's own family experiences might lead him to approve of very different relations between spouses than the ones he finds, or conversely to be reluctant about any judgment at all. The examples that can be cited are many. Suffice it to say that the profession is learning to take with increasing seriousness the cultural elements in any case diagnosis.

The sociologist or anthropologist must train himself to be objectively neutral regarding the societies he studies. The participants, of course, should not, indeed cannot, be objective about their own society and its culture. The social worker is faced with a paradox. To help, he must retain his objectivity. Yet to be neutrally aloof denies his own participantship in society and may even curtail his effectiveness with clients. Historically, social work has tended to see the role of the worker as an enabler in a process of self-determination, thus avoiding the dilemma head-on. Since this is now clearly an issue regarding social work intervention with individuals, groups and communities, the profession is engaged in a new, hard reexamination of this professional model.

NOTES

[1]For full discussion of the concept, see Robert Merton, "Manifest and Latent Functions," in *Social Theory and Social Structure*. New York: Free Press of Glencoe, 1957, pp. 19-84.

[2]William Graham Sumner, *Folkways*. Boston: Ginn, 1906.

[3]Nathan Glazer and Daniel Patrick Moynihan, *Beyond the Melting Pot*. Cambridge: MIT Press and Harvard University Press, 1963.

[4]Leslie A. White, "The Symbol: The Origin and Basis of Human Behavior," in *The Science of Culture*. N. Y.: Grove Press, 1949, pp. 22-39.

[5]George H. Mead, *Mind, Self and Society*. Chicago: University of Chicago Press, 1934, pp. 253-257.

[6]Freud's stress on the parent-child relationship is seen in his *Outline of Psychoanalysis*. (1940).

[7]See the work of Harry Stack Sullivan, Abram Kardiner, Erik H. Erikson and Karen Horney, each of which has a wider focus than the immediate family alone.

[8]Alex Inkeles and Daniel J. Levinson, "National Character: The Study of Modal Personality and Sociocultural Systems," in *The Handbook of Social Psychology*. 2nd ed., Vol. IV, ed. Gardner Lindzey and Elliot Aronson. Reading, Mass.: Addison-Wesley Publishing Co., 1969, p. 418.

[9]*Ibid.*, p. 419.

[10]See Y. Cohen, *Social Structure and Personality*. New York: Holt, 1961; F. L. K. Hsu, ed., *Psychological Anthropology: Approaches to Culture and Personality*. Homewood, Ill.: Dorsey Press, 1961; and B. Kaplan, *Studying Personality Cross-Culturally*. Evanston, Ill.: Row, Peterson, 1961.

[11]See Victor Barnouw, *Culture and Personality*. Homewood, Ill.: Dorsey Press, 1963, pp. 85-86.

[12]Robert Rosenthal and Lenore Jacobson, "Self Fulfilling Prophecies in the Classroom: Teachers' Expectations as Unintended Determinants of Pupils' Intellectual Competence," in *Social Class, Race and Psychological Development*. ed. Martin Deutsch, Irwin Katz and Arthur Jensen. New York: Holt, Rinehart, Winston, Inc., 1968.

MIRROR FOR MAN

CLYDE KLUCKHOHN

What good is the concept of culture so far as the contemporary world is concerned? What can you do with it?

Its use lies first in the aid the concept gives to man's endless quest to understand himself and his own behavior. For example, this new idea turns into pseudo problems some of the questions asked by one of the most learned and acute thinkers of our age, Reinhold Niebuhr. In his recent book *The Nature and Destiny of Man* Niebuhr argues that the universally human sense of guilt or shame and man's capacity for self-judgment necessitate the assumption of supernatural forces. These facts are susceptible of self-consistent and relatively simple explanation in purely naturalistic terms through the concept of culture. Social life among human beings never occurs without a system of conventional understandings which are transmitted more or less intact from generation to generation. Every individual is familiar with some of these and they constitute a set of standards against which he judges himself. To the extent that he fails to conform he experiences discomfort because his childhood training put great pressure on him to follow the accepted pattern, and his now unconscious tendency is to associate deviation with punishment or withdrawal of love and protection. This and other issues which have puzzled philosophers and scientists for so long become understandable through this fresh concept.

The principal claim which can be made for the culture concept as an aid to useful action is that it helps us enormously toward predicting human behavior. One of the factors limiting the success of such prediction thus far has been the naive assumption of a minutely homogeneous "human nature." In the framework of this assumption all human thinking proceeds from the same premises; all human beings are motivated by the same needs and goals. In the cultural framework we see that, while the ultimate logic of all peoples may be the same (and thus communication and understanding are possible), the thought processes depart from radically different premises—especially unconscious or unstated premises. Those who have the cultural outlook are more likely to look beneath the surface and bring the culturally determined premises to the light of day. This may not bring about immediate agreement and harmony, but it will at least facilitate a *more* rational approach to the problem of international understanding and to diminishing friction between groups within a nation.

Knowledge of a culture makes it possible to predict a good many of the actions of any person who shares that culture. If the American Army was dropping paratroopers in Thailand in 1944, under what circumstances would they be knifed, under what circumstances would they be aided? If one knows how a given culture defines a certain situation, one can say that the betting odds are excellent that in a future comparable situation people will behave along certain lines and not along others. If we know a culture, we know what various classes of individuals within it expect from each other—and from outsiders of various categories. We know what types of activity are held to be inherently gratifying.

Many people in our society feel that the best way to get people to work harder is to increase their profits or their wages. They feel that it is just "human nature" to want to increase one's material possessions. This sort of dogma might well go unchallenged if we had no knowledge of other cultures. In certain societies, however, it has been found that the profit motive is not an effective incentive. After contact with whites the Trobriand Islanders in Melanesia could have become fabulously rich from pearl diving. They would, however, work only long enough to satisfy their immediate wants.

Administrators need to become conscious of the symbolic nature of many activities. American women will choose a job as hostess in a restaurant rather than one as waitress at a higher salary. In some societies the blacksmith is the most honored of individuals while in others only the lowest class of people are blacksmiths. White children in schools are motivated by grades; but children from some Indian tribe will work less hard under a system that singles the individual out from among his fellows.

Understanding of culture provides some detachment from the conscious and unconscious emotional values of one's own culture. The phrase, "some detachment," must be emphasized, however. An individual who viewed the designs for living of his group with complete detachment would be disoriented and unhappy. But I can prefer (*i.e.,* feel affectively attached to) American manners while at the same time perceiving certain graces in English manners which are lacking or more grossly expressed in ours. Thus, while unwilling to forget that I am an American with no desire to ape English drawing-room behavior, I can still derive a lively pleasure from association with English people on social occasions. Whereas if I have no detachment, if I am utterly provincial, I am likely to regard English manners as utterly ridiculous, uncouth, perhaps even immoral. With that attitude I shall certainly not get on well with the English, and I am likely to resent bitterly any modification of our manners in the English or any other direction. Such attitudes clearly do not make for international understanding, friendship, and cooperation. They do, to the same extent, make for a too rigid social structure. Anthropological documents and anthropological teachings are valuable, therefore, in that they tend to emancipate individuals from a too strong allegiance to every item in the cultural inventory. The person who has been exposed to the anthropological perspective is more likely to live and let live both within his own society and in his dealings with members of other societies; and he will probably be more flexible in regard to needful changes in social organization to meet changed technology and changed economy.

Perhaps the most important implication of culture for action is the profound truth that you can never start with a clean slate so far as human beings are concerned. Every person is born into a world defined by already existing culture patterns. Just as an individual who has lost his memory is no longer normal so the idea of a society's becoming completely emancipated from its past culture is inconceivable. This is one source of the tragic failure of the Weimar constitution in Germany. In the abstract it was an admirable document. But it failed miserably in actual life partly because it provided for no continuity with existent designs for acting, feeling, and thinking.

Since every culture has organization as well as content, administrators and lawmakers should know that one cannot isolate a custom to abolish or modify it. The most obvious example of failure caused by neglect of this principle was the Eighteenth Amendment. The legal sale of liquor was forbidden, but the repercussions in law enforcement, in family life, in politics, in the economy were staggering.

The concept of culture, like any other piece of knowledge, can be abused and misinterpreted. Some fear that the principle of cultural relativity will weaken morality. "If the Bugabuga do it why can't we? It's all relative anyway." But this is exactly what cultural relativity does *not* mean.

The principle of cultural relativity does not mean that because the members of some savage tribe are allowed to behave in a certain way that this fact gives intellectual warrant for such behavior in all groups. Cultural relativity means, on the contrary, that the appropriateness of any positive or negative custom must be evaluated with regard to how this habit fits with other group habits. Having several wives makes economic sense among herders, not among hunters. While breeding a healthy skepticism as to the eternity of any value prized by a particular people, anthropology does not as a matter of theory deny the existence of moral absolutes. Rather, the use of the comparative method provides a scientific means of discovering such absolutes. If all surviving societies have found it necessary to impose some of the same restrictions upon the behavior of their members, this makes a strong argument that these aspects of the moral code are indispensable.

Similarly, the fact that a Kwakiutl chief talks as if he had delusions of grandeur and of persecution does not mean that paranoia is not a real ailment in our cultural context. Anthropology has given a new perspective to the relativity of the normal that should bring greater tolerance and understanding of socially harmless deviations. But it has by no means destroyed standards or the useful tyranny of the normal. All cultures recognize some of the same forms of behavior as pathological. Where they differ in their distinctions, there is a relationship to the total framework of cultural life.

There is a legitimate objection to making culture explain too much. Lurking, however, in such criticism of the cultural point of view is often the ridiculous assumption that one must be loyal to a single master explanatory principle. On the contrary, there is no incompatibility between biological, environmental, cultural, historical, and economical approaches. All are necessary. The anthropologist feels that so much of history as is still a living force is embodied in the culture. He regards the economy as a specialized part of the culture. But he sees the value in having economists and historians, as specialists, abstract out their special aspects—so long as the complete context is not entirely lost to view. Take the problems of the American South, for example. The anthropologist would entirely agree that biological (social visibility of black skin, etc.), environmental (water power and other natural resources), historical (South settled by certain types of people, somewhat different governmental practices from the start, etc.), and narrowly cultural (original discrimination against Negroes as "heathen savages," etc.) issues are all inextricably involved. However, the cultural factor is involved in the actual working out of each influence—though culture is definitely not the whole of it. And to say that certain acts are culturally defined does not always and necessarily mean that they could be eliminated by changing the culture.

The needs and drives of biological man, and the physical environment to which he must adjust, provide the stuff of human life, but given culture determines the way this stuff is handled—the tailoring. In the eighteenth century a Neapolitan philosopher, Vico, uttered a profundity which was new, violent—and unnoticed. This was simply the discovery that "the social world is surely the work of man." Two generations of anthropologists have compelled thinkers to face this fact. Nor are anthropologists willing to allow the Marxists or other cultural determinists to make of culture another absolute as autocratic as the God or Fate portrayed by some philosophies. Anthropological knowledge does not permit so easy an evasion of man's responsibility for his own destiny. To be sure, culture is a compulsive force to most of us most of the time. To some extent, as Leslie White says, "Culture has a life and laws of its own." Some cultural changes are also compelled by economic or physical circumstances. But most of an economy is itself a cultural artifact. And it is men who change their cultures, even if—during most of past history—they have been acting as instruments of cultural processes of which they were largely unaware. The record shows that, while situation limits the range of possibility, there is always more than one workable alternative. The essence of the cultural process is selectivity; men may often make a choice. Lawrence Frank probably overstates the case:

> In the years to come it is possible that this discovery of the human origin and development of culture will be recognized as the greatest of all discoveries, since heretofore man has been helpless before these cultural and social formulations which generation after generation have perpetuated the same frustration and defeat of human values and aspirations. So long as he believed this was necessary and inevitable, he could not but accept this lot with resignation. Now man is beginning to realize that his culture and social organization are not unchanged

cosmic processes, but are human creations which may be altered. For those who cherish the democratic faith this discovery means that they can, and must, undertake a continuing assay of our culture and our society in terms of its consequences for human life and human values. This is the historic origin and purpose of human culture, to create a human way of life. To our age falls the responsibility of utilizing the amazing new resources of science to meet these cultural tasks, to continue the great human tradition of man taking charge of his own destiny.

Nevertheless, to the extent that human beings discover the nature of the cultural process, they can anticipate, prepare, and—to at least a limited degree—control.

Americans are now at a period in history when they are faced with the facts of cultural differences more clearly than they can take with comfort. Recognition and tolerance of the deeper cultural assumptions of China, Russia, and Britain will require a difficult type of education. But the great lesson of culture is that the goals toward which men strive and fight and grope are not "given" in final form by biology nor yet entirely by the situation. If we understand our own culture and that of others, the political climate can be changed in a surprisingly short time in this narrow contemporary world providing men are wise enough and articulate enough and energetic enough. The concept of culture carries a legitimate note of hope to troubled men. If the German and Japanese peoples behaved as they did because of their biological heredity, the outlook for restoring them as peaceful and cooperative nations would be hopeless. But if their propensities for cruelty and aggrandizement were primarily the result of situational factors and their cultures, then something can be done about it, though false hopes must not be encouraged as to the speed with which a culture can be planfully changed.

THE SELF AND THE OTHER:
AN EMERGING FIELD OF SOCIAL PROBLEMS

FRANCIS E. MERRILL

This paper will explore some of the further implications of a shift in social problems resulting from recent changes in the social climate. An earlier paper examined some of the general relationships between social character and social problems and suggested that many traditional problems are on the way to amelioration and eventual solution. Among these problems are illiteracy, poverty, child labor, unemployment, undernourishment, old-age insecurity, infant mortality, endemic disease, and similar difficulties which have recently come within the purview of democratic government. These situations are by no means completely eliminated in the United States, much less in the underdeveloped parts of the world. But the technical knowledge and productive capacity to deal constructively with them are part of the heritage of modern democratic societies.

In place of these former concerns, a new type of problem situation has emerged, which likewise reflects a particular sociocultural climate with its own values and norms. This is the growing preoccupation with what might be called "self-other" problems, in which individuals and groups are concerned with interpersonal relationships in general and those involving the self and the other (s) in particular. Central to this preoccupation is the social self, as the product of the perceived and imagined appraisals of others. The investigation of the social self was pioneered by Baldwin, Cooley, and Dewey and given a systematic theoretical structure by Mead. Harry Stack Sullivan further developed this approach and made it the center of his conceptual system and therapeutic technique. In the present context, however, the self-other approach is applied to social problems, rather than to psychotherapy.

Reprinted from *Social Problems*, Vol. 4, No. 3, January, 1957, pp. 200-207, by permission of the Society for the Study of Social Problems and the author.

A social problem involves a situation, a value, and social action. The action is intended to alleviate or eliminate the situation and thereby enhance the value. Problems of the self and the other (s) are as crucial as they are intangible. Status is as important as material comfort and the deprivation of status as devastating as hunger. Technological and industrial development may eventually solve such problems as unemployment, but, for example, self-other problems of prejudice remain. Basic anxiety is the heritage of the new social climate, and the attempt to minimize this anxiety motivates social action. The latter ranges from informal efforts to win friends and influence people to formal attempts to understand small-group interaction.

THE SOCIAL SELF

The social self has been called "a subject which is its own object." Each person loves himself, hates himself, praises himself, blames himself, and punishes himself. Both the subject and the object of these verbs are the self. Motivation for this action is in large part derived from others, as each projects himself into the minds of others and takes their role toward himself. The social self thus arises in interaction with others, as the individual looks at himself through others' eyes. He feels happy or sad as he evokes praise or blame from those whose roles he takes in his imagination. In so doing, he develops self-attitudes, which range from blissful self-love to extreme self-denigration. The sources of these attitudes are the "significant others" in his environment, whose opinions about him matter very much.

The social self has been viewed in terms of the pronouns "I" and "me." The former is the subject of the self-attitudes, the latter their object. The "I" is the active part of the self, whereas the "me" reflects the attitudes of others. These elements are in constant interaction and give rise to what Sullivan has termed the "good-me" and the "bad-me." The former is the part of the self which reflects affection, tenderness, and generally pleasant treatment from others. The latter reflects dissatisfaction and anxiety arising from lack of affection and approval by the "significant others." People try to avoid thinking and talking about the "bad-me," because it makes them anxious and unhappy to do so. They prefer to think about the "good-me," because this gives them pleasure and generally enhances their self-feeling.

Both the "good-me" and the "bad-me" reflect the actual or imputed judgments of others. The nature of the social self therefore predisposes the person to a concern with these "reflected appraisals." In Mead's words: "The individual . . . enters his own experience as a self or individual . . . only insofar as he first becomes an object to himself . . . and he becomes an object to himself only by taking the attitudes of other individuals toward himself within a social environment . . . in which both he and they are involved."[1]

Under these conditions, the individual tries to maximize the "good-me" and minimize the "bad-me." Comparative inability to reach this goal, together with anxiety concerning the judgments of others, generates social problems of the self-other type. The individual does not receive as much love, affection, understanding, acceptance, or status as he has learned to expect. He desires more of these intangible but vital values so that he may incorporate them into his social self. He is somewhat like Arnold W. Green's unhappy middle-class male child, who has been reared in an atmosphere of comforting security and (sometimes) suffocating affection and is thenceforth unable to recapture this infantile paradise. Self-other problems are thus literally *social* problems, rather than economic, political, or moral problems. As people "take each other into account" and view themselves through the eyes of others, they are acting in a specifically social fashion.

SOCIAL STRUCTURE AND SELF-OTHER PROBLEMS

Social problems reflect social structure. As the patterned behavior of society has changed, the problems have changed accordingly, albeit with a time lag. Some of the traditional social problems reflected an economy of scarcity, in which technological knowledge, productive capacity, and distributive organization were inadequate. As suggested elsewhere, many of those problems are giving way before expanding industrial facilities. Other traditional social problems involved conflicts in social values. The way of life of the Old South incorporates values which are not the same as those of the American creed. Similarly, value conflicts are at the heart of such problems as child labor, slum clearance, sexual laxity, and divorce.

Each society has its own structure and its own accompanying problems. The present article suggests that social problems of the self-other type are emerging as increasingly important in American society. Among the structural factors responsible for this trend are the following:

Achieved status. The emphasis in our society upon achieved, as contrasted to ascribed, status needs no documentation. In an earlier day, achievement was gained by physical activity, whether clearing a wilderness, building a factory, or constructing a railroad. Although these activities actually required cooperation with others, the individual could entertain the illusion that he was acting as an independent and self-sufficient individual. Under present conditions, this illusion is no longer possible. In the bureaucratic structure of the large corporation, each man is at the mercy of his fellows, a fact of which he is acutely aware. From the moment he enters the bank, the railroad, or the plant, the aspiring young man is constantly taking the roles of others and viewing himself through their eyes.

Social mobility. In his movements up (or down) the status ladder, the individual is continually conscious of the attitudes of others toward himself. The "empathic responses" are at a premium, and the person who is deficient in the ability to take the role of the other is at a disadvantage. Both those going up and those going down derive their self-attitudes from the reflected appraisals of others. These self-attitudes tend to determine their attitudes toward the world in general. In their study of intolerance among veterans of World War II, Bruno Bettelheim and Morris Janowitz discovered that men who were losing status were much more prejudiced than those who were either gaining status or staying in the same place.

Competition. In societies which emphasize peaceful cooperation, the individul is presumably not so aware of other selves in opposition to himself. But the pervasive emphasis in our society upon competition for scarce goals means that self-appraisal is dependent upon competitive success, which in turn directly affects the attitudes of others. Money is the most important of these goals, and the status of the breadwinner is dependent upon his skill and acumen in this respect. Individuals also compete for status, love, and prestige, which can be gained only from others. Attitudes of others toward the self thus enter into many relationships which are arranged by custom in other societies. Manipulation of others is another element in competitive interaction, and here again each person is made aware of other selves and his own in relation to them. He must take others consciously into account, which increases his awareness of self-other relationships. The more bitter the competition, the more aware he is.

Class differentials. In their study of communication differences between classes, Leonard Schatzman and Anselm Strauss found that the lower class showed a deficiency in the ability to take the role of the other. Persons on this social level communicated with others in terms interesting and significant only to themselves, rather than to their listeners, who were middle-class. In another study, class differences appeared in the tendency to blame, censure, and otherwise act aggressively toward the self. Middle-class persons indicated a strong degree of self-aggression, which appeared as self-discipline, self-blame, and even self-hatred. In contrast, lower-class persons directed their aggressions against others. A society with middle-class values would thus presumably be more concerned with self-other relationships than one where either lower-class or upper-class values predominated.

Mass media. In their depiction of "personalities" and celebrities, the mass media make private emotions and self-conceptions a matter of public interest. The movies, radio, television, and the mass-circulation magazines are concerned, in one way or another, with the glorification of the self as seen through the eyes of others. In this case, the "others" comprise the bulk of the reading, listening, and viewing population. The love-life of a prominent movie actress becomes a matter of national importance, and millions of persons rapturously identify themselves with her. Interpersonal relations become vitally important and adolescents of both sexes and all ages view their own self-other problems as crucial. The mass media depict interpersonal situations because of the informal taboo against "controversial" topics, such as politics, religion, prejudice, or power. The least common denominator is the problem theme which stresses the self and the other.

TYPES OF SELF-OTHER PROBLEMS

Problems of the self and the other are thus intensified by the nature of the culture and the social structure. In one sense, these relationships are basic in *any* social setting, in that the social self is necessarily the product of the reflected appraisals of others. Under present conditions, however, this situation has been intensified by the emphasis upon these relationships and the corresponding individual self-consciousness. Examples of these emerging social problems have been anticipated in the foregoing discussion; they may now be discussed in more detail.

Role-playing. A generic problem of a self-conscious society is the inability of the individual to play the roles expected of him. Social roles are an integral part of the social self, and self-feeling reflects the ability to fulfill the expectations of one's roles. The more complex the society, the more difficult this feat becomes. The person who is chronically anxious about his role-*playing* ability (as distinguished from his role-*taking* ability) is often inadequate in the performance of a role, which further increases his anxiety. He thus becomes prey, in Sullivan's words, to an "anticipated unfavorable appraisal of one's current activity by someone whose opinion is significant." This is an interpersonal, rather than an individual, situation, inasmuch as both the conception of the role and the sense of adequacy (or inadequacy) in playing it come from other persons. Failure in role-playing may cause the individual to distrust his status, his motives, his fellows, and hence, himself. Many of the most pressing problems of the present society derive from role-failure. These roles include those of parent and child, peer-group member, adolescent, lover, mistress, husband, wife, group member, and "100 percent American."

Parent-child relationships. In an earlier generation, parents were primarily concerned with the physical safety, material comfort, and intellectual development of their children. For all practical purposes, these matters are no longer of immediate concern, because they are substantially under control; infant mortality, childhood disease, and material deprivation have been alleviated or virtually eliminated. In this self-conscious generation, however, parents are increasingly aware of the impact of their own personalities upon those of their children. Permissive or nonpermissive training, methods of discipline, relations with other children, and demonstrations of affection are still vital questions.

Peer-group acceptance. In his relations with the peer-group, the child is first introduced to self-other problems in all their stark reality. In the peer-group, from an early age through high school and college, the interactionist conception of the self is perhaps more clearly demonstrated than in any other context. The child is soon made aware of the attitudes of his peers toward himself, and these attitudes are often brutally expressed with no effort to soften the blow. Parents and siblings are ordinarily restrained by affection, custom, and in-group loyalty from expressing their true feelings toward the child. Not so his peer-group. Acceptance by this body is vital to self-respect, and status is made very clear. The child is provided with a virtual running market report on his status. The peer-group reaches its greatest influence during adolescence, when the child is trying to break away from his parents and has not yet attained adult status. In his marginal world, the adolescent looks largely to his peers for guidance, moral support, and self-realization.

Dating. Dating is a competitive game, in which the winner is "loved" because he is successful and successful because he is "loved." Boys and girls who are in demand as dates have prima facie evidence of their acceptance. High self-appraisal follows such acceptance and low self-feelings accompany a failure in this respect. Nothing succeeds like success, and an initial convergence of favorable self-judgments is prolonged into subsequent relationships with the opposite sex. The practice of "going steady" at an early age is a cautious attempt (which has become increasingly structured) to insure the adolescent of at least a modicum of success in dating. Boys and girls who are going steady are always assured of a date and need not run the risk of rejection.

Love and marriage. Closely related to self-other problems of dating are those of love and marriage. In both cases, the self is bolstered by the affectionate responses of another. When one is loved, he feels that he is a better person than before and is correspondingly grateful to the other for thus bolstering his self-attitudes. Lovers enhance each other's self-feelings, a process which may continue throughout their lives. Conversely, those who are unilaterally in love suffer an impairment in self-attitudes and self-respect. Romantic love as a prelude to marriage is one form of this desire for self-approval. Lost or frustrated love after marriage is a major self-other problem.

Conformity and nonconformity. In a stable society, adaptation to group demands is comparatively spontaneous and unreflecting. The members have the same general cultural patterns and are not *consciously* concerned with conformity. In a heterogeneous society, conceptions of the self require a more deliberate and self-conscious adjustment to the group. The mobile population is so large that, in many urban neighborhoods, a large proportion of the residents are and will continue to be "strangers" to each other. This is as true in middle-class suburbs as in lower-class slums. Acceptance requires (or is believed to require) a strong conformity to the superficial patterns of the mass culture. Those who conform will presumably be accepted, and those who do not, will not. This emphasis upon conformity has a stifling effect upon the society and increases intolerance on the part of those who are uneducated and provincial. The most pressing future social problems will involve acceptance of the individual by the group.

Minority-group status. The problem of minority-group status has ramifications ranging from the marginal status of some third-generation Americans to overt ethnic and racial discrimination. In each case, a self-constituted in-group rejects a designated out-group, with resultant impairment of self-feelings. Members of minority groups view themselves through the eyes of the majority, inasmuch as the latter, by definition, dominate the society and impose their definitions upon it. The Negro in America has for generations viewed his social self in terms of the white man's appraisal. The practice of segregation—whether formal or informal, legal or illegal, overt or covert —reacts negatively upon the self-attitudes of the segregated individual. The member of the majority group who holds a violent prejudice is himself marked by insecurity and self-hatred. His own self-feelings form the basis for his hatred of the minority group. In the resulting deprivation of status, the self-feeling of the minority group suffers accordingly. This situation constitutes perhaps the most widespread and corrosive social problem of our society.

SOCIAL ACTION AND SELF-OTHER PROBLEMS

Social problems are believed capable of solution by human action, whether or not any solution has demonstrably been reached. Many of the problems of an earlier day are in a fair way to ultimate elimination in the United States, although not yet in the rest of the world. Problems of the self and the other, however, are infinitely more difficult, if indeed they can ever be "solved" in any meaningful sense. Love, happiness, acceptance, and the rest are "infinite" values, which cannot be gained once and for all, as many of the "old-fashioned" material values can. The quest for self-other values is a never-ending one, and the related problems can perhaps never be completely "solved."

But this does not keep people from trying. A basic goal of the individual, in this or any other society, is to gain status from his fellows and, through reflected self-appraisals, enhance his own self-feelings. In our society, as noted, this process is more self-conscious and contrived. From play-group to the board of directors, the individual spends much of his energy in the sedulous cultivation of his social self.

Each individual works in a number of ways to solve this problem to his own satisfaction. The methods may be classified into two general types: common-sense action and scientific action. This distinction is clearly not absolute and considerable overlapping is apparent. But approaches to problems of the self and the other take two basic forms—the one spontaneous and empirical, the other derived from the sciences of human behavior.

Common-sense action. In his efforts to solve problems of the self and the other, the individual engages in a variety of activities, some deliberate and conscious and others spontaneous and haphazard. The reflected nature of the self provides the rationale behind efforts to "win friends and influence people," to sell oneself, to make oneself the center of group attention, to call the attention of the boss (or the boss's daughter) to one's qualifications, to be "popular" with the boys (or the girls), to be a charming and knowledgeable hostess, and to excel in the leisure arts of an increasingly leisure-conscious society. The individual is no longer judged by his ability as a producer but by his knowledge and skill as a consumer. Leisure is an important consumption commodity, and this consumption requires considerable *savoir faire* and *savoir vivre*.

Problems of the self and the other are at the heart of much of modern advertising copy. The unhappy person who is afflicted with halitosis, dandruff, body odor, or dishpan hands is continually exhorted (a) to beware of his self-image, and (b) to do something about it. Men are reminded that they must dress for other men as well as for women, if they are to retain their male self-image. Women need little urging to accept their obligation to look attractive, seductive, or smart, depending upon the time and circumstance. The buyer of a Cadillac is happily secure in the knowledge that he owns a prominent status-symbol, and prospective owners are lured in the same way. Other automobiles are made to look as much like a Cadillac as possible, so that their owners may bask in this reflected glory.

In the field of industrial relations, much "personnel" work is devoted to individual adjustment to the group and hence to bolstering the worker's self-feeling. In this endeavor, the personnel director makes use of some of the insights of applied psychology, but his efforts are still largely common-sense. The satisfied worker is presumably the efficient worker, and one way to bring about satisfaction is to make him happy about his role in the production process. Although recent research has questioned this all-out self-identification with the job, most programs still act as if a strong self-involvement were a vital prerequisite to industrial efficiency.

Scientific action. Much of the work in the behaviorial sciences involves, directly or indirectly, social action toward the amelioration of self-other problems. To be sure, most scientific work is geared to the *understanding* of interpersonal relations rather than to the application of this knowledge to self-other problems. At some point, however, the ordered knowledge will presumably be applied to the basic values of society. Science has a reason for being that is more than idle curiosity, however remote this reason may be from the day-to-day processes of scientific investigation. In their efforts to appear "scientific," the behavioral sciences have protested too much their indifference to human values and goals. The older sciences have no such compulsion to declare themselves remote from all consideration, proximate or remote, of human welfare.

Whether they like it or not, therefore, the researches of the "pure" scientists in the behavioral area will be applied to the enhancement of social values. One of these values is the social self. Among the specific subject matters related to ordered knowledge of self-other relationships are the following: (a) the study of social interaction in the small group; (b) investigations subsumed under the general title of sociometry; (c) empirical work on dating among high school and college students; (d) the study of the personality needs, both conscious and unconscious, that determine marital choice; (e) the extensive research in child psychology; (f) the investigation of interpersonal relations in marriage and the family; (g) the study of the relationships between culture and personality; (h) the study of social stratification; (i) the analysis of minority-group relationships; and (j) the study of ethnic, religious, and racial prejudice.

These fields of scientific investigation are by no means concerned exclusively with problems of the self and the other. But they all bear upon this field in one way or another. The most direct use of this information is made by psychiatrists and case workers, who are concerned directly with strengthening and rehabilitating individual self-feelings in an increasingly self-conscious society. Marriage counselors, clinical psychologists, clergymen, teachers, doctors, and lawyers are likewise called upon to deal with self-other problems with or without the knowledge derived from the above scientific disciplines.

In final analysis, however, therapeutic activities involve skills and insights which are related only indirectly to applied science. Those who deal with the social self require temperamental qualities which cannot be transferred. Compassion, insight, empathy, and the ability to take the role of the other are at least partially genetic, although they may be enhanced by scientific training. These practitioners will need all the help they can get. Ordered scientific knowledge will be increasingly in demand in the decades to come. In his search for self-fulfillment, man is faced with new and baffling social problems of the self and the other.

Personality is often defined as the totality of biogenic, psychogenic, and sociogenic reaction patterns that develop in human beings. And social psychologists always maintain that the human debt to sociogenic factors (social and cultural influences) in personality development is largest of all. Man, they insist, has relatively little that is fixed genetically; he is extremely flexible, having been born only with random, unco-ordinated vocal and muscular movements. Unlike animals, he remains dependent on others for a relatively long time, and this dependence provides a greater range of personality development.

For years, social psychologists have referred to human cases of extreme isolation in childhood to demonstrate how the lack of socialization and language makes personality development impossible. The cases have typically been "feral" children allegedly reared by wolves in India and subsequently recovered by people, thus making feasible concrete separation and evaluation of the biogenic and sociogenic factors which had heretofore only been analytically separable.

Ramu the Wolf Boy of India, the most recent case, had been recovered in 1954 at which time he walked like a quadruped, lapped food and water like an animal, and made incoherent vocalisms like a wild beast. Unable to sit, he cowered before humans. After seven years of human care in a hospital in Lucknow and at an estimated fifteen years of age, Ramu acquired many human personality traits. But because the years between two and nine are considered vital to personality development, there was virtually no hope that he would ever become completely human.

The difficulty in using such cases of feral children to illustrate scientifically the effect of extreme social isolation on personality development is that there has never been anything more than circumstantial evidence for the claim they were reared by animals and lacked human contact and socialization during the formative years of infancy and early childhood.

Since 1940, however, two other cases of extremely isolated children, both directly traceable from earliest infancy, have overcome the scientific inadequacies of the feral cases. In an article Kingsley Davis presents evidence about Anna and Isabelle which reveals that extreme isolation is deleterious to personality. However, if it does not continue beyond age six it need not permanently impair socialization and personality development.

NOTES

[1] Mead, George Herbert, *Mind, Self, and Society* (Chicago: University of Chicago Press, 1943), p. 138.

THE TASKS OF SOCIALIZATION

ROBERT ENDLEMAN

We can formulate the tasks of socialization in any society as the following: the channeling of libidinal forces, dealing with the unconscious, dealing with anxiety, the handling of aggression, life-cycle progression, learning of social roles, attainment of identity, internalization of values, dealing with play, provision of diversity, and the provision of integration. Let us briefly consider each of these in turn.

Channeling libidinal forces. Socialization must deal with the fundamental libidinal forces at the mainsprings of the human animal. Each society must provide some degree of gratification for these drives and at the same time impose some restraints. No social system can handle a complete freedom of the potential polymorphous eroticism of human beings. But neither can it dam up these forces completely without risking destructive consequences. On one side, complete permissiveness of libidinal expression conflicts with any society's need for structured patterns of cooperation and control. On the other, the blocking of these powerful libidinal forces produces aggression with its great potential for either destructive constriction or explosive disruption of social order.

Dealing with the unconscious. Socialization must handle the unconscious forces in man and tie them in with meaningful social experience with cultural validation. It must provide some channeling for the unconscious fantasy life of man that is so crucial and often fateful a part of childhood development. To say that socialization must deal with the unconscious is almost a tautology, for inevitably the socialization process involves unconscious molding, pressuring, and manipulating of the new human animals by the regular agents of socialization—parents, siblings, other kin, teachers, preachers, and the rest. In the earliest stages of socialization unconscious communication of the socializers is an essential part of the whole process. The child learns not only what the socializers say, but also what they communicate non-verbally, by tone, gesture, stance, expression, the whole repertoire of phatic communication, as already discussed. The commonalities among the socialization agents, at this unconscious level, are an important part of the process. There must be, paradoxically, some coherence within this area of irrationality and non-rationality, and between it and the areas of conscious verbalized directions. Where they are at odds, the socialization process needs to provide some kinds of bridges and reconciliations among these conflicting forces.

Dealing with anxiety. Socialization must deal with anxiety. There are universal conditions that create or exacerbate anxiety. These conditions include the inevitable frustration of the human infancy situation, the conflict in infancy between magical omnipotence and almost total helplessness, the ever-present danger of regression; the perpetual danger of breakthrough of forbidden inner strivings, the conflict among the inner, unconscious, or barely conscious drives themselves and between these drives and the outer controls and restrictions; and the uncertainty and ambiguity of that outer world itself. The latter is a problem of perhaps unprecedented complication in the modern industrialized world.

Socialization has to provide for a repertory of mechanisms for handling such anxieties. It must further tie these mechanisms in with the learning and playing of meaningful roles and the acquisition of values at costs that are not too excessive. Psychoanalysis has taught us much about the mechanisms for dealing with anxiety, and it has pointed out the enormous inner costs that these devices and strategies can have. Socialization involves the social and cultural patterning of such mechanisms and their reinforcement by (often unverbalized) cultural validation. Not that the goal is simply "peace of mind." Under certain kinds of social conditions, it may be that the most positive device a socialization system can offer is the sheer capacity to *face* anxiety rather than defending against it by costly unconscious maneuvers.

Handling aggression. Socialization must provide patterned means of dealing with aggression, a universal human force. Whatever its relationship to instinctual forces, *aggressive feeling* is aroused in any human society by the blocking of libidinal expression, by the imposition of outer and inner controls upon behavior, by conflicts and rivalries with others, and generally by the blocking of attainment of any kind of goals human beings may strive for. Some forms and degrees of such frustration are inevitable in any human society. The problem for socialization then is how to deal with and channelize aggressions: when, how, and how much shall be turned back inwardly against the self of the individual personality; when, how, how much, and against what objects shall be turned outward against objects, human and other, in the outside world, at what costs and with what consequences. Here again, socialization must furnish some patterned ways. It cannot leave the channeling to the special vicissitudes of each individual personality. Whatever the patterns, there are inherent difficulties and dilemmas involved.

Life-cycle progression. Socialization must provide some meaningful pattern of movement or progression through the stages of the life cycle. The pattern must take into account universal aspects of the psychobiological changes and crises of the periods of growth, maturity, and decline, and it must consider the special situational and social pressures of the particular time and place. It needs also to allow for idiosyncratic differences among individuals in stage development. It must provide for some patterning of the psychosexual development that deals with inevitable conflicts in this sphere, provide culturally approved ways of dealing with such conflicts, and offer viable means of going on to the next stages. It must deal with the various maturational tasks confronted in the process of growth and provide stable guidelines for developing the relevant capacities and strengths for these tasks. At each stage it must give necessary social supports and permissions. In all of this there is the dilemma of providing stability without rigidity, permissiveness without chaos.

Role learning. Socialization must provide meaningful *roles* and role learning which brings the child and developing adult into satisfying relationships with his society. This involves orientation to proximate goals that make sense in terms of the economy, history, and current situation of the particular society. It also involves orientation to the future, either assumed as stable continuation of the past or as something expected to be different in certain definable directions. This is not simply the task of preparing the young for the social roles that exist and keep the system going, for such a formulation assumes the integrity of the ongoing society and culture as a "going concern" and implicitly makes a positive value judgment of presently existing social arrangements. Rather we assume that any system, no matter how apparently well worked out and balanced by tradition, is a tentative arrangement, susceptible to change. There-fore, the question of what kind of socialization anticipatory of future adult roles that any particular society needs to have is problematical. This matter is open to evaluation, according to how well any given system reconciles societal or cultural "necessities" with the "necessi-ties" dictated by the nature of the human animal.

Identity. A related problem is that socialization must provide for some reasonably stable identities for males and for females, at various ages, and must facilitate the psychological mechanisms by which in-fant, then juvenile, human beings can arrive at such identities. Identity is, of course, a social product, its range of possibilities lim-ited, if not determined, by the social and cultural forces of a particu-lar society. But it is not only that. Identity for the individual means a uniquely personal configuration of his own choices among a range of models provided by the society. Socialization must provide the models, the standards for choosing among them, and the mechanisms for the pursuit of such choices, with all the intrapsychic and inter-personal difficulties involved in these processes. It must provide some coherence between expected or available social roles at different stages for each of the sexes, and the psychological dynamics of the individ-ual personality. The problems involved are variably acute in dif-ferent civilizations (and there is chorus of consensus that they are especially acute in our own at the present time). The socialization process must provide a repertory of viable solutions.

Internalization of values. Socialization must provide a meaningful system of values and mechanisms for learning these values. Some degree of internalization is necessary for any system, and socializa-tion must supply the psychosocial mechanisms for such internaliza-tion. Significant here is *what* is internalized, and how, and at what psychic and social costs. What is the balance between such costs and the gratifications provided by the system? Internalization involves some kind of superego formation, and this implies some kind of intra-psychic mechanisms for handling aggression, partially at least by turning it against the self. The 'social contract' always involves some kind of bargain, the giving up of some kinds of gratification or some times for gratification, in favor of others. But not all bargains are of equal value. A further complication is that much of the process is unconscious, rooted in early life experiences not easily recalled and therefore not easily open to deliberate change.

Play. Another task for socialization is to make room for *play*. This is related to the problem of dealing with unconscious processes, and to the problem of psychosexuality as an aspect of libidinal forces and of life-cycle stages. Man's protracted, indeed perpetual, infantilism includes his potential for play, not only in infancy and childhood, but throughout all of life. This is a basic, though not sufficient, condition for his enormous creativity. Socialization needs to provide for play as both an individual and a social need. Socially, play involves not only recreation — relaxation from required performances — but also the seeds of innovation, essential to keep any system adaptable to changing situations and changing character needs. Personally, play provides for expression of otherwise neglected or suppressed unconscious powers. It is not only a safety valve from the restrictiveness of any socially structured system of constraints, but also a positive creative force that can be channeled culturally into the arts and sciences or the molding of new social forms; or simply, and importantly, give expression to the sheer exuberance of the human animal.

Diversity. Socialization must provide for human diversity. It must be able to take into account the whole range of genetically given temperament variation, innate potentialities, and accidents of individual history that make for variability in the "human material" with which the society is working to mold its role practitioners. This means that there must be enough role variability to match the variability of the actors and sufficient areas of leeway and permissiveness in how, when, on what terms roles are undertaken and played.

It may seem at first glance that most systems do nothing of this kind, but rather seem to try to mold the variable "human material" into a single, narrow pattern, or at most two or three alternative ones. On closer examination, however, even many primitive societies, which by some accounts seem monolithic in structure and to demand only a single social type for all the population, reveal an internal range of diversity in ways of conforming to the social demands or in patterns of feeling about the standard ways. In any case, it needs to be raised as a question: *How much range* does the society give for different kinds of persons to be their different kinds of selves—recognizing the paradoxes and ambiguities of such a question, since both differences and similarities are partially social products, and not merely expressions of inherent genetic potential.

Integration. Lastly, socialization has to provide for integration: of the person within himself, of the person with social forms and necessities, of the person with the convolutions of the culture. The fulfillment of this requirement may work against the fulfillment of some of the other demands, notably the need for recognition of diversity, the need for play, the need for expression of unconscious forces, and, in general, all those demands that bear on the quality of human freedom. Further, there is the inherent difficulty that the integration of some persons deeply into the fabric of the society and culture may have to be achieved at the expense of the integration of others.

With these "tasks of socialization" in mind, then, let us examine several varieties of childhood socialization systems. About each we can ask how it works to deal with each of the kinds of problems that we have sketched: who are the primary agents of socialization, and how is the socialization process socially structured at each stage? What cultural norms apply to it at various stages and in various situations? And what are the effects, the costs, as well as the positive productivities, of each system in relation to universal human needs?

A LOOK BACK IN WONDER

RITA KRAMER

Are permissive parents to blame for the violence of some of today's campus protesters? Many consider this nation's extremist youth an impulse-ridden generation, too impatient to work toward long-range goals and with no respect for authority or for the past, and a number of recent articles have suggested that the trouble is that, in Stewart Alsop's words, they were "Spocked when they should have been spanked."

Recently, a Long Island reader wrote to this magazine:

> It's becoming more and more tiresome and disturbing to read accusations by psychiatrists and psychologists that middle-class parents, because of their false interpretation of Freud (i.e., extreme permissiveness) are to blame for today's way-out, violent, NOW generation.
>
> What they neglect to mention is this: who originally interpreted Freud to these misguided middle-class parents? Who wrote volumes of permissive advice? The child-rearing "experts," of course. I know. I used to read them.

All right, what were "the experts" advising parents back in those dear dead days when presumably children still wanted to grow up to be firemen and nurses, not revolutionaries? To find out, we dipped into the pages of some of the mass-circulation women's magazines of the mid-forties to mid-fifties that told millions of mothers how to handle their children.

Children's diseases were still dangerous and a regular summer feature article was the dangers-of-polio piece. A "problem child" meant one with diarrhea. By the late forties almost all the articles on children dealt with emotional development, and psychiatrists and psychologists had replaced pediatricians as the authors of most of them.

Reprinted from *The New York Times Magazine*, June 8, 1969, by permission of The New York Times and the author.

In 1945, the Woman's Home Companion was advising readers of its Child Guidance Series that "when your child has a tantrum . . . lies down on the floor, bangs his head and screams, or may kick and bite, scratch and cry . . . it is a perfectly natural thing for him to do. In most cases the reason for the tantrum lies not with the child but with the adult. He makes an issue over some insignificant situation and the child objects." The doctor-author tells parents to deal with tantrums by preventing them. "Divert the child by saying 'Let's go out and play' or by starting a favorite game." What if it doesn't work and Junior prefers to throw himself on the floor, kick and scream? "My advice," the doctor says, "is to do nothing at all." While the screaming and kicking are going on, he offers parents the comforting thought that, after all, "no tantrum will go on indefinitely," and when it's all over, he cautions, "Don't scold or punish your child. Try to make him happy, do what he is interested in. Punishment will only harm his development."

Nowhere in this glib statement is the kind of punishment that will harm a child's development distinguished from the kind of discipline the lack of which will *also* harm a child's development. There must have been a good number of mothers who put down the Companion with the idea that interfering with any discharge of impulses on their child's part would "harm his development."

The following month a lady Ph.D. was telling them, in a Companion article on "When Your Child Won't Obey," that "the child who has strong drives is more resistant to learning your ways, more forgetful and consequently more likely to be disobedient. It is essential that his impulses be patiently redirected rather than broken, for in them lies the secret of courage, scientific curiosity and boundless energy." We can't really blame a mother who, reading that, is afraid that if she says a firm "no" and stops her tyke from turning the sugar bowl upside down and pouring its contents on the floor, she will be depriving the world of a future Nobel-Prize-winning scientist.

The emphasis in these articles always seems to be on not breaking a child's will—assumed to be a very fragile thing—rather than on teaching him to control it. A psychologist writing about the bossy, belligerent child (whom she defines as "the one who must always be the marine while the others must be Japs") says he may be suffering from overstrict discipline. Nowhere is it even considered a possibility that he might be suffering from understrict discipline.

To some extent, this seems to have been an expression of the

Zeitgeist. All during the war we had talked about freedom, and after the war we were full of plans for building a better world. And it was going to be a world of participatory democracy. When the Companion's child-guidance expert advises mothers whose children are deliberately breaking dishes or rules that "what the child really needs is a lessening of demands" what she has in mind is that "If a parent succeeds in getting strict unquestioned obedience he has a child better adapted to live in a Nazi society than in a democratic one . . . We want children who will choose to cooperate with others, not those who are subservient to the arbitrary personal command of an adult."

The idea that the instinctual side of behavior should be given a freer rein went beyond tolerance to active encouragement. A psychiatrist writing about thumb-sucking advised parents "If a very young infant has trouble in getting his thumb into his mouth, and seems to be distressed, it's a good idea to help him."

The great age of clay and fingerpaints was dawning, perhaps in reaction to past restrictions. Everyone seemed to have the idea that undesirable behavior was a sign that what the child needed was "a picnic, a long hike in the country . . . clay to punch, finger paints to smear, etc." Their grasp of the facts of urban family life seems to have been weak. The prescription of picnics and hikes for discipline problems by the authors of articles like "When Your Child Won't Obey" seems about as relevant to many city readers as those schoolbooks about Dick and Jane, their picket-fenced yard and their dog Spot must have seemed to their children.

A 1945 Ladies' Home Journal article on "Preventing Children's Problems" warns parents against "undermining his sense of security by making him feel that our affection for him depends on how well he performs" and advises them to "find something to appreciate and don't hang on his mistakes." Another writer says, "The child needs constant encouragement. Whatever increases the courage of a child is helpful — and whatever discourages, harmful." One wonders how this was interpreted. Never criticize? Never correct? Praise him or else keep quiet? Is the kind of confidence a child would get from treatment like this a realistic basis for meeting the outside world on its own terms?

When the experts' advice is least ambiguous, it is liable to be most contradictory. For example, on the subject of how to handle children's fears, Expert A writing in the Journal in September 1946, says to "handle fears, especially ones which seem in danger of being fixed or prolonged, as you would any bad behavior—as something never to be rewarded by attention or affection." But here is Expert B, on the same subject, in a later issue of the same magazine: "It's better to give him sympathy—to make him feel he isn't facing his fears alone." Who is a parent to trust?

And while one Journal writer tells us the American Mom is a menace ("She is not mothering her son—she is smothering him"), another writes, "I question whether 'moms' exist in significant numbers. There are more youngsters who suffer from neglect because their parents are too busy with their own pursuits than from over-attention." Pity the poor mother who reads both articles, immobilized outside her son's door, not knowing whether she should go in and try to give him more attention or go away and get off his back.

Parents of gifted children were being given equally conflicting advice. A writer for this magazine reported: "For each educator who recommends acceleration there is another who holds that such practice can lead to maladjustment." She also informed readers that while "a bullying youngster may have a domineering, overstrict father . . . in another child bullying may be traced to weak, overindulgent parents."

Some of the advice that was being given in the forties has a vintage flavor today. Comparative strangers called Daddy were returning to many families, and mothers were advised to "avoid shifting your entire attention suddenly to your husband," as well as to try to keep the kids' clutter down. "The Battle of the Bulge hasn't prepared him for the Battle of the Bathroom."

What drove parents frantic in 1946? Then as now, listening to an adolescent girl on the telephone. The vocabulary has changed (did anyone ever really say things like "What a heaven man—he's simply atomic—but definitely"?) but Companion's advice to parents in this situation is probably still valid: "Close the door and try to concentrate on a good book."

Another cause of parental anguish that sounds familiar was "those dreadful programs." But it wasn't television. "Every afternoon from 5 to 6," we read in 1947, "some 5 million children sit before a magic box in their homes. Deaf to everything else, their attention is riveted on the sounds pouring from the radio." Parents are advised that when the programs are too exciting they should recommend a good book or send the children outdoors to play—advice that was probably as effective then as it is now—but they are also reassured that "these youngsters of the radio age may have developed brand-new habits of concentration." We are told that in their radio programs the kids of the late forties "meet the most exciting characters: cowboys and air pilots, savages (*savages?*), sea captains and G-men." If that doesn't make you feel old, you are probably well under 40 and shouldn't be reading this piece at all.

The experts gave it to parents straight from the shoulder on the radio question. "There's no escaping the fact that radio has won our children." (Little did they know what was coming!) On the whole, their advice was to make the best of it, to listen with them to some of their favorite programs, and to try to "widen the areas of their appreciation."

You don't realize how much older the young have gotten until you look through the articles about Our Youth in the postwar years. Idealism took the form of campaigning (very politely) for world government; teen canteens were going to help solve the problem of juvenile delinquency, and parents were told, in an issue featuring ads for the year's biggest movie — "The Best Years of Our Lives"— that "today children are assailed on all sides by sexual suggestions and excitement." You look through the illustrated stories, the photographs accompanying the articles, the ads for Ipana and Mum. Everyone is clean and wearing clothes. Lots of clothes. After a while, you get the feeling they're all wearing the same clothes. The picture-of-the-month starred Lassie, and Herbert Hoover was writing about "The Miracle of America" in the space that current magazines devote to the miracle of the pill.

Whatever passed for "sexual suggestions and excitement" twenty-two years ago is hard to imagine getting waxed up about in a time when kids know about—even if they haven't read or seen—"Portnoy's Complaint," "The Story of O," "I Am Curious (Yellow)," "Geese," and the New York Review of Sex.

It may not have been as exciting a world to grow up in, but it seems to have been a less pressured one. In 1946 it was felt that "a child should have mastered the essentials of reading by the end of the third grade." Today, parents are more likely to feel he had better have mastered them by the end of his third year if he's going to get into nursery school. One is almost touched by the proselytizing tone of 1940's articles *selling* parents on the idea of nursery schools for their young.

Advice to parents of teenagers from the Companion in 1947:

"Avoid the I-simply-won't-put-up-with-it tone. Ask what *they* think is reasonable; accept their plan if you can."

In that same year, an article by an up-and-coming pediatrician-author named Benjamin Spock urged "brotherhood on a planet which will soon be destroyed unless there are enough friendly people to prevail." Part of his prescription for raising friendly people: instead of letting a fight develop and punishing the malefactors, "Try to forestall trouble or suggest something else to do."

The emphasis on preventing the outbreak of hostilities is understandable in a world so recently ravaged by hostility, but one wonders if diverting children is always the best thing—if perhaps their education shouldn't also include some lessons in the consequences of certain kinds of actions. How else will they learn to avoid destructive behavior for themselves when we're no longer around to change the subject for them or take them on a picnic? It's perhaps in this sense that children "brought up by the book" in the late forties were "overprotected."

Many family problems of the middle to late forties were those of the veterans with wives and children going back to school on the G.I. Bill, living in quonset huts and trailers, or sometimes with in-laws. The Journal advised mothers to "Relax with your baby. In these days of housing shortage, crowded living quarters may be a constant source of irritation and upset to the busy mother. When mother and father have to get along in one room, or when families are doubled up so that privacy is impossible to achieve, the wear and tear on nerves may be severe. In doubled up families there are only too often conflicting opinions about how to care for the baby."

These were the years when "reliable nurses demand 50 cents an hour," when an article on "junk" could only refer to old things found in an attic, and one on "Possible Presidents" included Harold Stassen and Robert A. Taft. And the Journal described "an excellent small home for $3750."

In facing articles in September of 1947 two authors tell "Why I *Like* My Parents" and "Why I *Can't Like* My Parents" (italics theirs), as though the most important thing for parents was to be popular. Needless to say, the reason the second author couldn't like her parents was because they were too strict. And in another issue of that same year we find that "the girl who goes wrong is the girl who is seeking love, which she has not found in her home." Over and over we hear about the child's needs. And "love" is never very clearly distinguished from indulgence.

In 1948 a Journal child-care expert wrote: "The child should have many opportunities to express his feelings, even when they are hostile. These feelings will be less disturbing if they are fully expressed." And a pediatrician counsels, "Avoid making direct suggestions or requests which give the child an opportunity for overt refusal. Instead, offer a choice of desirable behaviors. Instead of announcing that it is naptime, ask him if he wants to nap with Teddy Bear or Fuzzy Elephant." Again, one wonders how this advice was taken. How, exactly, are hostile feelings "fully expressed"? Does anything go? And how, one wonders, will the child ever be able to cope with external demands in school or later at work if he is given the idea that all choices are his, and the expectation that all of them will be "desirable."

Other words of advice from the Journal in the late forties: "The cause of behavior problems in children often proves to be a lack of love or understanding on the part of the parents." "Try to understand him if you can, but when you can't understand him, let him alone."

Throughout these articles, the emphasis is on what "parents should" or "parents shouldn't" do. For better or for worse, the emphasis has definitely shifted from the "children should do this or that" of an earlier moralistic age to "parents should do this or that." One occasionally suspects the children might have been better off with parents who were less informed but more secure.

The New York Times Parent-Child editor reported having heard about "one mother who won't even change her two-and-a-half-year-old's diapers without asking him first if he wants her to."

In 1950 the Companion is telling us "There's a powerful new magic in the air. Any afternoon from 5 o'clock on you are likely to find your children in front of that magic box." This time, the magic box is a TV set, but the problem is the same: how to help youngsters organize their time so TV doesn't eat up all of it, and how to be selective about what they watch.

Now the war that fathers are coming home from is Korea, and parents are concerned about brutality and sadism in comic books. The comedy seems to consist mostly of half-naked girls being beaten, whipped, strangled, choked or treated in similarly impolite ways.

Teen-agers were already thought of as a problem for parents in 1950, although they had a long way to go yet before taking over the front pages. According to a writer for this magazine, a 1950 study of 15,000 high school students found only 10 per cent of them felt "There is a barrier between me and my parents." Obviously, they hadn't heard about the generation gap yet. And according to a writer for Companion, "The hardest part in learning to get along with young people is to make the first real contact—to break through the cellophane." How to make contact? "Ask their opinion on current topics. Controversial subjects, in particular, interest young people. You will be refreshed by the phrasing of their answers and often astonished by their penetration and wisdom." (Up against the wall, Woman's Home Companion!)

Another 1950 article, entitled "Be Popular with Your Daughter," advises mother, "Unless you have a sprained ankle, go upstairs and get your knitting bag yourself" instead of expecting daughter to get it for you. "Being undemanding will pay dividends in daily harmony." What price daily harmony?

The emphasis is on the need for patience, understanding, letting the child go at his own pace, making everything from mealtimes to learning "fun." Nothing suggests that maybe not everything in life can be fun.

This approach seems to have peaked in the years around 1950, when this magazine informed us that while permissive parents reported more damage to the living room furniture, that their children interfered more with adult privacy, and that they didn't mind very well, "they were convinced, along with most child specialists, they were rearing their children in a way that would produce the best results in the long run."

In a 1951 McCall's article co-authored by Dr. Frances L. Ilg of the Gesell Institute, titled "At 2½ They're All Little Tyrants," we are told "to get along with her (or him), try to let her go at her own speed, in her own way, as much as you can. She can't be forced. If you scold or make an issue of discipline, you won't win your point; you only start a battle of wills that may last a lifetime. But if you treat her like a queen, if you bow and scrape, with humor and whimsy, chances are pretty good that you'll both have a wonderful time. If she wants to take her galoshes to bed with her, let her. . . . When you can, set the stage so that she will think she's boss."

The philosophy of not thwarting the child finds one of its most fascinating spokesmen in the author of a 1951 Journal article called "Never Correct Your Child's English," who advises, when a child uses or pronounces words incorrectly, "Don't correct him—he is not looking for. criticism. He is making an experiment in communicating an idea; and unless you are intent on wrecking his self-assurance, accept his idea and his new word with dignity and keep your superior knowledge to yourself."

The author of this remarkable advice goes on to say "Continued correction is likely to produce loss of security. The result may be hidden for many years. It may not manifest itself until your child is an adult and has to visit a psychoanalyst.

"Perhaps," he adds, "you have never heard of neurotic children, but believe me, they exist." Yes, and one of them even now is probably penning the next great American novel, shocking us all with *his* complaint, which is of course that *his* mother was always correcting his English.

But in the early fifties the pendulum is already starting back in the other direction, toward a less permissive approach to bringing up baby. A later 1951 Journal article—"My Children Won't Obey" —describes a mother who "wanted free, untrammeled children who were not silent and repressed. She had a fear that if she used any strict discipline, the children would develop 'inferiority complexes.'" Well, we have a pretty good idea where she got *that* idea! Anyway, we are told these children, who do a lot of screaming, fighting and having temper tantrums, are so awful that their own father has "even wondered if the children might be abnormal." The author's diagnosis of the situation: "With all her good intentions and child-training reading and trying to follow progressive books, her children have developed such bad qualities that nobody seems to like them—not even their parents."

But by now the new message of the fifties is clear: a return to discipline. A 1952 article in this magazine titled "How Far Permissive Attitudes?" quotes one authority as saying "too extreme a permissive handling of infants and children may be as disastrous in effect as rigid control." Another says, "Children need limits and definite rules." And a third adds, "Limitations and responsibilities are as necessary to a child's social adaptation as is early fulfillment of his basic needs."

The postwar babies were already in grammar school (they're in college now, in case you haven't noticed) when the Journal printed these words for parents in 1953: "In their zeal to avoid harsh, rigid rules, some parents have abandoned all efforts to establish discipline. In these families, the tyranny of the parents has been supplanted by the tyranny of the child. Children need authority, as long as it is reasonable and kindly." Oh.

In the early fifties Dr. Spock wrote in McCall's, "There are many conscientious parents today who are afraid to give their children clear guidance. They think modern psychology preaches that children's freedom must not be cramped. This is a misunderstanding. There is a big difference between not forcing a child to do something that's unnatural for his age and letting him get away with murder."

In 1954 Dr. Spock began writing a monthly column for the Journal, and one looks in vain for the mythical overpermissive Dr. Spock, who on this charge at least seems to be more sinned against than sinning. The earliest edition of his book may have bent over backward to encourage parents to relax some of the rigid ideas of the twenties and thirties on feeding and training, but by the mid-fifties he was telling parents "a child needs to feel that his mother and father, however agreeable, still know how to be firm."

"Firmness," says Dr. Spock in 1956, is one of the aspects of parental love." And thus the age of tyranny of children seems to be drawing to a close.

Today most child-care authorities advocate what sounds like a middle ground between the rigid schedules of the twenties and thirties and the laissez-faire policy of the forties and early fifties. Be kind but firm, we are told. Understand your child, but don't let him become a tyrant. How good is *this* advice? We'll have to wait for some time around 1984 to see.

A CRITIQUE OF CULTURE-PERSONALITY WRITINGS

A. R. LINDESMITH
ANSELM STRAUSS

This paper is concerned with an analysis and criticism of what have come to be known as "culture and personality" writing, including among others the work of Benedict, Mead, Gorer, Kluckhohn, DuBois, Linton, La Barre, Erikson, and Kardiner. The scholars who have contributed to this movement have a common general orientation although some differences of opinion and emphasis exist. One wing of the movement includes psychoanalytically trained persons like Fromm, Erikson, and Kardiner. Another wing, represented by a writer like Benedict, places the main emphasis upon descriptions of cultural configurations and personality types, but puts relatively little emphasis upon genetic explanations or on psychoanalytic concepts. Most of the writers fall between the extremes, using a sprinkling of psychoanalytic terminology, sometimes in combination with ideas derived from other areas.

The interdisciplinary nature of this approach is often stressed but it is, in actual fact, sharply limited. For example, the theory and research of most psychologists, social psychologists, and sociologists who are concerned with personality and psychological processes are virtually unaffected by the culture-personality writings. Conversely, in the latter there is rarely any reference to the research of social psychologists or psychologists other than clinicians and psychiatrists of Freudian persuasion, and almost no references to the writings of foreign psychologists.

The major preoccupations of the culture-personality writers are: (a) the description and psychological characterization of cultural configurations and the delineation of personality types associated with them, and (b) the explanation of given personality types as

Reprinted from the *American Sociological Review*, Vol. 15 (1950), pp. 587-600, by permission of the American Sociological Association and the authors.

products of cultural influences and especially of interpersonal relations in early childhood. We shall discuss each of these major interests in turn.

CULTURAL CONFIGURATION AND
MODAL PERSONALITY POINT OF VIEW

The traditional method of ethnology emphasized the exhaustive description of primitive societies with relatively little emphasis upon psychological characterization as such or upon the total configuration or gestalt. The emphasis was rather upon specific modes of behavior in definitely delineated situations and upon the "psychological" features mainly as exhibited in the overt behavior and verbalization of the natives. The change in viewpoint initiated by the culture-personality school is well indicated by Kroeber's comment: "As late as 1915 the very word 'personality' still carried overtones chiefly of piquancy, unpredictability, intellectual daring. . . ." Influenced by conceptions borrowed from Gestalt psychology and psychoanalysis, and by Sapir's early stress on the need to study the individuals in a society, some ethnologists have attempted to characterize societies in psychological terms as functioning wholes or configurations. The observer seeks to characterize what may be called the "essence" of the culture in psychological terms, i.e., the people's view of the world and of human relations. Such characterization of peoples and nations is not a totally new enterprise. Long before the rise of modern anthropology, writers and scholars attempted the same sort of description of what was called the "genius" or "ethos" of a people. As Kroeber notes: "More than eighteen hundred years ago Tacitus gave to posterity one of the masterpieces of this genre in his analysis of German custom and character."

Following logically from this emphasis on cultural configurations is the idea that given cultural configurations have their counterparts in the individuals of each society. Given cultures produce one or more types of personality designated by such terms as "modal personality," "basic personality structure," "character structure," and so oon.

In arriving at their characterization of cultures and personality types the investigators rely upon conventional ethnological techniques and data, but seek to go beyond them by utilizing them in combination with studies of individuals. Much attention is paid to interpersonal relations, childhood training, projective and objective tests, and sometimes even to photographing people in specified situations.

The investigator immerses himself in a given society as far as the barriers of language, time, available informants, and his own personality permit. From the welter of data he arrives at his characterizations through acts of abstraction, selection, and synthesis. Some characterizations are made vicariously, the writer utilizing materials collected by others, supplemented usually by interviews with emigrants.

The investigators do not describe very clearly or in detail how given characterizations are arrived at. Stress is placed upon offering the reader a mass of data concerning those aspects of behavior which are the focus of the characterizations.

It should be noted that anthropologists often view the culture-personality approach as something in the nature of a fad, although it is generally conceded that it offers interesting and potentially significant knowledge. In terms of total output, culture-personality writings constitute only a small portion of anthropological writings. Current popularity of the point of view is attested by Kroeber who remarks: "Personality is the slogan of the moment . . . the prospect may look dire to those who are interested in culture as such. But with experience one learns that these waves go much as they come."

The works of the culture-personality writers, widely read outside of academic circles, offer a valuable antidote to provincialism and ethnocentrism. The implications of the cultural relativity principle have not by any means been fully taken into account either by social scientists or by the general public. The point, no doubt, needs to be hammered home as these writers are doing. Their works amply demonstrate the enormous range of variation in the organization of societies and human responses. The criticisms which follow are not intended in any way to detract from this substantial accomplishment.

CRITICISM

Oversimplification and the homogeneity postulate. The attempt to make psychological characterizations of cultures "may be regarded as attempted short-hand translation of the more general patterns of a culture." This procedure raises questions having to do with selectivity, neglect of inconsistent data, proof of assertions, and the possibility of corroboration by other investigators. No one, of course,

questions the existence of gross differences between cultures. The
question is rather that of the scientific precision of specific characterizations and the methods of obtaining them.

Anthropologists have questioned the accuracy of the boiling-down
process when carried too far. Benedict, for example, was criticized
for describing Zuni, Kwakiutl, and Dobu peoples too simply. In short,
one notes that the number of questions that are raised concerning
any characterization tends to increase with the number of investigators familiar with the society. The question was raised whether many
non-literate societies might not be characterized more profitably in
terms of multiple patterns or "themes." A similar point has been
made with respect to the numbers of personality types within given
societies. The earlier culture-personality writings often understressed
or ignored individuals who did not conform to the personality type
assumed as typical of the culture. This explaining away or ignoring
of negative evidence has given way to

> . . . the study of the *range* of personalities in a society. . . . Characteris-
> tic personality sub-types may develop from the differing situations of the
> life of persons who play different roles in a given group.

This trend toward studying the "range of personalities" and of
multiple themes within a culture, if carried out to its logical limits,
implies a radical revision of the original ideas, as we shall show later.
It represents a healthy tendency to move toward more limited and
specific problems which can be handled by the established techniques of analysis and proof, rather than dealing with the impossible
task of handling entire cultures in one fell swoop, as "wholes." A
good many of the questions now being raised will no longer be pertinent when the tendency described by Herskovits is carried further.
When this is done, however, stricter standards of proof will have to
be met, and many other theories besides the neo-Freudian will have
to be taken into account. The dangers inherent in gestalt descriptions of societies are graphically brought out by culture-personality
efforts to describe complex modern societies. Any social scientist who
seeks to characterize a modern nation, even in a whole volume, to say
nothing of a few pages, has to handle a host of detailed problems and
meet a number of exacting requirements. These are so numerous and
so complex that to one not imbued with the culture-personality fervor
the task looks impossible. These problems and requirements have to
do with such matters as sampling, statistical distributions, regional

differences, migration, ethnic differences, social classes, diverse group affiliations, standards, social change, culture conflict, and enormous bodies of literature and historical materials. One may admire the boldness of the attempts to make broad general characterizations of such peoples as the Americans, Japanese, and Germans, but one must view the results and methods of proof with a generous measure of skepticism. The same strictures apply with even greater force to attempts to characterize Western character and culture in general.

The applications of culture-personality methods to modern societies—especially the American, with which we are reasonably well acquainted—have fared so badly at the hands of competent critics that one wonders along with Bierstedt whether the effect has not been "to stimulate the growth of skepticism concerning the information which anthropologists have given us about nonliterate peoples."

Undoubtedly the heterogeneity of modern nations, as many of the writers themselves have pointed out, offers a considerable obstacle to the application of present configurational methods. It is hoped, however, that after the techniques have been perfected in the study of simpler, more "homogeneous" societies they may be extended successfully to more complex groups. A more fundamental question must, however, be raised concerning the general validity of the homogeneity assumption itself, even as applied to the larger groupings of nonliterate peoples. One suspects, as Bernard has said, that too much attention is being paid to "the blond Swede."

Psychic Entities vs. Behavior. The homogeneity-configuration postulates savor strongly of Aristotelian conceptions of "essence" and "accident." The "essences" (configuration, basic personality structures) are given high status in the realm of "being," whereas the behaviors which "express" these essences are of an inferior status. Even though the behavior may vary from one individual to the next, and from one generation to the next, it is thought of as an emanation or manifestation of the same essence. Current recognition of a range of personality types and of multiple configurations within a single society is an effort to deal with negative evidence and deviations often ignored by earlier writers, but the accident-essence framework is still retained since the number of essences is merely increased. The range idea also has the effect of making it doubly difficult, if not impossible, to prove that the generalizations reached are either true or false.

There is a tendency in these investigations to deduce psychic entities from overt behavior in specific situations, and then to explain the overt behavior in terms of these reifications. There is a search for something like the "real inner personality" or "authentic individual" conceived as something apart from behavior. The inner reality thus becomes a force which manifests itself in the behavior from which it is inferred. Linton explicitly states this position:

> The nature and even the presence of psychic needs are only to be deduced from the behavior to which they give rise. . . .
>
> Personality will be taken to mean 'the organized aggregate of psychological processes and states pertaining to the individual.' [This definition] rules out the overt behavior resulting from the operation of these processes and states, although it is only from such behavior that their nature and even existence can be deduced. . . .
>
> In general, all the individuals who occupy a given position in the structure of a particular society will respond to many situations in very much the same way. . . . Until the psychologist knows what the norms of behavior imposed by a particular society are, and can discount them as indicators of personality, he will be unable to penetrate behind the facade of social conformity and cultural conformity to reach the authentic individual.

What is meant by "authentic individual"? Do not cultural roles and internalized norms connected with them (e.g., sex roles) influence the "authentic individual"?

The search for the "real motives," the "deep inner core," the "authentic individual," conceived as something separate from behavior leads to circularity of proof and immunity to negative evidence. Thus, if there is no available evidence that ascribed reactions actually take place, it can always be assumed that they are "unconscious" reactions. If the persons seem to have no knowledge of them, or deny the imputed motives, or give other interpretations of their behavior, these objections are easily disposed of by calling them "rationalizations" or by pointing out that, after all, the people are not usually aware of the premises of their culture which as motivations underlie their daily conduct.

A gross example of this procedure is provided by G. Roheim, who argues with regard to knowledge of procreation among primitives, that:

> If we see, on the one hand, that the Arunta deny knowing anything of the matter, and on the other that they have beliefs and rites that are only explicable on the assumption that such knowledge exists some-

where and makes itself felt in their psychic system, we shall say that they are unconscious of their own instinctive knowledge of procreation and that the concepts that enter consciousness are symbolic substitutes of a physiological account of the process of procreation.

The above may be dismissed as an extreme psychoanalytic fantasy, but, with some differences, the same technique of calling on unconscious ideas when the evidence fails, or is disputable, is widespread. Thus Benedict in her book on the Japanese says that: "In this task of analysis the court of authority is not necessarily Tanaka San, the Japanese 'anybody.' For Tanaka San does not make his assumptions explicit, and interpretations written for Americans will undoubtedly seem to him unduly labored." Such a procedure allows the interpretive framework of the investigator to persist undisturbed in the face of negative evidence and criticisms, even from intelligent and trained members of the group being characterized.

Trait psychology lends itself very readily to the use of reified psychic elements to explain behavior of which these traits are, in reality, merely names. Thus, when aggressive behavior is explained in terms of a "fund of aggression," or of a "trait of aggressiveness," this amounts to saying that behavior is aggressive because it is aggressive. These traits are often not self-evident, and at the beginning of his research the investigator often is uncertain of the "meaning" of specific acts. The "meanings" that are finally found are thus the investigator's inferences from behavioral data. The final psychological characterizations often leave this behavioral or situational basis of the inferred psychic elements or traits out of consideration.

Confusion of Fact and Interpretation. The terms that are used in these characterizations are inevitably taken from Western psychological vocabularies, and inevitably lead the reader to think of the people according to the Western models with which he is familiar. A description of the psychological responses of people within the behavioral context of the society does not run into the same dangers of unchecked inference. In this regard a remark of Titiev's, a Southwest specialist, is pertinent:

> Dr. Thompson . . . exhibits an unfortunate tendency to distort various items taken from literature. A girlish pursuit game somewhat comparable to follow-the-leader, is magnified into a faithful portrayal of "the guidance role of the mother and the difficult and centripetal life course of the Hopi girl."

Titiev's criticism may be extended to many culture-personality inferences. Thus, whenever it is postulated that a given people have a
given trait such as "aggressiveness," "passivity," "withdrawnness,"
"impulsiveness," as part of their "basic personality structure," it is
easy to take the unwarranted step of regarding specific behavior as a
manifestation or effect of the given trait. Conclusions of this type
are buttressed not so much by evidential proof as by the piling up
of illustrations which are unlikely to convince anyone who is not
already sold on the underlying ideology.

No one is likely to quarrel seriously with characterizations of a
people when these descriptions are couched in objective behavioral
terms, as in conventional ethnological accounts. But when ethnologists interpret the "meanings" of behavior in psychological terms, it
becomes exceedingly difficult for the reader to separate facts from interpretations. An interesting comment bearing on this point was
made by the Murphys in a review of Mead-Bateson's *Balinese Character*. They conclude that "in spite of the photographic record, the
study still shows some lack of systematic framework, the lack of sharp
distinction between hypotheses and fact."

The extensive use of photographs in the Mead-Bateson book made
it possible for the reviewers to question some of the authors' interpretations. The reviewers go on to say that the photographs allow
the reader to observe incidents in the backgrounds of the pictures
which raise questions about matters in the foregrounds. They add
that "as a device for cultural study this has very important advantages over one which presents data and interpretations so intertwined
that they are impossible to handle independently."

The necessity for presenting "data" and "interpretations" sepa-
rately becomes greater the more remote and inaccessible the culture.
The closer a society is to us and the more that is known about it,
the easier it becomes to dispute interpretations of it. One wonders
what would happen to the various characterizations of psychologically
remote societies if the natives, as well as the investigator's own colleagues who happen to have some knowledge of the society, were able
to answer back! We know what happened when the "natives" read
the Mead and Gorer material on the United States.

Two interesting incidents that bear upon this point may be cited.
Herskovits writes that "Li, a Chinese anthropologist, whose own
physical traits made him inconspicuous among the Indians [Zuni],
found them, as people, to be quite different from the picture of them-

selves they had presented to white students." Li spent a mere two and one-half months of moderately intimate participation in Zuni life—the Zuni being among the most studied and most characterized non-literate peoples in the world. Another relevant case is that of the anthropologist Peter Buck, of Maori descent, who called into question some of the fundamental interpretations of Maori character and culture made by the Beagleholes.

The recent tendencies to present more documentation of conclusions is certainly a step in the right direction since it allows the reader to form some opinions of his own. This documentation usually consists of autobiographies and test results. The utilization of these materials has, however, raised additional questions. For example, there is the question of sampling that arises when autobiographies are gathered. DuBois' study of the Alorese employs this method and illustrates the problem very well. H. Powdermaker suggests that the autobiographies do not represent Alorese modal character because DuBois was apparently able to interview only relatively unsuccessful Alorese, "those who did not approximate the goals of their culture." She also raises the question of the influence of the investigator upon the interview situation. "We know of no society where people will talk about their private inner feelings upon request [and for pay], and in response to questions from a relative stranger at regular periods each day." The use of autobiographical documents is of course desirable but does not in itself prove anything. The critical reader is not convinced that the persons used in obtaining the documents constitute a representative sample, or that the documents cannot be interpreted in a variety of ways.

The claim that projectives and other tests may be used to validate analyses made by other ethnological methods must be qualified by noting that test results are not self-explanatory, but must themselves be interpreted like other data. The tests are certainly useful, but they are not an open-sesame to the truth. All of them were devised and validated by Western investigators operating within the confines of Western culture, and even within that culture their significance is a matter of controversy. This is especially true of the projectives. The discrepancies between Kardiner's interpretations of Alorese character and Overholzer's inferences from Rorschach results raise some doubts about the use of projectives in culture-personality research.

The use of tests may prove to be misleading by suggesting an illusory precision and definitiveness. This is especially true when the usual statistical precautions are not followed. Thus, in a review of the *Children of the People,* M. Kuhn remarks:

> . . . a defect is the failure of the researchers, after espousing the use of quantitative methods, to apply even the minimum sampling standards, such as tests of representativeness, adequacy, and statistical significance of difference which are required by these methods.

An idea of the inadequacy of some of the interpretations of the tests may be obtained from the fact that in *The Hopi Way* conclusions about Hopi animism are based on the answers to a single question! And this is done in spite of the extensive controversial literature on methods of testing animism in children. As other examples, Powdermaker notes that the thirty-seven Alorese who took DuBois' Rorschach test were unidentified and probably unrepresentative, and Titiev questions how the Hopi way, "which is a subtle, complex, and mature outlook on life, can be properly interpreted or clarified on the basis of tests administered to 190 school children, of whom no less than 45 per cent were 10 years of age or younger."

The Operation of Western Biases. The use of projective tests points up one of the fundamental and pervasive weaknesses of many of the interpretations of non-Western peoples; namely, that Western biases must inevitably find expression in the inferences made about the psychological characteristics of given peoples. As R. Benedict has said:

> No man ever looks at the world with pristine eyes. He sees it edited by a definite set of customs and institutions and ways of thinking. Even in his philosophical probings he cannot go behind these stereotypes; his very concept of the true and the false will still have reference to his particular traditional customs.

Herskovits makes a similar point. *"Judgments are based on experience, and experience is interpreted by each individual in terms of his own enculturation."* (Italics his.)

Anthropologists constantly warn their readers against Western biases, and quite rightly. They are generally aware that these biases can, and perhaps must, unwittingly influence their own research. This warning has not been taken into account in anything like its full implications by culture-personality writers. Admittedly the problem of describing non-Western peoples without including one's own biases in the account is a difficult undertaking. One cannot help but feel that many conclusions reached about non-Western character structures and their genesis should have been couched in much more tentative and cautious terms. This is especially relevant to characterizations which seek to get at "inner psychic realities" and their origins.

A comment from Li, whose short participant-observer residence among the Zuni we have previously mentioned, portrays vividly the culture-personality writer's difficulties:

> We find another one-sided statement on . . . the problem of interpretation of Zuni life. Avoidance of leadership in social life is a corollary of the lack of personal feelings in religion. If one is not interested in vision quest . . . what is more natural than the supposition that leadership among men is not desired. But here is just a case in which the premise is correct enough while the conclusion does not necessarily follow. Dr. Benedict reports that a Zuni is afraid of becoming "a leader of his people" lest he should "likely be persecuted for sorcery," and that he would be "only interested in a game that a number can play with even chances" for "an outstanding runner spoils the game." The basic fallacy seems to lie in *the tendency to reason with the logical implications of one's own culture.* [Our italics.] In the competitive Western world where one is brought up to assume that the world is made for his exploitation, and where if one does not push ahead, one is surely pushed behind, it is certainly logical that lack of personal acquisitiveness implies the denial of leadership.

One of the aspects of anthropological thinking which tends to neutralize the wholesome emphasis on cultural variability and the dangers of ethnocentric bias, is the out-of-hand dismissal of the hypothesis that intellectual processes may vary in different societies and even within different groups within the same society. This is part of the reaction against the writings of some scholars like Levy-Bruhl, who have attempted to give brief, simple characterizations of primitive thought in general. Linton perhaps summarizes a fairly usual position when he asserts categorically:

> As far as we can ascertain, the intellectual processes themselves are the same for all normal human beings in all times and places. At least individuals who begin with the same premises always seem to arrive at the same conclusions.

Linton has inconsistently assailed his own view by elsewhere describing language as "a tool for thinking" (note the characteristic dualism which separates language behavior from thinking behavior by animistically designating the former as a tool of the latter); and asserting that "concepts which are an integral part of all linguistic forms have a subtle influence upon individuals' ways of thinking. The concepts are even more compulsive because they are totally unconscious." His primary criticism of linguistics appears to be that it has ignored this problem of how linguistic forms condition different ways of thinking.

Since virtually all readers of characterizations of non-literate peoples are themselves Westerners, unacquainted with the peoples in question, there are few competent critics to point out any but the most flagrant instances of the influence of Western "projective systems" on the ethnologists' accounts. It is, for example, relatively easy to detect La Barre's wartime pro-democratic feeling in his unsympathetic account of Japanese "compulsive" character, and it is easy to agree with J. Honigmann that Kardiner has placed a rather gross evaluation upon Alorese "narrowness" and "unfitness for cooperation"; and one may readily agree with Kroeber's statement that DuBois' characterization of the Alorese:

> . . . . seems one-sidedly repellant. . . . The appraising observer comes from a culture that values internalization, conscience, reliance, scruple, courage, consistency of feeling and relations, dignity, and achievement, qualities that are under-developed in Alor. Hence the picture is black.

The detection of more subtle biases awaits the scrutiny of other trained observers—especially natives and cultural hybrids—and the development of more objective techniques of evaluation. Thomas and Znaniecki's *Polish Peasant* might be taken as a suggested model in that one of the authors was a native Pole.

Kroeber, having the Western bias in mind, has suggested that although some of the characterizations of non-Western peoples are undoubtedly partially correct, there is not at present any way of distinguishing what is valid from what reflects merely "personalized reactions." He even suggests that the basic assumptions of culture-personality studies may be unwarranted since "the categories of psychological characterization developed among Occidentals for Occidentals break down, tend to lose their meaning when applied to Asiatics." He suggests that comparative studies of Western societies may be a necessary preliminary to valid configurational and personality studies of non-Western peoples. D. Haring's caution on drawing conclusions about Japanese character might well be extended to all works in this field:

> . . . those who do such research should spend years, not months, in Japan. The writer "learned all the answers" in his first year in Japan. The next six years taught him that practically all of those answers were misleading or false. Perhaps another seven years would have indicated the wisdom of saying nothing at all.

DEVELOPMENT OF MODAL OR BASIC PERSONALITY POINT OF VIEW

In culture-personality writings, personality is conceived largely as the product of interpersonal relationships in childhood. Various degrees of emphasis are placed upon different types of experience. The more psychoanalytically-oriented writers, such as Gorer, Roheim, Kardiner, La Barre, and Erikson, stress the earliest years as the most crucial; whereas others, like Thompson, Kluckhohn, Goldfrank, Mead, and Benedict place considerable emphasis upon later experiences. Some of the genetic explanations employ a straight neo-Freudian terminology, and most of them use at least a few psychoanalytic concepts. Virtually the only hypotheses which are generally regarded as worthy of checking are the modified Freudian ones. A. I. Hallowell gives the rationale for this tendency:

> This problem [personality] could not be appreciated by either anthropologists or students of human psychology until a working hypothesis about the nature of human personality as a structural whole had been developed. Neither academic psychologists nor psychiatrists of a generation ago had much to offer. It is here that psychoanalysis enters the picture.

There has been some recent attention paid to the possible applicability of learning theories in this field, but in general the work of social psychologists and the mass of critical material on Freudian concepts are ignored.

CRITICISM

Effects of Infant Experience Are Undemonstrated. The lack of attention to alternative hypotheses and the neglect of criticism and negative evidence concerning various aspects of psychoanalytic theory give the culture-personality writings the characteristics of illustration and documentation of a point of view already assumed to be true. The principal problem merely seems to be to show how the view may be extended to other cultures and perhaps modified in minor ways in the process.

A point of view that looms very large in these writings is the one that emphasizes the predominant character-forming efficacy of the infant disciplines: bowel and bladder training, nursing, weaning, mothering, restraint of motion, punishment, amount and kinds of frustration, and so on. Thus, La Barre virtually ascribes the main features of Japanese personality to the rigid bowel training of infants; C. Kluckhohn and O. Mowrer state that too precipitous training of the child in weaning, cleanliness, sex taboos, and aggression control lays the groundwork for "obsessive ambition" and "severe competitive behavior" in adults. E. Erikson carries this type of explanation to an absurd limit:

> The Yurok child . . . is weaned early and abruptly, before the full development of the biting stage, and after having been discouraged from feeling too comfortable with his mother. This expulsion may well contribute to the Yurok character a residue of potential nostalgia which consequently finds its institutionalized form in the Yurok's ability to cry while he prays in order to gain influence over the food-sending powers behind the visible world. . . . The Yurok, in order to be sure of his food supply, feels it necessary to appear hallucinatory, helpless, and nostalgic, and . . . to deny that he has teeth or that his teeth can hurt anybody.

The general unproved assumption lying behind this type of interpretation is expressed as follows by Erikson:

> We hold that a child absorbs through his needy senses the cultural modalities of what happens in, to, and around him long before he is provided with a vocabulary. . . . Adults . . . selectively accelerate and inhibit the sensual maturation of body orifices and surfaces, and they encourage and restrict the gradual expansion of sensory, muscular, and intellectual mastery. In doing so, they systematically though unconsciously establish in the infant's nervous system the basic grammar of their culture's patterns.

H. Orlansky, in an excellent recent paper, has critically evaluated the data and assertions bearing on the question of the influence of infant care on personality development. He has shown that there is no body of evidence to support assertions like those given above. Some of his main points may be summarized as follows: (a) various writers attribute different and contradictory effects to the same or similar childhood experiences; (b) the alleged influences of given infant disciplines or types of experience on personality have not been proven within our own society, to say nothing of others; (c) the method of "proving" that early infancy is of primary importance is shot through with anthropomorphism and unsupported assumptions; and (d) post-infantile childhood experiences are probably of more vital importance in shaping personality than the prelingual ones.

Most psychologists and social scientists agree that there is a special significance attached to first or early learning. There is good evidence for this assumption. What we do not know, and are unable to discover from the culture-personality writings, is what precisely it is that is learned in early infancy and what its exact significance may be for later training. As D. O. Hebb tersely remarks: "In such matters, our ignorance is virtually complete."

Ineffectual Attempts to Salvage Infantile Determination. In an attempt to bring post-infantile experiences into the picture and to salvage remnants of the original doctrine it is commonly asserted (a) if post-infantile experiences tend to reinforce the personality trends established in infancy, then the resulting adult traits will conform to the infantile pattern; however, (b) if later experiences run counter to earlier ones the resulting adult character may be something not predictable from infantile experiences alone.

Thus E. Beaglehole distinguishes between the "primary character structure" formed in infancy and "secondary character structure" formed later if later experiences do not reinforce the earlier ones. Similarly, Kluckhohn and Mowrer assert that:

> It should be emphasized that, like biological heredity, infant experiences, while placing certain constraints upon personality, give mainly potentialities. . . . Whether these potentialities become actualized or not, or the extent to which they become actualized, depends upon later social and other conditions which structure the individual's experience.

Kardiner makes the same point when he notes concerning the effects of infantile experiences: "The . . . question that arises is whether these attitudes need remain permanent. They need not, if other factors are introduced into the child's life which would tend to counteract them. However, if they are not counteracted, they tend to continue."

These statements raise serious methodological problems that are not dealt with adequately, if at all, in this literature. A verifiable theory is one which can be proved to be right, and this implies that conceivably it might be proved wrong by exceptional cases. The latter possibility is not allowed for in the doctrine since, as Kluckhohn and Mowrer state:

> Substantially the same personality trait may be caused by different patterns of childhood experience. . . . The same basic discipline or event in early life may result in quite different personality trends, depending upon the juxtaposition of various other disciplines, the problems which individuals in each particular society have to meet, and, always, the differing biological equipment of different individuals.

Thus, whatever happens, the theory is confirmed in a heads-I-win-tails-you-lose procedure. Orlansky has made a similar point in speaking of infantile disciplines:

> . . . the same childhood experience is arbitrarily read as having one significance for personality formation in one society and the opposite significance in another. . . .

The concept of causation which we are criticizing might be called "proof by juxtaposition." Using this method, culture-personality writers describe two sets of phenomena widely separated in time, and assert a causal relation. The *post hoc* nature of this reasoning is clearly exemplified by Kardiner's own account:

> It is well nigh impossible to tell in advance what particular elaborations will take place in a given culture of such a basic pattern. However, once we are told by the Rorschach that certain end results can be identified, it is a relatively easy matter to reconcile them with the more basic traits.

This *post hoc* method apparently does sometimes have its difficulties, for, as Kardiner tells us: "I feel somewhat ashamed to confess that some of the main points in Alorese personality did not become clear to me until four years after I originally got to know the material."

Some writers stress not only that culture shapes personality, but also that personality affects culture. Though the latter assertion is not of concern in this paper, it may be noted that the same sort of *post hoc* reasoning is used. Thus DuBois suggests that institutions and child training techniques should be regarded as interdependent variables, and advances the thesis that institutions should be altered indirectly through changes in child-rearing practices.

In an excess of enthusiasm, Gorer carries the *post hoc* method to an all-time high when he offers twentieth-century urban middle-class fads in child training as the basis for the American form of government established in the eighteenth century.

Anthropomorphism. Culture-personality explanations of the development and fixation of personality in early infancy and childhood are pervaded by anthropomorphism, as Orlansky has amply shown. The main reasons for this appear to be (a) that little direct study of infants or children is undertaken to determine whether the reactions attributed to them actually occur, and (b) it is assumed that the reaction of infants to a given type of experience "must be" of a certain character without any effort to prove that such is the case, and (c) the dualistic procedure, which postulates psychic "processes and states" as forces or "first causes" that produce behavior, invites the investigator to attribute motives and reactions which appear reasonable or plausible to him. The following quotation nicely illustrates the last two of these points:

> To the white child, whose feedings and other routines are rigidly scheduled, the mother or nurse *must appear incalculable.* He finds that there are rules of behavior which are above and beyond his needs or wishes. No matter how hard he cries, he does not get his bottle until the clock says he should. *He must develop a feeling that each individual is alone in life.*
>
> To the Navaho baby, on the other hand, other persons *must appear warmer and more dependable,* for every time he cries, something is done for him. . . . [Our italics.]

What is "Basic"? Everyone will agree that persons in adult life change occupations, learn new skills, change their status, and so on. It will be admitted that such changes involve personality alterations of some kind. What objective grounds are there for stating that such changes are or are not "basic"?

The idea that basic personality patterns are established in the first couple of years of life or in pre-adolescent childhood involves the assumption that personality does not change, or changes only in minor ways, in response to later experiences and cultural influences. This view of the matter involves a considerable commitment on an issue that must still be regarded as unsettled, and requires that some kind of objective statement about the so-called "basic" elements of the personality be made. It may be pointed out that if personality is conceived as a system of responses arising in a cultural matrix, the individual lives his entire life within such a matrix and is never independent of it. Why, then, unless one assumes that learning and the organization of responses takes place only in childhood, should later experiences be largely ruled out? Most of the culture-personality studies by their very emphases are only partially situationally oriented —that is, with respect to childhood—and take the relative insignificance of later experience for granted. Though this assumption appears to be generally plausible to most social scientists, it is nevertheless necessary to show empirically which response systems change readily and which do not, and under what conditions.

Indirect vs. Direct Learning. The belief that personality patterns are fixed unconsciously and early involves a corollary assumption that these patterns cannot be directly taught, or that they can be taught later only if the childhood training has been favorable. The latter argument is another heads-I-win-tails-you-lose proposition; the former argument rests upon an invidious comparison of different types of behavior, some being judged as more basic than others without specification of the grounds for these conclusions. At times the argument assumes a purely circular form: those patterns which come first are most important because they are the earliest ones.

In reports of research on non-literate peoples considerable data are of course given on direct teaching, but in the interpretation of the deeper meaning of the data and in offering genetic explanations of personality there is a clear tendency to stress the major influence of indirect and unconscious learning. For example, the Beagleholes explain the free spending habits of the Maori in terms of childhood frustrations. The fundamental motive operating here is said to be the "buying of love" which the individual is afraid of losing because of the impact of certain childhood experiences. Peter Buck denies this interpretation, suggesting that patterns of handling money are directly taught—a point that is also made by B. Mishkin.

The Beaglehole interpretation is rendered untenable anyhow by the fact that, regardless of types of childhood training, most non-literate peoples were resistant to the introduction of European economic practices and ideas.

Though this particular interpretation by the Beagleholes is more obviously vulnerable than others of like character, it is, nevertheless, a good example of the emphasis on cumbersome and unverifiable theories of indirect learning where much simpler explanations are available. Admittedly the hypothesis of direct learning is not always applicable, but whenever it is, it is attractive by contrast in its simplicity and verifiability. The predilection for indirect explanations no doubt stems from stresses placed upon "unconscious" processes, upon emotional aspects of interpersonal relations, and upon the deep, hidden, inner reality called "personality." We agree with Linton who says:

> . . . how far is the personality formed by these factors which operate on the child without the child really understanding what is happening, and how far is it formed by actual instruction? I think this is a question we have not solved at all at the present time.

SUMMARY AND SUGGESTIONS

The bulk of this paper has been concerned with negative criticisms, raised by us and others, concerning the conclusions, evidence, methods, and general conceptual framework offered and used by culture-personality writers. These criticisms seem to us to indicate quite clearly that available evidence offered by the writers in support of their conclusions is inadequate and does not justify their conclusions. Positive generalizations made in this area are generally based upon unwarranted confidence in rather loose unscientific methods of interpreting data, and upon a relatively uncritical acceptance of a particular conceptual scheme.

Research on the psychological responses of non-Western people needs to be made more specific and concrete. Culture-personality writers have, on the whole, tended to avoid this kind of limited investigation for a number of reasons having to do with the danger of viewing a given segment of behavior out of its cultural context. The emphasis upon cultural configurations was in part a reaction against such segmental interpretations. Moreover, ethnologists have not been concerned with specific psychological problems because they have been urgently concerned with gathering descriptive materials about non-literate societies before they vanished or were distorted by Western influences.

In his role as a psychologist the anthropologist needs to integrate his work as a careful ethnologist with a large body of psychological theory and research, including the non-clinical. The study of limited, specific, and verifiable propositions does not necessarily run counter to the ethnologist's insistence that a culture must be understood as a whole before specific psychological studies are undertaken. The cultures best suited for these purposes should be those concerning which a considerable amount of ethnological material is available. Such investigations would be valuable, not only as correctives of certain ethnocentric tendencies in psychological theorizing, but should also make constructive theoretical contributions on specific issues. Aside from the obvious benefits accruing to anthropology from this "gearing-in," another advantageous effect might be to arouse much more interest in anthropological work on the part of the great majority of psychologists and social psychologists.

A concern with more concretely limited and traditionally emphasized psychological problems would broaden the culture-personality ethnologist's range of choice of conceptual schemes and hypotheses. As it is now, the substantial choice is between no psychology at all and a brand of neo-Freudianism. The emphasis should not be on committing oneself to one school of thought or another, but of checking all rival hypotheses on specific problems by accepted scientific procedure.

ADULT SOCIALIZATION AND SOCIAL WORK PRACTICE

PHILIP BERG

In the early stages of its history social work was so intimately bound up with the discipline of sociology that often the two were indistinguishable from each other, either by the general public or by academicians. In the early twentieth century, however, there occurred a schism between the two fields that grew to such proportions that by the 1920's the "do-gooders" and the "nose-counters" regarded each other with mutual disdain. In seeking recognition as a "pure" science, sociology zealously followed the path of positivism and empiricism, concentrating primarily on the accumulation of "raw" data and the refinement of research techniques. Finding itself increasingly hard put to utilize such alien endeavors in the formation of its knowledge base, social work turned to psychoanalytic theory as its chief authority in explaining human behavior. Psychoanalysis helped fortify an already existing trend in social work toward treating the "individual." Although Freudian theory could hardly be considered less esoteric than sociological theory, it did at least provide social work with a therapy-centered focus and a fairly coherent theory of personality structure.

During the past decade or so, there have been indications of a "theory-sharing process" occurring among the fields of sociology, anthropology, psychology, and psychiatry. The traditional academic boundaries, so vigilantly guarded for decades, show signs of disintegration at certain points.

The traditional earmark of sociology and cultural anthropology has been the concern with such concepts as the group, the community, or society. Psychology and psychiatry, on the other hand, have been concerned primarily with the individual. Now, all the behavioral sciences are coming to agree that the distinction between "in-

Reprinted with permission of the author and of the National Association of Social Workers, from *Social Work*, Vol. 12, No. 2 (April, 1967), pp. 89-94.

dividual" and "society" is an arbitrary one, and that knowledge of the one is inconceivable without some knowledge of the other. New interest is being taken in the concept of socialization, which has been defined as "the process whereby personality is acquired through social interaction."[1] This "encounter" between the individual and his sociocultural milieu is coming to be a "common denominator" for discussions among behavioral scientists.

It is from this concern with socialization that sociologists and anthropologists have contributed new insights into not only the developmental aspects of personality but also those aspects relating to personality change. The socialization of adults is a comparatively recent topic of investigation, yet it is a most pertinent one for the practicing social worker. For the worker ought to recognize that even though his professional goals are usually articulated by such phrases as "helping clients help themselves," his actual "societal" function, in many cases at least, involves a directed attempt to modify certain values and to redirect the behavior patterns of his clients. And since adults undoubtedly comprise a fair proportion of the total clientele served by social workers, it seems logical to conclude that the social worker's knowledge base must include a realization that (1) adult personality is subject to change and (2) social and cultural factors can act as potent stimulants to such change.

ADULT SOCIALIZATION

The concept of adult socialization has, until very recently, been the object of neglect by behavioral scientists. The most sophisticated efforts to account for personality development—those of Freud and Sullivan—follow the child's path of development to the point at which he is about to become an adult. At that point the theories come to an abrupt halt and seem to imply that whatever personality changes might occur in adulthood will be only inconsequential variants of earlier development.[2] As Sarnoff comments:

> This neglect is puzzling, especially when we consider that novelists, those nonscientific brothers under the skin of students of personality, have not shared the psychologist's apparent disinterest in this realm. On the contrary, it would appear that the changes in personality occurring in adulthood have been the foremost preoccupation of literary geniuses such as Dostoyevski, Tolstoi and Proust.[3]

Many sociologists have been sharply critical of psychological theories in general and of psychoanalytic theory in particular, arguing that such explanations are excessively individualistic, physiology-bound, and childhood-deterministic. The formulations that have proved most acceptable to sociologists as explanations of personality development have arisen from such sources as the "symbolic interactionist" school of social psychology, "culture and personality" studies by anthropologists, and that rather amorphous school of thought that has been labeled "neo-Freudian" psychology. All of these approaches tend to share at least one common element, namely, "situational" factors and their influence on human personality. A number of researchers have noted the far-reaching effects of these factors (including statuses, roles, values, and reference groups) on an individual's attitudes and actions at any given time. These studies have been concerned with such problems as the "conditioning" effects of poverty, the influence of economic affluence on American "national character," the effects of prejudice and discrimination on members of minority groups, the psychological consequences of modern business organization, and the effects of occupation on personality.[4] Moreover, these investigations serve to confirm the idea that human personality is not a rigid structure as much as it is a dynamic, changing phenomenon.

DEVELOPMENT AND CHANGE

One of the crucial areas of adult socialization is the concept of development. Inherent in the definition of the term is the idea of progressive movement, in which each stage has some discernible connection to the other stages. The problem is to determine precisely the nature of this relationship that exists between early and later stages of development. The following metaphor may be used to illustrate this:

> We have before us an uncooked egg. We may choose to boil, scramble or poach it, or make it into a dozen different kinds of omelet. Regardless of the treatment this egg receives, it remains an egg. To the extent that any claim is made that "this egg is now cooked," all that this can mean is that in more or less degree the egg is finished. Up to the point where it becomes converted into charcoal and is really finished, the cooking of the egg represents a matter merely of degree: no matter how the egg changes in appearance, it is still essentially an egg.[5]

Therefore, one may say that a person may experience extensive changes during his lifetime, but the "essential" person remains. The metaphor suggests that the core of personality is formed in early childhood and that any subsequent changes are simply variations on a theme. To lend support to this notion, it is not necessary to resort to such concepts as needs, identifications, or ego defenses. A strictly sociological interpretation views the source of human behavior as values that have been determined by society, implanted within the young child, and thereafter nurtured and preserved by a variety of institutional constraints. Thus, even from a sociological viewpoint it would be possible to regard personality change in adulthood as something quite superficial.

Freud's theory wrestles with complex issues, such as the changes in the growing child's physiological functioning and the effects on his personality that stem from his need to adapt to these changes. He also stresses the importance of the long period of child rearing, during which the child is exposed to another set of unavoidable stimuli—this time from his immediate environment—in the form of parental and sibling influences. The personality development of the child may, therefore, be traced, in a general way, by exploring the dual impact of physiological factors and the agents of socialization.

ADULTHOOD AS A SOCIAL PHENOMENON

After he has passed through puberty, the individual comes to be recognized as an adult, having arrived at his new status with a rather well-structured personality configuration. But if it is conceded that his personality has been shaped by a process of social interaction with his environment, it would seem unjustifiable to conclude that as he continues to interact with the external world he will no longer be subject to personality change. It is obvious that the adult is not the weak, helpless creature he once was, and thus is not a passive recipient of environmental stimuli. As an adult, therefore, he must constantly deal with new and changing conditions in his social life.

If it is granted that the adult's personality may continue to change, there still remains the problem of conceptualizing such change. Psychoanalytic theory affirms that "the child is father to the man." It sees adulthood as a relatively stable period, although it seems implicit in the very existence of psychoanalytic therapy that one's personality continues to develop after the attainment of biological maturity. Despite this recognition, it is evident from the length and complexity of psychoanalytic therapy that the analyst considers the task of altering the basic structure of the adult personality extremely formidable.

To Freud, the concept of maturity or adulthood was almost wholly physiological. The attainment of genital sexuality, according to psychoanalytic theory, is reflected in various types of social attitudes and behavior.[6] However, anthropologists have discovered that adulthood is really as much a social condition as it is a biological one, and is characterized by constellations of social roles as well as by certain physical realities. Cultural anthropologists have noted, for example, that in some cultures adulthood is defined in ways that run counter to Freud's expectations of the "genital character." Kluckhohn reports that among the "Siwana and Keraki, all males practice homosexuality as boys (passively) and as men (actively)."[7] This pattern of adult male sexuality is so conventional among the Keraki that a male adult would be regarded as seriously abnormal if he chose to abstain from homosexual relations prior to marriage.[8]

"NORMAL" TRANSFORMATIONS

Membership in any group or social structure almost inevitably involves the passage from one status to another. Many such passages are institutionalized, so that the individual moves through them in an orderly sequence. This serves to provide continuity to the group as well as to the individual's experience. In various ways the person is prepared for what is to come and is reminded of the transition from one status to the next. Such status transformations often involve not only changes in actions, but also changes in the "reasons" given for these changes. Motivations that were suitable to previous, lower statuses tend to be cast aside in favor of newer, more "appropriate" motivations.

This process was illustrated by Arensberg and Kimball, who described family transition in Irish peasant culture.[9] The marriage of a son brings about a sudden transformation in status, action, and motivation. The father is expected to yield control of family policy and to cease active work; the son must not only assume chief responsibility, but strongly desire to do so; the mother is then expected to become the teacher of the son's wife; and the son's wife becomes, for the time being, subservient. The younger woman is also expected to be strongy motivated to become a mother as soon as possible, and after the birth of her first son, she is expected to assume full household responsibility and to do it with enthusiasm. At this point the older couple becomes recognized socially as "aged."

Not all personal transformations are as neatly institutionalized as family transition in Irish peasant culture. Some changes in perspective occur outside of, and even in spite of, influences from the major social institutions. Drastic transformations of identity are rare, but when they do occur they tend to be accompanied by a psychological reorientation in which the person develops a new set of values and new criteria for judging himself and his world. For example, an adult may undergo considerable change after a traumatic experience. The death and bloodshed of combat often cause soldiers to perceive the world in a very different light; some of them develop psychoses. The sudden loss of fortune by one who has always been wealthy can be a shattering experience, although it is often reported that a man "really finds himself" for the first time after such an experience. A woman may become a "different woman" after her marriage, cheerfully assuming duties of which her friends thought her totally incapable. After the birth of their first child, one or both parents may change noticeably when they suddenly realize their new social responsibilities. In all such cases there are modifications in self-conceptions that, in turn, are accompanied by changes in interpersonal relationships.

Conversion

Conversion may occur in a variety of contexts, of course, though the term has been used most frequently in referring to religious experiences. In dealing with the question of which persons tend to be converted to "esoteric cults," Niebuhr refers to those who are "disinherited," and other scholars have similarly asserted that the disgruntled, maladjusted, and frustrated are those who tend to be most receptive to this type of experience.[10] Many converts come to reject their families and former friends, and state that their "experience" makes them feel appreciated and restored the prestige they lacked.

Rapoport's study of the Mormon missions in Rimrock, Arizona, shows that the Indians who were converted to Mormonism were those who, for one reason or another, failed to fit into Navaho social life. Some were young people who wanted to identify themselves with the dominant American culture, others were women who were dissatisfied with their subordinate social roles.[11]

Recovery from mental disorders also may have many of the characteristics of conversion. Burke has referred to successful psychoanalytic therapy as "secular conversion," in the sense that the patient is persuaded to redefine himself from a new standpoint. He contends that psychoanalysts have constructed their own symbolic environment, complete with a special "vocabulary of motives," which enables the patient to alleviate his stress by attaching new names to his faults. Burke labeled this process "exorcism by misnomer."[12] Before a patient can be persuaded to accept a new perspective, an interpersonal tie must be established between the patient and therapist — a process known as "transference." The therapist thereby becomes a "significant other," who teaches the patient a new outlook and then supports it. It is interesting to note that therapists trained in different schools of psychoanalysis claim approximately the same degree of success. This seems to indicate that therapeutic techniques based on "doctrine" probably have a minor influence on the rate of recovery. The crucial element seems to be the establishment of warm, personal ties with the patient.

Viktor Frankl, a contemporary Austrian psychotherapist, founded the system of logotherapy. His approach, which is less retrospective and introspective than Freudian theory, holds that man's primary motivation is not the will to pleasure or to power (in Freudian or Adlerian terms), but the "will to meaning."[13] Frankl attempts to change a person's attitudes by persuading him to perceive his current situation from a new vantage point, without the lengthy process of recounting childhood experiences. This existentialist psychotherapy, although arising and operating entirely outside of a sociological framework, is nonetheless a clear recognition of the importance of one's immediate interpersonal situation.

SITUATIONAL ADJUSTMENT

Brim has argued that there are no really "deep" personality characteristics that persist across any or all situations and social roles.[14] Kallen expressed a similar view:

> Personal accounts of progress uncover no single pattern, no straight in-
> evitable line, developmental or other. They speak of regressions and
> other shifts of interest and direction.[15]

If a person is a transient rather than a permanent or long-term
participant in a social situation, his perspectives can be expected to
shift with his movement. This was shown by Wheeler, who observed
that prisoners tended to become more "prisonized" the longer they
were in prison, but when they approached their time of release they
became increasingly law-abiding.[16] The inmate finds that he must
adjust himself to the criminally oriented social structure of the prison
in order to get along satisfactorily, but when he approaches the time
of release from prison he realizes that the values that put him in good
stead in prison simply are not practicable on the outside. To imply,
however, that values are purely situational in nature would be un-
justifiably extreme. It could be argued, for instance, that in Wheeler's
study the prisoners' behavior reflected no real change in values, but
rather a tactful role-playing by persons forced into a highly restrictive social situation.

COMMITMENT

The process of situational adjustment helps to account for much
of the change that an adult experiences when he encounters shifting
social and psychological demands during his lifetime. Yet it is common knowledge that human behavior is not so flexible as to be
chaotic or random. People tend to exhibit, in other words, a certain
consistency as they pass from one situation to another. Sociologists
have used the concept of "commitment" to explain this consistency.[17]
Although a person may engage in a wide range of unrelated disparate actions, it is still likely that he perceives these acts as fundamentally integrated and consistent with his pursuit of certain goals.
It is quite possible that he may choose to ignore the pressures of situational adjustment in order to follow a consistent pattern of behavior in the many areas of his life; he may do this even though his
decision may result in a short-term loss.

Adulthood, therefore, may be described as a period in which a
person gradually acquires a variety of commitments that constrain
him to follow a consistent direction of behavior throughout his life.

Certain events, such as the choice of an occupation, finding a wife, or having children, tend to produce relatively lasting commitments and thus constrain a person's behavior. One sociologist suggests that the concept of commitment

> . . . accounts for the fact that juvenile delinquents seldom become adult criminals, but rather turn into respectable, conventional, law-abiding lower-class citizens. It may be that the erratic behavior of the juvenile delinquent is erratic precisely because the boy has not yet taken any actions which commit him more or less permanently to a given line of endeavor.[18]

The concepts of commitment and situational adjustment are related, but not identical, processes. Situational adjustment encourages change; commitment encourages stability. The two concepts are complementary to the extent that one's immediate situation is viewed as having definite connections to anticipated future situations.

The most promising area for further research into adult socialization lies in the little-explored territory of the relationship between the social structural "imperatives" and individual behavior. For it is social structure that creates the conditions for *both* change and stability in adult personality. The concepts of situational adjustment and commitment, by affirming that values are not inflexible and unalterable in adult life, provide a much-needed supplement to traditional theories of personality. As Erikson noted: "Identity is never gained nor maintained once and for all. Like a good conscience, it is constantly lost and regained."[19]

NOTES

[1] Francis E. Merrill, *Society and Culture* (Englewood Cliffs, N.J.: Prentice-Hall, 1961), p. 151.

[2] Anselm Strauss, *Mirrors and Masks: The Search for Identity* (Glencoe, Ill.: Free Press, 1959).

[3] Irving Sarnoff, *Personality Dynamics and Development* (New York: John Wiley & Sons, 1962), p. 401.

[4] *See,* for example, William Whyte, Jr., *The Organization Man* (New York: Doubleday & Co., 1956); and Maurice R. Stein, Arthur Vidich, and David M. White, eds., *Identity and Anxiety* (Glencoe, Ill.: Free Press, 1960).

[5] Strauss, *op. cit.,* pp. 90-91.

[6] Sarnoff, *op. cit.*

[7] Clyde Kluckhohn, "Culture and Behavior," in Gardner Lindzey, ed., *Handbook of Social Psychology* (Cambridge, Mass.: Addison-Wesley Publishing Co., 1954), p. 928.

[8] C. S. Ford and F. A. Beach, *Patterns of Sexual Behavior* (New York: Harper & Bros., 1951).

[9] Conrad M. Arensberg, *The Irish Countryman* (Magnolia, Mass.: Peter Smith, 1937); Arensberg and S. T. Kimball, *Family and Community in Ireland* (Magnolia, Mass.: Peter Smith, 1959).

[10] H. Richard Niebuhr, *Social Sources of Denominationalism* (New York: Henry Holt & Co., 1929).

[11] Robert Norman Rapoport, *Changing Navaho Religious Values*, A Study of Christian Missions to the Rimrock Navahos, "Reports of the Rimrock Project, Values Series No. 2," Vol. 41, No. 2 (Cambridge, Mass.: Peabody Museum of American Archaeology and Ethnology, 1954).

[12] Kenneth Burke, *Permanence and Change* (Los Altos, Calif.: Hermes Publications, 1954).

[13] Viktor E. Frankl, *Man's Search for Meaning* (New York: Washington Square Press, 1963).

[14] Orville G. Brim, Jr., "Personality as Role-Learning," in Ira Iscoe and Harold W. Stevenson, eds., *Personality Development in Children* (Austin: University of Texas Press, 1960), pp. 127-159.

[15] Horace Kallen, *Patterns of Progress* (New York: Columbia University Press, 1936), p. 26.

[16] Stanton Wheeler, "Socialization in Correctional Communities," *American Sociological Review*, Vol. 26, No. 5 (October 1961), pp. 697-712.

[17] Howard S. Becker, "Notes on the Concept of Commitment," *American Journal of Sociology*, Vol. 66, No. 4 (July 1960), pp. 32-40.

[18] Howard S. Becker, Blanche Geer, Everett C. Hughes, and Anselm Strauss, *Boys in White: Student Culture in Medical School* (Chicago: University of Chicago Press, 1961), p. 51.

[19] Erik H. Erikson, *Childhood and Society* (New York: W. W. Norton & Co., 1950), p. 57.

SECTION III

Family: Change and Dysfunction

INTRODUCTION

Institution and Functions:

Family is generally acknowledged to be the most significant social institution devised by man. If any supporting evidence of this is necessary, we need only consider that the institution is all but universally found in human society around the world. Despite the many changes taking place in our society, it remains the most important contemporary social institution as well.

The significance of family rests largely on the fact that we all spend considerable spans of our lives within its framework. Usually, this includes our most formative and dependent years. Because of its universality, family accomplishes a number of necessary tasks on behalf of the society and its individual members.[1]

The family is the ideal setting for reproduction of the group, thus fulfilling the basic quest of all living species to leave behind them a next generation. Then, too, it provides a suitable setting for the maintenance of the individual. This, of course, regards children in their extended dependency. The female also finds protection during pregnancy, when she is tied down with her young, and generally from the physically more powerful males of her society. For all family members, however, help and care during illness, injury or old age is facilitated by the usual loyalty and attachment which mark human family groups.

Having brought children into the world, family is also the most significant socializing agency of society. It provides the rewards and punishments which shape the next generation's values, understanding of society and its expectations. William Goode refers to family as the "transmission belt by which the culture is kept alive."[2] Not only does the family socialize the next generation, it provides the social and sexual controls necessary to keep the society functioning on a day-to-day basis. Through it, the individual can give expression to those wishes and desires which his society deems acceptable. At the same time, its complex interpersonal relations enable other family members to exercise informal sanctions, persuasion, influence or even punishment to forestall culturally defined unacceptable behavior, before it

139

brings down upon the recalcitrant, public sanction and severe community reaction.

THE CHANGING FAMILY

These basic functions, of course, may explain the sociological roots and universality of the family, even though some may apply more literally in one society than another. However, human ingenuity being what it is, it doesn't take long to discover that the various functions can conceivably be parceled out to specialized instrumentalities of society. Children can be born out of wedlock, sexual favors can be purchased through prostitution or entered into by mutual consent of unmarried individuals, children have been raised institutionally and socialized with the help of specialized educational expertise, the maintenance of the individual is entrusted to medical personnel, and support for the aged provided by the government. Such variations are indeed found when we study family cross-culturally. We also know that in many ways, certain of the traditional functions of the family have been transferred. So, the family as the basic economic unit of production has all but passed out of existence in our society. To a somewhat lesser degree, this holds true for its function as a unit of consumption and entertainment, while bio-medical technology and its application to contraception, make it feasible that the sexual and the reproductive functions also be separated from one another. It is not surprising that many have concluded from these and other changes that family is a declining institution in the Western world.[3]

In reaching such conclusions, these students of family have overlooked such contradictory evidence as the continued high rate of married persons in the adult population.[4] Statistical evidence on second marriages supports the view that even those who divorce are soured, not on marriage per se, but on the particular marriage partner.[5]

To grasp the motivation behind this seeming contradiction, one needs to recognize the one function of family which clearly takes on more significance, rather than less, in our modern specialized mass society. This has to do with the intense emotional quality of family relations. While just about all other aspects of our interpersonal contacts become increasingly secondary, that is utilitarian, objectified, devoid of affect, family remains an island of primary relationships —

deep, personal, emotionally involved.[6] Here one must come to grips with intense emotions of love and hate, loyalty and commitment. There is no room for objectivity in the family group.

Extended family attachments have declined, thus placing extreme burdens on the nuclear family (parents and children). All these intense emotions are concentrated on a small group of objects and cannot effectively be diffused. In light of this, one can understand the high incidence of intrafamily violence which occurs annually. If a particular family fulfills its function as a haven of emotional satisfaction, the individual is indeed fortunate to have a base from which to cope with the emotional sterility of anonymous mass society. If not, he is in trouble and may seek to break his family ties more readily than in previous generations. On the other hand, some dysfunction does stem from the fact that the setting which socializes the individual for our society, with its secondary relationships, is one which is so emotionally intense. At each stage in expanding his social horizons, the individual faces the potential trauma of relating on successively less personal planes. This is often quite marked when the child must learn to relate to a teacher and classmates on the basis of his earlier experiences with mother and perhaps a couple of siblings.[7]

The changing nature of family has also changed the nature of courtship and marriage. When family fulfilled various traditional functions, the bonds which held the spouses together were intimately connected with the wishes and expectations of many others in the couple's family and community who had a stake in the success of their marriage, sometimes literally. If, for example, many relatives have contributed to the bride price, the groom will think twice before sending her packing over a small argument. Too many of his own kinsmen would feel he had cheated them without good cause. Thus he is likely to hesitate. The appropriate spouse was not only chosen on the basis of personal preferences of the individuals directly involved, but on a range of social and economic considerations as well. Compatibility was only part of the story. The perspective of the other relatives was likely to be far less influenced by personal and emotional judgments and more by the question of whether these two were amalgamating two suitable family lines.

It should be pointed out that courtship is a kind of bargaining or bartering process, with each side seeking to enter into that partnership which offers the "best deal." Even when families in traditional societies signed contracts and engaged in exchanges of gifts or actual payments, it is a cultural bias which causes us not to notice the ritual nature of such business arrangements. Brides were usually "sold" since in simple societies, sale and barter was the model for all social affairs. Besides, it is pretty clear that in traditional society one only conducts business with appropriate counterparts. Economic and social relations are not specialized activities in the folk society, as they are with us.[8] Thus every marriage entailed a system of interconnections which fostered its success.

Although it may shock those who are more romantically inclined, modern courtship has not changed the basic nature of this barter. The terms and commodities considered have changed. The woman's physical attractiveness, always a factor, has become paramount. The man's potential earning power, socio-economic status and to a lesser degree physical characteristics, are important. Since the industrial revolution, families play a decreasing role in judging the suitability of potential spouses. This is partly due to the greater mobility of the young and partly due to the unavailability of data and criteria on which to base more mature judgments. Who knows anything about the family of a date until the two are already quite involved? This has been especially true for girls who rarely met their future in-laws before engagement or at least "engagement to be engaged." Boys used to meet the girl's family in calling for their dates at home. Today, even that is a fading custom of the past, if for no other reason than the fact that so many young women no longer live at home. Modern conditions have conspired to reduce the criteria for selection to the point where young people are left to make choices on their own. Often, away from family, in such artificially contrived environments as college campuses, a different set of values operates than in their own society, and an emotional romantic aura is created by our dating and courtship oriented entertainment industry. Linton, in a particularly sharp analysis, put it as follows:

> All societies recognize that there are occasional violent emotional attachments between persons of opposite sex, but our present American culture is practically the only one which has attempted to capitalize these and make them the basis for marriage. Most groups regard them as unfortunate and point out the victims of such attachments as horrible examples. Their rarity in most societies suggests that they are psychological abnormalities to which our own culture has attached an extraordinary

value just as other cultures have attached values to other abnormalities. The hero of the American movie is always a romantic lover, just as the hero of the old Arab epic is always an epileptic. A cynic might suspect that in any ordinary population the percentage of individuals with a capacity for romantic love of the Hollywood type was about as large as that of persons able to throw genuine epileptic fits. However, given a little social encouragement, either one can be adequately imitated without the performer admitting even to himself that the performance is not genuine.[9]

One reaction to this may be seen in the computer dating fad, with our technology replacing earlier family judgment. Another may be engagement in sexual release, without the finality of a wedding ceremony. This is facilitated by advances in modern contraceptive techniques as well as new attitudes, especially on the part of the women, regarding sexuality as a value in and of itself. That the latter has fostered promiscuity tends to be exaggerated of late since most research reveals that significant rises in premarital sexual behavior have not occurred since the 1920's! Most young women who do become involved in premarital intimacy genuinely seem to believe at the time that they were fulfilling a "meaningful relationship."[10] As expected, fewer males hold such a belief. Thus far, at least, there is reason to believe that it is talk, not action, which has radically changed for most Americans. Even evidence from emancipated Sweden supports the view that young people are essentially not promiscuous.[11] Yet the loss of other factors takes sexual gratification, a highly volatile characteristic, out of perspective. The remarkable feature of modern marriage is therefore its stability, not its instabilty.

A major component of family change in our society involves the change we have seen this century in the place of women in the Western world and their status relative to men. These matters reach to the very concept of sex role in our society. One of the most fundamental types of division of labor found in human societies entails the recognition of appropriate sex roles for males and females. While the particulars of such socially defined roles may differ cross-culturally, no society fails to take cognizance of the differences between males and females, and to reserve for each certain sanctioned forms of behavior. Traditionally, Western Christian society has largely been marked by a greater or lesser degree of masculine dominance, ambivalence toward sexuality, a dual standard with regard to sexual freedom and an image of the male as the aggressive, wage earner and the female as the passive housewife and mother. These traditions have been undermined by the emancipation of women socially and sexually.

The early Hebrews viewed premarital sexual activity as a rather natural consequence of the unchaperoned association of the sexes. To them, such license would undermine the girl's attractiveness in the bargaining process for a prestigious marriage. Thus, they handled the question of sexual controls through family supervision and early, family negotiated, unions.[12] Early Christianity seems to have taken a somewhat less natural view of sexual behavior, seeing it, even in marriage, as a kind of necessary evil.[13] It was Greco-Roman influence on Western civilization which provided the real cultural sources for our dual standards. One married a wife suited to his station in order to continue his family line and provide for a home, but felt no compulsion to "love" or be faithful to her. For erotic gratification, one could maintain a courtesan or, if less prosperous, purchase the favors of a prostitute. It would seem from prominent figures in the ancient world that it was also quite respectable to resort to homosexual contacts with young males if one's tastes ran in that direction.[14] In the Middle Ages, the chivalric code refined this split, giving rise to "romantic love." The object was someone other than one's own wife, who was idealized as perfection itself. That someone was often someone else's wife, in whose honor the knights performed great acts of valor, but with whom they ostensibly had no physical contact.[15] Wearing the lady's colors or scarf in battle may actually have had some relationship to fetishism. However, that these "romances" were really so chaste is dubious. At any rate, the Industrial Revolution did away with chivalry and direct family control over courtship. We were left only with a dual standard for conduct: Girls to be ostensibly "pure" while men were free to roam. This, of course, is related to physiological realities. Such attitudes are described by Whyte with regard to even working class boys.[16] Few of us are aware that the merger of the two figures, the fantasied erotic object and the proper spouse and mother is a recent invention of American metropolitan society, promoted by our mass media. Not too long ago, as even now in most circles, a dual standard prevailed. The words of that clever toast, "Here's to our wives and sweethearts — may they never meet," have had some literal significance in our emerging values.

The life of the married woman has changed sharply in recent years, reflecting her changing status. Today she is less likely than ever before to be limited to the role of homemaker. This is partly attributable to the high prestige of the temptress image and the low prestige of home-making and partly to an education which acts as if women should be prepared for every occupation, save housewife. This unpreparedness along with that of young men for fatherhood, may explain some of the resentment which feeds our growing child abuse records. In every aspect possible, our formal education tries not to notice boys and girls. This is unfortunate since in growth, learning and emotions there seem to be somewhat distinctive patterns. However, a major factor in the decline of housewifery is our level of technology which obviates the need to invest long hours, great energy, and skill in homemaking tasks which consumed the time of our mothers and grandmothers. Besides, commercial processors are better at these jobs than the average house-wife today. Women do feel a touch of guilt about neglecting these wifely virtues, but psychologists have convinced food processors to leave just enough processing to the little woman to take care of that. Thus she is assured that, "Nothin' says lovin' like somethin' from the oven — and Pillsbury says it best!"

One-third of all married women are now in the labor market.[17] The percentage of working mothers is admittedly higher as you go down the socioeconomic ladder. However, in the middle income brackets it is not necessity but an advertising generated desire for "extras" which motivates them. Substantial numbers of married women, however, either work or engage in other non-salaried activities out of the home out of sheer need to escape their homes. With fewer children, im-proved health and longevity, one also finds women returning to the job market when children are no longer dependent. Even those who are not employed have changed from producers and processors of goods to administrators and managers of consumption.

All of these changes have created a "climate" of equality between the sexes which is new in the Western world. The stress must be placed on climate because, in reality, the sexes remain far from equal. However, the earlier dimension of clearly defined sex roles has been obscured to the point where Odenwald[18] could discuss the decline of sexual differences and more recently Winick could, with much justice, discuss desexualization in our society.[19] We don't sense this process too readily despite the transvestite styles, autoerotic dancing, cosmetics, jewelry and housework for men, jobs and buying power for women, because our attention has been focused on the more blatant expressions of sensuality. We rarely consider that behind the "sexy" miniskirt is the childlike exhibitionism of preadolescence, just as behind the American male's enchantment with boyish styled clothing and hair may be his somewhat less complicated latency period. This, more than anything else, might explain why changing attitudes have entailed many immature forms of sexual expression as well as our enchantment with perpetual youth.

Class Factors in Illegitimacy and Broken Homes

While neither adultery nor extramarital promiscuity seem to have risen sharply, premarital intimacy on the part of single women is popularly identified with rising illegitimacy rates. It should be pointed out that the illegitimacy rate is very much linked to social class phenomena in our society. Rates are inversely correlated with socioeconomic status. Of Negro births in the United States (substantially a lower class population), an estimated 25% are illegitimate![20] This figure, however, is problematic, since legal marriage as an institution in the lower class is limited and common law unions frequent. The distortion is also connected with the repeated "illegitimate" births by mature women and does not reflect only youthful, premarital conduct. The black community also suffers from the special legacy of slavery and continued impoverishment.

Low illegitimacy rates in the middle class reflect more than sexual morality although this remains a part of it. The rates reflect greater availability of and readiness to use contraceptives. In dire emergencies, they reflect our rising national abortion rate. However, one cannot dismiss the apparently greater anxiety evoked in the middle class by the specter of an illegitimate child. This doesn't mean greater abstinence. In a society which has thrown young people together with so many opportunities for intimacy, abstinence would be near miraculous. Instead, the anxiety apparently diverts the sexual intimacy from actual coitus to other forms of sexual release. This may reflect a greater responsibility regarding the conception of a child who will not be raised in a completed natural family. However, one may question whether this behavior really reflects any different sexual morality, per se.

Some have challenged the assumption that high illegitimacy rates in the black population reflect differing values concerning sexual promiscuity and out-of-wedlock births. Even the higher percentage of unwed mothers keeping their babies may simply result from the absence of adoptive homes. One thing is indisputable, however. When so many out-of-wedlock children are born in a segment of society, there must be a great reduction in the social control which can be exercised by rumor, scandal and other informal sanctions usually leveled at those who violate group mores. Only in this setting could it be proposed that concern about illegitimacy is not a "black value". Concern about legitimacy seems to be a value of all peoples. However, Malinowski points out that legitimacy is closely linked to social placement and lineage, especially as related to inheritance. Therefore, the lower an individual's place in the socioeconomic structure, the less concerned is the society with irregularity and lack of clarity in his lineage.[21]

Many similar considerations enter into discussions of broken, matricentric, lower class homes. With all of the attention on what happens to lower class children because of the father's abdication, little attention has been directed to an essentially similar trend in the middle class. Work and home in the suburbs being separated by great distances, most of the suburban world is dominated by females, with the father's work totally unrelated to the lives of the children. Of course, all of this remains within the context of an existing family, thus making it a subtler problem.[22]

For those of higher socioeconomic status, illegitimate birth seems to be the result of the individual's definite need for an experience which is, after all, avoidable. One frequent observation made by professionals, is that middle class boys act out through delinquency, while the girls act out through promiscuity and illegitimacy. Given our present values, such behavior still makes the girl as unacceptable for other than casual exploitation. There is little evidence of much change in these attitudes.

INTERGENERATIONAL CONFLICT

Never before, it would seem, has conflict between generations seemed to occupy so much public attention. A special term, generation gap, has even been coined to express the schism between the young and their elders. In a sense, to each of us, the world begins when we are born and ends when we have passed from the scene. No child ever grew or discovered as each of us grows and discovers. Each couple who court and marry would believe that never before has there been such immortal love. We are often convinced that no predecessor shared our insights or understood as well as we do how to right the world's wrongs. So, too, the temptation is strong to see our current woes without an historical perspective.

We know, of course, that some tension between generations has marked most ages of mankind. The elders of many civilizations have no doubt had occasion to worry about the predictably dire consequences they expected when their children's generation took over the reins. As with so many social phenomena, however, one must ask whether our current predicament is unique to our own age or the contemporary expression of an age-old pattern.

Theories concerning intergenerational conflict have tended to stress the patterned recurrence of such phonomena. Perhaps this is attributable, in part, to the age at which thinkers begin to theorize. At any rate, Freud's widely accepted Oedipal myth about primitive man represents a symbolic base for such a cyclical view.[23] His formulation, however, lacks verification in analysis of the societies of either primitive men or higher mammals. It can perhaps best be understood in light of the Social Darwinism current in the intellectual climate of his time. A more useful psychological formulation might be found in Erikson's view of the developmental tasks faced by the individual,[24] particularly in adolescence, or Parsons' psychosocial formulation which seeks to bring together the individual systems and the societal framework.[25]

However, Kingsley Davis' *Sociology of Parent-Youth Conflict*[26] continues to have the most insightful ring about it. He stresses the differing rates of socialization and past-future orientation at different stages of the life-cycle as related to the degree of change occurring during any one generation. Another point in his analysis with a contemporary ring to it has to do with the reaction of young people to the adolescent discovery of their elders' clay feet. Lacking the emotional capacity to live with imperfection, they are readily attracted to the totalities of alienated cynicism or idealistic revolution. Davis stresses the inadequacy of our competitively oriented society's mechanisms to forestall direct confrontation over authority. There is an old Jewish folk saying that two are not envious of the achievements of others — a father of his son and a teacher of his student. By contrast, reading student papers on the generation gap leads one to conclude that the topic may as well be class war, intergroup conflict, or international relations. Davis is extremely helpful in understanding intergenerational conflict over authority. Yet to explain why even in our own society there seems to be more pronounced conflict than there was in the past, we need to acknowledge certain additional contributing factors.

Although Davis sees parent-youth conflict as an age-old process, he recognizes our peculiar circumstances, especially the competitiveness and rapid social change. However, we should note how the values of our society are intricately tied in with our technological development. It encouraged a new hedonism among the children of our affluence which their elders have more difficulty taking in stride. Even more, our technological innovation, stressing as it does the new over the old, has carried over from gadgetry to people and ideas. Thus, in a society where experience is believed to lose its relevancy, so are its bearers. It should not surprise us that those over thirty are easily intimidated from imposing their views on those under thirty. As a matter of fact, adolescents have set the pace in many phases of American life in recent years. Permissiveness is perhaps the wisest course when your own perspective is so questionable. One must recall that this is not a rigid, tradition-oriented society faced by youthful rebellion, but a changing, liberal, even permissive one. Those most actively engaged in rebellion are not the society's victims, but gifted, satiated young people from prosperous homes, marked perhaps, by excessive achievement expectations and demands.

Not only are the normal authority figures in our society undermined by our technology, other competing authorities result from the institutional specialization which marks our technological society. Thus there are a multiplicity of potential sources of values and role models. These are given a broader audience than ever before conceivable through our modern means of communication. Many observers of American life since Davis, have commented on the potential harm arising from the absence of "rites of passage" in American life. Gioscia has recently related this "achrony" to the growing drug use among our youth.[27]

In general, one can characterize the arenas in which intergenerational friction comes to the fore largely as the areas of authority, sexuality and drugs. All three can be seen as ambivalent aspects of our culture in general. Authority invites challenge when it is so unsure of itself. Sexuality for its own sake is promoted at every turn by a society which officially frowns at such a point of view and illegal drug use is just one phase of a burgeoning consumption of chemical agents affecting the individual's sense of reality in varying degrees. It might be that the young are giving expression in their naive, youthful exuberance to the subtle, ambivalent suggestions of their society.

Because of the highly emotional quality of these issues, here precisely are the battlegrounds on which social workers may expect to see family conflict expressed. Many troubled young people from unhealthy families find in these channels the means of striking back at their parents with the ultimate weapon — destruction of the parents' dream for their child. This is a highly seductive situation for the professional. Not every innovative or rebellious soul is in trouble. Not infrequently the complaining parent needs more help than the child. However, as a participant in our youth oriented society, often with more "liberal" views than is typical, there is a strong temptation to identify with the intellectualization of a highly emotional situation, rather than search for the roots of conflict within the family constellation.

A MENTAL HEALTH APPROACH TO FAMILY STRIFE

All that has been said suggests that one is likely to find in family very intense feelings which can, of course, be negative as well as positive. Thus, conflicts between spouses and between parents and children are unlikely to be faced rationally. Furthermore, it is only recently that those with better educational background have sought professional help, although such help often comes at a point too late in the deterioration of relationships. Our legal system, which has insisted on assigning blame to one or another spouse in divorce cases, further works against the best possible resolution of marital difficulties. In this aspect of law, there is a vested interest on the part of the legal profesion in maintaining the fiction of an aggrieved and a guilty party. Nevertheless, recent years have seen an increase in the mental health approach to many phases of family strife which were formerly seen as strictly legal issues.

NOTES

[1]A fuller description of the family's functions may be found in William Goode, *The Family*. Englewood Cliffs, N.J.: Prentice-Hall, Inc., 1964, pp. 4-6.

[2]*Ibid.*, p. 5.

[3]This view has been shared by those who express concern over the breakdown of family stability, as well as those who advocate new freedoms in sexual and other family matters.

[4]Murray Gandell and Hans L. Zetterberg, *A Sociological Almanac for the United States*. New York: Bedminster Press, 1961, p. 37.

[5]For a discussion of some of the influences in our society which promote remarriage, see Willam Goode, *After Divorce*. Glencoe: The Free Press, 1956, pp. 206-216.

[6]C. H. Cooley, *Social Organization*. New York: Scribner's, 1909, Chapter 3.

[7]See Talcott Parsons, "The Kinship System of the Contemporary United States," *The American Anthropologist* (January 1943), pp. 22-38.

[8]Melville J. Herskovits, "Before the Machine," *Readings in Anthropology*. Vol. II. Morton Fried, ed. New York: Thomas Y. Crowell Co., 1959, pp. 157-158.

[9]Ralph Linton, *The Study of Man*. New York: Appleton-Century, 1936, p. 175.

[10]A good review of trends in premarital sexuality is found in Gerald R. Leslie, *The Family in Social Context*. New York: Oxford University Press, 1967, pp. 376-419.

[11]J. Robert Moskin, "The New Contraceptive Society," *Look*, Feb. 4, 1969, 50-53.

[12]See Raphael Patai, *Sex and Family in the Bible and the Middle East*. Garden City, N.Y.: Dolphin Books, especially p. 50.

[13]Leslie, *op. cit.*, pp. 177-179.

[14]*Ibid.*, pp. 169, 175, 176; Charles E. Winick, *The New People*. New York: Pegasus, 1968, pp. 342-350.

[15]Leslie, *op. cit.*, pp. 188-189.

[16]William Foote Whyte, "A Slum Sex Code," *American Journal of Sociology*, Vol. 49 (July 1943), pp. 24-31.

[17]See Esther Peterson, "Working Women," *Daedalus* (Spring 1964), pp. 671-699.

[18]Robert P. Odenwald, *The Disappearing Sexes*. New York: Random House, 1965.

[19]Winick, *op. cit.*

[20]Daniel Moynihan, *The Negro Family*. Washington, D.C.: Office of Policy Planning and Research, U.S. Dep't. of Labor, March 1965, p. 59.

[21]Bronislaw Malinowski, *Sex and Repression In Savage Society*. Cleveland: Meridian Books, 1955, pp. 187-190.

22Alice S. Rossi, "Institutional Levers for Achieving Sex Equality," in *Vital Problems For American Society.* ed. J. Alan Winter, Jerome Rabow, Mark Chester. New York: Random House, 1968, p. 167.

23Freud's views on these roots of society are expressed in *Totem and Taboo.* (1913), in *Moses and Monotheism.* (1939).

24Erik H. Erikson, *Childhood and Society,* 2nd ed. New York: W. W. Norton, 1963.

25Parsons, *op. cit.*

26Kingsley Davis, "The Sociology of Parent Youth Conflict," *American Sociological Review,* Vol. 5 (1940), pp. 523-534.

27Victor J. Gioscia, "Adolescence, Addiction and Achrony," *Personality and Social Life,* ed. Robert Endleman. New York: Random House, 1967, especially pp. 341-345.

MARRIAGE IS NOT A PERSONAL MATTER

JOHN FINLEY SCOTT

The newest wrinkle in the old game of courtship is match-making by computer. It goes something like this: a young man lists in a "data bank" what he most desires in a prospective female companion and supplies information about his own characteristics. The computer compares the qualities and interests desired against those of a (presumably vast) inventory of candidates who have also put themselves on file. After some adjustment and compromise, our young man is presented with the name, address and telephone number of a "Miss Just-Right-and-very-nice-too." Since electronic match-making is not quite yet an exact science, he may also be informed of a few alternates (who are also very nice) in case something goes wrong and he doesn't quite hit it off with Miss Just-Right.

The fact that many "computerized introduction services" are pretty much fly-by-night operations does not mean that computer match-making is unworkable in principle. If marital felicity can be accurately defined, then it would seem that a compatible marriage partner would more likely be found among the thousands of candidates to which a computer could refer than among the handful that any one person could ever meet face to face.

But the problem is identifying "marital felicity"; what on earth *is* a successful marriage? Can any kind of successful matching be based on the verbal responses of the largely adolescent segment of the population that is on the verge of matrimony? Any programmer will tell you that a computer is no better than the information put into it. In many respects, the verbal professions of persons facing marriage are the last things on which to base predictions about the future condition of the families thus formed. That a number of marriages—a minority, to be sure, but a substantial one—will terminate in divorce within three years will hardly be revealed through polling the expectations of brides-to-be.

Reprinted from *The New York Times Magazine,* October 30, 1966, by permission of The New York Times and the author.

Part of the problem with the sort of individualistic mate-selection that computer match-making proposes derives from the fact that marriage, though often regarded as an intensely personal affair, is one of the least individualistic of all social institutions. The family—which is, by the way, surprisingly invariant among societies in its basic features—has evolved not because it satisfies individual preferences but because it is socially useful. It combines the functions of reproduction, child care, sexual gratification and economic cooperation with an over-all efficiency that no alternative arrangement has so far been able to match. Since marriage is such a good thing from the society's point of view, it is convenient to make young people want to get married by teaching them that marriage satisfies their *own* needs, and to soft-pedal the demands of the larger society. This is why marriage (like the armed forces) is easier to enter than to leave. Young people are recruited to matrimony, but at the same time their hopes come to depend on frequently unrealistic aspirations and their ability to predict what lies ahead becomes limited.

Here lies the problem with any scheme of matchmaking that relies solely on the expressed preferences of the young people involved. This is hardly anything new: many parents, and most professional match-makers—from Japanese villages to American suburbs—have known it for years. It would be interesting to see what kind of matches a computer would arrange if it interviewed parents as well as their eligible children.

We live in a society where unprecedented numbers of young people, aided by rapid social change, higher education, urbanization and widespread geographical and social mobility, negotiate marriages on their own, without the help of kith and kin. But the notion that the process as a whole is primarily an individual matter is a myth. When two people date who did not know each other beforehand, it is called a "blind date"—a name which stresses the fact that most dates are not blind. Wherever dating customs are studied closely—from church socials to Army barracks — intermediaries and "fixer-uppers" are found busily at work, pairing off the boys and girls in roughly the same way as the new computers. Considering the cost involved, it is economical for persons who date to rely on some outside help. For a young man, expected to take the initiative, dating is one of the most ruthless and unprotected forms of competition in which he can engage. He must put himself up for acceptance or rejection, and rejection can produce severe psychic wounds.

For a young woman, masculine attention in dating and courtship is the greatest social reward she will ever receive, and she therefore desires it to an extreme degree. But for her to accept dates indiscriminately is to run a variety of risks from boredom to sexual assault. The services of intermediaries, who present young men with invitations already accepted and young women with escorts already screened, are therefore greatly appreciated and widely practiced. But intermediaries bring their own interests into the transaction as well as those of the boy and girl whom they introduce. And since the dating career of any person is likely to make use of several intermediaries over time, dating and courtship thus become a thoroughly social process, affected by prevailing norms of mate selection even when the dating partners are not themselves committed to them. When young people today talk in all sincerity about their freedom to date anybody they please, they simply are not describing the entire process, of whose many controls they are often artfully kept unaware.

One very general answer can be given to the question of who marries whom: Most people marry someone pretty much like themselves. (If opposites do attract it has yet to show up in the statistics.) But scientific and garden-variety curiosity alike concentrate on the unexpected and unlikely combination. It is rather like asking the question in a college classroom: "Which girls are going to get pregnant this semester?" Our curiosity runs so much to the irregular, the exotic and the immoral that we usually overlook the one obvious answer that covers almost all cases: "The ones who are married."

Unexpected marriages, like unexpected pregnancies, catch our attention when they deviate from social norms. The salient thing about marriage in this society—indeed, in any society with an organized system of kinship—is that it is regulated by the kinship-based groups which it affects. On the one hand, rules against incest drive young adults out of their own families; yet everywhere these young adults are expected to marry someone from a quite similar family. The anthropologist A. R. Radcliffe-Brown put the matter well when he referred to marriage as a "crisis."

Norms of mate selection—as sociologists rather coarsely phrase it—can be looked at as a classification of social groups in some of which marriage is to be preferred and in others is to be avoided. The practice of marriage within a group is called endogamy. All large groups formed by inheritance—what we call "ethnic groups"—will prefer endogamy to some degree. Since two parents who share the same ethnic traditions can pass them on more consistently than two whose backgrounds differ, endogamy makes a good deal of sense if one wishes to preserve traditions. And the more traditions are cherished, the stronger is the urge toward endogamy. American Jews, for example, voice great concern over the extent of Jewish exogamy—the opposite of endogamy — although, from a comparative point of view, it is amazingly small—probably less than 10 per cent of all marriages involving a Jew. But it seems that the only way for Jewish traditions to survive is through lifelong training of persons born into the group. (A Yiddish aphorism puts it: "A converted Jew is no Jew and no gentile.") Jewish control of endogamy is therefore remarkably strong, and the democracy and indulgence that seem characteristic of Jewish family life usually end abruptly when the prospect of intermarriage looms. Similar rules can be found among American Oriental population groups, the Mormons and, in weaker form, Roman Catholics (who more willingly accept converts) .

One of the strictest rules of endogamy applies to "Negro-white" inter-marriage. It is an essential part of the caste-like status of the black man and the innumerable rigid, two-class distinctions that derive from it. If, for a few generations, there had been practiced in America a degree of intermarriage amounting to 10 per cent of all marriages involving blacks, with the wife assuming the status of the husband and the children combining the genetic and social characteristics passed on by their parents, the contemporary racial situation would be profoundly different. "Black" and "white" would not be two discrete categories of color and (more important) of status, but a widely dispersed continuum, and the two-color caste system, with all its social consequences, would have crumbled in the face of the multiplicity of distinctions that in practice would have to be made. So patterns of marriage have historical consequences.

Predicting whether a certain proportion of marriages will be endogamous or exogamous actually depends on a few rather obvious variables. The relative numbers of the two sexes—the "sex ratio"— is one of the most obvious. It is historically important because men are more likely to migrate than women. This is largely why America, as a land of migrants, has been as much of a melting pot as it has. Many immigrant men who felt strongly about "Marrying a nice (Jewish-Polish-Irish-Armenian, etc.) girl" found there wasn't enough of the kind they wanted to go around. Faced with the choices of marrying out or not marrying at all, many of them married out. The same thing goes on inside America today because men migrate to one place and women to another (there are usually more unmarried women than men in big cities, for example), so that rules for some sort of endogamous marriage get slighted in the competition for anyone to marry at all.

Another factor is the degree of parental control. This is important because it is the older generation that most respects the traditional rules of endogamy, while young people are easily swayed by personal attractions. Here residence is important. A young lady who lives at home and receives her suitors there cannot easily entertain young men of whom her parents strongly disapprove. Even when she is given much freedom, the elders can still influence her choice. Daughters can hardly fall in love with unsuitable men they never meet, and the chances of their not meeting them are greatly increased if the parents happen to have moved (for the children's sake, of course) to a class-homogeneous suburb. When a girl becomes infatuated with a boy beneath her station, parents can use the old strategem of inviting him to a rather formal dinner, the better that his incorrigible unfitness for symbolically important occasions will be forced on the daughter's attention.

Today, however, parental control faces the peculiar threat of college education. When children live at home, parents can keep track daily of whom they are dating. But college often requires "dependent" and "irresponsible" children to live away from home. To be sure, a few young people have been going away to college for generations. But three trends combine to make college today a major threat to endogamy: (1) More persons of college age are in college (currently about 40 per cent); (2) An increasing proportion of students are women; and (3) The average age at marriage has dropped (especially for women) to a point where it falls for many in the traditional undergraduate years.

College and matrimony thus combine to render the campus the most active marriage market of modern times. Even when children live at home while attending college (a growing trend as new campuses and junior colleges are built) the dating situation on the campus is hard for parents to control. Student bodies tend to be large and heterogeneous, and almost any of the many campus activities can be used for making contacts and thus beginning the process of dating and courtship. Not that parents have not fought back. College fraternities, and especially sororities, embody many ingenious arrangements whereby the courtship of young persons is kept in line with the desires of an older generation. Yet it is safe to predict that an increasing number of American marriages will be between persons who meet in college, and they are likely to meet under conditions largely indifferent to older rules of endogamy. A third factor affecting the maintenance of endogamy is social mobility—the process by which members of a generation achieve a higher class position than that into which they were born. In America this movement is intimately related to higher education, for we widely believe that upward mobility is a good thing and that higher education contributes to it. But to the extent that young people start moving up before they are married, and that boys move up in different ways, or at different rates, than girls, then the traditional ways of pairing them off endogamously no longer work.

The most basic difference here is that a man gains his status mainly through his job, whereas a woman's status is mainly conferred on her by her husband. We often speak as if occupational success were equally important for both sexes, but actually it is much less important for women. Women *can* gain a tolerable status through work, but a better one can usually be gained more easily through marriage. Where men move up most directly by competing for good jobs, women move up mainly by marrying men who move up. Marriage thus becomes the means of mobility for women. Insofar as she responds to the American dream of upward mobility, every unmarried American girl has a bit of the gold-digger in her.

Consider the situation of American Catholics. Catholic girls are expected to marry Catholic boys, but they also want to marry successful men. And it just so happens that, for most of the country, Protestant men on the average hold higher-ranked positions than do Catholic men. If the Catholic girl marries up, she is likely to marry out. And evidently this does occur, because more Catholic women marry outside their faith than do Catholic men. Among Jews, however, the situation is reversed. Men in this group are eminently successful and are "good catches" for girls of any faith who want to marry up. Evidently they do get caught, for many more Jewish boys marry gentiles than do Jewish girls.

The pressure for marrying up among women produces a kind of imbalance in marital bargaining, to the advantage of high-status men and low-status women and the disdvantage of low-status men and high-status women. A low-status man has little wealth or prestige to offer a wife. In addition, he must compete for a wife not only with others in his own station but with higher-ranked men as well.

A well-born woman, if she is to maintain through marriage the status conferred on her by her parents, must marry a man at least equally well-born—but for such men she faces a deadly competition from lower-status female rivals who also regard them as desirable husbands. As a result, low-status men are more likely to remain bachelors, and high-status women are more likely to remain spinsters. This is the "Brahmin problem," so named because it reached its most extreme form among the high castes of Hindu India (but it can be observed among Boston Brahmins as well).

If a sociologist is so artlessly blunt as to ask young women whether they marry for money or for love, he will be lucky to escape with his questionnaire forms. Love, the girls indignantly tell us, conquers all. Lovable personal qualities eclipse Philistine wealth. But this is too simple by far.

On the one hand, there is a strong statistical tendency for women to marry up. If our hypothetical sociologist returns, suitably chastened, with a subtler set of questions on what makes men lovable, he will receive a list of characteristics of which many—urbane good manners, sensitivity, sophisticated good taste, interesting conversation, and so on—depend on expensive education and are thus associated with wealth. Money, in short, tends to be despised only in the abstract: in concrete form, enjoyed by the unmarried scions of a rich family, it is highly admired.

On the other hand, there probably never has been a society in which all lovable attributes were monopolized by one class. Love thus becomes a potentially random factor in marriage, one contrary to all rules of endogamy. In societies with stronger rules of endogamy than our own, love is not unknown, but it is strongly controlled and is regarded as irrelevant in the choice of marital partners.

The emotions of love are strong, but they are also ambiguous and volatile, and are therefore subject to deception and fraud. This places an emphasis on sincerity, but sincerity in love is very hard to assess. Young women are besieged with professions of love which they suspect are voiced simply to facilitate a quick seduction—and this is not what "love" means to most of them.

Especially where courtship tends to be individualistic, so that suitors cannot be effectively held to account for their promises, young women tend to measure the love of a young man not simply by what he says, but also by what he invests in the relationship. Often this is his money, but more often it is his time. Because any marriage market involves a wide age range of men competing for the smaller range of women in the years when they are young and pretty, the investment required in courtship gets bid up to a high level. Feminine nubility, thus rewarded, becomes a veritable institution in its own right. The extravagance of attention that young girls expect, however, paradoxically limits their chances for marrying well. Regardless of his income, the *time* of a successful man is always dear, while the adult male who is "still finding himself" is the one with the leisure to invest in courtship.

This applies also at the college level, where the pre-professional student who is going places occupationally has little time for dating and leaves most of the social life to the less ambitious campus playboys. This means that women who expect their suitors to spend a great deal of time in dating are likely to marry men of modest achievements in other areas.

Now: How can all this be put in a matchmaking computer? It would be easy to specify the information that would be required, but awfully hard to find any way of digging it up. Getting it by simple interrogation—which is what the computers use now—would make the money-or-love question look like a masterpiece of diplomacy.

The problem, of course, is that the factors that do explain who is likely to marry whom are systematically obscured for the young people directly involved, the better to inspire them to get married in the first place. And if the parties involved *do* take a calculating attitude toward the bargaining and exchange that is part of any system of marriage, they are likely to practice fraud and deception, systematically misrepresenting their age, income, background and other assets and liabilities, just as in face-to-face contact they tell tall tales and white lies and wear elevator shoes and falsies.

The marriage practices of human society embody both ancient traditions and novel responses to changing times. The broad patterns of marriage—movement across class lines, the age at which it occurs, its impact on education and work—can be pretty well predicted, and in fact are predicted by sociologists, demographers and insurance actuaries. But the narrow practical questions—"Will he marry her?" or "Will they be happy together?"—are likely to remain inexplicable, at least to the people involved. And the mystery is what gives these questions their abiding appeal. Successful computer matching—unlikely, anyway—would only spoil the fun.

THE SEVENTH VEIL
FROM
THE NEW PEOPLE

CHARLES WINICK

Salome's taking off of each veil revealed another aspect of herself, and a look at each dimension of our social milieu can clarify a different facet of the style of life of the New People. Just as removal of Salome's seventh veil revealed the total of all that had been exposed by each previous covering, an examination of sexual behavior is one way of understanding the many changes in sexual identity and social role that have occurred since World War II. How a person behaves in a sexual relationship is a result of how he views himself, his partner, and their mutual roles. Bedrooms accurately reflect what is happening in other rooms in the house of society.

LOVE IN RUNES

We are moving toward the permissiveness, non-mystery, equalitarianism between men and women, and early sex interest that already exist in Denmark, and a comparison of the two countries provides some clues to future levels of sexual behavior in America. The reputation of Scandinavian countries for permissiveness is closely linked to legislative measures like the legalizing of homosexuality and abortion.[1] Such laws date from the 1940's, but reflect attitudes that have evolved there over the last half-century. Young Danes give considerable sanction to premarital coitus and the desire to meet peer standards is an important motive for sexual activity.[2]

Denmark has the third highest population density in Europe, insuring considerable opportunity for contact between men and women. Although the relatively large size and small population of Sweden and Norway provide fewer opportunities for sexual contact, sexual

Reprinted from *The New People*, by Charles Winick, by permission of Pegasus.

patterns in the Scandinavian countries appear to be fairly similar.[3] A scale of attitudes toward sexual permissiveness and a questionnaire dealing with sexual behavior were administered to samples of male and female students at a university in (a) the intermountain region of the United States that has a predominantly Mormon student body; (b) the midwest; and (c) Denmark.[4] The Danish students had the highest scores on permissiveness and the most accepting attitudes toward premarital coitus and premarital pregnancy. The Danes were more liberal than the midwesterners, who in turn were significantly more open-minded than students from the intermountain area.

When the students were asked about the length of acquaintance-ship that would be appropriate for sexual intimacy, the Danes favored the shortest and the intermountain group recommended the longest time spans for various degrees of intimacy, with the midwestern sample again occupying the intermediate position. Male students in all three cultures tended to have more permissive attitudes than females, although the difference was smallest in Denmark.

Information was available, for each student, on attitudes as well as actual premarital coital activity, and the relationship could be expressed as a ratio of those endorsing premarital sex to the number experiencing it. A ratio greater than 1 suggests that more students approved than experienced premarital coitus, less than 1 that fewer students approve than have premarital relations. The ratios for the three groups are:

SAMPLE	MALES	FEMALES
Danish	1.47	1.35
Midwestern	.92	.82
Intermountain	.59	.33

More Danes expressed approval of premarital coitus than experienced it. But the reverse was true for the midwesterners and was even more so for the intermountain students. A similar pattern for both sexes represents additional evidence that the ratios reflect real cultural differences. It would seem that the less permissive a culture, the greater is the likelihood that persons who disapprove of premarital coitus will nevertheless have engaged in it. The more permissive a culture, the greater is its proportion of persons who approve of premarital coitus but have not experienced it. Median age at the time of the first intercourse tended to be lower and premarital petting was more frequent in the less permissive cultures. In spite of more emancipated attitudes, Danish students start petting and initial coital relationships at a later age than Americans.

Another comparison comes from a report on the sexual behavior of Danish women which was published in the same year as the Kinsey volume on women.[5] Although the attitudes of Danish women toward sex were far more permissive than their American counterparts, the former had substantially fewer coitions per month than the comparable American sample. There appears every reason to believe that Americans have more coital activity than Danes, although the latter's attitudes are much more permissive.

Why should people with a liberal outlook have less sex than those with conservative viewpoints? One reason could be that American attitudes toward sex included ambivalence and tension that made it opaque, forbidden, and secretly prized. Sex as forbidden fruit could be attractive, by operation of the Godiva Principle. Contrariwise, the relative absence of ambivalence and tension in Denmark may have led to taking sex for granted, with a resultant diminution in actual sexual behavior.

It is also necessary to consider factors like the availability of sexual partners, economic and housing conditions, the occasions and circumstances in which sexual intercourse is possible or appropriate, national levels of activity-passivity, and similar aspects of social life. In spite of such caveats, countries with a rigid culture and repressive religion, (e.g., Presbyterianism in Scotland) generally have a high level of sexual activity. Scandinavians represent the most conspicuous western example of an emancipated culture, and there seems little doubt about their comparative sexual inactivity.

It should also be possible to demonstrate a decline in the frequency of sexual intercourse in Denmark, parallel with the development of permissive attitudes. Although modern survey techniques did not exist a half-century ago, trends in the incidence of coition in Denmark can be approximated by a study of the venereal disease rate, which should be especially sensitive to non-marital sex. Such data may be regarded with confidence in Denmark, where one laboratory conducts all serological testing and venereal disease is reportable under law. Except for participation in the worldwide increase during war, Denmark has had a steady drop in gonorrhea and syphilis over the last half-century, a decline that can be extrapolated to suggest less sexual activity as the country's attitudes toward sex became more emancipated.[6]

Although we do not have any substantial post-Kinsey data on the incidence of sexual activity in this country, we can speculate that as Americans develop more liberal attitudes, they will not necessarily behave more permissively. Paradoxically, discussing sex and having information about it do not necessarily influence actual sexual behavior. College students in California, Minnesota, and Indiana were questioned about their beliefs and behavior before and after a semester devoted to discussion of sex.[7] By the semester's end, attitudes were more tolerant and understanding but there was no change in the students' sexual behavior. Less than one-tenth of a New York State sample of high school and college students with permissive attitudes toward premarital intercourse had actually engaged in it.[8] Columbia University's guidance director noted that most of the students were not achieving much sexual expression, although 83 percent of them believed in premarital sexual intercourse.[9]

In America as in Denmark, permissive attitudes do not mean permissive behavior. The campus orgies that are regularly denounced in mass media are simply not occurring to any significant extent. Several independent studies have reported that a minority (20-25%) of college girls are non-virgins and a far smaller proportion (2-3%) are promiscuous.[10] All available evidence suggests that these proportions have been fairly constant since the 1920's and that there has been an acceptance and consolidation of attitudes toward sex in the last 40 years. Worrying about the alleged promiscuity of youth may titillate some older people but the liberation of sexual attitudes and conversational freedom do not necessarily imply behavioral changes. Inhibition and cautiousness still characterize the behavior of most college students.

Even teenagers may be engaging in less sexual intercourse than is commonly believed. Frequently cited as "proof" of the growing incidence of teen-age sexual activity is the increase in teenage illegitimacy. It would seem, however, that disproportionate publicity has been given younger unwed mothers. Between 1938 and 1957, females under the age of 20 had a *smaller* percentage of increase in illegitimacy than any other age group. Between 1957 and 1963, the greatest percentage increases in illegitimacy were for women over 20, while the teen-age rate *decreased.*[11]

Illegitimacy is not running rampant among teenagers, although their attitudes are becoming more liberal. Additional evidence of an inverse relationship between sexual attitudes and behavior is provided by a comparison of interview data with the findings of Kinsey and his associates. Roper and other polls conducted at the same time as the Kinsey interviews suggest that persons of low socioeconomic status are more likely to express disapproval of extramarital intercourse than the middle or upper classes.[12] Yet male Kinsey interviewees with a grade-school level of education engaged in 10.6 times as much extramarital intercourse as college men, with the high school group occupying an intermediate position.

In sex it seems relatively easy to "go away a little closer" and adapt to an incompatibility between attitudes and behavior: those who do, say they don't; those who don't, say they do. Those who coo, don't bill and those who bill, coo less.

THE TROUBADOUR'S FAREWELL

The comparison with Denmark underscores the vast importance of cultural factors in modifying biological forces. War, depression, or social change may catalyze, modify, or mask some determinants of sexual behavior. Attitudes of contemporary middle class Americans who enjoy "black novels" are quite different from those of the ruling-class Provençals who were exposed to troubadour lyric poetry and romantic gallantry.

People who live under the threat of imminent death or disaster may engage in more sex than under ordinary circumstances, like the men and women in the *Decameron* distracting themselves by revelry in a large country house during the plague.[13] An urgently felt danger may enhance sex by adding a dimension of guilt, but one difference between the Black Death and today's problems is the plague's visibility as it killed one-fourth of Europe's population between 1348 and 1350. We become so little exercised about the less tangible problems of our day that one experienced discussion leader who talked to many groups of young people concluded that they respond to themes of war and death with " . . . always a shrug of the shoulders."[14]

Our comparative diffidence toward basic problems contrasts with the growing importance of sex in advertising and mass media, which probably drains off much libidinal energy that formerly found outlets in sexual activity. Paradoxically, our society's near-satiation with sex may lead to a decline in its direct expression, as in the classical example of the *Thousand and One Nights*. The Sultan Shahriyar had a policy of killing every woman with whom he spent a night of love, so that Scheherezade knew she was to die on the morning after her bridal night. But she told so interesting a story to the Sultan that he wanted her to finish it on the following night. She would always stop her tale at its most provocative moment. For a thousand nights, stories about love were so gratifying to the Sultan that he fell asleep every morning fully satisfied, but without having had intercourse. The Sultan's satiation gives the *Thousand and One Nights* a special relevance for the many American homes in which the condition of a television tube is often more important than the functioning of a fallopian tube.

Satiation can involve both the underlying drive and specific expressions of sexual appetites.[15] The underlying drive, which Freud regarded as constant and described as libido, is biological although its outlets are influenced by social and cultural factors. Several lines of evidence suggest that many young people who date early, go steady, make love during the dating years, and are subject to a continuing barrage of sexual stimuli from mass media, may lose interest in sex at a relatively early age. The Godiva Principle implies that persons who begin dating later, do not go steady as adolescents, eschew love-making on dates, and are uninvolved in popular culture, would maintain a very substantial level of sexual activity in later life. A careful study of the latter group concluded that its members actually do engage in a very high level of sexual activity as adults.[16]

Growing up in a repressive situation may, ironically enough, have contributed to interest in the opposite sex being sustained for longer than is likely under current conditions of sexual hyperstimulation of the young. As libido becomes more diffuse, any one source of its gratification tends to become less fulfilling. Traditional procedures for romantic courtship almost insured its taking place on an intense emotional level that helped to give its participants the energy to play their parts. It provided mystery and an atmosphere conducive to later sexual expression, as in a story told about Victor Hugo, who was addressing the French Senate in his eightieth year. "It is as difficult for a man of my years to address this august body as it is for me to make love three—no, four times in a single afternoon," he remarked. One reason Hugo could maintain such a high level of activity was his society, which was intensely committed to the romantic ethos of which the writer was such a splendid example.

THE AGE OF TIRESIAS

One possible gain resulting from women's new leadership could be the ability of some to achieve more satisfying sexual response. The Indiana researchers concluded that peak frequency of orgasm was reached by late adolescence in males but did not occur in women until their thirties.[17] Society's acceleration of girls' interest in sex may help to bridge a gap that has been described as "nature's joke" by making the frequency and age of onset of women's orgasms more compatible with men's.

Any new similarity between the sexual behavior of men and women may reflect deep-rooted correspondences that had previously been masked by cultural stereotypes. The Indiana investigators found that both sexes can achieve orgasm in approximately the same time, and also that the female does not seem to be as slow as had been believed. Another myth punctured by their data was that post-orgasm excitement recedes more slowly in women than men. More recently, Masters and Johnson have suggested that the vaso-congestive and pelvic-genital contraction phenomena which constitute orgasm are quite similar in both men and women.[18]

Wide dissemination of such findings and greater acceptance of women's sexuality are modifying stereotypes about the need for men to initiate psychological and other sexual stimulation of the woman. Helene Deutsch's classic study assumed that "the awakening of the vagina to full sexual functioning is entirely dependent upon the man's activity."[19] Van der Velde cautioned the husband about how he played "this delicate human harp" and Balzac had earlier warned the man not to be an orangutan playing a violin. Balzac rhapsodically compared the man to an orchestra conductor who gradually elicits a response from otherwise muted instruments. Tender was the night and non-responsive his lady.

Cross-cultural studies have amply demonstrated that the initiative in sexual intercourse is evenly distributed between the sexes.[20] Some popular folklore, however, still deals with the traditional passivity of American women, as in a once popular story. A Cannes policeman who came across a dead woman on the beach went to telephone for a physician. He returned to find a man making love to the woman. This was too much for even the sophisticated gendarme, and he angrily restrained the man. "Stop! That woman is dead!" "My God!" gasped the man, "I thought she was an American."

Such stories would not get a response in our time of Bedwoman-ship. Men are far less likely to read Balzac and Helene Deutsch than women are to study marriage manuals, which demonstrate remarkable ingenuity in suggesting quasi-military erotic maneuvers for the in-struction of women. They are reminiscent of a remark of George Sand: "Last night I had Mérimée; there is not much to him."

Women readers of the manuals may ultimately help to reestablish Tiresias' evaluation of the relative pleasure that men and women derive from sex. On the basis of having been first a man and then a woman, Tiresias estimated that women got nine-tenths and men only one-tenth of love's pleasure. Women who diligently apply the man-uals' wisdom may not do quite so well, but will receive instructions detailed enough to embolden the most Timid Wife. After all, a woman who is active and aggressive during the day can hardly be expected to rely on her husband's ministrations at night.

Psychoanalyst Ralph R. Greenson has commented that: "Today I rarely see a woman patient who accepts her frigidity. In fact, most of them demand orgasms and feel they are cheated by their sexual partners if they do not obtain them readily. . . . Today it is the women who complain that their husbands do not seem to be eager for sexual relations."[21] It is not the man but the woman who is increas-ingly urged toward a regime of cold showers and hard physical exercise.

Typical of many a wife's desire for the ecstasy without the agony are techniques like the "ice-spurred special."[22] The wife brings a plate of ice cubes to her night table for use if the husband responds Too Quickly. She cools his ardor with the ice cubes, and then pre-sumably reestablishes a mood of romantic receptivity. Turning knobs and switching levers have replaced the poetic and rapturous efful-gences of the *Kama Sutra* and D. H. Lawrence's warm mysticism.

Manuals also exist for the unmarried girl who needs instructions in how to remove her clothes while turning out lights, etc. Books and articles set forth instructions on how to trap the wary male, in a prose that has all the precision of a cookbook. The goose being cooked is the male, married or unmarried. Judge Woolsey permitted *Ulysses* into the United States in 1933 because, among other reasons, ". . . his locale was Celtic and his season Spring," but it is a Celtic Spring 365 days a year in the writings of our new female predators. Small won-der that a perfume which failed when it was called "Lady" became a success when its name was changed to "Hussy."

Another effect of the new climate is a decrease in hypocrisy. For her whole life prior to marriage, a young woman had been urged and exhorted to maintain a stainless-steel virginity, although she was expected to become a woman of passion overnight, through participation in a marriage ceremony. By exposing her to sexual stimulation and information from childhood, society is preparing her to be a better sexual partner, although not necessarily a more romantic wife. The audience of *Luv* laughs when the wife unrolls a chart that records how much sex she has been getting, but it is the nervous laughter of recognition.

Relationships between youthful women and older men constitute themes of recent popular humor. One story deals with a seventeen-year-old girl in bed with a sixty-five-year-old man. As he reached for a condom, she said, "That won't be necessary. I take pills." The man replied, "I'll use it anyhow; the moisture is bad for my arthritis." The listener does not know if the girl is really using pills or thinks that the man is impotent. She is expressing age-graded expectations that are appropriate for her role in today's culture, and so is the man, but he displaces and denies his declining sexual powers by calling attention to the arthritis that is associated with old age. The two groups in the population that repeat the story most enthusiastically are teen-age girls and older men. Girls enjoy the aggressiveness and superiority of its heroine and men identify with defensiveness and passivity. Reversal of traditional sex roles, which is implicit in the story, could be one important reason for fellatio's appeal to both sexes.

All available evidence indicates a shift from the use of mouth and anus in forepleasure play to their replacing coitus for many persons. What is the emotional loading of such a change? Instead of being tributary to genital sexuality, the mouth and anus are used to bypass genitality, and replacement of coitus by the use of neutral organs may have profound effects. Coitus permits each sex to reflect complementary roles and use unique and reciprocal organs that are identical in both sexes. But in oral and anal sex, at least one partner has a genderless stimulus or response.

One positive unanticipated consequence of increased use of neuter organs is an insight into the treatment of homosexuals. Some psychiatrists have been able to move homosexual patients toward heterosexuality by suggesting that they might engage in oral or anal sex with women if they have done so with men. The patient is reassured that the mouth and rectum are similar in men and women. Once the patient can begin to contemplate such activity with a woman, he may ultimately engage in coitus with her.[23] The new orality and anality also, of course, express our greater freedom, increased leisure, and greater regard for sex as play. The growing use of neuter organs, however, may be related to a blurring of feelings of personal identity. It is possible that devaluation of craftsmanship due to automation and the loss in significance of work are contributing to an erosion of personal identity that makes coitus too demanding for some people.

PLEASURE VERSUS PROPAGATION SEX

Advances in contraceptive techniques should be making it easier for men and women to combine the tender with the sensual and cope with the problems which arise from the separation of propagation from pleasure sex.[24] Some of our current difficulties still derive from the lack of a model for sexual activity that is conducted for non-procreative purposes.

It is possible that some Americans are also losing their model for procreative sex. Both the marriage rate and age composition of the female population are favorable to a higher level of fertility than actually exists.[25] Our birth rate has declined continuously for ten years. The 3,767,000 births in 1965 represented the smallest annual total since 1951, and a 24 percent decline since 1957. Although predicting the birth rate with complete confidence is impossible, one of the most thorough investigations of American fertility patterns has seen a downward trend for the next twenty years.[26]

Dr. René DuBos has suggested that Americans will soon be seeking values to substitute for those previously provided by offspring. A second car may take the place of a third or fourth child in many homes. The proportion of Americans regarding four or more children as the "ideal" number declined from 49 percent in 1945 to 35 percent in 1966, according to a Gallup poll. The drop in our birth rate also involves the draft, unemployment among young people, and a growing demand for higher education, which may discourage early marriage and childbearing. A population shift from rural to urban areas and from large, stable families to smaller, movable families is also a factor along with greater acceptability of birth control. But another reason may be that asserting one's sex role, implicit in the decision to have a child, is more difficult when so much of the personal and social environment reflects depolarization and neuterization.

The decision to have fewer children may represent one way in which some people respond to confused sex roles. Others may run away into a reaction formation, i.e., an excess of sexual activity. Relatively few are likely to move toward homosexuality, which is not likely to be fostered by our society's blurred sexual identification. Societies with little or no homosexuality, like the Arapesh, Lepcha, and Mundugumor, have blurred goals of masculinity and femininity.

Even though homosexuality is not a single clinical entity but a symptom with different meanings, there would seem to be less occasion for it when masculinity and femininity are not idealized values. Children whose parents' gender is ambiguous will probably demonstrate decreased identification with the parent of the same sex and lesser likelihood of becoming homosexuals.[27] Homosexuality resulting from rebellion against the repressions of an anti-sexual society is also less likely to be found in our libidinized America.

Homosexuals really may be fewer at the very time that they seem to be becoming more numerous. What could be the illusion of numbers may reflect more tolerant attitudes which encourage many homosexuals to identify themselves, increased sympathy of mass media, and the missionary activity of homophile organizations. The Indiana researchers estimated that about 4 percent of men and 2 percent of women are exclusively homosexual, but these proportions may actually have dwindled somewhat over the last twenty years.

Homosexuality could also be declining because of the mannish aspects of women's appearance. A fashionable woman of today could sport a hard, boyish Vidal Sassoon haircut and a crash helmet, with a chin-strap framing her colorless face. Her pants suit would minimize the display of breasts and buttocks. A relationship with such a woman could displace or sublimate homosexual impulses, especially now that oral and anal sex are achieving heterosexual popularity.

And with the hand on a rotating hip the starting position for the frug, some of the more flamboyant gestures of the male homosexual are being taken from him. At just about the same time, the gaiety and genital and hip display of modern men's clothes and their use of perfume have provided additional avenues of homosexual sublimation for the "straight" man. Heterosexual and homosexual represent a far less differentiated choice than they did a generation ago.

Another response to ambiguous sexual identification may be an acting out of a depolarized sex by persons who engage in both heterosexual and homosexual activity. There is reason to suspect an increase in the amount of bisexuality or "switch-hitting" or "AC-DC" sex, with an estimated 14 to 16 percent of American men now responding to either males or females.[28] We can only hope that men and women of the future will have the sangfroid of Joe E. Brown in *Some Like It Hot*. When told that the woman he loves is really a man, he unabashedly replies, "Well, nobody's perfect."

THE PRUDENT AMORISTS

One reason for the thread of neutering that runs through the fabric of our time is the dissociation among mind, body, and emotions in response to sex. One pre-jet but still current American story deals with the man and woman who met in the club car of a transcontinental train, had a few drinks, and retired to the man's compartment. By the time he awoke on the following morning, the woman had gone. The man went to the dining car for breakfast and was delighted to see his companion of the previous night. "Hello, honey," he said as he slid into the seat opposite her. She indignantly snapped, "I beg your pardon, but since when does sexual intercourse constitute a formal introduction?" Such separation of emotional closeness from physical gratification suggests one way in which sex can be compartmentalized. For some new Puritans, sex is a duty and an injunction to be lived up to; for others it is prudent.

One reflection of our sexual fractionation is the enormous popularity of the two magazines most directly concerned with impersonal sex: *Confidential* and *Playboy*. In its heyday, *Confidential* dealt primarily with the sexual activities of the famous and did less to provide a sexual catharsis for readers than to deplete and enervate them. *Confidential's* documentation of mindless and emotionless sex attracted many Americans who were confused about their sexual identity.

The magazine presented gossip about sex; a reader learned something other people didn't know. If he felt somehow dissatisfied with his sexual identity, what could better reinforce such dissatisfaction than having inside information on the confused sexual identity of the famous?[29] Stories about celebrities in ambiguous sex situations showed readers that their own fantasies might be less unworthy. Impressive documentation of *Confidential's* broad appeal is provided by its having become the most successful magazine ever published in this country in terms of newsstand sales.

Another reason for its success was the public's desire to think less of contemporary heroes, in response to the same needs that led to the hero's disappearance from the arts. A reader who read about a celebrity's unbuttoned private life in *Confidential* had a leash on him, in revenge for his *hubris.* "I know what you're doing but you're not getting away with it—I know all about your feet of clay."

Although the editors of *Playboy* seem to have some awareness of differences in gender, they present sex as an aspect of leisure to be handled with detachment. The magazine straddles the dichotomy by making sex a pleasant consumption item and the Playmate a servant who represents an infantile ego boost. Probably the only feature differentiating *Playboy* from innumerable similar magazines is its presentation of a fully clothed Playmate who is shown nude on the next page, so that the reader can strip her just by turning a page.

The Playmate's very nudity is non-sexual because her whorish pose is in sharp contrast to the demure, fully clothed appearance at her regular job, e.g., graduate student of Sanskrit. Even though the Playmate looks as if she ought to be available, she turns out to be a pearl unattainable at any price. Readers' fantasies about her are likely to be non-genital and are conveyed by the quip that many young men subscribe to *Playboy* in order to keep abreast of the times. The magazine epitomizes the prudery and thrill-seeking of our time and the guilt with which the latter is spiced because of the former. Almost every issue carries editorials and philosophical musings that try to reassure the reader.

Confidential and *Playboy* represent impressive tributes to the appeal of voyeuristic and uninvolving sex and an archeologist of the future would get more insight into the New People from such modern graffiti than from the official documents that are usually included in time capsules. Any impressions suggested by the magazines would be strengthened by books that ask *What Are You Doing After the Orgy?*[30]

The magazines' popularity is hardly surprising in a country that made burlesque more popular than it ever has been elsewhere. Before World War II, every large city in America had one or more burlesque theatres, patronized primarily by lower- and middle-class men who came alone.[51] Other cultures have produced erotically stimulating spectacles that were preludes to more solid pleasures, but burlesque is unique in providing a visual satisfaction complete in itself. The frozen-faced strippers would alternate with comedians whose jokes had the dual theme of women rejecting men and the probability that something would always interfere with consummation.

Burlesque has made a successful comeback in our frugging and voyeuristic age, and there are now about sixty theatres devoted to it and many more that show burlesque and other public stag films. Americans' desire to look without touching also expresses itself in the popularity of topless waitresses. There is probably no other country where such waitresses could go about their business, confident that men would not even try to touch them.

American homes have proportionately more windows to space than in any other country with comparable climate. Our desire to look finds other outlets in the picture windows which began staring out at suburban streets in the 1940's, and led to the glass cages inside which go-go girls "shake it out" at discotheques.

Peep magazines have flourished during a decade that saw new popularity for voyeuristic jokes. A representative story concerns an attractive woman who had been prepared for surgery and was lying nude under a sheet in a hospital corridor. Three men walked by within a few minutes of one another. Each raised the sheet, looked, and nodded to the woman. When the fourth man similarly lifted the sheet, she asked him: "Doctor, when will they operate on me?" The man replied, "I don't know, lady. We're only the painters."

Such detached voyeurism leads to anti-sentimentality and avoiding strong emotions, even in greeting cards. Greetings that communicate a pleasant if frequently soppy sentiment are giving way to clever cards that minimize rather than celebrate an occasion. A sharp reminder of the change is provided by the holiday, birthday, and anniversary "studio cards" which now account for over two-fifths of all greeting-card sales and convey an unconventional, frequently hostile greeting. A typical card to be sent to a sick friend shows a frog on its outer jacket. Above the frog is the legend "Don't tell me." The person receiving and opening the card will find the rest of the legend, "You're gonna croak?"

The boom in studio cards suggests that the simple communication of warmth toward a relative or friend may be as difficult to express in writing as in direct contact. Similar impulses have made the wisecrack a uniquely American form of humor. Wisecracks are often cruel and deny gentleness and feeling, in contrast to the softer, flickering, and subtle wit of other countries.

Our acceptance of psychoanalysis has undoubtedly contributed to the climate. Once we could dissect and explain love in terms of its constituents, we began to think in terms of relationships and defense mechanisms. Falling in love becomes much less spontaneous when people are more evaluative about their own feelings. A person who might once have been embraced with feeling may now be studied at fingertip length.

Living is most worth its cost when it includes the enlargement of experience and joyfulness in which each sex explores the other and simultaneously discovers new depths in the self. A genuine I-Thou encounter between a man and woman involves a communion, an exchange, giving and taking. It is a unifying and sharing experience, evocative of creative depths. Awareness of such meanings can help to bridge the gap between sex and passion and lead to relationships in which sex is an authentic and vital experience between human beings.

Patterns of love and sex in America vary not only within a community but on the same street, and even in adjacent apartments in the same building. There is also considerable intra-person variation, and the situation is compounded by the lack of established symbols for the expression of passion. A modern concept of love may build on connotations and fantasies related to meanings that are relevant today. How distant some of these meanings are from romance can be seen in the guidance which many marriage manuals offer the husband suffering from premature ejaculation, who is often advised to develop fantasies about an unpleasant experience, while making love to his wife.

As the husband recalls a disagreeable experience, it is likely that the fantasies of his wife will not be overly romantic. An American woman might well be the contemporary hero of a story told about Gustave Flaubert, who won a bet that he could achieve orgasm in intercourse without disturbing the ash on a cigar he was smoking Flaubert's detachment may be congenial to the modern wife who studies technocratic prescriptions in the manuals and for whom sex is as lyrically rapturous as assembling an Erector set.

Truly personal and meaningful connotations and fantasies could help reestablish polarization of the sexes. Extensive new knowledge of the self has led to many associations that are humanistic and not based on fear or sanctions. They stem from the unique appositeness of each sex, deal with the present, build on the past, point to the future, and include the many-meaninged irrationality that is part of being human.

NOTES

[1] G. Van Emde Boas, "Sex Life in Europe," in A. Ellis and A. Abarbanci, editors, *The Encyclopedia of Sexual Behavior*, Vol. I. New York: Hawthorne, 1961. pp. 373-383.

[2] R. T. Anderson and G. Anderson, "Sexual Behavior and Urbanization in a Danish Village," *Southwestern Journal of Anthropology*, 16, 1960, pp. 93-103; H. Hoffmeyer, "Anti-conception," *Ugeskrift for Laeger*, 113, 1951, pp. 569 ff.

[3] G. Jonsson, "Sexual vanor has avensk ungdom," *In Ungdomen Moter Samhället.* Ungdomsvardskommittens sluthekankarde. Stockholm: 1951; C. Melbye, *Studentmoral.* Oslo: *Universitas*, No. 7-8. 1946; K. Svalastoga, "The Family Life in Scandinavia," *Marriage and Family Living*, 16, 1954, pp. 374-380.

[4] The scale was a ten-point Guttman type; see H. T. Christensen and G. R. Carpenter. "Value Discrepancies Regarding Premarital Coitus in Three Western Cultures," *American Sociological Review*, 27, 1962, pp. 66-74; and "Timing Patterns in Premarital Sexual Intimacy, an attitudinal report on three modern western societies," *Marriage and Family Living*, 24, 1962, pp. 30-35.

[5] Alfred C. Kinsey, W. B. Pomeroy, C. E. Marin, and P. H. Gebhard, *Sexual Behavior in the Human Female.* Philadelphia: Saunders, 1953, pp. 288-307; Kirsten Auken, *Undersogeleer over Unge Kvinders Sexualle Adfaerd.* Kebenhaun: Rosenkilde og bagger; Oslo: Olaf Norlis Bokhandel; Stockholm: Almguist and Wiksell, 1953. The subsample consisted of 235 women between 20 and 35, with a mean age of 26.

[6] The 1920's average of 335 cases of gonorrhea per 100,000 dropped in the 1930's to 262, and in the mid-1950's to 174 per 100,000. Comparable figures for syphilis are 70 per 100,000 in the 1920's, 21 in the 1930's, and 5 per 100,000 in the 1950's. See *Medical Report for the Kingdom of Denmark*, 1960. Copenhagen: National Health Service of Denmark, 1963, pp. 51-53.

[7] Wardell B. Pomeroy, *New York Mattachine Newsletter*, 9 (4), 1964, pp. 3-4.

[8] Lillian B. Redcay, "Adolescent Reactions to a Film Regarding Premarital Sex Experiences," doctoral dissertation, Pennsylvania State University, 1964.

[9] *New York Times,* March 14, 1964; *Columbia Spectator,* November 22, 1963, p. 1.

] [10] Mervin B. Freedman, "The Sexual Behavior of American College Women: An Empirical Study and An Historical Survey," *Merrill-Palmer Quarterly,* 11, 1965, pp. 33-48.

[11] The 1938-1957 percentages applied in all three basic indicators of illegitimacy: number, ratio, and rate. Number indicates the total volume; ratio is the number of illegitimate births per 1,000 live births; rate is the number of illegitimate births per 1,000 unmarried females of childbearing age and is the most reliable measure because it considers the total number of unmarried females in each age group. The 1957-1963 change applied to ratio and rate. During this six-year period, the increase in the number of illegitimate births to teen-agers reflected an increase in teen-age females in the population as a result of the 1945-1947 baby boom. See Clark E. Vincent, "Teen-Age Unwed Mothers in American Society," *Journal of Social Issues.* 22, 1966, pp. 22-33.

[12] Stanton Wheeler, "Sex Offenses: A Sociological Critique," *Law and Contemporary Problems,* 25, 1960, pp. 267-268; Alfred C. Kinsey, Wardell B. Pomeroy, and Clyde E. Martin, *Sexual Behavior in the Human Male.* Philadelphia: Saunders, 1948, p. 354; J. Dreyfus-Moreau, "A Propos de Quelques Facteurs Favorisant l'Impuissance," *L'Evolution Psychiatrique,* 29, 1964, pp. 437-458.

[13] William L. Langer, "The Black Death," *Scientific American,* 210, February 1964, pp. 114-121.

[14] Udo Derbolowsky, "Two Years of Discussion Groups." Paper presented to First International Congress on Social Psychiatry, London, August 1964.

[15] A. Margoshes and S. Litt, "Sexual Appetite and Sexual Drive," *Psychological Reports,* 16, 1965, pp. 713-719.

[16] F. Rigney and D. Smith, *The Real Bohemia.* New York: Basic Books, 1961.

[17] Kinsey, 1953, *op. cit.,* pp. 257-258, 587; Kinsey, 1948, *op. cit.,* 176-187.

[18] William S. Masters and Virginia E. Johnson, *Human Sexual Response.* Boston: Little Brown, 1966.

[19] Helene Deutsch, *Psychology of Women.* New York: Grune and Stratton, 1944, Vol. I, p. 233.

[20] Clellan S. Ford and Frank A. Beach, *Patterns of Sexual Behavior.* New York: Harper, 1951, p. 105.

[21] *Medical Tribune,* October 18, 1965, pp. 1, 8.

[22] John E. Eichenlaub, *The Marriage Art.* New York: Dell, 1962, pp. 107-108.

23 Dr. Herbert Holt first called this approach to the author's attention.

24 Dr. Meyer Maskin suggested this terminology.

25 Joseph A. Loftus, "Postwar Population Leap Is Dwindling to a Brisk Hop," *New York Times,* January 17, 1966.

26 The crude birth rate goes from 24.7 per 1,000 in 1955-60 to 22.3 in 1980-85, in the projections reported in Pascal K. Whelpton, Arthur A. Campbell, and John E. Patterson, *Fertility and Family Planning in the United States.* Princeton: Princeton University Press, 1966, p. 401. No discussion of fertility can ignore changes in socioeconomic status: see Ronald Freedman, "The Sociology of Human Fertility," *Current Sociology,* 10, 1961, pp. 53-59.

27 Charles Winick, "Dear Sir or Madam, As the Case May Be," *Antioch Review,* 23, 1963, pp. 35-49.

28 Bruce Ogilvie, "The Social Setting of Homosexuality," California Health Department Venereal Disease Control Informational Report #8, 1964, p. 8.

29 Charles Winick, "Celebrities' Errancy as a Subject for Journalism: A Study of *Confidential," Gazette,* 7, 19962, pp. 329-334; "Thoughts and Feelings of the General Population as Expressed in Free Association Typing," *American Imago,* 19, 1962, pp. 67-84.

30 By Henny and Jim Backus. New York: Prentice-Hall, 1962.

PSYCHOLOGICAL MISCARRIAGE: AN END TO MOTHER LOVE

MARIAN GENNARIA MORRIS

Not long ago a mother in the Midwest, while giving her baby its bath, held its head underwater until it drowned. She said that there was something wrong with the child. Its smell was strange and unpleasant; it drooled; it seemed dull and listless. It reminded her of a retarded relative, and the thought of having to spend the rest of her life caring for such a person terrified her. Her husband was out of work, and she was pregnant again. She said she "felt the walls closing in." When, in her confused and ignorant way, she had asked her husband, a neighbor, and a doctor for help, she got promises, preachments, and evasions. So she drowned the baby.

This mother said she had felt "so all alone." But, unfortunately, she had plenty of company. Many thousands of American women do not love or want their babies. Although few actually kill their infants, the crippling effects of early maternal rejection on children can hardly be exaggerated—or glossed over. The number directly involved is large. The social harm, for everybody, is great. An idea of the size of the problem can be gained from the following figures, taken from federal, state, and local sources:

50-70,000 children neglected, battered, exploited annually;
150,000 children in foster homes for these reasons;
over 300,000 children in foster care altogether;
8 to 10 percent of all school children in one twenty-county study

in need of psychiatric examination and some type of treatment for their problems.

But even these figures can hardly begin to describe the violence, deprivation, and dehumanization involved.

Reprinted by permission of the author and publisher from *Trans-action*, New Brunswick, N. J.

Recently we concluded a study of thirty rejecting mothers and their children who can serve as examples. Our findings are supported by a number of other studies of parents and their children who have various physical and psychological disorders. Although the poor are hardest hit by family and emotional problems it should be noted that the majority of these families were not poverty-stricken. Psychological miscarriage of motherhood attacks all classes and levels.

Twenty-one of the thirty mothers demonstrated clearly from the time of delivery that they could not properly mother or care for their babies—could not even meet their basic needs. Yet no one who had had contact with them—neither doctors, nurses, nor social workers— had apparently been able to help, effectively, any one of them, nor even seemed aware that severe problems existed.

The entire population of mothers was characterized by old troubles and hopelessness, stretching back to the previous generation—and in one-third of the cases, back to the third generation. Half the children were illegitimate, or conceived before marriage. Sixty per cent of the families had been in juvenile, criminal or domestic courts at some earlier time. Two-thirds of the children were either first-borns, or first-borns of their sex—and lack of experience with children increased their mothers' insecurities.

All thirty children needed intensive psychiatric treatment. Only two of the thirty were "well" enough—from homes that were "stable" enough—for out-patient care to even be considered. The remaining twenty-eight were headed for institutions. Their prognoses are grave, their chances doubtful. They will cost us a great deal in the years to come, and their problems will be with us a long time. Some will never walk the streets as free men and women.

Actually, the children were so disturbed that they could not be diagnosed with great accuracy. For instance, it was impossible to tell how intelligent most really were because they were in such emotional turmoil that they could not function properly on tests, and seemed retarded. A fifth of them had been so beaten around the head that it is quite possible their brains were damaged. (One baby had been thrown across the room and allowed to stay where it fell.) Women who feel neglected and less than human in turn neglect their children and treat them as less than human.

In our supposedly interdependent society, we are close together in violence, but apathetic to each other's needs. But apathy to their needs constitutes a violence to women facing labor, delivery, and the early and bewildering adjustments of motherhood. And it is in these days and weeks that psychological miscarriage occurs.

During pregnancy, labor, and delivery the basic fears of childhood —mutilation, abandonment, and loss of love—are vividly revived for a woman, and with double force—for herself and the baby. Nor are these fears simply fantasies: mothers *are* frequently cut, torn, and injured, babies *are* born with congenital defects.

The entire pregnancy period, with its lowering of defenses, makes the mother more capable of loving and feeling for her baby. But whether she finds his needs pleasing or threatening depends on what happened to her in the past, and the support she gets in the present.

After delivery, still in physical and emotional stress, under great pressure, she must make the most important, difficult adjustments of all. She must "claim" her baby. That is, she must make it, emotionally, part of herself again; identify it with the qualities and values in herself and her life that she finds good, safe, reassuring, and rewarding. After all the dreams and fears of pregnancy, she now must face and cope with the reality—the baby and its needs. If she miscarries now and rejects the child as something bad that cannot be accepted, then the child cannot grow to be normal. Nor can its society be normal, since the mothers must hand down to each generation the values by which society survives.

In older days, when most women had their babies at home, these adjustments were made in familiar surroundings, with such family support as was available. Now they are made largely in the hospital. What actually happens to mothers in today's hospitals?

Childbirth, once a magnificent shared experience, has increasingly become a technical event. Administrative and physical needs get priority. Emotional needs and personalities tend to get in the way of efficiency. Administrators and medical personnel, like everyone else, respond most readily to those pressures which affect them. Since they are in charge, they pass them down to the patient, whether they help the patient or not.

The mothers of the poor in particular arrive faceless, knowing no one on the ward, with little personal, human contact from before birth until they leave. Increasingly, they arrive already in labor, so that the hospitals cannot turn them away. They also come at this late stage so that they can avoid the constant procession of doctors and the three and four-hour clinic waits, during which they are called "mother" because their names have been lost in the impersonal clinic protocols. In the wards, they may be referred to simply by their bed numbers.

Birth itself may be subordinated to the schedule: some doctors schedule their deliveries, and induce labor to keep them on time. Even "natural" labor may be slowed down or speeded up by drugs for convenience.

A Public Event

Mothers say that they are allowed little dignity or modesty. Doctors strange to them may, and do, examine them intimately, with little attempt at privacy. They say that without their permission they are often used as live lecture material, giving birth before interested audiences of young interns and students while the obstetrician meticulously describes each step and tissue. How apathetic we have become to the routine dehumanization of mothers is well illustrated by the story of an upper-middle-class woman I know. She was in labor, almost hidden by drapes preparatory to vaginal examination, light flooding her perineum (but not her face). Approached by a nurse and gloved physician she suddenly sat up in her short-tailed hospital gown and said, "I don't know who *you* are, doctor, but *I* am Mrs. Mullahy." Good for Mrs. Mullahy! She has a strong sense of personal identity, and is determined to preserve it.

Mothers say they are isolated and humiliated. They say that in addition to their own anxieties they must worry about what their doctors think, and be careful to please and propitiate the staff members, who may have power of life and death over them and their babies.

They say that they are kept in stirrups for hours—shackled in what reduces them to something subhuman—yet afraid to complain.

Is it increasingly true, as mothers say, that babies are not presented to them for from four to twelve hours after birth? Social histories show that prompt presentation is necessary for the mental health of the mothers; studies of other mammals indicate that such delay interrupts mothering impulses and may bring on rejection of the young. Is this happening to human mothers and babies? How necessary, medically, is such a delay? Is it worth the price?

Many women become deeply depressed after childbirth. Is this at least partly a reaction to hospital experiences? Is it an early distress signal of psychological miscarriage? There is very little research that attempts to assess early maternal adaptation, and we need such research badly. Are the violent mothers, so brutal to their children, violent at least in part because of our faceless and impersonal birth practices? Clinical studies show that the less sense of identity and personal worth a mother has, the more easily she displaces her aggressions onto others—*any* others. Are we scapegoating our children?

STAKING A CLAIM

To a mother, the birth of her baby is not a technical event. It starts in intimate contact with the father, and has deep roots in her feelings for and relationship with him, whether positive or negative. It reflects her personality, her state of maturity, the experiences of her most intimate anxieties and special hopes, and her associations with the adults who have had most influence on her. She enters the hospital prey to childhood insecurities, and stripped alike of defenses and clothes. Attitudes and cues from the hospital personnel, and from others, strongly affect her self respect and her feelings about her own and her baby's worth.

It is difficult to observe most normal claiming behavior in a hospital. But some of it can be observed. Most mothers, for example, do find ways to make contact with their babies' bodies — touching and examining them all over delightedly, even to the tiny spaces between fingers and toes—cooing and listening to them, inhaling their odors, nuzzling and kissing them.

Socially, a major way to claim a child is to name it. Names suggest protective good magic; they establish identity and suggest personality; they emphasize masculinity or femininity; they affirm family continuity and the child's place in it.

Nevertheless, it is usually difficult to follow claiming behavior for two reasons. First, because hospital routines and tasks interfere. To the staff, the process of mothers becoming acquainted with infants is seen as merely cute, amusing, or inconvenient. Babies are presented briefly, pinned and blanketed tightly, making intimate fondling— for women who have carried these infants for months—difficult and sometimes even guilt-producing.

The second reason is related to the nature of normal motherhood. The well-adjusted mother is secure within herself, content to confine her communications mostly to her baby, rather than project them outward. As Tolstoy said of marriage, all happy ones tend to be happy in the same way, and relatively quiet. But the unhappy ones are different and dramatic—and it is by observing unhappy mothers that the pathological breakdown of maternal claiming can be most easily traced.

Let us consider a few examples:

Tim—Breakdown in Early Infancy. When Tim's mother first felt him move in her, and realized then that all evasion and doubt about her pregnancy was past, she blacked out (she said) and fell down a flight of stairs.

Tim was her second child. Her first pregnancy was difficult and lonely and, she had been told, both she and the baby had almost died during delivery. She suffered from migraine headaches, and was terrified of a second delivery.

For the first four months of Tim's life, she complained that he had virulent diarrhea and an ugly odor, and took him from doctor to doctor. Assured by each one that there was nothing wrong with the child (in the hospital the diarrhea cleared up in one day), she took this to mean that there was something wrong with *her*—so she sought another doctor. She took out thirteen different kinds of cancer insurance on Tim.

During an interview, she told a woman social worker that it was too bad that doctors could not look inside a baby and know he was *all* O.K.

The social worker decided to probe deeper: "You would have a hard time convincing me that you *deliberately* threw yourself down those stairs."

"Who, me? Why I told my mother all along that I would never *willingly* hurt a hair of one of my children's heads."

"But suppose you had, unwillingly. Would you blame someone else for doing it, under the circumstances?"

"No. I was sick and don't even know how it happened."

After that, the demon that had haunted her was in the open, and recovery began. She had felt that she was both criminal and victim, with the child as the instrument of her punishment. (Only a "good" mother deserves a good baby; a "bad" mother deserves a "bad"— damaged or sick—baby.) The implied criticisms of her mother and doctor had aggravated these feelings. She identified Tim not with the good in her but the "evil"—he was something faulty, something to be shunned.

Under treatment she learned to accept herself and regain her role of mother. She was not really the bad little girl her critical mother and doctor had implied; neither, therefore, was Tim bad—she could accept him. It was no longer dangerous to identify with her. She let Tim see her face; she held him comfortably for the first time; she did not mention his "ugly" smell; she stayed by his bed instead of restlessly patrolling the corridors. She referred to our hospital as the place she had "got him *at*," instead of the hospital, ninety miles away, where he had actually been born.

Jack—Effects on an Older Child. Shortly after Jack was born, his mother asked her obstetrician whether Jack's head was all right. Gently touching the forceps marks, he said, *"These* will clear up." Thinking that she had been told delicately that she had a defective child, she did not talk to Jack for five-and-a-half years—did not believe he could understand speech.

At five-and-a-half, approaching school, he had never spoken. A psychologist, thinking that the child was not essentially retarded, referred the mother to a child guidance clinic, where the social worker asked whether she had ever found out if the obstetrician had meant the *inside* of Jack's head. For the first time in all the years it occurred to her that there might have been a misunderstanding. Three months later Jack was talking—though many more months of treatment were still necessary before he could function adequately for his age.

Behind this, of course, was much more than a misunderstanding. Behind it was Jack's mother's feelings of guilt for having caused her own mother's death. Guilt went back many years. During an auto ride long ago, she had an accident in which her mother suffered a mild blow on the head. In the early months of pregnancy with Jack, she had found her mother dead in the tub. The cause was cancer, which had nothing to do with the bump. But deep down she could not believe this, and she developed the fear that Jack's head, too, was damaged—a fitting punishment for a woman who feared she had killed her mother. When her obstetrician seemed to confirm it, she did not question further.

For almost six years Jack was not so much an infant or child as a damaged head. Like her mother he was silent—from "brain injury." It was only under treatment that she accepted the possibility that she might have "misunderstood."

Babs—Hell Revisited. Babs was fourteen months old when she was flown to our hospital from South America, physically ill with diarrhea and dehydration, and emotionally badly withdrawn. In South America, her mother had trouble getting proper drugs and talking effectively with Spanish-speaking doctors—and when she had had to face Bab's pleading eyes with little relief to offer, she had gone into acute panic. She hadn't been able to comfort her child, but had drawn away and could hardly look at her or touch her. From this rejection Babs had in turn withdrawn, and a mutual vicious cycle of rebuff and retreat had come about.

The mother felt that she had lived through all this before in her own childhood. When she was five, she had had a little brother, aged three. Her sick mother often left him in her charge. ("He was *my* baby.") One day both ate sprayed peaches from a tree. Both came down with severe diarrhea. She survived. She remembers vividly seeing him in "his little white coffin."

The pregnancy period with Babs had been stormy, full of family crises; she felt guilty about "not feeding Babs right." She could not accept the reassurances of her obstetrician. After Babs was born she was overmeticulous about cleaning her after bowel movements.

During treatment she shook visibly when asked whether Babs resembled her in any way. But when asked: "Could you have been Jim's *real* mother when you were only five?" she relaxed, and grew radiant. Later she said: "I know *now* that I couldn't have known that the peaches were poisoned."

"Nor that Babs would get sick with diarrhea if you went to South America to live with your husband?"

"No. I know now that the *place* is not good for any of us. I didn't know that before."

In a few days she was admiring in Babs the very qualities she had said she admired in herself—her sense of fun, and her determination. The positive identification between them had been made.

CLUES TO MATERNAL HAZARDS IN MOTHERING

There are several criteria that can be used to assess the adequacy of a mother's behavior during the early weeks of an infant's life. Mother-infant units can be said to be *satisfactory* when a mother can: find pleasure in her infant and in tasks for and with him; understand his emotional states and comfort him; read his cues for new experience, sense his fatigue points.

For example she can receive his eye contact with pleasure; can promote his new learnings through use of her face, hands and objects; does not overstimulate him for her own pleasure.

In contrast, there are specific signs that mothers give when they are *not adapting* to their infants:

See their infants as ugly or unattractive.
Perceive the odor of their infants as revolting.
Are disgusted by their drooling and sucking sounds.
Become upset by vomiting, but seem fascinated by it.
Are revolted by any of the infants' body fluids which touch them, or which they touch.
Show annoyance at having to clean up infants' stools.
Become preoccupied with the odor, consistency and number of infants' stools.
Let infants' heads dangle, without support or concern.
Hold infants away from their own bodies.
Pick up infants without warning by touch or speech.
Juggle and play with infants, roughly, after feeding, even though they often vomit at this behavior.
Think infants' natural motor activity is unnatural.
Worry about infant's relaxation following feeding.
Avoid eye contact with infants, or stare fixedly into their eyes.
Do not coo or talk with infants.
Think that their infants do not love them.
Believe their infants expose them as unlovable, unloving parents.
Think of their infants as judging them and their efforts as an adult would.
Perceive their infants' natural dependent needs as dangerous.
Fear death at appearance of mild diarrhea or cold.
Are convinced that infants have defects, in spite of repeated physical examinations which prove negative.
Often fear that infants have diseases connected with "eating", leukemia, or one of the other malignancies; diabetes; cystic fibrosis.
Constantly demand reassurance that no defect or disease exists, cannot believe relieving facts when they are given.
Demand that feared defects be found and relieved.
Cannot find in their infants any physical or psychological attribute which they value in themselves.
Cannot discriminate between infant signals of hunger, fatigue, need for soothing or stimulating speech, comforting body contact, or for eye contact.

Develop inappropriate responses to infant needs: over or under-feed; over or under-hold; tickle or bounce the baby when he is fatigued; talk too much, too little, and at the wrong time; force eye contact, or refuse it; leave infant alone in room; leave infant in noisy room and ignore him. Develop paradoxical attitudes and behaviors.

MOTHERS AS PATIENTS

How can we prevent such psychological miscarriages—and how can we limit their ravages once they have already occurred?

The dynamics of maternal rejection are not completely known—we need far more research, far more detailed and orderly observation of early maternal behavior. Nevertheless, enough is known already about the symptoms for us to be able to work up a reliable profile of the kind of woman who is most likely to suffer damage, and to take steps to make sure that help is offered in time. After all, the ultimate cause of maladaptation is lack of human sympathy, contact, and support, even though the roots may go back for more than one generation. We must, therefore, offer that support. We may not be able completely to heal old, festering wounds, but we can palliate their worst effects, and keep them from infecting new babies.

Mothers in our study identified the periods of greatest danger as just before and after delivery. It is then—and swiftly—that intervention by a psychiatric team should occur. What can be done?

We must have early recognition of trouble. Early signs of maternal maladaptation are evident in the mutual aversion of mother and child. But these signs have to be watched for—they cannot be ignored because of hospital routine that is "more important."

Let the mother have enough time to see and become acquainted with the hospital personnel with whom she will experience birth. Length of hospital stay is geared to technical requirements—five days for middle-class mothers, down (in some places) to twenty-four hours or less for the poor. Therefore, acquaintance should start before birth, at least with the physician, so that when delivery comes the mother will not be faced with a stranger in cap and gown, but a human being she already knows. Nurses and social workers should also be included. (The Hahnemann Medical College and Hospital in Philadelphia already assigns resident physicians to the pre-natal clinics to provide this continuity.)

Mothers of young infants suffer from geographical and psychological isolation. Services should work toward reducing both of these isolations. Ideally such services should come from a team, including not only the doctor and nurses, but a sympathetic pediatrician, psychiatric and medical social workers, of both sexes, who could also act as substitute parents. This help should be as available to the middle-class as to the poor (middle-class patients are sometimes denied hospital social services).

Help should carry over into home care. *Make sure that each mother has someone to care for her at home.* After their too brief hospital stay, poverty-stricken women, many without husband or family, are often more helpless and lost at home than in the hospital.

Mothers should not be left alone for long periods, whether under sedation or not. Schedules should and must be modified to allow them to have normal family support as long as possible. If they have none, substitutes—volunteers—should be found. Isolated mothers, cut off from support or even contact with their physicians, and treated as objects, much too often displace their loneliness, depression, resentment, bitterness, humiliation, rage, and pain onto their babies.

Get rid of the stirrups—and the practice of using them to hang mothers' legs in the air for hours. Find some other way to hold women on the delivery table until the last moments. Women often spend months recovering from backaches caused by stirrups.

Present the baby as soon as possible. The most frequent comment from mothers who remain conscious in the delivery room is, "The doctor gave him to me." This is psychologically very sound; when the father-image (doctor) presents the baby with the obvious approval of the mother-image (nurse), latent feelings of guilt about having a baby and about the acceptability of the baby—and of motherhood—are lulled and dispelled. Too often, however, the nurse is cast, or casts herself, in the role of unwilling, stingy, critical giver of the baby—in fact the whole institution lends itself to this. Presentation should precede and not depend on feeling; it should be made gladly and willingly; it should allow time and ease of access for the mother to examine her baby's body.

Doctors, nurses, and aides should understand and come to know pregnancy, labor, delivery, and early growth as a continuing process, rather than in bits and pieces, a series of techniques. They need to understand and see it from the mothers' viewpoint, as well as in terms of bottles, diapers, rooms, instruments, and procedures.

Reassure mothers about their infants. This includes understanding the real meanings of their questions. If a mother continually discounts good reports, rejection may be underway, and psychological miscarriage imminent.

First-born children, and the first-borns of each sex, are the ones most commonly rejected; their mothers need special care—as do the mothers of the poor and those without family, husband, or outside human supports.

None of these proposals are radical—even administratively. Most are quite simple, and could be done directly in the wards and the private rooms.

Overall, we need more research. We do not know enough about the earliest signals of psychological miscarriage; we have not trained ourselves, nor taken the trouble, to watch for these early signs. Nor do we know enough about the long-term effects of maladaptation. Are the older children completely lost? Is the process irreversible? Cannot something be done to bring them back to productive life?

There is nothing more important in a maternity pavilion, nor in a home, than the experiences with which life begins. We must stop the dehumanization of mothers. We must give all children a chance for life.

THE SOCIOLOGY OF PARENT-YOUTH CONFLICT

KINGSLEY DAVIS

It is in sociological terms that this paper attempts to frame and solve the sole question with which it deals, namely: Why does contemporary western civilization manifest an extraordinary amount of parent-adolescent conflict?[1] In other cultures, the outstanding fact is generally not the rebelliousness of youth, but its docility. There is practically no custom, no matter how tedious or painful, to which youth in primitive tribes or archaic civilizations will not willingly submit.[2] What, then, are the peculiar features of our society which gives us one of the extremest examples of endemic filial friction in human history?

Our answer to this question makes use of constants and variables, the constants being the universal factors in the parent-youth relation, the variables being the factors which differ from one society to another. Though one's attention, in explaining the parent-youth relations of a given milieu, is focused on the variables, one cannot comprehend the action of the variables without also understanding the constants, for the latter constitute the structural and functional basis of the family as a part of society.

The Rate of Social Change. The first important variable is the rate of social change. Extremely rapid change in modern civilization, in contrast to most societies, tends to increase parent-youth conflict, for within a fast-changing social order the time-interval between generations, ordinarily but a mere moment in the life of a social system, become historically significant, thereby creating a hiatus between one generation and the next. Inevitably, under such a condition, youth is reared in a milieu different from that of the parents; hence the parents become old-fashioned, youth rebellious, and clashes occur which, in the closely confined circle of the immediate family, generate sharp emotion.

Reprinted from *American Sociological Review,* Vol. 5 (1940), pp. 523-534, by permission of the American Sociological Association and the author.

That rapidity of change is a significant variable can be démonstrated by three lines of evidence: a comparison of stable and nonstable societies;[3] a consideration of immigrant families; and an analysis of revolutionary epochs. If, for example, the conflict is sharper in the immigrant household, this can be due to one thing only, that the immigrant family generally undergoes the most rapid social change of any type of family in a given society. Similarly, a revolution (an abrupt form of societal alteration), by concentrating great change in a short span, catapults the younger generation into power—a generation which has absorbed and pushed the new ideas, acquired the habit of force, and which, accordingly, dominates those hangovers from the old regime, its parents.[4]

The Birth-Cycle, Decelerating Socialization, and Parent-Child Differences. Note, however, that rapid social change would have no power to produce conflict were it not for two universal factors: first, the family's duration; and second, the decelerating rate of socialization in the development of personality. A "family" is not a static entity but a process in time, a process ordinarily so brief compared with historical time that it is unimportant, but which, when history is "full" (i.e., marked by rapid social change), strongly influences the mutual adjustment of the generations. This "span" is basically the birth-cycle—the length of time between the birth of one person and his procreation of another. It is biological and inescapable. It would, however, have no effect in producing parent-youth conflict, even with social change, if it were not for the additional fact, intimately related and equally universal, that the sequential development of personality involves a constantly decelerating rate of socialization. This deceleration is due both to organic factors (age—which ties it to the birth-cycle) and to social factors (the cumulative character of social experience). Its effect is to make the birth-cycle interval, which is the period of youth, the time of major socialization, subsequent periods of socialization being subsidiary.

Given these constant features, rapid social change creates conflict because *to* the intrinsic (universal, inescapable) differences between parents and children it adds an extrinsic (variable) difference derived from the acquisition, at the same stage of life, of differential cultural content by each successive generation. Not only are parent and child, at any given moment, in different stages of development, but the content which the parent acquired at the stage where the child now is, was a different content from that which the child is now acquiring.

Since the parent is supposed to socialize the child, he tends to apply the erstwhile but now inappropriate content (see Diagram). He makes this mistake, and cannot remedy it, because, due to the logic of personality growth, his basic orientation was formed by the experiences of his own childhood. He cannot "modernize" his point of view, because *he* is the product of those experiences. He can change in superficial ways, such as learning a new tune, but he cannot change (or *want* to change) the initial modes of thinking upon which his subsequent social experience has been built. To change the basic conceptions by which he has learned to judge the rightness and reality of all specific situations would be to render subsequent experience meaningless, to make an empty caricature of what had been his life.

Though the birth-cycle remains absolutely the same, it does not remain relatively the same, because it occupies, as time goes on, a successively smaller percentage of the total time lived. Furthermore, because of the decelerating rate of socialization, the difference in the total amount of cultural content as between parent and child becomes less pronounced. After the period of adolescence, for example, the margin is reduced to a minimum, which explains why a minimum of conflict is achieved after that stage.

Although, in the birth-cycle gap between parent and offspring, astronomical time constitutes the basic point of disparity, the actual sequences, and hence the actual differences significant for us, are physiological, psycho-social, and sociological—each with an acceleration of its own within, but to some degree independent of, sidereal time, and each containing a divergence between parent and child which must be taken into account in explaining parent-youth conflict.

Physiological Differences. Though the disparity in chronological age remains constant through life, the precise physiological differences between parent and offspring vary radically from one period to another. The organic contrasts between parent and *infant,* for example, are far different from those between parent and adolescent. Yet whatever the period, the organic differences produce contrasts (as between young and old) in those desires which, at least in part, are organically determined. Thus, at the time of adolescence the contrast is between an organism which is just reaching its full powers and one which is just losing them. The physiological need of the latter is for security and conservation, because as the superabundance of energy diminishes, the organism seems to hoard what remains.

Such differences, often alleged (under the heading of "disturbing physiological changes accompanying adolescence") as the primary cause of parent-adolescent strife, are undoubtedly a factor in such conflict, but, like other universal differences to be discussed, they form a constant factor present in every community, and therefore cannot in themselves explain the peculiar heightening of parent-youth conflict in our culture.

The fact is that most societies avoid the potential clash of old and young by using sociological position as a neutralizing agent. They assign definite and separate positions to persons of different ages. thereby eliminating competition between them for the same position and avoiding the competitive emotions of jealousy and envy. Also, since the expected behavior of old and young is thus made complementary rather than identical, the performance of cooperative functions as accomplished by different but mutually related activities suited to the disparate organic needs of each, with no coercion to behave in a manner unsuited to one's organic age. In our culture, where most positions are *theoretically* based on accomplishment rather than age, interage competition arises, superior organic propensities lead to a high evaluation of youth (the so-called "accent on youth") , a disproportionate lack of opportunity for youth manifests itself, and consequently, arrogance and frustration appear in the young, fear and envy, in the old.

Psychosocial Differences: Adult Realism versus Youthful Idealism. The decelerating rate of socialization (an outgrowth both of the human being's organic development, from infant plasticity to senile rigidity, and of his cumulative cultural and social development), when taken with rapid social change and other conditions of our society, tends to produce certain differences of orientation between parent and youth. Though lack of space makes it impossible to discuss all of these ramifications, we shall attempt to delineate at least one sector of difference in terms of the conflict between adult realism (or pragmatism) and youthful idealism.

Though both youth and age claim to see the truth, the old are more conservatively realistic than the young, because on the one hand they take Utopian ideals less seriously and on the other hand take what may be called operating ideals, if not more seriously, at least more for granted. Thus, middle-aged people notoriously forget the poetic ideals of a new social order which they cherished when young. In their place, they put simply the working ideals current in the society.

There is, in short, a persistent tendency for the ideology of a person as he grows older to gravitate more and more toward the status quo ideology, unless other facts (such as a social crisis or hypnotic suggestion) intervene.[5] With advancing age, he becomes less and less bothered by inconsistencies in ideals. He tends to judge ideals according to whether they are widespread and hence effective in thinking about practical life, not according to whether they are logically consistent. Furthermore, he gradually ceases to bother about the *untruth* of his ideals, in the sense of their failure to correspond to reality. He assumes through long habit that, though they do not correspond perfectly, the discrepancy is not significant. The reality of an ideal is defined for him in terms of how many people accept it rather than how completely it is mirrored in actual behavior.[6] Thus, we call him, as he approaches middle age, a realist.

The young, however, are idealists, partly because they take working ideals literally and partly because they acquire ideals not fully operative in the social organization. Those in authority over children are obligated as a requirement of their status to inculcate ideals as a part of the official culture given the new generation.[7] The children are receptive because they have little social experience—experience being systematically kept from them (by such means as censorship, for example, a large part of which is to "protect" children). Consequently, young people possess little ballast for their acquired ideals, which therefore soar to the sky, whereas the middle-aged, by contrast, have plenty of ballast.

This relatively unchecked idealism in youth is eventually complicated by the fact that young people possess keen reasoning ability. The mind, simply as a logical machine, works as well at sixteen as at thirty-six.[8] Such logical capacity, combined with high ideals and an initial lack of experience, means that youth soon discovers with increasing age that the ideals it has been taught are true and consistent are not so in fact. Mental conflict thereupon ensues, for the young person has not learned that ideals may be useful without being true and consistent. As a solution, youth is likely to take action designed to remove inconsistencies or force actual conduct into line with ideals, such action assuming one of several typical adolescent forms—from religious withdrawal to the militant support of some Utopian scheme —but in any case consisting essentially in serious allegiance to one or more of the ideal moral systems present in the culture.[9]

A different, usually later reaction to disillusionment is the cynical or sophomoric attitude; for, if the ideals one has imbibed cannot be reconciled and do not fit reality, then why not dismiss them as worthless? Cynicism has the advantage of giving justification for behavior that young organisms crave anyway. It might be mistaken for genuine realism if it were not for two things. The first is the emotional strain behind the "don't care" attitude. The cynic, in his judgment that the world is bad because of inconsistency and untruth of ideals, clearly implies that he still values the ideals. The true realist sees the inconsistency and untruth, but without emotion; he uses either ideals or reality whenever it suits his purpose. The second is the early disappearance of the cynical attitude. Increased experience usually teaches the adolescent that overt cynicism is unpopular and unworkable, that to deny and deride all beliefs which fail to cohere or to correspond to facts, and to act in opposition to them, is to alienate oneself from any group,[10] because these beliefs, however unreal, are precisely what makes group unity possible. Soon, therefore, the youthful cynic finds himself bound up with some group having a system of working ideals, and becomes merely another conformist, cynical only about the beliefs of other groups.[11]

While the germ of this contrast between youthful idealim and adult realism may spring from the universal logic of personality development, it receives in our culture a peculiar exaggeration. Social change, complexity, and specialization (by compartmentalizing different aspects of life) segregate ideals from fact and throw together incompatible ideologies while at the same time providing the intellectual tools for discerning logical inconsistencies and empirical errors. Our highly elaborated burden of culture, correlated with a variegated system of achieved vertical mobility, necessitates long years of formal education which separate youth from adulthood, theory from practice, school from life. Insofar, then, as youth's reformist zeal or cynical negativism produces conflict with parents, the peculiar conditions of our culture are responsible.

Sociological Differences: Parental Authority. Since social status and office are everywhere partly distributed on the basis of age, personality development is intimately linked with the network of social positions successively occupied during life. Western society, in spite of an unusual amount of interage competition, maintains differences of social position between parent and child, the development gap between them being too clearcut, the symbiotic needs too fundamental, to escape being made a basis of social organization. Hence, parent and child, in a variety of ways, find themselves enmeshed in different social contexts and possessed of different outlooks. The much publicized critical attitude of youth toward established ways, for example, is partly a matter of being on the outside looking in. The "established ways" under criticism are usually institutions (such as property, marriage, profession) which the adolescent has not yet entered. He looks at them from the point of view of the outsider (especially since they affect him in a restrictive manner), either failing to imagine himself finding satisfaction in such patterns or else feeling resentful that the old have in them a vested interest from which he is excluded.

Not only is there differential position, but also *mutually* differential position, status being in many ways specific for and reciprocal between parent and child. Some of these differences, relating to the birth-cycle and constituting part of the family structure, are universal. This is particularly true of the super- and subordination summed up in the term *parental authority*.

Since sociological differences between parent and child are inherent in family organization, they constitute a universal factor potentially capable of producing conflict. Like the biological differences, however, they do not in themselves produce such conflict. In fact, they may help to avoid it. To understand how our society brings to expression the potentiality for conflict, indeed to deal realistically with the relation between the generations, we must do so not in generalized terms but in terms of the specific "power situation." Therefore, the remainder of our discussion will center upon the nature of parental authority and its vicissitudes in our society.

Because of his strategic position with reference to the new-born child (at least in the familial type of reproductive institution), the parent is given considerable authority. Charged by his social group with the responsibility of controlling and training the child in conformity with the mores and thereby insuring the maintenance of the cultural structure, the parent, to fulfill his duties, must have the privileges as well as the obligations of authority, and the surrounding community ordinarily guarantees both.

The first thing to note about parental authority, in addition to its function in socialization, is that it is a case of authority within a primary group. Simmel has pointed out that authority is bearable for the subordinate because it touches only one aspect of life. Impersonal and objective, it permits all other aspects to be free from its particularistic dominance. This escape, however, is lacking in parental authority, for since the family includes most aspects of life, its authority is not limited, specific, or impersonal. What, then, can make this authority bearable? Three factors associated with the familial primary group help to give the answer: (1) the child is socialized within the family, and therefore knowing nothing else and being utterly dependent, the authority of the parent is internalized, accepted; (2) the family, like other primary groups, implies identification, in such sense that one person understands and responds emphatically to the sentiments of the other, so that the harshness of authority is ameliorated;[12] (3) in the intimate interaction of the primary group control can never be purely one-sided; there are too many ways in which the subordinated can exert the pressure of his will.

When, therefore, the family system is a going concern, parental authority, however, inclusive, is not felt as despotic.

A second thing to note about parental authority is that while its duration is variable (lasting in some societies a few years and in others a lifetime), it inevitably involves a change, a progressive readjustment, in the respective positions of parent and child—in some cases an almost complete reversal of roles, in others at least a cumulative allowance for the fact of maturity in the subordinated offspring. Age is a unique basis for social stratification. Unlike birth, sex, wealth, or occupation, it implies that the stratification is temporary, that the person, if he lives a full life, will eventually traverse all of the strata having it as a basis. Therefore, there is a peculiar ambivalence attached to this kind of differentiation, as well as a constant directional movement. On the other hand, the young person, in the stage of maximum socialization, is, so to speak, *moving into* the social organization. His social personality is expanding, i.e., acquiring an increased amount of the cultural heritage, filling more powerful and numerous positions. His future is before him, in what the older person is leaving behind. The latter, on the other hand, has a future before him only in the sense that the offspring represents it. Therefore, there is a disparity of interest, the young person placing his thoughts upon a future which, once the first stages of dependence are passed, does not include the parent, the old person placing his hopes vicariously upon the young. This situation, representing a *tendency* in every society, is avoided in many places by a system of respect for the aged and an imaginary projection of life beyond the grave. In the absence of such a religio-ancestral system, the role of the aged is a tragic one.[13]

Let us now take up, point by point, the manner in which western civilization has affected this *gemeinschaftliche* and processual form of authority.

1. Conflicting Norms. To begin with, rapid change has, as we saw, given old and young a different social content, so that they possess conflicting norms. There is a loss of mutual identification, and the parent will not "catch up" with the child's point of view, because he is supposed to dominate rather than follow. More than this, social complexity has confused the standards *within* the generations. Faced with conflicting goals, parents become inconsistent and confused in their own minds in rearing their children. The children, for example, acquire an argument against discipline by being able to point to some family wherein discipline is less severe, while the parent can retaliate by pointing to still other families wherein it is firmer. The acceptance of parental attitudes is less complete than formerly.

2. Competing Authorities. We took it for granted, when discussing rapid social change, that youth acquires new ideas, but we did not ask how. The truth is that, in a specialized and complex culture, they learn from competing authorities. Today, for example, education is largely in the hands of professional specialists, some of whom, as college professors, resemble the sophists of ancient Athens by virtue of their work of accumulating and purveying knowledge, and who consequently have ideas in advance of the populace at large (i.e., the parents). By giving the younger generation these advanced ideas, they (and many other extrafamilial agencies, including youth's contemporaries) widen the intellectual gap between parent and child.[14]

3. Little Explicit Institutionalization of Steps in Parental Authority. Our society provides little explicit institutionalization of the progressive readjustments of authority as between parent and child. We are intermediate between the extreme of virtually permanent parental authority and the extreme of very early emancipation, because we encourage release in late adolescence. Unfortunately, this is a time of enhanced sexual desire, so that the problem of sex and the problem of emancipation occur simultaneously and complicate each other. Yet even this would doubtless be satisfactory if it were not for the fact that among us the exact time when authority is relinquished, the exact amount, and the proper ceremonial behavior are not clearly defined. Not only do different groups and families have conflicting patterns, and new situations arise to which old definitions will not apply, but the different spheres of life (legal, economic, religious, intellectual) do not synchronize, maturity in one sphere and immaturity in another often coexisting. The readjustment of authority between individuals is always a ticklish process, and when it is a matter of such close authority as that between parent and child it is apt to be still more ticklish. The failure of our culture to institutionalize this readjustment by a series of well-defined, well-publicized steps is undoubtedly a cause of much parent-youth dissension. The adolescent's sociological exit from his family, via education, work, marriage, and change of residence, is fraught with potential conflicts of interest which only a definite system of institutional controls can neutralize. The parents have a vital stake in what the offspring will do. Because his acquisition of independence will free the parents of many obligations, they are willing to relinquish their authority; yet, precisely because their own status is socially identified with that of their offspring, they wish to insure satisfactory conduct on the latter's part and are tempted to prolong their authority by making the decisions themselves. In the absence of institutional prescriptions, the conflict of interest may lead to a struggle for power, the parents fighting to keep control in matters of importance to themselves, the son or daughter clinging to personally indispensable family services while seeking to evade the concomitant control.

4. Concentration within the Small Family. Our family system is peculiar in that it manifests a paradoxical combination of concentration and dispersion. On the one hand, the unusual smallness of the family unit makes for a strange intensity of family feeling, while on the other, the fact that most pursuits take place outside the home makes for a dispersion of activities. Though apparently contradictory, the two phenomena are really interrelated and traceable ultimately to the same factors in our social structure. Since the first refers to that type of affection and antagonism found between relatives, and the second to activities, it can be seen that the second (dispersion) isolates and increases the intensity of the affectional element by sheering away common activities and the extended kin. Whereas ordinarily the sentiments of kinship are organically related to a number of common activities and spread over a wide circle of relatives, in our mobile society they are associated with only a few common activities and concentrated within only the immediate family. This makes them at once more instable (because ungrounded) and more intense. With the diminishing birth rate, our family is the world's smallest kinship unit, a tiny closed circle. Consequently, a great deal of family sentiment is directed toward a few individuals, who are so important to the emotional life that complexes easily develop. This emotional intensity and situational instability increase both the probability and severity of conflict.

In a familistic society, where there are several adult male and female relatives within the effective kinship group to whom the child turns for affection and aid, and many members of the younger generation in whom the parents have a paternal interest, there appears to be less intensity of emotion for any particular kinsman and consequently less chance for severe conflict.[15] Also, if conflict between any two relatives does arise, it may be handled by shifting mutual rights and obligations to another relative.[16]

5. *Open Competition for Socioeconomic Position.* Our emphasis upon individual initiative and vertical mobility, in contrast to rural-stable regimes, means that one's future occupation and destiny are determined more at adolescence than at birth, the adolescent himself (as well as the parents) having some part in the decision. Before him spread a panorama of possible occupations and avenues of advancement, all of them fraught with the uncertainties of competitive vicissitude. The youth is ignorant of most of the facts. So is the parent, but less so. Both attempt to collaborate on the future, but because of previously mentioned sources of friction, the collaboration is frequently stormy. They evaluate future possibilities differently, and since the decision is uncertain yet important, a clash of wills results. The necessity of choice at adolescence extends beyond the occupational field to practically every phase of life, the parents having an interest in each decision. A culture in which more of the choices of life were settled beforehand by ascription, where the possibilities were fewer and the responsibilities of choice less urgent, would have much less parent-youth conflict.[17]

6. *Sex Tension.* If until now we have ignored sex taboos, the omission has represented a deliberate attempt to place them in their proper context with other factors, rather than in the unduly prominent place usually given them.[18] Undoubtedly, because of a constellation of cultural conditions, sex looms as an important bone of parent-youth contention. Our morality, for instance, demands both premarital chastity and postponement of marriage, thus creating a long

period of desperate eagerness when young persons practically at the peak of their sexual capacity are forbidden to enjoy it. Naturally, tensions arise—tensions which adolescents try to relieve and adults hope they will relieve, in some socially acceptable form. Such tensions not only make the adolescent intractable and capricious, but create a genuine conflict of interest between the two generations. The parent, with respect to the child's behavior, represents morality, while the offspring reflects morality *plus* his organic cravings. The stage is thereby set for conflict, evasion, and deceit. For the mass of parents, toleration is never possible. For the mass of adolescents, sublimation is never sufficient. Given our system of morality, conflict seems well nigh inevitable.

Yet it is not sex itself but the way it is handled that causes conflict. If sex patterns were carefully, definitely, and uniformly geared with nonsexual patterns in the social structure, there would be no parent-youth conflict over sex. As it is, rapid change has opposed the sex standards of different groups and generations, leaving impulse only chaotically controlled.

The extraordinary preoccupation of modern parents with the sex life of their adolescent offspring is easily understandable. First, our morality is sex-centered. The strength of the impulse which it seeks to control, the consequent stringency of its rules, and the importance of reproductive institutions for society, make sex so morally important that being moral and being sexually discreet are synonymous. Small wonder, then, that parents, charged with responsibility for their children and fearful of their own status in the eyes of the moral community, are preoccupied with what their offspring will do in this matter. Moreover, sex is intrinsically involved in the family structure and is therefore of unusual significance to family members *qua* family members. Offspring and parent are not simply two persons who happen to live together; they are two persons who happen to live together because of past sex relations between the parents. Also, between parent and child there stand strong incest taboos, and doubtless the unvoiced possibility of violating these unconsciously intensifies the interest of each in the other's sexual conduct. In addition, since sexual behavior is connected with the offspring's formation of a new family of his own, it is naturally of concern to the parent. Finally, these factors taken in combination with the delicacy of the authoritarian relation, the emotional intensity within the small family, and the confusion of sex standards, make it easy to explain the parental interest in adolescent sexuality. Yet because sex is a tabooed topic between parent and child,[19] parental control must be indirect and devious, which creates additional possibilities of conflict.

Summary and Conclusion. Our parent-youth conflict thus results from the interaction of certain universals of the parent-child relation and certain variables the values of which are peculiar to modern culture. The universals are (1) the basic age or birth-cycle differential between parent and child, (2) the decelerating rate of socialization with advancing age, and (3) the resulting intrinsic differences between old and young on the physiological, psychosocial, and sociological planes.

Though these universal factors *tend* to produce conflict between parent and child, whether or not they do so depends upon the variables. We have seen that the distinctive general features of our society are responsible for our excessive parent-adolescent friction. Indeed, they are the same features which are affecting *all* family relations. The delineation of these variables has not been systematic, because the scientific classification of whole societies has not yet been accomplished; and it has been difficult, in view of the interrelated character of societal traits, to seize upon certain features and ignore others. Yet certainly the following four complex variables are important: (1) the rate of social change; (2) the extent of complexity in the social structure; (3) the degree of integration in the culture; and (4) the velocity of movement (e.g., vertical mobility) within the structure and its relation to the cultural values.

Our rapid social change, for example, has crowded historical meaning into the family time-span, has thereby given the offspring a different social content from that which the parent acquired, and consequently has added to the already existent intrinsic differences between parent and youth, a set of extrinsic ones which double the chance of alienation. Moreover, our great societal complexity, our evident cultural conflict, and our emphasis upon open competition for socioeconomic status have all added to this initial effect. We have seen, for instance, that they have disorganized the important relation of parental authority by confusing the goals of child control, setting up competing authorities, creating a small family system, making necessary certain significant choices at the time of adolescence, and leading to an absence of definite institutional mechanisms to symbolize and enforce the progressively changing stages of parental power.

If ours were a simple rural-stable society, mainly familistic, the emancipation from parental authority being gradual and marked by definite institutionalized steps, with no great postponement of marriage, sex taboo, or open competition for status, parents and youth would not be in conflict. Hence, the presence of parent-youth conflict in our civilization is one more specific manifestation of the incompatibility between an urban-industrial-mobile social system and the familiar type of reproductive institutions.[20]

NOTES

[1]In the absence of statistical evidence, exaggeration of the conflict is easily possible, and two able students have warned against it. E. B. Reuter, "The Sociology of Adolescence," and Jessie R. Runner, "Social Distances in Adolescent Relationships," both in *Amer. J. Sociol.*, November 1937. 43:415-16, 437. Yet sufficient nonquantitative evidence lies at hand in the form of personal experience, the outpour of literature on adolescent problems, and the historical and anthropological accounts of contrasting societies to justify the conclusion that in comparison with other cultures ours exhibits an exceptional amount of such conflict. If this paper seems to stress conflict, it is simply because we are concerned with this problem rather than with parent-youth harmony.

[2]Cf. Nathan Miller, *The Child in Primitive Society*, New York, 1928; Miriam Van Waters, "The Adolescent Girl Among Primitive Peoples," *J. Relig. Psychol.*, 1913, 6:375-421 (1913) and 7:75-120 (1914); Margaret Mead, *Coming of Age in Samoa*, New York, 1928 and "Adolescence in Primitive and Modern Society," 169-188, in *The New Generation*, ed. by V. F. Calverton and S. Schmalhausen, New York, 1930; A. M. Bacon, *Japanese Girls and Women*, New York and Boston, 1891 and 1902.

[3]Partially done by Mead and Van Waters in the works cited above.

[4]Soviet Russia and Nazi Germany are examples. See Sigmund Neumann, "The Conflict of Generations in Contemporary Europe from Versailles to Munich," *Vital Speeches of the Day*, August 1, 1939, 5:623-28. Parents in these countries are to be obeyed only so long as they profess the "correct" (i.e., youthful, revolutionary) ideas.

[5]See Footnote 11 for necessary qualifications.

[6]When discussing a youthful ideal, however, the older person is quick to take a dialectical advantage by pointing out not only that this ideal affronts the aspirations of the multitude, but that it also fails to correspond to human behavior either now or (by the lessons of history) probably in the future.

[7] See amusing but accurate article, "Fathers Are Liars," *Scribner's Magazine*, March, 1934.

[8] Evidence from mental growth data which point to a leveling off of the growth curve at about age 16. For charts and brief explanations, together with references, see F. K. Shuttleworth, *The Adolescent Period*, Monographs of the Society for Research in Child Development, III, Serial No. 16 (Washington, D.C., 1938), Figs. 16, 230, 232, 276, 285, 308.

Maturity of judgment is of course another matter. We are speaking only of logical capacity. Judgment is based on experience as well as capacity; hence, adolescents are apt to lack it.

[9] An illustration of youthful reformism was afforded by the Laval University students who decided to "do something about" prostitution in the city of Quebec. They broke into eight houses in succession one night, "whacked naked inmates upon the buttocks, upset beds and otherwise proved their collegiate virtue. . . ." They ended by "shoving the few remaining girls out of doors into the cold autumn night." *Time*, October 19, 1936.

[10] This holds only for expressed cynicism, but so close is the relation of thought to action that the possibility of an entirely covert cynic seems remote.

[11] This tentative analysis holds only insofar as the logic of personality development in a complex culture is the sole factor. Because of other factors, concrete situations may be quite different. When, for example, a person is specifically trained in certain rigid, other-worldly, or impractical ideals, he may grow increasingly fanatical with the years rather than realistic, while his offspring, because of association with less fanatical persons, may be more pragmatic than he. The variation in group norms within a society produces persons who, whatever their orientation inside the group, remain more idealistic than the average outsider, while their children may, with outside contacts, become more pragmatic. Even within a group, however, a person's situation may be such as to drive him beyond the everyday realities of that group, while his children remain undisturbed. Such situations largely explain the personal crises that may alter one's orientation. The analysis, overly brief and mainly illustrative, therefore represents a certain degree of abstraction. The reader should realize, moreover, that the terms "realistic" and "idealistic" are chosen merely for convenience in trying to convey the idea, not for any evaluative judgments which they may happen to connote. The terms are not used in any technical epistemological sense, but simply in the way made plain by the context. Above all, it is not implied that ideals are "unreal." The ways in which they are "real" and "unreal" to observer and actor are complex indeed. See T. Parsons, *The Structure of Social Action*, 396, New York, 1937, and V. Pareto, *The Mind and Society*, III:1300-1304, New York, 1935.

12 House slaves, for example, are generally treated much better than field slaves. Authority over the former is of a personal type, while that over the latter (often in the form of a foreman-gang organization) is of a more impersonal or economic type.

13 Sometimes compensated for by an interest in the grandchildren, which permits them partially to recover the role of the vigorous parent.

14 The essential point is not that there are other authorities—in every society there are extrafamilial influences in socialization—but that, because of specialization and individualistic enterprise, they are *competing* authorities. Because they make a living by their work and are specialists in socialization, some authorities have a competitive advantage over parents who are amateurs or at best merely general practitioners.

15 Margaret Mead, *Social Organization of Manua*, 84, Honolulu, Bernice P. Bishop Museum Bulletin 76, 1930. Large heterogeneous households early accustom the child to expect emotional rewards from many different persons. D. M. Spencer, "The Composition of the Family as a Factor in the Behavior of Children in Fijian Society," *Sociometry*, (1939) 2:47-55.

16 The principle of substitution is widespread in familism, as shown by the wide distribution of adoption, levirate, sororate, and classifactory kinship nomenclature.

17 M. Mead, *Coming of Age in Samoa*, 200 ff.

18 Cf., e.g., L. K. Frank, "The Management of Tensions," *Amer. J. Sociol.*, March 1928, 33:706-22; M. Mead, *op. cit.*, 216-217, 222-23.

19 "Even among the essentially 'unpressed' Trobianders the parent is never the confidant in matters of sex." Bronislaw Malinowski, *Sex and Reproduction in Savage Society*, 36 (note), London, 1927, p. 36n. Cf. the interesting article, "Intrusive Parents," *The Commentator*, September 1938, which opposes frank sex discussion between parents and children.

20 For further evidence of this incompatibility, see the writer's "Reproductive Institutions and the Pressure for Population," (*Brit.*) *Sociol. Rev.*; July 1937, 29:289-306.

STUDENT REBELLION AGAINST PARENTAL POLITICAL BELIEFS

RUSSELL MIDDLETON
SNELL PUTNEY

The nation's press has proclaimed a surge of political interest among American college students. The beat, silent, apolitical generation of the 1950's is said to have been succeeded by a politically awakened, impatient, and iconoclastic generation of college students in the 1960's. This popular image is based both upon the proliferation of political clubs on college campuses[1] and upon an increasing tendency for students to engage in direct political action — sit-ins, freedom rides, peace marches, and demonstrations against the House Committee on Un-American Activities.

Traditionally it has been assumed that the usual political pattern was a liberal or radical rebellion during youth, followed by a gradual return to conservative orthodoxy in later life. As Robert Frost expressed it, "I never dared be radical when young/For fear it would make me conservative when old." At least two studies, however, have cast doubt on the assumption that conservatism increases with age. Lazarsfeld and associates found that older people were not necessarily more conservative than younger people, but were merely more closely aligned with the political attitudes prevalent in their ethnic or religious group,[2] and Centers failed to find a tendency for older people to be more conservative than younger people among laboring groups, although there was a slight tendency in this direction among the upper occupational groups.[3]

But whether or not youthful liberal rebellion has predominated in the past, most of the nation's press sees a reversal of this pattern today. It is contended that there is an upsurge of conservatism among students, who are rebelling from what is described as the current liberal establishment. The keynote was sounded by *Time:*

Reprinted from *Social Forces* (May, 1963), pp. 377-383, by permission of The University Press of North Carolina and the authors.

The new trend is youth's natural rebellion against conformity, and to many the liberalism of their New Deal-bred elders is the most iron-bound conformity. "My parents thought Franklin D. Roosevelt was one of the greatest heroes who ever lived," says Y.A.F. Chairman, Yale Law Student Robert Schuchman, 22. "I'm rebelling from that concept." Says President Roger Claus of Wisconsin's Conservative Club: "You walk around with your Goldwater button, and you feel the thrill of treason."[4]

Elms, on the other hand, writing in *The Nation,* maintains that there has been no mass conversion to conservatism among college students. The greater interest in conservatism, he argues, is merely a part of a wider political awakening among youths, and it is over-shadowed by a stronger but less publicized resurgence of liberalism on the campus. He also suggests that most student conservatives come from solidly conservative families and conservative milieux: "Conformity to socio-economic class roles is a more likely reason for student conservatism than reaction against the conformity of liberalism."[6]

Lacking comparable data from an earlier period, we cannot here determine whether college students are more interested in politics than formerly, or whether students are less inclined to rebel toward liberalism than in the past. However, it is possible to shed some light on the controversy between Elms and the Editors of *Time* by comparing the political viewpoints of college students with those of their parents. Accordingly, this study is focused on two questions: (1) Is the prevailing direction of political rebellion among college students today toward conservatism? and (2) Is there evidence that those who espouse conservative viewpoints are predominantly rebels against liberal parents?

METHODS

The data for this study were collected by means of anonymous questionnaires administered during 1961 to classes of students in 16 colleges and universities in the United States. The sample of institutions includes a private university, a private liberal arts college, a state college, and a state university in each of four regions: Far West, Middle West, Northeast, and South. Four of the eight private institutions are church affiliated. Thus the students represent a variety of regions and types of institutions although intact classes were selected within the institutions and caution should be used in generalizing the findings of this study to all American college and university students.

Completed and usable questionnaires were obtained from 824 males and 616 females, a total of 1,440 students. Approximately 28 percent of the students were freshmen, 23 percent sophomores, 23 percent juniors, 21 percent seniors, and 5 percent graduate students.

A major problem in any study of political attitudes is the definition of a continuum of political positions. Political party preference is a questionable index because of the wide range of ideological variation within American parties. Another approach, often used in the past, is a scale based on certain substantive issues, such as the role of government in the regulation of the economy. A typical example is the Politico-Economic Conservatism Scale developed in the California studies of the authoritarian personality.[7] Although such a scale may be of considerable utility for classifying people in regard to the substantive issues, the broader significance of these may be problematic. The components of variation in the political spectrum are both complex and controversial, and many substantive issues are not related in a linear fashion to a political continuum ranging from extreme left to extreme right. Moreover, many people who have political views nevertheless have no crystallized position on specific issues, particularly if they are complex.

At the other extreme, McClosky has developed a conservatism scale which taps an underlying conservatism in the personality structure, but is so far removed from particular political issues that many aspects of ideological variation are likely to be obscured.[8]

In this study we sought to avoid the problems inherent in the use of party identification or inferential scales by utilizing a set of familiar political labels, or categories, and asking the subject to choose the one most closely corresponding to his own political views. Although most Americans are by no means ideologues, they frequently think in terms of political labels and they appear to have much less difficulty in categorizing their own position than in spelling out their substantive views.

However, selecting categories which are familiar and meaningful to American college students and at the same time are free of evaluative bias is no simple task. Several sets of categories were tried and discarded during the pretesting. One set, for example, presented a series of current political figures ranging from left to right, and the subjects were asked with which figure they most closely agreed. The results, however, were distorted by the students' lack of familiarity with even major political figures, their ignorance of the political positions of figures whom they did know, and the purely personal appeal of some of the figures. In one pretest involving a class of seniors and graduate students in social science, for example, 25 percent said that they were not familiar enough with Senator Hubert Humphrey to classify his political position, even though he had conducted a vigorous and much publicized campaign for the Democratic nomination for President less than a year before. Another 14 percent classified him as a conservative. Similarly, 21 percent classified Senator Barry Goldwater as a liberal. President Kennedy, enjoying great personal popularity immediately following his election (this pretest was in the spring of 1961), attracted support from all camps—socialists, liberals, and conservatives.

It was necessary to avoid labels which are often used in a pejorative sense or as epithets. The labels "fascist" and "communist" are obvious examples, and the label "reactionary" failed to attract a single student during the pretesting (though some applied it to their parents). Despite evident pejoration the label "socialist" appeared to retain utility: a plausible minority of students applied it to themselves, and only rarely was it applied to others in an implausible manner (e.g., "most people in the United States are socialist").

The set of categories which proved to be most meaningful to American college students was an extremely simple left-to-right continuum. The students were presented with socialist, liberal, and conservative categories, the latter two being further subdivided by a qualifying adverb. Thus each subject was asked, "Which of these political positions is closest to your own views?"

(1) Socialist
(2) Highly liberal
(3) Moderately liberal
(4) Moderately conservative
(5) Highly conservative
(6) I have no political views.

The final category was added to avoid forcing the student with no real political views to make a choice which would not have been meaningful. Any Communists who might have been included in the sample would probably have been willing to accept the socialist label. Reactionaries, or members of the "radical right," generally refer to themselves as conservatives,[9] and they would seem most likely to choose the highly conservative category.

The meanings attached to these labels, particularly the moderately liberal and moderately conservative labels, may vary considerably from one individual to another. However, the problem of this study does not require the definition of an objective political continuum which is interpreted in precisely the same way by all subjects. It is sufficient that the subject be able to compare his position on the continuum with the positions he attributes to others, particularly his parents. It is not even essential that this attribution be accurate; for the purposes of this study what the parents or others actually believe is far less important than what the student thinks that they believe.

Many investigators have concentrated merely on the influence of one parent.[10] This procedure greatly simplifies the analysis, but as Hyman points out, ". . . familial influence involves a contribution from each of the parents."[11] We therefore developed the following classification of ways in which the views of the students could be related to those they attribute to their parents:

(1) *Rebels to the left of parents.* The student places himself to the left of both parents, or to the left of one parent when the other parent has no political views or when his views are unknown to the student.

(2) *Rebels to the right of parents.* The student places himself to the right of both parents, or to the right of one parent when the other parent has no political views or when his views are unknown to the student.

(3) *Conformists.* The student shares the beliefs of one or both of his parents or takes a compromise position between the views of disagreeing parents.

(4) *Independent crystallizers.* The student has arrived at a political position although both his parents either have no political views or have views of which he is unaware.

(5) *Uncrystallized.* The student has no explicit political views.

This classification of students in relation to their parents forms the basis of most of the analysis which follows. The chi-square test of significance was applied throughout the analysis, and the rejection level for the null hypothesis was set at .05.

FINDINGS

The distribution of the political views of the students, and of the viewpoints they perceive in their mothers and fathers, is presented in Table 1. The great bulk of the cases are moderately liberal or moderately conservative, the former constituting the modal category for students and the latter the modal category attributed to parents. Relatively few cases are to be found in the extreme categories—socialist and highly conservative. The students tend to be farther to the left politically than they think their parents are, either fathers (P < .001) or mothers (P < .001). Male students are farther to the left than female students (P < .001), and the females are more likely than males to have no crystallized political views (P < .001). The distributions for fathers and mothers are similar although the fathers show more tendency toward the extreme positions than do the mothers (P < .02).

In Table 2 the views of the students are compared to the views they attribute to their parents. In terms of the categories defined above, approximately two-fifths of the students are rebels, about an equal number are conformists, and the remaining fifth are about equally divided between the independent crystallizers and the uncrystallized. The students are far more likely to move to the left of their parents than to the right (P < .001), and this is true for both males (P < .001) and females (P < .001). Our findings thus contrast with those of Nogee and Levin who found in a 1956 study of 314 Boston University students that those who deviated from the political

REBELLION AGAINST POLITICAL BELIEFS

TABLE 1.   POLITICAL VIEWS OF STUDENTS AND PERCEPTIONS OF PARENTAL VIEWS

Political Views	Percent Holding Views			Percent Perceived to Hold Views	
	Male Students	Female Students	Total Students	Mothers	Fathers
Socialist	2.7	.8	1.9	.8	.4
Highly liberal	13.7	6.5	10.6	5.8	3.6
Moderately liberal	46.8	49.2	47.8	24.7	24.0
Moderately conservative	29.2	29.9	29.5	37.4	38.1
Highly conservative	3.3	2.6	3.0	13.1	10.0
No political views	4.3	11.0	7.2	1.4	6.5
Unaware of views	—	—	—	16.8	17.4
Total	100.0	100.0	100.0	100.0	100.0
N	824	616	1440	1440	1440

TABLE 2. POLITICAL VIEWS OF STUDENTS IN RELATION TO PERCEIVED PARENTAL VIEWS

Relation of Student Views to Perceived Parental Views	Percent of Students		
	Male	Female	Total
Rebels to left of parents	37.3	27.3	33.0
Rebels to right of parents	8.0	7.0	7.6
Conformists	41.4	44.3	42.6
Independent crystallizers	9.1	10.4	9.7
Uncrystallized	4.2	11.0	7.1
Total	100.0	100.0	100.0
N	824	616	1440

party preference of their parents were as likely to do so in a conservative direction as in a liberal direction.[12]

It is also evident from Table 2 that male students are more likely to rebel to the left than are female students $(P < .001)$, and that female students are more likely than males to remain uncrystallized $(P < .001)$. Otherwise the patterns for males and females are not significantly different.

In Table 3 the students adhering to each political position are broken down into rebels to the right, rebels to the left, conformists, etc. About one-half of the highly conservative students are conforming to the position held by their parents. On the other hand, only about one-sixth of the socialists and highly liberal students are conforming to the position of their parents. Thus, highly conservative students are far more likely to be conformists than socialist and highly liberal students $(P < .001)$.

Moreover, about two-thirds of the highly conservative students who are rebels had parents who were themselves moderately conservative rather than liberal. It is possible that such deviation should be viewed more as over conformity than as rebellion. The moderately conservative group of students also shows by far the greatest degree of conformity, with two-thirds of the students agreeing with at least one parent or taking an intermediate position between disagreeing parents.

In contrast, the largest single group of socialist students—37 percent—report that their fathers are highly conservative. Among highly liberal students only 7 percent say that their fathers are highly conservative, but another 33 percent consider their fathers to be moderately conservative. Thus highly conservative students, even when rebels, are more likely than socialist or highly liberal students to have parents who are on the same end of the political continuum.

TABLE 3.   POLITICAL VIEWS OF STUDENTS IN RELATION TO PERCEIVED PARENTAL VIEWS

Relation of Student Views to Perceived Parental Views	Percent of Students				
	Socialist	Highly Liberal	Moderately Liberal	Moderately Conservative	Highly Conservative
Rebels to left of parents	81.5	73.2	43.1	10.4	——*
Rebels to right of parents ..	——*	.7	4.4	13.6	46.5
Conformists	11.1	18.3	40.8	66.4	45.6
Independent crystallizers ..	7.4	7.8	11.7	9.6	7.0
Total	100.0	100.0	100.0	100.0	100.0
N	27	153	689	425	43

* No cases possible by definition.

Most of the students claim to be at least moderately interested in politics. About 26 percent say that they are very much interested in political matters all of the time, 48 percent are moderately interested most of the time, 22 percent are only slightly interested most of the time, and 4 percent admit that they are not at all interested in politics most of the time. Interest in politics is strongly associated with rebellion from parental political beliefs, as is shown in Table 4. The

TABLE 4.   STUDENT POLITICAL REBELLION, BY INTEREST IN POLITICS

Degree of Interest in Politics	N	Percent of Students		
		Political Rebels	Political Nonrebels	Total
Very much interested	368	54.6	45.4	100.0
Moderately interested	687	40.0	60.0	100.0
Slightly interested	307	29.6	70.4	100.0
Not interested	59	18.6	81.4	100.0

greater their interest in politics, the greater is the likelihood that the students are rebels from the political views of their parents (P < .001). Those with little or no interest in politics tend to accept their parents' political positions or fail to develop any identifiable position at all, whereas more than half of those who are very much interested in political matters reject the views of their parents in favor of other views.

It might be expected that the direction of rebellion from parental beliefs would be influenced by the student's conceptions of the predominant or conventional political position. Thus, if his parents diverged from the conventional, he might rebel from their views as a means of conforming to the society around him. In a somewhat parallel study of rebellion of college students from the religious views of their parents, we found a clear tendency for rebels against parental beliefs to move toward a more conventional position than that of their parents.[13]

TABLE 5.   STUDENT POLITICAL REBELLION, BY PARENTAL AGREEMENT WITH PERCEIVED CONVENTIONAL POLITICAL VIEWS IN THE UNITED STATES

Relation of Perceived Parental Views to Perceived Conventional Political Views	N	Percent of Students		
		Political Rebels	Political Conformists	Total
One or both parents in agreement with perceived conventional position	534	44.0	56.0	100.0
Neither parent in agreement with perceived conventional position	550	55.3	44.7	100.0

Analysis of the data in Table 5 reveals that students are less likely to rebel against the political views of their parents when at least one parent holds what the student regards as the conventional position, than when neither parent is seen as conventional ($P < .001$). However, analysis of the data in Table 6 reveals that when students do rebel against the political position of their parents, they tend to move away from the position which they perceive as conventional ($P < .001$). This pattern was present for both male rebels ($P < .01$) and female rebels ($P < .01$). Students are thus less likely to rebel politically if their parents seem to hold conventional views, but those who do rebel are likely to move away from the conventional position rather than towards it. Conformity to the society around them does not emerge as a basic factor in student rebellion against parental political beliefs, as it did in the case of rebellion against parental religious beliefs. A possible interpretation of this finding would be that students tend to rebel religiously largely as a means of adjusting

TABLE 6.   STUDENT POLITICAL REBELLION, BY RELATION TO PERCEIVED
CONVENTIONAL POLITICAL VIEWS IN THE UNITED STATES.

Direction of Rebellion on Conventionality Continuum	Percent of Students		Total Students
	Males	Females	
Rebellion toward perceived conventional position	36.5	33.2	35.3
Rebellion away from perceived conventional position	50.1	50.7	50.3
Rebellion to position equi-distant from perceived conventional position	7.0	6.2	6.7
No perception of conventional position	6.4	9.9	7.7
Total	100.0	100.0	100.0
N	373	211	584

themselves to society, whereas political rebellion is more likely to be associated with a generalized disenchantment with their social milieu.

CONCLUSION

In this sample of 1,440 American college students we find that nearly as many deviate from their parents' political views as conform to them. Rebellion is particularly likely among those students most interested in politics and among those students who see their parents as holding unconventional political views. There is no evidence in this study that the prevailing direction of political rebellion is toward conservatism, the contentions of the popular press to the contrary notwithstanding. Indeed, the students are considerably more liberal than their parents due largely to the fact that rebels are about five times as likely to move to the left as to the right. Lacking comparable data from the past, we cannot rule out the possibility that rebellion to the right is increasing, but the prevailing direction of rebellion today would seem distinctly leftward.

Neither is there evidence in this study to support the contention that the current campus conservatives are predominantly the offspring of liberal parents. A few of them are, but the great majority of the conservatives in our sample came from conservative family backgrounds, and those who have rebelled at all have usually moved only from "moderately conservative" to "highly conservative." The greater vigor which has been observed among conservative student organizations is probably due primarily to an awakening of latent political interest among conservative students from conservative backgrounds, not to recruitment of students from liberal backgrounds. The student rebels do tend to move away from the position they regard as conventional, but it is typically the conservative position that they see in this light.

NOTES

[1] *Time* reported that in 1961 on 353 campuses a total of 315 new political groups were formed — 169 conservative and 146 liberal — and that the pace was even faster in 1962. "The Need to Speak Out," *Time*, 79 (February 23, 1962), p. 74.

[2] Paul F. Lazarsfeld, Bernard Berelson, and Hazel Gaudet, *The People's Choice* (New York: Harcourt Brace, 1952), p. 44.

[3] Richard Centers, *The Psychology of Social Class* (Princeton: Princeton University Press, 1949), p. 165.

[4] "Campus Conservatives," *Time*, 77 (February 10, 1961), pp. 34, 37. The same theme has been stressed by a number of other news magazines and authors as well.[5]

[5] Raymond Moley, "Youth Turns to the Right," *Newsweek*, 57 (March 13, 1961), p. 100; "Conservatism in the U.S. . . . And Its Leading Spokesman," *Newsweek*, 57 (April 10, 1961), pp. 28-38; "Behind the 'Conservative' Movement in Colleges," *U.S. News and World Report*, 51 (December 25, 1961), p. 64; and M. Stanton Evans, *Revolt on the Campus* (Chicago: Henry Regnery Co., 1961).

[6] Alan C. Elms, "The Conservative Ripple," *Nation*, 192 (May 27, 1961), pp. 458-460, 468. George Gallup has recently commented in a similar vein: "We hear it said that there is a 'great, conservative movement' sweeping the college and university campuses today. We find no evidence of any great conservative movement on the campuses. That doesn't mean that if Goldwater, who is an interesting and exciting person, came to campus he wouldn't draw a big crowd. He most certainly would. But right-wing Republicans, I believe, are engaging in wishful thinking." "Opinion Polls: Inter-

views by Donald McDonald with Elmo Roper and George Gallup," pamphlet issued by the Center for the Study of Democratic Institutions, Santa Barbara, California, 1962, p. 34. Michael Harrington also sees little evidence of any conservative trend among college students: "From reading the journals one might think that there is a wave of campus conservatism. As far as I can tell, that is simply not true. I have been North, South, East and West, and I have yet to find a chapter of Young Americans for Freedom which is playing a really vital role on campus . . . Generally speaking, YAF is less of a force on the big campuses than the Young Peoples Socialist League—and no one has been writing about a socialist sweep among the young. . . . The young conservatives are the product of some good copy writers, not the campus scene." Michael Harrington, "The American Campus: 1962," *Dissent*, 9 (Spring 1962) , p. 167.

[7] T. W. Adorno et al., *The Authoritarian Personality*, (New York: Harper, 1950), pp. 163, 169.

[8] Herbert McClosky, "Conservatism and Personality," *American Political Science Review*, 52 (March 1958) , pp. 27-45.

[9] See Senator Barry Goldwater's statement of philosophy, *The Conscience of a Conservative* (New York: Hillman Books, 1960), the title of which indicates his choice of political labels. Far from advocating the conservation of the status quo, however, Senator Goldwater argues for radical political changes: "I have little interest in streamlining government or in making it more efficient, for I mean to reduce its size. I do not undertake to promote welfare, for I propose to extend freedom. My aim is not to pass laws, but to repeal them. It is not to inaugurate new programs, but to cancel old ones that do violence to the Constitution, or that have failed in their purpose, or that impose on the people an unwarranted financial burden." (p. 23).

[10] See, for example, Robert E. Lane, "Fathers and Sons: Foundations of Political Belief," *American Sociological Review*, 24 (August 1959) , pp. 502-511.

[11] Herbert H. Hyman, *Political Socialization* (Glencoe, Ill.: Free Press, 1959) , p. 82.

[12] Philip Nogee and M. B. Levin, "Some Determinants of Political Attitudes among College Voters," *Public Opinion Quarterly*, 22, Winter 1958-59, pp. 449-463. As Hyman points out, however, political party preference is probably more subject to family influence than political ideology, and this may account for part of the difference. Hyman, *op. cit.*, pp. 74-76.

[13] Snell Putney and Russell Middleton, "Rebellion, Conformity, and Paternal Religious Ideologies," *Sociometry*, 24 (June 1961) , pp. 125-135.

PARENT-CHILD CONFLICT IN SEXUAL VALUES

ROBERT R. BELL

The old cliché that as one grows older he becomes more conservative may be true, if premarital sexual values held by parents are compared with the values they held when they were younger. In this
paper, the interest is in the nature of sex value conflict between parents and their unmarried late adolescent and young adult children.
Our discussion will focus on values held by parents and by their unmarried children toward premarital sexual intimacy.

Conceptually, our approach focuses upon values related to a specific
area of sexual behavior held by individuals from two very different
role perspectives. The perspectives differ because parents and children are always at different stages in the life cycle, and while parents
are highly significant in the socialization of their children, other social
forces increasingly come to influence the child as he grows older. The
various social values that influence the child's sexual behavior are
often complementary, but they may also be contradictory. Furthermore, various types of influences on the acceptance of a given set of
values may operate on the child only during a given age period. For
example, the youngster at age fifteen may be influenced by his age
peers to a much greater extent than he will be at age twenty.

Given their different stages in the life cycle, parents and children
will almost always show differences in how they define appropriate
behavior for a given role. Values as to "proper" premarital sexual
role behavior from the perspective of the parents are greatly influenced by the strong emotional involvement of the parent with his
child. Youth, on the other hand, are going through a life cycle stage
in which the actual behavior occurs, and they must relate the parent
values to what they are doing or may do. There is a significant dif-

Reprinted from *The Journal of Social Issues*, Vol. XXII, No. 2, pp. 34-44, by permission of The Society for the Psychological Study of Social Issues, and the author.

ference between defining appropriate role conduct for others to follow and defining proper role conduct to be followed by oneself. Even more important for actual behavior, there is often more than one significant group of role definers to which the young person can turn to as guides for his sex role behavior. Therefore, our discussion will focus more specifically on parent values related to premarital sexual intimacy, the peer group values of youth, and how these two different age groups, as role definers, influence the sexual values and behavior of unmarried youth.

Limits of Discussion. For several reasons, our discussion will center primarily on the middle class. First, this class level has been highly significant in influencing changes in general sexual values and behavior. Second, and on a more pragmatic level, what little research has been done on parent-child conflict over sexual values has been done with middle-class groups. Third, the general values of the middle class are coming to include an increasing proportion of the American population. This also suggests that the values and behavior of college youth are of increasing importance as this group continues to expand in size and influence within the middle class.

A further limit is that our main focus is on the generational conflict between mother and daughter. The history of change in sexual values in the United States has been complexly interwoven with the attainment of greater sex equality and freedom by the female (2). Also, the relationship between the mother and daughter tends to be the closest of the possible parent-child relationships in the family socializing of the child to future adult sex roles. Furthermore, whatever the value system verbalized and/or applied by the girl, she often has more to gain or lose personally than the boy by whatever premarital sexual decisions she makes.

We also believe that any analysis of conflict over premarital sex between generations should center on *value* changes rather than *behavioral* changes. On the basis of available evidence, it appears that there have been no significant changes in the *frequency* of premarital sexual petting or coitus since the 1920's. Kinsey has pointed out that "there has been little recognition that the premarital petting and coital patterns which were established then (1920's) are still with us" (15, p. 300). Therefore, it is important to recognize that the parents and even some of the grandparents of today were the youth who introduced the new patterns of premarital sexual behavior about forty years ago.

PARENT VALUES ABOUT PREMARITAL SEX

The transmission of sexual values by parents to their children is only a small part of all parent values passed on during the family socialization process. Most parents do a more deliberate and comprehensive job of transmitting values to their children in such areas as educational attainment, career choice, religious beliefs, and so forth than they do with reference to any aspect of sexual values. Often when parents do discuss sex with their children it may be from a "clinical, physiological" perspective with overtones of parental embarrassment and a desire to get a distasteful task over with.

But perhaps more important than the formal confrontation between the parent and child in sexual matters are the informal values transmitted by the parent. In the past girls were often taught that premarital sexual deviancy was dirty and shameful, and that nonconformity to premarital sexual chastity values would mean suffering great personal and social shame. This highly negative view of premarital sex is undoubtably less common today, but the newer, more "positive" values may also have some negative consequences. Very often today the mother continues to place great value on the daughter's virginity, and stresses to the daughter the great virtues of maintaining her virginity until marriage. But the "romantic" view of the rewards for the girl who waits for coitus until after marriage are often highly unrealistic and may sometimes create problems by leading the girl to expectations that cannot be realistically met in marital sex. Morton Hunt writes with regard to this approach that "if the woman has been assured that she will, that she ought, and she *must* see colored lights, feel like a breaking wave, or helplessly utter inarticulate cries, she is apt to consider herself or her husband at fault when these promised wonders do not appear" (13, 114). Whether or not the "romantic" view of marital sex is presented by her mother the girl often encounters it in the "approved" reading list suggested by the adult world, which tells her about the positive delights of waiting for sex until after marriage. So, though premarital sexual control may be "positive" in that it is based on rewards for waiting, it can be "negative" if the rewards are unrealistic and unobtainable.

For many parents, a major problem as their child moves through adolescence and into early adult years centers around how much independence to allow the child. Because they often recall the child's younger dependency, it may be difficult to assess the independency of the same child who is now older. Also, over the years the growing child has increasingly become involved with reference groups outside —and sometimes competing with—the family. In other words, the self-role definitions by the child and the parents' definitions of the child's role undergo constant change as the child grows older. For example, "The daughter in her younger years has her role as daughter defined to a great degree by her mother. But as she grows older she is influenced by other definitions which she internalizes and applies to herself in her movement toward self-determination. The mother frequently continues to visualize the daughter's role as it was defined in the past and also attaches the same importance to her function as mother in defining her daughter's role. But given the rapid social change associated with family roles the definer, as well as the definitions, may no longer be institutionally appropriate" (5, 388).

Parents may also be biased in their definitions of their child as less mature than they, the parents, were when they were the child's age. One can not recall experiences earlier in the life cycle free from influence by the events that have occurred since. This may result in many parents' thinking of their younger selves as being more mature than they actually were. At the same time the parents' view of their child's degree of maturity may be biased by their recall of him when he was younger and less mature. Thus, from the parents' perspective they may recall themselves as youngsters within the context of what has occurred since (more mature) and may see their offspring within the context of their earlier childhood (less mature).

There also may be some symbolic significance for parents who must define their children as having reached the age when something as "adult" as sexual behavior is of relevance. In part, viewing one's children as too young for sexual involvement may contribute to the parents' feeling young, while seeing their children as old enough to be involved in sexual activity may lead to some parents feeling forced to view themselves as aging. For example, the comment about a man seen out with a young woman that "she is young enough to be his daughter" may have implications for his self-role image if the young woman *is* his daughter. We have little research data on how the aging process of parents influences their definitions of appropriate behavior for their young adult children.

In general, it is probable that most parents assume that their children, especially their daughters, accept the traditional restrictive values about premarital sexual behavior unless they are forced to do otherwise. Also, because of the great emotional involvement of parents with their own children, there is a common parental tendency to attribute sexual "immorality" to other youngsters. For many parents to face the possibility that their children do not conform to their values is to suggest some failure on the part of the parents. Often, rather than admit failure, the parents may define their children as having been forced to reject the parent values by other social influences or that their children have willfully let them down.

Youth Views About Premarital Sex

The importance of age peer group influence on the values and behavior of young people has been shown by a number of social scientists (see: 6, 9, 10, 11, 12, 14, 19, 20, 21, 22). Because youth subcultures are to some degree self-developing, they often have conflict points in relation to some dominant adult values. However, the inconsistency and lack of effective adult definitions for adolescent behavior have also contributed to the emergence of youth subcultural values. That adults often view the adolescent with indecision as to appropriate behavior means that sometimes given adolescent behavior is treated one way at one time and in a different way at another time. Since the young person desires some decisiveness and precision in his role definitions, he often develops his own role prescriptions. Often when he creates his own role expectations, he demands a high degree of conformity by other adolescents as "proof" of the rightness of his definitions. It is ironical that the adolescent often thinks of himself as a social deviant. What he fails to realize is that his adolescent group deviates from the adult world, but that the requirements for conformity within his youth subculture are very strong (1, 369-74).

Youth subcultures have developed great influence over many aspects of premarital male-female interaction. The patterns of dating and courtship, appropriate behavior, success and failure are for the most part patterns defined by the youth group and not by the adult world. Yet, heterosexual relationships of youth are often based on adult role patterns, and they are therefore an important part of the youth world because they are seen by the youth as symbolizing adult status. To many young people, who are no longer defined by the adult world as children, but are not yet given full status as adults, their involvement in what they see as adult roles is important to them in seeking for adult status and recognition.

A part of the American youth subculture has been the development of new values related to premarital sexual intimacy. Reiss suggests that "It might well be that, since the 1920's, what has been occurring is a change in attitudes to match the change in behavior of that era" [premarital sexual behavior] (16, 233). The evidence suggests that for at least some college students new sex norms are emerging at the various stages of dating and courtship. One study found that "on the dating level necking is the norm for females and petting for males. During going steady and engagement, petting seems to be acceptable for both sexes. This would suggest that the young people both act and accept a higher level of intimacy than has generally been suggested by courtship norms." (3, 63).

In the past, emphasis was placed on the girl's virginity at the time of marriage; but today, many young people may only emphasize her being a virgin until she is in love, which may mean at the stage of going steady or engagement (8, Ch. 5 and 16, Ch. 6). If the girl is in love, some premarital sexual relations may be acceptable by peer group standards, although the dominant adult values—that love *and* marriage are basic prerequisites for coitus—continue. In the United States love as a prerequisite for sexual relations has long been a necessary condition for most middle-class females. The condition has not changed; rather, the point in the courtship-marriage process where it may be applied to sexual involvement has shifted. Hence, the major point of parent-child conflict over premarital sex centers around the parent value that one should be in love *and* married before entering coitus and the modified value system of youth that an emotional and interpersonal commitment is important, but that this may occur before marriage.

There are two recent studies that provide some evidence on the nature of generational conflict; one study is of youth and adults in general and the other study is specifically concerned with mothers and their daughters. Reiss, in his extensive study of premarital sexual permissiveness, provides data on values held by adults as contrasted with values in a sample of high school and college students. The respondents were asked to express their beliefs about different combinations of intimacy and degree of interpersonal commitment for both unmarried males and females. Respondents were asked if they believed petting to be acceptable when the male or female is engaged.

In the adult sample the belief that petting during engagement was acceptable for the engaged male was the response of 61 per cent, and for the engaged female the response was 56 per cent. Of the student responses 85 per cent approved for the engaged male and 82 per cent for the engaged female (17, 190-91); thus adult attitudes about petting during engagement were more conservative than those of the student population. It may also be noted that for both the adult and student groups there was a single standard—that is, the acceptance rates were essentially the same for both males and females.

Reiss also asked his respondents if they believed full sexual relations to be acceptable if the male or female were engaged. Approval was the response given by 20 per cent of the adult group for males and 17 per cent for females. In the student group acceptance was given by 52 per cent for the male and 44 per cent for the female (17, 190-91). Here, as with petting, there are significant differences between the adult and the student samples, and once again both respondent groups suggest a single standard of acceptance or rejection for both males and females.

A study by Bell and Buerkle compared the attitudes of 217 coeds with those of their mothers. Both mothers and daughters were asked to respond to the question, "How important do you think it is that a girl be a virgin when she marries?" Of the mothers, 88 per cent answered "very important", 12 per cent "generally important", and 0 per cent "not important"; compared to 55 per cent, 34 per cent and 13 per cent of the daughters (4, 391). Both the mothers and daughters were also asked: "Do you think sexual intercourse during engagement is: very wrong; generally wrong; right in many situations?" The percentages for each response category were 83 per cent, 15 per cent and 2 per cent for the mothers; and 35 per cent, 48 per cent, and 17 per cent for the daughters (4, 391).

Both of the above questions show sharp differences between the value responses of the mothers and daughters with reference to premarital chastity. Many mothers were undoubtedly influenced in their responses by having a daughter in the age setting where the questions had an immediate and highly emotional application. Nevertheless, the differences in mother and daughter responses indicate that the area of premarital sexual behavior is one of potentially great conflict. One means of minimizing conflict is for the daughter not to discuss her sexual values or behavior with her mother. In the Bell and Buerkle study it was found that only 37 per cent of the daughters, in contrast with 83 per cent of the mothers, felt daughters should freely answer questions from their mothers in regard to attitudes toward sexual intimacy (4, 392).

The area of sexual values appears to be highly influenced by emotion, especially for the mother with reference to her daughter. Generational conflict with regard to premarital sexual intimacy has a variety of implications. First, the conflict in values clearly suggests that the traditional morality is often not socially effective as a meaningful determinant of behavior. Social values have behavioral influence when they emerge as social norms with significant rewards and punishments. In the case of sexual norms, however, there are rarely clearly-articulated rewards, or positive consequences, for the conforming individual. In almost all situations the effectiveness of sexual norms is dependent upon their negative sanctions, or punishments. For example, the traditional norm of female premarital chastity bases its behavioral influence primarily on negative consequences for the girl who fails to conform. This negative means of control is most commonly found as a part of the adult value system. In effect, the major sanctions over premarital chastity are based upon punishments for the girl and for her family if she deviates. Yet, in most cases the girl who has premarital coitus is not discovered by her parents or by the community. The real danger for the girl often centers around premarital pregnancy, because if that occurs and becomes known there can be no denying premarital coitus. Vincent has suggested that an important part of the negative sanction toward premarital pregnancy is not the pregnancy itself, but rather that it symbolizes premarital coitus *and* getting caught (23, Ch. 1).

The available studies indicate that fear of pregnancy is not the major deterrent for most girls (7, 344 and 15, 315). The personal values of the girl appear far more important in restricting her from engaging in premarital coitus. Yet, within the privacy of the youth world, there may operate for some girls certain values positive toward premarital coitus. For example, there may be a strong emotional desire and commitment to the boy and a positive feeling by the girl of wanting to engage in greater sexual intimacy.

There is a tendency by parents, as well as by many who give professional advice, to overlook the pleasurable aspects of sex at all ages, especially for the young who are experiencing sexual pleasure for the first time. Undoubtedly many girls engage in premarital sexual intimacy to "compensate" for some need and many may suffer some negative consequences. But it is foolish to state categorically that the "artificial" setting of premarital sex always makes it negative and unpleasant for the girl. We would be much more honest if we recognized that for many girls premarital coitus is enjoyable and the participants suffer no negative consequences. This was illustrated in the Kinsey research; it was found that "69 per cent of the still unmarried females in the sample who had had premarital coitus insisted they did not regret their experiences. Another 13 per cent recorded some minor regrets" (15, 316). Kinsey also found that "77 per cent of the married females, looking back from the vantage point of their more mature experience, saw no reason to regret their premarital coitus" (15, 316).

The Extent of Generational Conflict

With the evidence suggesting strong conflict between generations with regard to premarital sexual values, our final consideration is: how permanent is this generational conflict? We can provide some evidence on this question by examining the values of college-educated females of different ages. This appears justified because higher educated females are generally the most liberal in their views about sexual rights and expectations for women.

The evidence suggests that the premarital sexual liberalism of the college girl may be a temporary phenomenon. The coed's sexual liberalism must be seen as related to the interactional context of her being emotionally involved, and to a future commitment to an ongoing paired relationship. The Bell and Buerkle study (4) found that the values of daughters toward the importance of premarital virginity were very similar to those of their mothers, until they had spent some time in college. However, at "around age 20 there emerge sharp differences between mothers and daughters in regard to premarital sexual attitudes. Behavioral studies indicate that it is at this point that sexual activity is greatly intensified, perhaps because it is at this age that college girls are entering engagement. A suggested pattern is that the college girl of 20 or 21 years of age, in her junior or senior year and engaged, has a strong 'liberal' pattern toward premarital sexual behavior and attitudes" (4, 392 nd 18, 696).

We can get some indication of the persistence of premarital sexual liberalism by comparing the values of mothers by education. In the mothers' views as to the importance of premarital virginity it was found that the college educated mothers were actually as "conservative" as those mothers with lower levels of education (4, 392). It is quite possible that in the future the coeds will become as conservative as the college educated mothers. This may occur when the coed's attitudinal rationales are not related to herself, but as a mother to her own daughter. It is therefore possible that the "sexual emancipation" of the college girl exists only for a short period of time, centering mainly around the engagement years.

Yet, even if the girl becomes more conservative as she grows older, and especially with reference to her own daughter, her temporary "liberalism" probably is contributing to some shift in adult values about premarital sexual intimacy. Certainly, today's parental generation accepts greater sexual intimacy as a part of the premarital heterosexual relationship. Probably most parents assume that their adolescent and young adult children are engaging in necking and even some petting. Most parents, as long as they don't actually see the sexual intimacy, don't concern themselves about it. However, to suggest that parents may be more liberal (or tolerant) of premarital sexual intimacy does not necessarily suggest that parents are liberal if the intimacy reaches coitus.

It also appears that there has been some reduction in the severity of negative sanctions by parents if the daughter deviates and is caught. Among middle-class parents today it may be less common to reject the unwed daughter if she becomes pregnant than in the past, and more common for the parents to help her. This is not to suggest that today's parents offer any positive sanctions for premarital pregnancy, but that they may be able to adapt (often painfully) to it, rather than respond with high rejection and anger.

If our suggestion is correct (that parents take a less totally negative view of "discovered" premarital coitus), then this further suggests that traditional sexual values are being altered, since, as we have suggested, in the past the values of premarital chastity were primarily based on the negative consequences for those who deviated and were caught. If these negative consequences have been reduced, then the social force of the traditional values has been reduced as a means utilized by parents to control premarital sexual deviancy.

CONCLUSIONS

Based on the available evidence, there are several general specu-

lations that may be made about future generational conflict over premarital sex. In general we would suggest that conflict between parents and their adolescent-young adult children with regard to premarital sexual intimacy may decrease in the future, because of several trends.
1. The trend in the United States is toward a more liberal view of sexual behavior in general. This is reflected in the generally accepted professional opinion that the woman has a right to sexual satisfaction, and that sexual satisfaction is a desirable end in itself. The trend toward a belief in a single sexual standard for both men and women, even though within the setting of marriage, is bound to influence the beliefs and behavior of the unmarried. For the unmarried, there may be an increasing tendency to attach less importance to the marriage act as the arbitrary dividing line between socially approved and socially disapproved sexual intimacy.
2. Since the evidence suggests that over the past three or four generations the rates of female premarital coital experience have not changed, and since the younger generation has developed some value frameworks for its behavior, modification of traditional values and behavior may increasingly influence the values of parents to be more liberal. That is, it may become increasingly difficult for many parents to hold their children to a set of conservative values which they, the parents, did not hold to when they were younger.
3. Parents seem increasingly unwilling to strongly punish their daughters who sexually deviate and are caught. This parental reduction of punishment may be influenced by the increasing public attention directed at such social problems as illegal abortion. For example, many parents may be more willing to accept and help an unmarried pregnant daughter than take the risk of her seeking out an illegal abortion. The possible negative consequences of abortion may appear more undesirable than the premarital pregnancy.
4. Less generational conflict will occur if parents know less about the sexual activities of their children. A great part of the social activity of young people is carried out in the privacy of their age peer setting; what they do in the way of sexual intimacy is increasingly less apt to be noted by their parents. With the development and marketing of oral contraceptives, the risks of premarital pregnancy will be greatly reduced. In the future the rates of premarital coitus may remain the same, but with the chances of pregnancy reduced parents may be less aware of their children's premarital coitus.

Over time, then, the values of parents and the adult community in general may become more liberal and the conflict between generations reduced. (There seems little possibility that the opposite will occur; i.e., the younger generation's reducing the conflict by becoming more conservative.) But in the meantime, and certainly in the near future, it appears that parents and their children will continue to live with somewhat different value systems with regard to premarital sexual values. Parents will probably continue to hold to traditional values, and assume that *their* child is conforming to those values unless his actions force them to see otherwise. The youth generation will probably continue to develop their own modified value systems and keep those values to themselves, and implicitly allow their parents to believe they are behaving according to the traditional values of premarital sexual morality. For many parents and their children, the conflict about premarital sex will continue to be characterized by the parent's playing ostrich and burying his head in the hand, and the youth's efforts to keep the sand from blowing away.

NOTES

1   Bell, Robert R. *Marriage and Family Interaction*, Homewood, Ill.: The Dorsey Press, 1963.

2   Bell, Robert R. *Premarital Sex In A Changing Society*, Englewood Cliffs, N.J.: Prentice Hall (in press).

3   Bell, Robert R. and Leonard Blumberg. "Courtship Stages and Intimacy Attitudes," *Family Life Coordinator*, 1960, 8, 60-63.

4   Bell, Robert R. and Jack V. Buerkle. "Mother and Daughter Attitudes to Premarital Sexual Behavior," *Marriage and Family Living*, 1961, 23, 390-92.

5   Bell, Robert R. and Jack V. Buerkle. "Mother-Daughter Conflict During The 'Launching Stage,'" *Marriage and Family Living*, 1962, 24, 384-88.

6   Bernard, Jessie (Editor). "Teen-Age Culture," *Annals of the American Academy of Political and Social Science*, November, 1961, 338.

7.   Burgess, Ernest and Paul Wallin. *Engagement and Marriage*, Chicago: J.P. Lippincott, 1953.

8   Ehrmann, Winston. *Premarital Dating Behavior*, New York: Henry Holt, 1959.

9   Ginsberg, Eli. *Values and Ideals of American Youth*, New York: Columbia University Press, 1962.

10   Gottlieb, David and Charles Ramsey. *The American Adolescent*, Homewood, Ill.: The Dorsey Press, 1964.

11   Grinder, Robert. *Studies in Adolescence*, New York: Macmillan, 1963.

12   Hechinger, Grace and Fred. *Teen-Age Tyranny,* New York: Crest, 1962.

13   Hunt, Norton M. *The Natural History of Love,* New York: Alfred A. Knopf, 1959.

14   Kelley, Earl C. *In Defense of Youth,* Englewood Cliffs, N.Y.: Prentice-Hall, 1962.

15   Kinsey, Alfred C., Wardell B. Pomeroy, Clyde E. Martin and Paul H. Gebhard. *Sexual Behavior in the Human Female,* Philadelphia: W. B. Saunders, 1953.

16   Reiss, Ira L. *Premarital Sexual Standards in America,* Glencoe, Ill.: The Free Press, 1960.

17   Reiss, Ira L. "The Scaling of Premarital Sexual Permissiveness," *Journal of Marriage and the Family,* 1964, 26, 188-98.

18   Reiss, Ira L. "Premarital Sexual Permissiveness Among Negroes and Whites," *American Sociological Review,* 1964, 29, 688-98.

19   Remmers, H. H. and D. H. Radler. *The American Teenager,* New York: Charter, 1957.

20   Seidman, Jerome. *The Adolescent,* New York: Holt, 1960.

21   Smith, Ernest A. *American Youth Culture,* New York: The Free Press, 1963.

22   Symonds, P. M. *From Adolescent to Adult,* New York: Columbia University Press, 1961.

23   Vincent, Clark. *Unmarried Mothers,* Glencoe, Ill.: The Free Press, 1961.

THE GOLDEN YEARS
FROM
THE OTHER AMERICA

MICHAEL HARRINGTON

> An aged man is but a paltry thing,
> A tattered coat upon a stick . . .

The poverty of old age in America is rooted in a biological revolution. There are more aging people today than ever before, and they are still on the increase. In 1850, 2.5 per cent of the nation was over sixty-five; in 1900 the figure had risen to 4.1 per cent. In 1960 almost 9 per cent of the American population was over that limit, and the statisticians of the Department of Health, Education, and Welfare estimate that in 1975 nearly 10 per cent of the United States will be over sixty-five. It is not so much that the upper limits of life have been extended as that a great many more people are living to become old.

The causes of this great change are fairly obvious. There have been enormous strides in medicine, and if cancer and heart disease are dealt with in the immediate future there will be still another gigantic lunge. The mortality rate has gone down. The fertility rate is lower than it was. And there are no great waves of immigrants bringing youth to America. The result is a society that is becoming older.

Yet it would be a mistake to pose the general problem of age as if it could be described in terms of life expectancy or medical problems. Even when the old are not poor, they are the victims of the very technology that has given them longer life. The very advances that have created the basis for a widespread old age have also destroyed the traditional props of the declining years. The "three generation family" uniting grandchildren, parents, and grandparents under a single roof is disappearing from the nation. Even on the farm, where the old used to have some light household chores to pass the time of day, mechanization and change have wiped out various functions.

So it is that, even without poverty, the aged are lonely and isolated. The image of a querulous, nagging, meandering old age is not a description of an eternal condition of human nature. It is, in part, the impression of what society has done to people by giving them meaningless years in which to live.

Indeed, it is an irony that leisure is a burden to the aged. (How many times does one hear the remark, "He will die if he stops working"?) In 1890, 70 per cent of the males over sixty-five were still working; in 1959 the figure had fallen to 34 per cent. Today, as noted before, some industries consider a factory worker obsolete when he passes forty. Business enforces retirement. So basic is this problem that there has been discussion of including the aged under the provision of antidiscrimination laws, of treating them as a minority group like the Negroes or the Mexican-Americans.

Loneliness, isolation, and sickness are the afflictions of the aged in every economic class. But for those who are poor, there is an intensification of each of these tragedies: they are more lonely, more isolated, sicker. So it is that a Government report unwittingly stated a social paradox. It noted that only a society of abundance could produce such a higher proportion of old people. We can afford them, we create them, because we are so rich. But later, in discussing the reality of life for the aged, the same report noted that these human products of abundance were denied its fruits. We tolerate them as long as they are poor.

The 1960 Senate report stated the issue clearly enough: ". . . at least one-half of the aged—approximately eight million people—cannot afford today decent housing, proper nutrition, adequate medical care, preventive or acute, or necessary recreation." The same grim picture emerged from the White House Conference on Aging in 1961. As on volume put it, "Many states report that half their citizens over 65 have incomes too low to meet their basic needs."

Here are the statistics. They are some of the most incredible figures to be found in American society:

The Bureau of the Census figures for 1958 show almost 60 per cent of the population over sixty-five with incomes under $1,000 a year. This must be measured against the Government computation that an adequate budget for a retired couple in the autumn of 1959 would range from an urban low of $2,681 in Scranton to a high of $3,304 in Chicago. In short, the top couples in the 60 per cent would have a budget 20 per cent below adequacy in the cheapest city, and almost 40 per cent below adequacy in the most expensive.

Over half of these people are covered by some kind of Federal program (social security, old-age assistance, and so on). Yet, the social security payments are, by Federal admission, completely inadequate to a decent life. In 1959, for instance, they averaged a little better than $70 a month. Or, to take another expression of the same fact, the Senate report concluded that if aged couples could live within the low-cost minimum food budget of the Department of Agriculture, a quarter of them would be spending more than half their income on food alone.

Some people try to soften these statistics by noting that old people receive money from children and relatives, that money income gives a false, overly pessimistic picture. Yet in 1961 one of the White House Conference reports estimated that the total contribution from relatives and friends was $3,000,000,000, which was only 10 per cent of the money income of these people. And the bulk of this, it can be assumed, comes from the most well-off children and goes to the better-off aged. The basic fact remains: at least 8,000,000 Americans over sixty-five are poor.

But even these statistics conceal the gravity of the situation. By one of the predictable paradoxes in the culture of poverty, it is the people with the lowest incomes among the aged who have the least resources in every sense of the term. Quite a few old people own houses, but not those at the bottom of the income pyramid. Of the people who get social security benefits, it has been estimated that 25 per cent of them have no savings at all and that over half have assets of less than $1,000.

Who are these people? How did they come to the culture of poverty?

Many of them are those who have been poor before. The misery of their old age is simply the conclusion of a life of misery. They are the ones who have grown up, lived, and will die under conditions of poverty. In New York State in the mid-fifties, for example, a legislative report found that a good number of people who were among the aged poor had been driven off the land and come to the cities. They had never made a success, and the impoverishment of their declining years was a result of their having been born in the wrong group in the first place.

Another factor making for continuous poverty is ill-health. The greatest single disability of the aged poor is chronic disease. Those who have been poor all their lives are sicker than anyone else in America. As a result, they have an almost guaranteed misery at the end of their lives.

But even if all the citizens who are young and middle-aged in the other America remain poor to the end of their days, that does not account for the enormous proportion of poverty among those over sixty-five. Fifty per cent of the elderly exist below minimum standards of decency, and this is a figure much higher than that for any other age group. So it is that a good many of these people are recruited to poverty after relatively decent working lives.

One obvious group among these new poor are the workers. There are unskilled and semiskilled workers who, with luck, can stay above the poverty line when they are young and strong. But each advancing year threatens whatever they have achieved. For them, old age comes as a permanent depression. Then there are the technologically displaced workers who are suddenly dropped out of the skilled work force. There are women who are forced back into the labor force at the lowest-paying jobs because they must have money to supplement their inadequate income when they reach sixty-five. And there are the workers whose health breaks down but who must keep on working.

Some of these recruits to poverty had known days of good wages and working conditions. Then they were caught in a technological cross fire. On the one hand, technology renders them economically superfluous, fit only for the economic underworld. On the other hand, technology gives them life. To them, progress comes to mean a bitter, desperate end to their lives.

And finally, the depressed areas are suffused and overwhelmed with poverty, and the aged are caught in them more than anyone else. Agricultural workers, for instance, are sentenced to work for starvation wages in the best of times. When they get old, they are among those in the society not covered by social security. They have never had a real chance to prepare for old age, and no one helps them when the terrible moment comes.

Here perhaps is the most shocking statistic of what happens at the bottom of the society, of how the poor are persistently penalized for the original sin of poverty. Somewhere between two-thirds and three-fourths of the aged in America are covered by social security; but the poorest of the poor, the "unrelated individuals" (those living alone, quite often aged widows) with incomes of less than $1,000, had only a 37 per cent coverage in 1957.

In the same vein there is the classic report from the State of Mississippi to the White House Conference: "Mississippi's older people are a low income people in a low income state." Indeed, the White House Conference noted that the huge band of rural poverty was an area of acute suffering for the aged. Here live people who are not covered by Federal programs, who find themselves in states and counties without adequate funds for relief.

The welfare state, in short, is upside-down in the subculture of aged poverty as it is everywhere else in the other America. The protection, the guarantees, the help all tend to go to the strong and to the organized. The weakest in the society are those who are always disposed of in some congressional logrolling session. And this simple lack of income persisting into old age becomes the basis for a structure of misery and loneliness. Once this is given, medical problems become insuperable, housing becomes impossible to find, and perhaps most importantly there is a growing feeling of being a useless, functionless human being in a land where youth is worshiped and death is rarely mentioned by name.

There is a connection between all these statistics and psychological depression. It can be made specific by considering where the aged poor live.

A high proportion of America's aged live with children, out of necessity rather than from choice. This results in tensions and difficult personal situations, but it is probably the best arrangement for living in the minimal choices the nation offers the elderly. Two-thirds of the people over sixty-five live with a spouse or a relative in a two-person household. They signify the breakdown of the old patterns of family living in the United States.

Like many of the poor, these people are particularly hurt by the transformation of the city. The young and middle-aged middle class is fleeing to the suburbs. The grandparents are often left behind. They might own a fairly decent house, but the neighborhood community of their early years has been destroyed. Now they are strangers on a street they have known for forty or fifty years. Forced to cope with the difficult problems of transitional neighborhoods, they are the least equipped to do so.

The aged widows are particularly badly off. A good percentage of them, the Senate Committee reported, live alone. In 1960 there were 6,000,000 Americans over seventy-five, most of them women, most of them on their own. Government statisticians calculate that in 1980 there will be 9,000,000 people over seventy-five years of age. If the present trend continues, they will face the most extreme conditions of loneliness and of poverty.

The lonely aged poor are, as noted before, the most impoverished single group in their subculture of poverty. A quarter of them have under $580 in money income a year. That is just above the minimum low-cost food budget of the United States Department of Agriculture, and it must provide for rent, clothing, and other things as well. For most of these people, amusement will be restricted to an occasional walk to the corner in good weather.

One consequence of this isolation is that the United States has some tendencies to produce age ghettos as well as racial ghettos. In most big cities there is a rooming-house area, often a place of decayed gentility, with a high concentration of the elderly. In St. Louis, for instance, there is a neighborhood of old houses that have been cut up into furnished rooms and tiny apartments for the poor. Scattered throughout the area are old people living in rooming houses.

Public housing is another problem for the aged. With slum clearance, the old neighborhoods are torn down. But there are no real guarantees that the elderly will find a new place. They are, as the Senate report noted, the special victims of the relocation problem, and they are the ones least able to fend for themselves in finding new accommodations. The suburbs are closed to them because they lack funds; the low-income projects have yet to take real notice of their special needs.

All of this is grim enough on the surface, but the facts and the figures do not really communicate the way in which social isolation is built into the "golden years." For the younger slum dweller there is some kind of street society, even if it takes the form of gangs. But for the old person, trapped in the decaying central area of the city and living among strangers, there is a terrifying lack of simple human contact. The whole problem might be summarized in a Government statistic that, in a way, is a measure of the loneliness of the aged poor: one-third of the aged in the United States, some 5,000,000 or more human beings, have no phone in their place of residence. They are literally cut off from the rest of America.

SECTION IV

Religion in a Secular Society

INTRODUCTION

How to Study Religion

Within the purview of the behavioral scientist is careful examination of the various human institutions which are related to individual and societal needs. In the course of such examination, one phenomenon has drawn the attention of anthropologists and sociologists in particular: Religious behavior, in one form or another, may be observed in just about all known societies. This fact has especially intrigued those who are alert to possible "universals" of human nature and behavior. To the sociologist, religion represents one, albeit ubiquitous social institution, like family or government. Thus he is interested in the social and individual significance of this, among other institutions.

Presented in this way, the scientific study of religion seems innocent enough. Yet we mustn't overlook the tensions engendered by such study in the past and perhaps even now. It would be naive not to recognize the emotionality of religious involvement. Certainly in the Western world, few, if any, individuals are neutral regarding the topic of religion. Thus, some who have studied religion have done so for the purpose of substantiating it, while others have undertaken the study of religion to prove it false. Even the sociologist who doesn't have an axe to grind but objectively seeks to explore religious behavior, begins typically with the scientist's perspective. Thus Canadian sociologist Frank Jones writes:

> If religion is regarded as part of the natural order of things, you can expect it to be found in all societies; you would necessarily be surprised if religion were not found everywhere. We, however, regard religion as man-made and when we observe such persistent forms of behaviour, we expect to find that they make contributions to the society and to its members which outweigh any negative consequences.[1]

Many "religionists" have been wary of scientific investigation in this area. Setting aside, for the moment, comments regarding religion as man-made, simply subjecting religion to the rules of scientific investigation could be construed to imply that intellectually, the scientific category is superior in scope to that of religion. Furthermore, the minute you step back to identify the components, to label, in short, to subject behavior to scientific scrutiny, one may imply that the sophisti-

241

cated judge is not only outside his subject's realm, but even above it. Looking at religion comparatively further suggests that religions are roughly of equal significance, and composed of similar elements, perhaps undermining the adherents' beliefs in the divine or unique origins of their own religion. Added to the thinly disguised hostility toward religion expressed by many past investigators, one can understand the wariness whether or not he agrees.

In our own society, such religious education as is given is typically terminated at some point in childhood. Many young people, with a child's Sunday School perspective, register for courses in the sociology of religion, seeking to resolve their personal doubts and confusion. Given the sociologist's frame of reference, such courses usually resolve very little. Where there is no commitment, one may question whether there are many scientific facts which would produce it and where there is commitment, then it would not seem to rest as directly on factual data as it does on faith and philosophy.

Thus we are led to ask how indeed can there be scientific investigation of such an ethereal subject? In what context can one study religion? If the essence of religion is belief, we must look to its literal meaning. "Belief means that statements are accepted without proof in the form of evidence, and religious belief in its pure form must be so, even though the faithful may point to humble events, such as the growth of trees, or to dramatic events such as miracles, to support their belief in some religious entity." One of the major shortcomings in the sociology of religion stems from attempts to investigate such metaphysical affairs as belief with the scientist's yardstick. We need to think of such study in the context of C.P. Snow's *The Two Cultures*. For discussion, let us take as axiomatic two distinct modes of intellectual processes by which man confronts his experiences. Call them Positivism and Idealism, if you will. On the one hand may be grouped such humanities as art, music, literature, philosophy, religion, on the other, mathematics and the physical and behavioral sciences at their various stages of development. Nineteenth century evolutionary thinking geared us to view the two realms as different stages of the same continuum. In such a context, religion was viewed as a prelude for science. Not lending itself to quantified measurement, it appeared to be obviously less advanced. Today, we need only assume two distinct systems of myth making, each with its own frame of reference. If we accept this as axiomatic, we are then in a position to proceed with objective analysis.[2] It means that the scientists' tools will enable us to probe only the penultimate questions in religion as they can only do so in the humanities. The sciences can no more verify the ultimate truth of religious belief than ultimate beauty in the arts. However, given a particular belief, the behavioral sciences can determine how widely the belief is held, as well as probe the relationship of that belief to other aspects of individual and group behavior.

Early researchers concentrated on trying to identify the origins and evolutionary stages of religion in much the same way they sought the origin and evolution of other institutions, like family. Their efforts, as in other areas, boiled down to a frustrating exercise in speculation. To explain the universality of religious behavior, each discipline has sought to find the source of religion in its own sphere. Traditional theologians were satisfied to leave the issue with doctrinal statements regarding revelation. Schmidt and others would then explain that primitives have a less perfect grasp of true religion.[3] Psychologists and psychiatrists have been interested, by and large, in the individual. This was the approach of William James[4] before Freud and this is the more current approach of Gordon Allport.[5] In seeking the universal motivation toward religious behavior, existentialist theologians have also stressed religion as a response to individual, presumably divinely implanted, emotions. So Kierkegaard emphasized man's search to overcome longing and despair,[6] Schleiermacher stressed a sense of dependency or "creature consciousness,"[7] and Rudolph Otto, the "numinous," that mysterium tremendum which moves man, in awe, to a sense of the "holy."[8] By contrast, Wobbermin stressed security.[9]

Freud was consistent in treating religion as he did other social institutions, especially family. He was influenced a great deal by evolutionary ideas in other fields and relied upon available early investigations of primitive society. This evolutionism led him to view magic, religion and science as a developmental continuum. Freud's historical and psychological reductionism led him to see societal religion primarily as an expansion of individual reactions to personal emotional need. Thus religion to him was the invention of men who sought to shield themselves from the painful realities of life (and death). He saw religion as a mass neurosis. The evolutionary stages, for him, paralleled the stages of psychosexual development. Religion, in his view, would be well dispensed with when modern man attained the final, heterosexual, mature stage of rational science. Then he would be able to face the harsh realities of the human condition without the need for neurotic illusions.[10]

A full discussion of these views is unwarranted here. Aside from his use of the Oedipal myth, describing events in a "primal horde" (there is no evidence that man ever lived in such arrangements), suffice it to say that Freud's views on culture and social institutions were generally inadequate, if not inaccurate.[11]

One point, however, does call for some amplification. Malinowski pointed out that even in primitive societies, magic and religion often exist side by side, meeting different needs.[12] Other anthropologists have also identified both, although classification isn't always clear. There is little reason for assuming that magic is the predecessor of religion. Since, where both exist, magic tends to be more of an applied technique for influencing nature while religion relates to larger issues, magic is probably the primitives' science more than anything else.

While psychology and many theologians have stressed individual aspects of religion, sociologists and anthropologists, as one would expect, have tended to emphasize the group as the source of religious behavior in mankind. In this they are following the lead of Emile Durkheim. In *The Elementary Forms of Religious Life,* Durkheim concluded that the totem phenomenon in primitive groups actually represents society as a whole. For him, society itself is the object of religious veneration and the source of the "sacred." The purpose of religion is thus believed by him to be the preservation of group solidarity through beliefs and practices.[13]

The problem with this, and many other attempts to understand the origin of religion, is that they fail to consider the differences between manifest and latent functions of the institution. William Goode presented this idea as follows:

Positive Function		Negative Function		Irrelevant	
Manifest	Latent	Manifest	Latent	Manifest	Latent

Functional anthropologists have concentrated upon those positive functions which are not usually known to the members of the society, i.e., the positive, latent functions. The rebels and debunkers among modern economists and historians have concentrated upon the negative latent functions. It is clear that much exploration remains to be done among the remaining cells.[14]

Promotion of group solidarity may be a positive latent function of religion, but it would be doomed to failure if that were the beginning and the end of it. What is true of the sociological functions is equally true of the psychological or emotional and. alas even the broadest multifunctional theory can help us resolve neither the question of origin nor of metaphysical truth. However, sociologists have long recognized the intimate connection between the form of religious expression in a society and other aspects of its social behavior. Outstanding among such theories is the work of Max Weber who, for example, called attention to the economic implications of the Protestant Ethic.[15]

From our discussion thus far it should be evident that religious behavior finds expression on both an individual and a group level. To see it from only one perspective is to examine only one side of the coin. Such behavior also involves a number of levels of expression. Belief, in the form of mythology, doctrine or actual theology, is but one facet of religious behavior. Cultus or the practices of the religion are an integral part of religious behavior. Religions typically involve their adherents with rituals, symbols and sacraments (sometimes sacrifices) which enable the practitioners to translate thought and verbal behavior into prescribed actions. These are, of course, part of the carefully transmitted culture of all societies. Earlier attempts to determine which came first, Belief or Cultus, are no doubt like other such quests, a futile effort.

Finally, religion involves the adherents in a community. Wach sites Dimond who wrote, "Vital religion, by its very nature, must create and sustain a social relationship." In folk society, with its lack of specialized function, that community may simply be the cult of family, village or tribe. While some of this is known in modern society (e.g., grace at family meals), specialized religious organization is typical. A sect is the least formal of contemporary religious organizations. It is typically a group in conflict with existing mores. For its different orientation it claims divine authority. Its adherents are at one with its purposes while in conflict with the outside world. When this conflict aspect passes, the sect is transformed into a denomination. Now personal attachments which promote group solidarity are institutionalized. The size, leadership and organizational structure now promote a decline in primary group affiliation and controls. These developments, in some societies, give rise to a genuine universal or established church, termed Ecclesia.[17]

The leadership of the family or tribal group is usually spontaneous, following general lines of social leadership. The cult may already have a specific leader even though he is not exclusively involved in religious leadership. With the development of a sect, the founder is distinguished by an inspiring personal charisma. At his death, the sect may actually disintegrate. Often, from his circle of disciples, emerges one who claims the founder's mantle by reason of special association with the founder rather than his own qualifications. The original circle is now transformed into a brotherhood which may still venerate the founder but must now define a new direction for itself. As a sect moves along the path toward denominational status, the charismatic leadership changes from the original personal charisma to the charisma of office. Finally, as an established, accepted social institution, hierarchical and administrative considerations lead to a professional leadership distinguished from the general population of adherents.

Organized Religion in American Life

Religious behavior in the United States has emerged from the involved history of immigration and ethnicity in our country dating back to colonial times. Even before independence, what was to become the United States already bore the heritage of the Dutch, Spanish and French and their religious forms, in addition to the dominant English Colonies. Even among the English, those who emigrated over dangerous seas to the hardship of colonial life were not likely to be the most prominent homeland citizenry. More typically, they were the disenfranchised seeking their good fortune. The religion they brought with them, except in the South, was by no means the established Church of England. The various groups of dissenters who settled tended to become the local establishments. As one travels through New England, he realizes that the same "meeting house" which served as the seat of government during the week was on the Sabbath the house of worship. The same officials, under different titles, governed both church and community.

The large number of highly competitive denominations and sects made one established church unfeasible, particularly in the heterogeneous Middle Atlantic colonies. It is with great difficulty that some would claim that the separation of church and state enunciated by the founding fathers other than Jefferson, was intended to do any more than prevent such establishment. The country and its government, however, was clearly non-denominational Protestant, with a dash of deism which typified the climate of those days. Nothing in this orientation should be construed as intending religious liberty for Jews (anti-

Christs) or Catholics (Papists), and many legal battles were required to win for non-Protestants equality before the law. Yet our nation has never experienced Ecclesia as it exists in other countries. The Catholic, Lutheran, Episcopal churches all had to accommodate to that reality. Perhaps the closest we have come to that experience is the special connection of the Morman Church to the State of Utah.

As the nation grew and the sources of immigration shifted primarily across Europe — from North to South, from West to East — the religions of the immigrants began to reflect the broader spectrum of Eastern faiths. By the time open immigration was effectively stifled, around World War I, we had substantial minorities of ethnic Catholics, Jews and some Eastern Orthodox Church adherents, in addition to ethnic Protestants.

Exact figures on religious communities in the United States are difficult to obtain since religious affiliation is not part of the usual census data and churches use varying enumeration criteria for determining membership. However, information from a special census sample in 1957 and extra-governmental sources suggest that about 31 million Americans, the largest single religious body in our nation, are at least nominally Catholic. Over 5 million Americans are believed to be Jews.[18]

Due to the closing of the frontier before their arrival as well as a number of other sociocultural factors, adherents of various religious bodies in the United States are not equally distributed throughout the country. Some are regionally based, some are especially urban or rural in composition.[19] Thus in many of the great metropolises of the United States, white Protestants are outnumbered by Jews, Catholics and Negro Protestants who have higher rates of urbanization.

The shift from rural to urban has had many effects on organized religion in this country. Religious innovation and drifting away from established religions tends to spread from urban to rural society so that increases in urbanization would lead to religious change. City dwellers, surrounded as they are by their man-made environment, are less likely to find religious inspiration in the forces of nature, thus the weakening of tradition.

Participation in religious life also reflects age and sex differences. Active religious participation in the United States is greater among females than males, greater among children and married adults than among unmarried young adults. The sex differences are widest in the lower classes, reflecting their general single sex peer group orientation and sharper traditional division of sex role than among those with better education. These patterns, incidentally, have not coincided with the religious traditions of Jews, whose women's active religious leadership has focused on home ritual and children's education. With the Protestantization of American Judaism and the accompanying decline in ritual, desire for equality in public worship became a major theme in challenging the older tradition.[20]

In light of the historic place of Protestantism and the strength of its influence on all religious behavior in the United States, "the Triple Melting Pot," Protestant, Catholic, Jew, with each as an equal constituent, is actually a liberal conceptualization superimposed on the historic tensions between American Protestantism and other religious bodies, especially Catholicism.[21] These contentions have frequently come to the surface around the issue of public school prayer, financial aid to parochial schools, vis-a-vis Jews particularly around public Christmas and Easter observations.[27] In these symbolic conflicts over community power, there is rarely any sense of equal partnership such as one sees on state occasions.

Nevertheless, the Americanization of both Catholicism and Judaism, essentially a liberal Protestantization, with its emphasis on humanism and patriotism rather than creed and ritual, has served as a vehicle for such genuine interfaith sentiment as does exist. Within the Catholic Church, the rise of American clergy has been one of the generating forces behind ecumenism and liberal reform.

One would think, in a society where one finds a basically secular orientation and decrease of interest in doctrinal and cultic expression, that religion itself would decline in significance. In actuality, the opposite is true. Larger percentages of Americans maintain religious affiliations than previously or in comparable industrial countries.[23] Religious endogamy remains the prevailing pattern. Prevailing judgments concerning this paradox have stressed organized religion's associational significance. In our mass society, religious communities have provided a framework for identity otherwise difficult to attain. With the rewards of work reduced to the salary and not identification with a product, one's trade is no longer a focus of belonging. Ethnicity, too strongly held to, is an unhappy reminder of one's lower class immigrant background. Heterogeneity of modern society, the decline of regional differences and frequent movement from one place to another, make it difficult to identify with one's home town. When traveling, one may proudly see himself as a Texan or New Yorker.

But at home, what distinction does this provide? For many, religion provides this sense of belonging. Participation in church affairs provides social expression for its members. Through the church's organization, one can achieve a sense of belonging which was formerly derived from participation in organic community. This observation is most true for American Jews whose religious behavior is bound up with their status as an ethnic minority, but applied in differing degrees to Catholics and ethnic Protestants as well.

With so much of our social and political life touched by our religious organization, the atheist, the secularist and even the unaffiliated are at a distinct disadvantage.[25] By way of illustration, it is always fascinating to follow the increase in religious activity of American political figures in their ascendency. To be "churched" is understood by our society to be a mark of good citizenship.

RELIGIOUS STRATIFICATION

While just about any church will do from the perspective of American participation-oriented religion, clearly the various religious bodies enjoy differing socioeconomic status in the hierarchy of American social structure.

Liston Pope, in a classic report, showed that the members of different religious communities differ in their distribution of upper, middle and lower class membership.[26] Various researchers have been able to identify different churches with special strata of society. Generally, ethnic churches, storefront churches and a plethora of sects are at the lower end of the socioeconomic scale. Churches like the Episcopal, Presbyterian or Congregational stand high, with Methodists and Baptists intermediary.

Within the Jewish group, Orthodox, Conservative and Reform divisions, over and above their theological significance, reflected socioeconomic standing. Until this generation, they marked recency of immigration to the United States and rise in standing.[27] With the virtual end of immigration, these characteristics are beginning to fade. Among Catholics, each parish has reflected the socioeconomic standing of its parishoners. On the whole, however, their recent immigrant background, along with certain sociocultural characteristics of the various Catholic ethnic groups, combined to depress the Church's ranking. Until recently, primarily some Irish and German

Catholics had begun the upward climb, and one notes that it is these groups, not the Italian or Spanish American Catholics, who still provide the bulk of the Church's religious.

Not only does church participation differ by class, the social meaning of religious behavior becomes colored by other class interests. Thus, for the wealthy, participation on governing boards of metropolitan churches and national church bodies is a natural carryover from leadership in other spheres of commercial, industrial and civil achievement. In the light of the Protestant ethic, their success makes them the rightful leaders of religious sentiment in our sociey. For the middle class, church participation represents respectable membership in the community. It is one more mark of the responsible citizen.

For the lower classes, participation in denominational churches is too expensive and too formal. Some groups retain official membership in the Catholic Church, for example, and participate in less formal churches and sects. Cathartic release of emotions through shouting, singing, clapping and rhythmic dancing marks the services in the revival meetings of the rural poor and the storefront sects and churches of the urban slums. The preacher, typically self-ordained, is of the same unlettered background as his flock. His sermon is couched in the allegory and fables of the simple folk, his message, fire and brimstone. Such religious expression permits the channeling of the pent-up emotions of the suffering poor. They can leave not only exhausted by the activity, but satisfied in their belief that the rich will pay for ill treating the good, poor folk while the poor will ultimately gain their just reward.[28]

The Negro church has within it a stratification parallel to that of the white Protestant churches. For decades it has been the most stable of social institutions in the black community. Its latent functions include provision of escapist outlets, similar to lower class white churches, to channel frustration and hostility. The dynamics of its position made its stance regarding civil rights and social action ambiguous.[29] For a long time, it was clear that the black clergy would lose their "monopoly" should the unlikely occur and churches be integrated. With the ascendancy of better educated, professional clergymen who would have every opportunity to compete with white clergy for truly integrated pulpits, this reservation declined. Now the significant factor to be considered was the peculiar insulation Southern black clergymen enjoyed. They were just about the only occupational group responsible to and paid by the black community, not whites. As a result we see the emergence of the black church, Martin Luther King, the SCLC in Southern civil rights activism during the 1950's.[30]

ISSUES FOR THE SOCIAL WORKER

Although sects, in conflict with society, have historically tended to draw younger people to them, established denominations and churches have not. As a rule, religion is concerned with the conservation and continuity in a society's values. Its nature is thus not highly attuned to youthful character. It is therefore hard to say whether today's alienation from religious organizations is a phase or lasting phenomenon.

In our society, religion is faced with the additional problem of relevancy, in a period of rapid change. Old answers do not appear to address themselves to new questions. By way of a simple illustration, the Protestant Ethic, stressing diligence and frugality, has little place in an economy based on consumer credit, planned obsolescence and extensive leisure. Christianity, a missionary faith, has had to face the reality that the overwhelming majority of the world's population are neither Christian nor have they any inclination toward Christianity. Other doctrines of Western religion have been taken for granted without exploring their contemporary significance. Regarding specific values, the Catholic Church is so powerful in Western tradition that its position on such issues as celibacy, birth control, original sin, salvation outside the Church, etc., creates an atmosphere in which laymen believe all religion shares identical views. That the Catholic Church has itself been experiencing upheaval is seen in ecumenism and movement toward liberalization, no matter how halting. A culture which stresses participation, disregards doctrine, and proclaims the equivalency of all religious expression is bound to run headlong into sharply divided religious bodies. Sooner or later, someone is sure to ask why bother? Particularly in the United States, belonging has not met the full range of human needs which total commitment and genuine belief can achieve. We therefore experience a crisis of values in which youthful alienation is matched by adult lip service.

In the midst of rejecting the seeming superficiality of organized religion, a significant number appear to be turning, not to nineteenth century rationalism, but to other emotional, "idealist" expressions to encounter our technology. We see the emergence of such searching for new emotional experience in the phenomenal growth of drug use by those of middle class background and rising interest in religions of the "exotic" East, meditation, scientology, astrology, witchcraft and seances. Apparently, when religion began to fit itself into the bureaucratized rationality of the day, its ability to relate to the non-rational needs of man waned.

The distinction we have drawn between magic and religion is highly pertinent for American religious practice. Americans have taken to heart the instrumentalist lessons of the scientists about what religion can do for man. However, these functions can only operate when they are by-products of religious commitment. Thus commitment leads to practice, which in turn, may result in certain qualities of individual or group life. If you begin by asking what will be instrumental in producing the desired qualities, one may question whether the behavior will have that imperative backing to achieve the goal. This is, incidentally, one of the major shortcomings of those theories which see in religion simply another functional "man-made institution." The need for closure apparently leads some sociologists to transcend the scope of their instruments in much the same vein as it leads the devout to their absolute faith. Secondly, the nature of the sequence is thus transformed from a stance regarding the great philosophical questions to a magical manipulation for the control of nature, in this case, the nature of individual and societal behavior. Such has been the message of popular American religion. Religion will keep the family together, grant peace of mind, prevent juvenile delinquency, drug addiction, community disharmony, in short, anything but heal warts (unless you happen to believe in faith healing).

It is wise to remember that the social worker is himself a product of the secular environment which has produced the religious forms prevalent in our contemporary society. His attitudes, like his contemporaries', are those shaped by his culture. Some years ago Niebuhr pointed out that many quite secular social workers are moved by concerns for their fellow man which in other ages would have probably directed them to religious vocations and missionary orders.[31] Like their more devout predecessors, the helper and the helped can become separated from one another by a dividing line. In Christianity, that line often focused on the sinfulness of the poor. Although these attitudes may remain today, for the social worker the dividing line may be professionalism itself. On the other hand, social work seeks to retain the human quality in our machine age and in this task it may find a valuable ally in man's religious sentiment.[32]

Many social workers continue to work under the aegis of church-related social agencies. These often operate under policies shaped by doctrinal considerations. The organization of social services under religious structures often affects their availability as well. Thus old, high status, WASP church groups in cities often find that they are taxed to serve the predominantly Protestant Negro slum, while other agencies try to decide whether they should concentrate on quality services or pitch in. Sometimes, Catholics and Jews are predominantly served by their own private agencies, leaving provision of services to the Protestant population to public agencies. When both public and private denominational agencies are available, one must consider what one or another choice represents to the client (as well as the worker).

On an individual level, the professional must be prepared for the emotionality of religious sentiment in himself and his client, particularly at times of personal crisis. At such times, even the confused, childhood conceptions which emerge may have great force for the client. These include natural events as well as symbolic issues like intermarriage or child rearing. To use such a moment to score a point for one's own religious or anti-religious philosophy seems obviously inappropriate although one frequently encounters such unprofessional behavior. Workers also may overlook the resource possibilities of religion in times of personal crisis. Often the worker can utilize the charisma of a clergyman where his own efforts fail to move the client, although care needs to be exercised regarding the client's attitude and the careful selection of a clergyman. Social work can ill afford to disregard both the functional and dysfunctional aspects of religious behavior since it seems that much personal unhappiness is generated by the breakdown of our values in the face of changing environmental demands.

REFERENCES

1 Frank E. Jones, *An Introduction to Sociology*. Toronto: CBC Publications Branch, 1961, p. 41.
2 The author acknowledges the contribution of Samuel Z. Klausner of the Bureau of Social Science Research to the formulation of his own thoughts in this area.
3 Paul Schmidt, *The Origin and Growth of Religion*. New York: The Dial Press, 1931.

4 William James, *The Varieties of Religious Experience.* New York: Mentor Books, 1958. See especially p. 41 where he explains his intent to ignore organized religion.

5 Gordon W. Allport, *The Indvidual and His Religion.* New York: Macmillan Paperbacks, 1960.

6 Soren Kierkegaard, *Fear and Trembling and Sickness Unto Death.* New York: Doubleday Anchor, 1954, pp. 146-168.

7 Friedrich Schleiermacher, *On Religion: Speeches To Its Cultured Despisers.* New York: Harper Torchbook, 1958.

8 Rudolf Ott, *The Idea of the Holy.* New York: Oxford University Press, 1958.

9 G. Wobbermin, *The Nature of Religion.* New York: Thomas Y. Crowell, 1933.

10 Freud's view on religion are expressed most clearly in his *Totem and Taboo,* 1913; *The Future of An Illusion,* 1927; *Civilization and Its Discontents,* 1930; and *Moses and Monotheism,* 1939.

11 For two opinions of the significance of Freud's views of society, see Calvin S. Hall and Gardner Lindzey, "The Relevance of Freudian Psychology and Related Viewpoints for the Social Sciences," in *The Handbook of Social Psychology.* 2nd ed., Vol. I., ed. Gardner Lindzey and Elliot Aronson, Reading, Mass.: Addison-Wesley Publishing Company, 1968, pp. 294-302; and J. Milton Yinger, *Religion, Society and the Individual.* New York: Macmillan Co., 1957, pp. 110-114.

12 Bronislaw Malinowski, "Magic, Science and Religion," in *Magic, Science and Religion and Other Essays.* New York: Doubleday Anchor Books, 1955, pp. 17-92; also highly instructive in understanding of ancient religion and magic are Yehezkiel Kaufmann, "Pagan Religion" and "Israelite Religion," in *The Religion of Israel,* tr. Moshe Greenberg. Chicago: University of Chicago Press, 1960, pp. 21-121.

13 Emil Durkheim, *The Elementary Forms of the Religious Life.* tr. Joseph W. Swain, New York: Collier Books, 1961.

14 William Goode, *Religion Among the Primitives.* Glencoe: The Free Press, 1951, p. 33.

15 Max Weber, *The Protestant Ethic and the Spirit of Capitalism.* New York: Charles Scribner's Sons, 1930. In this classic essay Weber stresses his views that an ideology might shape economics rather than the contrary Marxist view of economic determinism.

16 Joachim Wach, *Sociology of Religion.* Chicago: Phoenix Books, p. 27.

17 Wach, *ibid.,* has an excellent discussion of the social organization and leadership of religion.

[18] Murray Gendell and Hans L. Zetterberg, A Sociological Almanac for the United States. New York: Bedminster Press, 1961, pp. 76-77.

[19] Stuart A. Queen and David B. Carpenter, *The American City.* New York: McGraw-Hill, 1953, p. 289.

[20] Marshal Sklare, "Aspects of Religious Worship in the Contemporary Conservative Synagogue," in *The Jews: Social Patterns of an American Group.* Marshall Sklare, ed. Glencoe, Ill.; Free Press, 1958, pp. 358-361.

[21] James Coleman, "Social Cleavage and Religious Conflict," in *Religious Conflict in America,* ed. Earl Raab. New York: Anchor Books, 1964, pp. 90-100.

[22] See "Community Conflict: Christmas Observance in the Public School," *ibid.,* pp. 198-208.

[23] Gendell and Zetterberg, *op. cit.,* pp. 76, 78.

[24] Clark E. Vincent, "Interfaith Marriage," in E. Raab, *op. cit.,* pp. 50-59.

[25] In "Religious Liberty From the Viewpoint of a Secular Humanist," Sidney Hook speaks for an oft overlooked minority in American society. See E. Raab, *ibid.,* pp. 138-151.

[26] Liston Pope, "Religion and the Class Structure," *The Annals* (March 1948), pp. 84-91.

[27] Marshall Sklare, *op. cit.,* pp. 357-358.

[28] Charles S. Braden, "The Sects," in *The Annals* (March 1948), pp. 84-91.

[29] See E. Franklin Frazier, *The Negro Church in America.* New York: Schoken, 1963, for a good analysis of the social dimensions of the Negro church.

[30] Louis E. Lomax, *The Negro Revolt.* New York: Signet, 1963, p. 59.

[31] Reinhold Niebuhr, *The Contribution of Religion to Social Work.* New York: Columbia University Press, 1932, pp. 61-62.

[32] Herbert Stroup, "The Common Predicament of Religion and Social Work," *Social Work,* Vol. 7, No. 2 (April 1962), pp. 89-93.

THE RELIGIOUS FACTOR

GERHARD LENSKI

God is concerned with the whole of men's lives: on at least this one point all the churches agree. He is not merely the Lord of the Sabbath, but is equally concerned with men's activities the other six days of the week: their work, their play, their politics, their family life.

But how does this doctrine work in practice? Does a man's religious commitment *really* influence his everyday actions, especially a man who lives in the highly secularized environment of the modern American metropolis? Is there *really* a difference between the believer and the unbeliever in the market place or in the voting booth? Does the *type* of religious commitment make a difference: do the actions of Protestants differ from those of Catholics and Jews in the fields of politics, economics, and family life? If so, are these differences due to the influence of their religion, or to something else?

The study was carried out in the Midwestern metropolis of Detroit, fifth largest community in America today, and probably eleventh largest in the world. Here, by means of personal interviews with a carefully selected cross-section of the population of the *total* community (i.e., suburbs as well as central city), we sought to discover the impact of religion on secular institutions. Strictly speaking, the findings set forth in this volume apply only to Detroit. However, in view of the steady decline of localism and regionalism in America during the last century, it seems likely that most of these findings could be duplicated by similar studies in other communities. This is a matter to which we shall return later.

BACKGROUND OF THE STUDY

The basic problem with which this study is concerned, the influence of religion on secular institutions, has long been debated by laymen and scholars alike. One school of thought denies that religion has any significant influence on politics, economics, or other important secular areas of modern society. This view has gained considerably in popularity during the last century and is very evident in the many social science textbooks which largely ignore religion, apparently thinking it irrelevant to the problems at hand. For example, in a leading textbook on American politics, published as recently as 1958, there are only minor scattered references to religion, none of which suggest that religion is, or could be, a factor of importance on the contemporary American political scene.[1] What is even more significant, none of the major reviewers of this book thought this omission deserving of comment.

By contrast, a second school of thought asserts that religion has been, and continues to be, a force in human history. For example, many of the proponents of this point of view maintain that American civil liberties rest ultimately on the foundation provided by the Judaic-Christian conception of the nature of man. Others, in a more critical vein, see religion as a force fostering superstition and retarding the progress of science.

This lack of consensus is hardly surprising in view of the limited amount of serious, systematic research devoted to the problem. Less systematic sociological research has been devoted to religion than to any other major institution of our society. Particularly lacking are studies of the *interrelations* between modern religious institutions and other basic institutional systems.

POSITIVISM AND ECONOMIC DETERMINISM

For those familiar with the history of sociology, there are obvious reasons for this neglect. Sociology is essentially a child of the French Enlightenment, and from its inception was committed to the positivist view that religion in the modern world is merely a survival from man's primitive past, and doomed to disappear in an era of science and general enlightenment. From the positivist standpoint, religion is, basically, institutionalized ignorance and superstition.[2]

While still in its formative years sociology was also strongly influenced by the theory of economic determinism. For the economic determinist, the economic institutions of society are the ultimate source of all social change.[3] Changes in all other social institutions represent nothing more than adjustments to prior changes in the economic institutions on which they are dependent for their very existence.

Neither positivism nor economic determinism was conducive to sustained sociological research in the field of religion, since both theories viewed religion as a negligible force in the modern world. Furthermore, both tended to provide solutions, not problems, and research flourishes only where the existence of unsolved problems is recognized.

DURKHEIM AND WEBER

It was not until the early twentieth century that any serious challenge to either of these two systems of thought developed within sociology. The challenge, when it finally came, was raised chiefly by two men: the German sociologist Max Weber, and his French contemporary, Emile Durkheim. Shortly after the turn of the century each of these men published a major work concerned with the place of religion in human society, which brought them into sharp conflict with the older sociological viewpoints.

In *The Elementary Forms of Religious Life,* Durkheim opposed the positivists with a provocative analysis in which he argued that the roots of religious belief and practice lie in the very fabric of society itself and in the nature of human interrelations, not in ignorance and superstition as the positivists maintained. The religion of primitive man is the symbolic expression of his awareness of the social system on which he depends not only for the material necessities of life, but for psychic necessities as well. According to Durkheim, the religious man who feels dependent upon some external moral power is not the victim of an hallucination. Such a power exists, in the form of society itself. In short, religious institutions embody in symbolic form some of the most profound insights of men. Far from being an unfortunate survival from man's primitive past, they are an integral and necessary element in any stable social system. The form which religious symbols take may change, but there is something basic underlying the forms, and this basic element is destined to survive so long as human societies continue.

About the same time, Weber offered an equally significant challenge to the economic determinists.[4] In his famous essay, *The Protestant Ethic and the Spirit of Capitalism,* he sought to demonstrate that without the Protestant Reformation modern Western capitalism would never have developed.[5] This form of economic enterprise, according to Weber, is unique in human history, since the driving force behind it is not the spirit of greed (for men have always been avaricious) but a spirit of *dedication and commitment to work.* For Weber, the "spirit of capitalism" is distinguished by three main characteristics:

    (1) a conviction that work is a worthwhile activity in its own right, and not merely as the means to material comfort or wealth;

    (2) a belief that economic judgments should be made on purely rational grounds, without regard to traditional criteria;

    (3) a distaste for personal indulgence.

Once established, Weber argued, capitalism can be expected to be self-perpetuating; but the critical problem is to discover its origin in precapitalist society. Only by discovering the source of the spirit of capitalism can we discover the source of modern capitalism itself.

Weber found this source in Protestantism in general, and more especially in Calvinism and Puritanism. He saw the spirit of capitalism as an unintended by-product of these important religious movements, which contained in their theology the seeds of a radical reorientation of men's thinking concerning economic activity. For example, for the followers of Luther and Calvin, work was to be viewed not as a penalty for sin, but rather as a means of glorifying God. For Calvinists and Puritans, self-indulgence was among the most deadly sins. For Calvinists and Puritans, and later for Methodists as well, life was not to be lived on a day-to-day basis; rather, God demanded a rationalized, unified system of life and the elimination of magic as a means to salvation. In these and other ways, Protestantism laid the foundation for the emergence of the spirit of capitalism.[6] Thus, economic institutions are *not* the uncaused cause of all social change. Rather they are part of a complex social system in which change may originate at various points, with significant consequences for all other parts of the system.

Weber was careful to point out that he was not trying to replace economic determinism with a theory of religious determinism, nor was he even denying the tremendous importance of economic institutions in the process of social change. His goal was simply to challenge what he regarded as the unrealistic and oversimplified theory of social change advocated by the economic determinists and to suggest a more adequate alternative.[7]

While the work of Durkheim and Weber has generated much discussion and debate, unfortunately it has led to little systematic, empirical research. Furthermore, most of the work that has been done has been limited to investigations of problems of an historical character, with all of the attendant methodological difficulties.[8] There have been no major studies of the problems raised by the theories of Durkheim and Weber as they apply to the modern metropolitan community.[9] As a result we do not know much more today about the influence of religious institutions on secular institutions in modern society than was known half a century ago.

WEBERIAN THEORY AND THE PRESENT STUDY

From its inception this study was designed with the Weberian controversy in mind. No one who has read Weber's analysis of the historical significance of religion for economics can help wondering what relevance his theory has for the contemporary scene. Are the major religious groups in America today the carriers of distinctive economic ethics? Do the economic values and actions of Protestants and Catholics in mid-twentieth-century America differ as much as Weber suggests they did in post-Reformation Europe? Are Protestants more inclined to view their work as a sacred calling? Do they practice the pattern of worldly asceticism Weber identified with the Puritans and Pietists of an earlier era?

Since Weber's concern was with the origins of the capitalist system, he has little to say explicitly about religion's role in a mature capitalist society. What he did say tended to be brief asides rather than carefully developed analyses.[10] However, his basic theoretical position strongly suggests that here, as in all other types of societies, religion is a factor to be reckoned with. Underlying the whole of his writings on the sociology of religion we find two basic postulates which point to this conclusion. First, he assumes that every major religious group develops its own distinctive orientation toward *all aspects of life,* and that these orientations profoundly influence the daily actions of its adherents and hence the institutional structure of society.[11] Second, Weber assumes that these orientations are partially independent of the social situation of the group.[12] On the basis of these postulates we would expect differences between religious groups in mature capitalist (or even post-capitalist) societies as well as in precapitalist societies. And we would expect them not only in economic behavior, but in political behavior, family life, and all other areas of human activity. Furthermore, we would expect these differences to be more than mere reflections of the differences in the economic situations of the religious groups.

THEORIES OF URBANISM AND THE PRESENT STUDY

While Weberian theory leads one to expect religion to have a significant effect on secular institutions in contemporary America, other theories point to a different conclusion. This is true not only of positivism and economic determinism; it is equally true of the theories of urbanism.

During the last century and a half the Western world has undergone a dramatic transformation. In 1800 the people of Western Europe and the United States were predominantly agrarian, and scattered among thousands of small towns and villages. Today they are largely city dwellers, increasingly concentrated in a small number of massive metropolitan centers. As long ago as 1950, nearly one third of the American population was concentrated in fourteen great metropolitan communities, each with a population of a million or more. There is every indication that this trend will continue for years to come.

This trend is significant for our study, because urban living produces a distinctive way of life.[13] Among the many important features of urbanism, two deserve special attention in the present context, since both suggest that, in the modern metropolis, the influence of religion on secular institutions is substantially reduced, or even eliminated altogether.

To begin with, urban conditions bring people of diverse backgrounds into constant and close association with one another. More than that, they find that they are obliged to cooperate in the production of goods and services, the maintenance of law and order, and a variety of other tasks essential to the well-being of the total community. As a consequence they find it necessary to ignore the differences which divide them, at least while they are engaged in those activities requiring co-operation. Eventually, what began as a mere *modus vivendi,* or temporary arrangement for specific situations only, becomes generalized into a basic value applicable to all kinds of situations. In short, norms of *tolerance* and *secularism*[14] inevitably arise in urban centers. Norms peculiar to one religious group or another are de-emphasized, leaving a common core of moral norms which are shared by all the various faiths represented in the community.

The second characteristic of urbanism which suggests that religious institutions may have little impact on secular institutions is the pronounced tendency toward *specialization* and *compartmentalization.* Specialization in the work of both individuals and organizations has been carried to a level undreamed of in simpler communities. As specialization increases, people tend to view life less and less as a unified whole, and more and more as a series of discrete parts relatively unrelated to each other. Thus, in the modern metropolis work and family life tend to become two distinct aspects of life, a sharp contrast with the situation in agrarian communities, or even in urban communities of an earlier era.

Similarly, religion becomes increasingly a highly compartmentalized activity rather than an integral part of the daily round. The more compartmentalized religion becomes, the less influence we should expect it to have on secular institutions. One of the main channels for exercising influence, the membership of the faithful in secular organizations, can no longer be used. Transformation from within (such as Weber was concerned with) ceases to be a possibility in a world of persons accustomed to thinking of religion in compartmentalized terms. In such a situation, religious organizations can only influence secular organizations through pressure-type tactics from without.

If this view of urbanism is valid, one can only conclude that, while Weberian theory may have had validity in other times and places, it is largely irrelevant to the secularized, specialized, and compartmentalized modern metropolis.

A decade ago few sociologists doubted the basic tenets of the classical theory of urbanism, but today the situation is changing. Research during the last decade has made it increasingly evident that, while the rise of the modern metropolis has certainly led to many radical changes in behavior, there are also many striking evidences of continuity with traditional ways of life which prevailed in simpler communities of an earlier era. For example, recent research has shown that kinship roles in particular, and primary-type relationships (i.e., close or intimate social relations) in general, have proven far more resistant and durable than earlier urban theorists ever imagined they could be.[15]

The traditional view of urbanism as it affects religion has recently been questioned by several writers. Most notable among these is Will Herberg. In his provocative essay, *Protestant-Catholic-Jew*, Herberg asserts that urban conditions of life promote what we shall here call *communal* religion, as contrasted with *associational* religion.[16] According to the classical theories of urbanism, religion in the modern metropolis becomes a highly specialized aspect of life. The church itself becomes a highly specialized formal association, and ceases to be a nucleus around which a variety of social relationships is organized, as in the typical agrarian community. Herberg suggests, however, that the very impersonality of so much of modern life creates in individuals a need for communal relationships, broader than the family, but narrower than the total society.

Earlier in American history ethnic groups served such a function, and individuals were able to enjoy this sense of communal identification and participation as members of the German, Polish, Italian, or other ethnic colonies established in this country. Today such groups are rapidly disintegrating, but many of the needs they served continue to be felt. In this situation, Herberg argues, Americans are turning increasingly to their religious groups, especially the three major faiths, for the satisfaction of their need for communal identification and belongingness. In brief, the specialization and compartmentalization inherent in the urban way of life drive men to transform their religious groups from narrow, specialized associations into groups which are more communal in character.[17]

In view of the increasing recognition of the elements of continuity between the patterns of life in the modern metropolis and in the simpler communities of an earlier era, we can be less confident of the irrelevance of Weberian theory in the modern setting. On the contrary, recent changes in the sociological theory of urbanism are almost all of such a nature as to *increase* our expectation that religious institutions have a significant impact on secular social institutions. In the last analysis, however, the issue can only be settled by systematic, empirical research.

IMPLICATIONS FOR THE FUTURE

THE CHANGING COMPOSITION OF THE AMERICAN POPULATION

This study has many implications not only for general sociological theory, but also for our understanding of American society and its future course of development. In this final section it may be well if we briefly examine some of the latter.

To begin with, it should be noted that the religious composition of this country is constantly changing. At the beginning of Washington's first term as president, the white Protestant group constituted from three quarters to four fifths of the population.[18] The Negro group constituted about one fifth, while Catholics and Jews combined made up no more than one per cent of the American population.[19] Since Negroes were disenfranchised, white Protestants constituted 98 per cent of the electorate.

Today the situation is radically changed. In 1957 the U. S. Bureau of the Census found that among Americans aged 14 and over only 58 per cent belonged to the white Protestant group. Negro Protestants accounted for only another 9 per cent. White Catholics, by contrast, had increased to the point where they constituted 27 per cent of the total, and Jews 3 per cent.[20]

Of equal significance was the finding that in the large metropolitan communities of this country (i.e., urbanized areas with populations of 250,000 or more) white Protestants constituted only 39 per cent of the population. In these same areas Catholics now constitute 38 per cent of the population, Negro Protestants 11 per cent, and Jews 8 per cent. In short, in these influential centers of our society the white Protestant group, which once formed a large and effective majority of the population, now barely enjoys a tiny plurality.

To a considerable degree this transformation of the religious composition of the American population occurred in the interval between 1825 and 1925, the era of mass immigration from Europe. During this period large numbers of Catholic and Jewish immigrants came to this country, settling chiefly in the urban centers of the North. However (on the basis of research carried out by the present writer in another context), it appears that the process of population composition change is still going on today, though at a slower rate than in the period before the First World War.[21] For example, it appears that since 1920 the Catholic segment of the population has grown by about one percentage point per decade, due both to continuing immigration and high rates of fertility. Since World War I there has been little change in the relative sizes of the Negro Protestant and Jewish groups. Hence, the growth of the Catholic population has been accompanied by a corresponding decline in the relative size of the white Protestant group, reflecting both low fertility rates and limited immigration. Available evidence indicates that these trends are likely to continue for the foreseeable future.

If this is true, this means that behavior patterns linked with the Catholic group are likely to become somewhat more prevalent while patterns linked with the white Protestant group are likely to become less common. More specifically, we may expect these gradual changes in population composition to encourage many, or most, of the following developments:

1. Rising rates of church attendance in American society;
2. Strengthening of religious group communalism;
3. Strengthening of both the nuclear and extended family systems;
4. Declining emphasis on intellectual independence;
5. Increasing support for welfare state policies;
6. Increasing support for the Democratic Party;
7. Shifting focus of interest from work group to kin group;
8. Slowing rate of material progress, and perhaps also of scientific advance;[22]
9. Rising birth rates;
10. Narrowing latitude for exercise of the right of free speech;
11. Increasing restraints on Sunday business and divorce, and possibly birth control;
12. Declining restraints on gambling and drinking.

It should be understood that *we are not predicting that these developments* will *occur, but only that these are developments which are likely to be encouraged by the growth of the Catholic segment of the American population and the decline of the white Protestant segment.* Major social changes are seldom attributable to the influence of any single factor. Rather, such changes usually represent society's response to the workings of multiple forces, many of which largely cancel out each other. Therefore, the changes which occur represent the net balance which remains. Our concern here is to identify some of the more important pressures likely to be generated by one significant factor in American life: the slow but steady alteration of the socio-religious composition of the population.

DRIFT TOWARD COMPARTMENTALIZATION?

Among the possible trends cited above, one deserves special comment both because of its far-reaching implications and because many of these implications have received so little attention from the general public. This is the possible trend toward increased religious group communalism. As we noted in Chapter 2, communalism along socio-religious group lines seems to have been gaining in strength in recent years, and promises to continue to gain in the foreseeable future.

This development is one which has been greatly hastened by the rapid decline of the older ethnic subcommunities in recent years—a development noted by Herberg and others. Until about a generation ago, the American population was sharply divided into a rather large number of relatively small ethnic subcommunities which, in the northern part of the country at least, served as basic points of reference for the masses of Americans. These groups, however, were unable to preserve their organizational integrity in the face of the powerful and pervasive pressures to Americanize the immigrant, and intermarriage across ethnic lines has now become quite common.[23] As a result, loyalties to the various ethnic subcommunities cannot be maintained. The successor to the ethnic subcommunity is the socio-religious subcommunity, a group united by ties of race and religion. As our own and various other studies have shown, while intermarriages across ethnic subcommunity lines are occurring with increasing frequency, there is no trend toward increasing intermarriage across socio-religious group lines. Hence, while Poles now marry Irish with greater frequency, these are marriages of Catholics with Catholics. Even where religious intermarriages occur, our study has shown they lead increasingly to the conversion of one partner or the other, and hence the reestablishment of religious units within the family.

These facts are especially significant in view of Weber's important distinction between classes and status groups, and subsequent work relevant to this distinction.[24] In classical Marxian theory, the chief units of social organization are classes. In Marx and Engels' famous phrase, "The history of all hitherto existing society is the history of class struggles."[25] By this they meant not merely that classes and class struggles are ubiquitous features of human history, but rather that classes and class struggles alone *make history*.

In reacting against this theory of social change, Weber developed the thesis that societies are organized not merely in terms of classes, but also in terms of status groups. These units are differentiated from one another on the ground of social honor or prestige rather than (like classes) on economic grounds. Furthermore, Weber maintains that they are normally communal groups characterized by distinctive subcultures, whereas classes are not. While there is usually some relationship between the class system of a society and its system of status groups, the two are by no means the same.

There seems little doubt that socio-religious groups are rapidly replacing ethnic groups as the basic units in the system of status groups in American society. Of the four major socio-religious groups, the white Protestants enjoy the greatest social honor, Catholics rank second, Jews third, and Negro Protestants fourth.[26] As the position of the Jewish group indicates, status-group rank by no means parallels class position.

In recent years sociologists have increasingly recognized the importance of status and status groups in the life of industrialized societies.[27] More especially, they have come to recognize that political controversy in modern industrial societies has a tendency to change in character from one decade to the next. Sometimes the basic controversies are between classes; other times they are between status groups. Class-based controversies normally dominate politics in periods of economic crisis, while controversies involving status groups tend to dominate in periods of prosperity.[28]

If our analysis is correct up to this point, it indicates that in the foreseeable future we can expect that economic prosperity will be accompanied by heightened tensions between socio-religious groups, and political controversies during such periods will be closely linked with the hopes, fears, and aspirations of these groups. Only severe economic and international crises seem likely to alter the situation. In short, the controversies surrounding John Kennedy's candidacy in 1960 may well mark the beginning of a new era in American life, not the end as many people imagine.

The findings of this study force us to consider the possibility that American society is moving (though admittedly slowly) towards a "compartmentalized society" of the type found in contemporary Holland and Lebanon, to cite but two of the more prominent examples. In these societies most of the major institutional systems are obliged to take account of socio-religious distinctions. Hence, political parties, families, sports teams, and even business establishments are often identified with one or another of the major groups. The Dutch even have a word, *verzuiling*, to describe this kind of social arrangement. Literally translated it means "columnization," since society is organized like a series of parallel columns or pillars.[29]

American society has a long way to go before it will even approach the degree of compartmentalization attained by Holland or Lebanon, but the trend itself is a matter of importance. The old American ideal of a great melting pot out of which would someday emerge a new, unified nation seems to have been abandoned, and increasingly we hear discussions about "pluralistic society." "Pluralistic society" may be a real alternative to "compartmentalized society," but present-day proponents of pluralism do not seem greatly concerned with making the distinction. This suggests that "pluralistic society" may turn out to be merely another term, a polite euphemism, for "compartmentalized society," or at best a stepping stone leading to it.

It may well be that compartmentalization along socioreligious group lines is the best we can hope for in a society which is religiously divided as ours is, if at the same time we are to preserve the values linked with the various subgroups. However, if given the group loyalties of Americans compartmentalization is the best arrangement we can achieve, it would seem desirable that this alternative be chosen *after rational exploration and consideration of the alternatives.* Currently we seem merely to be drifting into a type of social arrangement which Americans of all faiths might well reject if they became fully aware of all it entails.

This problem should be of special concern to religious leaders. Our current drift toward a "compartmentalized society" could easily produce a situation where individuals developed a heightened sense of religious group loyalty combined with a minimal sense of responsibility for those outside their own group. In a more compartmentalized society there is good reason to fear a weakening of the ethical and spiritual elements in religion and a heightening of the ever dangerous political elements. Such a development would be a serious departure from the basic ideals of all of the major faiths in America, sharing as they do in the Biblical tradition. Hence, on both religious and political grounds, Americans might do well to study more critically than they yet have the arguments advanced by advocates of pluralistic society.

NOTES

[1] V. O. Key, *Politics, Parties, and Pressure Groups.* New York: Thomas Y. Crowell, 1958, 4th edition. Otherwise this is an excellent textbook.

[2] Properly speaking, the positivists applied this generalization only to *traditional* religion. Some, like Comte, sought to establish a new religion of Humanity, which would perform the socially useful functions of traditional religions. However, since this new religion never found acceptance except among a small minority, our description of their view seems only a slight overstatement, at least so far as the implications for research are concerned.

[3] Except, of course, change originating in the physical environment, or outside the social system. From the standpoint of the economic determinists, such change would normally be "filtered" into the social system through the economic institutions of society, since they would be the first to adjust to the changed environment.

[4] For an excellent summary and analysis of the work of Weber, see Reinhard Bendix, *Max Weber: An Intellectual Portrait.* Garden City: Doubleday, 1960, Parts I and II, or Talcott Parsons, *The Structure of Social Action.* New York: McGraw-Hill, 1937, Part III.

[5] *The Protestant Ethic and the Spirit of Capitalism.* Translated by Talcott Parsons. New York: Charles Scribner's Sons, 1958.

[6] Weber conceded that prior to the Protestant Reformation, isolated individuals had exhibited the spirit of capitalism, but he maintained that this was not enough to permit the emergence of capitalism as a dominant economic system. The dominance of capitalism presupposes whole groups of men committed to the spirit of capitalism, and prior to the Reformation this was lacking. Ibid., p. 55.

[7] Throughout his career Weber was greatly concerned with this important problem which he attacked by means of a broadly comparative study of China, India, ancient Israel, and Western Europe. Originally published as *Gesammelte Aufsätze zur Religionssoziologie.* Tübingen: J. C. B. Mohr, 1920-21, 3 volumes, these materials are now available in English translation as follows: (1) *The Protestant Ethic and the Spirit of Capitalism,* op. cit.; (2) *From Max Weber: Essays in Sociology.* Trans. by H. H. Gerth and C. Wright Mills. New York: Oxford University Press, 1946, Part III; (3) *The Religion of China.* Trans. by H. H. Gerth. Glencoe: The Free Press, 1951; (4) *The Religion of India.* Trans. by H. H. Gerth and Don Martindale. Glencoe: The Free Press, 1958; and (5) *Ancient Judaism.* Trans. by H. H. Gerth and Don Martindale. Glencoe: The Free Press, 1952.

[8] See, for example, Ernst Troeltsch, *The Social Teachings of the Christian Churches.* Trans. by Olive Wyon. London: Allen & Unwin, 1931, 2 vols.; Werner Sombart, *The Jews and Modern Capitalism.* Trans. by M. Epstein. London: T. Fisher Unwin, 1913; R. H. Tawney, *Religion and the Rise of*

Capitalism. New York: Harcourt, Brace, 1926; Amintore Fanfani, *Catholi-cism, Protestantism, and Capitalism.* London: Sheed and Ward. 1951. For an interesting new study, see David S. Landes, *Religion and Enterprise: The Case of the French Textile Industry.*

9 At the present time G. E. Swanson is engaged in a study of the relevance of Durkheim's theory to the contemporary religious scene, and is utilizing materials from the Detroit Area Study. A monograph based on this study should be forthcoming in the next several years.

10 See, for example, *The Protestant Ethic,* op. cit., pp. 55 and 72. Here Weber specifically rejects the hypothesis that Protestantism is a *necessary* condition for the *survival* of capitalism (though elsewhere, as in Chapter I, he indicates that significant differences in the economic ethics of religious groups persist). He states that a mature capitalist society will possess its own institutionalized arrangements for educating and selecting individuals to perform the various functions required by the system, so that assistance from the churches will no longer be required.

In conceding the irrelevance of religious institutions to the survival of capitalism, Weber seems to have supposed that capitalism represents the end product of economic evolution. It apparently did not occur to him *at this point* that capitalism might have to contend with a revival of anti-capitalistic values and might ultimately be destroyed or substantially modi-fied, and that the outcome of this struggle might be profoundly affected by non-economic factors such as religion.

Actually, however, it is unfair to examine Weber's views on this matter too closely since it is evident from the context of his remarks that his chief purpose in making them was to define the limits of his own problem and thereby avoid entanglement in what he regarded as a very different problem: that of determining the conditions necessary for the survival of capitalism.

11 While Weber is noted chiefly for his analysis of the impact of religious institutions on *economic* institutions, it is clear that he believed they in-fluenced *all* of the major institutional systems of society. For example, in a number of places Weber speaks of the impact of Christian groups on the kinship system, undermining its traditional position of centrality in human affairs. See, for example, *The Religion of China,* op. cit., pp. 236-37, or Weber, *The City.* Translated by Don Martindale and Gertrud Neuwirth. Glencoe: The Free Press, 1958, pp. 102-3. Elsewhere he speaks of the im-pact of religion on art, science, government, and education (*The Protestant Ethic,* op. cit., pp. 13-17, 168, 249, etc.).

12 It is this second assumption which brings Weber sharply into conflict with the economic determinists. They are very willing to grant the first of his assumptions, but regard the differences between religious groups as mere reflections of differences in their economic situation. For a more de-

tailed discussion of this point, see *From Max Weber,* op. cit., pp. 267-70, or Bendix, op. cit., especially Chapter 8.

[13] See, for example, Louis Wirth, "Urbanism as a Way of Life," *The American Journal of Sociology,* 44 (1938), pp. 1-24; Georg Simmel, "The Metropolis and Mental Life," in *The Sociology of Georg Simmel.* Trans. by Kurt H. Wolff. Glencoe: The Free Press, 1950, pp. 409-24; Pitirim Sorokin and Carle C. Zimmerman, *Principles of Rural-Urban Sociology.* New York: Holt, 1929. In large measure all of the modern theories of urbanism are derived from the pioneering work of Ferdinand Tönnies, entitled *Gemeinschaft und Gesellschaft.* This volume has now been translated into English by Charles P. Loomis under the title *Community and Association.* London: Routledge and Kegan Paul, 1955.

[14] Secularism is used here in the sense of religious neutralism.

[15] See Morris Axelrod, "Urban Structure and Urban Participation," *American Sociological Review,* 21 (1956), pp. 13-18, or Floyd Dotson, "Patterns of Voluntary Association Among Urban Working Class Families," ibid., 16 (1951), pp. 687-93.

[16] Garden City: Doubleday, 1956.

[17] This is a rather free translation of Herberg's views, and tends to make explicit ideas which are left implicit in much of his discussion of the subject.

[18] This is not to say that three quarters or four fifths of Americans were churchgoers or even church members. Then, as now, large numbers of Americans were not active in religious associations.

[19] See, for example, Gerald Shaughnessy, *Has the Immigrant Kept the Faith?* New York: Macmillan, 1925.

[20] U. S. Bureau of the Census, *Current Population Reports: Population Characteristics,* Series P-20, No. 79, February 2, 1958.

[21] A preliminary report on this other study was read as a paper at the annual meeting of the American Sociological Society in Washington, D.C., in 1957. It was entitled, "The Growth of Catholic Population in the United States Since 1920." Similar conclusions are suggested by an analysis of the age pyramids of the major groups based on the 1957 census report, ibid.

[22] It seems much less likely that the gradual growth in numbers in groups which are weak in the qualities required for success in science will slow scientific advance, since the numbers of scientists who make the really creative breakthroughs are small and these could easily be recruited from other segments of the population in ample numbers, if society as a whole continues to provide the necessary financial support.

[23] See especially Ruby Jo Reeves Kennedy, "Single or Triple Melting Pot? Intermarriage Trends in New Haven, 1870-1940," *American Journal of Sociology,* 49 (January 1944), pp. 331-39. Her findings concerning the mid-twentieth century situation are confirmed by Detroit Area Study findings

which are as yet largely unpublished. However, see our data concerning intermarriage in Chapter 2. See also John C. Leggett, *Working Class Consciousness in an Industrial Community* (unpublished doctoral dissertation, The University of Michigan, 1962), p. 141.

24 *From Max Weber,* op. cit., pp. 180-94.

25 Karl Marx and Friedrich Engels, *Manifesto of the Communist Party.* 1848.

26 This fact has been demonstrated numerous times in studies of social distance. For example, see Emory S. Bogardus, *Immigration and Race Attitudes.* Boston: Heath & Co., 1928, or Daniel Katz and Kenneth Braly, "Racial Stereotypes of 100 College Students," *Journal of Abnormal and Social Psychology,* 28 (1933) pp. 280-90. More recently the author together with Werner S. Landecker conducted a study of the status of ethnic groups in Detroit which reconfirmed earlier findings.

27 In addition to the vast literature on the American caste system (referring to the racial cleavage), there is a growing literature on the tripartite religious division among whites. In addition to Herberg's classic analysis, there is Ruby Jo Reeves Kennedy's pioneering work, op. cit., A. B. Hollingshead's article, "Trends in Social Stratification: A Case Study," *American Sociological Review,* 17 (December 1952), especially pp. 685-86, and Mhyra S. Minnis' article, "Cleavage in Women's Organizations: A Reflection of the Social Structure of a City," ibid., 18 (February 1953), pp. 47-53 to cite but a few. It is perhaps significant that much of the literature on this subject comes from the New England area where the Catholic proportion of the American population is greatest and the white Protestant proportion the smallest. If population trends are as our research indicates, and if the drift toward compartmentalization is stimulated by these trends, other secions of the country can be expected to display more of the pattern which is now relatively marked in that one section of the country.

28 See, for example, S. M. Lipset, "The Sources of the 'Radical Right.'" and Richard Hofstadter, "The Pseudo-Conservative Revolt," in Daniel Bell, ed., *The New American Right.* New York: Criterion Books, 1955, pp. 166-235 and 33-55 respectively.

29 For a discussion of the Dutch pattern see David O. Moberg, "Religion and Society in the Netherlands and in America," *American Quarterly,* 13 (Summer 1961), pp. 172-78. See also J. A. A. Van Doorn, "Verzuiling: Een Eigentijds Systeem van Sociale Controle," *Sociologische Gids,* 3 (1956), pp. 41-49; I. Schöffer, "Verzuiling, Een Specifiek Nederlands Probleem," ibid., 3 (1956), pp. 121-217; or see the special issue of *Socialisme en Democratie* devoted to the subject of *verzuiling,* January 1957, all cited by Moberg. See also John W. Dykstra, "Holland's Religious Segmentation," *Christian Century,* October 19, 1955, pp. 1207-8 and the special issue of *Social Compass,* 9 (1962) on "vertical pluralism."

RELIGION IN AMERICA IN THE PERSPECTIVE OF FAITH

WILL HERBERG

Jewish-Christian faith[1] is God-centered. All being finds its beginning and its end in God, and its unity, reality, and order in its ordination to Him. Jewish-Christian faith sees man's proper life, the life for which he was created and which corresponds to his "essential nature," as the life of responsive love of God and hence love of fellow man. But it also knows that man's actual life is corrupted by idolatrous self-love, which disrupts and perverts all human relations. We are always prone to idolize ourselves and our works, to attribute quite uncritically final significance to our interests, ideas, and institutions, to make of our achievements an instrument of pride, power, and self-aggrandizement. Such perverse egocentricity is not without its consequences. "Thus saith the Lord God: Because you count yourself wise as a god, behold I bring strangers against you. . . . Your heart was proud because of your beauty; you corrupted your wisdom by reason of your splendor. [Therefore] I cast you to the ground . . ." (Ezek. 28.6-7, 17). The prophets trace all the evils of life to this kind of human self-idolatrization, which is at the heart of what the theologians know as "original sin."

Sinful egocentricity invades all areas of life, including the religious. Man is *homo religiosus,* by "nature" religious: as much as he needs food to eat or air to breathe, he needs a faith for living. He is always striving to find a center of life beyond life, a larger whole transcending the self in which to ground the meaning and security of existence; he is always searching for some god and some way of salvation from the fears, futilities, and frustrations of life. But—and this is the challenging word of Jewish-Christian faith—so long as he pursues this search in self-sufficiency, relying on his own virtue, wisdom, or piety, it will not be God that he finds, but an idol—the self, or some aspect of the self, writ large, projected, objectified, and worshiped. The living God of Jewish-Christian faith is to be found not through self-sufficient "searching," but through "meeting" Him as He discloses Himself in the divine-human encounter of which Scripture and the tradition of the believing community are the witness. He is a God Who goes forth to "visit" man in the midst of life, and discloses Himself in the encounter.

The God of the Bible makes His unconditional demand upon men, calls them to total love and obedience, and therewith also judges them in their self-interest and self-aggrandizing pretensions. In Jewish-Christian faith, the word of redeeming grace comes only after the word of judgment has shattered all human claims to security and self-sufficiency. "I dwell in a high and holy place, saith the Lord, but also with him that is of a contrite and humble spirit" (Is. 57.15).

The word of judgment upon human self-sufficiency is also a word of judgment upon human religion, or the human element in religion. "There is nothing in the Bible to support the view that religion is necessarily a good thing. Scripture has no ax to grind for religion; on the contrary, it is highly suspicious of much that passes for religion."[2] "Religion qua religion," says Reinhold Niebuhr, "is naturally idolatrous, accentuating rather than diminishing the self-worship of men, [institutions] and nations by assuring them of an ultimate sanction for their dearest desires. . . . Religion per se and faith per se are not virtues, or a cause of virtue. The question is always what the object of worship is, and whether the worship tends to break the pride of the self so that a truer self may arise, either individually or collectively."[3] To the man of biblical faith, religion is not self-validating or self-justifying; it has to be tested, critically examined, and evaluated in terms of its authenticity in mediating the will, judgment, and redeeming grace of the God Who can be "met" only in repentance and the abandonment of all claims to human self-sufficiency.

The ambivalence of religion extends to the church. Biblical faith is defined by, and expressed through, community: the Jew or Christian finds access to his God from within the People of God. "The individual Israelite," Alan Richardson points out, "approached God in virtue of his membership in the holy people. . . . In the whole of the Bible, in the Old Testament as well as the New, there is no such thing as a private, personal relation between an individual and God apart from his membership in the covenant-folk."[4] Biblical faith is thus the faith of man-in-community, and both Judaism and Christianity place strong emphasis on the corporate dimension of the religious life. In this sense, the church—of which the equivalent in Judaism is the People Israel—is divine, with a divine vocation.

But in another sense, in the temporal, institutional sense, the church is, of course, human, and subject to all of the temptations and corruptions of human institutions. Indeed, precisely because in the church man confronts God in a quite unique way, the church may well become the "final battleground between God and man's self-esteem,"[5] where "the hostility of men against God is brought to a head."[6] Since there is nothing human that self-interest and irresponsibility may not attempt to exploit for its own purposes, the church too (in its human aspects, at least) stands under judgment.

Religion, then, is an ambiguous and doubtful thing, requiring careful scrutiny on the part of the man of faith. And what is true of religion in general is particularly true of religion in contemporary America, where the great and almost unprecedented upsurge of religiosity under way today stems from so many diverse sources and manifests itself in so many contradictory forms.

The outstanding feature of the religious situation in America today is the pervasiveness of religious self-identification along the tripartite scheme of Protestant, Catholic, Jew. From the "land of immigrants," America has, as we have seen, become the "triple melting pot," restructured in three great communities with religious labels, defining three great "communions" or "faiths." This transformation has been greatly furthered by what may be called the dialectic of "third generation interest": the third generation, coming into its own with the cessation of mass immigration, tries to recover its "heritage," so as to give itself some sort of "name," or context of self-identification and social location, in the larger society. "What the son wishes to forget" —so runs "Hansen's Law"—"the grandson wishes to remember." But what he can "remember" is obviously not his grandfather's foreign language, or even his grandfather's foreign culture; it is rather his grandfather's *religion*—America does not demand of him the abandonment of the ancestral religion as it does of the ancestral language and culture. This religion he now "remembers" in a form suitably "Americanized," and yet in a curious way also "retraditionalized." Within this comprehensive framework of basic sociological change operate those inner factors making for a "return to religion" which so many observers have noted in recent years—the collapse of all secular securities in the historical crisis of our time, the quest for a recovery of meaning in life, the new search for inwardness and personal authenticity amid the collectivistic heteronomies of the present-day world.

Self-identification in religious terms, almost universal in the America of today, obviously makes for religious belonging in a more directly institutional way. It engenders a sense of adherence to a church or denomination and impels one to institutional affiliation. These tendencies are reinforced by the pressures of other-directed adjustment to peer-group behavior, which today increasingly requires religious identification and association with some church. Thus a pattern of religious conformism develops, most pronounced, perhaps, among the younger, "modern-minded" inhabitants of Suburbia, but rapidly spreading to all sections of the American people.

The picture that emerges is one in which religion is accepted as a normal part of the American Way of Life. Not to be—that is, not to identify oneself and be identified as—either a Protestant, a Catholic, or a Jew is somehow not to be an American. It may imply being foreign, as is the case when one professes oneself a Buddhist, a Muslim, or anything but a Protestant, Catholic, or Jew, even when one's Americanness is otherwise beyond question. Or it may imply being obscurely "un-American," as is the case with those who declare themselves atheists, agnostics, or even "humanists." Sidney H. Scheuer, a leading Ethical Culturist, was expressing a genuine concern when he stated recently: "There is a tendency to regard all people who are not committed to one of the three great faiths as being disloyal to American principles and traditions."[7] Americanness today entails religious identification as Protestant, Catholic, or Jew in a way and to a degree quite unprecedented in our history. To be a Protestant, a Catholic, or a Jew are today the alternative ways of being an American.

This religious normality implies a certain religious unity in terms of a common "American religion" of which each of the three great religious communions is regarded as an equi-legitimate expression. America has emerged as a "three-religion country,"[8] in which the Protestant, the Catholic, and the Jew each finds his place. Insofar as America knows of a church in the Troeltschean sense—a form of religious belonging that goes along with being a member of the national community—it is this tripartite unity of Protestant-Catholic-Jew. Each on his part—the Protestant, the Catholic, the Jew—may regard his own "faith" as the best or even the truest, but unless he is a theologian or affected with a special theological interest, he will quite "naturally" look upon the other two as sharing with his communion a common "spiritual" foundation of basic "ideals and values"—the chief of these being religion itself. America thus has its underlying culture-religion—best understood as the religious aspect of the American Way of Life—of which the three conventional religions are somehow felt to be appropriate manifestations and expressions. Religion is integral to Americanism as currently understood. "Recognition of the Supreme Being," President Eisenhower declared early in 1955 in his address launching the American Legion's "Back to God" campaign, "is the first, the most basic, expression of Americanism. Without God, there could be no American form of government, nor an American way of life."[9] In uttering these words, Mr. Eisenhower was speaking for the great mass of American people and affording an important insight into one aspect of contemporary American religiosity.

The religious unity of American life implies an institutional and ideological pluralism. The American system is one of stable coexistence of three equi-legitimate religious communities grounded in the common culture-religion of America. Within this common framework there is persistent tension and conflict, reflecting the corporate anxieties and minority-group defensiveness of each of the three communities. To mitigate these tensions and prevent the conflicts from becoming too destructive, American experience has brought forth the characteristically American device of "interfaith," which, as idea and movement, has permeated broad areas of national life. Interfaith, as we have seen, is a religiously oriented civic co-operation of Protestants, Catholics, and Jews to bring about better mutual understanding and to promote enterprises and causes of common concern, despite all differences of "faith." The interfaith movement is not secularistic or indifferentist but in its own way quite religious, for it is conceived as a joint enterprise of representative men and women of the three religious communities dedicated to purposes of common interest felt to be worthwhile from the religious point of view. Interfaith is thus the highest expression of religious coexistence and co-operation within the American understanding of religion.

NOTES

[1] The theological critique and evaluation here undertaken is carried out in terms of "Jewish-Christian faith," by which is meant the basic theological

outlook underlying both Judaism and Christianity as biblical religions. In this view, Judaism and Christianity are understood as two religions sharing a common faith. For a statement of this position, see Paul Tillich, "Is There a Judeo-Christian Tradition?", *Judaism,* Vol. I, No. 2, April 1952. In defining the unity of Judaism and Christianity, Tillich speaks of their "identity of structure at all points and identity of content in most." See also Will Herberg, "Judaism and Christianity: Their Unity and Difference," *The Journal of Bible and Religion,* Vol. XXI, No. 2, April 1953. For statements of biblical faith, see G. Ernest Wright, *The Challenge of Israel's Faith.* University of Chicago Press, 1944; Martin Buber, *The Prophetic Faith.* Macmillan, 1949; Paul Minear, *Eyes of Faith: A Study in the Biblical Point of View.* Westminster, 1946; J. Guillet, *Thèmes bibliques.* Aubier, Paris, 1950.

2 A. Roy Eckardt, "The New Look in American Piety," *The Christian Century,* November 17, 1954. See also the vivid account of "The Religion That Is No Religion" and "A Religion to End All Religion" in Alexander Miller, *The Renewal of Man* (Doubleday, 1955), chaps. ii and iii.

3 Reinhold Niebuhr, "The Peril of Complacency in Our Nation," *Christianity and Crisis,* Vol. XIV, No. 1, February 8, 1954; "Religiosity and the Christian Faith," *Christianity and Crisis,* Vol. XIV, No. 24, January 24, 1955.

4 Alan Richardson, "Instrument of God," *Interpretation,* Vol. III, No. 3, July 1949.

5 Reinhold Niebuhr, *The Nature and Destiny of Man.* 2 vols. Scribner's, 1941, 1943, Vol. I, p. 200.

6 "In the Church, the hostility of men against God is brought to a head; for there human indifference, misunderstanding, and opposition attain their most sublime and also their most naive form," Karl Barth, *The Epistle to the Romans.* tr. by Edwyn C. Hoskyns, Oxford, 1933, p. 418.

7 Sidney H. Scheuer, a vice president of the American Ethical Union, in an address to the annual assembly of that organization, St. Louis, April 1954; reported in *Information Service* (National Council of the Churches of Christ), October 30, 1954. Revealing of the universal American attitude is the outraged disapproval expressed by a ninth-grade girl at a suburban New Jersey junior high school in a composition entitled "Matilda": "Not the least bit patriotic, Matilda does not even go to church . . . !"

8 This illuminating term comes from an article, "A 3-Religion Country," by Max Lerner commenting on the original edition of this book (*New York Post,* November 6, 1955). References to the United States as a "Christian country," once so common, are now extremely rare. The appropriate designation today is contained in Justice Douglas' celebrated dictum, speaking for the Supreme Court, in the New York released-time case: "We are a religious people whose institutions presuppose a Supreme Being" (Zorach *v.* Clauson, 72 S. Ct. 679, 1952).

ETHICAL FAILURE OF THE DIVIDED CHURCH

H. RICHARD NIEBUHR

One element in the social sources of theological differentiation deserves especial attention. Max Weber and Ernst Troeltsch have demonstrated how important are the differences in the sociological structure of religious groups in the determination of their doctrine. The primary distinction to be made here is that between the church and the sect, of which the former is a natural social group akin to the family or the nation while the latter is a voluntary association. The difference has been well described as lying primarily in the fact that members are born into the church while they must join the sect. Churches are inclusive institutions, frequently are national in scope, and emphasize the universalism of the gospel; while sects are exclusive in character, appeal to the individualistic element in Christianity, and emphasize its ethical demands. Membership in a church is socially obligatory, the necessary consequence of birth into a family or nation, and no special requirements condition its privileges; the sect, on the other hand, is likely to demand some definite type of religious experience as a pre-requisite of membership.

These differences in structure have their corollaries in differences in ethics and doctrine. The institutional church naturally attaches a high importance to the means of grace which it administers, to the system of doctrine which it has formulated, and to the official administration of sacraments and teaching by an official clergy; for it is an educational institution which must seek to train its youthful members to conformity in thought and practice and so fit them for the exercise of rights they have inherited. The associational sect, on the other hand, attaches primary importance to the religious experience of its members prior to their fellowship with the group, to the priesthood of all believers, to the sacraments as symbols of fellowship and pledges of allegiance. It frequently rejects an official clergy, preferring to trust for guidance to lay inspiration rather than to theological or liturgical expertness. The church as an inclusive social group is closely allied with national, economic, and cultural interests; by the very nature of its constitution it is committed to the accommodation of its ethics to the ethics of civilization; it must represent the morality of the respectable majority, not of the heroic minority. The sect, however, is always a minority group, whose separatist and semi-ascetic attitude toward "the world" is reenforced by the loyalty which persecution nurtures. It holds with tenacity to its interpretation of Christian ethics and prefers isolation to compromise. At times it refuses participation in the government, at times rejects war, at times seeks to sever as much as possible the bonds which tie it to the common life of industry and culture. So the sociological structure, while resting in part on a conception of Christianity, reacts upon that conception and re-enforces or modifies it. On the other hand the adoption of one or the other type of constitution is itself largely due to the social condition of those who form the sect or compose the church. In Protestant history the sect has ever been the child of an outcast minority, taking its rise in the religious revolts of the poor, of those who were without effective representation in church or state and who formed their conventicles of dissent in the only way open to them, on the democratic, associational pattern. The sociological character of sectarianism, however, is almost always modified in the course of time by the natural processes of birth and death, and on this change in structure changes in doctrine and ethics inevitably follow. By its very nature the sectarian type of organization is valid only for one generation. The children born to the voluntary members of the first generation begin to make the sect a church long before they have arrived at the years of discretion. For with their coming the sect must take on the character of an educational and disciplinary institution, with the purpose of bringing the new generation into conformity with ideals and customs which have become traditional. Rarely does a second generation hold the convictions it has inherited with a fervor equal to that of its fathers, who fashioned these convictions in the heat of conflict and at the risk of martyrdom. As generation succeeds generation, the isolation of the community from the world becomes more difficult. Furthermore, wealth frequently increases when the sect subjects itself to the discipline of asceticism in work and expenditure; with the increase of wealth the possibilities for culture also become more numerous and involvement in the economic life of the nation as a whole can less easily be limited. Compromise begins and the ethics of the sect approach the churchly type of morals. As with the ethics, so with the doctrine, so also with the administration of religion. An official clergy, theologically educated and schooled in the refinement of ritual, takes the place of lay leadership; easily imparted creeds are substituted for the difficult enthusiasms of the pioneers; children are born into the group and infant baptism or dedication becomes once more a means of grace. So the sect becomes a church.

Religious history amply illustrates the process. An outstanding example is the "Half-Way Covenant" of the New England churches, which provided for the baptism of the children of second-generation, unconverted parents who had "owned the covenant" and submitted to the discipline of the church without being able to attain full membership because of their lack of the experience of salvation. The rise of "birth-right membership" in the Society of Friends shows the same process at work while the histories of Mennonites, Baptists, and Methodists offer further illustrations. Doctrines and practice change with the mutations of social structure, not vice versa; the ideological interpretation of such changes quite misses the point.

The evils of denominationalism do not lie, however, in this differentiation of churches and sects. On the contrary, the rise of new sects to champion the uncompromising ethics of Jesus and "to preach the gospel to the poor" has again and again been the effective means of recalling Christendom to its mission. This phase of denominational history must be regarded as helpful, despite the break in unity which it brings about. The evil of denominationalism lies in the conditions which makes the rise of sects desirable and necessary: in the failure of the churches to transcend the social conditions which fashion them into caste-organizations, to sublimate their loyalties to standards and institutions only remotely relevant if not contrary to the Christian ideal, to resist the temptation of making their own self-preservation and extension the primary object of their endeavor.

The domination of class and self-preservative church ethics over the ethics of the gospel must be held responsible for much of the moral ineffectiveness of Christianity in the West. Not only or primarily because denominationalism divides and scatters the energies of Christendom, but more because it signalizes the defeat of the Christian ethics of brotherhood by the ethics of caste is it the source of Christendom's moral weakness. The ethical effectiveness of an individual depends on the integration of his character, on the synthesis of his values and desires into a system dominated by his highest good; the ethical effectiveness of a group is no less dependent on its control by a morale in which all subordinate purposes are organized around a leading ideal. And the churches are ineffective because they lack such a common morale.

The measure of their ethical weakness, of course, is taken especially in the crises, in wars and social revolutions. Divided against themselves they must leave the work of social construction to those forces which can develop an effective morale, which have for their basis the common and all too human interests in acquisition, in national and racial prestige, and which are unified by the common purposes and common fears of mankind at its lower levels. Under these circumstances it is almost inevitable that the churches should adopt the psychologically more effective morale of the national, racial, and economic groups with which they are allied. Hence they usually join in the "Hurrah" chorus of jingoism, to which they add the sanction of their own "Hallelujah"; and, through their adeptness at rationalization, they support the popular morale by persuading it of the nobility of its motives. The specifically Christian ethics is allowed to fade into the background while the ethics of the social classes takes its place, unless, indeed, it is possible to re-interpret the Christian ideal in such a way that its complete accord with social morality is demonstrated.

The lack of an effective, common, Christian ethics in the churches is illustrated by the manner in which they have divided their loyalties in each national crisis in the history of America and allied themselves with the struggling partisans of parliament and marketplace. During the American Revolution the rector of Trinity Church, New York, wrote to an English confrere, "I have the pleasure to assure you that all the society's missionaries without excepting one, in New Jersey, New York, Connecticut, and, so far as I learn, in the other New England colonies, have proved themselves faithful, loyal subjects in these trying times; and have to the utmost of their power opposed the spirit of disaffection and rebellion which has involved this continent in the greatest calamities. I must add that all the other clergy of our church in the above colonies though not in the society's service, have observed the same line of conduct." On the other hand, he testifies, the Presbyterian ministers, with singular uniformity, are promoting by preaching and every other effort in their power "all the measures of the congress, however extravagant." In any case, and this applies also to Congregationalists, Baptists, Methodists, and the other churches in the revolutionary colonies, one hears no word of a common Christian system of values to which all can express allegiance. Each religious group gives expression to that code which forms the morale of the political or economic class it represents. They function as political and class institutions, not as Christian churches.

The case was not different in the slavery crisis. Methodism had carried an anti-slavery doctrine in its platform from the very beginning, but even Whitefield urged the desirability of eliminating from the charter of Georgia the prohibition of slavery and when Methodism became the church of the slaveholder as well as of the poor tradesman it soon divided into a Northern and a Southern branch although the gradual emasculation of the anti-slavery clause in the old program was designed to maintain peace at the expense of principle. So it was also with Baptists and Presbyterians. Again the interests of economic class bent to their will the ethics of the Christian church and it was unable to speak a certain word on the issue of slavery. When the irrepressible conflict came the various denominations, as was to be expected, showed themselves to be the mouthpieces of the economic and sectional groups they represented.

The role played by the churches in the World War is too well known to require comment. Even when resistance was offered to wartime psychology it was often apparent that such resistance was not animated by Christian principles but by the social attitudes of immigrant groups, in whom the Old World heritage had not lost its force. Almost always and everywhere in modern times the churches have represented the ethics of classes and nations rather than a common and Christian morality. Evident as this is in the crises, it is no less true of the times between crises. In the issues of municipal and national elections, on the questions of industrial relationships, of the conservation or abrogation of social customs and institutions—including the prohibition issue—the denominations have been the religious spokesmen of the special non-religious groups with which they are allied.

For the denominations, churches, sects, are sociological groups whose principle of differentiation is to be sought in their conformity to the order of social classes and castes. It would not be true to affirm that the denominations are not religious groups with religious purposes, but it is true that they represent the accommodation of religion to the caste system. They are emblems, therefore, of the victory of the world over the church, of the secularization of Christianity, of the church's sanction of that divisiveness which the church's gospel condemns.

Denominationalism thus represents the moral failure of Christianity. And unless the ethics of brotherhood can gain the victory over this divisiveness within the body of Christ it is useless to expect it to be victorious in the world. But before the church can hope to overcome its fatal division it must learn to recognize and to acknowledge the secular character of its denominationalism.

INSPIRATIONAL RELIGIOUS LITERATURE:
FROM LATENT TO MANIFEST
FUNCTIONS OF RELIGION[1]

LOUIS SCHNEIDER
SANFORD M. DORNBUSCH

Inspirational religious literature is known to be enormously popular. The books of Norman Vincent Peale today, of Bruce Barton a generation ago, and of numerous of their close intellectual relatives and imitators have achieved staggering sales.[2] Sociologists have left comment on the literature to journalists or theologians or gifted outsiders.[3] But it is of significance for the analysis of "cultural drift," with broad general implications. In this article, a brief survey of the literature and a summary of its dominant trends and themes, attention is given to a special phase which is of considerable sociological import.[4]

The literature is by no means entirely unitary, but strains or trends in it exhibit prominent elements of unity.[5] Ralph Waldo Trine's *In Tune with the Infinite*, Bruce Barton's *The Man Nobody Knows*, Henry C. Link's *The Return to Religion*, and Peale's *A Guide to Confident Living* and *The Power of Positive Thinking* suggest for purposes of definition four criteria to which the items of literature should conform: (*a*) they assume the general validity of the Judeo-Christian religious tradition; (*b*) they aim to inspire with the hope of salvation here or in an afterlife; (*c*) they recommend use of techniques to achieve salvation, in whatever sense salvation might be understood; and (*d*) they address themselves to the "everyday problems" or "everyday people." The books vary in the balance among the four points.

Reprinted from *The American Journal of Sociology*, Vol. LXII, No. 5, March 1957, pp. 476-481, by permission of The University of Chicago Press. Copyright 1957 by The University of Chicago.

The general validity of the Judeo-Christian tradition is assumed in these works with significant vagueness. Specific theological doctrines, such as of Christ's soteriological mission, or specific theological discussions, as of Christ's status as a member of the Trinity, are hard to find. More likely, there will be found discussion of a transcendent "something" about which a professed theologian could say practically nothing. Daniel Poling confesses, "I began saying in the morning two words, 'I believe'—those two words with nothing added."[6]

The literature also holds forth the hope of some kind of salvation. In the seventy-five years covered in the survey eschatological interest has declined. But, while concern with the next world fades increasingly, salvation comes quite conclusively to mean salvation in this world: release from poverty or handicapping inhibition in personal relations or from ill health or emotional disequilibrium. But salvation in this secular sense is held forth as a definite hope and even a promise.[7]

The inspirational literature bristles with techniques to attain peace and power which range from putting one's self "in tune with the infinite" by some intuitive twist of the psyche to sensing a deity in the chair by one's bed at night; from reconstructing failures as trifles or even as successes to whispering to one's self a promise of good things to come. These practices, finally, are represented as helpful to ordinary men and women in solving their everyday problems, but this point needs no elaboration here.

Elements of this kind may be found in a variety of other places, for example, in Augustine's *Confessions* or Thomas à Kempis' *Imitation of Christ*. But these documents differ in affirming faith unequivocally. Moreover, the salvation they envisage is not of this world. The ends they set out lack the concrete, tangible quality of such goals as business success or emotional "adjustment," and, consequently, they hardly bristle with the techniques with which the modern literature is filled. True, in a certain sense there is some overlap, as, for instance, in the case of prayer, which is often recommended; but there are obvious differences between devotional prayer and prayer that, not very subtly, is instrumental.[8] On the other hand, the literature, not only on its own recognizances, is in some sense "religious." Advertisements that promise to add six inches to the chests of scrawny men are "inspirational" in tone, but they make no pretensions to being religious and cannot qualify as inspirational religious literature.

A dominant trend in the literature through the decades is secularization; for instance, suffering has lost its "meaningfulness" and more and more is described as senseless misery, best gotten rid of. No longer divinely or transcendentally significant, suffering figures as a pathological experience calling for a psychiatrist or a minister trained in counseling. Again, the deity as represented in the literature is in process of transformation: his existence in some objective sense is no longer insisted upon, and he often approximates a consciously useful fiction. The "hero" appears more and more as the "well-adjusted" man, who does not question existing social institutions and who, ideally successful both in a business or in professional sense,[9] feels no emotional pain. Finally, there is a strong bias against the "unscientific" and for equating religion and "science."[10]

In American thought William James,[11] in effect, substituted, "I believe because it is useful" for "I believe because it is so"—or even, with Tertullian, "because it is impossible"—an idea which abounds in the inspirational religious literature. Or the best is made of both worlds in a combination such as, "I feel it is absurd; but, since it is useful, I shall insist that it is true." Thus, Henry Link avers, "I believe in God because I have found that without the belief in someone more important than themselves, people fail to achieve their own potential importance." And he adds later: "Agnosticism is an intellectual disease, and faith in fallacies is better than no faith at all."[12] Writers like Harry Emerson Fosdick will go only a certain distance in this direction. Fosdick asserts:

> The explanation of the rise of cults like Christian Science and New Thought is obvious. While the old-line churches were largely concerning themselves with dogma, ritual, and organization, multitudes of folk were starving for available spiritual power with which to live. These cults arose to meet this need, and with all their mistaken attitudes . . . they have genuinely served millions of people by *translating religion into terms of power available for daily use.*[13]

But if Fosdick is willing to go only thus far, others are willing to go beyond him. The literature consistently emphasizes "God-power" as divine flow into men, sustaining and aiding them in some materially useful sense to the point where the deity often becomes simply a psychological device. The strain toward instrumentalization is so strong in Peale, for example, that one must by inference from his work assign to God as a primary function the dispensing of divine vitamins to men eager for health and wealth.

A kind of spiritual technology has also been developed, inseparable, of course, from the instrumental element. Standard religious procedures like prayer are constantly recommended, although often with a characteristic twist, as in Peale when he urges: "Learn to pray correctly, scientifically. Employ tested and proven methods. Avoid slipshod praying."[14] Self-exhortation, another frequently suggested procedure, undoubtedly has affinities with more "classical" religious procedures, as in "I do believe," "Christ is with me," "In everything I do God helps," "I cannot lose." Again, stress is placed on special psychic states, perhaps with physical props simultaneously suggested —for example, a state of receptivity to "God-power." A notable set of recommendations depends upon converting spiritual principles into magic. Thus, as in some of the work of Lloyd Douglas, which is frequently only a fictional transcript of inspirational religious literature, he who gives without letting anyone know it is repaid a thousandfold, both magically and materially; he becomes a great success. An outcome not only of impossible physics but—in the light of the principle, "cast your bread upon the waters" and cognate exhortations— of a dubious spirituality, this can be described as spiritual technology.

Other trends include, as the quotation above from Fosdick illustrates, a definitely antiritualistic,[15] antidogmatic, antiinstitutional (antiorganizational) strain. The stress is most emphatically on religious "experience," as might be expected.

In marking the transition from latent to manifest functions of religion, one must distinguish between a *primary* and a *secondary* religious sequence. A good enough text for the primary sequence is afforded by the biblical prescription and promise, "Seek ye first the Kingdom of God, and all these things shall be added unto you." "Faith" is thus urged, but it is urged as primary; its possible "fruits" are only hinted at. The notion that Job might have been seeking to be "well adjusted" simply on the basis of the Book of Job is incongruous. The primary religious sequence may be roughly rendered, then as follows: Faith → Action → "Results" (for example, emotional equanimity.)[16]

But the modern inspirational literature more or less deliberately reverses this sequence. It starts from the observation (here assumed to be correct) that what is loosely called "faith" *can* bring about "peace of mind" and cognate desired ends. It does not, so to say, start with "the Kingdom of God," that is, with what may be called "classical" religious belief, because the belief is thought to be *true*. (Of course, it may incidentally hold out for the truth of such doctrine as it happens to retain.) It relies on a secondary sequence that begins with a projection or presentation of the desirability of all manner of "good things," mainly wealth and emotional or physical health. This secondary sequence becomes, then, "Results" (in prospect) → Action → Faith (or, possibly, also "Results" → Faith → Action), "action" being largely on the lines of spiritual technology. The modern spiritual technology may in a number of ways be a substitute for older religious ritual. If it is acknowledged that at times, when men have believed sincerely and devotedly, serenity or calm has come to them, it has clearly often come as a *by-product*. Serenity, calm, and the like have been latent functions of religious faith and devotion. It is not necessary to claim that they have been *unqualifiedly* latent; differences of degree may well be crucial. But the inspirational religious literature makes these latent functions of religion manifest and pursues them as aims.

The shift from latent to manifest raises the question: Can the same "results" be obtained? A task facing sociological theory is the classification and explanation of cases in which the transition has different kinds of results. If, say, factory workers can be inspired by a demonstration of the full nature and final uses of the product to which their seemingly disjointed individual efforts have led, it does not follow that an analogous service will always be performed by a demonstration to the religious that their efforts to "find God" afford them "peace of mind." Nor is there any reason to think that faith will be enhanced if it is also shown, directly or by implication, that gaining peace of mind is the point of religious practice in the first place. Here, too, differences of degree are important. That the inspirational religious literature does not always make an outright and unqualified shift from latent to manifest but often stops short of an uninhibited assertion that the *object* of faith is to attain power or peace of mind is of sociological interest.

But the sheer fact that there has been a shift on the lines indicated is easily documented and, for that matter, not only in the inspirational religious literature. Thus, Marshall Sklare notes a similar development in Conservative Judaism:

> According to tradition, the Jew should observe the Sabbath because it is God's will that he do so. In appealing for a reinvigoration of the

holiday. Conservatism, however, speaks in terms of *social utility*—in this case the potential contribution of observance to better mental health. Only secondarily is it suggested that the Sabbath may have something more than therapeutic significance, and, furthermore, no Divine sanctions are inferred. The performance of a religious obligation becomes a technique for achieving personality adjustment.[17]

Thus, curiously, the religious begin to look on their own activity in the manner of functionally oriented sociologists and psychologists. The question is whether, in doing so, they do not endanger the religious function; or perhaps these are all signs that faith has already lapsed, the efforts to exhibit its virtues being proof. In this connection it is pertinent to look back to a recent paper by William Kolb, who poses a "moral dilemma" for sociologists of religion who affirm the "integrating" function and necessity of belief in ultimates while themselves holding that belief to be illusory:

> To spread the idea that a belief in ultimate validity of values is necessary but illusory would be to destroy society through destroying or confusing this belief. Yet to urge people to accept the idea that there is an ontic realm of values while believing oneself that such an idea is false is deliberately to deprive people of the knowedge necessary for their freedom and dignity.[18]

Many of the purveyors of inspirational religion may represent a kind of halfway house. At one extreme we would find followers of the "old-time religion," unreserved believers that their creed has objective validity, who, at times, incidentally reap material benefits from it. At another extreme, are "positivistic" functional sociologists, quite prepared to find religion increasing the solidarity of the group, drawing the deviant individual back to it, and so on, while unconvinced themselves. Inspirational religion is somewhere between these extremes, somewhat fluctuating and unsure, yet with a powerful instrumental bent. Faith, again, is "the answer"—enjoined in the first instance not because the religious content that it affirms is above all "true," but just because it is "the answer." The concentration on "the answer," the results, already half-suggests an "illusion." The presumed primary "truth," put into the background from the very absence of attention to it, becomes the more dubious the less stress it receives and the vaguer it gets. The impulse to make religion "useful" is understandable, but the deliberate effort to do so may be self-defeating.

NOTES

[1] Grateful acknowledgment is made to the Center for Advanced Study in the Behavioral Sciences, Inc., and to the Laboratory of Social Relations of Harvard University for their support of the project which this paper reports in part. We are also grateful to Miriam Gallaher, Margaret Swenson, David Feldman, and Bruce Finney.

[2] A two-page advertisement in the *New York Times Book Review* (April 8, 1956) announces that Peale's *The Power of Positive Thinking*, "the best-loved inspirational book of our times, reaches its 2,000,000 copy anniversary." A generation ago it could be remarked that "few realize that the field of religious books often furnishes the most spectacular and continuing records in book sales. While novelists may vie with each other for records of a hundred thousand, there are continually springing up in the field of religious books titles that go far beyond that, and even into the million" (*Publisher's Weekly*, February 19, 1921, p. 513).

[3] See, however, Everett C. Parker, David W. Barry, and Dallas W. Smythe, *The Television-Radio Audience and Religion* (New York: Harper & Row, 1955), for a sociological analysis of the output of inspirational religion on television and radio in New Haven. Other discussions are: William Lee Miller, "A Passionate Faith in the Great Whatever" (review of Edward R. Murrow's *This I Believe*), *The Reporter*, X (April, 1954), 46-48, and "Some Negative Thinking about Norman Vincent Peale," *ibid.*, XII (January, 1955), 19-24; and Gustave Weigel, "Protestantism as a Catholic Concern," *Theological Studies*, XVI (June, 1955), 214-32.

Detailed statistical verification of some points made here will be provided in a forthcoming paper, "American Inspirational Religious Literature, 1880-1955."

[4] The article reports part of a study of a sample of over thirty best-sellers published since about 1880.

[5] Individual writers differ; e.g., there are marked differences between Peale and Harry Emerson Fosdick and between them and Bruce Barton or between all three and British writers who have found a sizable American public, like Harold Begbie, who in *Twice-born Men* (Boston: F. H. Revell, 1909) praised the "inspiration" afforded the poor of the London slums by the Salvation Army more than a generation ago, or like Daphne du Maurier, who ranges herself, in *Come Wind, Come Weather* (New York: Doubleday, & Co., 1940), with the followers of Frank Buchman. Catholic writers, like Bishop Sheen, are in quite a different universe, to which the characterization below will not apply well. This should not, however, suggest that there are no important resemblances between Catholic and other writers; many, for example, share the view that "social salvation" or social reform is to be achieved more or less exclusively through the reform of the individual and

increased numbers of reformed individuals. Thus, Bishop Sheen, who avers that "world wars are *nothing but* macroscopic signs of the psychic wars waging inside microcosmic muddled souls" (*Peace of Soul* [New York: Perma-books, 1954], p. 8) (italics ours), allies himself on this point with Daphne du Maurier and Henry C. Link.

6 Quoted from *Parade: The Sunday Picture Magazine*, September 19, 1954, by Will Herberg; *Protestant—Catholic—Jew*, New York: Doubleday & Co., 1956, p. 282.

7 So Emmet Fox: "If only you will find out the thing God intends you to do, and will do it, you will find that all doors will open to you; all obstacles in your path will melt away; you will be acclaimed a brilliant success; you will be most liberally rewarded from the monetary point of view; and you will be gloriously happy" (*Power through Constructive Thinking* [New York: Harper & Row, 1932]), p. 23.

8 A qualification rather unusual in the literature is: "Too often the whole value of a prayer is judged by emotional awareness of change in one's inner states, and if one does not feel differently after having prayed, he begins to wonder if there is anything to it." The writer adds, in even more unusual vein, that "to make such a test is to forget that prayer is directed toward God, not toward ourselves" (Georgia Harkness, *Prayer and the Common Life*. Nashville: Abingdon-Cokesbury Press, 1948, p. 66).

9 Bruce Barton in one strategic sentence sets off two dominant strains in the literature in speaking of the life of Christ: "Stripped of all dogma, this is the grandest achievement story of all" (*The Man Nobody Knows*. Indianapolis: Bobbs-Merrill Co., 1925, p. 9). Surprisingly little attention has been given by sociologists to the success theme and the support for it in American religion, especially in view of the leads given by Weber and Tawney. The Reverend Russell H. Conwell's "Acres of Diamonds" speech, with its forthright assertion that "the foundation principles of business success and the foundation principles of Christianity, itself, are both the same" (*Acres of Diamonds*. New York: Modern Eloquence Corp., 1901, pp. 138-68 at p. 148) is a pertinent and well-known item, but Weber would also have been interested in numerous cognate items, such as the contention of Mrs. Stetson, the Christian Scientist, that poverty is a form of evil and error, while prosperity is both symbol and consequence of spirituality (see E. S. Bates and J. V. Dittemore, *Mary Baker Eddy: The Truth and the Tradition*. New York: A. A. Knopf, 1932, p. 381).

10 Perhaps simply an exaggeration of an already fundamental strain in Protestant philosophy of religion and theology (cf. George F. Thomas, *Protestant Thought in the Twentieth Century*. ed. Arnold S. Nash, New York: Macmillan Co., 1951, pp. 99-100).

11 Cf. his *Varieties of Religious Experience*. New York: Longmans, Green & Co., 1902 and *Essays on Faith and Morals*. New York: Longmans, Green

& Co., 1949. From Ja. :s comes, apparently, much of whatever intellectual stock in trade the inspirational literature manifests. "Believe," he says, at one point, "that life *is* worth living, and your belief will help create the fact" (*Essays on Faith and Morals*, p. 31). However, the literature, taking the stance that "faith is the answer," hardly bothers with instances in which the most devoted faith has not brought emotional calm or brought it only after long struggle, such as are often found in James.

12 *The Return to Religion.* New York: Macmillan Co., 1936, pp. 34, 63. This may also be simply an exaggeration of trends found throughout American Protestantism (cf. Willard L. Sperry, *Religion in America.* New York; Macmillan Co., 1947, pp. 153-54.

13 *As I See Religion.* New York: Harper & Bros., 1932, pp. 17-18 (italics ours).

14 *A Guide to Confident Living.* Englewood Cliffs, N.J.: Prentice-Hall, Inc., 1948, p. 114.

15 Cf., e.g., E. Stanley Jones: "Nothing is essential but God, and no rite or ceremony is essential in finding him" (*The Christ of Every Road.* Nashville: Abingdon Press, 1930, p. 150).

16 An anthropologically or psychologically simplistic view is not being suggested. If "faith" can lead to "action," under "action" including ritual or ceremonial behavior, there is no implication that this is a *necessary* sequence. It is quite possible for "action" to reinforce "faith" or for each to reinforce the other. Moreover, it is not suggested that a *necessary* outcome of "faith" is "peace of mind"; merely that this is *sometimes* the outcome.

17 *Conservative Judaism* (New York: The Free Press, 1955), pp. 121-122. Sklare also quotes from a wall poster that avers the Sabbath has afforded the Jew "a blessed opportunity for personality adjustment" and the opportunity, furthermore, "to preserve our psychological, physical, and spiritual equilibrium" amid the tensions of daily stress (*ibid.*, p. 122).

18 W. L. Kolb, "Values, Positivism, and the Functional Theory of Religion: The Growth of a Moral Dilemma," *Social Forces,* XXXI (May, 1953), 309.

RELIGION AS A SOURCE OF
MENTAL AND SOCIAL HEALTH

REINHOLD NIEBUHR

We may readily assume that three-fourths of our social workers in this country function under secular auspices. The percentage for case workers is probably even higher. Those who work under religious auspices are prompted, both by their own convictions and by the traditions of the organization to which they belong, to take cognizance of religion as a force in the lives of the people to whom they minister. The secular social workers are more inclined to disregard religion. Some of them, who have come in contact with the deleterious effects of certain types of religion are even hostile to it. In another chapter we shall consider the validity of this critical attitude toward religion. But a discriminating attitude toward the forces of religion which we find among those entrusted to us is of equal importance for all of us, lest we destroy or remain oblivious to resources which we might well use for the redemption of human life from chaos to order.

Religion is first of all a force of order and unity in the lives of individuals. Men differ from brutes, in that the impulses of their lives do not possess a natural and inevitable harmony and unity. There are dozens of different ways in which the forces with which we are endowed by nature may be integrated. The dynamics of life may be directed into many different channels, according as personal inclination and family and national tradition, prompt the choice of a dominant interest or sanction a particular type of behavior. Any one of many varying impulses may become the organizing center of a life, and the other impulses may be grouped around it in many patterns and configurations. The unity and order of a life depend upon the

Reprinted from Reinhold Niebuhr, *The Contributions of Religion to Social Work*, N. Y., Columbia University Press, 1932, by permission of Columbia University Press.

emotional power and the moral inclusiveness of that life's guiding principle. If the character of an individual be centered on a primary impulse, such as sex, for instance, the principle of unity may be powerful, but may lack the inclusiveness to bring order into life. If loyalty to the family be the unifying principle of life's impulses, the sex impulse will take its important, but subordinate, place among many others, though family loyalty may not be inclusive enough to give a satisfactory organization of life for all purposes. Ideally, religion is the commitment of life to the highest values, conceived as the will of God. The moral potency of Christ in the Christian religion is derived from the fact that he is to the religious imagination the symbol of the best that life can be. The individual who commits himself to Christ usually does not, and may never, fully understand the significance of all the ethical positions which are associated with the historical Jesus. Sometimes the symbol remains devoid of any specific moral meaning. It stands in general only for the good life, the specific meaning of which is given by the problems which the individual faces and the circumstances in which he stands. To a converted drunkard, the conversion experience, in which Christ is accepted as the savior, simply means that the will to be master over an anarchic impulse is supported by the whole emotional force of the individual. The more purely personal the religious symbol, and the more immediate the relation between the religious object and the individual, the more powerful is the emotional force which is placed behind the integrating force of religion.

Miss Beatrice Hinkel observes:

> From a study of the lives of mystics and from many other recorded experiences we may discover, in the struggles and emotional states which involve the total being, a use of religious forms and beliefs as a special reconciling medium, through which there was gained a deepened consciousness and a more harmonious functioning on a level higher than that of the former discordant tendencies. When, however, instead of an interior personal relationship toward religious symbols, they represented merely a collective dogma or traditional form into which the person was born, their value was only that of an authority and discipline imposed from without.[1]

The religion with which we usually come in contact is of the dogmatic and traditional variety. While Miss Hinkel is right in suggesting that this kind of conventional belief is not powerful enough to resolve active conflicts in the lives of individuals, it is nevertheless serviceable in averting such conflicts and preserving lives from disorder. Its therapeutic value may be small, but it is nevertheless potent as a preventive. Stereotyped religion is a very conservative force. It is therefore frequently dangerous to a soicety which must face new situations, and is at the same time inhibited from changing its *mores* because these are sanctified by religion. This very religion, may, however, be a wholesome force in the lives of individuals who, but for it, would become victims of life's anarchic impulses, with no force strong enough to direct the multifarious impulses of life into a central channel. Irwin Edman, in analyzing the chaos in which many modern individuals live, has wisely observed that a crazy pattern for life is better than no pattern at all.[2] It is a significant fact that the percentage of crime in our cities is much higher among children of immigrants than among immigrants themselves. The moral and religious traditions of the newcomers, usually formed in European peasant life, may be inadequate for the larger problems of an urban civilization, but they prevent the first generation, among whom they have not disintegrated, from making shipwreck of their individual lives. In the second generation, the "acids of modernity," the conflict of various competing cultures and religious traditions, and the disintegrating effect of urban life upon all religious and cultural traditions, emancipate the young people from any discipline powerful enough to order their lives. Oswald Spengler has made a convincing analysis of the decadence of culture and morals which inevitably results from the impersonal relationships of urban life, producing footloose and rootless individuals who fall into chaos because they are not integrally related to any great tradition.

It is always possible to a few individuals to live by a rational discipline, which borrows from various religious traditions but is subject to none. It may be doubted whether such discipline ever produces the vitality characteristic of a high religious mandate, except when it, as T. S. Elliot suggests, lives parasitically upon the religious convictions of the past. But whatever may be possible for a small group of intellectuals, the masses of men need to have their lives ordered by religious convictions. Sometimes, as in the case of communism, the convictions are avowedly nonreligious, but the avowal does not make them so. As long as they transcend the bounds of rationality, as must all ultimate affirmations about what life is and ought to be, they are religious. Life itself is not rational. Reason may refine and qualify our central convictions and redirect and divert our central loyalties, but the loyalties themselves are religious because they spring from either primary or inherited conceptions of the meaning of life and the goal of existence, these invariably implying an ultrarational affirmation.

A very wise social worker of my acquaintance, himself quite irreligious, has always made it a practice, when dealing with problem boys, to strengthen their religious heritage. He has felt that this offered him a fulcrum which could not be replaced by any other force. The crime problem of American cities, which we try to solve by ever greater police vigilance, is really only a symptom of the spiritual chaos in which the average urbanite lives. It is more accentuated in American, than in European cities, because in Europe the city is still organically alive to a national religious and cultural inheritance, which does not exist for the sons and daughters of immigrants in our American cities. It is a question whether a mechanical civilization like our own, which destroys the cultures of the past, will be able to form a new religious culture, relevant to the problems of our own life. If it cannot, we had better hold to traditional disciplines as long as we may, lest confusion become worse confounded.

If traditional religion is able to prevent chaos, a vital religion is able to resolve it. The experience of conversion which rationalized types of religion tend to discredit and which conventionally unified and integrated personalities find irrelevant to their needs, has always been a potent force in bringing order out of confusion for those who, having become victims of their passions, have failed to achieve a decent order and unity in their lives. Modern psychotherapy may be superior to the religious evangelist, in that it makes a scientific analysis of the conflicts which need to be resolved in the lives of individuals. The religious revival created a powerful emotion which sometimes dissipated conflicts without analyzing them, but which at other times failed because it did not deal accurately with the specific problems which individuals faced. Nevertheless, this failure was not always so fateful as one might believe. Religion, with its sense of dependence upon a Supreme Being, with its emotional commitment to the will of that person, with its belief in the benevolent aid of that person for the achievement of our highest aims, is able to create a white heat of sublime emotion which devours all lesser passions and interests, leaving the soul purged of its distracting and confusing preoccupations and redirected toward the highest goal that it is able to conceive. This goal, regarded as determined by the will of God, may not be the highest possible goal which the rational analysis of a particular moral problem would offer; on the other hand, it may on occasion be higher. It may suggest an altruism which prompts a giving of the self beyond anything that a cool and calculating reason would suggest.

Real religious conversion, if it follows the certainties and assurances implied in the Christian religion, contains another element of great therapeutic value, though this is an element which sophisticated people understand very little—the assurance of grace and forgiveness. Modern thought is too deterministic and too impressed with the sequence of cause and effect to have any great confidence in this assurance. It is particularly critical of it because religious grace has so frequently degenerated into magic. It must be admitted that even when this does not occur, even when the religious experience of grace and forgiveness is preserved as a personal mystical experience, it has its moral dangers. It easily hampers moral effort, and offers men a short cut to that peace which ought to come only to those who have made a valiant effort. Nevertheless, it rests upon experiences of life and satisfies necessities, much more real than the sophisticated modern can realize. The idea of the love of God, which forgives sins and gives us the assurance that "though your sins be as scarlet they shall be as white as snow," is not purely a figment of the imagination. It is the religious symbol for a real force which reveals itself in life, the healing force. Even in nature there are healing and redemptive forces. The tree struck by lightning need not always perish: the rent in its side may be covered and its bleeding stopped by nature's own forces. How could a great urban community exist without asphyxiating itself, were it not for a generous alchemy of nature which purifies the polluted air? In the sphere of human and moral relations, the love of those who are nearest and dearest to us and who do not lose confidence in us in spite of our weaknesses and failings, is, and has always been regarded by the religious imagination, as a symbol of the benevolence and the forgiving love of God. What religion does is to heighten and to give cosmic significance to the fact that there are healing and redemptive forces at work in life, and that Omar's mournful conclusion:

> The moving finger writes; and having writ,
> Moves on, nor all your piety nor all your wit
> Shall lure it back to cancel half a line
> Nor all your tears wash out a word of it,

is not really true. For all who have fallen into confusion and who have become the victims of circumstances and of their own passions, there is a tremendously helpful and therapeutic value in the assurance of religion that the past can be conquered and need not tyrannize over the present or the future. The social worker who does not understand the mysteries of life out of which this assurance is born, and who regards this whole aspect of the religious life as a relic of a superstitious past, will never be able to make the redemptive forces in religion fully available to those who are in need of them.

Religion may be a resource not only to those who suffer from inner confusion, but to those who have become the victims of untoward circumstances and who face the perils of an uncertain and an insecure existence. There is a sense of security in religion. The religious person is able to cultivate an optimism, which, in its more decadent forms, creates romantic illusions about the goodness of life, with which the facts do not square but which in its purer and more classical aspect is simply a kind of heroic courage which appeals from the immediate to the ultimate in life. About the therapeutic value of this religious sense of security, it would be well to let a psychotherapist speak:

> In this place I need only indicate the close connection between restfulness of mind, so essential to the cure of nervous ills, and that characteristic of religious devotion. "They that *wait* on the Lord shall *renew* their strength." There is the alternation of repose and work, and the insistence of the source of strength being of a psychical and not a physical character. Christianity also teaches that to learn to rest, not only in moments snatched from our work but by keeping a mind free from worry and anxiety, neither caring for the morrow nor fearful of the forgiven past, is to give ourselves the opportunity of drawing on that "ample re-supply" which comes to those who do not fear to expend their energy for others. Life will throb within and through us, but our souls will be in repose.
>
> The religious writings of men of old constantly emphasized confidence and cheerfulness as the keynote to strength. "In quietness and confidence shall be your strength." "Let not your heart be troubled." "Be not anxious." "Be of good cheer, I have overcome the world."

"Say unto them of a fearful heart, 'Be strong, fear not.'" Such words as the following are literally fulfilled before our eyes in a shell-shock hospital of the present day. "The eyes of the blind shall be opened, and the ears of the deaf be unstopped. Then shall the lame man leap as an hart and the tongue of the dumb shall sing. They shall obtain gladness and joy, and sorrow and sighing shall flee away." Accurately and wonderfully these words describe both the treatment by the suggestion of confidence and its effects, as well on the body as on the mind.

This power which the Church has lost is being rediscovered, but along different lines. The psychotherapist, who is a physician of the soul, has been compelled to acknowledge the validity of the practical principles of the Christian religion, though he may or may not accept the doctrines on which they are said to be based.

Speaking as a student of psychotherapy, who, as such, has no concern with theology, I am convinced that the Christian religion is one of the most valuable and potent influences that we possess for producing that harmony and peace of mind and that confidence of soul which is needed to bring health and power to a large proportion of nervous patients. In some cases I have attempted to cure nervous patients with suggestions of quietness and confidence, but without success until I have linked these suggestions on to that faith in the power of God which is the substance of the Christian's confidence and hope. Then the patient has become strong.[3]

The critic of religion will pounce upon this aspect of the religious life and make some rather telling charges against it. He will say that it propagates illusion and offers men the opportunity to escape from the real, into an imaginary world, that it perpetuates a childish sense of dependence and prevents men from reaching full emotional maturity; and that it tempts men to accept untoward conditions in social life with greater equanimity than is good for them. All these charges contain a measure of truth, but the religious sense of security is not so easily to be disposed of. There is illusion in religious optimism only if the hard facts of life are denied, and there is escape only if the difficulties of the moment are not met. In the face of history, with its evidences of the splendid heroism of men and women who have believed that "underneath are the everlasting arms," it would be foolish to maintain that confidence in the ultimate beneficence of life and the cosmos incapacitates men from dealing realistically with their immediate problems. It may give them the very serenity and poise which they require to deal with them adequately. Their very faith in the goodness of life may be self-validating by releasing within themselves and within other men energies which will make them more nearly equal to the tasks which confront them. Human resources are never of fixed quantity or potency, and what men are potentially is just as real as what they are at a given moment. The ultimate affirmation of religion about the goodness of God remains, of course, a hypothesis of faith which can never be proved to those who are preoccupied with the chaos and evil which life reveals; neither can it be disproved to those who have felt it validated in their own inner experience. That is the character of religious faith; it must remain ultrarational to the end, because it makes the world that is external to man revelant to his enterprise, an absurdity according to every canon of pure rationality, but an absurdity which has in it the root of ultimate wisdom, and which is perpetrated by many unconsciously, even while they disavow it.

The charge that the optimism and the sense of security of religion inhibit men from dealing realistically with, and resisting bravely, the social evils from which they suffer, is perhaps the most serious and most plausible indictment which can be brought against it. The fact is that the religious strategy of life is admirable for dealing with circumstances which are immutable, but not so admirable when conditions are mutable and wait upon the will of man to change them. It is a virtue to know how to bear adversity bravely and to know "how to be abased and how to abound"; but if adversity should be due, not to capricious circumstance or the blindness of nature, but to the stupidity of man and the injustice of society, the virtue of religion becomes dubious. The fact is that the religious approach is much better suited to cope with the problems of man in nature, than those of man in society, *i.e.*, it is more nearly adequate to the task of wresting victory from defeat in man's unequal struggle with the hostile forces of the natural world, than to the task of making human society habitable for the human spirit. The radicals who insist that religion is an opiate for the people are partly right; and they will never know that they are partly wrong until they have built their ideal society. Then they will discover that even there men will suffer from disease, face death, confront untoward fortune, and endure many indignities from a world which is partly beneficent, but also hostile to human enterprise. "Man," said Robert Louis Stevenson, "is not destined to succeed; failure is the fate allotted to all men." In the sense that this is true, religion will always have a word to say about the manner in which failure can be turned into victory; and it will be scorned by men only in those brief periods in which they imagine that all the ills of mankind can be eliminated by building a new social order. All this does not change the fact that in those particular periods of history when old societies are crumbling and new ones must be constructed, periods such as the one we are living in now, religion will frequently be a force of reaction, because the tranquility and security which it creates may transcend all vicissitudes of time and tempt men to an attitude of detachment from the historical and social problems which they ought to face. Yet religion is not the only force, the virtues of which may be turned to vices by undue emphasis or inopportune application. The virtues remain virtues, whatever perils may inhere in them.

> Religious faith [declares Dubois, of Berne, himself an agnostic] would be the best preventative against the maladies of the soul and the most powerful means of curing them, if it had sufficient life to create true Christian stoicism in its followers. Feeling himself upheld by his God, he fears neither sickness nor death—he remains unshaken in the midst of suffering and is inaccessible to the cowardly emotion of nervous people.[4]

Thus far we have dealt only with the resources of religion for the mental and spiritual health of individuals; yet religion may be a source of social health as well. In the larger community problems, the limitations already observed operate, of course; and in addition there are the denominational divisions of religion, which frequently rend the life of the community with strife and prejudice. Religion too easily endows with undue sanctity, in its social influence in intergroup relations, the group with which it is associated. But the fact that it hallows the life of the group in this way, makes it a wholesome influence in intragroup relations. A community which feels its customs and ideals to be derived from religious principles, which expresses its communal spirit in religious terms on festive occasions, such as seedtime and harvest and the anniversaries of an heroic past, has its entire life lifted to higher levels and gains a stability which a secular culture can never supply. Furthermore, there is in religion an emphasis upon mutual forbearance and forgiveness which may, if there is any real vitality in religious life, operate to mitigate the inevitable frictions which occur in community life. In all true religion there is a sense of humility and contrition which operates to destroy the natural moral conceit from which all men suffer, or to which all men are tempted. "Why," said Jesus, "beholdest thou the mote that is in thy brother's eye, and considerest not the beam that is in thine own eye?"[5] That insight which prompts to a more critical appraisal of the self and a more sympathetic appraisal of the neighbor, is a true and authentic attribute of high religion, and it reveals how naturally contrition and forgiveness are related to each other. We can deal lovingly with our brothers, only if we have discovered the analogues of their limitations in our own souls. Any searching analysis of human motives and human actions should make it possible for us to realize the common and universal roots of all human frailties; but the fact is that only religious insight provides a sufficiently rigorous analysis for this purpose. It alone looks at human nature from a perspective high enough to discover the insignificance in the differences in virtue and attainment between men, and to know that "in Thy sight no man living is justified."

The sanifying influence of the religious spirit in communal life is nowhere more apparent than in family life. Religion operates best in intimate communities, because the impulses of religion lose some of their virtue when they cannot find a direct and immediate application; they must be wedded to the astute social intelligence which is needed to guide the moral will through complex social relations. In the family, where relations are intimate but where points of friction are therefore correspondingly frequent, nature herself provides forces which soften these points of friction. Yet the natural attraction of sex is not always sufficient to prevent calamity in family life. Where religion encourages attitudes of mutual forbearance and forgiveness, and where it emphasizes the sacramental character of the family union, thereby assuming its permanence, an atmosphere is created in which difficulties are resolved much more easily than in a purely secular atmosphere. It might not be too strong an assertion to say that religion has achieved its highest triumphs in family life. While divorce is steadily increasing and is quite frequent among those who are nominally religious, it is an unchallenged fact that divorce is a very rare occurrence among families in which vital religion is maintained.

Social workers must deal increasingly with the problems of broken homes, and homes near the breaking point. It is not suggested that they can supply the religious resources where the unfortunate family is in need of them. But they can make use of whatever religious resource still exists in the family; and sometimes, if they realize how powerful this may be, they may be enabled to strengthen it sufficiently to make of it a redemptive force in the imperiled unity of the family.

FOOTNOTES

1 *The Recreating of the Individual*, p. 424.
2 *The Contemporary and His Soul.*
3 J. A. Hadfield. *The Psychology of Power*, pp. 50-52.
4 Hadfield, *op. cit.,* p. 52.
5 Matthew 7:3.

THE COMMON PREDICAMENT OF RELIGION AND SOCIAL WORK

HERBERT STROUP

The usually profound, often turbid Alfred North Whitehead put the substance of rapid cultural change succinctly for his own special interests when he remarked in maturity that "every single generalization respecting mathematical physics which I was taught at the University of Cambridge during my student period from the years 1880 to 1885 has now been abandoned."[1]

What Whitehead said about mathematical physics is largely true about several prime departments of culture. Fantastically rapid changes have transformed certain aspects of human culture so drastically within the last half-century that very few, if any, persons have the intellectual power to comprehend the radically new situation confronting mankind. In addition, there looms the shadow of nuclear warfare—that ultimate human threat. Men are frightened at this juncture in history and there is little to comfort them. Religion is now much like the sleeve of an outer garment worn thin through too much wiping of a sniffling nose. Social work has lost its lofty vision of a redeemed society and has become content with itself as a profession. Science itself is no longer the jaunty peacock of men's minds. The stonemason who engraved the headstone of an infant in an English churchyard did not know that he well might have written the epitaph of the human race:

> It is so soon that I am done for
> I wonder what I was begun for.

In this present period of vast and intense upheaval life's old markers have been erased, and the game scarcely can be played intelligently. This predicament affects both men as individuals and men in

Reprinted from *Social Work*, Vol. 7, No. 2 (April, 1962), pp. 89-93, by permission of the National Association of Social Workers and the author.

their social organizations. Now more than ever they feel, and feel deeply, that they are cut off from the traditional sources of security and well-being. They are like fishermen who after an unsuccessful day find that their outboard motor has broken down and that they are adrift in the face of a fierce storm gathering on a far horizon. They are, in the parlance of today, "alienated beings."

Religion and social work, along with all sectors of society, have felt the challenge of the widescale unsettling.[2] Like persons, they have been affected by this sense of alienation.[3] They have come to realize that the traditional society which comfortably nurtured them has been transformed. They have perceived the urgent need for change on their part. The changes that are required, moreover, are profound and manifold; a mere effort at patchwork is not enough. This is an "age of reconstruction" in which the basic requirement is that men "seek truth in its ultimate depths."[4]

Both religion and social work, then, are faced with a common predicament. The rapid cultural changes of the last decades, the rise of international threats to human existence, the decay of vital reliance upon transcendent belief systems, the rising impersonality of urbanized living, the failure of politics to win the "good life" for all peoples, the growing fragmentation of professionalism, the overpowering influence of rampant bureaucracy, and other features of an age in transition—these have created the common predicament for religion and social work. As social institutions, both affecting and affected by the surrounding culture, they now must seek truth "in its ultimate depths."

The common predicament which religion and social work face today contains both concrete and theoretical elements. For present purposes three concrete issues will be discussed briefly to illustrate their nature and range: (1) relations to other professions, (2) relations to problems within themselves, and (3) relations to each other.

RELATIONS TO OTHER PROFESSIONS

As clergymen and social workers look beyond themselves they find a plethora of professions with related and overlapping responsibilities. Social work classifies itself as a "helping profession," and religion at times is happy to accept the same classification. The fact is, however, that even the helping professions—those which seek to contribute to human welfare—have greatly increased in number during recent decades. At present there are so many with such divergent and confusing mandates that it is difficult even to recall them all. There are, among others, social workers, clergymen, psychologists, psychiatrists, therapists, morticians, group therapists, community welfare organizers, nurses, occupational therapists, adult educationalists, speech therapists, physical therapists, counselors, physicians, clinical psychologists, student personnel workers, public welfare workers, administrators, researchers, policemen, firemen, counseling psychologists, government workers. Their number is legion.

The tremendous growth in the number of professions is due in part to historical factors.[5] Professionalism began under the sponsorship of the medieval church, broke away from its spiritual premises and controls as the relations between church and society changed in the Renaissance, and developed into patchwork fragmentation on a secular basis in more recent times. The substitution of the pastoral for the sacerdotal conception of the Christian ministry following the Reformation was one of the most powerful influences in the development of present-day professionalism. Instead of a unitary conception of the nature of man, society, and truth, a pluralistic and nonreligious view arose which encouraged the development of heteronomous experts. The rise of professional education apart from religion firmly established the professions. The universities, having lost their unifying vision and function, also abetted schismatic professions by providing the necessary training for each and all. Since the professions hardly had the inclination or the effective means to control themselves, they faced the prospect—and later the fact—of community regulation through governmental licensing.

The prolific growth in the number of professions also reflected the high regard Americans have for specialization of function. Emile Durkheim elaborated the principle of the "division of labor," but the United States made it into a fetish.[6] If specialization pays off on the Detroit assembly line, as it has been reasoned, then it should be an advantage for those who wish to help people. The free enterprise system and the libertarian notions that shaped the society also had their impact upon the professions.

One of the shibboleths of modern professionalism is the "whole person." Every profession seeks to aid the "whole" individual. The clergyman is not content to give assistance to less than the "whole" person. The social worker claims the same goal. Easy acceptance of this objective, however, is belied by the partisan and competitive activities and ideologies of the several professions.

The ultimate recipient of the specialized services a rampant professionalism seeks to serve is currently in a state of bewilderment, Almost any need an individual may have must be gauged against the extreme variety of persons and agencies that exists to help him.

Clergymen and social workers are faced with this concrete predicament: How shall they relate to those who also profess professional competence and authority? Can they be content to bury their heads in the morass of professionalese? Should they too seek ever higher and, therefore, more restrictive, standards for their practice? Can they rightfully claim both expertise and generic competence? How shall they conceive their function in the community in relation to the other professions?

RELATIONS TO PROBLEMS WITHIN THEMSELVES

Perhaps clergymen and social workers would be in a better position to deal with the problem of relations with other professions if they were first able to isolate and solve some of the problems they face internally. In recent years a number of instructive studies have been made of clergymen. These have uncovered the debilitating ambiguities and outright conflicts that exist within that profession. For example, the clergyman today is called upon to assume such a variety of roles as to macerate him. He suffers as did Bishop Basil of old, whose body was "torn every day in seven different parts until his skin and flesh were entirely mangled."[7] Clergymen have much to do before their house is put in order.

But social workers, too, are confronted with a number of internal problems. A few will be mentioned as illustrations of the totality, although others exist.[8] First, to what degree do the canons of scientific adequacy and objectivity obtain in social work? For the longer part of the history of social work this question was not genuinely pertinent. Social work historically was a "cause," in the terminology of Porter Lee.[9] Now it is a "function." Formerly it was a kind of applied religion or secular humanitarianism. Now it pretends to have a "functional" or scientific part to play within the field of community forces. But is it truly scientific? And by what conception of the term?

Second, in what ways is social work to be differentiated from neighboring, scientific disciplines. Social work obviously is related to, and different from, sociology, psychology, anthropology, economics, biology, and other disciplines.[10] But in what way is it related to each and all of these? What is the meaning of "social" in social work? Is social work an autonomous profession, or is it an applied science bearing the same relation to the sciences as engineering does to physics and other disciplines?

Third, what are the describable consequences of separating the "scientific" from the "skill" elements in social work? Currently, as in the past, social workers speak of their profession as combining both scientific knowledge and artistic skill. Is this a valid distinction? What results have been achieved to retard or advance the profession as a result of this dichotomy? What is the relation of social work to the non-scientific aspects of culture?[11]

Fourth, is the traditional agency organization adequate? Social work agencies are as separatistic, competitive, divisive, and specialized as the religious agencies of the community. Social work theory and education have in the past lent active support for these divisions. But social work theory and education have advanced beyond the forms by which social work is presently expressed in American urbanized communities. Do the relations between voluntary and governmental agencies require radical analysis and realignment?[12] How can the separateness of sectarian and specialized agencies be overcome for the benefit of uninitiated clients? How should concepts of "generic social work" and "teamwork" affect agency organization?

The mere presentation of these internal problems illustrates another facet of the predicament confronting social work. Similar dilemmas also are apparent for religion.

RELATIONS TO EACH OTHER

Social work and religion have for many centuries shared a common history.[13] The Golden Rule, formulated originally in the Hebrew tradition, constituted the core of expression in many forms of social concern that characterized the Jews of former times as well as now.[14] The "mighty deeds" of Jesus illustrate for the Christian the basic nature of his obligation. The early Christians also perceived the importance of caring for widows, the homeless, ransomed prisoners, the physically handicapped, and the sick. The "xenodochia" were the forerunners of all later Western institutions for the aid of the needy. Similarly in later periods the expression of religious obligations and aspirations was embodied in social service activities. The growth of social work in the United States cannot be fully understood without constant recourse to the contributions of religious persons and organizations.

In this respect, Nathan Cohen presents a sadly incomplete account of social work in the American tradition.[15] He is right in claiming that a secular humanitarianism has prominently characterized the American development. This development largely accounts for the present cleavage between social work and religion. But he is wrong in finding no other urgent, persistent, and powerful force in the development of American social work than enlightened humanitarianism.

In fact, even at present there is a strong interrelationship between religion and social work. The sheer quantity of services offered by Jewish, Protestant, Roman Catholic, and other religious agencies requires respect and understanding.[16] Moreover, many social workers not employed by sectarian agencies cherish religion—as does the citizenry generally—and seek to interpret its significance for their lives and professional practice.

The important question for religion and social work is not the fact of their relationship, but how concretely and in what detail they can and do relate to each other. This problem is pertinent, for example, in a day when social workers are concerned with urgent recruitment programs. What does motivate a person to enter the profession of social work? Are there legitimate bases in religion whereby social work could enhance its appeal to uninformed but otherwise qualified college students who both seek a challenging career and wish to satisfy non-social work values?[17] Or, what light can professional social work throw upon the work of the pastoral counselor? Can the clergyman fulfill his role as shepherd without a careful understanding of, and training in, social work?[18] In which areas should the clergyman and the social worker co-operate for their mutual benefit and that of their clients or parishioners?

By and large, clergymen and social workers today maintain cordial, sentimental, helpful, but vague relations to each other. Yet the common predicament of each requires consideration of the more precise ways in which their specialized knowledge and experience can relate to each other.

NOTES

[1] A. H. Johnson, ed., *Whitehead's American Essays in Social Philosophy* (New York: Harper & Brothers, 1959), p. 160.

[2] By religion and social work the author means religion and social work as they currently exist in the United States. Religion should be construed to include the various organized expressions of the Judeo-Christian tradition, social work the various forms of casework, group work, community welfare organization, and related aspects of professionally conceived and practical social work.

[3] Father W. Norris Clarke has described the impact of current notions of alienation upon contemporary sculpture and painting. *See* "New Images of Man," *America* (November 21, 1959), pp. 232-235.

[4] Alfred North Whitehead, *Science and the Modern World* (New York: The Macmillan Company, 1945), p. 52.

[5] For more details, *see* Herbert Stroup, "Professionalism and the Christian Faith," *The Lutheran Quarterly* (February 1956), pp. 33-42.

[6] Emile Durkheim, *The Division of Labor in Society.* Trans. by George Simpson. (Glencoe, Ill.: The Free Press, 1947).

[7] William Forbush, ed., *Fox's Book of Martyrs* (Philadelphia: The John C. Winston Company, 1926), p. 35.

[8] A stimulating account of some of these problems may be found in Alfred J. Kahn, ed., *Issues in American Social Work* (New York: Columbia University Press, 1959).

[9] Porter Lee, *Social Work as Cause and Function, and Other Papers* (New York: Columbia University Press, 1937), pp. 3-5. The following is a summary description of the differences: "The emblazoned banner and the shibboleth for the cause, the program and the manual for the function; devoted sacrifice and the flaming spirit for the cause, fidelity, standards, and methods for the function; an embattled host for the cause, and efficient personnel for the function."

[10] An illustration of the nature of one of these relations is outlined in Herbert Stroup, "The Contribution of Anthropology to Social Work Education," *Social Casework*, Vol. 31, No. 5 (May 1950), pp. 189-194.

[11] *See*, for example, Herbert Stroup, "The Use of Biography in Preprofessional Social Work Education," *Social Casework*, Vol. 33, No. 5 (May 1952), pp. 179-186.

[12] An instructive beginning can be made by reading and applying the concepts developed by Hannah Arendt, *The Human Condition* (New York: Anchor Books, 1959), pp. 23-69.

[13] An instructive history of one phase of the relation is provided by J. T. McNeill, *A History of the Cure of Souls* (New York: Harper & Brothers, 1951).

14 Lev. 19: 18-34.

15 Nathan Cohen, *Social Work in the American Tradition* (New York: Dryden Press, 1958).

16 *Social Work Year Book 1960* (New York: National Association of Social Workers, 1960), contains accounts of Jewish, Protestant, and Roman Catholic social work.

17 Reinhold Niebuhr has said: "I wonder how many social workers in America once dreamed in their youth of being missionaries." *See The Contribution of Religion to Social Work* (New York: Columbia University Press, 1932), p. 61. Novelist Morris L. West tells about a Monsignor Blaise Meredith, a dry, self-contained English priest dying of cancer. It was his profession to prepare other men for death; it shocked him to be so completely unready for his own. *See The Devil's Advocate* (New York: William Morrow & Co., 1959).

18 Seward Hiltner fully develops the idea of the clergyman as a shepherd, although he includes the social worker and others under this idea. *See Preface to Pastoral Theology* (Nashville: Abingdon Press, 1958), p. 25.

SECTION V

Stratification and Poverty

INTRODUCTION

Stratification is, in a sense, an extremely subjective topic because each of us individually has many concerns about where we fit in our society. As a matter of fact, the profession of social work as a whole has had some very strong feeling about its placement as an occupational category in our society. There is much evidence that stratification, the class placement of individuals, has a great deal to say about various aspects of their psychological or social functioning in society.

In our society, stratification, along with family and ethnic group, is one of the three major social influences shaping the personality of the individual. In addition, one would have to be quite naive not to recognize the political implications of the stratification structure of a society, particularly our own. We know very well that at this point real or imagined stratification is a major slogan or motto of political movements around the world, and of course we recognize that the major divisions of world or international political movements revolve in one way or another around diverse conceptualizations of the social class system.

Despite these political and economic implications, two things are evident: that there is no unstratified modern society, and that sociologists tend to look at stratification from a very different perspective than do, say political scientists or economists. With regard to the first, every society has a built-in stratification based on certain kinds of obvious differences in human beings. That is, every society recognizes and acknowledges differences based on what we are physiologically. The two major categories into which even the most primitive society places people are sex (all societies acknowledge that there are males and females) and age groupings. There is no society that fails to recognize that there are infants and children and young adults (whatever age groupings fall into that), full adult members of the society, and older people, depending upon just how long people live. Now this is not to say that every society does the same thing with this recognition. One society chooses to take old people and put them on an ice floe, disposing of them so that they do not become a burden, other societies choose to make old people elders who lead decision-making in the society, and some societies put them into golden age clubs so that they are away from the real, active world. However, we all

315

recognize that there are age differences. We also recognize differences in sex. What do we do about this? Once again, we don't see cross-cultural uniformity.

This is not the kind of stratification that the sociologist is interested in as far as class structure is concerned. The sociologist is interested in stratification which does not place individuals as individuals into categories, but places them as members of the family which in itself is part of a group of families which can be identified on a particular stratum. In light of this, stratification depends not only on the individual's characteristics, but in the more complex society, it depends on certain indicators or variables which we use in order to arrive at placement.

STRATIFICATION SYSTEMS: CRITERIA

What are the clues or the variables that a society might use? Berelson & Steiner list a few for us. It may not be a complete listing, but it is useful:

1. Authority — just how much authority people of a particular stratum can exercise in a society;
2. Power — political, economic, or military control;
3. Ownership of property, relation to means of production, control over land (in a feudal state). These, of course, are the criteria that Marx singled out as his main concern;
4. Economic — amount, type and resources, related to 3;
5. Consumption pattern and style of life;
6. Occupation or skill and achievement in that occupation or skill;
7. Education, learning, wisdom. We know there have been societies that have placed the scholar at the highest rung. This was the case in ancient classical China, and there was a tendency toward this in Eastern European Jewish life of the more recent past;
8. Divinity, relationship to the supernatural. Obviously, if a man can influence the gods, it is worth paying a certain tribute to him;
9. Altruism, public service, morality;
10. The individual's place in "high society," kinship connection, ancestry. This could mean inherited position;
11. Associational ties and connections, whom you know;
12. An ethnic status — one's religion, or race or nationality background.[1]

The way you see your society depends on the criteria that are used for measuring stratification. Some analysts of stratification have suggested one or another of these dimensions. Some have tried to be eclectic and include many or all. As already pointed out, Marx's thinking tended to exclude or to subsume all others under a purely economic relation to the means of production.

Sociologists in the main tend to be very strongly influenced by a classical sociological thinker, a contemporary of Marx, Max Weber. Weber could not personally, intellectually and politically accept Marx's monistic view of society and its stratification. Weber tried to refine Marx's ideas by talking not of just social class, but by talking about three distinct dimensions of stratification. These are what Weber called class, status and party.[2]

Generally in one way or another, sociologists use this triple analysis. Weber included a part of Marx's view and would say, Yes, there is a purely economic way of grouping people according to their market position. This is something like Marx's economic determinism. but Weber singled this out as purely economic. It has nothing to do with consciousness of where you stand or what group you belong to. It has nothing to do with any interclass struggle. There is economic interaction of classes, but basically this is limited to the economic way of looking at stratification. The significance of class in this sense is its effect on "life chances." He understood very clearly that if you could command a higher market value on your work, or because you have inherited wealth, you obviously had superior life chances. You could go to better schools, you had better health services, greater comforts, longer life expectancy, and such advantages. However, it did not automatically mean to Weber that people with similar life chances identify as a group. On the contrary, to him this was simply a statistical category, all those with a similar income having similar life chances. They may not even be conscious of these factors.

By contrast, Weber recognized a grouping into which society is stratified, particularly industrial society, which he called status, or prestige groups. Unlike class, status groups are highly conscious of their placement. They know very well where they belong in the stratification of the society. As a matter of fact, they guard their placement zealously.

In light of this, the key element in status groups is not that they identify certain life chances as being part of their lives, status groups relate themselves not to what they can command on the labor market, but rather the kind of lives they can lead as consumers of goods and services, which reflect their prestige level. He used for this the term "life style." The life style of status group members was very similar, and in this similarity they consciously sought out others of similar style. This was not the unconscious placement into a statistical category; this was the real thing. It was calculated. For example, if I lead my life in a certain style, I want my children to associate with others of similar life style.

The third element of stratification which Weber saw in society is what he called party and we would call power. This was the political organization of a society. Basic to the idea of power is the ability to make others in a society conform to what you want people to do, that is, to exercise influence over the behavior of other members of a society. When it comes to party, said Weber, society does not necessarily follow either the economic or the status arrangements. There are other kinds of maverick influences which operate to disrupt the neat package Marx had suggested. If a purely economic influence operated in Europe at the time of the First World War, for instance, France would never had fought Germany because the workers of France and the workers of Germany had agreed that they would not fight each other. Somehow nationalism doesn't particularly lend itself to this kind of class identity. Nationalism was not the only factor in European politics which could not be neatly subsumed, as Marx had, under economics. Marxism had conceptual problems with nationality groups, with religious parties like Christian Democrats, who for one reason or another could not affiliate with National Democrats, and ideological schisms generally. People divided on ideological grounds which somehow just did not appear to fit neatly into the Marxist model of stratification.

Weber was an astute observer of social phenomena. He recognized that whatever one of these three he looked at — whether it is class or status or power — they are not equally distributed among all members of a society. As a matter of fact, except for idealistic reasons of a temporary nature, we can't find a society where the various dimensions of stratification are equitably distributed. Be that as it may, he insisted that one could observe different pyramids of class, status and power groups, recognizing that in many, or maybe even in most cases, the three may overlap. So you may find that the same individual who is very wealthy has tremendous prestige in society because his name may be Rockefeller, and also can wield tremendous power on the social system. He can pick up the phone and get things to happen.

On the other hand, one can observe discrepancies in these areas, one can observe a wealthy criminal who does not enjoy high prestige in a society although he might wield certain kinds of power. One might observe certain kinds of occupation groups which have prestige but really do not command great economic return, such as university professors or clergymen. In a democratic society it is quite conceivable that by using democratic mechanisms, an individual politician might wield considerable power, his base coming from a large number of votes. You cannot dislodge him, yet he may have neither high status nor even personal wealth. Conceptually, then, said Weber, we are really looking at not a single stratification system, but three important variables that operate in an industrial society.

If we accept this tri-partite view of stratification, then we can understand the United States' historical view of social class. It is perhaps more than coincidence that the two industrial nations which have historically insisted that they do not have social classes have been the United States and the Soviet Union, both of which obviously do have social class structures. Once United States behavioral scientists began to analyze our stratification structure, most of what attention was paid to social class had to do with prestige: who enjoys high status and who enjoys a lower status in American society. The classical studies of American stratification, such as those of Warner and Hollingshead,[3] have rested on the presumption that prestige is the most important element to consider. A second observation that one can make historically is that most analysis of American society of a purely occupational, economic nature has been under government auspices. Few American researchers have looked at this dimension independent of the federal, state or local authorities.

The power dimension, which was neglected all these years, has become a central concern in American society today. Who really wields power in American society? It is interesting to note that no one really knows. There is considerable difference of opinion among researchers as to whether there is, as assumed, a military-industrial complex or, for that matter, any kind of unified power structure, even locally. One thing seems clear: American research in the area of stratification has tended to move away from theory and stress empirical research, to stress what is the situation in town "X" and community "Y", in this place or that. With regard to power, findings have been quite contradictory depending on where you have looked.[4] Yet the central struggle in our society today, it would seem by picking up any newspaper, is the struggle of those who feel themselves disenfranchised, whether they are students or the poor or Negroes or Mexican Americans, with the "power structure" real or imagined, of their community. There are some, of course, who would insist that there is an international power structure; others don't go that far and insist there is a national power structure; some will say that in every city there is a power structure. It must, however, be noted that the jury is really out with regard to whether there is a single power structure in any community or whether the distribution of power is a phenomenon which is peculiar to particular communities.

ROLE, STATUS AND MOBILITY

Since the question of status is of such importance in stratification, we should examine briefly Ralph Linton's concept of status and role.[5]

Status, as we have said, is related to prestige. It is the relative ranking of an individual in his society measured against all other individuals in the society. It is a conscious process even though we may not think of it all the time. Where do I stand compared to a lawyer, an M.D., a ditchdigger, a bookbinder? It is the classification that NORC has examined several times, finding considerable consensus regarding well-known occupations. The better known the occupation, the more consensus is found. Social workers, along with other secondary status professions, play the prestige game. This is one of the subtle implications of private practice and the desire to identify with the higher status model of the M.D.-patient relationship rather than that of an employee in a social agency.

The concept of status needs to be contrasted with the related concept of role. Role refers not to the prestige that a person has relative to everybody else in a society, but to the esteem he enjoys within his peer group, among his colleagues. It extends from how well a person fulfills his particular status functioning. As seen by Linton, it is the actualization of one's status, so you can have, within broad limits, a very good social worker and a very poor social worker, not in income but in how well she fulfills the role expectations of her job. The esteem of the social worker stems from how well she performs at work. No matter how well that social worker performs her task, it doesn't change her status in the society barring a change of job. She remains a social worker of whatever status is attached to that. All of us in our role enactment are not just social workers or teachers or clerks. We have a variety of statuses in the repertoire that we play at different times, depending on the context. Nevertheless, successful role enactment can only lead to esteem within our ranking in the society vis-a-vis others of similar ranking. Prestige has to do with placement in this vertical system. Thus being a Supreme Court Justice (at least until recently) involved considerable high prestige. How good a Supreme Court Justice one was had to do with one's esteem.

One gains status in two different ways. The first has been called ascribed status. Ascribed status has to do with characteristics which we do not govern individually. One is born a male — and most of us retain the sex that we were born with — so that whatever status is attached to maleness in our society stays as an ascribed characteristic in American life. There are certain ascriptions that we outgrow, for instance — teenager. There isn't much you can do about it. You may be unhappy but presumably sooner or later you outgrow it. However, there are other kinds of ascription which can be much more permanent and are related to that kind of stratification, as already pointed out, in which sociologists are particularly interested. For instance, what does one do with the ascriptive category "Negro" in American society? Can ascription ever be changed or does it automatically relegate a person to a particular stratification level? What about one's religion? What does your family name signify about you? We have mentioned Rockefeller — that's a good name. No matter what John D.'s sons do short of changing their name, they remain Rockefellers. They can be anthropologists or lawyers or bankers or governors. There is magic in a hereditary title. This is ascription. It plays a role even in our stratification placement.

There is a second way in which one's status is determined, not by ascription but achievement. This has nothing to do with whether I was born on the right or the wrong side of the tracks, whether my parents are fifth generation Americans, or whether they just got off the boat, whether they are of one religion or another or what color skin I have. It has to do with what I, as an individual, can make of myself. Thus, if one way or another I can struggle my way through school and come out at the top of the ladder, I too may enjoy high status. Status can be attained in either of these two ways. There appear to be no utopian societies where nothing follows ascription. Every child that is born begins with whatever silver spoon he has been born with. That's the first step, certainly in American society, no matter how idealistically we look at what American society ought to be. The first step is that ascription. However, we know very well that there are vast differences in whether a society places its main emphasis on the ascribed characteristics of an individual or whether it places its main emphasis on the achieved characteristics of the individual. How bright is he? How much schooling did he get under his belt? Who cares what his parents were? As a matter of fact, it's a great compliment — he was born in a log cabin and look at him now!

There is this range in all societies and the model of the extreme ascription-conscious society has been called by various terms — a caste system, a closed society or a closed class society. All three of these terms have been used. Basically, what is it they are describing? They are describing a social order in which it is predictable on the day you are born how you will die. Whatever your father was, that is what you will be. The model for this, of course, is classical India, though even in classical India there were modifications. There was some movement possible, but basically a caste system reenforced through law and custom the ascribed characteristics of the individual, built around what he was born with, utilizing a whole formalized system of what education one needs in order to live according to the ascribed status one had on the day of his birth: whom you will marry, what kind of occupation you will have, what kind of religious reenforcements will keep you in place. Variations within the religious system reflect caste lines. In classical India, the Untouchables were the only Hindus to eat meat.

It was precisely such abhorrent qualities which made them untouchable. In any case, there were formalized, legal reenforcements for this ascribed placement which kept the person in his position. Lest anyone erroneously think that the participants in a caste system were beaten and intimidated in order to accept their inferior position, we should remember that no social system can work if the participants within it are not ready to accept the system as having an inherent logic and sense to it. The members of that system who are at the bottom accept it as being correct with almost the same zeal as the members at the top of that system. Otherwise it wouldn't work. They may have come to accept it because they were afraid of the repercussions of trying to fight it, but they must have internalized and accepted its values.

In classical India, the reenforcement for this system seems to have been the religio-philosophical beliefs of the people.

In our own society, there was some remarkable intellectual juggling required to square a conception of all men as equal with rationalization of slavery based on a view of the slave as less than human. Although we needn't emphasize the religio-philosophical base for this, the caste-like features of American race relations mar the otherwise largely open class model. Especially in the South, caste lines were institutionalized with support from the laws and mores of the society. Although with hindsight we might today see evidence of resistance to this system on the part of the powerless slaves, the estimation of that resistance seems currently to be overemphasized. The percentage of slaves in uprisings was small while Elkins points out that the slave would naturally tend to identify with his master in much the same way that more recent inmates of concentration camps tended to identify with their Nazi guards.[6] There are many subtle ways in which the American Negro, even as a slave, fought this kind of overpowering dehumanization. One is the last resort of the powerless, "I am so incompetent, you can't expect much from me." That kind of presentation to the white master was very effective, so effective, it did two things. It reenforced the white master's belief in the incompetency of the slave and unfortunately blacks said this about themselves and acted accordingly so often that it reenforced the Negro's belief in his own incompetency. Thus there is a kind of self-defeating side to this ploy.

In our country, even within the caste lines, one can observe class divisions within in each racial community in a way which clearly differs from the Indian caste model. There is an interplay of caste and class rather than one or the other.

The second kind of society, as an ideal type, is one which stresses achievement as the basic criterion by which it places individuals. That is the ideal model of what we think of as American society. In reality, one must recognize, we are far from that ideal. But this is the ideal model just as we have an ideal of what the caste system was when we think of classical India. In this ideal system we would put great stock in the individual and his characteristics and worry less about inherited characteristics such as his family ancestry. If this is the model that you use, then there is much more room for a gifted person to move in the society based on his achievement. He is not held down; as a matter of fact he is not buoyed up either. You can have not only upward mobility, but greater downward mobility as well. A society marked by this great concern for achieved status rather than ascribed status will have within it a substantial percentage of individuals whose placement in the society is in a state of flux. There is reason to believe that such individuals, and as a matter of fact such a competitive society as a whole, will display less security and self-assurance than will a society where everyone has his place because of the deep-rooted traditional inherited ascribed placement. There is much more room for status anxieties and concerns.

Now this introduces the concept of social mobility, a difficult characteristic to measure. How does one determine the degree of mobility in a society? If we propose that high mobility contributes to more anxiety, how do you know where there is more mobility and where there is less? There are several measures or types of mobility that · sociologists have used. A basic measure of mobility is intergenerational, and this is perhaps the most useful measure. By checking the occupational position of an individual compared with the occupational position of his father, you can tell whether this individual has remained on a similar level, has dropped or moved up. Given this measure, you can still see that it leaves us room for considerable variability in explaining mobility trends.

For one thing, there is reproductive mobility. If you analyze Western society in general, and American society until quite recently, you will find very sharp differences in fertility among socio-economic classes. The higher you go, the smaller the number of children per family. Even if nothing else happened in the society, the fathers who are doctors and lawyers and big industrial magnates do not have a sufficient number of children to replace themselves in these higher status positions especially in an expanding economy. As a result there has been room at the top. The fertility differential is diminishing, so this kind of mobility is being cut back..

Then there is, what at least in the United States has been a very strong influence, immigration mobility. Each subsequent group coming into American society has served to push up the group ahead of it. New immigrants, whether they are migrants from overseas or in-migrants from rural areas to urban areas, have historically played this role. However, this is very much subject to both demographic trends and to our immigration laws. As we cut down the number of immigrants, obviously we diminish this pressure. If you have an increase in the rate of migration from rural to urban areas, then you get an increase in immigration generated mobility. So you can attribute a percentage of the upward mobility of those who are in the Northern cities of the United States to in-migration at present primarily of Southern rural Negro population. This trend will depend very much on just what happens in the current racial situation.

You can attempt to measure individual mobility considering only the fact that an individual is able to move from one social class to another in the course of his life. It has been suggested that individual mobility in American society has slowed down. This is related to Turner's classical theory with regard to the frontier. As long as we had a frontier and our society was open, there was always room for people to rise; now that we have no frontier, it has changed.

Berelson and Steiner have cited assembled comparative data on mobility rates in a number of countries and come up with an interesting observation. Roughly speaking, in the United States, Germany, Sweden, Japan, France and Switzerland, between a quarter and 31% of the population have a different socio-economic status than the one their fathers had. How many of these have moved up and how many have moved down does vary in these industrial nations. For the United States, 33% of our males in the non-farm labor force have been upwardly mobile. This represents sons in non-manual categories whose fathers were in manual occupational categories. The figure rarely cited, 26% are in manual occupational categories whose fathers were in non-manual categories. Comparable data from other industrial societies show some variation in upward and downward mobility rates.[7] Such international data, it must be remembered, are not necessarily accurate. Nevertheless, the mobility rate in American society does not seem to be especially slow. It also supports the view that American society does not seem to be either a classical caste system or the ideal model of an achievement class structure. There are studies which confirm that the financial backing a family has will determine how many of their children finish college and what colleges they attend, thus achieving what is already ascribed to them.

Certain features emerge with regard to the stratification in our society. The range from the top to the bottom would appear to have narrowed compared to the range in earlier American history. Secondly, we have in American society a significant gap in between the strata occurring near the bottom and the rest of society. If you want to visualize American class structure, it is something like a diamond with the top part moving further and further away from the separated bottom all the time. The division between the people below this "poverty line" and those above grows larger, not necessarily because the lot of the poor gets worse, but because they just cannot in any way catch up in society where the uneducated and unskilled are obsolete.

To understand just why this split leads to such current dissatisfaction, one must understand at least two other sociological concepts, one old and one relatively new. The old one is Veblen's idea of conspicuous consumption which we have all heard about or at least practiced.[8] Conspicuous consumption refers to the desire for status symbols, status-conveying behavior or objects (particularly material goods) which reflect one's prestige position or the prestige position that one would like to show others that he enjoys. It could involve owning a Cadillac or vacationing in the right places, or skiing or water skiing, or jumping out of airplanes, or whatever the craze is. When this operated in a community, it could be vicious enough, but now that it is broadcast from coast to coast into all our homes by television, it really gets to be a powerful force.

The second concept is a more recent one, "relative deprivation."[9] This concept suggests that it is not just how cold you are, it is how cold you think you are compared to the next individual. Even if you are better off than you were, if the other fellow has gained even more than you, you still feel worse about it. Again, thanks to our technology, we are now in a position to know more about what the other fellow has than we ever were and we can feel worse about it, too. Even if he doesn't let you into his home, society lets you know. These two ideas contribute greatly to our understanding of the urgent realities of stratification in American society.

Class Related Behavior

When we examine the literature concerning the significance of belonging to the different socio-economic classes, we walk right into a considerable difference of opinion. It is remarkable that social workers have glibly moved ahead as if this difference did not exist.

We begin with an assumption that groups of families of similar occupational levels were identified by others in their society as having certain common characteristics which they in fact actually develop through in-group identification and repeated associations. It is not too hard to visualize how this would work. For example, all the cobblers might have common interests in the price of shoes. When one's trade was the result of life-long preparation and apprenticeship of children at the side of their parents, it might not be too unexpected that the son of a cobbler will at least tend to marry the daughter of a cobbler. Whatever the specifics are, it is not unreasonable to conclude that prestige groups in society display a strong tendency to associate not only because of placement in society, but also on account of styles of life which make the members of different strata identifiable. Therefore, sociological literature developed an elaborate description of the social classes seen as idealized models, stereotypes, if you will.[10] A quick overview of the traditional descriptions of the social classes will allow us to consider some questions about this approach.

If any particular phrase is to describe the life of the upper class, it would probably be gracious living or graceful living. We know that every American community has a larger or smaller group of the wealthiest, most powerful, most exclusive families. In large metropolitan areas, they tend to cluster in specific neighborhoods or specific suburban sections. Membership is not just based on income, but also an elaborate system of associations. In reality there seems to be a dual quality that American society has identified with the upper class, perhaps even two upper classes. To people who are not upper class, the two don't matter very much. But the real upper class, themselves seem to have a fine line drawn between those whose position is inherited, stemming from their forebears, and those whom you might call self-made men who have worked their way up by means of some new undertaking, a new industrial process, "striking it rich" on the market, or whatever. This difference is a temporary one; it does not last more than a generation, and outsiders often fail to notice the differences. However, those who have an inherited position, whose forefathers were among the founders of the New England town or were plantation owners or the true Texas ranchers, cannot overlook this factor. They are not the new wealthy, like former President Johnson, who turn around and legitimate their wealth by buying a ranch, but whose source of wealth is less historic, but those who always were wealthy ranchers. In each region this historical origin of wealth may be differently based. In New England, the typical founder was the old whaler, shipbuilder or merchant whose sailing ships plied the ocean. The members of the upper class sit together on Boards of

Directors of businesses and banks, universities, social agencies and community chests, boards of education and all the important circles of policy making. They are the important decision-makers outside of government, and, of course, government cannot afford to disregard them either formally or informally. The wives of these men appear regularly in the social column. The social register generally lists a substantial percentage of them. If you are looking to identify the new rich who are not quite equal, then you must add to the social register also those who appear in the "Who's Who" listing. This would include people who have gained prominence in their own lifetime as well as those who have come through either learned professions or industrial undertakings or the arts. These are the people whose children have attended the ivy league schools or the seven sister schools. They are extremely conscious of their identification as a group because it is a relatively small group which does not replace itself. That is one of the major reasons why the division between the new rich and the old rich is temporary. There just are not enough youngsters among the old rich to provide suitable choice of spouses for their children. Girls, especially unable to marry down, often remain unmarried. The old families set the pace for the upper class, and these values are readily copied by the new rich. As a matter of fact there is a tendency to overdo among the new rich in order to establish themselves as truly belonging.

Since true status in the upper class is related to family ties and the historical position of forebears, family ties in the upper class tend toward the extended family more than they do in the typical American family. The family gatherings around holidays, the traditions, the history of the family founder who crossed the ocean or the desert or did something noteworthy, the old pioneer who started the heritage, these are the things that tie a family together. In addition, the wealth of the family generally involves the larger family group. There are many subtle reasons for this tie, some of which are simply economic.

Individual behavior is a reflection not only on the immediate family, but on the family name. It is one thing for Greenberg's father to be an alcoholic and another thing for an upper-upper father to be. In the latter case, they might move heaven and earth to protect the children of the family, seeing to it that this misfortune does not become too public. Great stress is placed on the family's traditional ties with certain educational institutions. Some members of the family must be skilled

in maintaining the assets of the entire clan. But most are free to cultivate the arts and politics, philanthropic interests, gracious living in
general. The true upper class is not driven by the pressures of the
middle class to achieve, they have already achieved. They can relax
and enjoy, so to speak. To the upper class, the college experience
is not a channel for mobility as it is for most Americans. It is a social
experience allowing the children to associate with others of their kind
in order to seek out proper spouses, to make continuing ties with the
right families, for future reference. The upper-class male is quite
knowledgeable in many areas. Perhaps the most widespread difficulties that the upper class seems to get into are not missteps with regard
to personal behavior, but a tendency toward excessive consumption
of alcohol.

Newcomers, the most recently moved into the upper class, are accepted because the class is small, but they have to prove themselves
and in so doing they imitate very carefully, with a great deal of anxiety, the standards set by the true old wealthy of the upper-upper class.
In this country, more than in most, truly wealthy people are very
uncomfortable about their position. It is remarkable that they are, if
we can judge from the clues, very eager to be accepted for themselves
and not for their wealth. So you get them very eager to be seen as
just common men with a little more money rather than the inherited
upper, upper aristocrats that they truly are. The newcomers, on the
other hand, make sure that their children develop the proper polish
necessary to legitimate their position. This has to do with removal of
the final stigmas and barriers of having worked their way up. The
children must marry the descendants of inherited position.

In short, the upper class believe very strongly in tradition, in continuity with the past and history. They are very much concerned with
family ties and lineage, and this is cemented by the sources of family
wealth. Historically they have had the opportunity, the gracious living
and dilettantism, and if we can stylize this kind of orientation, there is
a value placed on the man more than on the accomplishment. Although the children of the inherited wealthy families are raised to
believe in their own superiority, there is a defensiveness in the United
States which one does not sense about the true upper class in other
countries. This seems to be related to the egalitarianism of stated
American ideals.

When you look below, the upper middle class view themselves, as
leaders in American work. They are the trained specialists of business

and professions who make the guiding decisions for all the little people that carry out their decision-making. Upper middle class people don't speak about holding jobs; they occupy positions. They don't work; they pursue careers. This idea of the career and achievement in one's career is perhaps the central theme of the upper middle class. The upper middle class can also be seen as composed of two elements which reflect what has been happening in American industrial and commercial enterprise. On the one hand, you have the "old" middle class which are basically entrepreneurs — those with the traditional independent attitude of self-employed business and professions, the people who would not under any circumstances make their corporation a subsidiary of General Motors and become vice-president-in-charge of . . ., and the older of the professions, the doctor or lawyer. The "new" middle class are the salaried bureaucrats and officials who operate our commerce, our industry, our new professions, who are involved not in individual occupations or careers, but who are part of the "massification" of our economic undertakings. Clearly, the old middle class is losing ground very rapidly and the age of the private enterprise professional is drawing to a rapid close. The AMA seems to be fighting a valiant rear guard stand but it would appear to anyone who takes a long-range view that it is doubtful whether non-group practice can survive. Doctors, lawyers, retail merchants, all of these with a long tradition of working for themselves, are rapidly (either because they cannot compete or because their own fields are becoming so complex that they must draw upon skills of others) being absorbed into mass corporations or institutions based on the rational division of specialized functions.

This upper middle class lives in respectable apartments or large single-family homes, primarily, in the suburbs. However, most large metropolitan areas have, somewhere near the commercial center, high-rise, highly exclusive apartment buildings for those who have tired of suburban living. The upper middle class, unlike the upper class are only vaguely conscious, it seems, of their class. They think of themselves as the educated, successful, respected leaders of their local communities. They are almost all white, American born. Those of immigrant background expend great efforts in avoiding such identity. Whatever ethnicity they may have carried with them as they grew up rubs off rapidly as a result of their college experience, and business competition does the rest. They are extremely interested in the latest fashions, cars, home decor, and this year's ideas. They have a strong sense of participation in their communities and the belief that they do play a role in world affairs. The central value of the upper middle class, seems to be careers since this is their vehicle for mobility. The whole way of life has been made dependent on the husband's career which is the central fact for the entire family's status. The career takes a good deal of education in specific professional or business skills. Aside from technical knowledge, it involves a great deal of skill in manipulating people. These are persons on decision-making and policy-making levels who must deal with others. They have to mix well with semi-strangers, talk at ease, and in general be men of the world, comfortable in all types of social settings. The prerequisites of success in this kind of life involve a certain minimum intelligence, outgoing, flexible personality, a great deal of motivation to make sacrifices in order to put up with long stretches of education and to tolerate other people over you, compensated only by your ability to make decisions concerning others. Aside from specific school education, general, intellectual and social skills are vital. This kind of background is greatly enhanced by birth into a middle class family. But our educational system does enable a substantial percentage of working class children to catch on, provided they start with certain talent and move up in the system starting early enough.

Once a man has started in the upper middle class direction, he needs the right wife. He must be a success for her while she, in turn, must be an asset to his standing in the community. She has to rear his children so that they should reflect the proper style of life on him. Ideally, his wife helps him construct an isolated oasis in a highly competitive environment to which he can escape from the tensions of his career anxieties. A career based on the subtleties of bureaucratic competition obviously involves a great deal of a man's personal life — not just what he does on the job, but how he gets along in his free time with others who are important to his successful climb upward. It involves his taste in clothing, his wife, the way he deals with his business acquaintances in his private social life, the community in which he lives, the causes he is involved in, and so on.

To prepare children for this kind of life in the shifting economy that we have is not easy because the base on which the career is built keeps changing. There is new technology, new industry. The parents who are eager to have their children move in a socio-economic system are not necessarily able to say to their child, "You should become a doctor," or "You should become a lawyer," because no one can predict whether being a doctor or a lawyer is a good career for twenty years from now. Therefore, the socialization of the middle class places stress on the general social values rather than on the specific technical skills. Formal education will provide the technical skill, but you have to learn how to hang loose, you have to learn how to be outgoing, how to have the necessary social graces. The boy's basic education revolves around developing the kind of outward characteristics which will make him acceptable regardless of the specific career that he later gets into. It does entail school success, and great pressure is on these children for school success, great anxiety over examination taking, but it also involves a general personality, a general extrovert behavior. The girls, on the other hand, are socialized with an eye to ensnaring an upwardly mobile young man, and so the positives involve developing the appropriate social graces while the negatives involve learning how to stay out of trouble which will make one undesirable as a spouse. The upper middle class family is basically nuclear: just the parents and their unmarried children count. It is almost necessary to have it that way because a substantial percentage of the upper middle class are people upwardly mobile from a lower middle or working class background. As a result, their relatives may well be moving in the social system at a different pace and too-close ties to the working class brother and his family would be inappropriate for an upwardly mobile business executive. The upper middle class seem to be marked by a considerable instability, a great deal of mobility, both geographic and occupational. There are pressures on these people because they have cut themselves loose from tradition. The upper class has traditions that have meaning to it. The upper middle class does not. These are the people who were the center of attention for sociologists of the 1950's — the *Organization Man*,[11] the *Lonely Crowd*,[12] suburbia trend of study. Because they have cut themselves off from tradition, there is a tendency to accept external symbols, imitation of others, to demonstrate one's position — the right car, the home in the right neighborhood, proper clothes, the status vacation, and so on. These individuals have tended, as seen by sociologists, to epitomize the conspicuous consumption mentioned briefly above.

There are many observers of our contemporary scene who have suggested that a great deal of the intergenerational ferment today is a reaction against this kind of Brahmin preparation in American life. It is the suburban upper middle class that seems to be giving rise to the most outspoken rebellion against the system.

In summary, we do have a growing upper middle class related to changes in our technology and the need for larger numbers or a larger percentage of people in the kinds of occupations in our bureaucratic structure — government, industry, education, commerce — which demand this level of decision-making. These are increasingly employed professionals and managers who are typified in suburban life, who believe primarily in themselves — highly individual-oriented, in an individual capacity to succeed or fail according to the individual's strengths. This is very much a modern adaptation of older American values, with modifications, to allow for bureaucratization.

If the upper middle class is oriented around careers, the lower middle class, whose occupations are not that promising, don't have that much to look forward to. The white collar workers who are the semi-professionals, the semi-managers, the petty business people, the petty farmers, these people are oriented more around respectability in their style of life. Today they include foremen in our industries and skilled craftsmen in our highly unionized blue collar occupations. These are people who tend to live either in small single- or two-family homes or in small, but reasonable, apartments in our cities. Most have completed high school and probably given today's circumstances, have additional kinds of specialized education or training. They seldom make basic decisions, but they do carry out intelligently, highly technical, responsible jobs. They strive to get ahead, but it becomes very clear to the lower middle class person once he has passed through his youth that he cannot move too far up and he can only hope for the greater success of his children. They have a strong sense of superiority to the working class who have no specialties and who are readily interchangeable, in our highly rationalized technological system. They have a feeling that they cannot, although objectively there is some doubt about it. They cannot live elegantly and one of the measures traditionally suggested is that the lower middle class cannot afford the luxury of discarding something that is still serviceable because they like something else. Education is highly valued for the children and it is this class which provides perhaps the bulk of the students in commuter colleges around the country. Children of this class traditionally have been educated at great expense and sacrifice to the family. Religion plays a very important role to the lower middle class. While a larger percentage of the upper middle class maintains membership in American churches, a much higher percentage of the lower middle class actually attend church services. Their attitudes stress family stability and respectability. They are highly suspicious of those both above them and below them in the area of sexual behavior and they put great stress on well-behaved children who will not be publicly embarrassing. If you will, it is more important to be good than to be self-expressive.

Home ownership is respectable. They pay mortgages, work on their homes and do things themselves. Their home furnishings tend to be of the kind that they read about in various magazines, with a tendency toward standardization. They have a history of self-denial in order to save for whatever it is they want, although this has undergone change in this age of consumer credit. It is the lower middle class that was portrayed in *Death of A Salesman* in the home life of Willie Loman. In the extreme, the lower middle class represents not just respectability, but an actual prudery and narrowness, but for most it represents the means for Americanization. There is a great deal of ethnic origin to be traced to lower middle class families, strong stable families especially in small towns where they consider themselves the respectable solid citizens with moderate success, moderate education. It may be dull, but it isn't necessarily devoid of its satisfactions.

The problems of the upper class have rarely become the problems of social workers (a) because they have a tendency to handle their difficulties within the extended family structure, and (b) because they have the financial resources to seek out private and secretive ways of handling difficulties. The problems of the middle class have been very much the problems that social workers have dealt with in the recent past because they have been very attuned to the psychoanalytical model that social workers have suggested but also have had relatively limited funds for the luxury of higher priced private analysis. The upper middle class seems to have been in the recent past the largest consumers of psychoanalysis.

The upper-lower class or the working class is the next stratum of the society. Working class people are those who have low-paying salaried jobs. They are primarily blue clollar workers with steady sources of earned income. Formerly they were high school dropouts. Now such wage earners are usually high school graduates. There aren't too many differences from job to job and much prospect for advancement. Life in this class is routinized both on and off the job. The semi-skilled worker has no real career plans nor does he derive satisfaction from the respectability of his work like the lower middle class. His personality and his outside life are not invested in the work setting; for him it remains a job. He derives pleasure from his home and family, and looks forward to increasing his comfort as he "gets ahead." He is an avid consumer of mass entertainment and has not been very involved in community activities. He is a spectator who just wants to get by without disruptions.

The working class family is distinguished by the dominance of the family circle. Gans suggests that everything outside this circle is viewed as potentially helpful or harmful to this extended family grouping. Between spouses, surprisingly little is shared.[13]

As automation takes hold in our economic system, the working class has been faced with increasing threats to its sources of livelihood.

THE POOR AND THEIR CULTURE

We turn now to the poor who began as our most frequent clients, were largely forsaken for a period of years and have now turned into perhaps our most troubling clients. Walter Miller has suggested a list of "focal concerns" of the lower class culture.[14] While he admits that these are by no means exclusive to the poor, he nevertheless says that these are dominant. He lists six ways in which the alternatives with regard to these areas of focal concern are perceived by poor people. To this list should be added a couple of others.

The first is trouble. Here, he says, the poor tend to perceive of trouble or their relationship to trouble as either law-abiding behavior or law-violating behavior and the poor are very much concerned with trouble and how to avoid getting into it. The second area of focal concern is what he calls toughness. In the Latin tradition, it may involve the idea of "machismo." The alternatives here are physical prowess, skill, masculinity, fearlessness, bravery, daring. Opposed to this is the idea of weakness, ineptitude, effeminacy, timidity, cowardice, caution. The third area of concern that he speaks about is what he calls smartness — notice he does not say intelligence. The alternatives here: the ability to outsmart, to dupe, to con, gaining money by one's wits, shrewdness, adroitness in repartee. Verbally it may take the form of "ranking out." There is a point at which all you can do is punch the other guy in the nose. The opposite of this is gullibility (if you will, "con ability"), gaining money by hard work, slowness, dull wittedness, verbal maladroitness. The fourth focal concern is excitement. Here he juxtaposes risk, danger, change, activity as opposed to boredom, deadness, safeness, sameness, passivity. He talks about fate and its alternative. As seen by the poor, to be favored by fortune or lucky on the one hand as opposed to being ill-omened or being unlucky. Finally, the concern about autonomy. Here the alternatives as seen by the poor, according to Miller, are freedom from external constraint, freedom from superordinate authority, independence, as opposed to the presence of external constraint, the presence of strong authority, dependence, being cared for.

One must add the idea of routine drawn from Herbert Gans's *Urban Villagers.*[15] Routine-seeking, as opposed to action-seeking, Gans claims, can draw the line in a predominantly lower-class neighborhood between those who are working class oriented and above (who did not want to rock the boat and wanted everything to go along routinely) and those who were bored stiff and wanted nothing better than a moment's peak of excitement to break the monotony. Gans has also stressed the centrality of single sexed peer groups to lower class at all ages. To other classes, peer groups decrease their significance after adolescence. Add to this the debate over deferred gratification. For a long time it has been claimed that the middle class and middle class oriented learn from very early in life to postpone gratification to attain future reward while the poor want it here, want it now.

There are other concepts that have been advanced with regard to the poor, such as the difference with regard to achievement orientation. It has been claimed that the middle class child displays a high achievement motivation and the poor child does not.

Over the years, many studies of child rearing patterns suggest a growth of permissive non-authoritarian child rearing. There is evidence that child rearing has been considerably modified by the mass media in the direction of similarity in child rearing behavior among mothers of all socio-economic classes, although middle class mothers are most susceptible to these influences. Because of TV portrayals of what families are like, because of popularized articles and constant watering down, many ideas filter across class lines in a society like ours. Therefore, we cannot be sure of the degree of difference in child rearing attitudes and practices at this time.[16]

In spite of the contradictory conceptualization of distinctive class-related cultures in American society or perhaps even universally, there are certain class-related behavior differences which seem to lend themselves to objective measurement. One of these is Kinsey's finding that there were differences in sex behavior among the different socio-economic classes. So distinctive did they seem to be that there was even a suggestion that one could predict upward or downward mobility by analyzing the nature of sexual behavior in an individual. This behavior reflects not necessarily the class to which the individual belongs, but even more so, the class to which the individual aspires or with which the individual identifies. Specifically, by way of illustration, Kinsey's material suggested that lower class individuals engaged in more actual heterosexual relations, while middle class individuals used other kinds of behavior short of actual coitus for release of sexual tensions.[17]

In the nature of criminality, those acts classified by the Crime Reports of violence, tend to be more typical of lower class crime, while what Sutherland has called "white collar crime" was more typical of the middle class.[18] This, of course, is related to differential opportunities as well as socialization. We know, of course, there are variations with regard to many other kinds of phenomena.

Proponents of the culture of poverty view believe that poor people, whether in Latin America or in India or in the United States, differ from the general society. The poor are more present-oriented, they have a divergent family life style, a resentment toward all authority figures, etc. The assumption that has spread through the behavioral sciences, and the outstanding spokesman for this assumption has been Oscar Lewis, has been that you are observing a class-related variation in values.[19]

Sociologists and psychologists have been all too committed to the idea that all of this is a real picture of what the poor are like. As a matter of fact, whether American society or indeed any society, is so divided by class-oriented values that you can pinpoint the values of different strata by their socio-economic position, had almost come to be taken for granted. This reopened question encompasses the idea of "culture of poverty." To use a pun, the two sides of the debate are really whether you believe there is a culture of poverty or whether you see a poverty of culture, whether we really have an alternative cultural pattern or whether what we see is the same cultural pattern as it is enacted by people of different classes perhaps for some very sensible adaptational reasons.

From the start, not everybody had agreed. Merton's view is a good example. He has suggested that in reality what you get is perhaps the same ideal goal shared by the poor and other classes, but without equal access to the means of attaining the goal. Merton has suggested that we have numerous examples where the legitimate means for achievement may be blocked. If these means are blocked, some individuals or groups may desert the achievement goal even though they really would like it while other groups may seek illegitimate means.[20] One can use this model to understand the differences between the style of life of one class and another. Thus we might say that the values are really similar, but the means for achieving those values differ and therefore the outcome appears to be different.

If you talk about powerlessness by way of example, the lower you go on the socio-economic ladder, the less power the population commands. They are further away from the seat of decision-making, which is true of any bureaucratic structure and is also true of our society as a whole. This can give rise to a compensating tendency or pressure for autonomy. The autonomy historically within the reach of the poor has not been the autonomy derived from power to make decisions in the system. It is the kind of autonomy that comes to play on the street in "chip-on-the-shoulder" behavior. This autonomy merely gives vent to the deep resentments over being pushed around. In reality, those who are truly powerless are pushed around a great deal but can only react to the overt, physical sphere which is least important but most visible.

Hyman Rodman has suggested what he calls the "lower class value stretch." He comes to this by reviewing the literature with regard to a culture of poverty. Is there really a culture of poverty? Obviously we have two diverse views of the lower class: one that they have a different value system, and the other that they have the same value system. Rodman tries to resolve this by suggesting that in a sense, both sides have observed accurately. The lower class actually do have similar values, but are unable to fulfill in reality the values that they seek. They stretch their image of what these values are, to encompass those goals which can be achieved. So, he suggests, a poor person would like to live in a comfortable house with a room for each member of the family, he would like to have a style of life that he sees on TV Lacking that, his interpretation of the desired style of life is broadened to include instead the purchase of a shiny automobile on time payments, or a moment's autonomy perhaps at the expense of a future jail sentence, or a moment's expression at the expense of a future of paying the piper.[21]

On the other side, the ideal images of the other social classes are also not accurate portraits of the way they actually live. The middle class, if they were so convinced of deferred gratification, would not be "in hock" as they are. The number of personal bankruptcies in American society would not be so high and rising. Our whole economy would not be based on the purchasing power of a working class and a middle class living on income that they won't earn for years to come—mortgaged to the hilt. Furthermore, we see increasing evidence of cross-class influence on values and not necessarily in only one direction. Particularly among young people, there is upward absorption, so that a great many of the "in" patterns — music, art forms, expressive behavior forms — are cross-class learned. So very often the medium for this is what has been called "upper Bohemia" or the artiste or intellectual elements in American life. There is a good deal to suggest, for example, that the pattern of drug use which may have begun among lower class young people because of the need to escape has been upwardly mobile so that it has been adapted to middle class suburbia for other kinds of reasons. Given these phenomena, we don't really see the closed class value divisions which many sociologists and psychologists have suggested since World War II. There is a good reason for second thoughts concerning class values and behavior.

Until recently, social workers, applying their own class values, have viewed illegitimacy, for example, as an individual's problem. They have just begun to question this as a universally individual problem. It may involve a problem in the nature of social organization which pushes this kind of behavior pattern on to a particular individual. That does not necessarily eliminate the fact that there is a behavior problem or that we need to understand the individual psychological dynamics as well. However, it means one thing to find a teenager from the lower class who turns up pregnant, and another for a girl from the middle class who becomes pregnant. The assumption we have to make is that the girl from a middle class background is saying some very different things about herself, her family, her society, than is the girl from a lower class background. One would accept more readily the tendency for the psychoanalytic interpretation with regard to this middle class client than he would regarding the lower class client. If the middle class girl did not want to be pregnant, or did not want to be faced with an illegitimate child, she had many different "outs" which the lower class girl may not have.

One other thing that needs to be pointed out with regard to these two different perspectives on class is that most of the measures that behavioral scientists have devised—whether psychological or social measures—have tended to have a middle class bias built into them. For example, measurement of intelligence has historically had this kind of middle class bias although the instruments used for measuring intelligence have been applied with a disregard of class background. Efforts at devising intelligence tests which were either "culture fair" or "culture free" and thus avoid this difficulty, have either proven inadequate or have wound up correlating too well with the existing tests to indicate that they are not tapping into other dimensions. One of the biases built into this is the very nature of the testing situation which differs in its motivating significance to the middle class and the lower class child.

IMPLICATIONS FOR POLICY

Your position regarding the culture of poverty debate theoretically should determine the kind of program you are going to undertake, what kind of help (assuming the society genuinely wanted to help) you are going to offer the poor. Consider the following: If you say there is no culture of poverty (some of the very peple who are inclined to say there is no culture of poverty would not like to follow the logic of this to its conclusion), then what you are really saying is that you have a poorly assimilated middle class style of life among the poor. Their life reflects an inadequately absorbed general culture. The way to correct it, therefore, is to feed into their lives more "middle classness." You therefore need poverty programs or social services which are rooted in the middle class. As a matter of fact, with all of our democratic pretensions, you could logically conclude that agencies need. not self-determination, but middle class direction. The aim of such programs would be to break a continuing cycle of inadequate assimilation of middle class values. If you say this then the total society has a kind of broad obligation toward the poor. If the general orientation of our society is middle class and we have a group within the society which has been inadequately absorbed due to some kind of barrier to communication of these values, then the general society has some very serious obligations to undertake steps to improve this communication of its values. We might perhaps say to the poor as social workers have often said, that you may verbally say certain things to satisfy an emotional need but as competent social workers we understand the underlying needs. We will help you overcome your feelings. We will help straighten you out. In a sense, one might conclude that the protests of the poor that they want to run their own agencies and exercise self-determination are really a manifestation of their syndrome as clients, and essentially our stance would be that we can help if the client lets us. That is what social workers have often implied to clients—if you will allow us, we can cure you of your inadequacies. This extreme presentation is one which still assumes a benevolent attitude. If you are other than benevolent, if you want to keep people down, you might really come up with the same argument. You could use this as a ploy to hide behind, but really mean to say, "If you people have not adequately absorbed the values and opportunities that our society has for you—all these good, middle class things to which you have not caught on—then whose fault is it?" Even if you are benevolent, if you are helpful, you could reach the conclusion suggested.

On the other hand, if you are an adherent of the culture of poverty position, then you open a Pandora's box of possibilities. American society, when it initiated anti-poverty legislation, never thought through these alternatives. If you repeatedly say, as was the motto, "maximum participation," you imply acceptance of an alternative culture that exists among poor people all over the world and that American society is big enough to live with various alternatives, including the alternative of the culture of poverty. Then you could conclude from this that poor people perhaps don't need guidance from above or direction from the middle class or from what has been called "the caretakers." The only thing that is wrong with poor people living their alternative is that they are poor, so give them some money, feed some more resources into their situation, raise the bottom of the poverty level, and poverty will take care of itself. The poor will develop their own fate in accordance with their own style of life. It certainly suggests who should determine the policy of agencies dealing with poor people. The poor themselves. Who else is more expert in "telling it like it is"?

What do you do with those social norms of the poor which run into conflict—even being nice and moving over and letting the poor shape their own thing? What do you do with conflict areas where the behavior of poor people clearly violates the expectations of middle class people? To illustrate with an example, what do you do when rich and poor live in close proximity, as they well may in the heterogeneous metropolis? What do you say about those nasty poor people on the corner who keep throwing beer cans out of the window? Cleanliness, for the middle class, after all, is next to godliness, and littering is probably one of our major problems in the city. That is only a small thing. Should the middle class taxpayer think pluralism when he feels that his tax money is being used to support illegitimate children among the poor? Doesn't he that pays the piper call the tune? All of our explanations have done nothing regarding the ill will bred by these interclass value clashes.

If the majority of our society sees it as middle class, and there are people who have a sub-culture which runs into conflict with the majority, it is fairly evident that at various points where they come into contact, you are going to have friction. At least one of those points is education where the children of the poor notoriously have difficulty behaving in school the way the teachers of the poor anticipate they should. So what happens? Even if you want to be nice about the whole thing and say, "OK, you have your way, we have ours." You run into conflict at points of contact. Society's institutions must be after all based on broad spheres of consensus if they are to function at all.

There is also a sinister side that may emerge from this conflict at points of contact, once you start from the perspective of acceptable alternative sub-cultures. If you have your own and I have mine, and my way entails a nice Protestant ethic of earning my own way and nice family units that keep their problems to themselves and don't take them out into the streets, and we don't run into conflict with authority, and I like it that way, then, the society as a whole, at least that part of it which adheres to the middle class value, could very well turn its back, could very well say all right, you want your own business, you run it your way and it's not my affair. The possibilities that we come to from what seems to be greater cultural pluralism or democratic choice are perhaps less democratic than the possibilities that might emerge from less pluralistic thinking.

What has happened in reality is that we have tried to weasle out of this situation. We have gotten into anti-poverty programs without considering what the alternatives would imply. At the very same moment that you have programs aimed at facilitating absorption of middle classness among the lower class, you have other programs often involving the same individuals, which are aimed at highlighting the cultural alternatives of the poor. We have had this contradictory and unconsidered policy in effect from the beginning of the War on Poverty. Having started with a neat political plan and a catchy motto, "War On Poverty," we then found ourselves in a dilemma since behind it all, one must ask: How much diversity can and will our society tolerate? One cannot be sure that anybody at the start of this political campaign against poverty raised that question. How much pluralism can a society absorb and still remain a society? Ultimately, the question rests on that elusive culture of poverty.

The alternative models may really be extreme. While it presents us the opportunity to examine the significance of our assumptions about the poor, such extremes may not reflect reality. It seems that money alone will not change many attitudes, although there is some evidence that those individuals who do become involved in the exercise of self-determination, say in welfare rights groups, do show changes in attitude vital to breaking the poverty cycle. Whether these experiences and changes can be translated into personal style of life is another matter. If it can, would not that individual really be taking an important step toward the middle class?

NOTES

[1] Bernard Berelson and Gary Steiner, *Human Behavior*. New York: Harcourt, Brace and Co., 1964, p. 454.

[2] See H. H. Gerth and C. W. Mills, *From Max Weber: Essays in Sociology*. New York: Oxford University Press, 1946, p. 180 and, Max Weber, *The Theory of Social and Economic Organization*, trans. A. M. Henderson and T. Parsons. London: William Hodge, 1947, pp. 390-395.

[3] W. Lloyd Warner and Paul S. Lunt, *The Social Life of a Modern Community*. New Haven: Yale University Press, 1941, and A. B. Hollingshead, *Elmtown's Youth*. New York: Wiley, 1949.

4. See Nelson W. Polsky, *Community Power and Political Theory*. New Haven: Yale University Press, 1963, especially p. 67 and p. 138.

[5] Ralph Linton, *The Study of Man*. New York: Appleton-Century-Crofts, Inc., 1936, pp. 113-131.

[6] Stanley M. Elkins, *Slavery*. Chicago: University of Chicago Press, 1959, pp. 103-115; also, Kenneth Clark, *Dark Ghetto*. New York: Harper & Row, 1965.

[7] Berelson and Steiner, *op. cit.*, p. 473.

[8]Thorstein Veblen, *The Theory of the Leisure Class.* New York: Macmillan Co., 1899, pp. 25-34, 68-69, 97-101.

[9]S. A. Stauffer, E. A. Suchman, L. C. DeVinney, S. A. Star, and R. M. Williams, Jr., *The American Soldier: Adjustment During Army Life.* Vol. I. Princeton: Princeton University Press, 1949, pp. 124-130.

[10]This material is based on Chapter VII of Joseph Kahl, *The American Class Structure.* New York: Rinehart & Company, Inc., 1957. However, most texts on stratification give attention to such ideal typologies.

[11]William H. Whyte, Jr., *The Organization Man.* Garden City, New York: Doubleday and Co., 1956.

[12]David Riesman, Nathan Glazer and Reuel Denney, *The Lonely Crowd: A Study of the Changing American Character.* Garden City, New York: Doubleday and Co., 1956.

[13]Herbert Gans, *The Urban Villagers.* New York: Free Press of Glencoe, 1962, pp. 45-53, 120-121.

[14]Walter B. Miller, "Implications of Urban Lower-Class Culture for Social Work," *Social Service Review,* Vol. 33 (1959), pp. 219-236.

[15]Gans, *op. cit.,* pp. 28-31.

[16]Urie Bronfenbrenner, "Socialization and Social Class Through Time and Space," in *Readings in Social Psychology,* ed. E. E. Maccoby, T. M. Newcomb, E. L. Hartley. New York: Henry Holt and Co., 1956, 3rd ed., pp. 400-425; and Suzanne Keller, *The American Lower Class Family.* Albany: N. Y. State Division for Youth, 1966, pp. 38-55.

[17]Alfred C. Kinsey, Wendell B. Pomeroy, and Clyde E. Martin, *Sexual Behavior in the Human Male.* Philadelphia: W. B. Saunders Co., 1948, pp. 374-384.

[18]Edwin H. Sutherland, "White Collar Criminality," *American Sociological Review,* 1940, No. 5, pp. 1-12.

[19]Oscar Lewis, "The Culture of Poverty," *Scientific American* (Oct. 1966), Vol. 215, No. 4, pp. 19-25.

[20]Robert K. Merton, "Continuities in the Theory of Social Structure and Anomie," in Robert Merton, *Social Theory and Social Structure.* New York: Free Press of Glencoe, 1957, pp. 170-181.

[21]Hyman Rodman, "The Lower Class Value Stretch," *Social Forces* (Dec. 1963), pp. 205-215.

SOME PRINCIPLES OF STRATIFICATION

KINGSLEY DAVIS
WILBERT E. MOORE

In a previous paper some concepts for handling the phenomena of social inequality were presented. In the present paper a further step in stratification theory is undertaken—an attempt to show the relationship between stratification and the rest of the social order. Starting from the proposition that no society is "classless," or unstratified, an effort is made to explain, in functional terms, the universal necessity which calls forth stratification in any social system. Next, an attempt is made to explain the roughly uniform distribution of prestige as between the major types of positions in every society. Since, however, there occur between one society and another great differences in the degree and kind of stratification, some attention is also given to the varieties of social inequality and the variable factors that give rise to them.

Clearly, the present task requires two different lines of analysis— one to understand the universal, the other to understand the variable features of stratification. Naturally each line of inquiry aids the other and is indispensable, and in the treatment that follows the two will be interwoven, although, because of space limitations, the emphasis will be on the universals.

Throughout, it will be necessary to keep in mind one thing— namely, that the discussion relates to the system of positions, not to the individuals occupying those positions. It is one thing to ask why different positions carry different degrees of prestige, and quite another to ask how certain individuals get into those positions. Although, as the argument will try to show, both questions are related, it is essential to keep them separate in our thinking. Most of the literature on stratification has tried to answer the second question (particularly with regard to the ease or difficulty of mobility between strata) without tackling the first. The first question, however, is logically prior and, in the case of any particular individual or group, factually prior.

Reprinted from *The American Sociological Review*, Vol. 10, No. 2, April, 1945, pp. 242-249, by permission of the American Sociological Association and the authors.

THE FUNCTIONAL NECESSITY OF STRATIFICATION

Curiously, however, the main functional necessity explaining the universal presence of stratification is precisely the requirement faced by any society of placing and motivating individuals in the social structure. As a functioning mechanism a society must somehow distribute its members in social positions and induce them to perform the duties of these positions. It must thus concern itself with motivation at two different levels: to instill in the proper individuals the desire to fill certain positions, and, once in these positions, the desire to perform the duties attached to them. Even though the social order may be relatively static in form, there is a continuous process of metabolism as new individuals are born into it, shift with age, and die off. Their absorption into the positional system must somehow be arranged and motivated. This is true whether the system is competitive or non-competitive. A competitive system gives greater importance to the motivation to achieve positions, whereas a non-competitive system gives perhaps greater importance to the motivation to perform the duties of the positions; but in any system both types of motivation are required.

If the duties associated with the various positions were all equally pleasant to the human organism, all equally important to societal survival, and all equally in need of the same ability or talent, it would make no difference who got into which positions, and the problem of social placement would be greatly reduced. But actually it does make a great deal of difference who gets into which positions, not only because some positions are inherently more agreeable than others, but also because some require special talents or training and some are functionally more important than others. Also, it is essential that the duties of the positions be performed with the diligence that their importance requires. Inevitably, then, a society must have, first, some kind of rewards that it can use as inducements, and, second, some way of distributing these rewards differentially according to positions. The rewards and their distribution become a part of the social order, and thus give rise to stratification.

One may ask what kind of rewards a society has at its disposal in distributing its personnel and securing essential services. It has, first of all, the things that contribute to sustenance and comfort. It has, second, the things that contribute to humor and diversion. And it has, finally, the things that contribute to self respect and ego expansion. The last, because of the peculiarly social character of the self, is largely a function of the opinion of others, but it nonetheless ranks in importance with the first two. In any social system all three kinds of rewards must be dispensed differentially according to positions.

In a sense the rewards are "built into" the position. They consist in the "rights" associated with the position, plus what may be called its accompaniments or perquisites. Often the rights, and sometimes the accompaniments, are functionally related to the duties of the position. (Rights as viewed by the incumbent are usually duties as viewed by other members of the community.) However, there may be a host of subsidiary rights and perquisites that are not essential to the function of the position and have only an indirect and symbolic connection with its duties, but which still may be of considerable importance in inducing people to seek the positions and fulfill the essential duties.

If the rights and perquisites of different positions in a society must be unequal, then the society must be stratified, because that is precisely what stratification means. Social inequality is thus an unconsciously evolved device by which societies insure that the most important positions are conscientiously filled by the most qualified persons. Hence every society, no matter how simple or complex, must differentiate persons in terms of both prestige and esteem, and must therefore possess a certain amount of institutionalized inequality.

It does not follow that the amount or type of inequality need be the same in all societies. This is largely a function of factors that will be discussed presently.

THE TWO DETERMINANTS OF POSITIONAL RANK

Granting the general function that inequality subserves, one can specify the two factors that determine the relative rank of different positions. In general those positions convey the best reward, and hence have the highest rank, which (a) have the greatest importance for the society and (b) require the greatest training or talent. The first factor concerns function and is a matter of relative significance; the second concerns means and is a matter of scarcity.

Differential Functional Importance. Actually a society does not need to reward positions in proportion to their functional importance. It merely needs to give sufficient reward to them to insure that they will be filled competently. In other words, it must see that less essential positions do not compete successfully with more essential ones. If a position is easily filled, it need not be heavily rewarded, even though important. On the other hand, if it is important but hard to fill, the reward must be high enough to get it filled anyway. Functional importance is therefore a necessary but not a sufficient cause of high rank being assigned to a position.

Differential Scarcity of Personnel. Practically all positions, no matter how acquired, require some form of skill or capacity for performance. This is implicit in the very notion of position, which implies that the incumbent must, by virtue of his incumbency, accomplish certain things.

There are, ultimately, only two ways in which a person's qualifications come about: through inherent capacity or through training. Obviously, in concrete activities both are always necessary, but from a practical standpoint the scarcity may lie primarily in one or the other, as well as in both. Some positions require innate talents of such high degree that the persons who fill them are bound to be rare. In many cases, however, talent is fairly abundant in the population but the training process is so long, costly, and elaborate that relatively few can qualify. Modern medicine, for example, is within the mental capacity of most individuals, but a medical education is so burdensome and expensive that virtually none would undertake it if the position of the M.D. did not carry a reward commensurate with the sacrifice.

If the talents required for a position are abundant and the training easy, the method of acquiring the position may have little to do with its duties. There may be, in fact, a virtually accidental relationship. But if the skills required are scarce by reason of the rarity of talent or the costliness of training, the position, if functionally important, must have an attractive power that will draw the necessary skills in competition with other positions. This means, in effect, that the position must be high in the social scale—must command great prestige, high salary, ample leisure, and the like.

How Variations Are to Be Understood. In so far as there is a difference between one system of stratification and another, it is attributable to whatever factors affect the two determinants of differential reward—namely, functional importance and scarcity of personnel. Positions important in one society may not be important in another, because the conditions faced by the societies, or their degree of internal development, may be different. The same conditions, in turn, may affect the question of scarcity; for in some societies the stage of development, or the external situation, may wholly obviate the necessity of certain kinds of skill or talent. Any particular system of stratification, then, can be understood as a product of the special conditions affecting the two aforementioned grounds of differential reward.

MAJOR SOCIETAL FUNCTIONS AND STRATIFICATION

Religion. The reason why religion is necessary is apparently to be found in the fact that human society achieves its unity primarily through the possession by its members of certain ultimate values and ends in common. Although these values and ends are subjective, they influence behavior, and their integration enables the society to operate as a system. Derived neither from inherited nor from external nature, they have evolved as a part of culture by communication and moral pressure. They must, however, appear to the members of the society to have some reality, and it is the role of religious belief and ritual to supply and reinforce this appearance of reality. Through belief and ritual the common ends and values are connected with an imaginary world symbolized by concrete sacred objects, which world in turn is related in a meaningful way to the facts and trials of the individual's life. Through the worship of the sacred objects and the beings they symbolize, and the acceptance of supernatural prescriptions that are at the same time codes of behavior, a powerful control over human conduct is exercised, guiding it along lines sustaining the institutional structure and conforming to the ultimate ends and values.

If this conception of the role of religion is true, one can understand why in every known society the religious activities tend to be under the charge of particular persons, who tend thereby to enjoy greater rewards than the ordinary societal member. Certain of the rewards and special privileges may attach to only the highest religious functionaries, but others usually apply, if such exists, to the entire sacerdotal class.

Moreover, there is a peculiar relation between the duties of the religious official and the special privileges he enjoys. If the supernatural world governs the destinies of men more ultimately than does the real world, its earthly representative, the person through whom one may communicate with the supernatural, must be a powerful individual. He is a keeper of sacred tradition, a skilled performer of the ritual, and an interpreter of lore and myth. He is in such close contact with the gods that he is viewed as possessing some of their characteristics. He is, in short, a bit sacred, and hence free from some of the more vulgar necessities and controls.

It is no accident, therefore, that religious functionaries have been associated with the very highest positions of power, as in theocratic regimes. Indeed, looking at it from this point of view, one may wonder why it is that they do not get *entire* control over their societies. The factors that prevent this are worthy of note.

In the first place, the amount of technical competence necessary for the performance of religious duties is small. Scientific or artistic capacity is not required. Anyone can set himself up as enjoying an intimate relation with deities, and nobody can successfully dispute him. Therefore, the factor of scarcity of personnel does not operate in the technical sense.

One may assert, on the other hand, that religious ritual is often elaborate and religious lore abstruse, and that priestly ministrations require tact, if not intelligence. This is true, but the technical requirements of the profession are for the most part adventitious, not related to the end in the same way that science is related to air travel. The priest can never be free from competition, since the criteria of whether or not one has genuine contact with the supernatural are never strictly clear. It is this competition that debases the priestly position below what might be expected at first glance. That is why priestly prestige is highest in those societies where membership in the profession is rigidly controlled by the priestly guild itself. That is why in part at least, elaborate devices are utilized to stress the identification of the person with his office—spectacular costume, abnormal conduct, special diet, segregated residence, celibacy, conspicuous leisure, and the like. In fact, the priest is always in danger of becoming somewhat discredited—as happens in a secularized society—because in a world of stubborn fact, ritual and sacred knowledge alone will not grow crops or build houses. Furthermore, unless he is protected by a professional guild, the priest's identification with the supernatural tends to preclude his acquisition of abundant worldly goods.

As between one society and another it seems that the highest general position awarded the priest occurs in the medieval type of social order. Here there is enough economic production to afford a surplus, which can be used to support a numerous and highly organized priesthood; and yet the populace is unlettered and therefore credulous to a high degree. Perhaps the most extreme example is to be found in the Buddhism of Tibet, but others are encountered in the Catholicism of feudal Europe, the Inca regime of Peru, the Brahminism of India, and the Mayan priesthood of Yucatan. On the other hand, if the society is so crude as to have no surplus and little differentiation, so that every priest must be also a cultivator or hunter, the separation of the priestly status from the others has hardly gone far enough for priestly prestige to mean much. When the priest actually has high prestige under these circumstances, it is because he also performs other important functions (usually political and medical).

In an extremely advanced society built on scientific technology, the priesthood tends to lose status, because sacred tradition and supernaturalism drop into the background. The ultimate values and common ends of the society tend to be expressed in less anthropomorphic ways, by officials who occupy fundamentally political, economic, or educational rather than religious positions. Nevertheless, it is easily possible for intellectuals to exaggerate the degree to which the priesthood in a presumably secular milieu has lost prestige. When the matter is closely examined the urban proletariat, as well as the rural citizenry, proves to be surprisingly god-fearing and priest-ridden. No society has become so completely secularized as to liquidate entirely the belief in transcendental ends and supernatural entities. Even in a secularized society some system must exist for the integration of ultimate values, for their ritualistic expression, and for the emotional adjustments required by disappointment, death, and disaster.

Government. Like religion, government plays a unique and indispensable part in society. But in contrast to religion, which provides integration in terms of sentiments, beliefs, and rituals, it organizes the society in terms of law and authority. Furthermore, it orients the society to the actual rather than the unseen world.

The main functions of government are, internally, the ultimate enforcement of norms, the final arbitration of conflicting interests, and the overall planning and direction of society; and externally, the handling of war and diplomacy. To carry out these functions it acts as the agent of the entire people, enjoys a monopoly of force, and controls all individuals within its territory.

Political action, by definition, implies authority. An official can command because he has authority, and the citizen must obey because he is subject to that authority. For this reason stratification is inherent in the nature of political relationships.

So clear is the power embodied in political position that political inequality is sometimes thought to comprise all inequality. But it can be shown that there are other bases of stratification, that the following controls operate in practice to keep political power from becoming complete: (a) The fact that the actual holders of political office, and especially those determining top policy must necessarily be few in number compared to the total population. (b) The fact that the rulers represent the interest of the group rather than of themselves, and are therefore restricted in their behavior by rules and mores designed to enforce this limitation of interest. (c) The fact that the holder of political office has his authority by virtue of his office and nothing else, and therefore any special knowledge, talent, or capacity he may claim is purely incidental, so that he often has to depend upon others for technical assistance.

In view of these limiting factors, it is not strange that the rulers often have less power and prestige than a literal enumeration of their formal rights would lead one to expect.

Wealth, Property, and Labor. Every position that secures for its incumbent a livelihood is, by definition, economically rewarded. For this reason there is an economic aspect to those positions (e.g., political and religious) the main function of which is not economic. It therefore becomes convenient for the society to use unequal economic return as a principal means of controlling the entrance of persons into positions and stimulating the performance of their duties. The amount of the economic return therefore becomes one of the main indices of social status.

It should be stressed, however, that a position does not bring power and prestige *because* it draws a high income. Rather, it draws a high income because it is functionally important and the available personnel is for one reason or another scarce. It is therefore superficial and erroneous to regard high income as the cause of a man's power and prestige, just as it is erroneous to think that a man's fever is the cause of his disease.

The economic source of power and prestige is not income primarily, but the ownership of capital goods (including patents, good will, and professional reputation). Such ownership should be distinguished from the possession of consumers' goods, which is an index rather than a cause of social standing. In other words, the ownership of producers' goods is, properly speaking, a source of income like other positions, the income itself remaining an index. Even in situations where social values are widely commercialized and earnings are the readiest method of judging social position, income does not confer prestige on a position so much as it induces people to compete for the position. It is true that a man who has a high income as a result of one position may find this money helpful in climbing into another position as well, but this again reflects the effect of his initial, economically advantageous status, which exercises its influence through the medium of money.

In a system of private property in productive enterprise, an income above what an individual spends can give rise to possession of capital wealth. Presumably such possession is a reward for the proper management of one's finances originally and of the productive enterprise later. But as social differentiation becomes highly advanced and yet the institution of inheritance persists, the phenomenon of pure ownership, and reward for pure ownership, emerges. In such a case it is difficult to prove that the position is functionally important or that the scarcity involved is anything other than extrinsic and accidental. It is for this reason, doubtless, that the institution of private property in productive goods becomes more subject to criticism as social development proceeds toward industrialization. It is only this pure, that is, strictly legal and functionless ownership, however, that is open to attack; for some form of active ownership, whether private or public, is indispensable.

One kind of ownership of production goods consists in rights over the labor of others. The most extremely concentrated and exclusive of such rights are found in slavery, but the essential principle remains in serfdom, peonage, encomienda, and indenture. Naturally this kind of ownership has the greatest significance for stratification, because it necessarily entails an unequal relationship.

But property in capital goods inevitably introduces a compulsive element even into the nominally free contractual relationship. Indeed, in some respects the authority of the contractual employer is greater than that of the feudal landlord, inasmuch as the latter is more limited by traditional reciprocities. Even the classical economics recognized that competitors would fare unequally, but it did not pursue this fact to its necessary conclusion that, however it might be acquired, unequal control of goods and services must give unequal advantage to the parties to a contract.

Technical Knowledge. The function of finding means to single goals, without any concern with the choice between goals, is the exclusively technical sphere. The explanation of why positions requiring great technical skill receive fairly high rewards is easy to see, for it is the simplest case of the rewards being so distributed as to draw talent and motivate training. Why they seldom if ever receive the highest rewards is also clear: the importance of technical knowledge from a societal point of view is never so great as the integration of goals, which takes place on the religious, political, and economic levels. Since the technological level is concerned solely with means, a purely technical position must ultimately be subordinate to other positions that are religious, political, or economic in character.

Nevertheless, the distinction between expert and layman in any social order is fundamental, and cannot be entirely reduced to other terms. Methods of recruitment, as well as of reward, sometimes lead to the erroneous interpretation that technical positions are economically determined. Actually, however, the acquisition of knowledge and skill cannot be accomplished by purchase, although the opportunity to learn may be. The control of the avenues of training may inhere as a sort of property right in certain families or classes, giving them power and prestige in consequence. Such a situation adds an artificial scarcity to the natural scarcity of skills and talents. On the other hand, it is possible for an opposite situation to arise. The rewards of technical position may be so great that a condition of excess supply is created, leading to at least temporary devaluation of the rewards. Thus "unemployment in the learned professions" may result in a debasement of the prestige of those positions. Such adjustments and readjustments are constantly occurring in changing societies; and it is always well to bear in mind that the efficiency of a stratified structure may be affected by the modes of recruitment for positions. The social order itself, however, sets limits to the inflation or deflation of the prestige of experts: an over-supply tends to debase the rewards and discourage recruitment or produce revolution, whereas an under-supply tends to increase the rewards or weaken the society in competition with other societies.

Particular systems of stratification show a wide range with respect to the exact position of technically competent persons. This range is perhaps most evident in the degree of specialization. Extreme division of labor tends to create many specialists without high prestige since the training is short and the required native capacity relatively small. On the other hand it also tends to accentuate the high position of the true experts—scientists, engineers, and administrators—by increasing their authority relative to other functionally important positions. But the idea of a technocratic social order or a government or priesthood of engineers or social scientists neglects the limitations of knowledge and skills as a basis for performing social functions. To the extent that the social structure is truly specialized the prestige of the technical person must also be circumscribed.

VARIATION IN STRATIFIED SYSTEMS

The generalized principles of stratification here suggested form a necessary preliminary to a consideration of types of stratified systems, because it is in terms of these principles that the types must be described. This can be seen by trying to delineate types according to certain modes of variation. For instance, most of the most important modes (together with the polar types in terms of them) seem to be as follows:

(a) *The Degree of Specialization.* The degree of specialization affects the fineness and multiplicity of the gradations in power and prestige. It also influences the extent to which particular functions may be emphasized in the invidious system, since a given function cannot receive much emphasis in the hierarchy until it has achieved structural separation from the other functions. Finally, the amount of specialization influences the bases of selection. Polar types: *Specialized, Unspecialized.*

(b) *The Nature of the Functional Emphasis.* In general when emphasis is put on sacred matters, a rigidity is introduced that tends to limit specialization and hence the development of technology. In addition, a brake is placed on social mobility, and on the development of bureaucracy. When the preoccupation with the sacred is withdrawn, leaving greater scope for purely secular preoccupations, a great development, and rise in status, of economic and technological positions seemingly takes place. Curiously, a concomitant rise in political position is not likely, because it has usually been allied with the religious and stands to gain little by the decline of the latter. It is also possible for a society to emphasize family functions—as in relatively undifferentiated societies where high mortality requires high fertility and kinship forms the main basis of social organization. Main types: *Familistic, Authoritarian* (*Theocratic* or sacred, and *Totalitarian* or secular), *Capitalistic*.

(c) *The Magnitude of Invidious Differences*. What may be called the amount of social distance between positions, taking into account the entire scale, is something that should lend itself to quantitative measurement. Considerable differences apparently exist between different societies in this regard, and also between parts of the same society. Polar types: *Equalitarian, Inequalitarian*.

(d) *The Degree of Opportunity*. The familiar question of the amount of mobility is different from the question of the comparative equality or inequality of rewards posed above, because the two criteria may vary independently up to a point. For instance, the tremendous divergences in monetary income in the United States are far greater than those found in primitive societies, yet the equality of opportunity to move from one rung to the other in the social scale may also be greater in the United States than in a hereditary tribal kingdom. Polar types: *Mobile* (open), *Immobile* (closed).

(e) *The Degree of Stratum Solidarity*. Again, the degree of "class solidarity" (or the presence of specific organizations to promote class interests) may vary to some extent independently of the other criteria, and hence is an important principle in classifying systems of stratification. Polar types: *Class organized; Class unorganized*.

EXTERNAL CONDITIONS

What state any particular system of stratification is in with reference to each of these modes of variation depends on two things: (1) its state with reference to the other ranges of variation, and (2) the conditions outside the system of stratification which nevertheless influence that system. Among the latter are the following:

(a) *The Stage of Cultural Development*. As the cultural heritage grows, increased specialization becomes necessary, which in turn contributes to the enhancement of mobility, a decline of stratum solidarity, and a change of functional emphasis.

(b) *Situation with Respect to Other Societies*. The presence or absence of open conflict with other societies, of free trade relations or cultural diffusion, all influence the class structure to some extent. A chronic state of warfare tends to place emphasis upon the military functions, especially when the opponents are more or less equal. Free trade, on the other hand, strengthens the hand of the trader at the expense of the warrior and priest. Free movement of ideas generally has an equalitarian effect. Migration and conquest create special circumstances.

(c) *Size of the Society.* A small society limits the degree to which functional specialization can go, the degree of segregation of different strata, and the magnitude of inequality.

COMPOSITE TYPES

Much of the literature on stratification has attempted to classify concrete systems into a certain number of types. This task is deceptively simple, however, and should come at the end of an analysis of elements and principles, rather than at the beginning. If the preceding discussion has any validity, it indicates that there are a number of modes of variation between different systems, and that any one system is a composite of the society's status with reference to all these modes of variation. The danger of trying to classify whole societies under such rubrics as *caste, feudal,* or *open class* is that one or two criteria are selected and others ignored, the result being an unsatisfactory solution to the problem posed. The present discussion has been offered as a possible approach to the more systematic classification of composite types.

CLASS AND OPPORTUNITY IN EUROPE AND THE U.S.

SEYMOUR MARTIN LIPSET
NATALIE ROGOFF

In an article that continues to be the subject of lively discussion ("Is America Still the Land of Opportunity," November 1953), William Petersen concluded — contrary to much recent opinion that the "rags-to-riches" tradition of the United States had become a myth — that the individual has much or more chance to rise in the world as he ever had in this country. In this present article, Seymour Martin Lipset and Natalie Rogoff examine another myth, that Europe, as compared to the U.S., has a "frozen class structure" which keeps individuals from rising out of their fathers' class. Marshaling recent studies of European social mobility, they find that our accepted notions of European society need to be considerably revised. As for the comparative opportunities open to the newly risen white-collar worker and middle class on the two continents — here, too, they have much new insight to contribute. Mr. Lipset is associate professor in the graduate department of sociology at Columbia University and the author of *Agrarian Socialism: A Study of the Cooperative Commonwealth Federation in Saskatchewan* (University of California Press), and the forthcoming *Union Democracy* (with Martin Trow and James Coleman). Miss Rogoff is a Research Associate at the Bureau of Applied Social Research of Columbia University. She has written *Recent Trends in Occupational Mobility* (The Free Press).

The new sociology has in recent years effectively destroyed a number of hallowed myths. Studies of election campaigns have demolished the civics-textbook image of the independent voter who decides the election after weighing all the arguments—we now know that the "independent voters," the men who make up their minds at the last moment, are for the most part the least informed and least interested section of the electorate, as Paul F. Lazarsfeld, Bernard Berelson, and Hazel Gaudet show in their book *The People's Choice* (Columbia University Press). In a recently published study, *Psychosis and Civilization* (The Free Press), Herbert Goldhamer and Andrew Marshall indicate that the almost universally accepted belief that insanity has increased during the past century is untrue. And in the November 1953 issue of COMMENTARY, William Petersen assembled the evidence from a number of studies to demolish the myth that opportunity to rise in the social scale in the United States is shrinking. Examining, among other things, the survey data on the relation between the occupational status of fathers and sons, Mr. Petersen concluded that the rate of social mobility is probably at its all-time high today, with more people rising above the occupational status of their fathers than ever before in American history.

I

If one were to find fault with Mr. Petersen's demonstration that America is still a land of opportunity, we think it would be in his implicit assumption that the United States has a higher rate of social mobility than other countries. High mobility is a relative term; we call the American rate "high" in comparison with what is assumed to be the "low" rate obtaining in the rigid, closed societies of Europe. But is this assumption, traditional and universal though it be, justified, or is it another one of those myths waiting to be destroyed by sociological analysis?

Until recently we simply did not have the data to answer this question. In the last few years, however, sociologists in Germany, France, Great Britain, Finland, Italy, The Netherlands, Sweden, and Japan have made studies of social mobility rates based on random samples of national populations. Unfortunately, it is not easy to compare these studies with one another, for in almost every country different systems of classifying occupations were employed. But every study (except the British) does differentiate between manual and non-manual (white collar, professional, managerial, etc.) occupations, and most (except the British and the Italian) separate rural from urban occupations.

Thus broad comparisons are possible; and having made them, we can hardly doubt that all of the European societies for which we have data, except Italy, actually have "high" rates of social mobility, if by a high rate we mean one comparble to the American. In each country, a large minority is able to rise above the occupational position of their fathers, while a smaller but still substantial minority falls in occupational status. Indeed, the data indicate hardly any substantial difference in the rates of mobility among France, Great Britain, Germany, Finland, Sweden, *and* the United States. In our opinion, even if the data were completely comparable, they still would not show a great difference among these six countries. The Italian data, it is true, indicate a somewhat lesser rate of mobility in that country than in the other six, but even here the difference does not appear to be great.

Three of the studies—the American, French, and German—permit a statistical comparison if we reduce the occupational classifications to three groupings: manual, non-manual, and farm.[1] The table below compares the proportion of sons in each country who remained in the occupational groupings of their fathers, and the proportion that shifted into different groupings—that is, it compares the occupational "destinations" of men of similar origins in each society. Thus, the first column of the table shows that of 100 sons of American non-manual workers, 71 are themselves engaged in non-manual work, 25 in manual work, and 4 in farming. Notice how similar are the figures for non-manual workers' sons in France and the United States and that the pattern of movement of manual workers' sons in all three countries is well-nigh identical.

Father's Occupation	Son's Occupation		
	Non-Manual	Manual	Farm
United States			
Non-manual: 100%	71	25	4
Manual: 100%	35	61	4
Farm: 100%	23	39	38
France			
Non-Manual: 100%	73	18	9
Manual: 100%	35	55	10
Farm: 100%	16	13	71
Germany			
Non-Manual: 100%	80	20	—
Manual: 100%	30	60	10
Farm: 100%	12	19	69

There can be no doubt that the data from these three studies refute any claim that social mobility in the United States is on the whole markedly greater than in Europe, where family status allegedly limits positions open to sons.[2]

There is, however, a significant difference revealed in the above table between the United States and the other countries: while the majority of the sons of American farmers have shifted to non-agricultural occupations, in France and Germany seven farmers' sons out of ten stay on the land. That is, the American urban economy has offered many more opportunities than the European, drawing large numbers of people from rural areas into cities, with the result that the number of people engaged in farming in the United States has declined at a far greater rate than in France or Germany. But this is not so much a reflection of the difference in the rate of social mobility between America and Europe, of any severer limitations imposed by class origins in Europe—after all, the pattern of occupational distribution for the sons of manual and non-manual workers remains approximately the same in France, Germany, and the U.S.; rather it reflects a difference in what is called the "opportunity structure" in these countries.[3] Not the alleged rigidity of European class lines—Europe's supposed lower rate of social mobility—but the ability of the expanding American urban economy to absorb much larger numbers of the sons and daughters of the American countryside, explains why America is more of a land of opportunity than Europe.

We have looked at the different social "destinations" of men of the same social origins. Now let us consider the different social origins of men who have arrived at the same destination. This is the conventional approach to the study of social and political elites, but it is just as enlightening when used to examine the origins of *all* strata in society.

We find that there is more movement from the manual worker and farm class into clerical, managerial, and professional jobs in the U. S. than abroad. A larger proportion (52 per cent) of American non-manual workers have manual or farm backgrounds than do their French and German counterparts (35 per cent and 30 per cent respectively). But this is only the other side of the above-mentioned decline of the proportion of Americans engaged in agriculture. The larger movement of Americans into the class of non-manual workers is due, again, not to *a higher rate of social mobility as such,* but to a greater increase in the proportion of non-manual "opportunities" in the U.S., which have expanded at a faster rate than in Europe.[4]

Returning again to the comparison of social mobility patterns, we should like to buttress our conclusion that much of Western Europe has as open a class structure as the U.S. with data from two provincial cities, Indianapolis, Indiana, and Aarhus, Denmark.[5]

Son's Occupation	Father's Occupation			
	Aarhus, Denmark			
	I	II	III	IV
I—Professionals, Bus. Exec. & Self Employed	38%	23%	14%	32%
II—Clerical & Sales	20	28	12	12
III—Manual	41	48	73	52
IV—Farm	1	1	1	4
	Indianapolis			
I	33%	21%	10%	11%
II	29	42	17	15
III	38	37	72	70
IV	—	—	1	4

It is clear that there is no substantial difference in the social mobility patterns of Aarhus and Indianapolis. The sons of manual workers have about the same chance of rising in both communities.

The Indianapolis study was primarily designed to find out whether mobility in the U.S. has decreased over time. As Mr. Petersen notes in his article, it demonstrates conclusively that the rate of social mobility in Indianapolis remained constant between 1910 and 1940.[6]

Happily, we have a somewhat similar comparison for a European city. One of the earliest quantitative studies of social mobility (Federico Chesaa, *La Transmissione Ereditoria delle Professione*, Fratelli Bocca, 1912) was made in Rome using marriage license statistics for 1908. In 1950 another survey of Rome was made using a representative sample of the population. (This study by Alessandro Lehner is reported in a paper presented to the 1953 meeting of the International Sociological Association.) These two studies suggest the same conclusion as the Indianapolis study: mobility rates have hardly varied in the forty-year period.

There are also a number of studies, made during the 20's, of social mobility in Germany, and these, too, indicate a rate of social mobility (both upwards and downwards) which is not much below contemporary findings. The largest single study was made by the German white-collar workers' union, which secured questionnaire data from over 90,000 white-collar workers in the late 1920's. Almost a quarter of the males in this group, 23.9 per cent, came from working-class families.

To sum up, our evidence suggests that in the United States, France, and Germany, somewhere between a fifth and a quarter of those with fathers in white-collar occupations become manual workers, whereas about one-third of those whose fathers are manual workers rise to a non-manual position, and that this has been the state of affairs since before the First World War.

II

Two questions present themselves. First, why do all the countries for which we have data exhibit similar patterns of social mobility? And second, why did everyone agree in seeing great differences in social mobility between Europe and America when the data in fact show none?

The answer to the first question is relatively simple. In each of these countries, the so-called new middle (white collar) class has grown at the expense of the rural population, and to a lesser extent of the manual working-class population, though this development has gone very much further and faster in the U. S. than in Europe. The "second industrial revolution" has brought about an increase in administrative, office, and paper work rather than in the number of industrial workers. More and more people are needed in each country to manage industry, distribute goods, provide the services required for leisure activities, and run the welfare state. Thus there has to be "upward" mobility within each society.

A second factor that tends to produce upward mobility is 'a differential fertility—the tendency of those with more money to have fewer children. While shifts in the economic structure have expanded the proportion of the non-manual prestige occupations, the families in such occupations have not been begetting their proportionate share of children. Consequently, even if every son of a high-status family keeps that status, room is left for others to rise into it.

There is also the fact that the ever growing cities in modern industrial countries cannot replenish and enlarge themselves except by receiving a steady stream of migrants from the countryside who take the least desirable positions. The implications of this fact emerge clearly from two studies, one of Stockholm, and the other of a San Francisco area.

In the first study ("Social Mobility in Sweden," a paper presented to the International Sociological Association at Liège in August 1953), two Swedish social scientists, Gunnar Boalt and Carl-Gunnar Jannsson, determined the name and father's occupation of every boy in the fourth grade of the Stockholm public schools in 1936. By checking these same names against the Stockholm electoral register for 1949, they were able to discover the occupations of 94 per cent of the 1936 schoolboy group. To their surprise, 69 per cent were employed in non-manual occupations; over half of the sons of manual workers had entered non-manual work, though the group was only about twenty-four years old in 1949.

The question naturally arose as to where the manual workers of Stockholm came from, since most of the children of manual workers were no longer in that class. To answer this, Boalt and Jannsson went back to the electoral register and recorded the occupations of all males born in 1925, the year in which their original group had been born. Comparing "natives" (those in Stockholm schools in 1936) with "migrants" (those who had *not* been in Stockholm that year), they found that over two-thirds of the "migrants" were manual workers, as compared with less than one-third of the "natives." Comparable findings are also reported for Finland.

This clearly suggests the existence of a cycle in which the children of workers in metropolitan areas are able to climb higher on the occupational ladder while their places below are taken by migrants from smaller communities and rural areas. A similar pattern in the U.S. was detected in a study of social mobility in Oakland, California, conducted by the Institute of Industrial Relations of the University of California. The smaller the community in which one was brought up, the greater the likelihood of remaining a manual worker. (In the U. S., the migrants taking up the lower positions in the rapidly growing cities come from Puerto Rico, Mexico, and Canada, as well as from the smaller American cities and the countryside.)

Since urban expansion is also characteristic of Western Europe, this pattern of migrants taking up the lower positions is probably uniform. No wonder the rate of social mobility differs so little at the present time among these countries.

III

Given the evidence that the social structure of the U. S. is actually no more fluid than that of Western Europe, the problem remains of explaining why everyone thinks that it is. This is a complex question. We have answered it in part by distinguishing between social mobility as such, and fundamental changes in the "opportunity structure" caused by the rapidly expanding American economy. Thus the precipitous decline in the absolute and relative size of the American farm class, the other side of which is a sharp increase in the number and proportion of non-manual urban occupations, has been mistakenly attributed to a more fluid class structure in the U. S. But this is only part of the answer. The rest of the answer is to be sought in two things: the differences in total national income and its distribution between the U. S. and Western Europe, and the different value systems of the American and European upper classes.

Income, in every class, is so much greater in America, and the gap between the living styles of the different social classes so much narrower that in effect the egalitarian society envisaged by the proponents of high social mobility is much more closely approximated here than in Europe. While Europeans rise in the occupational scale as often as we do, the marked contrast between the ways of life of the different classes continues to exist. Thus, in the United States, workers and middle-class people have cars, while in Europe only the middle class can own an automobile. In the world as a whole, the wealthier countries tend to have a more equitable distribution of income among their social and occupational groups than do the poorer ones, contrary to the view that sees the rich getting richer and the poor poorer under capitalism. (This more equal distribution of income has nothing to do with social mobility, strictly defined: a high rate of social mobility is compatible with wide discrepancies in standards of living, as we find in India and the Soviet Union today.)

This is what one might call the real, or material, explanation of the impression that the European class structure is rigid and the American fluid. However, there is also an "ideological" explanation, and this has not perhaps been given its due weight.

Until the emergence of the Communist societies, the U. S. was the only country in which the predominant conservative as well as liberal ideology asserted the equality of all men. Ideological egalitarianism in the U. S. has not denied or even challenged existing differences in rank and authority. It has, however, insisted that such differences are only justifiable as a reward for demonstrated ability: able men can and should rise. While family background and inherited social position play a role in the U. S., eminent businessmen of even upper-class background point in self-justification to the humble youthful origins from which they have risen. Walter Chrysler entitled his auto-biography *The Story of an American Workman,* and a recent maga-zine advertisement by the Crown-Zellerbach Corporation, one of the largest West Coast businesses, boasts that it started in a pushcart in the streets of San Francisco in 1870.

In Europe, on the other hand, the conservatives, at least until the present century, have rejected egalitarianism. Aristocratic values and patterns of inherited privilege and position are still upheld by much of the upper class of Great Britain, Germany, France, and many other countries. Thus the European conservative would wish to mini-mize the extent of social mobility. We would hazard that in much of Europe successful individuals of lower-class provenance would seek to conceal rather than publicize their origins.

In the previously cited French survey of social mobility, this mo-tive is considered a problem affecting the very data. The author of the survey says that "it is precisely among those who have experienced the greatest social mobility that reticence [in the interview] may be of most significance. One interviewer, commenting on the refusal of an interview by a respondent, adds: 'I think it was a question of self-esteem; though he is an industrialist, his father was a white-collar worker, and his grandfather's origins were humble.' "

Then, too, advocacy of equality in European society has largely been the function of the left, whose chief charge against capitalist so-ciety is that equal opportunity does not exist and class mobility is not possible. Thus European conservatives and radicals both find it to their interest to deny the existence of significant opportunity to rise out of one's class in Europe. In America, on the other hand, the conservatives argue that it has existed and still exists, and the radicals disagree with them solely as to whether there is sufficient opportunity, or whether the rate of mobility is declining.

This is undoubtedly an illustration of W. I. Thomas's sociological dictum, "If men define things as real, they are real in their conse-quences." Whatever the actual rate of social mobility has been in

Europe, it has been *experienced* by Europeans (and Americans) as low; and this illusory conviction of a lack of mobility has served as one of the major stimuli to political activity.

Is it possible that occupational mobility means less in Europe because there is more snobbery there, and one does not move up *socially* as fast, or as far, as one moves *occupationally?* Such data as we have do not support this view. We have German and American data[7] on marriages between persons classified according to their occupations, the former being based on all marriages in the state of Bavaria in 1927, and the latter on Philadelphia marriage licenses for the year 1913 to 1916.

Occupations of Marriage Partners
Bavaria and Philadelphia

Husband's Occupation	*Bavaria* 1927 Wife's Occupation		*Philadelphia* 1913-1916 Wife's Occupation	
	Non-Manual	Manual	Non-Manual	Manual
Non-Manual	59%	21%	60%	23%
Manual	41	79	39	77

One would have expected that the differences between the value systems of the European and American upper classes discussed above would make for higher barriers to inter-class marriage in Europe. In fact, however, if the limited and partly non-comparable data for Bavaria and Philadelphia are typical of European and American patterns, such differences do not exist. Indeed, the similarities in inter-class mobility patterns revealed by the above table are in some ways more startling than the similarities in occupational mobility patterns considered earlier.

Other evidence also suggests that social snobbery in Europe is perhaps not as strong a barrier as many believe. A recent British study reports little difference in the rates of marriage across class lines between Great Britain and America when occupations of the fathers of husbands and wives are compared. (David V. Glass, ed., *Mobility in Britain*, Routledge and Kegan Paul, 1954.) The fact that intermarriage between Jews and Gentiles tends to be higher in Western Europe

than in America (see "Jewish-Gentile Intermarriage: Facts and Figures," by Herschel Shanks, in COMMENTARY, October 1953) also suggests that status restrictions may be lower under certain conditions
abroad than in this country. It may be argued, in fact, that the more
aristocratic and secure an upper-status group, the less emphasis it
places on exclusiveness. Thus the patterns of rigid upper-class exclusion of *nouveau riche* families, which W. L. Warner has suggested is
characteristic of the highest status groups in American society, may
reflect the insecurity which is felt in a highly mobile society where
no one can feel that he has a permanent and irrevocable place in the
upper class.

But why is it that successful Americans, who are more open about
their lower-status origins than successful Europeans, nevertheless seem
to show great concern about origins in evaluating a man's status? The
answer may lie in the ability of men and groups successfully to up-
hold contradictory values in different life contexts. In economic contexts, ability is on the whole the criterion; in social contexts, inherited
qualities.[8] A recent study of race tensions among automobile workers exposes clearly this human ability to maintain "contradictory"
attitudes. Dietrich Reitzes reports (in *Journal of Social Issues,* Vol.
IX, No. 1, 1953) that many of the workers who strongly favored equal
job rights for Negroes took part in organized efforts to keep Negroes
out of their residential neighborhoods.

IV

Our finding that no significant differences exist between the rates
of occupational mobility in America and industrially advanced European countries suggests a need to modify the long held assumption
that a large socialist movement and class-conscious proletariat have
not developed in the U. S. because of the high rate of American social
mobility as compared with the presumed low European rate. Ambitious sons of lower-class fathers are able to rise in *all* Western societies.

What then makes for the difference in political behavior? Apparently, for one thing, the differences in total income as between America and Europe and the degree to which the different classes share
equally in that income, and the different definitions of the class structure. Socialism developed in countries whose dominant groups traditionally accepted rigid class differentiation as a basic social value.

Marxist doctrine, with its emphasis on class differences, reflected the realities of European society; it reflected less and less of the realities of the American status system as the productivity of the American economy surged upwards. The socialists in Europe did not have to underline the large variations in rewards for different services; this was, and is, an obvious feature of most non-American societies. It is the American assumption of egalitarianism, combined with the 20th-century fact of the greater economic productivity and more equal distribution of income and prestige symbols, that prevents the building up of proletarian class-consciousness in this country.[9]

Further evidence for this general thesis may be found in the fact that there was greater working-class radicalism and class-consciousness in 19th- and early 20th-century America than exists today. In the 19th century, the income and consumption gap between the urban classes was much greater than at present. And we find that workers were much more likely to respond to class appeals than today. The slogan, "a rich man's war and a poor man's fight," arose during the Civil War, not during the First or Second World Wars. Local labor and radical parties had greater success between 1865 and 1914 than they have had since. Trade unions were much more outspokenly anti-capitalist in the early period. The assembly line and mass production, with the higher wages and more equal distribution of wealth that they make possible, are thus probably more responsible for the development of the American "classless" society than trends in social mobility.

Notes

[1] The American study "Jobs and Occupation: A Popular Evaluation" was made by the National Opinion Research Center and appears in its bulletin *Opinion News* for September 1947. The French survey "Mobilité sociale et dimensions de la famille" was made by the Institut National d'Etudes Démographiques, and appears in *Population*, Vol. V, No. 3. The German data are from the files of the German Institut für Demoskopie. We assume for all three countries that a man's going from a manual to a non-manual job constitutes upward social mobility. For a justification of this assumption, see S. M. Lipset and Reinhard Bendix, "Social Mobility and Occupational Career Patterns," in *American Journal of Sociology* (March 1952).

[2] Pitirim Sorokin reached similar conclusions in the 1920's in his compre-

hensive survey of the then existing mobility data, *Social Mobility* (1927). A recent survey, *Mobility in Britain*, edited by David V. Glass, also concludes that Britain, France, and the U.S. have about the same rates of social mobility.

3 Country A may have more social mobility than country B, and still enjoy less equality of variation in the opportunity structure. For example, if a country's economy requires 90 per cent of a population to be peasants, even though absolute equality of opportunity prevails, most children of peasants must remain peasants; that is to say, even if every non-peasant position is filled by a peasant's son, only 10 per cent at best can change their occupations. On the other hand, if a country undergoes rapid economic change and the proportion of non-manual positions rises from 10 to 25 per cent—i.e., its "opportunity structure" changes — then even if every son of a non-manual father is provided a non-manual position, a large group must be recruited from some other occupational stratum. Thus one society may have very little inheritance of socio-economic privilege and still have little social mobility, while another society may place a great stress on the inheritance of privileged status and have a great deal of mobility. In any given situation, the "opportunity structure" must be taken into account.

4 The Finnish data show origins only, and suggest an extremely high rate of social mobility. For example, 29 per cent of the "middle class" (white-collar people) have "working-class" fathers, and an equal percentage have "farmer" fathers. "Upper-class" sons (business and industrial leaders and persons in positions which require a university degree) reported that 15 per cent of their fathers were workers, and 17 per cent farmers. The data are unfortunately not comparable with those from other countries, but they suggest that Finland may have an even higher rate of social mobility, as judged by destination, than the United States. (See Tauno Hellevuo, "Poimintatutkimus Säätykierrosta" [A Sampling Study of Social Mobility], *Suomalainen Suomi*, No. 2, 1952.)

5 The Indianapolis data are taken from Natalie Rogoff, *Recent Trends in Occupational Mobility* (The Free Press, 1953). The late Theodore Geiger made the Aarhus survey, which was published under the title of *Soziale Umschichtungen in einer Dänischen Mittelstadt* (University of Aarhus, 1951).

6 An excellent study of the social origins of the American business elite in 1870, 1900, and 1950 demonstrates that the amount of movement from the lower classes into the "upper crust" of business leadership is about the same today as it was in 1870 (Suzanne Keller, *The Social Origins of Three Generations of American Business Leaders,* an unpublished doctoral dissertation presented to Columbia University in 1953).

7 The German material is contained in *Sozialer Auf und Abstieg im*

Deutschen Volk. The American material is drawn from Donald Marvin, "Occupational Propinquity as a Factor in Marriage Selection," *Publications of the American Statistical Association,* 1918, one of the first and in many ways the best American study of social mobility.

[8] See "The Psychological Theory of Prejudice," by Paul Kecskemeti, in October 1954 COMMENTARY.

[9] Many sociological studies have been dismissed as "painful elaborations of the obvious." If the comparative studies cited in this article had shown that the U.S. had a much higher rate of social mobility than Europe, they too would have fallen under this general condemnation. But their results happen to challenge popular consensus and therefore are exciting. It should be obvious, however, that studies which validate popular opinion are as significant as those which suggest it is wrong—there is no way of telling beforehand: before, that is, a scientific determination of the truth has been made.

SOCIAL CLASS AND CHILDHOOD PERSONALITY[1]

WILLIAM H. SEWELL

INTRODUCTION

During the past twenty-five years there has been a great deal of
interest in the relationship between social class and personality—particularly in the bearing of social class on the personality of the child
and the relationship between social class and adult mental illness. Because of space and time limitations, this paper will concentrate on
social class influences on childhood personality and will not be concerned with the literature on youth and adults. The product of this
interest in social class influences on childhood personality has been
numerous books, monographs, research articles and essays—often with
contradictory emphases and conclusions depending on the convictions,
theoretical orientations, and research styles of the authors.[2]

The theoretical basis for expecting a substantial relationship between social class and personality rests on three major assumptions
upon which there seems to be widespread agreement among social
scientists. The first is that in all societies some system of social stratification exists whereby the members of the society are differentiated
into subgroups or classes which bear to one another a relationship
of social inequality. It is further generally acknowledged that persons
in the society can be more or less located in the stratification system
in terms of the characteristic social roles they play. Consequently it
is possible to infer crudely at least the social class position of most
individuals in terms of readily ascertainable criteria. The particular
criteria will be dependent on the culture of the society in question.[3]
There are rather wide differences among writers as to the origins of
stratification, the functions of stratification, the criteria of social classes,
the meaning of the term class,[4] the number of classes, the rigidity of
any particular stratification system, and almost any other aspect of

Reprinted from *Sociometry*, Vol. 24, No. 4 (December, 1961) pp. 340-356, by permission of the American Sociological Association and the author.

theory, substance, or measurement which could possibly be raised, but almost everyone seems agreed that some system of stratification based on social inequality is an inevitable product of organized group life. The empirical basis of this proposition is strong in that no society has yet been studied in which a stratification system, fulfilling at least the minimum requirements stated above, has not been found.

The second assumption is that the position of the child's family in the stratification system determines in considerable measure not only the social learning influences to which he will be subjected during the early period of his life, and in later life for that matter, but greatly affects also the access that he will have to certain opportunities that are socially defined as desirable. Certainly, there seems to be ample evidence that this is true even in societies in which the stratification structure is not particularly rigid or the differences between the social classes extreme. While many social scientists would deny that American society has fixed classes each with its own distinctive subculture, none would claim that the learning environment of the child whose family is highly placed in the stratification structure does not differ materially from that of the child whose social class position is low. Also it is readily apparent that the styles of life, the material comforts, the value systems and the instruction, both intentional and unintentional, which the child receives about the roles available to him in society differ depending on the social class position of his family. And finally even his treatment in the neighborhood, community and larger society will depend for some time, at least, on his social status origins.

The third assumption on which there is general agreement is that the early experiences of the individual will be of considerable importance in determining his later social behavior. To be sure, there is rather massive disagreement about the particular psychodynamics of the relationship between early experience and later behavior, the specific or patterned experiences which produce other patterns or traits of later personality, or even the critical periods in terms of days, months and years in which the individual is most susceptible to influence. However, these details and differences of theory and commitment have not led to any widespread rejection of the basic notion of the primary importance of early experiences in shaping later personality. The experimental evidence on animal behavior and the somewhat more inferential knowledge about human learning furnish the empirical foundation for this assumption.

On the basis of these assumptions, the reasonable expectation would
be that some distinct personality traits, configurations, or types might
be found which would differentiate the children of the several social
classes, or at least that the incidence of certain personality characteristics would be different for the children of the various social classes.
The results of research efforts to elucidate these relationships have
been disappointing for a number of methodological and theoretical
reasons. It would be impossible and is unnecessary to review each of
the numerous writings which have direct bearing on the problem, but
it does seem worthwhile to examine some of the most important of
them to see if it is possible to reach any valid conclusions on the extent and nature of the relationship between social class and childhood
personality, to point out some of the weaknesses of the research in the
field, and to make some suggestions for future research. This is the
purpose of the present paper.

AN EXAMINATION OF SELECTED STUDIES

A convenient point of departure might be to look at examples of
studies which illustrate various approaches to the problem. As a minimum these would seem to include (a) work based primarily on typo-
logical and informal observational procedures, (b) those in which detailed observations on class-related child-training procedures have
been made and personality characteristics inferred, observed or systematically assessed, and, finally (c) studies in which some measure of
social class position has been related directly to some independent
assessments of personality.

Perhaps the best-known example of the first type of study mentioned is Arnold Green's "The Middle-Class Male Child and Neurosis" (11) which was originally published in 1946 and has been re-
published in numerous collections of readings. Green, stimulated by
the neo-Freudian writers Horney and Fromm, and on the basis of his
recollections of his childhood and young adulthood in a Massachusetts industrial community of about 3,000 persons, delineated a set of
social psychological conditions that he had observed in middle-class
families which he believed predisposed middle-class male children to
neurosis. He observed that the middle-class parent is caught up in a
life-long struggle for improvement of personal position in the class

structure. The father's work takes him away from the home and involves the manipulation of others around him to further his personal career. He is ambivalent toward his son because the child takes time, money and energy that could be used for the father's social advancement and also interferes with his role as a partner and companion to his wife. The mother, too, is ambivalent toward her child. He interferes with her career aspirations and her individual pleasures. Also, he causes worries and demands great care and attention. Despite the socially structured ambivalence of both parents toward their son, they train him to love them for the care and sacrifices they have made for him and force him to feel lost without their love. Thus, the middle-class boy suffers "personality absorption" to such an extent that he cannot turn to others for genuine emotional satisfaction. Moreover, he is faced with the constant threat of withdrawal of parental love. Little wonder, then, that he feels small, insignificant, unworthy, inferior, helpless and anxious! He can never escape his parents' norms at home, in school or in his play groups—always he must try to live up to their high expectations of him, or he will lose their love. Thus, he lives "alone and afraid in a world he never made." The lower-class (Polish-American) child suffers no such fate. Although parental authority is often harsh and brutal, it is also casual and external to the "core of the self." The children avoid their parents, in fact have contempt for them and band together in common defense against their cruelty. Consequently the parents do not have the opportunity or the techniques to absorb the personalities of their children. Thus, the lower-class boys do not suffer from the guilt, anxiety and extreme sense of insecurity from which the middle-class boy suffers as a result of his extreme dependency on his parents.

This is possibly an all too brief portrayal of Green's argument, but it summarizes his main points. Although the paper purports to be based on careful observation, no indication is given about the number of observations made of the socialization practices of either lower- or middle-class families, nor is there any indication of the frequency of neurosis or neurotic behavior among either lower- or middle-class boys—much less any direct evidence on the incidence of neurotic behavior among those middle-class boys (or lower-class boys) who have, as against those who have not, been socialized in the "middle-class way." Consequently the article might well be dismissed as a provocative and speculative essay except for the fact that it has served as one of the principal supports for the currently widely-held stereotype of the neurotic middle-class child and has fostered the idea that the lower-class child in our culture is relatively less subject to neurotic tendencies and symptoms. It also illustrates something of the current state of the field in that a paper which is based essentially on speculation and retrospection should be widely accepted as portraying an accurate account of the influence of social class on childhood personality.

The second type of study is perhaps most conveniently illustrated by the research done by members of the Committee on Human Development at the University of Chicago and originally reported in 1948 in two articles, one by Allison Davis and Robert J. Havighurst (8),[5] "Social Class and Color Differences in Child Rearing," and another by Martha C. Ericson (10), "Child Rearing and Social Status." These studies were the first to report systematic empirical findings indicating that child-rearing practices of middle-class parents differ significantly from those of lower-class families. The findings of the Davis-Havighurst study were based on interviews with 98 middle-class (48 white and 50 Negro) and 102 lower-class (52 white and 50 Negro) mothers and dealt with a wide variety of child-training questions and the mothers' expectations concerning their children. Perhaps the most important finding of the study was the restrictiveness of the middle-class mothers in the critical early training of the child. They were shown to be less likely to breast-feed, more likely to follow a strict nursing schedule, to restrict the child's sucking period, to wean earlier and more sharply, to begin bowel and bladder training earlier and to complete toilet training sooner than were lower-class mothers. In addition, they generally ₋followed stricter regimes in other areas of behavior and expected their children to take responsibility for themselves earlier. From these results the inference was drawn that middle-class children encounter more frustration of their impulses and that this is likely to have serious consequences for their personalities. Their findings regarding the differences in nursing and toilet training between the middle and lower classes were widely heralded and served to strengthen the conviction, especially of psychoanalytically oriented workers in the field—particularly those at the forefront of the culture and personality movement—that the socialization of the middle-class child in America was producing neurotic middle-class children and adults.[6] Davis and Havighurst themselves did not make this assertion. Their own conclusions were rather equivocal concerning the supposed consequences of these differences in training for the middle-class child. Actually, the inference they drew regarding personality effects was that the training influences to which middle-class children are subjected are likely to produce an orderly, conscientious, responsible, tame, but frustrated child. The only direct evidence they presented about the personalities of the children studied was that thumbsucking, which may be seen as an evidence of oral deprivation, and masturbation, which may indicate general frustration, are both much more frequently reported for middle-class than for lower-class children.

The findings of the Chicago group and the inferences made from their findings as to the personality consequences of class-related child-training practices were widely accepted and held sway without competition for some time. However, they were finally challenged by the results of two carefully designed empirical studies with quite different research objectives. The first of these was the attempt by the present writer to determine the consequences of a variety of infant-training practices on independently assessed childhood personality characteristics and the second was the careful study of patterns of child rearing made by a group of behavioral scientists at Harvard under the leadership of Robert R. Sears.

The study of infant training and personality, published in 1952, was based on interviews conducted in 1947 with the mothers of 165 rural Wisconsin children concerning the practices they followed in rearing their children and subsequently relating the data thus obtained to the personality characteristics of the same children as these were determined from scores on both paper-and-pencil and projective tests of personality and ratings of the children's behavior by their mothers and teachers.[7] The specific infant-training practices studied were those most stressed in the psychoanalytic literature, including: feeding, weaning, nursing schedule, bowel training, bladder training and punishment for toilet accidents. These experiences were not found to be significantly related to childhood personality characteristics as assessed in the study. Moreover, two carefully constructed factor-weighted indexes measuring permissiveness in toilet training and feeding produced even less positive results.[8] In all only 18 out of 460 relationships tested in the study were significant at the .05 level and, of these, seven were opposite from the predicted direction.[9] These results, along with evidence from studies not so directly focused on the problem, tended to undermine the confidence of many who had made the inferential leap from class-determined early training practices to class-linked childhood personality characteristics and types.

Equally upsetting evidence came in 1954 with the publication of a preliminary report from the Harvard study (21) by Eleanor E. Maccoby and P. K. Gibbs on "Methods of Child Rearing in Two Social Classes," and later when the more complete report of the study (30) was published by Robert Sears, Eleanor Maccoby and Harry Levin in their well-known book, *Patterns of Child Rearing.* Their results, based upon careful interviews with 379 New England middle-class and lower-class mothers (labeled "upper-middle" and "upper-lower" by Maccoby and Gibbs), clearly indicated no differences in infant-feeding practices between the two social classes, more severity in toilet training in the lower-class families, less permissiveness in sex training in the lower-class families, more restriction of aggression toward parents and peers (and more punitiveness where such aggression took place) in lower-class families, greater imposition of restrictions and demands on the child in the lower-class family, more physical punishment, deprivation of privileges and ridicule by lower-class parents, but no differences between the two groups on isolation and withdrawal of love. Needless to say, these results were in important respects directly contradictory to the findings of the Chicago group and provided little factual basis for continued acceptance of the stereotyped version of the middle-class mother as a rigid, restrictive, demanding and punitive figure whose behavior can but result in frustrated, anxious, conforming and overly dependent children (30, Ch. 12). Neither was there any evidence whatever to support Green's contention about personality absorption of the child in the middle-class family or its supposed consequent—the neurotic middle-class child.

As might well be expected, the findings of the Harvard group provoked considerable debate and Havighurst and Davis did a comparison of the data of the two studies after adjusting to make the age groups more comparable, but they still found substantial and large differences between the results of the Chicago and Harvard studies (12). A number of other studies (16, 17, 20, 40) have appeared in recent years that generally confirm the findings of the Harvard group. Finally, Urie Bronfenbrenner (4), on the basis of an examination of a whole battery of studies, both published and unpublished, found a basis for explaining some of the differences, particularly in infant feeding and toilet training, in terms of a trend toward greater permissiveness in these areas on the part of lower-class mothers up to World War II but with a reversal since then, middle-class mothers subsequently becoming more permissive in infant training. The data gathered over the 25-year period on the training of the young child seem to him to show that middle-class mothers have been consistently more permissive towards the child's expressed needs and wishes, less likely to use physical punishment and more acceptant and equalitarian than have lower-class mothers. Finally, he sees indications that the gap between the social classes may be narrowing. While one might disagree with some of his interpretations and question some of the data on which his trends are based, it is clear from his review that in the present situation the evidence clearly supports the findings of the Harvard group and furnishes little basis for the belief that the training practices of middle-class parents are more likely than those of lower-class parents to produce neurotic personalities in their children.

One other important study which carries the analysis of class-related child rearing a step forward has recently been reported (1958) by Daniel R. Miller and Guy E. Swanson, in *The Changing American Parent* (23, 24). In their study of child rearing in Detroit, Michigan, they add to the stratification position represented by social class a second variable dealing with integrative position in the social structure which they have called "entrepreneurial-bureaucratic integration." Families with entrepreneurial orientations are those in which the husband works in organizations that are relatively small in size, with a simple division of labor, have relatively small capitalization, and provide for mobility and income through individual risk-taking and competition. Families with bureaucratic orientations are those in which the father works in a large and complex organization employing many specialists, paying fixed wages or salaries for particular jobs, and, in place of reward for individual risk-taking, provides security in continuity of employment and income for those who conform with organizational demands. Miller and Swanson feel there is reason to believe that this aspect of status interpenetrates the family and influences child-rearing practices. Consequently, in their analysis they classify their families not only by social class but also by entrepreneurial-bureaucratic position. The addition of this new dimension of status produced results which were not nearly as clear-cut and definite as they had expected. In keeping with their predictions, entrepreneurial middle-class mothers were not less permissive than

entrepreneurial lower-class mothers and there were no differences between bureaucratic lower-class and middle-class families in this regard.
Their prediction that entrepreneurial middle-class mothers would
be more likely to train their children in an active and manipulative
view of the world was not supported. Moreover, entrepreneurial and
bureaucratic lower-class mothers did not differ to any appreciable extent in the way they trained their children. If only the class differences are considered, their results are quite similar to those of the
Harvard group. It seems quite probable that the relative failure of
the new dimension to add much to the predictive power of social class
was to some extent due to the inadequacy of their scheme for determining entrepreneurial-bureaucratic orientation.[10] Consequently, in
future studies, better categorization and assessment of this dimension
may produce greater associations.[11] In any event the idea of intro-
ducing other dimensions of status than social class position seems to
be a good one and should be tested in other studies.

A third type of research bearing directly on the relationship between social class and personality involves the correlation between
measures of socioeconomic status (henceforth referred to as SES) and
children's scores on personality tests and is perhaps well illustrated by
a study by the present writer and A. O. Haller, "Social Status and
the Personality Adjustment of the Child" (34; see also 1, 5, 6). A
comprehensive review of the studies in which SES had been measured
objectively and correlated with independent assessments of the personality of the child indicated that middle-class children consistently
made a better showing than lower-class children. For the most part
the correlations were low or the differences were small and often
there was no indication that the association was statistically significant, that sampling was adequate, that the tests of status and personality were dependable, or that variables known to be related to status
or personality or both were controlled (34, pp. 114-115).

Consequently it was decided to make a rigorous test of the hypothe-
sized relation between SES and personality using a design in which
both variables were measured objectively and independently for a
large sample (1,462) of grade-school children in a culturally homogeneous community with a fairly wide range of SES. Correlation
analysis techniques were used to determine the relationship between
SES, as measured by father's occupation and a rating of the prestige
of the family in the community, and personality adjustment as indicated by a factor-weighted score on the California Test of Person-

ality. The zero-order correlation coefficients between the two status measures and the personality scores were determined. Then the multiple correlation coefficient of the two status measures and personality score was computed, and, finally, the relationship was determined with sibling position, intelligence, and age controlled. The results indicated a low but significant association between status and measured personality (.16 for father's occupation and child's personality score, .23 for prestige position and child's personality score, .25 for the multiple correlation of the two status measures and child's personality score). The combined effect of the two status measures was not significantly reduced when the controls were introduced. The direction of the correlations indicated that the lower the SES of the child's family the less favorable his personality test score.

Certainly these results indicate that only a relatively small amount of the variance in measured personality found in this group of children can be accounted for by their SES. However, the test of the hypothesis was stringent and the correlations might well be higher in communities with more distinct stratification systems, and if more refined measures of status and personality were used. In any event the correlations, particularly since they are not markedly different from those reported by others who have followed similar methods, should not be dismissed. They at least help to explain some of the variance in measured personality—an area in which little measured variance has been explained by other measured variables. However, the results do not provide much encouragement for the view that social class is a major determinant of childhood personality and they offer still another instance of evidence against the claim that middle-class children suffer greater personality maladjustment than lower-class children.

In an attempt to explore further the relationship between SES and personality, the writers (35) next did a factor analysis of the 30 personality test items which had been found to be most highly correlated with SES. The results of this analysis indicated that four factors explained approximately 90 per cent of the common variance among the items. These factors were tentatively identified as (a) *concern over status,* (b) *concern over achievement,* (c) *rejection of family,* and (d) *nervous symptoms.* Each factor was negatively correlated with SES, their respective correlations being —.31, —.18, .—12 and —.26, indicating that the lower the status of the child the greater the tendency to score high (unfavorably) on each of the factors. The inter-correlation between the factors ranges from + .25 to + .59. Thus, there seems to be a tendency for children who are concerned about their social status to worry about their achievements, to reject their families and to display nervous symptoms. The evidence from this study points to the fact that these characteristics are more common among lower- than higher-status children. Again the correlations between SES and the personality characteristics indicated by the factors, although statistically significant, are low and offer only limited support for the notion that the position of the child in the stratification system has bearing on his personality pattern. They are, however, suggestive of a line of attack on the problem which may be somewhat more rewarding than some of the approaches employed thus far.

Conclusions Regarding Social Class and Childhood Personality

On the basis of this brief review of studies of the bearing of social class on the personality of the child, the following conclusions seem justified:

First, there is a growing body of evidence from empirical studies of several types indicating a relatively low correlation between the position of the child in the stratification system (social class) and some aspects of personality, including measured personality adjustment. The relationship has not been shown to be nearly as close as might have been expected, but there is mounting evidence that at least some of the variance in childhood personality can be explained by the social status position of the child. Possibly when better measures are used the relationship will prove to be higher. The present crude techniques of measuring both variables doubtless result in underestimation of the correlation.

Second, the direction of the relationships found offer absolutely no support for the notion that middle-class children more commonly exhibit neurotic personality traits than do children of lower-class origins. Indeed all of the empirical evidence points to the opposite conclusion.

Third, the studies of child rearing in relation to social class, made since the publication of the Chicago studies, have found fewer class-related differences in infant training than might have been expected and those differences that have been found tend to indicate greater permissiveness in feeding and toilet training on the part of middle-class mothers rather than lower-class mothers. The findings in relation to early childhood training indicate less impulse control, less punitiveness, less reliance on strict regime, less restrictiveness in sex behavior and less restriction on aggression—in other words, generally greater permissiveness on the part of middle-class mothers.

Fourth, empirical studies of the consequences of child training have given a great deal of attention to such aspects of infant discipline as manner of nursing, weaning, scheduling, bowel and bladder training, but have found very little or no relationship between these experiences and childhood personality traits and adjustment patterns. Much less attention has been given to the consequences of other aspects of child training, but some low correlations have been found between such factors as patterns of punishment, permissiveness for aggression and mother's affectional warmth for the child and such aspects of personality as feeding problems, dependency and aggression. Although these correlations explain only a small portion of the variance in childhood personality, they cannot be entirely dismissed and, to the extent that the child-training practices are class-linked, they must be credited with having some bearing on the relationship between social class and personality. Certainly, however, the empirical evidence does not permit any lavish claims regarding the influence of the child-training variables studied on the personality of the child.

Fifth, a final inescapable conclusion from reading these and other writings on social class and childhood personality is that, with a few notable exceptions, the level of research and theoretical sophistication in this area has been appallingly low. Some of the most influential work has had little or no acceptable empirical basis. The evidence upon which widely accepted claims have been founded is sometimes from samples that are so small or so clearly biased that no reliable conclusions could possibly be reached. In fact there is not a single study that can claim to be representative of the whole society or any region of the country and only a small handful are clearly representative of any definable social system. The statistical techniques in some of the studies are clearly inappropriate for the data. The theoretical guide-lines for most of the studies are seldom specified and often are not even discernible. The chain of inference from theory to data, to conclusions, to wider generalizations is sometimes unclear and instances can be cited in which links in the chain are entirely missing. Great lack of conceptual clarity, particularly concerning the two principal variables, social class and personality, is generally apparent. Thus, statistical categories of socioeconomic status measured by crude techniques are treated as social classes in the broader meaning of that term, and inferences are drawn about sub-cultures, learning environments, value systems and other social class characteristics without the necessary empirical evidence of their existence. Likewise the term personality is used in a variety of ways but with little attention to definition and specification. Often inferences are made about deeper levels of personality from more or less surface variables. Because of these weaknesses in theory and method, more definitive conclusions about the relationship between social class and childhood personality must await better designed studies.

SUGGESTED DIRECTION FOR FUTURE RESEARCH

In the light of the present situation in the field and because of the basic importance of the problem, both from the theoretical and practical points of view, a few suggestions regarding future research may be helpful.

First, although the available evidence concerning the relationship between child training and personality does not provide much of a basis for explaining personality variation and despite the fact that the present evidence concerning the relationship between social class and child training does not seem to indicate a very close correspondence, further studies of social class and child rearing are desirable and necessary. With our present knowledge of sampling procedures, data-gathering methods, and analysis techniques, a carefully designed large-scale study using a sample of sufficient size to permit racial and ethnic breakdowns and other needed controls and concentrating on various aspects of child rearing ranging over the whole period of childhood is the indicated next step. In such a study additional attention should be given to assessment of the behavioral correlates of child-training practices and to appropriate delineation of larger personality configurations. Additional studies of small local communities with relatively narrow stratification systems or studies in larger communities with samples that are inadequate to represent the full range of the stratification system are not likely to add much to the knowledge already available from existing studies and could well be dispensed with.

Second, despite the fact that many studies have been made of the relationship between the SES and the measured personality of school children, there is still need for a definitive study in a large community with a heterogeneous population. Since it would be an over-whelming task to map the actual class structure of such a community, several objective SES indicators might be employed singly and in combination, using modern multivariate statistical analysis techniques to determine their relationship to measured personality as indicated by personality test results. With large samples, a number of variables could be controlled and some definitive conclusion might be reached regarding the relationship between SES and childhood personality. Further analysis, following the general model used by Sewell and Haller in their most recent study of test items having high correlations with SES, could be done to determine the factors which account for variance in responses to personality tests.

Third, there is need for an intensive study of the relationship between social class and personality in some community or society in which a functionally existing class system with well-established sub-cultures is present, if indeed such can be found. It is clear from the literature that classes in this sense have been assumed to be operative but in no case have they been properly delineated, validated and sampled in any study of social class and personality. Such a task would be a major undertaking and probably could be carried out only in a modest-sized community, but, if an appropriate community were found, this would provide a more critical test of the theoretical relationship between social class and personality than any yet attempted. Unless and until such a study is done, no one is really justified in implying that social class is more than a convenient statistical category in discussing its relation to personality.

Fourth, it now seems clear that scientific concern with the relation between social class and personality has perhaps been too much focused on global aspects of personality and possibly too much on early socialization. Therefore, it is suggested that the more promising direction for future research will come from a shift in emphasis, toward greater concern with those particular aspects of personality which are most likely to be directly influenced by the position of the child's family in the social stratification system, such as attitudes, values and aspirations, rather than with deeper personality characteristics. It also is suggested that instead of focusing so much attention on the very young child, more research should be done on older children and adolescents—on the assumption that whatever differences one's social class position makes to the above-mentioned aspects of personality are likely to be the product of later and more gradual socialization experiences rather than the more proximate effect of specific aspects of early experiences (39). Evidence already available from a number of studies seems to clearly indicate that adolescents' belief systems and values differ rather clearly in relation to their social status positions: adolescents of lower-class backgrounds appear to have lower need-achievement, lower achievement values (27, 28), are much less likely to place high value on a college education, less frequently aspire to high level achievement in educational pursuits and occupational activities (13, 36) and are less willing to defer their gratifications than are middle- and upper-class adolescents (7, 29). Recent studies by the writer and others have shown that there is a marked negative correlation between the socioeconomic status and the educational and occupational aspirations of high school seniors and that relationship remains even when sex and intelligence are controlled (36, pp. 70-72). As yet unpublished, results from a more recent study which the writer is currently conducting on a statewide sample of Wisconsin high school seniors indicate that other variables such as parental pressure, rural-urban background, community and peer group influences may also be introduced without negating the influencing of SES on these aspirations. It may well be that it is precisely in the area of attitudes, values, and aspirations that social class influences are most pronounced. If so, it would be profitable to study children of different social-class backgrounds to determine when and how these characteristics of personality develop and how responsive they may be to other influences.

Fifth, it is suggested that it might be more revealing and more promising in terms of the knowledge that may be gained about social influences on personality to focus some attention on intraclass differences instead of being concerned exclusively with interclass variations. The data of most empirical studies of social class in relation to personality and related variables indicate the existence of considerable intraclass variation. Thus in the writer's studies of social status and personality, there were many children in each social status level who made favorable scores on the personality measures and some at each level who made unfavorable scores. Even in the study of differences in educational and occupational aspirations, where sizable differences were found between SES groups, there were important differences within each status group (36). Obviously, it is not intelligence or sex which accounts for the within-class differences found in this study, because these variables have been controlled, but it may well be that family attitudes and values, peer-group influences, and community forces will be found to explain a sizable portion of the variance. Another interesting series of questions suggested by these results is: What are the personality effects of having values and aspirations that are deviant from those of one's social class? Does it mean that the lower-class child has to reject the values of his famliy and neighborhood in order to be socially mobile? If so, what are the dimensions and what is the nature of the stress experienced by the upwardly mobile lower-class child and what personality consequences flow from such striving? If he is successful in his mobility aspirations, will the lower-class child find it impossible to internalize the values of his new status position or will he be constantly plagued by the conflict between his old values and the new? These are just a few of the kinds of questions that could be studied in relation to intraclass differences in personality.

Sixth, it is suggested that, as basic a variable as social class is for social behavior, there are other important aspects and dimensions of social structure that cut across the social stratification system which should not be neglected in the study of the personality development of the child.[12] Among the more important of these are the mobility and the occupational orientations of the family. In addition, there are other traditional social structure variables such as age, sex, family size, sibling position, race, ethnic background and religion which probably play a significant role but have been taken into account insufficiently in studies of social structure and childhood personality. Moreover, much theoretical and analytical work is needed on the possible influence of various combinations of social structure variables, and their joint as well as independent influence on the personalities of children.

NOTES

[1] This paper was presented at the Berkeley Conference on Personality in Childhood, arranged by the late Professor Harold E. Jones, on May 5, 1960. It was prepared while the writer was a Fellow at the Center for Advanced Study in the Behavioral Sciences.

[2] An extensive bibliography, consisting of 195 items, has been depositd with the American Documentation Institute Auxiliary Publications Project, Photo Duplication Service, Library of Congress, Washington 25, D. C. Order

Document no. 6906 remitting $1.75 for 35 mm microfilm or $2.50 for photo copies. Advance payment is required. Make checks or money orders payable to: Chief, Photo Duplication Service, Library of Congress.

[3] A number of books, summarizing contemporary theory and research in social stratification, have appeared in recent years. See, for example, references 2, 3, 15, 19, 22, and 26.

[4] The writer is not convinced that social class is the best term for describing the socioeconomic levels treated in most of the literature covered in this paper. Actually, the term social class implies much more than has been established concerning the existence of classes with distinctive boundaries and subcultures. What is meant operationally by social class in most studies is simply a convenient category of socioeconomic status. While the writer would prefer to use the more accurate term socioeconomic status or simply social status, he bows to the trend in the literature and will use the term social class in this paper except in referring to those studies where the authors have themselves used socioeconomic status or social status.

[5] See also reference 9.

[6] For a summary and critique of personality and culture literature see references 14 and 18.

[7] For another paper dealing with the effects of feeding techniques on oral symptoms, see reference 36. Other papers reporting on theoretical, methodological and substantive aspects of this study include references 31, 33 and 37.

[8] For the indexes, see (37), page 144.

[9] A replication of the study in Ceylon (38) resulted in the same conclusions.

[10] Apparently the use of this variable was something of an afterthought and consequently its operational definition for purposes of the research had to be based on data available from the interview rather than what might have been more pertinent information. See (23), pp. 67-70.

[11] Possibly it would be a better test of the hypothesis to simply compare the personality characteristics, for a large number of cases, of children brought up in families more clearly representing the entrepreneurial and bureaucratic ends of the continuum, i.e., children of owner-operators of independent retail establishments vs. children of government clerks. It might even be more rewarding to drop the bureaucratic-entrepreneurial orientation entirely and to examine the influence of specific occupations on socialization norms and practices, on the assumption that occupations differ in the extent to which they interpenetrate family life and influence the behavior of members.

[12] Some provocative suggestions along these lines are given in (25).

REFERENCES

1. Angelino, H., J. Dollins, and E. V. Mech, "Trends in the 'Fears and Worries' of School Children as Related to Socioeconomic Status and Age," *Journal of Genetic Psychology*, 1956, 89, 263-277.

2. Barber, B., *Social Stratification*, New York: Harcourt, Brace, 1957.

3. Bendix, R., and S. M. Lipset (eds.), *Class, Status and Power: A Reader in Social Stratification*, Glencoe, Ill.: Free Press, 1953.

4. Bronfenbrenner, U., "Socialization and Social Class Through Time and Space," in E. E. Maccoby, T. M. Newcomb, and E. L. Hartley (eds.), *Readings in Social Psychology*, New York: Holt, 1958, 400-425.

5. Burchinal, L. G., "Social Status, Measured Intelligence, Achievement, and Personality Adjustment of Rural Iowa Girls," *Sociometry*, 1959, 22, 75-80.

6. Burchinal, L. G., B. Gardner, and G. R. Hawkes, "Children's Personality Adjustment and the Socio-economic Status of their Families," *Journal of Genetic Psychology*, 1958, 92, 149-159.

7. Davis, A., and J. Dollard, *Children of Bondage: The Personality Development of Negro Children in the Urban South*, Washington, D. C.: American Council on Education, 1940.

8. Davis, A., and R. J. Havighurst, "Social Class and Color Differences in Child-Rearing," *American Sociological Review*, 1946, 11, 698-710.

9. Davis, A., and R. J. Havighurst, *Father of the Man: How Your Child Gets His Personality*, Boston: Houghton Mifflin, 1947.

10. Ericson, Martha C., "Child Rearing and Social Status," *American Journal of Sociology*, 1946, 52, 190-192.

11. Green, A. W., "The Middle-class Male Child and Neurosis," *American Sociological Review*, 1946, 11, 31-41.

12. Havighurst, R. J., and A. Davis, "A Comparison of the Chicago and Harvard Studies of Social Class Differences in Child Rearing," *American Sociological Review*, 1955, 20, 438-442.

13. Hyman, H. H., "The Value Systems of Different Classes: A Social Psychological Contribution to the Analysis of Social Classes," in Bendix and Lipset (see 3 above), 426-442.

14. Inkeles, A., and D. J. Levinson, "National Character: The Study of Modal Personality and Sociocultural Systems," in G. Lindzey (ed.), *Handbook of Social Psychology*, Cambridge, Mass.: Addison Wesley, 1954. Ch. 26.

15. Kahl, J. A., *The American Class Structure*, New York: Rinehart, 1953.

16. Kohn, M. L., "Social Class and the Exercise of Parental Authority," *American Sociological Review*, 1954, 24, 352-366.

17. Kohn, M. L., "Social Class and Parental Values," *American Journal of Sociology*, 1959, 64, 337-351.

18. Lindesmith, A. R., and A. L. Strauss, "A Critique of Culture-Personality Writings," *American Sociological Review,* 1950, 15, 587-600.

19. Lipset, S. M., and R. Bendix, *Social Mobility in Industrial Society,* Berkeley: University of California Press, 1959.

20. Littman, R. A., R. A. Moore, and J. Pierce-Jones, "Social Class Differences in Child Rearing: A Third Community for Comparison with Chicago and Newton, Massachusetts," *American Sociological Review,* 1957, 22, 694-704.

21. Maccoby, E. E., P. K. Gibbs, *et al.,* "Methods of Child Rearing in Two Social Classes," in W. E. Martin and C. B. Stendler (eds.), *Readings in Child Development,* New York: Harcourt, Brace, 1954, 380-396.

22. Mayer, K. B., *Class and Society,* New York: Doubleday, 1951.

23. Miller, D. R., and G. E. Swanson, *The Changing American Parent,* New York: Wiley, 1958.

24. Miller, D. R., and G. E. Swanson, *Inner Conflict and Defense,* New York: Holt, 1960.

25. Morris, R. T., and R. J. Murphy, "The Situs Dimension in Occupational Structure" *American Sociological Review,* 1959, 24, 231-239.

26. Reissman, L., *Class in American Society,* Glencoe, Ill.: Free Press, 1959.

27. Rosen, B. C., "The Achievement Syndrome: A Psychocultural Dimension of Social Stratification," *American Sociological Review,* 1956, 21, 203-211.

28. Rosen, B. C., "Race, Ethnicity and the Achievement Syndrome," *American Sociological Review,* 1959, 24, 47-60.

29. Schneider, L., and S. Lysgaard, "The Deferred Gratification Pattern: A Preliminary Study," *American Sociological Review,* 1953, 18, 142-149.

30. Sears, R. R., E. E. Maccoby, and H. Levin, *Patterns of Child Rearing,* Evanston, Ill.: Row, Peterson, 1957.

31. Sewell, W. H., "Field Techniques in Social Psychological Study in a Rural Community," *American Sociological Review,* 1949, 14, 718-726.

32. Sewell, W. H., "Infant Training and the Personality of the Child," *American Journal of Sociology,* 1952, 58, 150-159.

33. Sewell, W. H., "Some Observations on Theory Testing," *Rural Sociology,* 1956, 21, 1-12.

34. Sewall, W. H., and A. O. Haller, "Social Status and the Personality Adjustment of the Child," *Sociometry,* 1956, 19, 114-125.

35. Sewell, W. H., and A. O. Haller, "Factors in the Relationship between Social Status and the Personality Adjustment of the Child," *American Sociological Review,* 1959, 24, 511-520.

36. Sewell, W. H., and P. H. Mussen, "The Effects of Feeding, Weaning and Scheduling Procedures on Childhood Adjustment and the Formation of Oral Symptoms," *Child Development,* 1952, 23, 185-191.

37. Sewell, W. H., P. H. Mussen, and C. W. Harris, "Relationships among

Child-Training Practices," *American Sociological Review,* 1955, 20, 137-148.

38. Straus, M. A., "Anal and Oral Frustration in Relation to Sinhalese Personality," *Sociometry,* 1957, 20, 21-31.

39. Strodtbeck, F. L., "Family Interaction Values and Achievement," in D. C. McCelland *et al., Talent and Society,* New York: Van Nostrand, 1958, Ch. II.

40. White, M. S., "Social Class, Child-Rearing Practices and Child Behavior," *American Sociological Review,* 1957, 22, 704-712.

THE CULTURE OF POVERTY

OSCAR LEWIS

Poverty and the so-called war against it provide a principal theme for the domestic program of the present Administration. In the midst of a population that enjoys unexampled material well-being—with the average annual family income exceeding $7,000—it is officially acknowledged that some 18 million families, numbering more than 50 million individuals, live below the $3,000 "poverty line." Toward the improvement of the lot of these people some $1,600 million of Federal funds are directly allocated through the Office of Economic Opportunity, and many hundreds of millions of additional dollars flow indirectly through expanded Federal expenditures in the fields of health, education, welfare and urban affairs.

Along with the increase in activity on behalf of the poor indicated by these figures there has come a parallel expansion of publication in the social sciences on the subject of poverty. The new writings advance the same two opposed evaluations of the poor that are to be found in literature, in proverbs and in popular sayings throughout recorded history. Just as the poor have been pronounced blessed, virtuous, upright, serene, independent, honest, kind and happy, so contemporary students stress their great and neglected capacity for self-help, leadership and community organization. Conversely, as the poor have been characterized as shiftless, mean, sordid, violent, evil and criminal, so other students point to the irreversibly destructive effects of poverty on individual character and emphasize the corresponding need to keep guidance and control of poverty projects in the hands of duly constituted authorities. This clash of viewpoints reflects in part the infighting for political control of the program between Federal and local officials. The confusion results also from the tendency to focus study and attention on the personality of the individual victim of poverty rather than on the slum community and family and from the consequent failure to distinguish between poverty and what I have called the culture of poverty.

The phrase is a catchy one and is used and misused with some frequency in the current literature. In my writings it is the label for a specific conceptual model that describes in positive terms a subculture of Western society with its own structure and rationale, a way of life handed on from generation to generation along family lines. The culture of poverty is not just a matter of deprivation or disorganization, a term signifying the absence of something. It is a culture in the traditional anthropological sense in that it provides human beings with a design for living, with a ready-made set of solutions for human problems, and so serves a significant adaptive function. This style of life transcends national boundaries and regional and rural-urban differences within nations. Wherever it occurs, its practitioners exhibit remarkable similarity in the structure of their families, in interpersonal relations, in spending habits, in their value systems and in their orientation in time.

Not nearly enough is known about this important complex of human behavior. My own concept of it has evolved as my work has progressed and remains subject to amendment by my own further work and that of others. The scarcity of literature on the culture of poverty is a measure of the gap in communication that exists between the very poor and the middle-class personnel—social scientists, social workers, teachers, physicians, priests and others—who bear the major responsibility for carrying out the antipoverty programs. Much of the behavior accepted in the culture of poverty goes counter to cherished ideals of the larger society. In writing about "multiproblem" families social scientists thus often stress their instability, their lack of order, direction and organization. Yet, as I have observed them, their behavior seems clearly patterned and reasonably predictable. I am more often struck by the inexorable repetitiousness and the iron entrenchment of their lifeways.

The concept of the culture of poverty may help to correct misapprehensions that have ascribed some behavior patterns of ethnic, national or regional groups as distinctive characteristics. For example, a high incidence of common-law marriage and of households headed by women has been thought to be distinctive of Negro family life in this country and has been attributed to the Negro's historical experience of slavery. In actuality it turns out that such households express essential traits of the culture of poverty and are found among diverse peoples in many parts of the world and among peoples that have had no history of slavery. Although it is now possible to assert such generalizations, there is still much to be learned about this difficult and affecting subject. The absence of intensive anthropological studies of poor families in a wide variety of national contexts—particularly the lack of such studies in socialist countries—remains a serious handicap to the formulation of dependable cross-cultural constants of the culture of poverty.

My studies of poverty and family life have centered largely in Mexico. On occasion some of my Mexican friends have suggested delicately that I turn to a study of poverty in my own country. As a first step in this direction I am currently engaged in a study of Puerto Rican families. Over the past three years my staff and I have been assembling data on 100 representative families in four slums of Greater San Juan and some 50 families of their relatives in New York City.

Our methods combine the traditional techniques of sociology, anthropology and psychology. This includes a battery of 19 questionnaires, the administration of which requires 12 hours per informant. They cover the residence and employment history of each adult; family relations; income and expenditure; complete inventory of household and personal possessions; friendship patterns, particularly the *compadrazgo,* or godparent, relationship that serves as a kind of informal social security for the children of these families and establishes special obligations among the adults; recreational patterns; health and medical history; politics; religion; world view and "cosmopolitanism." Open-end interviews and psychological tests (such as the thematic apperception test, the Rorschach test and the sentence-completion test) are administered to a sampling of this population.

All this work serves to establish the context for close-range study of a selected few families. Because the family is a small social system, it lends itself to the holistic approach of anthropology. Whole-family studies bridge the gap between the conceptual extremes of the culture at one pole and of the individual at the other, making possible observation of both culture and personality as they are interrelated in real life. In a large metropolis such as San Juan or New York the family is the natural unit of study.

Ideally our objective is the naturalistic observation of the life of "our" families, with a minimum of intervention. Such intensive study, however, necessarily involves the establishment of deep personal ties. My assistants include two Mexicans whose families I had studied; their "Mexican's-eye view" of the Puerto Rican slum has helped to point up the similarities and differences between the Mexican and Puerto Rican subcultures. We have spent many hours attending family parties, wakes and baptisms, responding to emergency calls, taking people to the hospital, getting them out of jail, filling out applications for them, hunting apartments with them, helping them to get jobs or to get on relief. With each member of these families we conduct tape-recorded interviews, taking down their life stories and their answers to questions on a wide variety of topics. For the ordering of our material we undertake to reconstruct, by close interrogation, the history of a week or more of consecutive days in the lives of each family, and we observe and record complete days as they unfold. The first volume to issue from this study is to be published next month under the title of *La Vida, a Puerto Rican Family in the Culture of Poverty—San Juan and New York* (Random House).

There are many poor people in the world. Indeed, the poverty of the two-thirds of the world's population who live in the underdeveloped countries has been rightly called "the problem of problems." But not all of them by any means live in the culture of poverty. For this way of life to come into being and flourish it seems clear that certain preconditions must be met.

The setting is a cash economy, with wage labor and production for profit and with a persistently high rate of unemployment and underemployment, at low wages, for unskilled labor. The society fails to provide social, political and economic organization, on either a voluntary basis or by government imposition, for the low-income population. There is a bilateral kinship system centered on the nuclear progenitive family, as distinguished from the unilateral extended kinship system of lineage and clan. The dominant class asserts a set of values that prizes thrift and the accumulation of wealth and property, stresses the possibility of upward mobility and explains low economic status as the result of individual personal inadequacy and inferiority.

Where these conditions prevail the way of life that develops among some of the poor is the culture of poverty. That is why I have described it as a subculture of the Western social order. It is both an adaptation and a reaction of the poor to their marginal position in a class-stratified, highly individuated, capitalistic society. It represents an effort to cope with feelings of hopelessness and despair that arise from the realization by the members of the marginal communities in these societies of the improbability of their achieving success in terms of the prevailing values and goals. Many of the traits of the culture of poverty can be viewed as local, spontaneous attempts to meet needs not served in the case of the poor by the institutions and agencies of the larger society because the poor are not eligible for such service, cannot afford it or are ignorant and suspicious.

Once the culture of poverty has come into existence it tends to perpetuate itself. By the time slum children are six or seven they have usually absorbed the basic attitudes and values of their subculture. Thereafter they are psychologically unready to take full advantage of changing conditions or improving opportunities that may develop in their lifetime.

My studies have identified some 70 traits that characterize the culture of poverty. The principal ones may be described in four dimensions of the system: the relationship between the subculture and the larger society; the nature of the slum community; the nature of the family, and the attitudes, values and character structure of the individual.

The disengagement, the nonintegration, of the poor with respect to the major institutions of society is a crucial element in the culture of poverty. It reflects the combined effect of a variety of factors including poverty, to begin with, but also segregation and discrimination, fear, suspicion and apathy and the development of alternative institutions and procedures in the slum community. The people do not belong to labor unions or political parties and make little use of banks, hospitals, department stores or museums. Such involvement as there is in the institutions of the larger society—in the jails, the army and the public welfare system—does little to suppress the traits of the culture of poverty. A relief system that barely keeps people alive perpetuates rather than eliminates poverty and the pervading sense of hopelessness.

People in a culture of poverty produce little wealth and receive little in return. Chronic unemployment and underemployment, low wages, lack of property, lack of savings, absence of food reserves in the home and chronic shortage of cash imprison the family and the individual in a vicious circle. Thus for lack of cash the slum householder makes frequent purchases of small quantities of food at higher prices. The slum economy turns inward; it shows a high incidence of pawning of personal goods, borrowing at usurious rates of interest, informal credit arrangements among neighbors, use of secondhand clothing and furniture.

There is awareness of middle-class values. People talk about them and even claim some of them as their own. On the whole, however, they do not live by them. They will declare that marriage by law, by the church or by both is the ideal form of marriage, but few will marry. For men who have no steady jobs, no property and no prospect of wealth to pass on to their children, who live in the present without expectations of the future, who want to avoid the expense and legal difficulties involved in marriage and divorce, a free union or consensual marriage makes good sense. The women, for their part, will turn down offers of marriage from men who are likely to be immature, punishing and generally unreliable. They feel that a consensual union gives them some of the freedom and flexibility men have. By not giving the fathers of their children legal status as husbands, the women have a stronger claim on the children. They also maintain exclusive rights to their own property.

Along with disengagement from the larger society, there is a hostility to the basic institutions of what are regarded as the dominant classes. There is hatred of the police, mistrust of government and of those in high positions and a cynicism that extends to the church. The culture of poverty thus holds a certain potential for protest and for entrainment in political movements aimed against the existing order.

With its poor housing and overcrowding, the community of the culture of poverty is high in gregariousness, but it has a minimum of organization beyond the nuclear and extended family. Occasionally slum dwellers come together in temporary informal groupings; neighborhood gangs that cut across slum settlements represent a considerable advance beyond the zero point of the continuum I have in mind. It is the low level of organization that gives the culture of poverty its marginal and anomalous quality in our highly organized society. Most primitive peoples have achieved a higher degree of sociocultural organization than contemporary urban slum dwellers. This is not to say that there may not be a sense of community and *esprit de corps* in a slum neighborhood. In fact, where slums are isolated from their surroundings by enclosing walls or other physical barriers, where rents are low and residence is stable and where the population constitutes a distinct ethnic, racial or language group, the sense of community may approach that of a village. In Mexico City and San Juan such territoriality is engendered by the scarcity of low-cost housing outside of established slum areas. In South Africa it is actively enforced by the *apartheid* that confines rural migrants to prescribed locations.

The family in the culture of poverty does not cherish childhood as a specially prolonged and protected stage in the life cycle. Initiation into sex comes early. With the instability of consensual marriage the family tends to be mother-centered and tied more closely to the mother's extended family. The female head of the house is given to authoritarian rule. In spite of much verbal emphasis on family solidarity, sibling rivalry for the limited supply of goods and maternal affection is intense. There is little privacy.

The individual who grows up in this culture has a strong feeling of fatalism, helplessness, dependence and inferiority. These traits, so often remarked in the current literature as characteristic of the American Negro, I found equally strong in slum dwellers of Mexico City and San Juan, who are not segregated or discriminated against as a distinct ethnic or racial group. Other traits include a high incidence of weak ego structure, orality and confusion of sexual identification, all reflecting maternal deprivation; a strong present-time orientation with relatively little disposition to defer gratification and plan for the future, and a high tolerance for psychological pathology of all kinds. There is widespread belief in male superiority and among the men a strong preoccupation with *machismo,* their masculinity.

Provincial and local in outlook, with little sense of history, these people know only their own neighborhood and their own way of life. Usually they do not have the knowledge, the vision or the ideology to see the similarities between their troubles and those of their counterparts elsewhere in the world. They are not class-conscious, although they are sensitive indeed to symbols of status.

The distinction between poverty and the culture of poverty is basic to the model described here. There are numerous examples of poor people whose way of life I would not characterize as belonging to this subculture. Many primitive and preliterate peoples that have been studied by anthropologists suffer dire poverty attributable to low technology or thin resources or both. Yet even the simplest of these peoples have a high degree of social organization and a relatively integrated, satisfying and self-sufficient culture.

In India the destitute lower-caste peoples—such as the Chamars, the leatherworkers, and the Bhangis, the sweepers—remain integrated in the larger society and have their own panchayat institutions of self-government. Their panchayats and their extended unilateral kinship systems, or clans, cut across village lines, giving them a strong sense of identity and continuity. In my studies of these peoples I found no culture of poverty to go with their poverty.

The Jews of eastern Europe were a poor urban people, often confined to ghettos. Yet they did not have many traits of the culture of poverty. They had a tradition of literacy that placed great value on learning; they formed many voluntary associations and adhered with devotion to the central community organization around the rabbi, and they had a religion that taught them they were the chosen people.

I would cite also a fourth, somewhat speculative example of poverty. On the basis of limited direct observation in one country—Cuba —and from indirect evidence, I am inclined to believe the culture of poverty does not exist in socialist countries. In 1947 I undertook a study of a slum in Havana. Recently I had an opportunity to revisit the same slum and some of the same families. The physical aspect of the place had changed little, except for a beautiful new nursery school. The people were as poor as before, but I was impressed to find much less of the feelings of despair and apathy, so symptomatic of the culture of poverty in the urban slums of the U.S. The slum was now highly organized, with block committees, educational committees, party committees. The people had found a new sense of power and importance in a doctrine that glorified the lower class as the hope of humanity, and they were armed. I was told by one Cuban official that the Castro government had practically eliminated delinquency by giving arms to the delinquents!

Evidently the Castro regime—revising Marx and Engels—did not write off the so-called *lumpenproletariat* as an inherently reactionary and antirevolutionary force but rather found in them a revolutionary potential and utilized it. Frantz Fanon, in his book *The Wretched of the Earth,* makes a similar evaluation of their role in the Algerian revolution: "It is within this mass of humanity, this people of the shantytowns, at the core of the *lumpenproletariat,* that the rebellion will find its urban spearhead. For the *lumpenproletariat,* that horde of starving men, uprooted from their tribe and from their clan, constitutes one of the most spontaneous and most radically revolutionary forces of a colonized people."

It is true that I have found little revolutionary spirit or radical ideology among low-income Puerto Ricans. Most of the families I studied were politically conservative, about half of them favoring the Statehood Republican Party, which provides opposition on the right to the Popular Democratic Party that dominates the politics of the commonwealth. It seems to me, therefore, that disposition for protest among people living in the culture of poverty will vary considerably according to the national context and historical circumstances. In contrast to Algeria, the independence movement in Puerto Rico has found little popular support. In Mexico, where the cause of independence carried long ago, there is no longer any such movement to stir the dwellers in the new and old slums of the capital city.

Yet it would seem that any movement—be it religious, pacifist or revolutionary—that organizes and gives hope to the poor and effectively promotes a sense of solidarity with larger groups must effectively destroy the psychological and social core of the culture of poverty. In this connection, I suspect that the civil rights movement among American Negroes has of itself done more to improve their self-image and self-respect than such economic gains as it has won, although, without doubt, the two kinds of progress are mutually reinforcing. In the culture of poverty of the American Negro the additional disadvantage of racial discrimination has generated a potential for revolutionary protest and organization that is absent in the slums of San Juan and Mexico City and, for that matter, among the poor whites in the South.

If it is true, as I suspect, that the culture of poverty flourishes and is endemic to the free-enterprise, pre-welfare-state stage of capitalism, then it is also endemic in colonial societies. The most likely candidates for the culture of poverty would be the people who come from the lower strata of a rapidly changing society and who are already partially alienated from it. Accordingly the subculture is likely to be found where imperial conquest has smashed the native social and economic structure and held the natives, perhaps for generations, in servile status, or where feudalism is yielding to capitalism in the later evolution of a colonial economy. Landless rural workers who migrate to the cities, as in Latin America, can be expected to fall into this way of life more readily than migrants from stable peasant villages with a well-organized traditional culture, as in India. It remains to be seen, however, whether the culture of poverty has not already begun to develop in the slums of Bombay and Calcutta. Compared with Latin America also, the strong corporate nature of many African tribal societies may tend to inhibit or delay the formation of a full-blown culture of poverty in the new towns and cities of that continent. In South Africa the institutionalization of repression and discrimination under *apartheid* may also have begun to promote an immunizing sense of identity and group consciousness among the African Negroes.

One must therefore keep the dynamic aspects of human institutions forward in observing and assessing the evidence for the presence, the waxing or the waning of this subculture. Measured on the dimension of relationship to the larger society, some slum dwellers may have a warmer identification with their national tradition even though they suffer deeper poverty than members of a similar community in another country. In Mexico City a high percentage of our respondents, including those with little or no formal schooling, knew of Cuauhtémoc, Hidalgo, Father Morelos, Juárez, Díaz, Zapata, Carranza and Cárdenas. In San Juan the names of Rámon Power, José de Diego, Baldorioty de Castro, Rámon Betances, Nemesio Canales, Lloréns Torres rang no bell; a few could tell about the late Albizu Campos. For the lower-income Puerto Rican, however, history begins with Muñoz Rivera and ends with his son Muñoz Marín.

The national context can make a big difference in the play of the crucial traits of fatalism and hopelessness. Given the advanced technology, the high level of literacy, the all-pervasive reach of the media of mass communications and the relatively high aspirations of all sectors of the population, even the poorest and most marginal communities of the U.S. must aspire to a larger future than the slum dwellers of Ecuador and Peru, where the actual possibilities are more limited and where an authoritarian social order persists in city and country. Among the 50 million U.S. citizens now more or less officially certified as poor, I would guess that about 20 percent live in a culture of poverty. The largest numbers in this group are made up of Negroes, Puerto Ricans, Mexicans, American Indians and Southern poor whites. In these figures there is some reassurance for those concerned, because it is much more difficult to undo the culture of poverty than to cure poverty itself.

Middle-class people—this would certainly include most social scientists—tend to concentrate on the negative aspects of the culture of poverty. They attach a minus sign to such traits as present-time orientation and readiness to indulge impulses. I do not intend to idealize or romanticize the culture of poverty—"it is easier to praise poverty than to live in it." Yet the positive aspects of these traits must not be overlooked. Living in the present may develop a capacity for spontaneity, for the enjoyment of the sensual, which is often blunted in the middle-class, future-oriented man. Indeed, I am often struck by the analogies that can be drawn between the mores of the very rich—of the "jet set" and "café society"—and the culture of the very poor. Yet it is, on the whole, a comparatively superficial culture. There is in it much pathos, suffering and emptiness. It does not provide much support or satisfaction; its pervading mistrust magnifies individual helplessness and isolation. Indeed, poverty of culture is one of the crucial traits of the culture of poverty.

The concept of the culture of poverty provides a generalization that may help to unify and explain a number of phenomena hitherto viewed as peculiar to certain racial, national or regional groups. Problems we think of as being distinctively our own or distinctively Negro (or as typifying any other ethnic group) prove to be endemic in countries where there are no segregated ethnic minority groups. If it follows that the elimination of physical poverty may not by itself eliminate the culture of poverty, then an understanding of the sub-culture may contribute to the design of measures specific to that purpose.

What is the future of the culture of poverty? In considering this question one must distinguish between those countries in which it represents a relatively small segment of the population and those in which it constitutes a large one. In the U.S. the major solution proposed by social workers dealing with the "hard core" poor has been slowly to raise their level of living and incorporate them in the middle class. Wherever possible psychiatric treatment is prescribed.

In underdeveloped countries where great masses of people live in the culture of poverty, such a social-work solution does not seem feasible. The local psychiatrists have all they can do to care for their own growing middle class. In those countries the people with a culture of poverty may seek a more revolutionary solution. By creating basic structural changes in society, by redistributing wealth, by organizing the poor and giving them a sense of belonging, of power and of leadership, revolutions frequently succeed in abolishing some of the basic characteristics of the culture of poverty even when they do not succeed in curing poverty itself.

THE POWER OF THE POOR

WARREN C. HAGGSTROM

On the average, the poor in the United States have bad reputations. They are regarded as responsible for much physical aggression and destruction of property; their support is alleged to be a heavy burden on the rest of the community; and they are said not even to try very hard to meet community standards of behavior or to be self-supporting. Poverty, it is said, is little enough punishment for people so inferior and so lacking in virtue.

Roughly speaking, these common opinions about the poor have some accuracy. Socially notorious varieties of deviancy and dependency do flourish in areas of poverty to a greater extent than in the remainder of our society. The middle classes, of course, have their own faults, which are sometimes perceptively observed and described by the poor. The relatively prosperous tend to use their verbal facility to conceal aspects of social reality from themselves and tend to use word-magic to make themselves comfortable about being in their generally undeserved positions of affluence, positions in which they manage to obtain the most pay and security for doing easy and interesting kinds of work.

Since the United States is a middle-class society, those who emphasize the bad reputations of the poor are regarded as hard-headed realists, while those who stress the phoniness of the middle classes are considered rather extreme and overly suspicious. When a social worker reports that the lower classes tend in the direction of schizophrenia and character disorders, he is viewed as having made a sober report of the existing state of affairs. Or when a social scientist discovers that the poor are unsocialized, childlike, occupy an early category in *his* category system of degrees of socialization, his discovery is treated as an important basis for further scientific work. But sup-

Reprinted with permission of The Macmillan Company from *Mental Health of the Poor*, edited by F. Riessman, J. Cohen, and A. Pearl. Copyright © 1964 by The Free Press of Glencoe, a division of The Macmillan Company.

pose that a leader of the poor announces that social workers tend to be "phonies" and "half-queer" as well, or suggests in his own language that social scientists are usually fuzzy-minded and socially irrelevant. This invidious description is not seen as a suitable hypothesis for investigation and research; it is rather said (without benefit of evidence) to be a symptom of the ignorance or of the personal or political needs of the person making the statement.

We cannot, of course, simply shed the presuppositions which attach to our social positions, and those of us who see the poor from above are likely not to have viewed them from the most flattering perspective. But let us, in the following discussion, attempt to be critical and scientific by orienting ourselves to reasons and evidence rather than to common-sense conceptual refinements of our current prejudices. We will first analyze a popular contemporary account of the psychology of poverty, and then advance a different orientation as a more precise explanation for available data.

PSYCHOLOGICAL CHARACTERISTICS OF THE POOR

Social scientists have arrived at a rough consensus about the modal personality in neighborhoods of poverty:

(1) The poor tend to have a keen sense of the personal and the concrete; their interest typically is restricted to the self, the family, and the neighborhood. There is a particular stress on the intimate, the sensory, the detailed, the personal. Not struggling to escape their circumstances, the poor often regard their ordinary lives as being of much intrinsic interest. This is related to their primary concern with the problem of survival rather than with the problem of moving up in society, and to the value which they attach to skills needed in coping with deprivation and uncertainty as distinguished from skills required to make progress. It has frequently been reported that persons in areas of poverty appear to be apathetic, to have little motivation, to be unable to cooperate with each other in the solution of problems which they regard as important, and to lack occupational and verbal skills and leadership traits; and are characterized by parochialism, nostalgic romanticism, and prescientific conceptions of the natural and social orders. Instead of having love for one another as fellow human beings, they achieve positive mutual attitudes through seeing themselves as all in the same boat together.

(2) Caught in the present, the poor do not plan very much. They meet their troubles and take their pleasures on a moment-to-moment basis; their schemes are short-term. Their time perspective is foreshortened by their belief that it is futile to think of the future. Thus, when the poor use conventional words to refer to the future, those words tend to be empty of real meaning. They have little sense of the past and they go forward, but not forward to any preconceived place. Their pleasures and rewards are sought in the present; they find it difficult to delay gratification, to postpone satisfaction.

(3) There is much egoism, envy, and hostility toward those who prosper. There is a feeling of being exploited. There are many negative attitudes and few positive ones. The unity of the poor comes about through suspicion of and resentment toward outsiders, through opposition to common enemies and hostility to powerful groups. Disillusion about the possibility of advancement stems from a victim complex in relation to the powerful. There is a sense of inability to affect what will happen, a lack of conviction that it is within their power to affect their circumstances. The outside world cannot be trusted; it must be defended against. Outsiders and the outside are seen as risky, likely to injure you when you least expect it. Pessimism and fatalism about being able to affect one's own situation stems from a feeling of being victimized by superordinate, capricious, and malevolent natural and social forces. Their lives appear to them to be fixed by the immutable forces of fate, luck, and chance. While well-to-do people tend to attribute causality to inner forces, the poor tend to make external attributes of causality, seeing themselves as subject to external and arbitrary forces and pressures.[1]

THE SOCIAL PROBLEM OF POVERTY AND ITS NATURAL SOLUTION

The poor, in short, are commonly seen as apathetic, childlike, not very competent, and hostile-dependent. Other research, emphasized in the past few years, has pointed out the extent to which the poor tend to occupy specific social categories (minority racial and ethnic groups, the elderly, ADC families, and the like), as well as the continuing large proportion of the population who have low incomes even in such an affluent society as the United States. It has been natural to get concerned about a large proportion of the population, the members of which have behavior patterns and psychological characteristics that tend to place them in opposition to or dependence on the remainder of the community.

Poverty has therefore again become a publicly recognized social problem in the United States. The general perception of a social problem leads to a search for its solution. Since a lack of money is the most universal characteristic of poverty, and since a general increase of income for some social groups would automatically abolish poverty, it seems clear to many persons that certain known steps are suitable to end poverty in the United States. Their view is that public policies should be developed and implemented that emphasize provision of jobs, increased access to education that leads to jobs, and higher minimum wage levels and welfare payments. Scientists, according to this view, can contribute by learning how to measure poverty with greater accuracy and by studying its adverse psychological and other consequences, and they should seek to understand how these consequences might be controlled.

In this natural line of reasoning it is assumed rather than demonstrated that the major problem of the poor is poverty, a lack of money. But this assumption is essential to the associated recommendations for scientific work and social policy. It may be well, therefore to inquire in a more searching fashion whether the problems of the poor primarily result from a lack of money.

There are a number of phenomena which one could hardly anticipate on the basis of such an assumption:

(1) A given level of real income has various consequences depending upon the circumstances in which a person receives the income.

Among the poor, there are many subgroups, the members of which do not display the presumed psychological consequences of poverty. These include most of that portion of the leadership of the poor which is itself poor, those low-income families with high educational aspirations for their children, low-income members of religious groups such as the Hutterites, university student families with little income; and the like. In the past, of course, members of the lower middle class have survived on real incomes below those received today by comparable public welfare families and without losing their capacity to struggle in the pursuit of distant ends. Many from the intelligentsia today in such countries as India and Japan have incomes that, in the United States, would place them with the poor. They may differ from educated Americans in personality characteristics, but they do not have the alleged psychology of poverty either.

(2) Increases in income often do not lead to a diminution of the expected psychological consequences of poverty.

For example, the rise in real per capita public welfare expenditures in the United States has not had a demonstrated effect on the psychological functioning of welfare recipients.

(3) Differences in income between otherwise comparable groups of poor do not appear to be accompanied by differences in psychological functioning.

For example, states vary greatly in the size of their payments to comparable welfare recipient families. Comparable families appear to resemble one another in psychological orientation regardless of relatively major differences in their incomes.

(4) When income remains constant, but persons in a neighborhood of poverty become involved in successful social action on important issues, in their own behalf, their psychological orientation does extend over a greater period of time, their feeling of helplessness does lessen, their skills and activities do gradually change.

For example, no one could have predicted on the basis of articles in the relevant scholarly journals that lowly Negroes from areas of poverty would, with some help, begin to organize with such effect that they would carry timid and ultra-conventional members of the Negro middle classes along with them into a militant struggle for freedom. It has also been reported that many "lower-class" Negroes, who have become part of the Muslim movement, have had their lives transformed in the direction of greater order and achievement.

During this past summer I gathered some data concerning The Woodlawn Organization (TWO), a primarily "lower-class," predominantly Negro organization which was initiated about two years ago in Chicago with the assistance of Saul Alinsky and the Industrial Areas Foundation. The poor constitute the bulk of active members, and are an important segment of the leadership of this community organization, which has already demonstrated its effectiveness and power. For example, TWO has delivered a majority of the votes from a Negro area to elect a white alderman who takes a strong civil rights position; the unsuccessful opponent was a Negro from the regular political organization. It has been able to secure its own conditions for implementation of an urban renewal development proposed by the University of Chicago for part of the Woodlawn area. TWO has carried out rent strikes and has taken other successful actions against owners of dilapidated slum buildings; it has organized picketing of

stores that sell merchandise to people who cannot afford the high interest on installments; it has organized successful city hall demonstrations of more than a thousand persons. Over this period of widespread
involvement, the poor appear to have gradually acquired skills of
organization, longer range planning, and other qualities contrary to
those which reputedly characterize areas of poverty. I observed a
similar process occurring in "lower-class" white neighborhoods in
Northwest Chicago, where the Northwest Community Organization,
another Alinsky-associated enterprise, has been in existence for less
than two years.

(5) When members of some groups lose or give up their wealth,
they do not thereby acquire the psychology of poverty.

One has only to consider the vows of poverty taken by members of
some religious orders to illustrate this assertion.

Since the psychology of poverty obtains only under specific and
describable circumstances, one cannot therefore use poverty as an
explanation for these psychological characteristics which often are
associated with poverty.

We might briefly mention other problems involved in the ready
identification of poverty as the major problem of the poor. First, it is
invalid reasoning to proceed without evidence from the fact that the
poor have distinctive failings to the assumption that poverty is important in the etiology of these failings. It is incorrect simply to take the
defining characteristics of a social category to which a group of people
belong (the category "poverty" in this case) and use it without
further evidence to account for the peculiar afflictions of that group of
people. Second, even if *all* poor today were to exhibit the psychology
of poverty, this may be merely an accidental connection, and the fact
of having little money could remain only distantly related, for example, to feelings of being dominated by irrational external forces. One
should not confuse an observed regularity with an inevitable regularity, a conventional law with a natural law. Third, when a scientist
observes that a group of persons, the poor, have adopted their own
patterns of behavior and systems of beliefs, this does not mean that
the behavior and belief patterns are cultural or that these patterns
represent durable characteristics of the people involved over a wide
variety of social situations. The patterns and beliefs may be situational, not internalized, and may shift readily as the situation changes.
Just when social scientists appear to be getting the poor firmly in
mind, the poor are transformed. Thus, the "psychology of the poor"

may be quite different from the psychology of a neurosis the basis of which *is* internalized.

It is therefore likely that the natural solution to the problem of poverty is naïve: it merely assumes the determinants of the psychology of poverty.[2]

THE SELF-HELP DOCTRINE AND ITS CONSEQUENCES FOR DEPENDENT PERSONS

In rapidly industrializing societies in which there are many opportunities for individual advancement there typically arises some form of the doctrine of self-help. The common core of self-help views can be stated as follows: a person is good to the extent to which he has assumed responsibility for and accomplished the realization of his potentialities for maximum use of his native capacities in a long, sustained, and arduous effort to reach a distant legitimate goal. With enough effort any normal person can attain such goals; no special ability is needed.

In the older Western industrial nations a growing appreciation of the limitations of opportunity has provided increasing support for modification of the traditional doctrine, with the qualification that ability as well as effort is necessary to success, and that some persons have been born with more ability than others. Also, since the nineteenth century, the common legitimate goal has changed from entrepreneurship of a prosperous independent business to a high position in a large work organization, and the struggle begins in the institutions of learning before the transfer to a work setting.

According to the doctrine of self-help, *anyone,* given enough time and enough effort, could achieve success. Thus, to be poor could have either of two meanings. On the one hand, poverty was regarded as the original accompaniment of the highest development of character, the struggling poor who were later to become successful were most worthy of respect. On the other hand, poverty indefinitely prolonged might mean a character defect, a lack of will power. Poverty, therefore, was ambiguous; from it alone one could reach no conclusion about virtue. However, an economy with limited opportunities for success plus the belief in equal opportunity for success according to merit made inevitable an assault on the self-esteem of the permanently unsuccessful.

Officially defined dependency was not usually regarded as ambiguous. The person on welfare has left the struggle altogether and has sat back to allow others to furnish his sustenance. It is true that some persons, the crippled, the very young, the seriously ill, and so forth, clearly could not have avoided dependency. But as for the rest, the presumption of their ability to work and succeed if they only tried hard enough led to the inevitable conclusion that those who have left off trying are bad. The intensity with which this conclusion was known was also related to the fact that dependent persons were seen to be living at the expense of the rest of the community. Not only did the scoundrels manage to exist without honest labor, but they actually made of the rest of the community a duped partner to their idleness. Inexcused dependency became a social symbol communicating defective character, toward which there was a feeling of superiority tinged with contempt. Even in the best of circumstances professional helpers were automatically considered morally as well as materially superior to those helped, and thus the helping relationship became a concrete carrier of the general meaning of dependency: the unworthiness of the dependent.

In affecting the psychology of dependency, the self-help doctrine has also, of course, affected the *behavior* of persons who are in need. One way to evade the unpleasantness of being dependent is to avoid getting help at all in a dependent situation. Families in trouble, as was discovered in various studies, often hide away when they need help the most. The stigma attached to receiving assistance prevents the use even of available resources.

Official dependency in modern society is a residual category of persons unable to enter into the normal types of income-producing relationships. Such persons are unable to relate to the normal avenues for gaining support, and the presence and location of such avenues is therefore the major immediate condition or cause of dependency in modern society. Inability to relate to normal avenues of support symbolizes failure, and perception by a dependent person of his own dependency is sufficient to produce shame and guilt and their complications. Official dependency is fundamentally the perception of the use of relative social power within a superordinate-subordinate relationship; the doctrine of self-help in a contractual economy made financial dependency the focal point for this definition in modern society. The official assumption is that all working adults are equal in that they have entered into work contracts on an equal basis, contracts which they could have chosen to enter or not to enter.

The financially self-responsible person is assumed to be responsible also in other areas of his life. For this reason dependency can concern any area of superordinate-subordinate relationship, and there is always some stigma associated with any dependency relationship, even though there is often pleasure in divesting oneself of the burden of self-responsibility. Even the relationship of citizen to expert can be distasteful since it makes the citizen intellectually dependent on the expert.

The sharpest psychological impact of dependency has occurred where it is officially defined and therefore clearly perceived and sanctioned by the community. However, most dependency is not so explicitly defined; most of the poor are not "on welfare." Even so, the poor are generally perceived, however unclearly, as having failed, and this perception has hardened the community against them. In the latter case, the doctrine of self-help has intensified the feelings of hopelessness among the poor.

The extent of self-support is only one measure of the extent of dependency, a measure stressed only in connection with the doctrine of self-help. More generally, dependency is the placement of one's destiny in other hands. It is therefore especially characteristic of the areas of poverty, but also characterizes many other aspects of society, including the low echelons of large organizations, organization men at any echelon, and so forth. In a general sense dependency is also destructive, but more subtly so. If extent of self-realization is a measure of personality development, then dependency, which erodes self-realization with loss of self-responsibility, is a measure of personality inadequacy. If the human personality develops as a decision process through self-responsible choices, then the taking away of self-responsible choices through assuming the subordinate position in a dependency relationship necessarily destroys personality.

THE SOCIAL SITUATION OF THE POOR

Most of the poor are heavily dependent on outside forces. In many places, a poor person is much more likely to be subject to police interrogation and search, or to public identification as the object of police activity, than is a member of a middle-class family. Urban renewal programs periodically disrupt the neighborhoods of poverty, scattering the families in several directions in accordance with standards which the poor do not understand or support. Schools function impervious to the concerns of the low-income families whose children attend, or else schools may seek themselves to "lead" in the areas of poverty in which they are located, that is, they seek to impose school standards and definitions on the neighborhoods. Settlement houses run recreation programs that meet their own traditional criteria, but neighborhood youth often do not understand these criteria, often cannot engage in accustomed and legal modes of behavior and still participate in settlement house activities, often, involuntarily and without understanding, have to disperse friendship groups in order to participate in a recreation program.

Many families, having bought more than they can afford, especially through high-interest installment financing, have no way to know whether or when their furniture will be repossessed or their check garnished. Medical and psychiatric care are inadequate, inadequately understood, and uncertainly available, especially to the poor who do not have connections through welfare. The securing of general relief or categorical assistance is a humiliating experience at best for people imbued with self-help ideas, but the deliberate rudeness intended to discourage as many applicants as possible, the complex agency rules which are not so much bases for action as after-the-fact rationales to provide support for decisions already made, and the subjective and unpredictable decisions of social workers representing agencies to the poor, all combine to place the economic foundation of many families at the mercy of completely incomprehensible forces.

The poor who seek employment must find it in a dwindling supply of jobs available to unskilled and semiskilled persons (including domestics), often seasonal or temporary work. In addition, the landlords of the poor are frequently discourteous, seldom inclined to make adequate repairs on their buildings, and likely to blame the tenants for the condition of the ancient and crumbling structures for which high rents are charged.

In other words the poor, by virtue of their situation, tend to be more dependent than other groups on a larger number of powerful persons and organizations, which are often very unclear about the bases for their actions and unpredictable in their decisions, and which further render the poor helpless by condescending or hostile attitudes, explicit verbal communications which state or imply the inferiority of the poor, and callousness or actual harassment. If we divide the powerful persons affecting the poor into two groups, the benevolent in intention on the one hand, and the callous or punitive on the other, we will find that the majority of both types of power figure treat the poor as inferior and reach down to relate to them.[3]

The situation of poverty, then, is the situation of enforced dependency, giving the poor very little scope for *action*, in the sense of behavior under their own control which is central to their needs and values. This scope for action is supposed to be furnished by society to any person in either of two ways. First, confidence, hope, motivation, and skills for action may be provided through childhood socialization and continue as a relatively permanent aspect of the personality. Second, social positions are provided which make it easy for their occupants to be implemented in their futures. Middle-class socialization and middle-class social positions customarily both provide bases for effective action; lower-class socialization and lower-class social positions usually both fail to make it possible for the poor to act.

Thus, the dependency of the poor is not primarily a neurotic need to occupy dependency positions in social relationships, but rather it results from a deprivation of those minimal social resources, at every period of their lives, which the poor need and therefore must seek. The poor are not victims of the social system in the sense that "organization men" are victims. They are rather, as Michael Harrington has emphasized, the *other* America, outsiders to the major society. In consequence, members of the majority society are usually outsiders to the poor.

The initial dependency and its consequences are reinforced by the hardening of a consensus in the majority community about the nature of the poor, stabilization of the patterns of behavior in areas of poverty, and partial internalization of ideas and patterns of behavior in the children who grew up in both communities. Thus, the positions of poor persons in relationship to superordinate forces are expressions of two communities, a superior and powerful community and an inferior and weaker community; two communities with institutionalized ways of living which prop up the superordinate position of the one in relation to the other.

People isolate and segregate those they fear and pity. The stronger of the two communities has traditionally acted to alleviate the results perceived to be undesirable without changing the relationship of the two communities or ending the division into two communities. Since persons designing and implementing such programs did not consider the consequences of the division for their aims, they were able to maintain an intention to bring the poor into their society. The recommendations have been for improved law enforcement; public welfare; public housing; social settlements; higher horizons educational programs; social work with "hard core" families; urban renewal, clean-up, paint-up, and fix-up programs; block and neighborhood organizations; and the like. All these plans and programs have usually shared two characteristics: (1) they are initiated and supported from outside the neighborhoods of poverty and imposed on the poor; and (2) they fail to make any lasting positive impact on neighborhoods of poverty. That is, although a few persons and families become affluent and leave the neighborhoods, the majority remain poor and continue in an atmosphere of apathy, disorganization, and hostility, toward the programs designed to rescue them. These programs, presupposing the inferiority of the people in the area, perpetuate and exacerbate the inequality. Definitions of the poor are carried by the institutionalized helping hands. Insofar as these agencies have any *social* impact, the definitions imbedded in them become self-fulfilling. But, although the powerful external social agencies—powerful in relation to the poor—are not very effective in carrying out their official tasks in areas of poverty, they do enable the stronger community to believe that something is being done about the social problem of poverty, reducing guilt and shame to such an extent that there remains little motivation to develop some effective means to bring the poor into the larger society.

On the basis of this sketch of the dynamics of the situation of the poor, the following classification can be made of the sources of the "psychology of poverty."

(a) In any modern industrial society the overall amount of power of the society tends constantly to increase, although the rate of increase may vary. Although everyone in the society may secure ownership of additional *material* goods as a result of technological progress, the additional *power* tends to be secured only by those persons and social systems with preexistent power. The poor boy with strong internalized drives and skills for success and the large corporation with effective control over technological advances in its field both illustrate the tendency for socially created power to attract to itself additional power. But the poor most often have neither the power created through childhood socialization nor that to be secured through attachment to a strong social system in which they have influence. In some countries, the population is predominantly poor, and this populace may have some power through the political process. But in the United States the poor are an unorganized or ineffectively organized minority, unable even to exert influence in the political sphere. Thus, increments in power tend to attach to those with power, and the balance of power in a country such as the United States tends naturally to tilt against the poor.

(b) The fact of being powerless, but with needs that must be met, leads the poor to be dependent on the organizations, persons, and institutions which can meet these needs. The situation of dependency and powerlessness through internal personality characteristics as well as through social position leads to apathy, hopelessness, conviction of the inability to act successfully, failure to develop skills, and so on.

(c) As a consequence of the self-help doctrine, this "psychology of poverty" arouses the anger of the affluent toward the poor. Thus, the affluent can avoid the necessity to alter the social situation of the poor by assuming that the poor are bad and deserve their situation. This additional meaning of poverty makes rigid the dependency aspects of the social situation of the poor, and, to some extent, the poor accept the prevalent view of themselves. However, since the poor are not together in an unambiguously clear social category, they, at the same time, may reject being placed in such a category subject to the assumption of their dependency and inferiority. For example, persons eligible to live in public housing are not affected only by the convenience, space, and other physical characteristics of their living quarters. A large proportion seem to prefer dilapidated private housing operated by an indifferent landlord to better maintained, less crowded, less expensive quarters in a public housing project in which the management is concerned with tenant needs. The meaning of living in such a project may offset the superiority of the physical living arrangements.

(d) Over time the dependency relationship of the poor becomes institutionalized and habits, traditions, and organizations arise in both the affluent community and in the neighborhoods of poverty, maintaining the relationship between them. The poor react in part to the institutionalization itself. For example, "lower-class" delinquency does not only stem from the fact that the poor have few and drab job opportunities. There is also the perception that the conforming poor tend to remain indefinitely in low social positions as well as the

angry rejection by the adolescent poor of attempts, through law enforcement and social agencies, to control and manipulate them without altering their situation.

Consequences of this social process for the poor have been indicated at several points in the preceding discussion; we will only briefly
recapitulate some of them here.

First, people tend either to retreat from or to attack forces controlling their lives which they cannot affect and which are not inescapable. For this reason the poor typically stand aloof from settlement
houses, get minimally involved with social workers, drop out of
school. Only forces too omnipresent to be escaped may ensure normative affiliation through identification with aggressors. It is easy to
see the poor as paranoid since they are so often hostile to and suspicious of powerful objects which they may perceive in a distorted
fashion. However, paranoia presumably requires origins in early
childhood, while the hostility and suspicion of the poor naturally
arise from their social position and their necessarily over-simplified
and naturally personified perceptions of it.

Second, with less of their selves bound up in their self-conceptions
than is the case with other groups, the poor do not entirely accept
these definitions of themselves, but protect themselves by various
psychological strategies from fully accepting the implications of their
situation. The impact of the definitions then is primarily indirect; the
definitions have consequences by creating the situation of the poor
through the meaning of poverty to those who possess power. The
situation gives rise to the typical absence of that hope which is associated with action and which gives salience to intentions and attitudes.
Thus, the poor frequently verbalized middle-class values without
practicing them. Their verbalizations are useful in protecting their
self-conceptions and in dealing with the affluent rather than in any
pronounced relationship to non-verbal behavior. This does not imply
deliberate falsification; a poor person may have the necessary sincerity,
intention, and skill to embark on a course of action but there is so
much unconscious uncertainty about achieving psychological returns
through success that the action may never be seriously attempted. As
has been discovered in social surveys, the poor may not only pay lip
service to middle-class notions, but may, for similar reasons, say to any
powerful person what they believe he wants to hear. That is, much of
the behavior of the poor does not relate primarily to their own basic
values, beliefs and perceptions held by others about the poor. The

poor are normally involved in partly involuntary self-diminution; their behavior may therefore be remarkably transformed when, as has happened through social action, they begin to acquire a sense of power, of ability to realize *their* aspirations. Thus, the so-called differential values of the poor, which are ill-defined at best, are more nearly comprehensible as the psychological consequences of a long continued situation of perceived powerlessness in contemporary industrial society. They become a subculture to the extent that the traditions, orientations, and habits of dependency become internalized.

Third, the situation of the poor, the inability of the poor to act in their own behalf, creates a less complex personality structure for them than is the case with affluent persons with more linguistic skills. This does not necessarily mean that the poor have less effective personalities, or are unsocialized in comparison, since the personalities of more highly educated persons are often partly constituted by social elaborated fantasies which conceal reality and rationalize avoidance of problem solving.

Fourth, awareness of their common fate typically leads the poor to engage in mutual aid activities, activities which, in spite of involving only very minor skills, are precursors to the joint social action which develops naturally as the poor acquire organizational skills and confidence in using them.

Fifth, because of the social situation of the poor and the fact that the majority society has relatively little normative basis for social control in areas of poverty, these areas are often characterized by high rates of publicly discernible types of deviance: juvenile delinquency, school dropouts, alcoholism, illegitimacy, mother-centered families, and the like.

Finally there are differential consequences of institutionalized, uncompensated powerlessness for the poor who have various social positions within areas of poverty. For example, because of the greater expectation for men to be powerful and to be sources of power, the consequences of powerlessness for "lower-class" men is usually greater than that for women.

All of this suggests that the problems of the poor are not so much of poverty as of a particularly difficult variety of situational dependency, a helplessness to affect many important social factors in their lives, the functioning or purpose of which they do not understand, and which are essentially unpredictable to them.

NOT ENOUGH MONEY VERSUS SITUATIONAL DEPENDENCY

With increased money the poor could at least be better able to cope with such forces, could be less dependent on some. What, then, is the relationship between the poverty of the poor and their situational dependency?

Money is a generalized source of power over people through a right to control over goods and services. As such, money is one of many kinds of power. Poverty, therefore, is one of many kinds of powerlessness, of being subject to one's social situation instead of being able to affect it through action, that is, through behavior which flows from decisions and plans. Since there are several varieties of generalized power, an absence of money is often replaceable *insofar as the psychological reactions to powerlessness are concerned.* An American Indian who lives in poverty may have considerable influence through authority relationships traditional in his culture. Members of religious orders who have taken vows of poverty remain able to exercise influence through their order and through relationships of interdependence with colleagues. The college student with a very low income has influence through the expectations of his future social position. When the poor engage in successful social action they gain power, even when their incomes remain unchanged.

In other words, when social scientists have reported on the psychological consequences of poverty it seems reasonable to believe that they have described the psychological consequences of powerlessness. And many persons without money have, or get, other varieties of power, or else identify with powerful persons or groups and therefore fail to exhibit these consequences. Even the poor do not react entirely on the basis of the social definition of them. There are counter institutions and traditions (churches, unions, and clubs) which deflect the impact of the majority definition. Primary groups (family and peer) also mediate and modify the community definitions they transmit. The behavior of the poor may not, therefore, reflect their self-conceptions; we should not suppose that the poor feel as would middle-class persons in their situations, or as their behavior suggests they feel. This very resistance of the poor makes it possible to attempt the otherwise herculean task of trying to get the major society to alter its relationship to poverty by helping the poor themselves to build a backfire, to become strong and effective enough to challenge the invidious definitions that have been made of them.

Human personality is a process of decisions and actions on the basis of decisions. One becomes fully human only through acting in important areas of one's life. All social arrangements which take responsibility out of the hands of the poor, which make decisions and action more difficult or operative over a more restricted area, feed the psychology of powerlessness which is so widely (and correctly) regarded as undesirable. For example, it is often noted that the poor lack a time perspective. But only through action (important decisions and behavior on their basis) does one acquire a history and, with the history, a practical concern with the future.

What consequences does the social situation of the poor have for programs to help the poor? We will next consider some general answers to this question.

Redefining the Social Situation of the Poor

We can reject two possible alternatives.

First, the solution most frequently suggested is to help the poor secure more money without otherwise changing present power relationships. This appears to implement the idea of equality while avoiding any necessary threat to established centers of power. But, since the consequences are related to *powerlessness,* not to the absolute supply of money available to the poor, and *since the amount of power purchasable with a given supply of money decreases as a society acquires a larger supply of goods and services,* the solution of raising the incomes of the poor is likely, unless accompanied by other measures, to be ineffective in an affluent society. Where the poor live in serious deprivation of goods and services, an increase in the supply of those goods and services would be an important source of power, that is, of access to resources which satisfy crucial needs. However, when the poor do not live in actual deprivation, increases in money make relatively little impact on the dependency relationships in which they are entangled. The opportunity to participate in *interdependent* relationships, as a *member* of the majority society, requires an increase in *power.*

Second, the *self-help* doctrine is normally related to conventional criteria of success, and persons who have not met these conventional criteria therefore are threatened with feelings of guilt and shame. One theoretically possible solution would seem to involve redefinition of success, allowing social support to lives which are now viewed as failures. This, however, presupposes an ability to meet some alternative criteria of success through action, a possible solution for philosophers, poets, or beatniks, but not now generally possible for the poor. It may, however, be that the meaning of the self-help doctrine could be adequately extended to reward the social action of the poor who can act successfully through their own organizations.

Along these lines the criteria for an effective solution are reasonably clear. In order to reduce poverty-related psychological and social problems in the United States, the major community will have to change its relationship to neighborhoods of poverty in such fashion that families in the neighborhoods have a greater stake in the broader society and can more successfully participate in the decision-making process of the surrounding community.

It is frequently said that we must provide opportunities for the poor. To render more than lip service to this objective demands more power and more skill and more knowledge than we now possess for the bureaucratic provision of such opportunities. For example, there are a finite number of jobs available, fewer than the number of people looking for work. There are severe limits to the extent to which the adult poor can be trained for existing openings. A large proportion of the poor have jobs which do not remove them from the ranks of the powerless. Any great shift in opportunities made available to the poor within the structure of the majority community will threaten more powerful groups with vested interests in those limited opportunities, and the proponents of creating opportunities for the poor cannot themselves affect the political or economic process enough to implement their good intentions.

It is important to develop opportunities in sensitive relation to the perception by the poor of their own needs. When this is not done, the poor are not likely to be able to use efficiently the opportunities created for them. And, most central of all, rather than to provide opportunities for the "lower class," the poor must as a group be helped to secure opportunities for themselves. Only then will motivation be released that is now locked in the silent and usually successful battle of the neighborhoods of poverty to maintain themselves in an alien social world. This motivation which will enable them to enter the majority society and make it as nurturant of them as it is at present of the more prosperous population.

The involvement of the poor in successful and significant social action provides both immediate and compelling psychological returns, and also the possibility of initiative to help the bureaucratic organizations related to the poor to fulfil their officially stated purposes. The institutions of the major community can be forced to establish relationship of interdependence, not of dependence, with the poor; professionals can help by accepting professional roles as employees of the organizations of the poor.

In our society, inner worth as expressed in action, striving, the struggle is held eventually to result in attainment of aspirations. If one is not successful, one is viewed as worthwhile so long, and only so long, as one struggles. The poor tend to be regarded as failures and not struggling, and hence as worthless. This perception of worthlessness is incorporated in the conception which others have of the poor and also, to some extent, in the conceptions which the poor have of themselves. One way in which the poor can remedy the psychological consequences of their powerlessness and of the image of the poor as worthless is for them to undertake social action that redefines them as potentially worthwhile and individually more powerful. To be effective, such social action should have the following characteristics:

1. the poor see themselves as the source of the action;
2. the action affects in major ways the preconceptions, values, or interests of institutions and persons defining the poor;
3. the action demands much in effort and skill or in other ways becomes salient to major areas of the personalities of the poor;
4. the action ends in success; and
5. the successful self-originated important action increases the force and number of symbolic or nonsymbolic communications of the potential worth or individual power of individuals who are poor.

The result of social action of this kind is a concurrent change in the view which the poor have of themselves and in the view of the poor by the outside world. There is a softening of the destructive social reality and immediate psychological returns to the poor, although not without hostile reactions from advantaged persons and organizations with known or hidden vested interests in maintenance of the areas of poverty.[4]

The only initial additional resources which a community should provide to neighborhoods of poverty should be on a temporary basis: organizers who will enable the neighborhoods quickly to create powerful, independent, democratic organizations of the poor. These organizations will themselves then seek from the rest of the community resources necessary to the neighborhoods for the solution of the problems they perceive. Agencies for the provision of training and education and opportunities can be developed under the control of the neighborhoods of poverty, thereby ensuring that the poor are in interdependent rather than dependent positions in relation to the agencies. This would meet the professed objectives of most communities since it would effectively motivate the poor to maximum use of opportunities, since the requirements of professional practice will ensure the quality of services rendered, and since the communities state their intention not to allow their help to become an instrument of domination.

The comment that "we know the needs of the poor" is accurate in a very general sense. But there is a great distance between this observation and a knowledge of how, in practice, those needs can be met. If a community is not merely giving lip service to meeting them, if a community wants to be effective as well as to have good intentions, then the way of meeting needs must be appropriate to the personal and social characteristics of those being helped. In this case, effectiveness requires that only *unilateral* additional help be given at the outset and in the form of temporary assistance in the creation of democratic and powerful organizations of the poor. Through such organizations, the poor will then negotiate with outsiders for resources and opportunities without having to submit to concurrent control from outside. The outcome will be maximal motivation to take advantage of resources and opportunities which are sensitively tailored to their needs.

SUMMARY

There are two alternative ways to understand the psychological characteristics of the poor. These characteristics can be naïvely understood as resulting from poverty. But there are a number of reasons why it is more precise to view them as the psychology of the *powerlessness* of the poor.

These alternative points of view have also different consequences for social policy. If the problem were only one of a lack of money, it could be solved through provision of more and better paying jobs for the poor, increased minimum wage levels, higher levels of welfare payments, and so on. There would be, in that case, no real need for the poor to undertake any social action on their own behalf. This view is consistent with the idea that the poor are unable to participate in and initiate the solution of their own problems.

However, since it is more likely that the problem is one of powerlessness, joint initiative by the poor on their own behalf should precede and accompany responses from the remainder of society. In practice this initiative is likely to be most effectively exercised by powerful conflict organizations based in neighborhoods of poverty.[5]

NOTES

[1] This summary social scientists' image of the psychological characteristics of the poor was prepared on the basis of a survey of articles and books relating to poverty published by social scientists during the past fifteen years. Any particular author would be likely to differ on one or more points and would probably want to add others not recorded here. For example, in *The Children of Sanchez* (New York, Random House, 1961), Oscar Lewis includes "a strong present time orientation with relatively little ability to defer gratification and plan for the future, a sense of resignation and fatalism based upon the realities of their difficult life situation, a belief in male superiority which reaches its crystallization in *machisme* or the cult of masculinity, a corresponding martyr complex among women, and finally, a high tolerance for psychological pathology of all sorts." (Pages xxvi-xxvii). Lewis, of course, restricted his account to urban Mexican poor.

[2] The personality characteristics of the poor may themselves be different from those reported. Much of the scientific literature is based on reports of verbal or other behavioral responses of the poor in the presence of researchers, usually middle-class persons of much higher status and greater power than those being studied. It is not easy for a powerful person accurately to understand one who is weak since the behavior of the latter in the research situation may depend very much on the behavior of the former. The massive failure of intelligent and educated Southern whites to understand Negroes with whom they had maintained years of presumably close relationship should provide reason for researchers to use caution in their claims based on a few hours' contact with persons much different from their usual associates.

[3] It should be remembered that not all sections of the poor are so much at the mercy of outside forces. The stably employed working-class poor are less dependent on mysterious, unpredictable, arbitrary, and capricious forces. There are degrees and kinds of poverty, and the differences among them will

be set forth elsewhere to supplement the general description contained in this paper.

4 The Syracuse University School of Social Work has developed a field placement in which graduate students are now receiving training in initiating social action projects by the poor to resolve problems of broad concern in neighborhoods of poverty. Experience indicates that social work students can learn to help the poor jointly to engage in efforts which meet these criteria. Social action efforts by the poor in areas of poverty have occurred in several places. For example, several years ago, Hope and Dan Morrow moved with their family into a block in East Harlem, New York City. With their help, the families in the block organized themselves formally and informally for a number of important purposes ranging from keeping streets clean to reducing juvenile delinquency. On a larger scale, some of the social action organizations originated by Saul Alinsky of the Industrial Areas Foundation have involved large numbers of people in neighborhood improvement through a conflict process around crucial neighborhood issues. IAF organizations have enabled areas to decrease or end exploitation by some absentee landlords and unethical businesses. They have also ended police brutality and secured police protection, street cleaning, and other services which low income neighborhoods had not previously received at a level equivalent to that of the remainder of the community. Several of the IAF organizations are engaging in "self-help" nonfederally assisted urban renewal. It remains true, however, that most social action programs in low income areas do not meet the above criteria. Such programs frequently attempt to mobilize neighborhoods of poverty without jeopardizing any existing power arrangement, even temporarily, and thus pursue two contradictory objectives simultaneously. They may, in any case, perform such useful functions as providing symbolic satisfaction for the conscience of the majority community and jobs for some estimable persons.

5 Because of the nature of this paper there has been no attempt in it to marshal the data relevant to the various assertions made in the discussion of the psychology of areas of poverty as the psychology of powerlessness. This paper has not been designed as a contribution to science in the sense in which science is understood to be a body of verified statements. In the area under consideration there is no such body of statements now available. Contributions to science remain possible, but must be put forward as relatively tentative formulations in the early stages of a process which will move to the collection of additional data relevant to specific points. It is my hope that the above formulation can serve such a purpose.

SECTION VI

Intergroup Relations

INTRODUCTION

This topic, intergroup relations, has become increasingly difficult to address. Public events show just how difficult it is for American society to deal rationally and objectively with questions related to the minorities and race. Even the choice of correct or acceptable racial designation is an emotionally charged issue to many. It has been pointed out that American Negroes are saying, "We want to be called by a name that we designate for ourselves rather than a name that somebody else has designated for us," a legitimate enough request. Spelled with a capital, "Negro" does represent an accepted designation around which there is reasonable consensus in the behavioral sciences. This debate reminds one of the period when nearly a century ago some Jews began referring to themselves as "Hebrews" to counter some of the connotative use of "Jew." The reader will find both black and Negro used here. Afro-American, Afram or African-American have not been used, although they do express, for some, their current orientation. However, this is not the big issue. The more important issue for us is the great concern that even a term generates. It reflects a climate that makes open discussion of issues extremely difficult. It is appropriate to search for the meaning behind this behavior. Given today's climate, such analysis is likely to evoke an emotional, as well as intellectual response.

RACE, ETHNICITY AND VISIBILITY

Before we actually try to place current tensions into some kind of a theoretical frame of reference, we should understand race as a concept. The idea of race, as used by anthropologists and biologists, is a reasonably defined concept which deals exclusively with hereditary physical characteristics.[1] These disciplines are not in a position to say very much about intelligence and even less in a position to say anything about culture, values or social relations.[2] Race as a biological concept is a tool that has been developed by physical anthropologists in order to allow them to apply to mankind the kind of classification system which biologists use with regard to all orders of life.

Despite differences of opinion, most systems of classification start with an assumption that all men are really part of one species, Homo Sapiens.[3] Given this, we can still classify people, on the basis of hereditary physical characteristics, not by one but clusters of characteristics, according to racial type. The most widely accepted classificatory system tends to identify three larger racial groups—Causasoid, Negroid and Mongoloid—and under each, a number of smaller subracial groups.[4] So, for example, biologists have identified the existence of several Negroid racial groups on the continent of Africa. One further observation is helpful: If you were to ask what's really so important about these racial divisions, what it means, most scientists, with few exceptions, would have to answer that it means very little, if anything in human terms.[5] There does not appear to be any significant differences between the functioning of one type of human being and another. This kind of division in other living creatures means, for example, that they cannot be interbred, that the offspring of a donkey and a horse, by way of illustration, would be sterile. There is no comparison here to human "races." We have no evidence at all of any difficulty or any harmful genetic results. Members of different races can, and always have, intermarried. As a matter of fact, this partly accounts for the rise of so many racial variations. The interrelation of races entails social questions that have nothing to do with biology. As far as is known, children of mixed marriages will be at least as fertile and will be at least as healthy, barring societal interference.[6] Furthermore, the most widely accepted concept of race does not view racial groups as fixed classifications as they always were and will always be. Instead, racial groups are essentially dynamic gene pools, composed of individuals sharing the current hereditary characteristics of their group. Those gene pools have not only been changing over the millennia, but will continue to do so through interracial mixing. Not in the next five years, but in the next 500 perhaps. Historically a racial group consists of a number of individuals sharing hereditary characteristics who, because of social or geographic isolation, inbred those characteristics. On the fringes, individuals of different gene pools have always, as far back as anyone can ascertain, been bringing into other gene pools their hereditary characteristics.[7] This is such an old, involved process of human breeding that, in a sense, one can no longer pick out clear-cut points at which one racial type ends and the next racial type begins. All that can still be said is that the different gene pools of the major racial groups have historically clustered in different parts of the world. The closer you get to the center of each of these clusters, the more you find isolation of their particular genes and the further away you get from the sources or the centers of these gene pools, the more you find evidence of considerable mixing. The racial background of Americans, whether they are white or black or any other type, is especially mixed due to the relative openness of our complex social order and extensive immigration. The American Negro, particularly, has been called a "social invention" quite unlike any one Negro group in Africa due to the racial amalgamation of individuals from various African tribes, whites and even some Amerindians.[8]

Our overriding concern with race is not because it is physically significant. We regularly choose to overlook even the most important physical characteristics of people, while singling out skin color, slanted eyes, the shape of lips and noses, or the texture of hair, for attention. One of the most significant hereditary physical characteristics about which we know a great deal is blood type, yet who has ever heard of a blood type racist advocating that the A's of the world should organize to fight off the B's, or that it is miscegenation for A's and B's to marry, although this is a truly important characteristic which could lead to death. No one, besides Lady Clairol, takes hair color too seriously nor has it been suggested that the talls of the world eliminate the shorts. Both of these are visible characteristics which we overlook. These examples should bring home the thoroughly cultural nature of our racial concerns, quite independent of race as a biological concept.[9]

The concept of race alone is not adequate to provide a frame of reference for the full range of minorities which may be encountered in a complex society such as ours. To do so, we must also consider such social and cultural collectivities as ethnic and religious groups. The nature of identity generally differs with regard to the racial on one hand and the ethnic or religious group on the other.

The sociologist uses the term "visibility" to describe those characteristics of groups which make them identifiable. Members of racial groups may be said to share physical visibility although these are still subject to social modification. Genotypical and phenotypical differences must both be considered.[10] Thus, an individual who has no visible Negroid features may nonetheless be so designated by a society which considers anyone with known Negro ancestry for such classification and not by a society which uses skin coloration exclusively as its criterion.

Ethnic groups generally exhibit social or cultural visibility. Their members may share a common language, type of name, style of dress, mutual association or predominance in certain occupations or residential areas. They may even share subtly learned mannerisms such as gestures, facial expressions and reaction to pain. Where they share a religion, this may provide the obvious criterion for visibility. Thus visibility is not limited to optical perception but encompasses anything which fosters awareness of group membership.

Members of minority groups with genuine physical visibility are largely limited in their ability to affiliate or disaffiliate at will. "Passing," even when desired, is possible only for those with the least pronounced group characteristics and generally entails considerable guilt and fear of detection. Groups with cultural visibility may initially be unable to divest themselves of identifying features. However, in a complex society, where opportunity for acculturation exists, group identification in succeeding generations begins to assume the quality of voluntary affiliation based on positive desire. Some groups are, of course, identifiable through both physical and cultural visibility, and some consciously stress certain characteristics over others.

AN END TO STATUS QUO

What has really unstuck the race situation in American society? After all, some white Southerners will tell you that "their blacks" were quite contented, that everybody got along very well until recently, when outside troublemakers started stirring things up, messing up a nice comfortable arrangement that seems to have been in effect for about 300 years. It is too simplistic to say that the whole nice, comfortable arrangement of race relations in America was upset by troublemakers from someplace. Instead, we need to examine those social forces operating in America which have led to the ungluing of old, neat arrangements.

The first thing that strikes us is the impact of World War II. It generated two forces in America. The first was an abhorrent reaction to the excesses of prejudice in general. Whether correctly or not, whether it was just a propaganda technique, the second World War was presented to Americans as a battle against anti-democratic racist doctrines overseas seeking to destroy democracy. On one level this caused behavioral scientists to look at prejudice as a social and a psychological phenomenon in a way they had not looked at it previously. A tremendously rich literature was generated through the end of World War II, continuing for about ten years. They began by asking what was wrong with prejudiced people, what hang-up lead them to have a need to persecute. They moved on to examining also what happens to the victims of persecution, emotionally as well as socially. Research productivity in this area was ultimately capped by the Supreme Court decision of 1954 which took into consideration behavioral science evidence regarding the concept of separate but equal. Thus, reaction to the Nazi excesses caused us to examine prejudice in a new light.

The second effect of World War II related to the tremendous upheaval in population it occasioned. In this country, it was represented not only by accelerated movement of entire segments of our civilian population, but also by those in the armed services, attaining ten percent of our population at its peak. In other countries it was often the movement of total populations. In the United States, the impact was especially on young adults, particularly men, away from home, away from the normal social settings, among people of different races, different cultures, and different religions. Contact with all kinds of people through African or Asian, or even European, service could not but affect their view of such diverse peoples and their cultures.

Since World War II, we have had subsequent changes in the way peoples around the world relate to each other. Although you still get anti-colonial rhetoric, the fact is that colonialism, in its original sense (not necessarily such concepts as neo-colonialism or economic spheres of influence), the government of "native populations" around the world by Europeans and Westerners for the exploitation of those governed countries, is essentially a thing of the past. It died with the second World War, giving rise to a large number of new, independent countries primarily populated by non-white peoples and to a vast world organization. Cross contact, at least on diplomatic, commercial, and cultural levels, has promoted the idea that modern nation states don't have to look like France or England or the United States to be going concerns. They could be populated by people with considerable divergency in racial background. This is not to deny that the new states tend to be largely the underdeveloped, unstable countries vis-à-vis the developed industrial countries. At least there is the format of an independent, autonomous, free nation. There is the possibility of positive identification with people of different racial backgrounds overseas.[12]

Finally, between the availability of instant mass communication and distance-shrinking transportation, generating a wanderlust, we no longer live in the kinds of parochial, isolated society that we once had. Perhaps, if you are particularly nostalgic, you might momentarily regret that. However, the significance of this cosmopolitan culture is profound. The Southerner, with all of his effort to hang on to his own old traditional way of relating to people, for good or bad, that Southerner has great difficulty showing network TV broadcasts that portray different attitudes; tremendous difficulty in his movie houses saying this film we are going to have but the other film we are not going to have; difficulty in avoiding exposure to what's happening around the world. At the same time, news is instantaneous. In the good old days, if a few coloreds or blacks were shot in South Africa, or the British landed in Anguilla, not many people would have noticed anywhere else. Now, the significance of local events is world-wide. Everybody may perceive the news in different ways, but the communication is there. It is very rare that something goes unnoticed. True, there are masses of people being killed every day that we don't know about. Only by a quirk do we learn of the Nigerians' Biafran genocide or the black-white imperialistic war being conducted by Egypt in the Sudan. One of the problems, of course, is that the communications industry can select what to reveal. Nevertheless, the potential is there and disclosure is inevitable. More than ever, "the truth will out." All of this has contributed greatly to building a backlog of resentment, dissatisfaction, unrest and impatience with what always was accepted and with "the way we have always done it around here." If you don't actually know, if you only suspect, that there is someplace else where life is different, that's one matter. If you see clearly that there are other places where the quality of life is different, it has a profound way of promoting a desire to initiate changes here as well.

This is related to what has been called the human rights revolution or the revolution of rising expectations and it operates not only here but around the world.[13] The starving peasant who must work like the devil to stand still, and still knows that he and his family will go to bed hungry, may have been willing to live with this in the past. Now he becomes aware that halfway around the world there is a man like himself who works no harder but whose family is not starving. He begins to ask himself, "Why is he better than I am?" This awareness overseas doesn't even approach the vivid way that it can exist in our own country. Given these factors, it is very hard to say that some kind of outside agitators have stirred people up. People have become stirred up by the larger social forces and are moved, at least potentially, by the thought of sharing in the better life.

Everything thus far stated essentially refers to the difference not only between racial groups, but between all have and have-not groups. Thus all social arrangements are being opened for review.

In this country, the major social arrangement that was not open for review, that was not considered throughout our history, from the time the problem was initiated, is the relationship between whites and blacks. It is a question that American society never faced squarely.[14] The question recurred in the earlier half of the nineteenth century and was not resolved.[15] Following the American Civil War there was a brief period during which it could have been believed that the question would be resolved and the good guys would come out on top, that democracy would prevail. Again, judicious compromises were worked out to enable the country to reunite.[16]

Two major points can be made with regard to the slave experience. First, that it served, in a primitive way, to Americanize the slave while destroying his African tradition; and secondly, that the history of slavery for Africans in America would be all but irrelevant by now, were it not that the end of slavery brought little, if any, genuine change in the conditions under which the freed slaves lived. Thus, contemporary situations have simply continued to reinforce the previous state of enslavement rather than counteracting it. Had it been otherwise, the history of slavery might have been a mark of distinction in American life somewhat akin to the idea that someone rose from birth in humble surroundings to become President. In reality, since our society did not allow for this kind of incorporation of black people, continued serfdom in the South and poverty in the North are more pertinent to current situations than the fact that up to 100 years ago most Africans living in America or in the Colonies were enslaved.

The question of the place of the Negro in American society was not faced when, after the turn of the twentieth century, American Negroes began at last to move from their rural Southern peasant state to Northern industrial centers because of the first World War and the attraction of industry. The depression brought retrenchment while the second World War again generated a migration, this time to a broader range of target cities, as Negroes moved out of the rural agricultural centers into Northern, Midwestern and West Coast industrial centers. The decline in industrial opportunities in the 1950's objectively should have made the attractiveness of cities decline as targets for people from an agricultural area. Yet they continued to move partly because of the decline in cotton production. Since migration patterns follow both expelling and impelling forces, we may conclude that there were pretty strong expelling forces which continued to propel Southern farm Negroes into cities despite the decline in their need for the unskilled. Finally we awake to an affluent technologically advanced society with a transplanted rural, agricultural population, racially identifiable and stranded in cities without the first rung of the ladder. No longer is there a need for unskilled labor, the starting place for past immigrants in U.S. cities. Three hundred years may be a false scale against which to measure the Negro's lack of progress since they have only recently entered the arena for mobility—the American city. Nevertheless, it is painfully clear that everything doesn't sit right with the American dream and all of the things that seem to have been appropriate for our nation of immigrants, no longer seem appropriate. The very complacent '50's with Eisenhower lulled us into believing that even race relations seemed to be moving ahead. Even then, dissatisfaction began to bubble up as the discrepancy between law and concrete changes became obvious in places like Little Rock.

THEORY AND APPLICATION

With this stress on the significance of the post-slavery condition of the American Negro, it is vital to look at majority and minority relationships and try to understand some of the dynamics of what goes on on both sides of the fence with regard to individuals who are members either of a majority of a society or members of the various minority groups. Most of the work generated by World War II was psychologically oriented, much of a psychoanalytic nature. Up to that time most attention seemed directed at elements in the nature of the minority which brought upon it majority abuse. In the second World War, behavioral scientists began to ask what in the nature of bigots leads them to be prejudiced or discriminatory. A number of very important concepts came out of this period.

Perhaps the most important concept, contributing a native American psychoanalytic theory, was conceptualization of "the authoritarian personality.[18]" The idea of authoritarian personality as a personality syndrome was extremely fruitful, permeating the behavioral sciences. It suggested that some individuals had unresolved family relationship problems with authority figures. These spilled over into the ambivalent way in which they related to authority in general, affecting the way in which they viewed society and the way in which they reacted to sociological phenomena, such as differences among people with whom they had contact. The California group which researched this area started with a psychoanalytic orientation, but related it to political, social and economic views and developed a series of testing instruments which seemed to tap the roots of these attitudes in the individual's personality. They found that the authoritarianism correlated with conservatism, ethnocentricity and deep seated prejudice.

While the original research stressed a rightist type of authoritarianism, recently Hoffer[19] and, even more importantly, Rokeach,[20] have stressed the inherent similarity of authoritarianism on either the political right or left. As a matter of fact, any extremism has been subject to suspicion. Rokeach has redrawn the lines as "Open and Closed Mindedness." In his terms it matters very little who it is that presents the non-negotiable conditions. *The Open and Closed Mind,* which contains a number of his researches, generally presents the view that authoritarianism can exist in many different guises, and the question is not so much whether one is politically right or left, but just how strongly one believes that his is the only point of view.

The literature of the time did not perhaps originate, but certainly gave emphasis to the concept of "scapegoating," pointing out that for the individual who had a sense of inadequacy and dissatisfaction with his own achievements, the availability of a handy outside group or individual to be blamed for everything is emotionally useful and comforting.[21] This was a particularly helpful analysis of German receptivity to Nazi thinking. This type of defense mechanism readily explains a good deal of observable behavior, where with varying degrees of justification, the blame for whatever happens to a country, or community, a group or an individual, is cast upon some readily identifiable outsiders.

Another, but related, concept is "stereotyping." Stereotyping provides us with shorthand clues to defining the social situation.[22] As we move into an urban environment with increasing secondary contacts, our tendency to stereotype about all the strangers that we deal with increases. We would be overwhelmed if we sought to know everybody personally. All of us stereotype in our daily lives and it is not necessarily sinister. It becomes sinister only when stereotyping doesn't permit us to look at reality or distorts reality, so that we jump to hasty or false conclusions with regard to a group, perhaps on the basis of some chance individual experience. Much examination went into what individual experiences might lend themselves to some kind of generalization about different groups.

One early psychoanalytic analysis of prejudice which is still of value, suggested that the major targets of prejudice in the United States, Jews and Negroes, were attacked by the deeply prejudiced for differing reasons, although the same individuals tended to be hostile toward both.[23] On the basis of research, Bettelheim suggested that the highly disturbed, prejudiced individual projects on to the Negro a kind of libidinal drive which he himself had difficulty controlling. Thus the Negro, as seen by such highly prejudiced and disturbed individuals, is promiscuous, hostile, lazy, dangerous, and so on. On the other hand, the image projected on to the Jew, as reported in this research, was more a reaction to one's own inadequacy in handling superego demands. So all of the positive, valued rules that had been absorbed—achievement orientation, success, legitimate goals of society—were projected in an exaggerated form on to this group. They were accused of being overly successful, overly achieving or controlling—often providing the individual himself with a rationalization of why he himself could not be successful.

Despite the psychological advantages which might accrue from prejudice, it would seem that individuals who actually use hostility in this way are a minority. They have a great need, and it serves as a tool to enable them to cope with their own emotions. However, for most Americans, prejudice is not necessarily a deeply rooted element of some personality disorder. Rather, the average American who either has prejudices or exhibits some form of discriminatory behavior, is simply conforming to cultural norms, living according to the rules of the society in which he lives, a society which does have various prejudices which it has only recently begun to recognize. To be a member of the majority might often allow the individual not to focus on any particular minority status problem. However, to be a member of a minority group—particularly a disadvantaged minority group—means that much more of the time, consciously and unconsciously, the individual relates to that phenomenon and reacts to it.

In a minority, there is potential exposure to varying intensity of both prejudice and discrimination. Prejudice is an attitude, while discrimination, a behavior pattern toward individuals of other groups and communities, can range from social distance and exclusion to outright persecution and genocide. Barring the presence of some positive, redeeming feeling about one's group, emotional damage may well result from being exposed to intense discrimination. The damage may take such forms as paranoia, frustration-aggression, a sense of impotence and lack of self-worth, sociopathy or other distorted ego defenses.[24] For the majority in institutionalized prejudice, such damage seems less likely. For that reason, one must suspect that the impact of minority-majority relations for members of minority groups is more significant than it is for majority for whom institutionalized discrimination may not even be visible.

In such circumstances it is a highly questionable tactic to promote, or pretend to promote, a feeling of guilt, or constantly refer to some kind of guilt-laden collective responsibility. In the long run this may lead simply to frustrated aggression on the part of the guilt ridden.[25] Probably more fruitful would be an attempt to get at the values and to look at the culture to which the society subscribes.

Membership in a minority involves the knotty problem of image. In point of fact, there is a rising percentage of American blacks who possess many of the features of middle-classness in their style of life and income. However, "Negro" in American society has been almost synonymous with poverty. Even the successful, upwardly mobile black person has been perceived as a poor slum dweller sharing with his less fortunate brother all of the social disorganization which frequently marks life in the racial slum. Thus, there are some very serious image problems encountered when we try to unravel the difficulties that American society is facing despite changing socio-economic realities.[26]

The idea of image is an extremely important one. We have examples of other racial minorities, Chinese and Japanese Americans particularly, whose image has changed radically since World War II and has been keyed not so much to racial characteristics as to other sociological characteristics perceived by the society. During the second World War, Japanese Americans certainly occupied low status to the extent of being forced to move to inland camps.[27] For their part, during the entire period of residence in the United States, the Chinese occupied a similarly low status, faced persecution, exclusion and disrupted family life.[28] Only in the last twenty years have these two groups become upwardly mobile, using education as their vehicle. They represent two groups with the highest average educational levels in American society.[29] As a result, Americans, in their mind's eye, increasingly see the Japanese or Chinese not as racial groups, but as a category of college professor, scientist or intellectual. There can thus occur changes in the socio-economic status and upward mobility of both groups, except perhaps, on the West Coast where the historic attitudes have tended to linger.

The Chinese and Japanese Americans are similar to any ethnic immigrant populations, with the added presence of physical visibility. Even more complicated is the situation of certain Latin American groups with mixed racial background, especially the Puerto Ricans. Here, the usual assimilation of immigrants is complicated by the ease of travel and communication with the island which reinforces the homeland and the racial background of the community which exposes some and not others to mainland racial prejudices. The deeper the individual's coloration, the greater has been the Hispanic emphasis, to distinguish himself from the American Negro.

Of course, not all individuals in any group are equally subject to the identical discrimination and where a society is complex enough to contain a number of sub-groups, they tend to be ranked in order of social distance and intensity of discrimination.[30] The nature of our social structure is such that it has tended to encourage a great deal of compromise and give and take in the past. This is due to the fact that perhaps 40% of our population belong to groups which at some point in history have faced discrimination in some form.

In many societies, the distance between their minority and majority populations is so great that there is need for an intermediary group. This may be a more assimilated segment of the minority or a segment of the population with mixed parentage. Often, however, a distinct minority is encouraged to take advantage of this marginal need. Such groups may develop a special propensity and skill at surviving in a hostile environment through assumption of this kind of marginality. Historically, the Jews have played such a role in the Western world, the Chinese for a shorter span of years in Southeast Asia and Asian Indians in the West Indies and in South Africa. Others, of course, have assumed such functions on local and less known bases. In the United States, some Jews have recently had such a marginal function vis-à-vis our non-white populations in Northern cities, but others such as Orientals and various ethnic immigrant groups can be found as "Middle-Man Minorities" in different regions of the country and in specific occupations.

The position of the middle-man minority is a very precarious one, since it is maintained only through the toleration of those with true power and at the expense of great animosity from those below. The middle-man group, lacking real power, is highly exposed when the put-upon minority finally rebels against its lot. At such times it is quite likely that the real "establishment" is pleased to have pent-up anger directed at the middleman, thus avoiding its own showdown.[31]

There are only a few options open to minorities in their interaction with majorities. Of the many conceptualizations of minority reaction, perhaps the most fruitful is a topological model such as Lewin's.[32] Lewin viewed the minority group member in what he called a psychological field. For the sake of examination, we can simply think in terms of an individual as Lewin would see this individual.

Think of a child who wants to achieve a particular goal: he wants to get at a cookie jar. If there is anything that impedes his progress in getting at the cookies, then he may react in several ways. If the cookies are on a shelf and he can't reach the shelf, he may try to overcome the barrier by drawing up a chair. When is he likely to try harder? When he perceives that in reality he can attain his goal by such effort. If, however, his perception of the field is that try as he will, he won't be able to get at that cookie jar, then he is unlikely to make the effort. He is prone to consider different alternatives. What are some of his other alternatives? For one thing, this child might physically leave the kitchen, "leave the field" and just give up. Instead of going for the cookies, he might become involved in playing with a toy or watching TV, or doing something else. There can be a physical or perhaps an emotional leaving of the field, an escape from the conflicted situation. "I don't need those cookies, they are no good," the fable of the sour grapes. Not always is it possible to escape from the field in which one finds himself, particularly if we are talking here about an emotional field. Caught in an unpleasant situation, you want to accomplish something and can't, or you want to escape from something and can't since you can't always just walk out. One can, instead of escaping, encrust himself or encyst himself in isolation, close himself in and say, "I reject all these goals, I am not going anywhere." If you can't escape the field, you can at least try to keep the field and its impact away from you. One can understand this as another defense against pressures one would normally face, being thwarted by having an unattainable goal. Such uncontrolled hostility can turn also into blind undirected anger.

Analysts of minority group relations have used a large variety of terms to refer to these various forms of behavior. One can react with aggression in trying to break down the barrier or aggression in trying to get over it—acceptance or avoidance. Such terms as assimilationist, isolationist, escapist race men, nationalist, chauvinist, have been applied. [33]

Whatever the terms used, we have to realize that individual members of minority groups will react individually to minority status on the basis of how they perceive the situation. The more they perceive the possibility of overcoming barriers, the more they are likely to show effort in that direction. The less they perceive such possibilities, the less likely they are to address themselves to the barrier and the more likely to choose some other alternatives. Most American minorities with cultural visibility have sought assimilation, while at the same time retaining certain circumscribed separate cultural group qualities. There are only certain limited number of options for the individual. The composite of what happens to various individuals of specific minority groups will give an overall picture of a group stance.

It should be pointed out that various motivations could be invested in seemingly similar forms of behavior. An individual might bring a great deal of hostility toward the barrier into a movement directed at his own group. Similar forms of behavior, however, might also represent escape or withdrawal from attack on the barrier. One might thus analyze the rise or the growth of black power or black nationalism within the American Negro community as perhaps a combination of several emotional investments in a particular change of attitude. We are often deceived by the more pronounced emotions into overlooking the subtler ones. Different minority groups have faced various kinds of barriers and since the strength or size of the barrier has differed, seem to have seen American society differently. In any case, the reaction of a particular group remains, despite the rhetoric concerning autonomy, just one combination of possible reactions to minority status.

There seems to have been a tendency for leadership and direction within minority groups to have been drawn from peripheral members.[34] That is, one can look at American society as a complex of a considerable number of minority groups. The reason that this kind of complex has worked well enough to give members of most minority groups a feeling that there was a possibility of upward mobility and acceptance into the mainstream, was that the interaction of all these groups was basically a kind of bartering. Their leadership tended to be drawn from the least ethnocentric, those with the least commitment to their own groups. Why is that? In all minority groups the impact of majority culture is overwhelming. That individual is most highly respected who is most highly respected by the majority of the society. Thus leadership of any minority you consider, would tend to be not the individuals who are most highly respected within the group for some internal distinction, but individuals who are most highly respected by the majority. These individuals are basically the ones who have moved most rapidly toward discarding group elements. One reason the majority respects them is that they can communicate. They are tuned in to the same wave length. For this reason, one generally would expect to find in all minority groups leadership drawn from those most advanced in their assimilation. This has also been so with regard to American Negroes. The latter has undergone some considerable attack. One early analysis of leadership or prominence in the Negro community was Frazier's *Black Bourgeoisie,* which was based primarily on a limited type of middle class individuals, given the limited opportunities that American society allowed the blacks at the time.[35] His sampling was composed primarily of teachers, civil servants and clergy. He saw them very much in the way we have thus far described minority leaders. As a matter of fact, so much did Frazier see this black bourgeoisie as assimilationist, that his description, with minor allowances, might be adapted to many ethnic communities.

Now there have been some very important changes. One of these is that the black bourgeoisie has changed. Middle class Negroes have changed. The percentage of this segment of the population is significantly enlarged.[36] Secondly, the economic base has broadened.

While our focus is overwhelmingly on poor blacks—slum residents and rural poor—there is a rapidly growing middle class which, though smaller than the white middle class percentage, nevertheless is apparently growing more rapidly than is generally recognized. The explosion of the college population in the Negro community is illustrative.[37] These individuals are not necessarily tied to the same kinds of attitudes or values that were described, correctly or wrongly, in 1948. A recent ad in the *Times* sought to attract advertising to *Ebony* magazine.

> All God's chillun got shoes, and coats and suits and dresses and furniture and food and dinnerware and tobacco and toys and appliances and beverages, but have they got your brand? Old myths die hard. Take the ones about the Negro as a consumer. A lot of people, even some good people, still have an image of all Negroes as bargain basement customers with neither the means nor the taste for quality merchandise. Except perhaps for a few flashy status items like Cadillacs. Ebony would like to chat with you. You may have been doing a disservice not only to Black people, but to your company as well. Each month Ebony reaches 3,650,000 urban black people with the taste for quality and the means to pay for it. Perhaps they can't always control where they live, but they can and do control how they live. And they live well. More than half own their own homes. More than $2/3$ own at least one car. Their median family income is nearly $7,000 and growing at a faster clip than the average white family income. When they buy shoes, for instance, they buy the best, spending at 32% more per pair than whites. When they buy clothing, they set trends. (According to one merchandise manager) "The Negro shopper is my guide. If I see him buy yellow shirts, I start to buy greater quantities of that color which filter down to the white men a little later." Ebony male readers buy almost twice as many suits per year as the average American male. 60.8% of Ebony males, by the way, have high school educations or better as compared with 55.7% in U. S. males. What's more, Ebony families spent 36% more of their income on personal care items, 4% or more on food, 29.4% more on tobacco, 7% more on housing, and 25% more on liquor than white families. Now, to dispel one more myth — that you can sell this lively market with your usual media. You may reach a portion of it that way, but you are not likely to influence it. To do so, you have got to talk to Negroes from their environment, and nothing reflects the Negro environment like Ebony, the magazine read by nearly 33% of all U. S. black families, families who are value-conscious and brand-loyal. But, we repeat, have they got your brand? If not, you have got our number.[38]

You can look at this in two ways. On the one hand this does represent the achievement orientation of the bourgeoisie. On the other hand, it represents an attempt to capitalize on a new sentiment, a changing sentiment, of in-group identification which Frazier did not find.

Liberal Americans have tended to look at the current race situation in our society in very much the same way that we have looked at all minority groups or all lower class groups; that is, they have attempted to apply welfare policies which was originated in the '30's to meet a specific and temporary need, to a situation that has very little to do with a temporary depression. They have continued to look at education as the tool for upward mobility in the way they saw it regarding every other group. Slum schools were probably never as good as non-slum schools. Urban teachers were rarely of the same ethnic background as their pupils, and suburban laymen, let alone those of slums, have never had an adequate say in school policy. One suspects that the inferior slum schools of today are really quite superior slum schools. This is something that we have not adequately explored. However, there were once enough entry jobs with high aspiration possibilities to make earlier groups believe that the system will work for them as it had worked for various other groups even when school did not work.[39] We have continued to see this in the very same way assuming that like all groups, Negroes must now get on line and work their way up as individuals. However, this model assumes an official, formal disregard of the existence of minority groups. While unofficially, minority groups were involved in the kind of give and take already discussed. This allowed those individuals who were least ethnocentric to rapidly discard their most distinguishing characteristics and become part of the mainstream. Thus others could see that there were channels for upward mobility. However, black people are here to stay. They cannot judiciously discard some of their most prominent identifying characteristics. To attempt it has led only to frustration and self-hatred. Since they will not be discarded, black people are saying to American society, "We want a reversal of the trend over the last fifty years. In order for us to be part of the society, we want, instead of an official disregard of the existence of minority groups, a recognition that different groups exist, particularly us." While other groups have progressed through assimilation and compromise, the Negro's inability to assimilate and be accepted has led to another reversal. (Whether the reversal is just a temporary position for argument's sake to get the most out of the situation or really intended, is hard to judge.) Certainly the public position increasingly expressed or implied by at least a segment of the Negro community is that compromise, not having worked, is to be replaced. Blacks have to be accepted on their own terms. Given this stance, we cannot really be sure that American society can or desires to reverse its field. For many progressive elements, aside from those who believe in the politics of confrontation, as well as those in the mainstream of American politics—many of whom elected Nixon and nearly elected Humphrey—it is quite difficult, perhaps even traumatic, to reverse field from what they believe has been increasing liberalization. Such specific items of contention as benign quotas are seen as a long-range threat, rather than an aid, to minority rights. After all, liberal elements in American politics had participated in the attack upon quota systems thus opening doors to minorities around World War II. They suspect that quotas potentially place the hard-won rights of the individual, regardless of background, into opposition with the demand for group advancement.

The American image of what happens to minority groups is that they are gradually absorbed into the mainstream, retaining certain quaint characteristics, but not particularly bothering anybody. The most "offensive" elements of being a minority group member tend to be rubbed off by increasing involvement and assimilation into mass society. Perhaps for the first time we have a sizable group in American society which will not rub off and which must, if it is going to be absorbed, be absorbed on the basis of true pluralism, a willingness to put up with variation. The feedback might be very useful to American society in general. Living in a time when there seems to be tremendous pressure for conformity in political views, in cultural practices, in occupation and behavior, it might be very valuable for American society in total that we do have a minority group within our society which is pushing us to reevaluate this kind of conformity. However, we face a period of delicate balance since extreme demands in any one direction are more likely to be met by extremity in the opposite direction, than achievement of rapid change.[40]

PROFESSIONAL STANCE IN THE CURRENT CRISIS

The current state of unrest with regard to intergroup relations has posed some very serious dilemmas for the social work profession. We can illustrate the question with the story of the well-meaning male case worker interviewing the mother of seven, pregnant with an eighth unwanted child, who complained of her illness. His response: "I know just how you feel." Social work has historically believed very much that there can be professional empathy, that you don't have to be a drug addict to work with addicts; you don't have to be an unwed mother to work with unwed mothers. Now, there are some serious problems for professionals who work increasingly with members of minority communities. If the question is one of empathy and learning, then the profession could conceivably apply its professional competence to working with such populations just as it worked with others in the past. If the question is one of a new sense of ingroup identity and ethnocentricism, of the need to unify within the group by rejecting the outside, then it is quite conceivable that it will become impossible for a white professional to establish rapport with a black client.[41] That the profession is seeking more minority group members may be motivated in part by this problem. Social work would rather not be seen as a profession engaged in patching up the damage wreaked by white society on American non-whites.

Lest we naively conclude that all social workers who work with black clients should themselves be black, other dangers must be borne in mind. It is quite conceivable that the black social worker also has status strivings which might sometimes have very strong, negative implications even worse than those of the white social worker. He may need to prove that he is not like his client, he may need to disassociate himself from the latter's pathology, rejecting and severely judging him. The opposite extreme is also possible. Like all minority groups in early stages of assimilation, the tendency to over-identify with one's client ethnocentrically, to be emotionally carried away, might also constitute a problem.

Recently, a Negro boy who was acting out in an urban school system, was referred to psychological services for a diagnostic interview. The youngster was first seen by a white psychologist, who couldn't do very much with the youngster because he refused to relate to the white professional. Finally the agency decided to call upon a black psychologist on their staff to relate to the boy, at least for an initial interview. This was done despite philosophical misgivings, in an effort to help the youngster. The black psychologist, after some hesitancy, conducted a brief interview and concluded that his assessment of the problem didn't differ from that of the white staff member before him. When they subsequently saw the youngster his comment was, "I'd rather talk to you than to that Uncle Tom." One suspects that we need to give some very serious consideration to this question of rapport and the ability of people to work with clients in helping professions of all kinds, both across minority group lines as well as within them. From that point of view, we have a national situation that is fraught with great anxiety, allowing many individuals to feed into group antagonisms unrelated personal emotional problems, thus complicating for themselves and society the quest for answers to both. The answers for the professional are not simply accepting or rejecting some civil rights position, but rather looking for useful strategies and consciously trying to develop professional approaches which recognize the underlying dynamics of minority-majority behavior. The need for professional image building, with clients as well as the society as a whole, may well be contradictory at times and doesn't always permit careful deliberation. This can give rise to the ambivalence of the 1969 National Conference of Social Welfare where many professionals seemed to have difficulty walking the line between legitimate and illegitimate minority expectations presented in a highly emotional context. This provided almost a microcosm of our national predicament.

REFERENCES

1. See the 1951 Unesco statement on race in *Race and Science,* (N. Y.: Coumbia University Press, 1961), p. 502.

2. *Ibid.,* 503-504.

3. M. F. Ashley Montagu, *Introduction to Physical Anthropology,* third ed., (Springfield, Ill.: Thomas, 1960), pp. 409, 410, 417, 419.

4. *Ibid.,* pp. 470-471.

5. See G. M. Morant, "The Significance of Racial Differences", in *Race and Science, op. cit.,* pp. 301-341. Very few scientists have taken the opposite stance. One such view is expressed by Stanley Garn, *Human Races,* (Springfield, Ill.: Thomas, 1961).

6. See Harry L. Shapiro, "Race Mixture" in *Race and Science, op. cit.,* 343-389.

7. L. C. Dunn, "Race and Biology", in *Race and Science, op. cit.,* pp. 281-286.

8. I. I. Gottesman, "Biogenetics of Race and Class", in *Social Class, Race and Psychological Development,* M. Deutsch, I. Katz and A. Jensen, editors,

(N. Y.: Holt, Rinehart and Winston, 1968), 15-22.

9. Ruth Benedict, *Race: Science and Politics*, (N. Y.: Viking Press, 1959).

10. Gottesman, *op. cit.*, pp. 29-35.

11. Mel Tumin, "Some Social Consequences of Research on Racial Relations", *The American Sociologist*, May 1968, Vol. 3, No. 2, pp. 117-124.

12. See Harold R. Isaacs, *The New World of Negro Americans*, (N. Y.: Day, 1963).

13. See Robert Perrucci and Marc Pilisuk, *The Triple Revolution*, (Boston: Little, Brown and Company), p. xiv.

14. The Constitutional compromise on the votes to be assigned to slaves failed to address the underlying philosophical question.

15. With each new territory admitted, the balance of slave and non-slave was maintained but still no basic decision was reached.

16. Only by backing down on Reconstruction could the bitter enmity of the war be healed enough for the country to face its new destiny as a world power.

17. See Dorothy K. Newman, "The Negro's Journey to the City, Part II", *Monthly Labor Review*, June 1965, Washington: Bureau of Labor Statistics, U. S. Department of Labor, 644-649.

18. T. W. Adorno, Else Frankel Brunswik, D. J. Levinson and R. N. Sanford, *The Authoritarian Personality*, (N. Y.: Harper and Row, 1950), and Richard Christie and Marie Jahoda, editors, *Studies in the Scope and Method of "The Authoritarian Personality"*, (N. Y.: The Free Press, 1954).

19. Eric Hoffer, *The True Believer*, (N. Y.: Harper and Row, 1951).

20. Milton Rokeach, *The Open and Closed Mind*, (N. Y.: Basic Books, 1960).

21. Gordon Allport, *ABC's of Scapegoating*, rev. ed., (N. Y.: Freedom Pamphlet, Anti-Defamation League, 1948).

22. For a good discussion of the functions of stereotyping, see Joshua A. Fishman, "An Examination of the Process and Function of Social Stereotyping", *Journal of Social Psychology*, Feb. 1956, pp. 27-64.

23. Bruno Bettelheim and Morris Janowitz, *Social Change and Prejudice*, (N. Y.: The Free Press, 1964).

24. The effect of severe discrimination has been widely examined. One landmark study was Abram Kardiner and Lionel Ovesey, *Mark of Oppression*, (N. Y.: Norton, 1951).

25. See John Dollard, Neal Miller, Leonard Doob, *et al.*, *Frustration and Aggression*, (New Haven, Conn.: Yale University Press, 1939); and Michael Halberstam, "Are *you* Guilty of Murdering Martin Luther King?", *The N. Y. Times Magazine,* June 9, 1968, pp. 27-29, 54, 59, 62, 64, 66.

26. *Recent Trends in Social and Economic Conditions of Negroes in the United States*, Current Population Reports, Series P-23, No. 26, Bureau of Labor Statistics Report No. 347, July 1968.

27. See Morton Grodzins, *Americans Betrayed*, (Chicago: University of Chicago Press, 1949).

28. See Rose Hum Lee, *The Chinese in the United States of America,* (Hong Kong: Hong Kong University Press, 1960).

29. Calvin Schmid and Charles Nobbe, "Socioeconomic Differentials' Among Non-white Races", *American Sociological Review*, Vol. 30, No. 6, Dec. 1965, p. 913.

30. The Social Distance Scale was first introduced in Emory S. Bogardus, *Immigration and Race Attitudes,* —————: Heath, 1928, pp. 13-18.

31. H. M. Blalock, *Toward a Theory of Minority-Group Relations,* (N. Y.: Wiley, 1967), pp. 79-84, 210-211.

32. Kurt Lewin, "Psycho-Sociological Problems of a Minority Group", in *Resolving Social Conflict* by Kurt Lewin, (N. Y.: Harper and Brothers, 1948), pp. 145-158.

33. For a full discussion of these possibilities, see George Simpson and J. Milton Yinger, *Racial and Cultural Minorities*, third edition, (N. Y.: Harper and Row, 1965), pp. 158-196.

34. K. Lewin, "Self Hatred Among Jews", in Lewin, *op. cit.*, pp. 195-197.

35. E. Franklin Frazier, *Black Bourgeoisie*, (Glencoe, Ill.: The Free Press, 1957).

36. See *Recent Trends in Social and Economic Conditions of Negroes in the United States, op. cit.*

37. *Social and Economic Conditions of Negroes in the United States*, Current Population Reports, Series P-23, no. 24, Bureau of Labor Statistics Report, no. 332, Oct. 1967, p. 47.

38. *The N. Y. Times*, Oct. 22, 1968, p. 96.

39. Selma Berrol, "The Schools of New York in Transition, 1898-1914," *The Urban Review*, (N. Y.: Center For Urban Education, Vol. 1, no. 5, Dec. 1966), pp. 15-20.

40. See "Ethnic Power", *The Center Forum*, (N. Y.: Center For Urban Education, Vol. 3, no. 6, May 15, 1969), p. 3.

41. See Donald Brieland, "Black Identity and the Helping Person", *Children*, Vol. 16, no. 5, Sept.-Oct. 1969, pp. 171-176.

ASSIMILATION IN AMERICA: THEORY AND REALITY

MILTON M. GORDON

Three ideologies or conceptual models have competed for attention on the American scene as explanations of the way in which a nation, in the beginning largely white, Anglo-Saxon, and Protestant, has absorbed over 41 million immigrants and their descendants from variegated sources and welded them into the contemporary American people. These ideologies are Anglo-conformity, the melting pot, and cultural pluralism. They have served at various times, and often simultaneously, as explanations of what has happened—descriptive models—and of what should happen—goal models. Not infrequently they have been used in such a fashion that it is difficult to tell which of these two usages the writer has had in mind. In fact, one of the more remarkable omissions in the history of American intellectual thought is the relative lack of close analytical attention given to the theory of immigrant adjustment in the United States by its social scientists.

The result has been that this field of discussion—an overridingly important one since it has significant implications for the more familiar problems of prejudice, discrimination, and majority-minority group relations generally — has been largely preempted by laymen, representatives of belles lettres, philosophers, and apologists of various persuasions. Even from these sources the amount of attention devoted to ideologies of assimilation is hardly extensive. Consequently, the work of improving intergroup relations in America is carried out by dedicated professional agencies and individuals who

The materials of this article are based on a larger study of the meaning and implications of minority group assimilation in the United States, which I have carried out for the Russell Sage Foundation and which is scheduled to be published as a book by the Foundation.

Reprinted by permission from *Daedalus*, Journal of the American Academy of Arts and Sciences, Boston, Massachusetts, Vol. 90, No. 2, Spring 1961, pp. 263-285.

449

deal as best they can with day-to-day problems of discriminatory behavior, but who for the most part are unable to relate their efforts to an adequate conceptual apparatus. Such an apparatus would, at one and the same time, accurately describe the present structure of American society with respect to its ethnic groups (I shall use the term "ethnic group" to refer to any racial, religious, or national-origins collectivity.), and allow for a considered formulation of its assimilation or integration goals for the foreseeable future. One is reminded of Alice's distraught question in her travels in Wonderland: "Would you tell me, please, which way I ought to go from here?" "That depends a good deal," replied the Cat with irrefutable logic, "on where you want to get to."

The story of America's immigration can be quickly told for our present purposes. The white American population at the time of the Revolution was largely English and Protestant in origin, but had already absorbed substantial groups of Germans and Scotch-Irish and smaller contingents of Frenchmen, Dutchmen, Swedes, Swiss, South Irish, Poles, and a handful of migrants from other European nations. Catholics were represented in modest numbers, particularly in the middle colonies, and a small number of Jews were residents of the incipient nation. With the exception of the Quakers and a few missionaries, the colonists had generally treated the Indians and their cultures with contempt and hostility, driving them from the coastal plains and making the western frontier a bloody battleground where eternal vigilance was the price of survival.

Although the Negro at that time made up nearly one-fifth of the total population, his predominantly slave status, together with racial and cultural prejudice, barred him from serious consideration as an assimilable element of the society. And while many groups of European origin started out as determined ethnic enclaves, eventually, most historians believe, considerable ethnic intermixture within the white population took place. "People of different blood" [sic]—write two American historians about the colonial period, "English, Irish, German, Huguenot, Dutch, Swedish—mingled and intermarried with little thought of any difference."[1] In such a society, its people predominantly English, its white immigrants of other ethnic origins either English-speaking or derived largely from countries of northern and western Europe whose cultural divergences from the English were not great, and its dominant white population excluding by fiat the claims and considerations of welfare of the non-Caucasian minorities, the problem of assimilation understandably did not loom unduly large or complex.

The unfolding events of the next century and a half with increasing momentum dispelled the complacency which rested upon the relative simplicity of colonial and immediate post-Revolutionary conditions. The large-scale immigration to America of the famine-fleeing Irish, the Germans, and later the Scandinavians (along with additional Englishmen and other peoples of northern and western Europe) in the middle of the nineteenth century (the so-called "old immigration"), the emancipation of the Negro slaves and the problems created by post-Civil War reconstruction, the placing of the conquered Indian with his broken culture on government reservations, the arrival of the Oriental, first attracted by the discovery of gold and other opportunities in the West, and finally, beginning in the last quarter of the nineteenth century and continuing to the early 1920's, the swelling to proportions hitherto unimagined of the tide of immigration from the peasantries and "pales" of southern and eastern Europe—the Italians, Jews, and Slavs of the so-called "new immigration," fleeing the persecutions and industrial dislocations of the day—all these events constitute the background against which we may consider the rise of the theories of assimilation mentioned above. After a necessarily foreshortened description of each of these theories and their historical emergence, we shall suggest analytical distinctions designed to aid in clarifying the nature of the assimilation process, and then conclude by focusing on the American scene.

ANGLO-CONFORMITY

"Anglo-conformity"[2] is a broad term used to cover a variety of viewpoints about assimilation and immigration; they all assume the desirability of maintaining English institutions (as modified by the American Revolution), the English language, and English-oriented cultural patterns as dominant and standard in American life. However, bound up with this assumption are related attitudes. These may range from discredited notions about race and "Nordic" and "Aryan" racial superiority, together with the nativist political programs and exclusionist immigration policies which such notions entail, through an intermediate position of favoring immigration from northern and western Europe on amorphous, unreflective grounds

("They are more like us"), to a lack of opposition to any source of immigration, as long as these immigrants and their descendants duly adopt the standard Anglo-Saxon cultural patterns. There is by no means any necessary equation between Anglo-conformity and racist attitudes.

It is quite likely that "Anglo-conformity" in its more moderate aspects, however explicit its formulation, has been the most prevalent ideology of assimilation goals in America throughout the nation's history. As far back as colonial times, Benjamin Franklin recorded concern about the clannishness of the Germans in Pennsylvania, their slowness in learning English, and the establishment of their own native-language press.[3] Others of the founding fathers had similar reservations about large-scale immigration from Europe. In the context of their times they were unable to foresee the role such immigration was to play in creating the later greatness of the nation. They were not at all men of unthinking prejudices. The disestablishment of religion and the separation of church and state (so that no religious group—whether New England Congregationalists, Virginian Anglicans, or even all Protestants combined—could call upon the federal government for special favors or support, and so that man's religious conscience should be free) were cardinal points of the new national policy they fostered. "The Government of the United States," George Washington had written to the Jewish congregation of Newport during his first term as president, "gives to bigotry no sanction, to persecution no assistance."

Political differences with ancestral England had just been written in blood; but there is no reason to suppose that these men looked upon their fledgling country as an impartial melting pot for the merging of the various cultures of Europe, or as a new "nation of nations," or as anything but a society in which, with important political modifications, Anglo-Saxon speech and institutional forms would be standard. Indeed, their newly won victory for democracy and republicanism made them especially anxious that these still precarious fruits of revolution should not be threatened by a large influx of European peoples whose life experiences had accustomed them to the bonds of despotic monarchy. Thus, although they explicitly conceived of the new United States of America as a haven for those unfortunates of Europe who were persecuted and oppressed, they had characteristic reservations about the effects of too free a policy. "My opinion, with respect to immigration," Washington wrote to John Adams in 1794, "is that except of useful mechanics and some particular descriptions of men or professions, there is no need of encouragement, while the policy or advantage of its taking place in a body (I mean the settling of them in a body) may be much questioned; for, by so doing, they retain the language, habits and principles (good or bad) which they bring with them."[4] Thomas Jefferson, whose views on race and attitudes towards slavery were notably liberal and advanced for his time, had similar doubts concerning the effects of mass immigration on American institutions, while conceding that immigrants, "if they come of themselves . . . are entitled to all the rights of citizenship."[5]

The attitudes of Americans toward foreign immigration in the first three-quarters of the nineteenth century may correctly be described as ambiguous. On the one hand, immigrants were much desired, so as to swell the population and importance of states and territories, to man the farms of expanding prairie settlement, to work the mines, build the railroads and canals, and take their place in expanding industry. This was a period in which no federal legislation of any consequence prevented the entry of aliens, and such state legislation as existed attempted to bar on an individual basis only those who were likely to become a burden on the community, such as convicts and paupers. On the other hand, the arrival in an overwhelmingly Protestant society of large numbers of poverty-stricken Irish Catholics, who settled in groups in the slums of Eastern cities, roused dormant fears of "Popery" and Rome. Another source of anxiety was the substantial influx of Germans, who made their way to the cities and farms of the mid-West and whose different language, separate communal life, and freer ideas on temperance and sabbath observance brought them into conflict with the Anglo-Saxon bearers of the Puritan and Evangelical traditions. Fear of foreign "radicals" and suspicion of the economic demands of the occasionally aroused workingmen added fuel to the nativist fires. In their extreme form these fears resulted in the Native-American movement of the 1830's and 1840's and the "American" or "Know-Nothing" party of the 1850's, with their anti-Catholic campaigns and their demands for restrictive laws on naturalization procedures and for keeping the foreign-born out of political office. While these movements scored local political successes and their turbulences so rent the national social fabric that the patches are not yet entirely invisible, they failed to influence national legislative policy on immigration and immigrants; and their fulminations inevitably provoked the expected reactions from thoughtful observers.

The flood of newcomers to the westward expanding nation grew larger, reaching over one and two-thirds million between 1841 and 1850 and over two and one-half million in the decade before the Civil War. Throughout the entire period, quite apart from the excesses of the Know-Nothings, the predominant (though not exclusive) conception of what the ideal immigrant adjustment should be was probably summed up in a letter written in 1818 by John Quincy Adams, then Secretary of State, in answer to the inquiries of the Baron von Fürstenwaerther. If not the earliest, it is certainly the most elegant version of the sentiment, "If they don't like it here, they can go back where they came from." Adams declared:[6]

> They [immigrants to America] come to a life of independence, but to a life of labor—and, if they cannot accommodate themselves to the character, moral, political and physical, of this country with all its compensating balances of good and evil, the Atlantic is always open to them to return to the land of their nativity and their fathers. To one thing they must make up their minds, or they will be disappointed in every expectation of happiness as Americans. They must cast off the European skin, never to resume it. They must look forward to their posterity rather than backward to their ancestors; they must be sure that whatever their own feelings may be, those of their children will cling to the prejudices of this country.

The events that followed the Civil War created their own ambiguities in attitude toward the immigrant. A nation undergoing wholesale industrial expansion and not yet finished with the march of westward settlement could make good use of the never faltering waves of newcomers. But sporadic bursts of labor unrest, attributed to foreign radicals, the growth of Catholic institutions and the rise of Catholics to municipal political power, and the continuing association of immigrant settlement with urban slums revived familiar fears. The first federal selective law restricting immigration was passed in 1882, and Chinese immigration was cut off in the same year. The most significant development of all, barely recognized at first, was the change in the source of European migrants. Beginning in the 1880's, the countries of southern and eastern Europe began to be represented in substantial numbers for the first time, and in the next decade immigrants from these sources became numerically dominant. Now the notes of a new, or at least hitherto unemphasized, chord from the nativist lyre began to sound—the ugly chord, or discord, of racism. Previously vague and romantic notions of Anglo-Saxon peoplehood, combined with general ethnocentrism, rudimentary wisps of genetics, selected tidbits of evolutionary theory, and naive assumptions from an early and crude imported anthropology produced the doctrine that the English, Germans, and others of the "old immigration" constituted a superior race of tall, blonde, blue-eyed "Nordics" or "Aryans," whereas the peoples of eastern and southern Europe made up the darker Alpines or Mediterraneans—both "inferior" breeds whose presence in America threatened, either by intermixture or supplementation, the traditional American stock and culture. The obvious corollary to this doctrine was to exclude the allegedly inferior breeds; but if the new type of immigrant could not be excluded, then everything must be done to instill Anglo-Saxon virtues in these benighted creatures. Thus, one educator writing in 1909 could state:[7]

> These southern and eastern Europeans are of a very different type from the north Europeans who preceded them. Illiterate, docile, lacking in self-reliance and initiative, and not possessing the Anglo-Teutonic conceptions of law, order, and government, their coming has served to dilute tremendously our national stock, and to corrupt our civic life . . . . Everywhere these people tend to settle in groups or settlements, and to set up here their national manners, customs, and observances. Our task is to break up these groups or settlements, to assimilate and amalgamate these people as a part of our American race, and to implant in their children, so far as can be done, the Anglo-Saxon conception of righteousness, law and order, and popular government, and to awaken in them a reverence for our democratic institutions and for those things in our national life which we as a people hold to be of abiding worth.

Anglo-conformity received its fullest expression in the so-called Americanization movement which gripped the nation during World War I. While "Americanization" in its various stages had more than one emphasis, it was essentially a consciously articulated movement to strip the immigrant of his native culture and attachments and make him over into an American along Anglo-Saxon lines—all this to be accomplished with great rapidity. To use an image of a later day, it was an attempt at "pressure-cooking assimilation." It had prewar antecedents, but it was during the height of the world conflict that federal agencies, state governments, municipalities, and a host of private organizations joined in the effort to persuade the immigrant to learn English, take out naturalization papers, buy war bonds, forget his former origins and culture, and give himself over to patriotic hysteria.

After the war and the "Red scare" which followed, the excesses of the Americanization movement subsided. In its place, however, came the restriction of immigration through federal law. Foiled at first by presidential vetoes, and later by the failure of the 1917 literacy test to halt the immigrant tide, the proponents of restriction finally put through in the early 1920's a series of acts culminating in the well-known national-origins formula for immigrant quotas which went into effect in 1929. Whatever the merits of a quantitative limit on the number of immigrants to be admitted to the United States, the provisions of the formula, which discriminated sharply against the countries of southern and eastern Europe, in effect institutionalized the assumptions of the rightful dominance of Anglo-Saxon patterns in the land. Reaffirmed with only slight modifications in the McCarran-Walter Act of 1952, these laws, then, stand as a legal monument to the creed of Anglo-conformity and a telling reminder that this ideological system still has numerous and powerful adherents on the American scene.

THE MELTING POT

While Anglo-conformity in various guises has probably been the most prevalent ideology of assimilation in the American historical experience, a competing viewpoint with more generous and idealistic overtones has had its adherents and exponents from the eighteenth century onward. Conditions in the virgin continent, it was clear, were modifying the institutions which the English colonists brought with them from the mother country. Arrivals from non-English homelands such as Germany, Sweden, and France were similarly exposed to this fresh environment. Was it not possible, then, to think of the evolving American society not as a slightly modified England but rather as a totally new blend, culturally and biologically, in which the stocks and folkways of Europe, figuratively speaking, were indiscriminately mixed in the political pot of the emerging nation and fused by the fires of American influence and interaction into a distinctly new type?

Such, at any rate, was the conception of the new society which motivated that eighteenth-century French-born writer and agriculturalist, J. Hector St. John Crèvecoeur, who, after many years of American residence, published his reflections and observations in *Letters from an American Farmer*.[8] Who, he asks, is the American?

He is either an European, or the descendant of an European, hence that strange mixture of blood, which you will find in no other country. I could point out to you a family whose grandfather was an Englishman, whose wife was Dutch, whose son married a French woman, and whose present four sons have now four wives of different nations. *He* is an American, who leaving behind him all his ancient prejudices and manners, receives new ones from the new mode of life he has embraced, the new government he obeys, and the new rank he holds. He becomes an American by being received in the broad lap of our great *Alma Mater*. Here individuals of all nations are melted into a new race of men, whose labours and posterity will one day cause great changes in the world.

Some observers have interpreted the open-door policy on immigration of the first three-quarters of the nineteenth century as reflecting an underlying faith in the effectiveness of the American melting pot, in the belief "that all could be absorbed and that all could contribute to an emerging national character."[9] No doubt many who observed with dismay the nativist agitation of the times felt as did Ralph Waldo Emerson that such conformity-demanding and immigrant-hating forces represented a perversion of the best American ideals. In 1845, Emerson wrote in his Journal:[10]

I hate the narrowness of the Native American Party. It is the dog in the manger. It is precisely opposite to all the dictates of love and magnanimity; and therefore, of course, opposite to true wisdom . . . . Man is the most composite of all creatures . . . . Well, as in the old burning of the Temple at Corinth, by the melting and intermixture of silver and gold and other metals a new compound more precious than any, called Cointhian brass, was formed; so in this continent,—asylum of all nations,—the energy of Irish, Germans, Swedes, Poles, and Cossacks, and all the European tribes,—of the Africans, and of the Polynesians,—will construct a new race, a new religion, a new state, a new literature, which will be as vigorous as the new Europe which came out of the smelting-pot of the Dark Ages, or that which earlier emerged from the Pelasgic and Etruscan barbarism. *La Nature aime les croisements.*

Eventually, the melting-pot hypothesis found its way into historical scholarship and interpretation. While many American historians of the late nineteenth century, some fresh from graduate study at German universities, tended to adopt the view that American institutions derived in essence from Anglo-Saxon (and ultimately Teutonic) sources, others were not so sure.[11] One of these was Frederick Jackson Turner, a young historian from Wisconsin, not long emerged from his graduate training at Johns Hopkins. Turner presented a paper to the American Historical Association, meeting in Chicago in 1893. Called "The Significance of the Frontier in American History," this paper proved to be one of the most influential essays in the history of American scholarship, and its point of view, supported by Turner's subsequent writings and his teaching, pervaded the field of American historical interpretation for at least a generation. Turner's thesis was that the dominant influence in the shaping of American institutions and American democracy was not this nation's European heritage in any of its forms, nor the forces emanating from the eastern seaboard cities, but rather the experiences created by a moving and variegated western frontier. Among the many effects attributed to the frontier environment and the challenges it presented was that it acted as a solvent for the national heritages and the separatist tendencies of the many nationality groups which had joined the trek westward, including the Germans and Scotch-Irish of the eighteenth century and the Scandinavians and Germans of the nineteenth. "The frontier," asserted Turner, "promoted the formation of a composite nationality for the American people . . . . In the crucible of the frontier the immigrants were Americanized, liberated, and fused into a mixed race, English in neither nationality nor characteristics. The process has gone on from the early days to our own." And later, in an essay on the role of the Mississippi Valley, he refers to "the tide of foreign immigration which has risen so steadily that it has made a composite American people whose amalgamation is destined to produce a new national stock."[12]

Thus far, the proponents of the melting pot idea had dealt largely with the diversity produced by the sizable immigration from the countries of northern and western Europe alone—the "old immigration," consisting of peoples with cultures and physical appearance not greatly different from those of the Anglo-Saxon stock. Emerson, it is true, had impartially included Africans, Polynesians, and Cossacks in his conception of the mixture; but it was only in the last two decades of the nineteenth century that a large-scale influx of peoples from the countries of southern and eastern Europe imperatively posed the question of whether these uprooted newcomers who were crowding into the large cities of the nation and the industrial sector of the economy could also be successfully "melted." Would the "urban melting pot" work as well as the "frontier melting pot" of an essentially rural society was alleged to have done?

ing pot" work as well as the "frontier melting pot" of an essentially rural society was alleged to have done?

It remained for an English-Jewish writer with strong social convictions, moved by his observation of the role of the United States as a haven for the poor and oppressed of Europe, to give utterance to the broader view of the American melting pot in a way which attracted public attention. In 1908, Israel Zangwill's drama, *The Melting Pot,* was produced in this country and became a popular success. It is a play dominated by the dream of its protagonist, a young Russian-Jewish immigrant to America, a composer, whose goal is the completion of a vast "American" symphony which will express his deeply felt conception of his adopted country as a divinely appointed crucible in which all the ethnic divisions of mankind will divest themselves of their ancient animosities and differences and become fused into one group, signifying the brotherhood of man. In the process he falls in love with a beautiful and cultured Gentile girl. The play ends with the performance of the symphony and, after numerous vicissitudes and traditional family opposition from both sides, with the approaching marriage of David Quixano and his beloved. During the course of these developments, David, in the rhetoric of the time, delivers himself of such sentiments as these:[13]

> America is God's crucible, the great Melting Pot where all the races of Europe are melting and re-forming! Here you stand, good folk, think I, when I see them at Ellis Island, here you stand in your fifty groups, with your fifty languages and histories, and your fifty blood hatreds and rivalries. But you won't be long like that, brothers, for these are the fires of God you've come to—these are the fires of God. A fig for your feuds and vendettas! Germans and Frenchmen, Irishmen and Englishmen, Jews and Russians — into the Crucible with you all! God is making the American.

Here we have a conception of a melting pot which admits of no exceptions or qualifications with regard to the ethnic stocks which will fuse in the great crucible. Englishmen, Germans, Frenchmen, Slavs, Greeks, Syrians, Jews, Gentiles, even the black and yellow races, were specifically mentioned in Zangwill's rhapsodic enumeration. And this pot patently was to boil in the great cities of America.

Thus around the turn of the century the melting-pot idea became embedded in the ideals of the age as one response to the immigrant receiving experience of the nation. Soon to be challenged by a new philosophy of group adjustment (to be discussed below) and always competing with the more pervasive adherence to Anglo-conformity, the melting-pot image, however, continued to draw a portion of the attention consciously directed toward this aspect of the American scene in the first half of the twentieth century. In the mid-1940's a sociologist who had carried out an investigation of intermarriage trends in New Haven, Connecticut, described a revised conception of the melting process in that city and suggested a basic modification of the theory of that process. In New Haven, Ruby Jo Reeves Kennedy[14] reported from a study of intermarriages from 1870 to 1940 that there was a distinct tendency for the British-Americans, Germans, and Scandinavians to marry among themselves — that is, within a Protestant "pool"; for the Irish, Italians, and Poles to marry among themselves—a Catholic "pool"; and for the Jews to marry other Jews. In other words, intermarriage was taking place across lines of nationality background, but there was a strong tendency for it to stay confined within one or the other of the three major religious groups, Protestants, Catholics, and Jews. Thus, declared Mrs. Kennedy, the picture in New Haven resembled a "triple melting pot" based on religious divisions, rather than a "single melting pot." Her study indicated, she stated, that "while strict endogamy is loosening, religious endogamy is persisting and the future cleavages will be along religious lines rather than along nationality lines as in the past. If this is the case, then the traditional 'single-melting-pot' idea must be abandoned, and a new conception, which we term the 'triple-melting-pot' theory of American assimilation, will take its place as the true expression of what is happening to the various nationality groups in the United States."[15] The triple melting-pot thesis was later taken up by the theologian, Will Herberg, and formed an important sociological frame of reference for his analysis of religious trends in American society, *Protestant-Catholic-Jew*.[16] But the triple melting-pot hypothesis patently takes us into the realm of a society pluralistically conceived. We turn now to the rise of an ideology which attempts to justify such a conception.

CULTURAL PLURALISM

Probably all the non-English immigrants who came to American shores in any significant numbers from colonial times onward — settling either in the forbidding wilderness, the lonely prairie, or in some accessible urban slum — created ethnic enclaves and looked forward to the preservation of at least some of their native cultural patterns. Such a development, natural as breathing, was supported by the later accretion of friends, relatives, and countrymen seeking out oases of familiarity in a strange land, by the desire of the settlers to rebuild (necessarily in miniature) a society in which they could communicate in the familiar tongue and maintain familiar institutions, and, finally, by the necessity to band together for mutual aid and mutual protection against the uncertainties of a strange and frequently hostile environment. This was as true of the "old" immigrants as of the "new." In fact, some of the liberal intellectuals who fled to America from an inhospitable political climate in Germany in the 1830's, 1840's, and 1850's looked forward to the creation of an all-German state within the union, or, even more hopefully, to the eventual formation of a separate German nation, as soon as the expected dissolution of the union under the impact of the slavery controversy should have taken place.[17] Oscar Handlin, writing of the sons of Erin in mid-nineteenth-century Boston, recent refugees from famine and economic degradation in their homeland, points out: "Unable to participate in the normal associational affairs of the community, the Irish felt obliged to erect a society within a society, to act together in their own way. In every contact therefore the group, acting apart from other sections of the community, became intensely aware of its peculiar and exclusive identity."[18] Thus cultural pluralism was a fact in American society before it became a theory — a theory with explicit relevance for the nation as a whole, and articulated and discussed in the English-speaking circles of American intellectual life.

Eventually, the cultural enclaves of the Germans (and the later arriving Scandinavians) were to decline in scope and significance as succeeding generations of their native-born attended public schools, left the farms and villages to strike out as individuals for the Americanizing city, and generally became subject to the influences of a standardizing industrial civilization. The German-American community, too, was struck a powerful blow by the accumulated passions generated by World War I—a blow from which it never fully recovered. The Irish were to be the dominant and pervasive element in the gradual emergence of a pan-Catholic group in America, but these developments would reveal themselves only in the twentieth century. In the meantime, in the last two decades of the nineteenth, the influx of immigrants from southern and eastern Europe had begun. These groups were all the more sociologically visible because the closing of the frontier, the occupational demands of an expanding industrial economy, and their own poverty made it inevitable that they would remain in the urban areas of the nation. In the swirling fires of controversy and the steadier flame of experience created by these new events, the ideology of cultural pluralism as a philosophy for the nation was forged.

The first manifestations of an ideological counterattack against draconic Americanization came not from the beleaguered newcomers (who were, after all, more concerned with survival than with theories of adjustment), but from those idealistic members of the middle class who, in the decade or so before the turn of the century, had followed the example of their English predecessors and "settled" in the slums to "learn to sup sorrow with the poor."[19] Immediately, these workers in the "settlement houses" were forced to come to grips with the realities of immigrant life and adjustment. Not all reacted in the same way. but on the whole the settlements developed an approach to the immigrant which was sympathetic to his native cultural heritage and to his newly created ethnic institutions.[20] For one thing, their workers, necessarily in intimate contact with the lives of these often pathetic and bewildered newcomers and their daily problems, could see how unfortunate were the effects of those forces which impelled rapid Americanization in their impact on the immigrants' children, who not infrequently became alienated from their parents and the restraining influence of family authority. Were not their parents ignorant and uneducated "Hunkies," "Sheenies," or "Dagoes," as that limited portion of the American environment in which they moved defined the matter? Ethnic "self-hatred" with its debilitating psychological consequences, family disorganization, and juvenile delinquency, were not unusual results of this state of affairs. Furthermore, the immigrants themselves were adversely affected by the incessant attacks on their culture, their language, their institutions, their very conception of themselves. How were they to maintain their self-respect when all that they knew, felt, and dreamed, beyond their sheer capacity for manual labor—in other words, all that they *were*— was despised or scoffed at in America? And—unkindest cut of all— their own children had begun to adopt the contemptuous attitude of the "Americans." Jane Addams relates in a moving chapter of her *Twenty Years at Hull House* how, after coming to have some conception of the extent and depth of these problems, she created at the settlement a "Labor Museum," in which the immigrant women of the various nationalities crowded together in the slums of Chicago could illustrate their native methods of spinning and weaving, and in which the relation of these earlier techniques to contemporary factory methods could be graphically shown. For the first time these peasant women were made to feel by some part of their American environment that they possessed valuable and interesting skills — that they too had something to offer — and for the first time, the daughters of these women who, after a long days work at their dank "needletrade" sweatshops, came to Hull House to observe, began to appreciate the fact that their mothers, too, had a "culture," that this culture possessed its own merit, and that it was related to their own contemporary lives. How aptly Jane Addams concludes her chapter with the hope that "our American citizenship might be built without disturbing these foundations which were laid of old time."[21]

This appreciative view of the immigrant's cultural heritage and of its distinctive usefulness both to himself and his adopted country received additional sustenance from another source: those intellectual currents of the day which, however overborne by their currently more powerful opposites, emphasized liberalism, internationalism, and tolerance. From time to time, an occasional educator or publicist protested the demands of the "Americanizers," arguing that the immigrant, too, had an ancient and honorable culture, and that this culture had much to offer an America whose character and destiny were still in the process of formation, an America which must serve as an example of the harmonious cooperation of various heritages to a world inflamed by nationalism and war. In 1916 John Dewey, Norman Hapgood, and the young literary critic, Randolph Bourne, published articles or addresses elaborating various aspects of this theme.

The classic statement of the cultural pluralist position, however, had been made over a year before. Early in 1915 there appeared in the pages of *The Nation* two articles under the title "Democracy *versus* the Melting-Pot." Their author was Horace Kallen, a Harvard-educated philosopher with a concern for the application of philosophy to societal affairs, and, as an American Jew, himself derivative of an ethnic background which was subject to the contemporary pressures for dissolution implicit in the "Americanization," or Anglo-conformity, and the melting-pot theories. In these articles Kallen vigorously rejected the usefulness of these theories as models of what was actually transpiring in American life or as ideals for the future. Rather he was impressed by the way in which the various ethnic groups in America were coincident with particular areas and regions, and with the tendency for each group to preserve its own language, religion, communal institutions, and ancestral culture. All the while, he pointed out, the immigrant has been learning to speak English as the language of general communication, and has participated in the over-all economic and political life of the nation. These developments in which "the United States are in the process of becoming a federal state not merely as a union of geographical and administrative unities, but also as a cooperation of cultural diversities, as a federation or commonwealth of national cultures,"[22] the author argued, far from constituting a violation of historic American political principles, as the "Americanizers" claimed, actually represented the inevitable consequences of democratic ideals, since individuals are implicated in groups, and since democracy for the individual must by extension also mean democracy for his group.

The processes just described, however, as Kallen develops his argument, are far from having been thoroughly realized. They are menaced by "Americanization" programs, assumptions of Anglo-Saxon superiority, and misguided attempts to promote "racial" amalgamation. Thus America stands at a kind of cultural crossroads. It can attempt to impose by force an artificial, Anglo-Saxon oriented uniformity on its peoples, or it can consciously allow and encourage its ethnic groups to develop democratically, each emphasizing its particular cultural heritage. If the latter course is followed, as Kallen puts it at the close of his essay, then,[23]

> The outlines of a possible great and truly democratic commonwealth become discernible. Its form would be that of the federal republic; its substance a democracy of nationalities, cooperating voluntarily and autonomously through common institutions in the enterprise of self-realization through the perfection of men according to their kind. The common language of the commonwealth, the language of its great tradition, would be English, but each nationality would have for its emotional and involuntary life its own peculiar dialect or speech, its own individual and inevitable esthetic and intellectual forms. The political and economic life of the commonwealth is a single unit and serves as the foundation and background for the realization of the distinctive individuality of each *natio* that composes it and of the pooling of these in a harmony above them all. Thus "American civilization" may come to mean the perfection of the cooperative harmonies of "European civilization"—the waste, the

squalor and the distress of Europe being eliminated—a multiplicity in a unity, an orchestration of mankind.

Within the next decade Kallen published more essays dealing with the theme of American multiple-group life, later collected in a volume.[24] In the introductory note to this book he used for the first time the term "cultural pluralism" to refer to his position. These essays reflect both his increasingly sharp rejection of the onslaughts on the immigrant and his culture which the coming of World War I and its attendant fears, the "Red scare," the projection of themes of racial superiority, the continued exploitation of the newcomers, and the rise of the Ku Klux Klan all served to increase in intensity, and also his emphasis on cultural pluralism as the democratic antidote to these ills. He has since published other essays elaborating or annotating the theme of cultural pluralism. Thus, for at least forty-five years, most of them spent teaching at the New School for Social Research, Kallen has been acknowledged as the originator and leading philosophical exponent of the idea of cultural pluralism.

In the late 1930's and early 1940's the late Louis Adamic, the Yugoslav immigrant who had become an American writer, took up the theme of America's multicultural heritage and the role of these groups in forging the country's national character. Borrowing Walt Whitman's phrase, he described America as "a nation of nations," and while his ultimate goal was closer to the melting-pot idea than to cultural pluralism, he saw the immediate task as that of making America conscious of what it owed to all its ethnic groups, not just to the Anglo-Saxons. The children and grandchildren of immigrants of non-English origins, he was convinced, must be taught to be proud of the cultural heritage of their ancestral ethnic group and of its role in building the American nation; otherwise, they would not lose their sense of ethnic inferiority and the feeling of rootlessness he claimed to find in them.

Thus in the twentieth century, particularly since World War II, "cultural pluralism" has become a concept which has worked its way into the vocabulary and imagery of specialists in intergroup relations and leaders of ethnic communal groups. In view of this new pluralistic emphasis, some writers now prefer to speak of the "integration" of immigrants rather than of their "assimilation."[25] However, with a few exceptions,[26] no close analytical attention has been given either by social scientists or practitioners of intergroup relations to the meaning of cultural pluralism, its nature and relevance for a modern industrialized society, and its implications for problems of prejudice and discrimination—a point to which we referred at the outset of this discussion.

CONCLUSIONS

In the remaining pages I can make only a few analytical comments which I shall apply in context to the American scene, historical and current. My view of the American situation will not be documented here, but may be considered as a series of hypotheses in which I shall attempt to outline the American assimilation process.

First of all, it must be realized that "assimilation" is a blanket term which in reality covers a multitude of subprocesses. The most crucial distinction is one often ignored—the distinction between what I have elsewhere called "behavioral assimilation" and "structural assimilation."[27] The first refers to the absorption of the cultural behavior patterns of the "host" society. (At the same time, there is frequently some modification of the cultural patterns of the immigrant-receiving country, as well.) There is a special term for this process of cultural modification or "behavioral assimilation" — namely, "acculturation." "Structural assimilation," on the other hand, refers to the entrance of the immigrants and their descendants into the social cliques, organizations, institutional activities, and general civic life of the receiving society. If this process takes place on a large enough scale, then a high frequency of intermarriage must result. A further distinction must be made between, on the one hand, those activities of the general civic life which involve earning a living, carrying out political responsibilities, and engaging in the instrumental affairs of the larger community, and, on the other hand, activities which create personal friendship patterns, frequent home intervisiting, communal worship, and communal recreation. The first type usually develops so-called "secondary relationships," which tend to be relatively impersonal and segmental; the latter type leads to "primary relationships," which are warm, intimate, and personal.

With these various distinctions in mind, we may then proceed.

Built on the base of the original immigrant "colony" but frequently extending into the life of successive generations, the characteristic ethnic group experience is this: within the ethnic group there develops a network of organizations and informal social relationships which permits and encourages the members of the ethnic group to remain within the confines of the group for all of their primary relationships and some of their secondary relationships throughout all the stages of the life cycle. From the cradle in the sectarian hospital to the child's play group, the social clique in high school, the fraternity and religious center in college, the dating group within which he searches for a spouse, the marriage partner, the neighborhood of his residence, the church affiliation and the church clubs, the men's and the women's social and service organizations, the adult clique of "marrieds," the vacation resort, and then, as the age cycle nears completion, the rest home for the elderly and, finally, the sectarian cemetery—in all these activities and relationships which are close to the core of personality and selfhood—the member of the ethnic group may if he wishes follow a path which never takes him across the boundaries of his ethnic structural network.

The picture is made more complex by the existence of social class divisions which cut across ethnic group lines just as they do those of the white Protestant population in America. As each ethnic group which has been here for the requisite time has developed second, third, or in some cases, succeeding generations, it has produced a college-educated group which composes an upper middle class (and sometimes upper class, as well) segment of the larger groups. Such class divisions tend to restrict primary group relations even further, for although the ethnic-group member feels a general sense of identification with all the bearers of his ethnic heritage, he feels comfortable in intimate social relations only with those who also share his own class background or attainment.

In short, my point is that, while *behavioral assimilation* or acculturation has taken place in America to a considerable degree, *structural assimilation,* with some important exceptions has not been extensive.[28] The exceptions are of two types. The first brings us back to the "triple melting pot" thesis of Ruby Jo Reeves Kennedy and Will Herberg. The "nationality" ethnic groups have tended to merge within each of the three major religious groups. This has been particularly true of the Protestant and Jewish communities. Those descendants of the "old" immigration of the nineteenth century, who were Protestant (many of the Germans and all the Scandinavians), have in considerable part gradually merged into the white Protestant "subsociety." Jews of Sephardic, German, and Eastern-European origins have similarly tended to come together in their communal

life. The process of absorbing the various Catholic nationalities, such
as the Italians, Poles, and French Canadians, into an American Catholic community hitherto dominated by the Irish has begun, although
I do not believe that it is by any means close to completion. Racial
and quasi-racial groups such as the Negroes, Indians, Mexican-Americans, and Puerto Ricans still retain their separate sociological structures. The outcome of all this in contemporary American life is thus
pluralism—but it is more than "triple" and it is more accurately described as *structural pluralism* than as cultural pluralism, although
some of the latter also remains.

My second exception refers to the social structures which impli-
cate intellectuals. There is no space to develop the issue here, but
I would argue that there is a social world or subsociety of the intellectuals in America in which true structural intermixture among
persons of various ethnic backgrounds, including the religious, has
markedly taken place.

My final point deals with the reasons for these developments. If
structural assimilation has been retarded in America by religious and
racial lines, we must ask why. The answer lies in the attitudes of
both the majority and the minority groups and in the way these
attitudes have interacted. A saying of the current day is, "It takes
two to tango." To apply the analogy, there is no good reason to
believe that white Protestant America has ever extended a firm and
cordial invitation to its minorities to dance. Furthermore, the attitudes of the minority-group members themselves on the matter have
been divided and ambiguous. Particularly for the minority religious
groups, there is a certain logic in ethnic communality, since there is
a commitment to the perpetuation of the religious ideology and since
structural intermixture leads to intermarriage and the possible loss
to the group of the intermarried family. Let us, then, examine the
situation serially for various types of minorities.

With regard to the immigrant, in his characteristic numbers and
socioeconomic background, structural assimilation was out of the
question. He did not want it, and he had a positive need for the
comfort of his own communal institutions. The native American,
moreover, whatever the implications of his public pronouncements,
had no intention of opening up his primary group life to entrance
by these hordes of alien newcomers. The situation was a functionally
complementary stand-off.

The second generation found a much more complex situation.

Many believed they heard the siren call of welcome to the social cliques, clubs, and institutions of white Protestant America. After all, it was simply a matter of learning American ways, was it not? Had they not grown up as Americans, and were they not culturally different from their parents, the "greenhorns?" Or perhaps an especially eager one reasoned (like the Jewish protagonist of Myron Kaufmann's novel, *Remember Me To God,* aspiring to membership in the prestigious club system of Harvard undergraduate social life) "If only I can go the last few steps in Ivy League manners and behavior they will surely recognize that I am one of them and take me in." But, alas, Brooks Brothers suit notwithstanding, the doors of the fraternity house, the city men's club, and the country club were slammed in the face of the immigrant's offspring. That invitation was not really there in the first place; or, to the extent it was, in Joshua Fishman's phrase, it was a " 'look me over but don't touch me' invitation to the American minority group child."[29] And so the rebuffed one returned to the homelier but dependable comfort of the communal institutions of his ancestral group. There he found his fellows of the same generation who had never stirred from the home fires. Some of these had been too timid to stray; others were ethnic ideologists committed to the group's survival; still others had never really believed in the authenticity of the siren call or were simply too passive to do more than go along the familiar way. All could now join in the task that was well within the realm of the sociologically possible—the build-up of social institutions and organizations within the ethnic enclave, manned increasingly by members of the second generation and suitably separated by social class.

Those who had for a time ventured out gingerly or confidently, as the case might be, had been lured by the vision of an "American" social structure that was somehow larger than all subgroups and was ethnically neutral. Were they, too, not Americans? But they found to their dismay that at the primary group level a neutral American social structure was a mirage. What at a distance seemed to be a quasi-public edifice flying only the all-inclusive flag of American nationality turned out on closer inspection to be the clubhouse of a particular ethnic group—the white Anglo-Saxon Protestants, its operation shot through with the premises and expectations of its parental ethnicity. In these terms, the desirability of whatever invitation was grudgingly extended to those of other ethnic backgrounds could only become a considerably attenuated one.

With the racial minorities, there was not even the pretense of an invitation. Negroes, to take the most salient example, have for the most part been determinedly barred from the cliques, social clubs, and churches of white America. Consequently, with due allowance for internal class differences, they have constructed their own network of organizations and institutions, their own "social world." There are now many vested interests served by the preservation of this separate communal life, and doubtless many Negroes are psychologically comfortable in it, even though at the same time they keenly desire that discrimination in such areas as employment, education, housing, and public accommodations be eliminated. However, the ideological attachment of Negroes to their communal separation is not conspicuous. Their sense of identification with ancestral African national cultures is virtually nonexistent, although Pan-Africanism engages the interest of some intellectuals and although "black nationalist" and "black racist" fringe groups have recently made an appearance at the other end of the communal spectrum. As for their religion, they are either Protestant or Catholic (overwhelmingly the former). Thus, there are no "logical" ideological reasons for their separate communality; dual social structures are created solely by the dynamics of prejudice and discrimination, rather than being reinforced by the ideological commitments of the minority itself.

Structural assimilation, then, has turned out to be the rock on which the ships of Anglo-conformity and the melting pot have foundered. To understand that behavioral assimilation (or acculturation) without massive structural intermingling in primary relationships has been the dominant motif in the American experience of creating and developing a nation out of diverse peoples is to comprehend the most essential sociological fact of that experience. It is against the background of "structural pluralism" that strategies of strengthening intergroup harmony, reducing ethnic discrimination and prejudice, and maintaining the rights of both those who stay within and those who venture beyond their ethnic boundaries must be thoughtfully devised.

NOTES

[1] Allan Nevins and Henry Steele Commager, *America: The Story of a Free People* (Boston, Little, Brown, 1942), p. 58.

[2] The phrase is the Coles's. See Stewart G. Cole and Mildred Wiese Cole,

Minorities and the American Promise (New York, Harper & Brothers, 1954), ch. 6.

³ Maurice R. Davie, *World Immigration* (New York, Macmillan, 1936), p. 36, and (cited therein) "Letter of Benjamin Franklin to Peter Collinson, 9th May, 1753, on the condition and character of the Germans in Pennsylvania," in *The Works of Benjamin Franklin, with notes and a life of the author,* by Jared Sparks (Boston, 1828), vol. 7, pp. 71-73.

⁴ *The Writings of George Washington,* collected and edited by W. C. Ford (New York, G. P. Putnam's Sons, 1889), vol. 12, p. 489.

⁵ Thomas Jefferson, "Notes on Virginia, Query 8;" in *The Writings of Thomas Jefferson,* ed. A. E. Bergh (Washington, The Thomas Jefferson Memorial Association, 1907), vol. 2, p. 121.

⁶ *Niles' Weekly Register,* vol. 18, 29 April 1820, pp. 157-158; also, Marcus L. Hansen, *The Atlantic Migration, 1607-1860,* pp. 96-97

⁷ Ellwood P. Cubberly, *Changing Conceptions of Education* (Boston, Houghton Mifflin, 1909), pp. 15-16.

⁸ J. Hector St. John Crèvecoeur, *Letters from an American Farmer* (New York, Albert and Charles Boni, 1925; reprinted from the 1st edn., London, 1782), pp. 54-55.

⁹ Oscar Handlin, ed., *Immigration as a Factor in American History* (Englewood, Prentice-Hall, 1959), p. 146.

¹⁰ Quoted by Stuart P. Sherman in his Introduction to *Essays and Poems of Emerson* (New York, Harcourt Brace, 1921), p. xxxiv.

¹¹ See Edward N. Saveth, *American Historians and European Immigrants, 1875-1925* (New York, Columbia University Press, 1948).

¹² Frederick Jackson Turner, *The Frontier in American History* (New York, Henry Holt, 1920), pp. 22-23, 190.

¹³ Israel Zangwill, *The Melting Pot* (New York, Macmillan, 1909), p. 37.

¹⁴ Ruby Jo Reeves Kennedy, "Single or Triple Melting-Pot? Intermarriage Trends in New Haven, 1870-1940," *American Journal of Sociology,* 1944, 49; 331-339. See also her "Single or Triple Melting-Pot? Intermarriage in New Haven, 1870-1950," *ibid.,* 1952, 58: 56-59.

¹⁵ ———— "Single or Triple Melting-Pot? . . . 1870-1940," p. 332 (author's italics omitted).

¹⁶ Will Herberg, *Protestant-Catholic-Jew* (Garden City, Doubleday, 1955).

¹⁷ Nathan Glazer, "Ethnic Groups in America: From National Culture to Ideology," in Morroe Berger, Theodore Abel, and Charles H. Page, eds., *Freedom and Control in Modern Society* (New York, D. Van Nostrand, 1954), p. 161; Marcus Lee Hansen, *The Immigrant in American History* (Cambridge, Harvard University Press, 1940), pp. 129-140; John A. Hawgood, *The Tragedy of German-America* (New York, Putnam's, 1940), *passim.*

¹⁸ Oscar Handlin, *Boston's Immigrants* (Cambridge, Harvard University Press, 1959, rev. edn.), p. 176.

19 From a letter (1883) by Samuel A. Barnett; quoted in Arthur C. Holden, *The Settlement Idea* (New York, Macmillan, 1922), p. 12.

20 Jane Addams, *Twenty Years at Hull House* (New York, Macmillan, 1914), pp. 231-258; Arthur C. Holden, *op. cit.,* pp. 109-131, 182-189; John Higham, *Strangers in the Land* (New Brunswick, Rutgers University Press, 1955), p. 236.

21 Jane Addams, *op. cit.,* p. 258.

22 Horace M. Kallen, "Democracy *versus* the Melting-Pot," *The Nation,* 18 and 25 February 1915; reprinted in his *Culture and Democracy in the United States* (New York, Boni and Liveright, 1924); the quotation is on p. 116.

23 Kallen, *Culture and Democracy. . . ,* p. 124.

24 *Op. cit.*

25 See W. D. Borrie *et al., The Cultural Integration of Immigrants* (a survey based on the papers and proceedings of the UNESCO Conference in Havana, April 1956), Paris, UNESCO, 1959; and Willliam S. Bernard, "The Integration of Immigrants in the United States" (mimeographed), one of the papers for this conference.

26 See particularly Milton M. Gordon, "Social Structure and Goals in Group Relations,"; and Nathan Glazer, "Ethnic Groups in America; From National Culture to Ideology," both articles in Berger, Abel, and Page, *op. cit.;* S. N. Eisenstadt, *The Absorption of Immigrants* (London, Routledge and Kegan Paul, 1954); and W. D. Borrie *et al., op. cit.*

27 Milton M. Gordon, "Social Structure and Goals in Group Relations," p. 151.

28 See Erich Rosenthal, "Acculturation without Assimilation?" *American Journal of Sociology,* 1960, 66: 275-288.

29 Joshua A. Fishman, "Childhood Indoctrination for Minority-Group Membership and the Quest for Minority-Group Biculturism in America," in Oscar Handlin, ed., *Group Life in America* (Cambridge, Harvard University Press, forthcoming).

SOCIOECONOMIC DIFFERENTIALS AMONG NONWHITE RACES

CALVIN F. SCHMID
CHARLES E. NOBBE

COMPARATIVE TRENDS

In 1960, the total population of conterminous United States (excluding Alaska and Hawaii) was reported as 178,464,236, of which 20,009,280, or 11.2 per cent, were classified as nonwhite. The nonwhite population included 18,860,117 Negroes, who represented 10.6 per cent of the total population.

Of the 20,009,280 nonwhites, 94.3 per cent were Negroes; 508,675, or 2.5 per cent, Indians; 260,059, or 1.3 per cent, Japanese; 198,958, or 1.0 per cent, Chinese; 106,426, or 0.5 per cent, Filipinos; and 75,045, or 0.4 per cent, "all other."

Figure 1 portrays comparative trends for the various nonwhite races along with the total white population in the U.S. from 1900 to 1960. The percentage of nonwhite population declined from 14.4 per cent in 1860 to 10.5 per cent in 1950, but rose again to 11.2 per cent in 1960. The nonwhite population increased from 4,520,784 in 1860 to 20,009,280 in 1960. Between 1940 and 1960, nonwhite races increased at a faster rate than the white population: the white population increased by 34.0 per cent; Negroes by 46.6 per cent; Indians, 52.6 per cent; Japanese, 104.8 per cent; Chinese 156.7 per cent; and Filipinos, 133.6 per cent.

Salient features regarding the growth and distribution patterns of the five nonwhite categories are as follows:

Negroes. Until 1930, the Negro population grew at a considerably slower pace than that of the white population. In recent years, however, owing to a continuous decline in Negro mortality, as well as to substantially higher fertility rates, this pattern has been reversed so

Reprinted from *American Sociological Review,* Vol. 30, No. 6 (December, 1965), pp. 909-922 by permission of the American Sociological Association and the author.

that the decennial growth rates for Negroes in the U.S. over the past 30 years have been larger than those for whites.

Data on the geographical distribution of Negroes in the United States are presented in Table 1 and Figure 2. The distributions over geographic regions, shown in Table 1, indicate the degree to which the Negro population has shifted out of the South during the past 20 years.

Indians. With reference to Figure 1, particular notice should be taken of the sizeable gain in the Indian population between 1950 (343,410) and 1960 (508,675), in striking contrast to the relatively meager growth of the 1930's and 1940's. The increment during the past ten-year period reflects, of course, an increase in fertility as well as a sharp decline in infant mortality. Another factor has been the influence of the self-enumeration procedure used by the Census Bureau in 1960 as well as the re-classification of many persons of mixed white, Negro, and Indian ancestry from "other races" to "Indian." Special mention should be made of the fact that more than seven out of every ten American Indians live on or near government reservations scattered through the country.

Japanese. Before the turn of the century, at approximately the same time that the Chinese population had attained its peak and begun to decline, large numbers of Japanese began arriving in pursuit of opportunities similar to those that had first attracted Chinese immigrants to this country. Figure 1 indicates that the increase among the Japanese population continued without interruption during each of the subsequent six decades, with the exception of the 1930's. The largest concentration of Japanese is in the West. In 1960,

TABLE 1.   REGIONAL DISTRIBUTION OF NEGRO POPULATION: 1940-1960

Region ᵃ	Percentage Distribution		
	1960	1950	1940
South	60.0	67.8	77.0
North	34.3	28.2	21.7
West	5.7	3.8	1.3

ᵃ "South" includes the South Atlantic and East and West South Central geographic divisions as defined by the U.S. Bureau of the Census; "North" includes the New England, Middle Atlantic, and East and West North Central geographic divisions; and "West," the Mountain and Pacific Geographic Division.

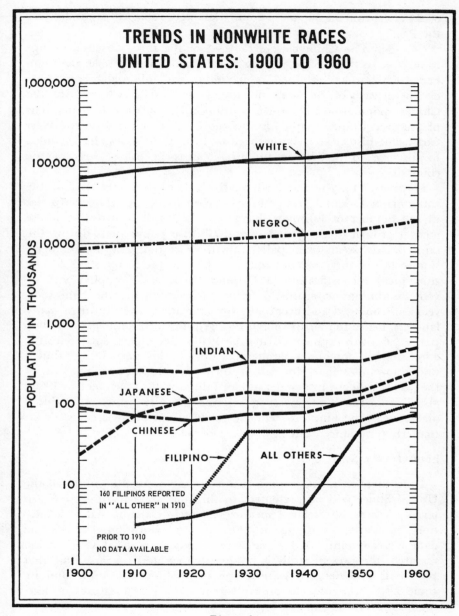

Figure 1

86.2 per cent of the Japanese population were reported as residing on the Pacific Coast, mainly in California.

Chinese. The Chinese were the first of the three Oriental groups to migrate to the U.S., beginning as early as 1850. By 1890, the number of Chinese had attained its maximum size, followed by a marked decline at each of the three subsequent census dates. Since 1920, the Chinese population has grown continuously. In 1960, 63.0 per cent of the total Chinese population in the U.S. was located on the West Coast, but historically, dating back to 1880, the Chinese have tended to disperse to predominantly urban areas in other parts of the country.

Filipinos. Filipinos arrived relatively late, being the last of the three major Oriental groups to appear on the scene. The sharp rise in the number of Filipinos during the 1920's, in contrast with the meager growth of the Japanese and Chinese populations during the same decade, stems principally from the fact that Filipino immigration to this country was not restricted by the Quota Act of 1924. The subsequent reclassification of Filipinos as "aliens," coupled with severe discrimination against Filipino laborers during the depression years, discouraged and eventually brought about the return of many laborers, hence the virtual absence of growth during the 1930 to 1940 period. Growth resumed during the 1940's, due almost entirely to the admission of non-quota immigrants during this period. Continued migration and a sharp increase in birth rates account for the gain of the past decade. A preponderance of Filipinos (82.0 per cent in 1960) also live on the West Coast, again largely in California. As Table 2 makes clear, the Filipinos' tendency to locate in urban areas was particularly pronounced during the past decade.

EDUCATIONAL STATUS[1]

Differences in socioeconomic status among nonwhite groups in the United States will be presented, in this and subsequent sections, in terms of three interrelated measures of socioeconomic status—education, occupation, and income. Occupation, education, and income data are commonly used as single-item indices in social stratification research; the present study is unique in that it is the first time that systematic and detailed statistics on occupation, education, and income have been used as multiple-item indices to measure socioeconomic differentials among nonwhite groups.[2]

Educational status is indicated by (1) proportion of the population

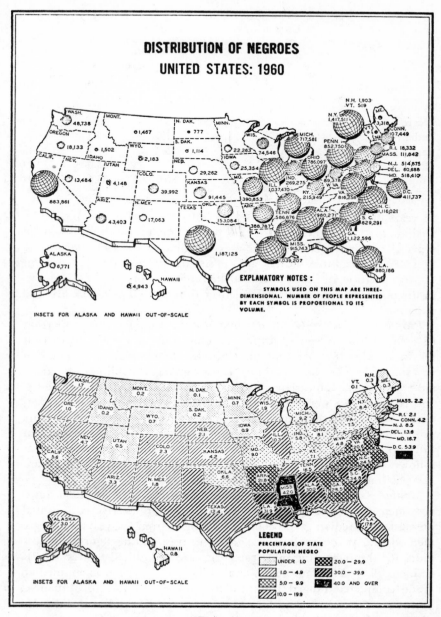

Figure 2

TABLE 2. URBANIZATION OF NONWHITE RACES
UNITED STATES: 1940-1960 [a]

Race	Percentage of Population Classified as Urban		
	1960	1950	1940
White	69.5	64.3	57.5
Negro	73.2	62.4	48.6
Indian	27.9	16.3	8.1
Japanese	83.2	71.1	54.9
Chinese	95.7	93.0	90.6
Filipino	80.6	66.4	60.6

[a] Excludes Alaska and Hawaii

25 years of age and over classified as college graduates or above, (2)
median grade completed, and (3) proportion of the population 25
years of age and over with four years of high school and above (Figures 3-5). The three indices are consistent; placing the Japanese in
the top position in the educational hierarchy, at present, and Indians
in the bottom position. Variations over time as well as by sex are also
apparent.

Proportion College Graduates and Above. In 1960, the proportion
of men with a college education or more ranged from 2.2 per cent
for Indians to 18.9 per cent for Chinese. The corresponding figures
in rank order for the remaining categories are as follows: Japanese
(18.4 per cent), Caucasian (10.3 per cent), Filipino (9.1 per cent),
and Negroes (2.8 per cent). For women, the disparity in the proportion of the population with a college education or more is even more
pronounced, ranging from 1.7 per cent for Indians to 19.6 per cent for
Filipinos. The corresponding figures for the other categories are as
follows: Chinese (14.4 per cent), Japanese (7.1 per cent), Caucasians
(6.0 per cent), and Negroes (3.3 per cent).

Median Grade Completed. Figure 4 indicates that in 1960 Japanese men and women were at the top of their respective educational
hierarchies. Median grade completed ranged from 7.4 years for Negro
men to 12.5 years for Japanese men. Corresponding figures in rank
order for the remaining male categories are as follows: whites (10.7),
Chinese (9.2), Filipinos (8.8), and Indians (7.5). For women, median
grade completed ranged from 7.6 for Indians to 12.4 for Japanese.
Figures for the remaining female categories are as follows: Filipinos
(12.2), whites (11.2), Chinese (10.7), and Negroes (8.2). The con-

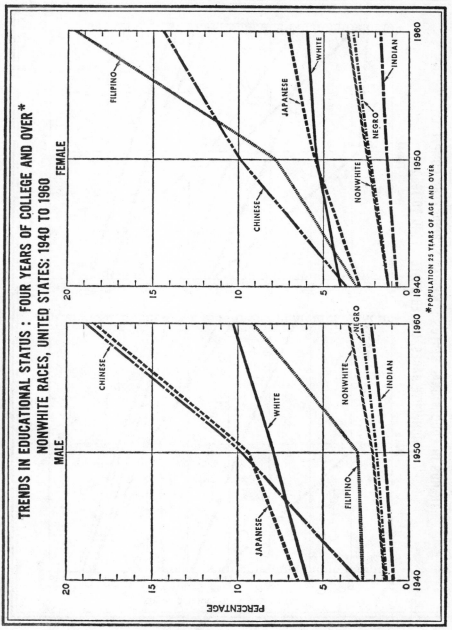

Figure 3

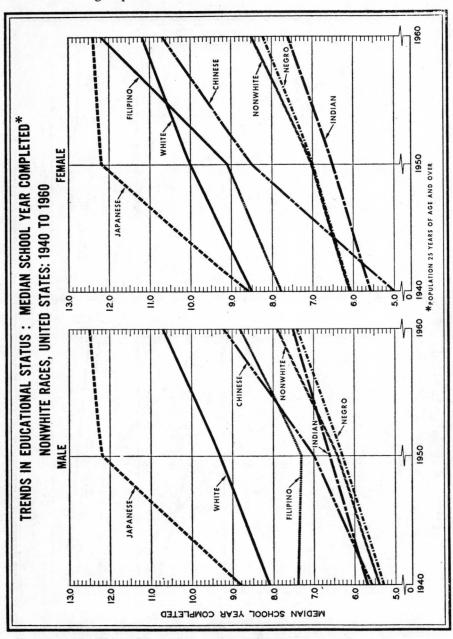

TRENDS IN EDUCATIONAL STATUS : MEDIAN SCHOOL YEAR COMPLETED*
NONWHITE RACES, UNITED STATES: 1940 TO 1960

Figure 4

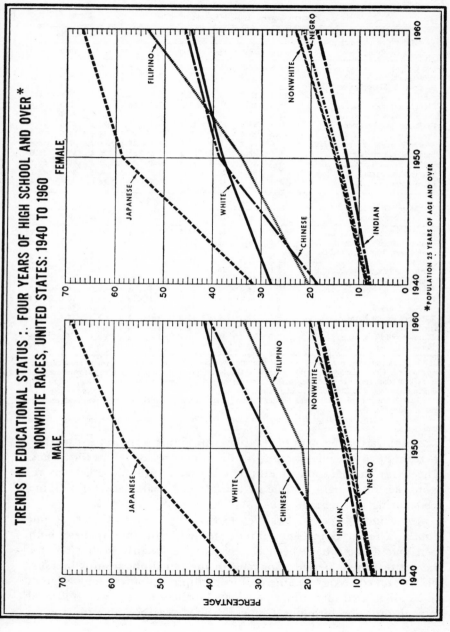

TRENDS IN EDUCATIONAL STATUS :. FOUR YEARS OF HIGH SCHOOL AND OVER*
NONWHITE RACES, UNITED STATES: 1940 TO 1960

Figure 5

TABLE 3. MAJOR OCCUPATIONAL GROUPINGS OF EMPLOYED MALE POPULATION BY RACE
UNITED STATES: 1960, 1950, AND 1940 [a]

Major Occupational Groupings	White			Negro			Indian		
	1960	1950	1940	1960	1950	1940	1960	1950	1940
White Collar[b]	42.1	39.2	39.1	13.8	11.4	8.7	16.6	14.4	17.5
Professional and Technical	12.5	9.3	7.6	3.9	2.9	3.1	6.5	4.8	6.7
Proprietors, Managers, and Officials	13.1	13.7	13.6	2.2	2.8	2.2	3.7	3.7	4.4
Clerical and Sales	16.5	16.2	17.9	7.7	5.7	3.4	6.4	5.9	6.4
Manual Workers[b]	57.9	60.9	61.0	86.3	88.5	91.3	83.5	85.7	82.4
Craftsmen and Foremen	23.3	23.3	20.1	12.2	10.3	7.6	20.2	20.6	17.9
Operatives	22.2	23.6	24.3	30.3	28.0	21.5	28.7	24.5	19.9
Service Workers	6.0	6.2	6.9	18.3	19.1	25.8	8.2	7.3	8.6
Laborers, except Farm	6.4	7.8	9.7	25.5	31.1	36.4	26.4	33.3	36.0
Farm[c]	8.3	14.5	21.3	12.3	24.1	41.3	23.5	46.6	66.5
Farmers and Farm Mgrs.	5.9	10.2	14.2	4.6	13.6	21.3	9.5	24.2	45.1
Farm Laborers	2.4	4.3	7.1	7.7	10.5	20.0	14.0	22.4	21.4

Major Occupational Groupings	Japanese			Chinese			Filipino		
	1960	1950	1940	1960	1950	1940	1960	1950	1940
White Collar[b]	56.0	36.2	44.5	50.7	41.5	35.3	25.7	11.9	9.2
Professional and Technical	26.1	9.6	5.4	20.3	6.6	2.5	13.3	3.1	3.0
Proprietors, Managers, and Officials	13.0	12.9	23.0	16.8	23.2	22.3	3.1	2.9	2.3
Clerical and Sales	16.9	13.7	16.1	13.6	11.7	10.5	9.3	5.9	3.9
Manual Workers[b]	44.0	63.9	55.5	49.3	58.4	64.7	74.4	88.1	90.7
Craftsmen and Foremen	15.3	11.5	4.8	5.1	3.5	1.4	9.9	8.1	2.3
Operatives	13.1	14.6	12.2	14.2	17.1	23.1	17.6	18.0	11.1
Service Workers	8.3	17.6	19.2	28.5	35.8	38.4	39.7	56.4	70.0
Laborers, except Farm	7.3	20.2	19.3	1.5	2.0	1.8	7.2	5.6	7.3
Farm[c]	25.7	32.5	43.1	1.3	2.9	4.2	23.8	43.1	49.4
Farmers and Farm Mgrs.	18.0	15.5	18.6	.8	1.4	1.4	2.9	5.9	1.6
Farm Laborers	7.7	17.0	24.5	.5	1.5	2.8	20.9	37.2	47.8

[a] Includes employed persons 14 years of age and over in civilian labor force for whom an occupation was reported. The unemployed are not included in this table, but they comprise an essential component of the civilian labor force. In 1960, the percentages unemployed were as follows: Indian 16.2; Negro 8.9; Filipino 6.3; White 4.7; Chinese 3.8; and Japanese 2.4.

[b] Base on which percentages for "White Collar" and "Manual" workers were computed excludes "Farm" category.

[c] Base on which percentages for "Farm" category were computed includes total employed civilian labor force.

sistent upward movement of the curves in Figure 4 indicates a marked increase in educational attainment for minorities as well as for whites. The heavy immigration of Filipinos between 1940 and 1950 was responsible for a slight decline in educational attainment for Filipino men during this period.

Proportion of Persons Completing Four Years of High School and Above. The curves in Figure 5 indicate that again the Japanese, both men and women, have been clearly and consistently at the top for the entire 20-year period. For men in the remaining groups in 1960, whites ranked second; Chinese, third; Filipinos, fourth; and Negroes and Indians tied for bottom position. Japanese women were followed in rank order by Filipinos, Chinese, whites, Negroes, and Indians.

OCCUPATIONAL STATUS

Table 3 summarizes under three broad categories—"white collar," "manual workers," and "farm"—the occupational distribution of male workers in the five nonwhite groups and in the white population for 1940, 1950, and 1960. The proportion of white-collar workers in 1960 is largest among Japanese (56.0 per cent), Chinese (50.7 per cent), and Caucasians (42.1 per cent). The corresponding figure for the Filipino population is 26.0 per cent; for Indians, 16.6 per cent; and for Negroes, 13.8 per cent. Increases in white-collar employment among Orientals, especially during the past ten years, have been most pronounced in the professional ranks, while the increase in white-collar occupations among Negroes has been largely in clerical and

TABLE 4. MEDIAN INCOME OF PERSONS BY SEX AND RACE
UNITED STATES: 1949 AND 1959

Race	1959		1949	
	Men	Women	Men	Women
White	$4,338	$1,509	$2,582	$1,139
Negro	2,254	905	1,356	703
Indian	1,792	1,000	a	a
Japanese	4,306	1,967	a	a
Chinese	3,239	2,067	a	a
Filipino	3,035	1,518	a	a

ᵃ Data not available.

sales positions. The proportion of white-collar workers during the same period has declined only among Indians.

Except for the Indians, all groups contained smaller proportions of manual workers in 1960 than in 1940. The proportionate declines have been most apparent among service workers and laborers, while the percentages for craftsmen, foremen, and operatives have increased in every group, except among white and Chinese operatives.

Despite the continued and steady decline in the proportion of non-whites engaged in agriculture, about one-fourth of the male Indian, Japanese, and Filipino labor forces are employed in farming activities, compared with 12.3 per cent of the male Negro labor force, 8.3 per cent of the whites, and only a token percentage of the Chinese.

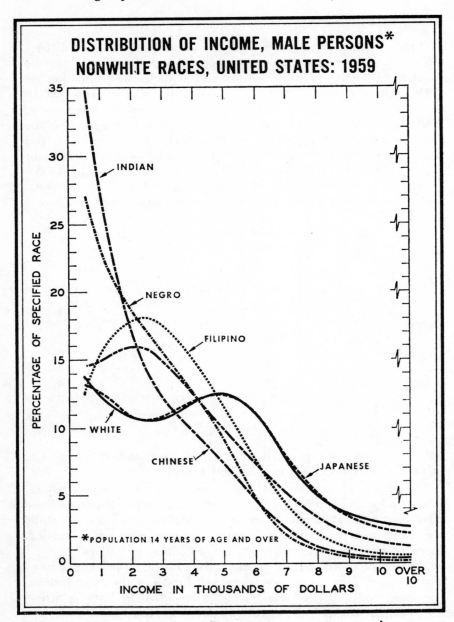

Figure 6

INCOME STATUS

Basic data for the third dimension of socioeconomic position—income—are presented in Table 4 and Figure 6.

Median Income. In 1959, median incomes for the male population in the various racial groups ranged from $1,792 for Indians to $4,338 for whites.[3] Although both Japanese and Chinese outrank Caucasians on the occupation dimension, and Japanese are above Caucasians in educational status, they rank second and third, respectively, in income. Apparently, members of nonwhite minorities are paid less for the same services than are members of the white majority. Discriminatory factors clearly enter into these differentials, but in addition, some minority groups have a smaller market for their goods and services than the whites do, and from a competitive standpoint with certain exceptions, Caucasians control key positions in the older, larger, and better established professions and businesses. In 1959, the median income of Japanese men was 99.3 per cent of the median income of Caucasian males. Corresponding percentages for the other groups are as follows: Chinese, 74.7; Filipino, 70.0; Negro, 52.0; and Indians, 41.3.

Frequency Distribution of Income. Figure 6 shows the income distributions of the five non-white groups and of the white population. Although the curves differ markedly from one another, they do emphasize the disparities of income distribution. For example, the pronounced J-shaped curve for Indians, with more than one-third of the population in the $0 to $1,000 interval and only a very small proportion in the upper brackets contrasts sharply with the whites' curve, which indicates a small proportion of the population in the lower income intervals and large proportions in the higher intervals. Further examination of Figure 6 supports the basic conclusion derived from the series on median income.[4]

SUMMARY INDICES OF SOCIOECONOMIC STATUS

These data clearly document large and consistent differences among the nonwhite racial groups and between whites and nonwhites generally, in education, occupation, and income.[5] To summarize the detailed data for each of the three dimensions into a single numerical index, weighted averages were computed on the basis of standardized scores developed by Nam.[6]

Profiles of Socioeconomic Status, 1960. To derive a series of comparable, generalized profiles for the various ethnic groups, the raw scores were transformed into percentages and portrayed graphically in Figure 7. The hierarchical positions of Japanese, Caucasians, and Chinese on all three dimensions—education, occupation, and income—are distinctly separate from those of Indians, Negroes, and Filipinos. The Japanese are far above any other group in educational status, with a raw score of 61.3, or a transformed score of 25.7 per cent. The corresponding scores for Caucasians are 44.8 and 18.8 per cent; for Chinese, 41.8 and 17.5 per cent; for Filipinos, 37.5 and 15.7 per cent; for both Negroes and Indians, respectively, 26.4 and 11.1 per cent. Japanese rank first in occupational status, followed in rank order by Chinese, Caucasians, Filipinos, Indians, and Negroes. Caucasians rank highest in income, followed in rank order by Japanese and Chinese. Indians and Negroes conform to a remarkedly consistent pattern toward the lower end of the scale on all three dimensions.

Trends in Socioeconomic Differentials, 1940 to 1960. To measure changes in socioeconomic status in the various groups during the past two decades, educational and occupational scores were computed for 1940, 1950, and 1960, and summarized in graphic form in Figure 8. The Japanese ranked highest in educational status throughout the past 20 years, and the disparity between their position and that of Caucasians has shown a marked increase. Similarly, Chinese have made significant strides in education during the same time period, and in 1960 they ranked third, just behind the whites. The rising levels of education among Japanese and Chinese reflect, at least in part, increased proportions native-born. A noticeable upward trend in educational status occurred in all other groups as well.

The occupational positions of all ethnic groups were higher in 1960 than in 1940. In 1940 and 1950, the white population ranked highest in occupational status, with the Chinese slightly below, but between 1950 and 1960, both Japanese and Chinese surpassed Caucasians in occupational status. The occupational order of the three remaining groups in 1960 was Negro, Filipino, and Indian.[7]

SUMMARY AND IMPLICATIONS

Well-defined and consistent patterns of socioeconomic status exist among nonwhites in the U.S. Japanese rank highest in educational status with whites and Chinese in second and third places, respectively; Filipinos rank fourth, and Negroes and Indians, with identical scores, lowest. The occupational hierarchy is similar: Japanese, Chinese, and

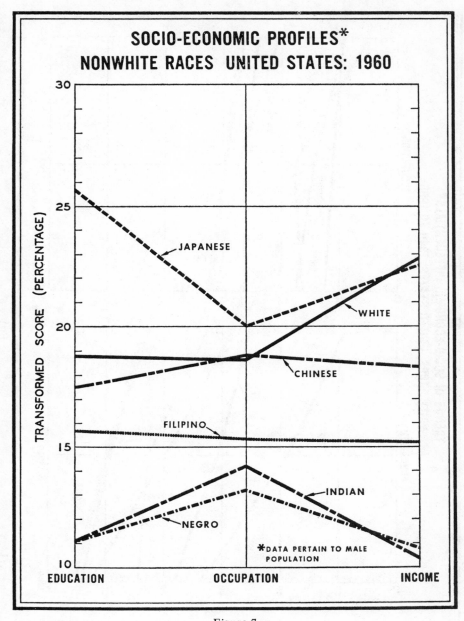

Figure 7

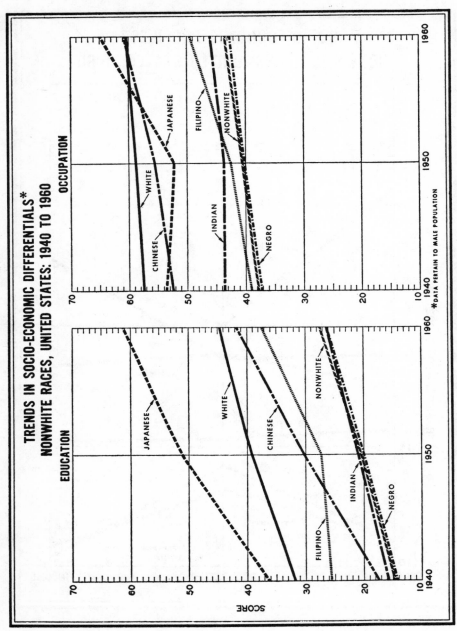

TRENDS IN SOCIO-ECONOMIC DIFFERENTIALS*
NONWHITE RACES, UNITED STATES: 1940 TO 1960

Figure 8

Caucasians hold first, second, and third positions, respectively. Filipinos are fourth; Indians, fifth; and Negroes, sixth. On the income dimension, the white male population is in first place, followed by Japanese and Chinese. Filipinos are again in fourth place, but the rank-order positions for Negroes and Indians are reversed.

Most shifts in the relative positions of the different racial groups in educational attainment and occupational status have been relatively minor. During the last two decades Caucasians, Japanese, and Chinese have maintained consistently high rank, while Negroes and Indians have held the lowest positions. Generally, Filipinos rank lower than the top three races, but distinctly higher than Negroes and Indians.

The implications of the basic patterns revealed by these data pertain not only to stratification, but especially to the process of assimilation, for the phenomena of assimilation and stratification are intimately related. The traditional model of the assimilation process assumes that an immigrant group will acquire, within a matter of several years, the language, habits, customs, and values of the dominant, native-born Anglo-Saxon population, and as a consequence its members will eventually move up in the social and economic hierarchies. Assimilation is expected to be completed by the third generation.

Such an explanation is highly over-simplified, and inadequate to account for the low degree of assimilation of nonwhite races, particularly Negroes.[8] Gordon, among others, has noted the complexity of the assimilation process. To clarify and make explicit various aspects of the assimilation process, he has developed the following classification: cultural, structural, marital, identificational, attitude receptional, behavior receptional, and civic.[9] "Not only is the assimilation process mainly a matter of degree, but obviously, each of the stages or subprocesses distinguished above may take place in varying degrees."[10]

As far as the cultural and civic dimensions are concerned, Negroes, for example, have evidenced a substantial degree of assimilation, but on the remaining five variables they have remained virtually unassimilated. Indians, with an overwhelming proportion segregated on reservations, are even less culturally and "civically" assimilated than Negroes. Filipinos have been handicapped in the assimilation process by their recent arrival to this country, as well as by language differences, and relatively low educational attainment. On the other hand, Chinese and especially Japanese show a higher degree of cultural and civic assimilation than any of the other minority races. Moreover, they have made some headway in the other dimensions of assimilation. As the Taeubers point out, the disappearance of ethnic colonies and the increased residential dispersion of the Japanese, compared with the relatively pronounced spatial segregation of Negroes, is indicative of their higher degree of assimilation. It should be evident that skin pigmentation alone—visibility—is not sufficient to explain the degree of assimilation or the social status of minority races.[11]

Although all of the dimensions are important and interrelated, Gordon hypothesizes that structural assimilation is the key dimension, for when a minority race participates in large numbers in primary group relations with the dominant white population, and enters fully into the societal network of groups and institutions, other forms of assimilation will be greatly facilitated.[12]

FOOTNOTES

[1] The basic 1940 and 1950 data apply only to the 48 conterminous states. Accordingly, to make the 1960 data comparable it was necessary to subtract figures for Alaska and Hawaii, as far as possible. It was not possible to eliminate all categories for Alaska and Hawaii, but the resulting discrepancies for the 1960 totals are relatively small: 0.1 per cent for Negroes, 2.8 per cent for Indians, 0.2 per cent for Japanese, 0.1 per cent for Chinese, and 0.5 per cent for Filipinos.

[2] For more detailed illustrative discussions and references pertaining to indices of socioeconomic status see: Albert J. Reiss, Jr., *et al., Occupations and Social Status,* New York: Free Press, 1961; Bernard Barber, *Social Stratification,* New York: Harcourt, Brace, 1957, esp. pp. 96-185; Joseph A. Kahl, *The American Class Structure,* New York: Rinehart, 1957, pp. 19-126; Harold M. Hodges, *Social Stratification, Class in America,* Cambridge, Mass.: Schenkman, 1964, pp. 78-101.

[3] Reliable and comparable data on income are not available for 1940, 1950, and 1960.

[4] Cf. Herman P. Miller, *Income of the American People,* New York: John Wiley, 1955, esp. pp. 34-96, and *Rich Man, Poor Man,* New York: Thomas Y. Crowell, 1964, esp. pp. 84-124.

[5] To attain strict comparability among the various races, age, sex, nativity, urban-rural residence, years of residence in the U.S., and other factors obviously should be held constant. Limitations of these data make this impossible, however, except perhaps for age and sex adjustment for educa-

tional status. Nevertheless, in spite of the variations in such factors as age, sex, nativity, urban-rural residence, and years of residence in the U.S., the basic patterns and trends in socioeconomic differentials among the several races are remarkably clear and consistent.

6 Charles B. Nam, *Methodology and Scores of Socioeconomic Status,* Working Paper No. 15, Washington, D.C.; U.S. Bureau of the Census, 1963. The computational procedures used in deriving the various scores discussed in this section are an adaptation of Nam's techniques and weighting system to grouped data. The Nam scores for major occupational groups, educational status, and income were applied to the appropriate categories of the several minority populations. The resulting scores represent weighted averages for each dimension for each racial group. The transformed scores for each group are percentages derived from the sum of the original scores of each dimension.

7 Although the Bureau of the Census does not classify Puerto Ricans and persons of Spanish surname (most of whom are of Mexican-American origin) as nonwhite, they are nevertheless large and distinctive American ethnic groups. Of the 892,513 Puerto Ricans recorded in 1960, approximately 70 per cent resided in New York City. Data on persons of Spanish surname were obtained only for the southwest portion of the United States including Arizona, California, Colorado, New Mexico, and Texas; in 1960 there were 3,464,999. Comparison of the Nam scores on education, occupation, and income in 1960 with those of the other racial groups indicates that Puerto Ricans and persons of Spanish surname rank slightly lower than Negroes and Indians on education but higher than these two groups on occupation and income, and lower than whites, Japanese, Chinese, and Filipinos on all three variables.

8 See Nathan Glazer and Daniel P. Moynihan, *Beyond the Melting Pot: The Negroes, Puerto Ricans, Jews, Italians, and Irish of New York City,* Cambridge, Mass.: The M.I.T. Press, 1963.

9 Milton M. Gordon, *Assimilation in American Life,* New York: Oxford University Press, 1964, pp. 70-75. "Cultural" refers to change of cultural patterns to those of the host society; "structural," to large-scale entry to cliques, clubs, and institutions of the host society; "marital," to widespread intermarriage; "identificational," to development of a sense of peoplehood based exclusively on the host society; "attitude receptional," to absence of prejudice; "behavior receptional," to absence of discrimination; and "civic," to absence of value and power conflict.

10 *Ibid.,* p. 71.

11 Karl E. Taeuber and Alma F. Taeuber, "The Negro as an Immigrant Group: Recent Trends in Racial and Ethnic Segregation in Chicago," *American Journal of Sociology,* 69 (1964), pp. 374-382.

12 Gordon, *loc. cit.*

THE NEGRO REVOLUTION:
POSSIBLE OR IMPOSSIBLE?

L. M. KILLIAN

From May 17, 1954 until the March on Washington and the passage of the 1964 Civil Rights Act, the battle over segregation forcibly reminded the American people that race relations constituted their foremost domestic problem. Just as the end of this battle seemed to be at hand, it became evident that there existed a crisis that was far graver than the desegregation controversy had ever been.

Fantastic gains had been made in terms of judicial interpretation of the Constitution, of federal legislation, and of public acceptance of the "qualified" Negroes of the black bourgeoisie. The federal antipoverty program represented a broad attack on the plight of the poor, white as well as nonwhite, not originally envisioned as part of the war on inequality. With the death of the doctrine of separate but equal, the nation had a new, albeit incomplete, commitment to an equality of opportunity that was color blind.

INTEGRATION: A FADING GOAL

Now it appeared, however, that integration had lost its luster as a goal. In practice it had turned out to mean the token integration of a minority of qualified Negroes into what remained a white man's society. For the majority of Negro Americans, handicapped by generations of isolation from the mainstream of American culture, the mere relaxing of racial barriers could not mean "Freedom Now." In acknowledgment of this new facet of the Negro's problem, Whitney Young called for "a decade of dedicated special effort" to close the gap created by three hundred years of preferential treatment of white

Reprinted from *The Impossible Revolution,* by L. M. Killian, by permission of Random House, Inc.

citizens. He said, "At this point when the scales of justice are so grossly unbalanced it is impossible to balance them by simply applying equal weight."[1] James Farmer, militant leader of CORE, soon to be replaced by the even more militant Floyd McKissick, expressed the same theme in stronger terms. He said of the impoverished Negro, "Offering him equal rights, even equal opportunity at this late date without giving him a special boost is the kind of cruel joke American individualism has played on the poor throughout history. And so CORE and the Movement of which we are part planned compensatory and remedial programs to provide the necessary boost."[2]

THE NEW CRISIS

The new crisis in race relations arose from this basic fact: an emergency program giving Negroes preferential treatment on the basis of their color, not just the mere cessation of crude color discrimination, was necessary to make equality meaningful for Negroes. Two years of experience with seemingly radical civil rights laws and with the much-vaunted War on Poverty revealed that both attempts fell far short of the kind of special effort that was needed. The near-rebellion of Negro leaders at the White House planning conference and the ghetto riots in the summers of 1965, 1966, and 1967 symbolized how far a decade of favorable court rulings, non-violent demonstrations, and federal legislation had fallen short of satisfying the rising expectations of the Negro masses. It was evident that the Negro protest movement was at a critical juncture. To continue to pick away at segregation, the symbol of the Negro's inferior social and economic position, was not enough. An assault on the *de facto* inequality of the Negro masses in employment, housing, and education was now mandatory. The tactics of protest that had been effective in desegregating lunch counters and parks and in producing federal legislation were being brought into question.

A NEW "NEW DEAL"

First, there was a widespread fear even among militant Negro leaders that the limits of reform through federal civil rights laws had been reached. Effective enforcement of existing laws, a spirit of compliance on the local level, and broader social legislation were now needed. The failure of Congress to pass the 1966 civil rights bill suggested that this law-making body, too, felt that there were enough civil rights laws on the books. There was also an obvious fear among civil rights leaders that demonstrations could no longer be disciplined and nonviolent. The riots of the summers of 1965, 1966, and 1967 had revealed to Negro leaders how little control they had over the inhabitants of the ghettos. This apprehension led to another fear that continuation of the strategy of protest would alienate significant white support of the Negro movement and lead to a pervasive and clear-cut definition of the movement as revolutionary.

Bayard Rustin, whose credentials as a militant leader were impeccable, stated the case for a new strategy and new tactics in his famous article entitled "From Protest to Politics; the Future of the Civil Rights Movement." The strategy that Rustin suggested was radical, for he called for a shift from civil rights as a target to a program of "qualitative transformation of fundamental institutions, more or less rapidly, to the point where the social and economic structure which they comprised can no longer be said to be the same."[3] In amplification he called for "radical programs for full employment, abolition of slums, the reconstruction of our educational system, new definitions of work and leisure. . . . Adding up the cost of such programs we can only conclude that we are talking about a refashioning of our political economy."[4] He suggested that the civil rights movement had run its course and would have to be replaced by a broader social movement devoted to economic and political reform. There should be, in effect, a new New Deal and an enlargement of the Great Society to gargantuan proportions.

Rustin's proposal for bringing about these reforms was also reminiscent of the early days of Roosevelt's New Deal. Reflecting an optimism generated by the democratic sweep in the elections of 1964 he said:

> The future of the Negro struggle depends on whether the contradictions of this society can be resolved by a coalition of progressive forces which becomes the effective political majority in the United States. I speak of the coalition which staged the March on Washington, passed the Civil Rights Act and laid the basis for the Johnson landslide: Negroes, trade unionists, liberals and religious groups.[5]

It was in the same vein that, a few months later, A. Philip Randolph called for a one hundred and eighty-five billion dollar Freedom

Budget to make possible full equality for Negroes. Randolph made it plain that he believed only a comprehensive, far-reaching federal program could accomplish the job. Both Rustin and Randolph emphasized the benefits that would accrue to the entire economy if Negro poverty were abolished and, along with it, the poverty of all deprived Americans.

Such a solution as Rustin and Randolph proposed would indeed provide an unprecedented model of peaceful social change as an alternative to revolution. The dream of the New Deal, revived as the vision of the Great Society, would become reality as poverty, poor housing, and inferior schools were abolished for all Americans. In the process of achieving this reality, race consciousness would also be abolished as ambitious, upwardly mobile whites and Negroes made common cause against the ancient, impersonal evils of poverty, disease, and ignorance. A utopian society would be created without the ordeal of either a class war or a race war, but through a marvel of social engineering.

GUNS OR BUTTER: A PROBLEM OF VALUES

Nowhere is there evidence, however, that the majority of the American electorate is disposed to pay the price for such a feat. That the price would be small as compared to the cost of Viet Nam or the space program does not change the fact that the American public is willing to pay for these latter ventures, but not for the former. The affluence of the majority of the population accounts in part for this phenomenon. In the words of two sociologists Sidney Willhelm and Elwin Powell: "Our society prospers without a redistribution of income in favor of the lower brackets—despite liberal slogans. In the military system we have an impersonal, omnipotent consumer of tremendous proportions that, in effect, supplants a mass purchasing power that could have been placed in the Negro's hands."[6]

Economists and sociologists who take a pessimistic view of the crisis of automation predict that the problems of "uselessness" that now confront the Negro masses will eventually be recognized as a problem of whites also. Willhelm and Powell comment, "For the Negro is merely a weathervane for the future. *His* experienec will be a common one for many whites now deprived of some sort of usefulness; *his* frustrations will become those for many others the longer we hesitate to confront the meaning of human dignity in an automated society."[7]

The time in which the anxiety of the Negro is generalized to a large segment of potential political allies in white society has not yet arrived. The congressional and gubernatorial elections of November 1966, showed the existence of a backlash against the welfare programs of the Great Society, not a readiness to expand these programs. At a time when a radical program of social and economic reform was needed, the American people opted for moderation. Daniel Moynihan observed after these elections, "It appears that the nation may be in the process of reproducing the tragic events of the Reconstruction: giving to Negroes the forms of legal equality but withdrawing the economic and political resources which are the bases of social equality."[8]

In the meantime, the urgent needs and the intense dissatisfaction of the aroused Negro masses remained a present fact. The Negro Revolution had to continue in some fashion unless race relations were to enter a new era of accommodation. This would be an era in which the black bourgeoisie would enjoy the fruits of the civil rights movement while a larger body of "unqualified" Negroes remained segregated and deprived until the next renewal of the Negro's struggle for equality.

GRADUALISM REVISITED

In addition to the doubt of whether a radical program of political and economic reform would be supported by the white majority, there was the question of whether it would gain the support of Negroes themselves. Gradualism is an inherent feature of a program of building a viable political coalition and then reforming a society through social engineering. Maximizing voter registration, winning victories at the polls, and then translating votes into policy is a tedious, often discouraging task lacking the drama of a demonstration.[9] It is questionable whether Negroes could be mobilized for the long pull required to make them a decisive political power in the nation. Victories would not be quick and sure and setbacks, such as those encountered in the November elections of 1966, would be recurrent. Even if an effective progressive coalition could be forged, the task of reshaping the economic order could be accomplished neither easily nor quickly within the framework of the American political structure. The system of checks and balances, horizontal and vertical, that has always emasculated bold, comprehensive programs of social reform would still operate to frustrate the grand designs of the social planners and to disillusion Negroes who place their faith in such programs. Most important, the shift of the Negro s struggle from protest to politics and then to social engineering would offer little hope of providing that sense of identity that he is still struggling desperately to achieve. It may be argued that during the first decade of demonstrations it has been the struggle itself that has sustained Negroes, not the token victories they have achieved. To suspend the protest in the hope that more significant victories would thereby be achieved in a remote future would be to deprive Negroes of their chief source of pride in the present time.

NEGRO PRIDE AND THE NEW NATIONALISM

It is to this emergent pride that the revolutionary alternative offered by the new radicals, the advocates of Black Power, appeals. It is the same sort of appeal offered by an earlier generation of new radicals when, beginning in 1956, they led Negroes into the streets in demonstrations rather than wait on the result of the long, unsatisfying, legalistic strategy of the NAACP. Not a diminution of conflict and tension, but an intensification of the struggle has always been the answer of the radicals to the impasses the Negro Revolution has seemed to meet. But this latest version of Negro radicalism is the most revolutionary that has appeared. It is defined by white Americans and even by erstwhile radical Negro leaders as unrespectable and revolutionary. This definition is accepted as valid by the new radicals; they make no obeisances to the idols of national unity, legalism, and nonviolence. Instead of a strategy of coalition politics within the framework of a two party system, they propose the creation of a black political party. The suggestion has even been advanced that the black ghettoes become separate cities within the metropolitan areas where they are located. Instead of the preparation of Negroes for integration into a prosperous and presumably expanding white economy, the creation of a parallel Negro economy and the expulsion of white capitalists from the ghettoes has been recommended. Most notably, an appeal to the white man's fear rather than to his love or his guilt is the underlying theme of Black Power. This theme is couched in terms of self-defense, but included in it is a total rejection of the white man's law. Stokely Carmichael made clear his rejection of white America and of its laws when he said:

> We can't be expected any more to march and get our heads broken to say to you that you are nice guys. You are not nice guys. We have found you out. You are rotten through and through, and that's what we are saying. And, Alexander the Great was really Alexander the Barbaric, and that's what we're going to start from.[10]

> I've had so much law and order, I swear before God I want some chaos! I want some chaos so bad I can taste it on the tip of my lips, because all I see is law and order everywhere I go. Law and order: from Canton, Mississippi to Watts, Los Angeles, to Harlem, to Chicago— nothing but law and order.[11]

Carmichael and SNCC are not the only new radicals to put their foot upon the path of black nationalism. With the election of Floyd McKissick as its leader, traditionally nonviolent CORE assumed a posture that could scarcely be distinguished from that of SNCC. The words written by James Farmer shortly before he left the leadership of CORE presaged this decision to continue the struggle without dependence on white allies or white love. Farmer spoke of a new "mood ebony" in CORE and explained it on the basis of three reasons. First, he spoke of the pride that had developed among Negroes through the achievements of the civil rights movement, saying, "We learned that what was needed was not *invisibility* but a valid and legitimate *visibility.*" Second, he spoke of the influence of the masses of black people who were attracted to the banner of CORE. He said, "The integration-which-would-end-in-assimilation has never been a prime goal of the Negro masses. . . . Garveyism remains latent in the Negro ghetto, as our new recruits taught us." Finally, and most significantly, he declared, "The present day black nationalist groups . . . and figures like the late Malcolm X have influenced us perceptibly."[12] Then he advanced the psychological justification for the new strategy of black nationalism, saying:

> Like the nationalists, we must try to conquer the Negro sense of inferiority. We feel this will be possible only when it is legitimate to be a black man in this country. And here CORE has a unique contribution to make. *CORE knows that Negro identity will emerge only in the midst of purposive and realistic effort in America. The nationalists offer doctrine. We must offer program as well.*[13]

Farmer proposed that CORE stick to its "proven techniques of nonviolent direct action." While he had praise for the Deacons for Defense and Justice, he saw more danger than advantage in Malcolm X's bolder doctrine of violence. But McKissick, Carmichael, Brown, and even more so the host of unheralded local Negro leaders who amass arsenals of small arms and Molotov cocktails in the ghettoes, apparently do not share Farmer's fear of a race war.

The prospects for the success of the appeal of the new radicals in producing a large following and drastically changing the structure of American society must be considered from three perspectives. The first considers the sort of psychological appeal that the spirit of total war against white society might have, particularly for the younger generation of Negroes. The second considers the societal conditions that might accentuate Negro impatience and enhance the appeal of the black nationalists. The third perspective requires an examination of the program that may be dimly discerned in the Black Power movement.

THE APPEAL OF CONFLICT

Peaceful, secure men usually look at conflict, particularly violent conflict, from a strictly utilitarian standpoint. Unless they are pacifists, they view conflict as a necessary evil that must always be justified in terms of achieving some greater good. Thus it is assumed that the conflict in which rational men will engage will be directed at an enemy who is responsible for the conditions that the aggressors desire to have corrected and that victory will have some logical chance of changing these conditions. Conflict that seems to have no such chance is seen as the blind striking out of irrational, frustrated people who, in their desperation, think not of the consequences of their actions. This sort of conflict would seem to serve no function for the participants beyond a temporary release of tension.

It is this sort of thinking that leads to warnings that an intensification of the Negro's struggle for identity and equality will only serve to bring down the wrath of a powerful white community upon the heads of Negroes. There is another theory that holds that seemingly hopeless conflict has value both for the individuals who participate in it and for the group of which they are a part. The gains for the

individual and the group are much greater than mere relief of tension. This doctrine holds that a prideful group identity must be
achieved through the birth pangs of conflict. It has been enunciated
by the Algerian revolutionist Frantz Fanon in his book *The Wretched
of the Earth*.[14] Although the book is about the colonized people of
the African continent, many similarities may be found between the
plight of the Negro masses in America and that of the native peoples
of Africa. Fanon argues that only by taking up arms against the
European powers in a total and violent struggle can the peoples of
the Third World achieve national identities, national cultures, and
national pride. In the preface to Fanon's book, Jean Paul Sartre
says:

> He shows clearly that this irrepressible violence is neither sound and
> fury, nor the resurrection of savage instincts, nor even the effect of re-
> sentment: it is man recreating himself. . . . The native cures himself of
> colonial neurosis by thrusting out the settler through force of arms. When
> his rage boils over, he rediscovers his lost innocence and he comes to
> know himself in that he himself creates his self. . . . The rebel's weapon
> is the proof for his humanity. For in the first days of the revolt you must
> kill: to shoot down a European is to kill two birds with one stone, to
> destroy an oppressor and the man he oppresses at the same time: there
> remains a dead man and a free man; the survivor, for the first time, feels
> a *national* soil under his foot.[15]

Fanon explains how in his view the struggle to achieve nationhood
is an essential ingredient of group consciousness and group unity.
He says:

> But it so happens that for the colonized people this violence, because
> it constitutes their only work, invests their characters with positive and
> creative qualities. The purpose of violence binds them together as a
> whole, since each individual forms a violent link in the great chain, a
> part of the great organism of violence which has surged upward in rec-
> ognition of the settler's violence in the beginning. The groups recognize
> each other and the future nation is already indivisible. The armed
> struggle mobilizes the people; that is to say, it throws them in one way
> and in one direction.
>
> The mobilization of the masses, when it rises out of the war of libera-
> tion, introduces into each man's consciousness the ideas of a common
> cause, of a national destiny and of a collective history. In the same way
> the second phase, that of the building-up of the nation, is helped on by
> the existence of this cement which has been mixed with blood and anger.
> Thus we come to a full appreciation of the originality of the words used

in these under-developed countries. During the colonial period the people are called upon to fight against oppression; after national liberation, they are called upon to fight against poverty, illiteracy, and under-development. The struggle, they say, goes on. The people realize that life is an unending contest.[16]

The new radicals of the Negro Revolution, in contrast to strategists such as Bayard Rustin and A. Philip Randolph, are following this philosophy in placing Black Power at the top of the agenda and the war on cultural deprivation at the bottom. They would no longer have Negro Americans come as supplicants seeking the crumbs from the white man's table, ever conscious of their own inferiority. Like Fanon, they argue that pride and a sense of peoplehood must be achieved first if the black man is to enjoy real equality in a society that heretofore has condemned him to inferiority simply on the basis of his blackness. Carmichael speaks of the need of Negro Americans to overcome their own feelings of inferiority when he says:

> Black people in this country have to move to a position of psychological equality and that is very, very important. And they can't do that with white people getting everything for them. They have to confront the white power structure themselves, so that means that white allies will have to be pushed aside; we can no longer have white people getting poverty money for you—you have to get it yourself so that you know black people can do those things on their own—so that they don't always need somebody white to do it for them.[17]

One of the charges most frequently thrown at Negro Americans is that having lost their native African culture in slavery they have developed no culture of their own of which they could be proud. The whole notion of cultural pluralism implies that within the framework of the white man's society Negroes should learn to develop and take pride in their own cultural forms. These should be more than pale, shoddy imitations of the white man's culture. Fanon addresses himself indirectly to this notion also. Speaking of the development of national cultures in the emergent nations of Africa, he says:

> A frequent mistake, and one which is moreover hardly justifiable is to try to find cultural expressions for and to give new values to native culture within the framework of colonial domination. This is why we arrive at a proposition which at first sight seems paradoxical: The fact that in a colonized country the most elementary, the most savage and the most undifferentiated nationalism is the most fervent and efficient means of defending national culture. . . . The nation is not only the condition of culture, its fruitfulness, its continuous renewal, and its deep-

ening. It is also a necessity. It is the fight for national existence which sets culture moving and opens to it the doors of creation. Later on it is the nation which will insure the conditions and framework necessary to culture.[18]

By the same token, it may be argued that a meaningful and satisfying Negro-culture can come into existence in a pluralistic American society only through an antecedent state of black nationalism. In turn, it is through the myth of Black Power that the new radicals are attempting to create this black nationalism.

This is the logic of Black Power as this philosophy might be seen through the eyes of one who views Negro Americans as a colonial people and who has lost all faith in the willingness of white America to grant him real equality. Certainly there are individual black leaders, some enjoying national notoriety, others known only within their own ghetto neighborhoods, who have accepted the major part of this philosophy. By their logic, Watts, Newark, and Detroit were not senseless tragedies of nonrealistic conflict but minor victories in the war by black Americans to achieve identity.

The next phase of the racial crisis will consist of a contest between such leaders and more moderate Negro leaders, such as Martin Luther King, Jr., for the allegiance of the activists within the Negro population. How big a following the new radicals can attract, both to a compact, organized hard core and to a diffuse reserve of adherents who will jump into the fray whenever violence breaks out, will depend upon changes in the social and economic context.

ECONOMIC FACTORS

One development that would increase the number of desperate Negroes who would be responsive to this doctrine of disillusionment would be a further deterioration of the economic situation of the Negro masses. Continued inflation combined with a lag in the wage scales of unorganized workers and in welfare stipends would have this effect. Even greater economic cramp would be produced, and more quickly, by an economic recession. Even in a period of unprecedented affluence for the society as a whole unemployment among Negroes, particularly young people, remains alarmingly high. For the ghetto youth for whom James Baldwin, LeRoi Jones, and Claude Brown attempt to speak, depression conditions already exist. Were a cutback in employment added to the effects of automation, the army of potential revolutionary fighters would be augmented rapidly. But in another depression it would not be communism, Buy Black campaigns, or the Double Duty Dollar that would beckon to Negroes; it would be Black Power.

One event that could lead to a drastic economic readjustment in the United States would be a return to a peace economy as a result of American disengagement in Viet Nam. Were a reduction in military spending followed quickly by a shift of federal funds to the Freedom Budget, the utopian dream of Rustin and Randolph might be realized and the Negro Revolution terminated peacefully. If this did not happen, however, the end of the Viet Nam war might set the stage for the most violent phase of the Negro Revolution.

THE WAR IN VIET NAM AND THE NEGRO REVOLUTION

Many students of revolution have emphasized the close relationship between the involvement of a nation in an external war and the occurrence of a revolution. Chalmers Johnson proposes the term "accelerator" to designate an occurrence that catalyzes or throws into relief "the already existing revolutionary level of dysfunctions." Accelerators "do not of themselves cause revolution; but when they do occur in a system already bearing the necessary level of dysfunction . . . they will provide the sufficient cause of the immediately following revolution."[19]

Johnson identifies defeat in a foreign war as one of the most potent accelerators, noting, "Defeat in war, as an accelerator, shatters the myth of sovereignty, exacts sacrifices—even the supreme sacrifice—from a society's members for an unpopular system, and completes the crippling of an already creaking system; most important, it opens the doors to revolution because of its effects on the army."[20]

It is difficult to speculate about the relationship between the Negro Revolution, which so few Americans recognize as a real revolution, and the Viet Nam war, which officially is not a war! Analysis of the potential relationship between these two rests upon the assumption that there *is* a revolutionary situation in the United States and that the nation *is* engaged in a war, one in which defeat is possible. The analysis is complicated further by the fact that the American army in the field in Viet Nam is the most thoroughly integrated force in United States history; yet it is fighting an enemy that is "colored" and, like the Negro masses in the ghettoes, poor. The Negro leaders most disenchanted with the American society have been quick to point this out.

American withdrawal from Viet Nam, if followed by a final victory for Ho Chi Minh, would constitute a military defeat for the United States, even though the divisions returned intact. It would appear that the United States, although still on its feet, had conceded a technical knockout after challenging Asian communism. Belief in the invincibility of the white hope of the West would be shaken, not only among other nations and peoples but perhaps among Americans themselves, including Negro Americans. The lives lost in battle, including a disproportionate number of Negro lives, would appear to have been sacrificed in vain. To the most alienated Negroes, the altar on which these black soldiers would have been sacrificed would be the white American's vain belief in white supremacy in world affairs.

Chalmers Johnson argues that it is the crippling effect on the army itself, making it an inadequate instrument for defense of the status quo, that makes defeat in war important as an accelerator. There are no indications that the regular army that might be retained after a reduction of overseas commitments would become an active or even passive abettor of revolutionary violence. It is more likely that the armed forces would remain a bulwark against the *success* of a revolution. But the citizen soldiers, those members of the wartime armed forces who are rapidly demobilized at the conclusion of hostilities, could very well be the precipitant for violent revolution. It is significant that all ten of the founders of the Deacons for Defense and Justice were veterans of Korea or World War II.[21]

Negro veterans might find that they had exchanged the deprivations of the battlefield for the poverty and the indignities of the ghettos. But these would be the most battle-hardened, heroic group of Negroes who had ever fought for America simply because they had been given the greatest opportunity for combat and heroism. Trained, battle-tested, and embittered they could be the source of the guerrilla army that a Negro leader would need for the task of disrupting an American society from which he was totally alienated. Thus any end of massive United States military involvement in Viet Nam, even one coming as a result of token victory, could serve as an accelerator for the Negro Revolution.

A BATTLE PLAN FOR REVOLUTION

But what if RAM (Revolutionary Action Movement) or a more violent version of SNCC did become a rallying point for such an army? By what conceivable tactics could the impoverished denizens of the slums attack the might of the civil police and the armed forces of a rich, powerful, white society?

In Los Angeles, Newark, Cleveland, Detroit, and other cities, ghetto residents have already shown how effectively they can defy the police in what were essentially spontaneous, unorganized uprisings. It is true that these uprisings have been brought under control by military forces. But that in so many cities the National Guard had to be employed to restore order is a tribute to the power of Negro violence. Every time the National Guard has been employed to put down a riot, their intervention represented a victory for the rioters over the civilian police, the normal guardians of social peace in an American city.

Although the urban riots of the 1960s have so far stopped with the destruction of millions of dollars worth of private property and an inordinate drain on municipal and state budgets for the restoration of order, at least one blueprint for more widespread social disruption exists. The author of this blueprint is Robert F. Williams, who has been described as the spiritual godfather of RAM and premier of the African-American government in exile.[22] It is impossible to know just how much of a domestic following Williams has had since his flight from a federal warrant in 1961 led him first to Cuba, and then to Red China. There is no question, however, that his tactical ideas for a violent internal struggle, a minority revolution which could succeed in powerful America, are known and quoted by Negro extremists within the country. His belief that a minority revolution has a chance of succeeding in the United States rests upon his analysis of the vulnerability of American society as it is presently constituted. He says:

> The American society is a highly industrialized complex. A highly industrialized and mechanized system is also a very sensitive one. The more machinery required to serve a community, the greater the incidence of mechanical breakdown. The more dependent a community is on mechanization, the more important it is for the wheels of industry to perpetually turn smoothly. The American mind has been conditioned to think of great calamities, wars, and revolutionary upheavals as taking place on

distant soil. Because of the vast upper and middle classes in the U.S.A. that have grown accustomed to comfortable living, the nation is not psychologically prepared for massive violence and a sudden disruption of the essential agencies of the affluent society. The soft society is highly susceptible to panic.[23]

To produce this mechanical breakdown and generate panic, Williams recommends urban guerrilla tactics reminiscent of the methods used in Budapest during the Hungarian uprising. His brief but detailed description of the weapons and tactics is worth repeating.

The weapons of defense employed by Afro-American freedom fighters must consist of a poor man's arsenal. Gasoline fire bombs (Molotov cocktails), lye or acid bombs (made by injecting lye or acid in the metal end of light bulbs) can be used extensively. During the night hours such weapons thrown from rooftops will make the streets impossible for racist cops to patrol. Hand grenades, bazookas, light mortars, rocket launchers, machine guns, and ammunition can be bought clandestinely from service men anxious to make a fast dollar. Freedom fighters in military camps can be contacted to give instructions on use.

Extensive sabotage is possible. Gas tanks on public vehicles can be choked up with sand. Sugar is also highly effective in gasoline lines. Long nails driven through boards attached with long ends are effective to slow the movement of traffic on congested roads at night. This can cause havoc on turnpikes. Derailing of trains causes panic. Explosive booby traps on police telephone boxes can be employed. High-powered sniper rifles are readily available. Armor piercing bullets will penetrate oil storage tanks from a distance. Phosphorous matches (kitchen matches) placed in airconditioning systems will cause delayed explosions which will destroy expensive buildings. Flame throwers can be manufactured at home. Combat experienced ex-service men can easily solve that problem.[24]

Some of the weapons Williams recommends have already been used in urban riots. Small extremist groups in several American cities have already demonstrated their ability to collect weapons. The continued failure of Congress to pass an effective law controlling the possession and sale of small arms makes the creation of such weapons caches a continuing possibility. Ironically, the National Rifle Association has given as one of its grounds for opposition to such a law the need for citizens to possess arms to defend themselves against mob violence.[25]

THE NEED FOR LEADERSHIP

But the mere availability of weapons and individuals desperate enough to use them is not sufficient for launching a revolutionary war. There must be centralized leadership and organization, what Chalmers Johnson has called "a rebel infrastructure" or "autonomous government."[26] Williams concedes this in his explanation of how his own small-scale insurrection in Monroe, North Carolina, in 1957 ended in failure after two days of violence. He said:

> The lesson of Monroe teaches that effective self-defense on the part of brutally oppressed and terrorized people requires massive organization with central coordination. External oppressive forces must not be allowed to relieve the besieged racist terrorists. The forces of the state must be kept under pressure in many places simultaneously. The white supremacy masses must be forced to retreat to their homes in order to give security to their individual families.[27]

There is no question that one reason Negro destructiveness has not reached greater heights is the absence of organization and central coordination. Negro leadership in the United States, much like the leadership of the native fascist movement of the late thirties, is fragmented. It consists of many individual stars who spend as much time competing with one another for eminence as they do in promoting their common cause.

The individual leader or the leadership group who might lead the Negro Revolution into a phase of mass insurrection is not yet discernible. Such a person would have to combine charisma with organizational ability. Had he lived, Malcolm X might have been the type of leader who, with his lieutenants, would have been the nucleus for the building of a revolutionary army. It remains to be seen whether SNCC or CORE will produce a charismatic leader who can effectively challenge Martin Luther King, Jr., in capturing the imagination of large numbers of Negroes. It is doubtful that SNCC will constitute an adequate organizational vehicle because of its self-conscious emphasis on internal democracy.

During the summer of 1967, against the background of the infernos of Newark and Detroit, Black Power advocates began a struggle to achieve coordination. In July a national conference on Black Power brought together in Newark not only the extremist groups, but some members of more conservative civil rights organizations. That there is a Black Power element even in the NAACP was demonstrated by an attempted revolt of a group of Young Turks at the 1967 national convention of the organization. Later in the summer, Black Power forces displayed at least temporary unity and strength in forcing concessions from white delegates of the New Left at the National Conference on New Politics in Chicago. Significantly, James Forman, who had been temporarily eclipsed by Carmichael and Brown as a SNCC leader, came to the forefront again in this convention. Among the other Negro leaders present were King and his lieutenant, Ralph Abernathy, veterans like Forman of the nonviolent, interracial phase of the Negro Revolution.

The spirit of Black Power first welled up out of the ghetto and was enunciated by latecomers to the Negro Revolution, to the dismay of these early leaders. If this spirit of desperation begins to inspire members of the black bourgeoisie, as it is slowly doing, the reservoir of capable leadership will be enlarged. Cool-headed, sophisticated strategists may become available to supplement the efforts of the reckless agitators who now dominate the Black Power forces. Then the Negro Revolution will develop the rebel infrastructure that it now lacks.

The emergencce of yet a new strong man of the Negro Revolution depends, however, not just upon the existence of capable leaders. It is also contingent upon the unpredictable occurrence of a dramatic event that might thrust one individual into the limelight. Such an event might create a new hero of a new phase of the Negro Revolution, just as King was propelled into a position of leadership by the drama of the Montgomery protest.

Such a leader, yet unknown, may be waiting in the wings for the incident that will make him the rallying point for the now divided radical Negro leadership. How much of a following would gather around such a strong man depends upon situational factors, both domestic and international. Even as he was denouncing the philosophy of Black Power, Martin Luther King, Jr. described one of the circumstances that might cause large numbers of Negroes to turn away from his relatively moderate and nonviolent leadership. He declared, "The burden now shifts to the municipal, state, and federal authorities and all men in seats of power. If they continue to use our nonviolence as a cushion for complacency, the wrath of those suffering a long chain of abuses will rise. The consequence can well be unmanageable and persistent social disorder and moral disaster."[28]

The desperation of King's appeals for a continued adherence to the tactics of nonviolence seem to suggest that he fears that his own star is setting. At the time his star was clearly rising, it was observed, "Negroes demand of protest leaders constant progress. The combination of long-standing discontent, and a new-found belief in the possibility of change produces a constant state of tension and aggressiveness in the Negro community."[29]

At this time certain situational factors giving the advantage to the more militant Negro leader were identified. One was "the tendency of Negroes and white liberals to lionize the leader who displays aggressiveness and courage in defying the white power structure in his community." A second was, "the nationwide and even worldwide press coverage that such a leader is likely to receive, particularly if his tactics are met by illegal violence or police brutality." Then as now, it was observed that Negro leaders "realize that they must combat the suspicion among their followers that they have sold out to the white community and are permitting themselves to be used to preserve the status quo."[30] Martin Luther King, Jr., must today contend against the same situational forces that brought him to prominence as the greatest Negro leader since Booker T. Washington. The demands for ever greater militance and for constant proof of willingness to defy the white man continue to produce increasingly radical Negro leaders. Today King must defend himself against the charge that he is a modern-day Booker T. Washington whose leadership depends upon his acceptability to the white people. If the demand for militance produces Negro leaders even more militant than King, all omens indicate that such leaders will be advocates of violent, not nonviolent, resistance.

As has been pointed out, continued inflation or the occurrence of an economic recession could enhance the advantage that the new radicals already enjoy in appealing to the Negro masses. Even if American society continues to enjoy its precarious prosperity, such leaders will still have an advantage. Emergency action, not a business-as-usual approach, is required to reduce the frustration that is generated by the problems of race and poverty. It is just such a complacent, business-as-usual philosophy that Negro leaders, both moderate and radical, are already denouncing. The moderate leaders, such as Young, Wilkins, King, and Randolph, show even greater concern about the lack of responsiveness of the American body politic to the great needs than do the new radicals. They realize that they cannot maintain their tenuously held positions of leadership unless the Negro Revolution moves off dead center. The movement took a sudden, but non-violent, spurt forward in 1960 when the sit-ins resolved the impasse created by the failure of the legal tactics of the NAACP to produce change at a greatly accelerated rate. The next spurt forward might well be in the direction of violence.

NEGRO AMERICANS AND INTERNATIONAL RELATIONS

The faith of the new radical leaders and their followers in the desirability and feasibility of more aggressive, violent power tactics will be related also to world affairs. Many of these leaders see the Negro Revolution as part of the rise of the Third World. In the words of Harold Isaacs:

> Negroes accustomed always to feeling the big winds blowing against them now begin to feel the new sensation of having the wind at their backs. . . . Great and important things happening to millions of people all over the world affected what was happening to them and what happened to them had become important to everyone.[31]
>
> Frustrated Negroes are not the only ones, after all, who fear that Western white society is plunging towards some unimaginable hell, but Negroes in America do have their peculiarly equivocal status to resolve in their minds as they contemplate these prospects. Negroes of every estate have at one time or another exulted when some outside force has dealt white America a blow, have seen the Japanese, the Russians, or the Afro-Asians at the U.N. as acting somehow for *us* against *them,* and at every crisis in our history for half a century they have had to steady themselves with reminders about which, after all, was which. The deep and abiding identification of Negroes with America that has been maintained despite these feelings has had to persist in the face of a society's deep and abiding refusal to identify itself with Negroes.[32]

Thus the relative strength, prestige, and popularity of the United States in reference to Red China, the Afro-Asian nations, the United Nations, the emerging nations of Africa and Southeast Asia, and the sometimes democratic, sometimes communistic, revolutionary parties of Latin America, will influence the extent to which Negro Americans are willing to give American society yet another chance to prove its willingness to count them in. Even if the United States can maintain its position of military might, *sans* popularity, Negro Americans would find it extremely difficult to maintain their identification with a white American fortress standing, like the Union of South Africa, in defiance of a world in which the colored two-thirds of the population play an increasingly influential role.

In 1967, a significant symptom of a possible weakening of Negro identification with what is perceived as an aggressive America appeared in the commitment of Martin Luther King, Jr., to the peace movement. Although his motives were different, King's move brought him closer to the anti-Establishment position of Stokely Carmichael. At the same time, it created a serious rift between King on the one hand, and Whitney Young and Roy Wilkins on the other, further dividing and weakening the moderate element of Negro leadership.

THE FAITH OF THE ANARCHIST

Barring an all-out war between Communist China and the United States, how could the most optimistic Negro revolutionaries, without prospect of outside aid, hope literally to overthrow the white man's rule? This is the question that logical, cautious men, not revolutionary leaders, might ask. Confident in the faith that, with organization and the tactics of urban guerrilla warfare, they could bring the American social system to a state of chaos, the revolutionary leaders leave to a later date consideration of what sort of social structure could be rebuilt from a disorganized America in which white supremacy had been proven untenable.

One of the major elements which Howard Elinson identifies in the new radical leadership of the Negro Revolution is the new anarchists who, he points out, play an important part in SNCC, and in the Congress of Racial Equality in some areas. The important thing to recognize about the new anarchists and the approach they represent is the *absence* of a program for societal reconstruction. As Elinson says, "The goals and principles of the new anarchists are extremely difficult to describe, partly because the movement is committed to an ideology of nonideology; they are prone to deny that they have any set program."[33] To the extent that a new generation of Negro revolutionary leadership accepts the philosophy of the new anarchists, their concern will be with tearing down the established order, not with devising a new order. The building of a new order would be left to the operation of their ideal of participatory democracy.

A RACE AGAINST TIME

The United States is engaged in a dangerous race against time. It is a race against the day that the majority of Negroes decide that the future must be better than the present that white America offers them. The new radicals among Negro leaders are playing an equally dangerous game, however. White America has not reacted to the social disruption and the threats of even greater violence by taking heroic measures to redress the grievances that every Negro leader points to as the basic cause of Negro protests. The demand for integration that dominated the movement for so many years has been met with an ingeniously engineered tokenism, so frustrating as to cause many Negro leaders to abandon integration as a value. The demand for relief of Negro poverty has been met by an antipoverty program that has become bogged down in the morass of patronage and power politics. This program now is threatened with retrenchment because of a popular demand to hold the line of federal expenditures while still maintaining the military efforts in Viet Nam. Hence, the warnings of continued and greater violence to come are likely to be fulfilled. The warning of de Tocqueville, voiced over a century ago, remains both timely and ominous:

> If ever the free institutions of America are destroyed, that event may be attributed to the unlimited authority of the majority, which may at some future time urge the minorities to desperation, and oblige them to have recourse to physical force. Anarchy will then be the result, but it will have been brought about by despotism.[34]

There is every indication that the white electorate and its elected representatives will react to continued threats and to more violence in the streets not by a renewed effort to understand and alleviate the plight of underprivileged Negroes, but by reactionary measure to suppress these disorders. Given a choice between a massive freedom budget and a police state, the American electorate is more likely to choose the latter. The tide may have turned in the direction of a police state when, in the Eighty-ninth Congress, the House of Representatives passed the so-called antiriot amendment to the civil rights bill while failing to pass the bill itself. Moynihan saw in the results of the elections of November, 1966, "a bruising declaration that the electorate is fed up to the teeth with demonstrations and riots. . . ."[35]

The simple truth, too often overlooked in optimistic analyses of the racial crisis in America, is that neither white nor black Americans are a breed of angels. They are not set aside from the people of other nations and other tribes by superior rationality or greater tenderness toward one another. Despite repeated exposés of the organization's utter perversion of Christianity and Americanism, white Americans have allowed the Ku Klux Klan to rise again and again to the point where it could terrorize whole communities. Less than twenty years ago, McCarthyism put the nation into battle against an enemy whose visibility was far less than that of the forthright, defiant black extremists of the present day. In the hard-core states of the Deep South, racist politicians still find it politically profitable to run on platforms proposing to turn back the clock of race relations, not just to stop further progress. In the city of Chicago, in the summer of 1966, white Americans responded to Martin Luther King's latest campaign of nonviolence by shouting "white power" and contributing to the war chest of the late George Lincoln Rockwell's American Nazi party.

During the nonviolent phase of the Negro Revolution the majority of those white Americans who pride themselves on their Christian love have found it difficult to extend this love to Martin Luther King, Jr., and the middle-class Negro youth of the sit-ins and the picket lines. In the future, they will face the ultimate challenge to their capacity for Christ-like love as they are confronted by Negro leaders who talk of hate, not love, for the white man, and by the unlovely publicans and sinners of the Negro lower class. There is no assurance that the commitment of the majority of white Americans to democratic values and the forgiving spirit of Christ can stand the challenge of Black Power.

Nor is there assurance that Negro Americans will accept the verdict of logic that a Negro Revolution is, indeed, impossible in twentieth-century America. How much longer will they settle for whatever white Americans are willing to give them? From the lips of a traditional hero of white America, they have the battle cry, "Give me liberty or give me death!" They have their own heroes in Nat Turner, Denmark Vesey, and Harriet Tubman, and even in the street fighters of Detroit, Newark, and Watts. The new radical leaders can point to the failure of the conciliatory strategy of Booker T. Washington and Martin Luther King, Jr., to achieve the goal of freedom for Negroes. They can couch their own appeals in terms of a return to the strategy of power advocated by Frederick Douglass and W. E. B. DuBois. Even faced with the possibility of a fascist America dedicated to preventing Negroes from achieving their goals regardless of the cost to American democracy, they can harken to the yet unheeded appeal of Claude McKay, voiced in the thirties:[36]

> If we must die, let it not be like hogs,
> Hunted and penned in an inglorious spot,
> While round us bark the mad and hungry dogs,
> Making their mock at our accursed lot.
> If we must die, O let us nobly die,
> So that our precious blood may not be shed
> In vain; then even the monsters we defy
> Shall be constrained to honor us though dead!
> O Kinsman! We must meet the common foe!
> Though far outnumbered let us show us brave,
> And for their thousand blows deal one death blow!
> What though before us lies the open grave?
> Like men we'll face the murderous, cowardly pack,
> Pressed to the wall, dying, but fighting back!

Assessment of the countervailing power that the white Establishment could muster to oppose even the best organized revolution of Black Power makes the Negro Revolution seem indeed to be the Impossible Revolution. That such a revolution might be attempted in the face of overwhelming odds and without regard to the terrible consequences is not at all impossible.

NOTES

[1] Whitney Young, Jr., *To Be Equal* (New York: McGraw-Hill, 1964), p. 247.

[2] James Farmer, *Freedom—When?* (New York: Random House, 1965), p. 170.

[3] Bayard Rustin, "From Protest to Politics: The Future of the Civil Rights Movement," *Commentary* (February 1965), p. 28.

[4] *Ibid.*

[5] *Ibid.*, p. 27.

[6] Sidney Willhelm and Elwin Powell, "Who Needs the Negro?," *Trans-Action*, Vol. 1 (September-October, 1964), p. 6.

[7] *Ibid.*

[8] Daniel P. Moynihan, "The President and the Negro: The Moment Lost," *Commentary* (February 1967), p. 31.

[9] See Donald R. Matthews and James W. Prothro, *Negroes and the New Southern Politics* (New York: Harcourt, Brace & World, 1966).

[10] Stokely Carmichael, "Black Power: The Widening Dialogue," *New South*, Vol. 21 (Summer 1966), p. 67.

[11] *Ibid.*, p. 76.

[12] Farmer, *op. cit.*, p. 92-93.

[13] *Ibid.*, p. 106.

[14] Franz Fanon, *The Wretched of the Earth*, trans. Constance Farrington (New York: Grove Press, 1963), p. 10. Quotations used by permission of the publisher.

[15] *Ibid.*, pp. 18-19.

[16] *Ibid.*, p. 73.

[17] Carmichael, *op. cit.*, p. 66.

[18] Fanon, *op. cit.*, pp. 196-97.

[19] Chalmers Johnson, *Revolution and the Social System* (Stanford: The Hoover Institution on War, Revolution, and Peace, 1964), p. 12.

[20] *Ibid.*, p. 14.

[21] See Charles C. Moskos, Jr., "Racial Integration in the Armed Forces," *American Journal of Sociology*, Vol. 72 (September 1966), pp. 132-48.

[22] See Russell Sackett, "Plotting a War on Whitey," *Life* (June 10, 1966), pp. 101-02.

[23] Robert F. Williams, "For Effective Self Defense," in Frank L. Broderick and August Meier, eds., *Negro Protest Thought in the Twentieth Century* (New York: Bobbs-Merrill, 1965), p. 329. Quoted by permission of the publisher.

[24] *Ibid.*, p. 331. Quoted by permission of the publisher.

[25] "Who Guards America's Homes?" editorial in *The American Rifleman* (May 1967), p. 16.

[26] Johnson, *op. cit.*, p. 62.

[27] Williams, *op. cit.*, p. 331. Quoted by permission of the publisher.

[28] Martin Luther King, Jr., "It is Not Enough to Condemn Black Power," advertisement in *The New York Times*, July 26, 1966.

[29] Lewis M. Killian, "Leadership in the Desegregation Crisis: An Institutional Analysis," in Muzafer Sherif, ed., *Intergroup Relations and Leadership* (New York: John Wiley and Sons, 1962), p. 159.

[30] *Ibid.*, pp. 160-61.

[31] Harold Isaacs, *The New World of Negro Americans* (New York: John Day, 1963), p. 50.

[32] *Ibid.*, p. 339.

[33] Howard Elinson, "Radicalism and the Negro Movement," in Raymond J.

Murphy and Howard Elinson, eds., *Problems and Prospects of the Negro Movement* (Belmont, Calif.: Wadsworth, 1966), p. 361.

[34] Alexis de Tocqueville, *Democracy in America,* trans. Henry Reeve (New York: D. Appleton, 1899), Vol. 1, pp. 286-87.

[35] Moynihan, *op. cit.,* p. 31.

[36] "If We Must Die," in Claude McKay, *Selected Poems of Claude McKay* (New York: Bookman Associates, 1953). Permission to reprint granted by Twayne Publishers.

WE DON'T HELP BLACKS BY HURTING WHITES

NATHAN PERLMUTTER

When in 1964 Barry Goldwater declared that extremism in defense of liberty was no vice, his Presidential candidacy, which the statement was intended to spur, promptly sagged. His words evoked a specter of conspirational Birchites, of rightist and righteous American Gothics, even of racists, all with a license to ride witches' brooms. The electorate recoiled, and its vote, as close to being one as ever it was, vindicated those earliest viewers-of-Goldwater-with-alarm, the liberal intellectuals.

In the four years since, a fundamental change has occurred in the nature of both political extremism and the response to it from liberal intellectuals. Indeed, from the perspective of 1968, the Arizonan's rhetoric has a kind of tintype, fading charm. After all, the extremism he condoned was that of "little old ladies in tennis shoes" planning the capture of school and library boards—by turning out en masse for elections; it was an extremism the shock troops of which were laying siege to Chief Justice Earl Warren at muzzle point of—highway billboard signs; it was an extremism which was assiduously attempting to brainwash America—by flooding letters-to-the-editor columns. One looks back to 1964, past the riots and the lootings of the poor and the black, past the sniper actions of bands of black guerrillas, past the Students for a Democratic Society's Columbia University rebellion, past the confrontation of young radicals with Mayor Daley's police force, and Goldwater's extremism seems about as dangerous as Juicy Fruit.

But the liberal intellectual community's response to the current racial extremism runs something like this: "Upending law and order in defense of justice is no vice; it must be understood in the light of 300 years of white racism." The accents are socio-psychological, but the syntax is early Goldwater.

It is a melancholy but mischievous fact that in the recent past in response to the race issue, liberals have increasingly assumed the characteristics of political chameleons. No implied hurrah that, for political consistency. The looming presence of the race issue, long vaguely sensed, never really felt, required our gut to know it, really know it, the eye of our reason having for too long blinked its nearness. But it is one thing to respond finally to racial injustice with pulsing compassion and quite another thing suddenly to cool on political rationalism. It is one thing to ease momentarily the rules of the game in order to accommodate expediency and a far different thing to throw out the rule book. And the latter is happening. Liberal principles which have survived political natural selection have already been abandoned by militant blacks and are now under fire from the very liberals whom they have nursed and in whose shelter American liberalism has thrived.

One such fundamental principle has been that the larger the political subdivision, the more likely will its disadvantaged minority blocs, ethnic as well as economic, receive a fair shake. When social standpatters barricaded themselves behind states' rights, liberals successfully relied on more inclusive, more progressive Federal powers. Where municipalities have refused to bestir themselves in order to meet the needs of Topsy-growing megalopolises, liberals have championed more inclusive, more progressive metropolitan government. In the past two years, however, compassionate liberals — pre-eminently Mayor John V. Lindsay of New York; federally, members of the Office of Economic Opportunity, and among the maharajah-rich treasuries, those of the Ford Foundation—have U-turned. They, it is, who are pushing "decentralization" in education, and "community control" of socio-political institutions.

The press-release rationale for this basic change in the liberal's political machinery has been that slum-trapped blacks must be given the sense that theirs is the captaincy of their own destinies. Conversationally, however, the change in strategy has been explained like this: "The system we have hasn't worked and isn't working," and "Let them try it their way; if it doesn't work, at least they'll have only themselves to blame."

Both rationales, the first shorn of its good intentions, the second of its cynicism, basically say: "Let's return government to the people!" This, of course, has been the plaintive and self-serving cry of right-wing Republicans since "That Man" moved into the White House

in 1932 and of Southern Democrats for more than a century. The reactionaries, at least, knew what they were talking about.

For, despite our romanticizing of yesteryear's Town Hall, localities
are far more likely to be provincial on matters of race and taxes than
are larger political subdivisions. The smaller the subdivision, the
more homogeneous is its social outlook. The larger, the more heterogeneous it is, and the greater the political requirement of its would-
be officeholders to be responsive to a mix of social interests. Consequently, the Mayor of Albany, Ga., is not nearly the liberal that
Atlanta's is, nor can he be and remain as Mayor.

So it is that our Presidents of all of the people have been more
liberal, as a rule, than have been our governors of some of the people.
Indeed, our Presidents have been more liberal than they themselves
had been. Witness a haberdasher become middleground United
States Senator, who turns left to the Presidency; a general of, to all
appearances, neuter politics, bears left to the same destination; a
United States Senator from Massachusetts, the very profile of courage,
sits out the McCarthy era, but turns left for Pennsylvania Avenue; a
Southerner, Texas-orthodox on issues of race, makes a sharper left
turn for the White House than did its previous Northern occupants.

The fact is that for all of its vulgarities and insensitivities, big government has served small people—racial minorities, religious minorities, political minorities, ethnic minorities, the poor. And, as an extra-
added dividend, it has rendered city bosses vestigial, so much so that
the few survivors are political anachronisms. Ironically, however,
the new direction in which liberal intellectuals are headed, albeit the
road signs read "decentralization," and "indigenous control," lead to
places to which we have been and from which they themselves have
wisely led us. Indeed, during the very week this past summer that
former Gov. George Wallace was calumniating liberals and intellectuals and urging the "return of your local schools to local control,"
Mayor John V. Lindsay was packing the New York City Board of
Education with appointees pledged to effect that precise end.

That the intentions of the two are vastly different, and that the
Mayor's are liberal, is readily evident. What is seemingly not so evident, or at least, persuasive, to either the Mayor or his fellow-think-
ers, is that the recent gains of black communities are a consequence
of black power (political leverage) on larger rather than on smaller
political subdivisions. There being infinitely many more white

neighborhoods than there are black ones, "local control," despite its intended responsiveness to blacks, must heavily favor white separatism and, perhaps even more mischievously, contribute to the Balkanization of our cities. In addition, we may fairly, even if tartly, inquire of liberals: If local control is good for the Harlem goose, why then is it bad for the Birmingham, Ala., gander?

The group stereotype, whether mouthed by bigots or uttered with no offense intended by the insensitive, has been responsible for much mischief. Jews, Negroes, members of ethnic groups, regional and political minorities have all suffered its sting. Today, the group stereotype is in low estate, thanks to educational campaigns waged by minority groups, and supported by liberal intellectuals. But, alas, the racial stereotype is newly astir, and ironically, liberals, intellectual ones at that, are its broadcasters.

The new liberal stereotype comes in two models. One is the "neo-Noble Savage." Habitat: inner city; occupation: telling it like it is. No matter that this stereotype has about as much verisimilitude as the depiction of an industrial worker in a Soviet poster it at least has the merit of being well-intended. Not so its companion, "white racism," recipient of the Kerner commission's seal as "essentially responsible for the riots."

As stereotypes go, white racism is a whopper. But it is not my purpose here to knock it down; it is my purpose to suggest that the liberal's litany, white racism, is actually deflecting the nation's attention from the horrors of slum life, is putting off our confrontation with our responsibilities to black America and engaging us, instead, in an emotional, perhaps yet political, resistance to the Negro community's needs.

It would seem obvious enough that when arguing with a group whose conversion is imperative to the realization of our viewpoint, we do not name-call them. After all, bad-mouth a group as being a "bunch of bigots," and do we really expect them to smile ruefully and allow as they hadn't quite seen themselves that way before, and that from here on in, "We'll do it your way"? White racism as a battle cry with which to wage war against black poverty is more than just ineffectual. To the extent that it lends itself to viewing the white man as an abstraction, essentially malevolent, and so defined by his pigmentation, it is itself dangerous racism. No longer are whites good guys or bad guys; we are neither radicals nor liberals, neither conservatives nor reactionaries; no matter that this white man freedom-rode the buses in Mississippi and that it was the other fellow who burned the cross. Instead, we are all cast as dub-ins for Ralph Ellison's "Invisible Man," playing the anguished role in white-face. Racist tit for racist tat.

When the Kerner commission issued its finding that white racism was responsible for the past several summers of riots, liberals reacted to it with an enthusiasm that contrasted sharply with the cynicism with which they awaited it. In the face of that enthusiasm, Bayard Rustin ventured that the commission "helped no one by blaming white racism for the riots." George Wallace's current opinion-poll ratings among low-income and low-middle-income whites, as well as among ethnic groups, suggest that Rustin was as perceptive as he was brave. For the polls are telling us that the charge of white racism has failed to move these whites to "Give a Damn." Quite the contrary, they're saying, "Damn you," instead.

The Kerner report discusses their identity. It asserts that European immigrants are often the quickest to block Negro efforts to enter unions, get better jobs, move into better neighborhoods. Significantly, ethnic Americans and overlapping low-income and low-middle-income white Americans are the very blocs which have traditionally voted liberal. Now it is being said of them that this year they are abandoning liberal candidates. It may, in fact, be that for some time now liberals have been abandoning them. They it is who populate metropolitan area neighborhoods that are frequently contiguous to Negro slums. When the sun goes down, they go in. Their concern with street crime is personal and it is daily. Liberals, however, while expressing concern for law and order, use code words like "justice," that are not inaccurately perceived by low-income whites as being intended to change the immediate subject at hand: their safety. Besides, the liberal's lecture on crime in the streets is delivered from the rear lines of suburbia or from fashionable neighborhoods in urban D.M.Z.'s.

Ninety-four per cent of working white Americans have no education beyond high school and 43 per cent have only completed the eighth grade. Liberal rhetoric, however, dwells on the educational disadvantages of blacks. Schools of higher learning from the University of the City of New York to the Ivy League regularly release figures on the increasing percentages of black students who have been enrolled. Black Peter's long overdue educational favors are not unnoticed by white, untutored and resentful Paul.

The career expectations of the white male earning between $7,000 and $10,000 a year have been fixed since he reached the age of 35, when his debts, his family's size and the disparateness between his skills and his ambitions combined to shape his tomorrows in the worn mold of his yesterdays. But, Urban Coalitions, liberal rhetoric, Great-Society press releases are heard as being preoccupied solely with the Negro's upward occupational mobility.

Wilbur Cohen, Secretary of Health, Education and Welfare, observed that Americans favor Medicare and are for social-welfare programs, but that they seem to be against the poverty program. The reason seems plain. They favor those programs which they understand to be in their interests. They are against those programs which they have been led to believe are for Negroes, exclusively. That this is not really the case is beside the point. What is to the point is that low-income and low-middle-income whites, ethnic Americans included, like the black poor, are also possessed by a sense of powerlessness, are also alienated, are also resentful, and they are telling it like it is to Messrs. Harris and Gallup. Between the backlashing lines of their answers to pollsters, however, they are really saying, "Why doesn't someone look after me?"

These are the same people whose votes made possible the launching of the liberal New Deal, Fair Deal and Great Society domestic programs. Traditionally, their needs and aspirations have been bespoken by liberal intellectuals. Today, only their frustrations are spoken for and, ironically, by strangers to their social and economic interests. Meanwhile, liberals, their erstwhile spokesmen, are scorning them as "white racists," "bigots" and miscellaneous euphemisms for "honky."

Sadly, liberal stereotypy is accomplishing the very antithesis of that which it is designed to bring about: whites giving a damn, to the point of voting for those Democrats and Republicans who would be responsive to our urban crisis. Moreover, there is, in liberal rhetoric, a case to be made for the proposition that socially empathetic progressives have recently been more caring of the black poor than of the white poor. Not only is selective compassion a brand of mercy that is strained, and therefore suspect, but pragmatically, so long as there are more poor white voters than poor black voters, liberals who alienate those whites are dealing defeat to those blacks.

That the end does not justify the means has been fundamental to liberal political philosophy. Today, however, on the issue of race, the liberal is backsliding from his political scripture.

Last August, the New York Board of Education sponsored a public hearing on school decentralization. The viewpoint of the witnesses, overwhelmingly Negro parents, was that the city's educational system had failed to educate their children. Its strident communication was, in view of the desperation only a parent can feel, understandable; further, it was not without persuasiveness. It was conveyed, however, with more than anger. It took the form of marathon and crude vilifications of white people, of anti-Semitism, of choanged jeering and hooting, and of physical interference with white witnesses whose viewpoints differed from theirs. Climactically, and in full view of TV cameras, Negro witnesses climbed atop the dais and occupied—the word "captured" suggests itself—the seats of board members. Some days later a foundation official whose liberal credentials are impeccable allowed, in conversation, that he did not condone the conduct of the Negro witnesses but that school decentralization was imperative to future racial peace. Of the scarifying hearings, he soothingly philosophized that, after all, "this is only a transitional phase we are in."

In early September several Negroes, in an ironic replay of George Wallace at the University of Alabama, stood before the door of a school in Brownsville, Brooklyn, to bar physically the entry of 10 white teachers. The teachers had been fired by the experimental community school board (black) but had been subsequently legally cleared of the charges brought against them. Television cameras picture-tubed the swirling sea of angry blacks and television sound crews carried the epithet "honky" (antonym: "nigger") into metropolitan New York homes. Unlike James Meredith, the teachers never did get into their classrooms. The following morning the rule of the mob was duly deplored, but again steadfast white liberal proponents of "community control" drew on the soothing qualities of the word "transitional" to suggest that the scene was an unpleasantness which, in time, would go away if only the teachers would now.

Earlier this year, the bulletin of the Afro-American School Teachers Association in New York carried an article by one John Hatchett which maintained that "Black Anglo-Saxons" and Jews were "poisoning" the minds of black children. Several months later, New York University announced that Mr. Hatchett had been appointed to the directorship of its Martin Luther King Jr. Student Center. Despite the smoldering controversy which ensued, and during which it was revealed that upon the article's appearance Catholic, Protestant and

Jewish organizations had joined to characterize it as "Black Nazism," N.Y.U. stuck to its appointment.

Admittedly an excruciatingly difficult one, the decision was explained as designed to avoid "another Columbia." The reference was to threats from black students that they would not countenance Mr. Hatchett's being fired. Again, "transitional," a word that may soon succeed "dialogue" as the liberal's 1968 "in" word, was offered as a tranquilizer to those who were dismayed by the students' political extortion and by N.Y.U.'s submission to it. Presumably when this "transitional" period passes, extremist blacks will cool, and cowed N.Y.U. will regain its dignity.

In these and untold like instances, liberal temporizing has validated political thuggery, on the grounds that its declared end was presumably related to racial justice. To be sure, the temporizing has been part hopefulness, part compassion, and part, let's face it, desperation, but no matter, it all adds up to "the end (hoped for racial justice) justifies the means (racial bullying.) "

The academic question of means and ends aside, however, the liberals who diagnose lawlessness as merely "transitional" are morally obligated to offer an interim prescription for the teacher who is fired or bumped from promotion lists because he is not black; to the firemen and policemen who have been—or fear being—ambushed; to the ghetto's intimidated and trapped small merchants; to their families and friends. In the absence of liberal prescriptions for these people, their rush to the right is as much responsive to the liberals' indifference to them as it is to their private fears.

Our new recognition that we are a nation of groups rather than of free-floating individuals represents a breakthrough in our national response to the Negro. But in the process of making this breakthrough we have begun showing signs of wandering astray.

If Negroes as a group require, as assuredly they do, more college-trained young people, and if the corollary response of a university is to enroll a larger quota of Negroes, what does this bode for Irish or Jewish or, in New York City, WASP *individual* youths? It will be sore solace to the Jewish youth who is passed over for college admission that his ethnic group has more than 3 per cent of its young people in college. As Daniel Moynihan has pointed out, quotas in favor of one group mean quotas against another group. Rather than urging bigger slices of the educational and employment pies for Negroes, liberals would more creatively serve the cause of liberalism by working at baking bigger pies, thereby helping the Negro community without punishing innocent white individuals.

Reasoning that packages persons as statistics in boxes labeled Jews, Italians, etc., too easily lends itself to viewing Negroes *qua* Negroes as responsible for muggings, knifings, dope addiction and hustling, all of which beset our cities. Statistics are dangerous, if not handled with care. They have been useful insofar as they have helped to convince Washington, academia and industry of the need for massive social reparations to black communities; but they are tinder boxes if we overlook the individual and the preciousness of his right to be judged on his own merits rather than by his group's averaged accomplishments, or quota of the general population.

In Arles one afternoon, Van Gogh displayed his morning's work to Gauguin. The latter, his eyes sweeping over the several canvases, said, "Vincent, you paint too quickly." Van Gogh shot back, "Paul, you look too quickly." The liberal intellectual's new conceptualization of the Negro as an inextricable part of his group is panoramic and therefore well-dimensioned, but he is "looking too quickly," and mistaking factions in the Negro community for the whole Negro community.

Witness the rote acceptance of the notion that the experimental community school board in Brownsville *is* the community.

Yet Louis Harris Associates, in a poll of the Ocean Hill-Brownsville district for the Board of Education's Neimeyer panel, found that 31 per cent of the respondents had a "positive" view of the district governing board, while 47 per cent had a "negative" view. Less topically, but perhaps more significantly, a survey conducted for C.B.S. by Negro poll takers of the Opinion Research Corporation recently inquired of a sample of 1,000 Negroes, "Which do you think is the main reason Negroes have not made more progress in this city? Discrimination because of their race? Negroes haven't worked hard enough? Both?"

Only 45 per cent, a figure stunningly less than would be expected in view of white liberal rhetoric, blamed discrimination. What should be even more disconcerting to liberals who mistakingly view the black community as monolithic, is that fully 22 per cent of the black interviewees said that Negroes have not worked hard enough. Another 18 per cent answered "both."

Were it simply a matter of mistaking factions for communities, the mischief wouldn't be so bad. But white liberals often also mistake the resonancy of factions for the voice of the majority. In so doing they strengthen the vocal and often extremist minorities, while weakening the softer spoken moderate majority.

Through all of the recently executed turn-abouts in liberal responses to the race issue, one factor is frightening above all others. Whether it is implicit in "indigenous control" and its tributaries of neotribalism and the yet-to-surface struggles for the tax dollar; whether it is hidden in the new racial stereotypy; whether it lies just beneath the surface of callousness to "transitional" chaos, or whether it is a distortion of the pluralist view of America, it reads "divisiveness"—and it is seeding our tomorrows.

Where are we at today? Recently, a Negro, walking in Harlem with a long-time white friend, mused, "If I killed you now, right here, nobody would turn me in. That's where it's at, baby. Dig?"

Meanwhile, back at the opinion polls, union and nonunion laborers, policemen and firemen, cab drivers, ethnics, low-income and low-middle-income whites, their friends, families and sympathizers are promising, in November, to look out for themselves. That's where they're at.

The liberal intellectual will explain black militancy as the wages of 300 years of racism, and white resistance as backlash bigotry. That's where he's at, encouraging one group and alienating the other.

WHOSE DUES FOR GOOD BLACK NEWS?
(SOME NOTES FROM A JOURNEY TO MOBILE)

ALBERT MURRAY

In conversation and particularly in meetings and open forums, Southern Negro civil rights spokesmen and activists are likely to make liberal use of many of the slogans and generalities about black identity, black pride, and black heritage heard everywhere in the North these days. So much so, as a matter of fact, that an inattentive outside observer could easily forget where he is. Indeed, unless he remains alert, a native born Southerner who has been away a number of years might also do the same thing; for when the subject turns to black consciousness even the traditional downhome barbershop bull session, which used to be anything but academic, has begun to sound somewhat like a Northern campus caucus of television-oriented black power panelists doing their thing for the Six O'Clock Report.

So much so that after a while you realize that you are the TV *and they're talking not with you and to you but at you and into you and seeing themselves zooming up as the titles breeze upward. So much so that you almost expect them to pause, not for your reply or the next question, but for the commercial.*

When they finally get down to the specifics of programing, however, black Southerners (who are really mostly various shades of brown and beige) are likely to formulate social, economic, political, and educational objectives which are significantly different from those which have recently been turned into such sensational news copy elsewhere.

When they get down to specifics they forget about television for a while and see you as yourself again or whoever they remember you as having been or whoever it pleases them to think you have become. Then they talk to you man to man, Negro to fellowman, homefolks

Reprinted from *The Center Forum*, Vol. 3, No. 5 (Mar. 1, 1969), N. Y., Center for Urban Education by permission of the author and his agent, James Brown Associates, Inc. Copyright © 1969.

to our boy back home from up yonder, and also homefolks to homefolks about other folks elsewhere — but not without doing a little
chicken butt signifying in the process either: "Now of course you
folks up North, you folks up in New York, y'all up there. . ." That
is an indispensable part of the ritual. Establishes perspective. Adds
proper (and anticipated) dimension of downhome ambivalence.
Then old home week can begin: *Now I'm for the brother everywhere
because we all members in this mess together you know what I mean.
But man some of these new Northern kiddies ain't nothing but new
style white folks you know what, you dig: And don't know it. That's
the killing part about it. All that big mouth talk about whities and
honkies and all that. Man that ain't nothing but exactly what the
man want to hear so he can have an excuse to do anything he want
to. OK. Remember them cattle prods? They didn't really hurt nobody, right? But they got Bull Connor and Al Lingo into all kinds
of trouble because everybody all over the country was talking about
what an outrageous thing that was, remember? So the man goes and
finds him somebody to go on TV and start bragging about Negroes getting up rifle clubs. But who you reckon manufactured all the rifles
in the god-dam world and who knows the serial number on every
rifle in the USA. Look we were finally getting white folks so even them
poor sap suckers from back up in the hills were getting careful about
how they were saying Neegrow. No more of that Nigra stuff, know
what I mean? So they find somebody to get up there and say Negro
is ugly because its white talk and black is beautiful because they just
found out. So now white folks up North out talking about blacks
like the old slave traders, talking about blacks, coloreds, and whites
like down in South Africa. . .*

More often than not—or so it seems—when black New Yorkers
get going on television about black identity, black pride, black heritage, and the need for what many now call black studies, they speak
as if the Schomberg collection of Negro History and Art, which as
many white students of Negro culture are well aware is located in
the very heart of Harlem, was either non-existent or off-limits to
black people. They make sweeping statements that suggest that they
are really only shucking for the networks (and the foundations, to
be sure) or are completely unaware of the pioneering, even if sometimes somewhat less than comprehensive, work of men like Carter
G. Woodson and Benjamin Brawley. They sound as if they never
heard of the Association for the Study of Negro Life and History

which has been publishing the Journal of Negro History since 1916 and the Negro History Bulletin since 1937.

Black polemicists are forever complaining that white historians have been omitting and deliberately suppressing important facts about Negro achievement, and justification for their outrage is overwhelming. But for some reason they themselves seldom if ever make even the slightest mention of the work of Negro historians like Rayford Logan, John Hope Franklin, and Benjamin Quarles, three contemporary scholars of the highest professional standing who have devoted long careers to correcting the historical perspectives on U.S. Negro life. Some may make vague references to Du Bois (or even to E. Franklin Frazier whose socio-political view of Negro heritage was emphatically negative!). Otherwise most likely to be mentioned or even quoted are Malcolm X and Marcus Garvey, both of whom were spokesmen of high purpose who aspired to be activists rather than historians, research specialists, and survey technicians. Both inspired black pride in thousands of their followers, but neither ever had either the time or the means to engage in primary research on u.s. Negroes, to say nothing of archeological, anthropological, or philological research on the infinitely varied black peoples and civilizations of Africa.

But then so many of the most militant black polemicists appear to have swallowed the assumption and conclusions of precisely those writers who, like Frazier, describe the black American experience as adding up to little more than a legacy of degradation and despair— writers whose concern for the welfare of black people may be beyond reproach but whose opinion or esteem for them is often so low that it moves beyond condescension to contempt! As a result you often hear some of the most scandalous statements about black people repeated by the same black militants who complain loudest about the negative regard in which black people are held.

In contrast, black Mobilians generally seem to become considerably less polemical than New Yorkers on the subject of black heritage. But after all black teachers in Mobile, like perhaps most others throughout most of the South have been observing Negro History Week (the week in February that includes Lincoln's and Frederick Douglass's birthdays) for decades. It must be said that Alabama teachers have been incredibly apathetic about the ridiculous materials on black people in the text book on Alabama history. But on the other hand their libraries have always tried to promote and spread interest in black publications of all kinds, and everybody is quick to point out that books like Woodson's "The Negro in Our History," Brawley's "Negro Builders and Heroes," and John Hope Franklin's "From Slavery to Freedom" have been used as standard references in Negro schools and colleges throughout the South all along.

Actually there never was a time when Southern Negro colleges were not aspiring to be the so-called Black University serving the special needs of black American youth. Thirty odd years ago, for instance, when the generation of parents and grandparents now in their fifties, were college age, almost every campus had teachers, scholars, or historic figures in residence who were widely known and honored for the role they played in matters relating to black heritage. At Howard, for example, there were Kelly Miller, Alain Locke, and Sterling Brown; at Tuskegee there was Monroe N. Work heading a Department of Records and Research and editing the Negro Yearbook; at Atlanta University there were Du Bois and later Ira De A Reid; at Fisk there were James Weldon Johnson and Charles S. Johnson, and so on.

Anyway, when involved Mobilians get down to specifics about black heritage they are likely to begin not with highly questionable theories about black emasculation and self-rejection but rather by saying that the special displays and programs of Negro History Week were never enough to remedy the omissions and distortions in the books used in regular courses in history and social studies. Then, in response to inquiries about offerings presently under consideration at the local school board, they summarize as follows: They do not want black heritage courses to be either extracurricular or elective. They not only want them required but required of all pupils. They do not want them restricted to "black" schools or to black pupils in "white" schools because they are convinced that white pupils need such studies even more urgently than Negroes—who in truth already absorb at least a smattering of black heritage from *Ebony, Jet,* and other national Negro publications. Moreover, as some of them see it, the problem of improving the Black Image has as much to do with teaching white school children to honor Denmark Vesey and Nat Turner as with anything else.

Then, because they are thinking and talking like teachers and supervisors and not like TV spokesmen, they begin speculating about what will really happen when the actual classwork begins and there is not so much publicity any more. So they start remembering how students respond to assignments and, being teachers, they also know how precious student enthusiasm always is but, being experienced teachers and in some instances parents to boot, they know enough about it not to exaggerate its significance. Nor do they confuse the emotional response to statements about black pride at political rallies with the academic motivation that comes from genuine historical curiosity. So they come back to specifics for school board policy: Perhaps the current emphasis will generate greater historical curiosity among larger numbers of black students (and white ones too), but meanwhile now is the time to add missing black dimensions to existing courses. Now is the time to revise and update existing text materials, no little job in itself.

As for race pride as such, there are those who think it is a good thing which has nothing to do with racism. But some others are not so sure. Some flatly reject it as a highly questionable educational objective. Others see it as representing a regression toward social provincialism and political chauvinism, of which the u.s. has far too much already. Still others point out that the most urgent problems facing u.s. Negroes just simply do not have very much to do with any demonstrated lack of black pride. To them all the television talk about blackness is mostly a misuse of valuable time and mostly adds up to a misdirection of valuable energies; and they frankly doubt whether those who are doing it have any practical standards by which to calculate what degree of black pride must be developed (and by what means and through what measurable stages) before Negroes can get the hell on with the business of employment, housing, and equal protection under the law.

Nor do many of the so-called brothers on the street, on the block, and in the barbershop disagree: *Now look you know good and well color aint what Rockefeller is proud of. Hell, the only time you ever hear real big white folks bragging about the color of their skin is when they got a good deep tan. You know what Rockefeller is proud of? All that money and power. And you know what Wallace and all the rest of them are proud of? The same thing. Hell, anybody get up there on tv talking about Negroes don't have no pride ain't talking about no Negroes I know. Because you see sometimes I think the whole trouble is we got too much pride. Because you see I been up to New York and I say them Negroes in Harlem got more pride than them white folks down on Fifth Avenue. I say them welfare Negroes just as proud and loud as the rest. And I say we don't need to be getting no louder and prouder because what I want to see is more of our young folks getting smarter and when you got that you*

*don't have to be up there bragging about it. Because as soon as you
start carrying on like that I got to start worrying about how come you
so loud because if you really proud you supposed to be cooling it.*

And after all the Indians never had any shortage of red pride. Their
red identity was unmistakable and their sense of red heritage had
long since become a part of their religion. But they needed more
than a legacy of bow and arrow confidence and barebacked courage.
They had every right to be proud of their hair as well as their feath-
ers and buckskin and so on, but they did not have any factories and
merchant fleets to be proud of. In other words, redskin pride was
never any problem. The war drums took care of that business very
well. Perhaps even too well, because they hopped up a number of
young braves to the point where they were only too willing to risk
dying for the cause. The troops were magnificent. But the combat
plans were out of date. Nobody in the councils of war knew enough
to shout World History, World Geography and Demography. The
failure to understand the connection between the pale face invaders
and the other side of the Atlantic was disastrous. Nor was paleface
pride a decisive factor since the terrified white colonists were able to
offset their insecurity and lack of dignity with superior technology,
among other things.

But of course when Negro or so-called black teachers and supervisors in New York get closer to the specifics of curriculum construction, they do not often confuse the stimulation of black pride with
the refinement and extension of historical insight either. Nor do they
mistake themselves as television spokesmen simply because the news
media might choose to create the impression that anybody making
statements about black studies is a fully qualified expert in the field
of education. Most seem to go along with the black consciousness
campaign as an activist tactic; and more often than not they also approve of black militancy despite the fact that some of it violates their
sense of scholarly integrity (philosophically hoodwinking gross oversimplification and wild exaggeration as the dues you pay for long
overdue revolutionary change). But even so they also know how easy
it is for self-pride to degenerate into self-inflation, empty arrogance,
and chauvinism; so they want good news that meets the highest tests
of reliability. They want courses in history and culture that will improve everybody's perspective on the universality of human experience and will enrich everybody's sense of context and identity.

The main difficulty, however, is the fact that black teachers in New

York have less authority in such matters than their colleagues in the South. In Mobile, those from the so-called black community who exercise most influence on school board policies relating to black heritage or the "black dimension" of American culture are likely to be teachers and principals, not all-purpose spokesmen and overnight experts. Perhaps in time the same will be true in New York. But as of now, black professionals in education seem to enjoy less scholarly prestige among top school officials and other powerful white-friends-of-black-causes than the very same black students who otherwise are considered to be suffering from the gravest academic deficiencies and who paradoxically are complaining precisely because they are inadequately trained. Indeed it is not at all unusual for white New Yorkers to allow themselves to be instructed in language usage, history, anthropology, economics, and even clinical psychology by sub-standard students, and then presume to instruct their black professional equals on the whys, wherefores, and needs of black experience.

THE WHITE WORKER AND THE
NEGRO CLIENT IN PSYCHOTHERAPY

JULIA B. RAUCH

The author presents a discussion of the possible countertransference of the white worker practicing psychotherapy toward a Negro client in relation to the worker's identification with the white middle class, his individual psychodynamics, and the symbolism attached to the Negro.

Although it is recognized that class and cultural differences between a social worker, psychiatrist, or psychologist practicing psychotherapy and his client influence the course of therapy, relatively little attention has been given in either the psychiatric or social work literature to factors involved in the psychotherapeutic treatment of Negroes by white mental health workers.[1] Existing literature stresses the transference of the black patient and the ways in which distrust of and hostility toward whites militates against a viable therapeutic relationship.[2] Less attention has been given to the worker's countertransference and its effect on the treatment process. Since racial differences complicate an already delicate situation, there can be no intensive exploration of countertransference within the limits of this paper since the racial problems must also be discussed. The focus, then, will be on selected aspects of the worker's countertransference, with special reference to (1) cultural factors assumed to operate in all white middle-class workers and (2) racial factors related to their individual psychodynamics. It is emphasized that countertransference is not the only possible impediment to the establishment of an effective interracial treatment relationship.

HYPERSENSITIVITY

In the cross-cultural treatment situation, there is danger of misin-

Reprinted with permission of the National Association of Social Workers, from *Social Work*, Vol. 13, No. 2 (April, 1968), pp. 36-42.

terpreting the client's dynamics. Responses that seem inappropriate to the worker may, in fact, be appropriate responses to social stress. Too, the client's responses that seem inappropriate to the worker may be correct in his subculture or the client may be responding appropriately to attitudes emanating from the worker, such as racial bias. In responding to whites, it is not uncommon for Negroes to be accused of hypersensitivity to racial slurs. In some cases, it may be so; more than one writer has written that the American Negro walks on the edge of paranoia. Before the worker can be sure, however, that the client is behaving inappropriately, he must have some understanding of the client's cultural milieu and be clear that he is not unconsciously transmitting a deprecatory attitude to the client, as in the following example:

> Mr. F, a Negro college graduate and teacher, objected to his worker's addressing him by his first name; he saw in this a reflection of white condescension toward him as a Negro. The therapist, a psychoanalyst, assured him that he did not share such attitudes and used the first name with all his patients. As a result of the therapist's continued use of his first name, the patient withdrew from treatment, although he was later able to establish a positive relationship with another white mental health worker.

CLASS DIFFERENCES

A lower-class Negro client and a white middle-class mental health worker come from quite different social backgrounds and the worker's countertransference will be affected by his more or less unconscious identification with white middle-class values. Whether born into middle-class status or having achieved it, the white worker usually incorporates the values of his class and accepts the rightness of certain behavior and attitudes as comfortably and naturally as he accepts the color of his skin. Among those values may be included a belief in individual responsibility, approval of education and achievement, and some measure of self-control. The white worker's identification with his class values may cause special discomfort with lower-class or ghettoized Negroes whose values and behavior may be quite different from his own. By the same token, the worker may feel relatively at ease with a middle-class Negro who is "like himself."

Such negative or positive reactions to the Negro client's class status and behavior may incline him to misinterpret the client's ego strengths and weaknesses. It has been suggested that among marginal groups, personal insecurity is greatest if the identification is with the dominant group, whereas those who identify with their own group, rejecting the dominant culture, have greater personal security.[3] The middle-class Negro seems to identify with the aggressor (the white middle class), which results in attitudes of passivity and hostility toward the self. (It is emphasized that the Negro who has suffered extreme social and emotional deprivation and whose psychopathology borders on ego impairment is differentiated from the lower-class Negro who may be relatively well integrated into his subculture, while still having mores different from those of the dominant culture.)

CRISIS OF IDENTITY

Few Negroes escape the crisis of identity that results from being a black man in a white world that deprecates him. James Baldwin in *Go Tell It on the Mountain* presents the conflict facing an adolescent Negro seeking to establish his identity.[1] John, the protagonist, is faced with identifying with his father, Gabriel, who has incorporated the white rejection of blackness, equating color with an evil and sin worthy only of damnation. Roy, John's brother, who directs his hostility actively against whites, is killed in a gang war. Richard, the man whom John's mother loved as a girl, attempts to achieve manhood through education but finds that he cannot escape his color. Falsely accused of a crime and beaten by the police, he chooses suiside rather than emasculation. The only choice left open to John is to accept the religious ecstasy identified with his mother—through which he can escape the material world altogether—accepting "nonbeing" and emasculation as the only means of survival.

In our culture, masculinity is associated with power, aggression, and assertiveness, which compounds the problem of the crisis of identity for the Negro man. Historically, overt expression of aggression by Negroes brought swift reprisal from the more powerful white community. This has led to a variety of ego mechanisms used to insure survival, of which one example is "tomming." An Uncle Tom uses flattery and subservience in order to cajole and manipulate whites. He may do so knowingly by "laughing on the inside," or the aggression may be so deeply embedded that he "accepts his place" and derives pleasure from white acceptance.

The ego mechanisms adopted by a Negro to cope with his ambiguous position in American society have different psychological and social meanings. Whites tend to accept an Uncle Tom, whereas many Negroes view such a person with distaste because of his apparent acceptance of servility. The worker, too, may find himself responding positively to tomming, especially if it appears in a sophisticated guise; he may tend to view the client's behavior as an ego strength, without recognizing that it may be emotionally self-destructive and, therefore, should be modified. Because whites and Negroes have different perceptions of how a Negro should act, caste-determined perceptions may influence the evaluation of the health or pathology of a particular ego mechanism.

BLACK MUSLIMS

How would one judge the Black Muslims, for example? They have rescued Negroes from jail and helped them to live a more constructive and dignified personal life by strengthening family ties and work habits and turning their aggression outward to the white world. However, most whites find themselves threatened by the hatred of which the Black Muslims have become a symbol and see the movement as pathological. Some Negro intellectuals, on the other hand, are sympathetic to the Black Muslims, partly because of their vicarious enjoyment of aggression and partly because they feel that the threat imposed by the movement is socially useful and accelerates social change. They are sympathetic, too, because it has given a sense of dignity to some of its members.[5]

The worker's dilemma may be that on the emotional level a movement like the Black Muslims may represent a healthier ego mechanism than apathy, intergroup aggression, or the self-destructive dilemma of trying to be white, but, because of the personal threat to the worker and the wider social implications, it is doubtful that a white worker would evaluate this kind of deliberate channeling of aggression to whites as relatively healthy.

WORKER'S ATTITUDES

The worker's identification with middle-class values and his resulting feelings about the behavior of a Negro client have great significance for the conduct of therapy. Therapy is an ambiguous situation. It may be regarded as a social interaction influenced by the worker's own unwitting emotional reactions to the client.

In Strupp's operational formulation, for example, the components of the worker's contribution to the treatment process are conceptualized as coming from within as well as from without.[6] The worker responds to the client's personality structure, his station in life, and his current and long-range needs. He also responds from his conceptual base—his theories about therapy and his attitudes. His personality, attitudes, and values are of sufficient importance that some workers stress relationship as the key to treatment.

Strupp also found that the worker's response to the client influenced the conduct of the interview, the activity or passivity of questioning, the focus chosen, and the warmth or coldness of the atmosphere. The conduct of interviews, diagnosis, and prognosis did not vary significantly with the training or experience of the workers he studied; rather, they varied with their feelings about the client.[7] Recognizing the relationship between the worker's attitudes and the conduct of therapy, it is incumbent on the white mental health worker to develop conscious awareness of his attitudes toward a Negro client, lest his therapeutic effectiveness be diminished.

> Mrs. P, a teacher, was in treatment at a child guidance clinic because of the aggressive acting out of her son. During the first year of treatment she was resistant, refusing to come on a weekly basis and frequently breaking her appointments. During the second year, after a change of workers, she continued to behave this way. However, when her worker consciously adopted an attitude of professional equality, making active reference to the knowledge of child development shared by them, Mrs. P became more actively involved with the clinic and accepted and kept weekly appointments.

What is a Negro? In an interracial treatment relationship, a primary characteristic is the client's racial visibility—a fact to which the white worker responds from his past interracial experiences as well as from his conscious and unconscious attitudes toward Negroes. This is not to suggest that mental health workers, as a group, are intolerant. On the contrary, by virtue of an interest in human beings, education, and professional training, they are predisposed to enlightened racial attitudes. This is the rub. It may be assumed that mental health workers as a group view racial prejudice and bias as both personally and socially unacceptable. The danger is that the very objection to prejudice may lead them to deny or suppress negative reactions toward Negro clients.

For example, following the admission of Negro children to Bellefaire, a residential treatment center for children under Jewish auspices, it was reported:

> Indeed, a sudden "color blindness" seemed to have beset the total staff. Only upon specific inquiry did they report that some white children had reacted angrily to the acceptance of the Negro child. Their reports lacked the usual astute observation in this area. Nor did they report anything about their own feelings and reactions. There was a period of denial of difference. . . .[8]

If it occurs, such denial militates against recognizing the distinctive characteristics of interracial therapy, including, of course, the possibility of a negative countertransference.

SYMBOLS

The emotions aroused by the color difference are not readily accessible to conscious awareness. Describing the symbolic processes related to the terms "Negro" and "white," Andrew Curry writes:

> In much of the world's mythology and religion, a frequent theme is that light and darkness, black and white, are complementary and/or inseparably related in some type of dynamic tension or equilibrium. Black represents darkness, sleep, death, the Devil, and evil—all somehow playing an important part in life's progression. For white, illumination, light, awareness, etc., cannot exist without these complements.[9]

Curry suggests that racial attitudes are expressed not only in institutionalized patterns of discrimination, but in the very modes of thought (myth, fantasy, and the like) that characterize our culture.[10] In Christianity, God and the Christ are associated with goodness and light; Satan and evil with black. This equation is reflected in our language with such expressions as "pure as the driven snow" and "the black hole of Calcutta." As a result, "Negro" and "white" are more than descriptive terms. They are emotionally laden symbols to which our feelings about black and white, good and evil, have become attached.

The symbol "Negro" is closely allied with sexuality and aggression. When a society or culture imposes taboos on such forces, as has occurred in Western Europe and the United States, the result is a split image. The dominant culture is seen as good and the instinctual drives (which the society wants to repress) are projected onto a lower caste or outgroup.[11]

This is especially so in the southern United States where the white woman is protected by the white male and at the same time there exists an elaborate mythology concerning the sexuality of Negroes.

Thus, the threatening, repressed drives are projected onto the Negro who is then perceived ambivalently, as both alluring and threatening.

Although this occurs in grosser forms in the South, the same phenomenon exists in other areas of the United States. The taboo against interracial marriage, for example, is still more or less intact, even among middle-class groups for whom Negroes do not pose a significant social or economic threat.

This suggests that in treating Negro clients, the worker may feel a threat to his own repressions. Also, the myth of looser sexual mores among certain groups of Negroes may symbolize a freedom to which he may aspire. Even more complicated may be the worker's reaction to a Negro's aggressive drives. Not only is there the projection of the repressed instinctual drive, but guilt about being white and fear of Negro retaliation may create rather intense discomfort in the presence of a Negro client, especially one who does not have his aggression under control. The Negro as a symbol may arouse acute anxiety in the worker, resulting in a skewed perception of the client's sexuality and aggression, with the possibility that the therapeutic exploration of these areas may be mishandled.

Thus far, two factors have been discussed: the worker's identification with the white middle class and the symbolism surrounding the Negro, which are assumed to operate in the countertransference of most workers since they are largely culturally determined factors. The countertransference will also consist of attitudes determined by the worker's individual psychodynamics. It is assumed that the worker does not view the Negro client as a gross social stereotype, but has some degree of sympathy with and understanding of his life situation.

SYMPATHY

A white person's sympathy for Negroes can be excessive, in which case it may stem from identification with the underdog, which could be an extension of an individual's masochistic pattern. This sense of victimization may cause him to identify or sympathize with the client in ways that perpetuate his ego weaknesses.

> Mr. P was receiving psychotherapy each week at a child guidance clinic in conjunction with the treatment of his son who was acting out aggressively at school and at home. Mr. P was rudely insulted by a member of the clerical staff. His worker became intensely angry, and when Mr. P graciously accepted her apology on behalf of the clinic, saying that he understood and had learned to live with "those kinds of things," she

was tempted to leave the matter there, because she, too, "understood those kinds of things." Later, Mr. P's son insulted the staff member involved and Mr. P reacted to this with vicarious pleasure. Exploration of these incidents proved to be the key to his feelings of emasculation and to the way he used his son to act out his aggression for him.

An overly sympathetic worker may also err in his zeal by applying his understanding of cultural differences to the individual situation. Knowing, for example, that Negro families tend to fall into a matriarchal pattern, a worker may tend to accept such a pattern as normal, without sufficiently exploring its psychological meaning, possible conflict, and possible pathology for a client in such a family. One popular, current, and valid sociocultural generalization is the Negro's hostility to whites. The assumption is made that such hostility is ipso facto detrimental to therapy and must be "handled" before a sound treatment relationship can be established. This may not always be the case. Whether or not the client's feelings about whites and toward the "whiteness" of his worker should be probed is a matter that requires some delicacy of judgment, depending on the goals of treatment and the patient's character structure.

Mr. P described himself as "eaten up inside"—fearing an ulcer—because the conforming, pleasant façade that he assumed in order to succeed as an executive in an otherwise all-white firm did not conform with his inner feelings. In therapy, many of the sessions focused on his being a black man in a white world and the ways he could effectively channel his angry feelings so that his son need not continue to be both a scapegoat and an agent of his father's aggression.

* * * * *

Mrs. P used obsessive-compulsive defenses of intellectualization, isolation of affect, and denial, all useful in her professional and social functioning. Associations during therapy indicated fear of mental illnnesses as well as of instinctual drives. It was felt that therapy should be primarily educative and supportive, moving cautiously toward a loosening of her defenses. Because her identification was with the white world, with preconscious rejection of Negroes, it was felt that an identification with the white worker could be used to give her a more relaxed and permissive model for handling her son.

The worker who feels guilty about his own racial and class identity in the presence of a Negro client may discover that he wishes to prove to the client that he is different from other whites. If he has channeled such feelings into an active identification with the civil rights movement, he may find himself indicating this identification to the client. Similarly, if he has channeled feelings of rebellion into the civil rights movement, he may convey his agreement when the client expresses hostility toward whites, perhaps by encouraging him to elaborate on these feelings when it is not relevant to the course of therapy. Even when the worker has dealt with these feelings in his own therapy or supervision, they may still be operative and, as in any therapeutic situation, he needs to be aware of them and conduct the therapy in relation to the client's needs rather than his own. Freud wrote:

> We shall always tend to consider people's distress objectively—that is, to place ourselves, with our own wants and sensibilities, in *their* conditions, and then to examine what occasions we should find in them for experiencing happiness or unhappiness. This method of looking at things, which seems objective because it ignores the variations in subjective sensibility, is, of course, the most subjective possible, since it puts one's own mental states in the place of any others, unknown though they may be.[12]

Although the special characteristics of the interracial treatment relationship complicate an already complex situation, the difficulties are not necessarily insurmountable. For example, Claude Brown, writing of his relationship with a white psychiatrist, says the following:

> I usually didn't tell Papanek what was really bothering me, I didn't think he could understand. He had come up in some place called Austria, and I figured there wasn't a colored person in the whole country. So what could he know about coming up in Harlem? . . . [but] I had to talk to this cat. He was real stable and everybody else was crazy. Papanek was the only one I knew who seemed to know what was really going on. When Papanek wasn't in the office, it used to really upset me, because I never went to see him unless there was something really bothering me. Most of the time, I never told him what was really bothering me, but we would talk about something. And regardless of what we talked about, it always made me feel better.[13]

CONCLUSION

The barriers to communication between Negroes and whites are such that ability of a white worker to reach a Negro client is circumscribed. It is not possible within the hour of therapy to change the social context in which the Negro lives, and the Negro client may often be caught in the dilemma that behavior socially adaptive to the white world is emotionally maladaptive. However, if the worker is to help at all, he needs not only an understanding of the Negro's oppression but an understanding of the dynamics of his countertransference to the Negro client and the significance this may have for the conduct of therapy. The interracial treatment situation differs from other therapeutic relationships in that the explosive and painful problem of Negro-white relationships is basic to it. The "rules" of therapy may not change, but the worker must apply them with special sensitivity. Just as some mental health workers find they cannot work to optimum effectiveness with certain clients, some may find that their countertransference is sufficiently detrimental for them to refuse to treat Negroes. For others, the countertransference can be handled, with control or supervisory help, but first it takes the willingness to acknowledge that feelings about Negro clients are colored by both the facts and mythology of the racial system in which we live.

NOTES

[1] The term "mental health worker" will be used from now on to indicate those helping persons who practice psychotherapy.

[2] For a discussion of interracial treatment relationships, *see* Luna Bowdoin Brown, "Race As a Factor in Establishing a Casework Relationship," *Social Casework*, Vol. 31, No. 3 (March 1950), pp. 91-97; Andrew E. Curry, "The Negro Worker and the White Client: A Commentary on the Treatment Relationship," *Social Casework*, Vol. 45, No. 3 (March 1964), pp. 131-136; Esther Fibush, "The White Worker and the Negro Client," *Social Casework*, Vol. 46, No. 5 (May 1965), pp. 271-277; Jean S. Gochros, "Recognition and Use of Anger in Negro Clients," *Social Work*, Vol. 11, No. 1 (January 1966), pp. 28-34; and Leonard C. Simmons, "'Crow Jim': Implications for Social Work," *Social Work*, Vol. 8, No. 3 (July 1963), pp. 24-30.

[3] Alan C. Kerckhoff and Thomas C. McCormick, "Marginal Status and Marginal Personality," *Social Forces*, Vol. 33, No. 1 (September 1955), pp. 48-55.

[4] New York: Grosset & Dunlap, 1952.

[5] For a discussion of the Black Muslims *see* C. Eric Lincoln, *The Black Muslims in America* (Boston: Beacon Press, 1961).

[6] Hans Strupp, "Toward an Analysis of the Therapist's Contribution to the Treatment Process," *Psychiatry*, Vol. 22, No. 4 (November 1959), pp. 349-362.

[7] Hans Strupp, "The Performance of Psychiatrists and Psychologists in a Therapeutic Interview," *Journal of Clinical Psychology*, Vol. 14, No. 3 (July 1958), pp. 216-226.

[8] Morton Chetnik, Elizabeth Fleming, Morris F. Mayer, and John Mc-Coy, "A Clinical Problem in the Treatment of Disturbed Negro Children in a Predominantly White Treatment Center." Unpublished manuscript, Cleveland, undated.

[9] Andrew E. Curry, "Myth, Transference, and the Black Psychoanalyst," *Psychoanalytic Review,* Vol. 51, No. 1 (Spring 1964), p. 7.

[10] *Ibid.*

[11] John Dollard, *Caste and Class in a Southern Town* (New York: Doubleday & Co., Anchor Books, 1957), esp. chaps. 7, 8, and 16.

[12] Sigmund Freud, *Civilization and Its Discontents,* James Strachey, trans. (New York: W. W. Norton & Co., 1962), p. 36.

[13] *Manchild in the Promised Land* (New York: Macmillan Co., 1965), p. 121.

SECTION VII

Our Changing Society

INTRODUCTION

IDENTIFYING TRENDS

The intent of this section is not only to "tell it like it is," but also to attempt some understanding of where it's going. Like other sciences, sociology must ultimately be interested in prediction and control. Only by grasping societal trends can we hope to direct, or at least to be prepared for, those social forces which will affect our lives and the lives of forthcoming generations. Grasping these trends is not always easy. It remains patently true that "the squeaky wheel gets the oil." Our attention is often drawn to public issues which may, or may not, reflect the most salient concerns of society. Furthermore, in the constantly changing specifics of public issues, it isn't difficult to lose sight of long range trends. Finally we are forever evaluating scientific findings subjectively, noticing the disgraceful faults of the next fellow while totally overlooking our own shortcomings.

DEMOGRAPHIC CHANGES

Perhaps the most fundamental order of trends to consider has to do with population. The post World War II baby boom is just now producing a jump in the childbearing adult population. In 1950 there were 150,000,000 Americans, by 1970 there will be an estimated 210,000,000.[1] What does it take to deal with 3,000,000 more people annually? How do you provide for a given level in the quality of life—pure food, water, air—needed to maintain public health? How do you dispose of waste? What portion of the gross national product must be devoted simply to maintaining the status quo in hospital care, educational services or housing, let alone improving them? There are reasonable grounds to believe that we have been losing in this race with population.

Coupled with our exploding population is internal migration.[2] In little more than a century, we have gone from a rural to an urban society. The agricultural center of our country has been losing its population to the metropolises which ring its borders and coastlines. A number of chains of metropolises already qualify as what Gottman called "Megalopolis." This movement reflects the rise in farm productivity. Mass production has made the family farm obsolete while at

547

the same time making opportunities available in urban based commerce and industry. This process in our country was, of course,
spurred by two world wars and the Korean Conflict.

The most widely discussed segment of migrators are the Negroes,
who outside the South, are by now all but totally urban. However,
Indians off the reservations, Appalachian mountain folk, white rural
Southerners, Puerto Ricans, Midwestern farmers and Spanish Americans from the Southwest have all contributed to the city-bound flow
of population. The influx of these groups, especially rural blacks,
into the urban arena has simply added to the already complex ethnic
composition of urban America. Some 30% of all Americans are still
the foreign born or their children. The percentage is much larger in
the cities. Reaction by these groups to black consciousness and demands has already begun to make itself felt in rising ethnicity. Challenge and response may make inter-group relations in this country
worse before they grow better. Close proximity and high density of
populations from various ethnic and socio economic backgrounds in
metropolises further serves to aggravate latent tensions.[4]

MASS SOCIETY AND POLITICAL STRUCTURE

Concentration of population in non agricultural urban centers
coupled with the communications and transportation revolutions
have given us an urban, national, if not cosmopolitan society distinguished by a national pop culture as well as contraculture. The
problems affecting us are increasingly beyond the scope of local or
state wide solution. People, professional crime, or air pollution, for
example, are no respectors of state lines. In such a situation, Jeffer-
sonian democracy and our traditional division of labor among city,
state and federal government are not only quaint—they are a potentially dangerous—anachronism. Local autonomy or state responsibility cannot cope with provision of welfare aid in one state to victims of another state's inadequate education, just to cite one such
problem.

One effect of the mass society is that the media can and do generate
instant public opinion while transportation and population density
provide the bodies for public demonstrations and even violence. Public opinion polls were once seen as a technique for informing politicians of the people's desires between elections.[5] However, democratic processes are still too slow and instant demonstration has be-

come the latest political form. There is a danger that a national arena for issues which were formerly dispersed and obscured may yet undermine our whole representative government system. In many parts of the world, rule rests in the hands of those who can mobilize the largest mob. This could well develop here as the level of disruptive tactics progresses. Such escalation tendencies are already evident.[6]

Our political structure has been described as government by lobby groups. While there are those who believe that Americans are frustrated because they cannot participate in their own governance, the opposite may be more accurate. They may be frustrated precisely because they now participate at an unprecedented level. However, due to the complexity of our heterogeneous society every lobby and pressure group has its opposite number. To carry through your program you have to enlist others not of like mind. The process of gaining a majority usually involves bargaining, compromise, and watering down. Rarely can any side on any issue claim real victory.

Adding to the frustration is the high degree of specialization required to make decisions for our society. The man on the street may know more quantitatively than ever before, but he is less competent than ever in voicing an unprofessional opinion. Tragically, this is also true of our elected officials. They too depend on professional advisors for expertise. While we vote for a TV image, packaged and marketed by advertising agents, script writers and cosmeticians, the candidate is little better than the voter at making technical decisions of utmost importance.

One trend we have already begun to feel is our unprecedented capacity for monitoring and ultimately controlling the individual. Thus far, Congress has resisted efforts to combine all governmentally known data on any individual, using the social security number as the entry. Such considerations as personal liberty and invasion of privacy will ultimately be overridden by economy and improved convenience to the citizen through more efficient provision of government service.

Control may come from a second direction as well. The behavioral sciences are moving toward better understanding and prediction of behavior though most behavioral scientists are themselves uncomfortable with these trends. Already social work is unsatisfied with its intuitive, practice experience and searching for more exact techniques. Untestable psychoanalysis is challenged by a new round of behaviorism as well as growing knowledge of the chemistry and physics of our mental, emotional and sensory systems. Group behavior is a declining mystery and mob control, for example, will predictably move away from violence and counter violence toward application of a new technology of mass behavior and communications. Who will use this knowledge and to what ends? It can, of course, be used to foment uprisings as well as prevent legitimate protest (however that's defined). We are wary of governmental controls yet we seem hardly aware of such subtle non governmental controls as planned obsolescence and appeals to our unconscious needs promoted by advertising and market research.[7]

Yet one more reflection of our massive scale may be involved in our recent emphasis on group rights rather than individual civil rights, sometimes even at the expense of the individual. Individual rights were fought for by liberal tradition over a long period of our political history. Bureaucracy is the ideal setting to permit individual advance according to individual merit without reference to extraneous criteria like race or ethnic origin. That's why government and big business have lent themselves to the upwardly mobile minority group member. Now we hear again about benign quotas which cannot, of course, escape setting different kinds of quotas on the merit of others. That individual rights may be sacrificed to group needs at this juncture reflects our current trend toward seeing people as blocs, not as individuals in groups.

The same reversal has occurred with regards to political units. Throughout our history the way to overcome political bossism, reaction, extremism, parochialism has been to provide a larger population base for elected officials and for effective government. Generally, the larger the population base the more progressive the tendency. Now as reaction to "big government" we are being told that local control is the answer. It may well be, but we really have no basis in experience for such an assumption. Big government grew in response to big demands. One must discount both simple frustration or sinister need to control before accepting the assurances of those who see salvation in smaller governmental units.

THE SILENT CONQUEST

Economically we are in the midst of what has been called "the silent conquest."[8] This is changing the nature of work. Basically economics has always revolved around the question of producing enough goods and services to meet demand. Although there are lags and inconsistencies, we are rapidly approaching the reverse—generation of enough demand to permit production at full capacity.

The second economic change is in the nature of work. Technology demands ever more professionals and technicians, while unskilled labor finds a continually shrinking market. Theoretically, there is a maximum to the percentage of the labor force which can fill an occupational category calling for at least the equivalent of a college education. Thus, for the predictable future these occupations will continue to overwork while, for most employees work will entail shorter hours, longer holidays and earlier retirement. The trend to professions has changed education from a reflection of status to a creator of status in our society. Much of the unrest among our current student population is a reaction to this new role of education.

Finally, for the first time in history more of us are engaged in the provision of services rather than in the production of goods.

In the midst of all our affluence we are troubled to find that poverty cannot readily be eliminated from the fiber of our society. While it is theoretically possible, in practice making the poverty ridden productive is highly uneconomical. We find ourselves questioning whether our society truly wants to undertake the task.

VALUE AND ATTITUDE CHANGES

The rational organization of society to cope with needs on an unprecedented scale is related to the loss of identity and bored restlessness experienced by modern man. We needn't explore here anomie and alienation in modern society, except to note that the detrimental effects of bureaucratized society have been observed since the early stages of the industrial revolution.[9] Today such effects are even more pervasive. We see many examples of man's attempt to counter these effects through irrational, emotional behavior. Some are serious such as drug use and various forms of violent thrill seeking, others more subtle like the hypnotism of TV—called by one wag "optical chewing gum"—our vacation mania, or identification with a baseball team. Those at the bottom of urban stratification as well as adolescents, have been most susceptible to such escapes from the reality of their powerlessness.

Contrary to popular view, mass society is more, not less tolerant of differences. (Who cares, as long as you don't bother the smooth functioning of our complex interdependency?) On the other hand, the scale of our economy makes it most profitable to achieve mass conformity. Under such pressures, ethnic, regional, or even class differences, tend to be flattened by our mass media. Hippies began to be passé when they could no longer be distinguished from the plastic hippie type. For many Jews, being Jewish is what *Portnoy's Complaint* says it is, about what it is to the Americans in general. The doom of "Soul" is already in the making. It began when white coeds went Afro. Chitterlin's may yet join pizza, the matzo ball and fortune cookies on that great American menu in the sky. That's not too bad in itself but beautiful black will no doubt fall victim to its own Madison Avenue image as have other cultural variations, not by force but by being engulfed by pop culture.

Our shift from rural to urban conditions has not only affected the location of people, but with equal drama, their values. While earlier social theorists and planners looked with nostalgia to the quality of life of the pre-industrial village and even sought to recapture that quality in our contemporary metropolis, we are now beginning to get a few thinkers seeking the positives of our new urban setting.[10]   In effect, the urbanites' values were in the past an attempt to translate rural living to the city. The communications revolution has made today's city the generator of a new style of life which is rapidly engulfing the most isolated rural areas.

The pressure to consume has fostered a kind of neo-hedonism based on our new technology which often conflicts with our older values. We seek constant stimulation of the senses. Those who teach children or even college students, find that one must always cater to shrinking interest spans and fading powers of concentration, jaded by ever-present professional performers. Never before has education been so-akin to entertainment.

Of course, a good part of the sensual is sexual in nature and here too, technology increasingly enables us to use sex as a diversion. The dissection of its component physiological parts, a la Masters and Johnson, has robbed even romance of its mystery. This is essentially the story of our gadgetry; we have done so well in objectifying that we have few mysteries left to enjoy. So why wonder that some of us go so far to find an emotion or two tucked away in an unanalyzed corner or to snatch an irrational moment's escape. For all our young peoples' popular talk about "love", genuine affection seems to have been replaced by just one more overworked four letter word.

One temporary influence on our attitudes which has turned into a permanent feature of our society is the ongoing cold war in the quarter century since World War II. We are now experiencing extreme reaction to prolonged war conditions, although focused on a confusing, costly involvement in Viet Nam. Underlying this focus is anxiety over living on the edge of a man-made volcano which could be touched off by a moment's miscalculation. Modern war, however, is but one more reflection of modern technology. The most pronounced difference is the urgency of its immediate dangers.

Dehumanization is the process which has been described as the reaction to war and its emotional burdens. The individual sees the enemy as a non-human category instead of a person like himself. Ethical considerations are put aside as each individual convinces himself that he is incapable of effecting major decisions. Attention is focused not on the significance of the job but on the technical details of getting the job done. On the other side, the scale of devastation within our capacity is so great that we practice a kind of reductionism. We devise affectionate terms for bombs, we talk of megatons of explosive force as though they were something petite and diminutive.

However, dehumanization as a defense mechanism in the face of war is but one aspect of the dehumanization in mass social organization. The nameless, faceless crowds of modern urban society lend themselves to categorization. Not only can the poor, the black, the stranger be taken in an impersonal functional vein but any perceivable in-group out-group line is grasped with alacrity for its emotional value in a barren, feelingless void of objective interaction. Thus the cop on the beat is reduced to a uniform and redefined "pig", the next man struggling with many of the same problems as the non-white slum dweller becomes "whitey", as faceless as the black man can be to the white. In other countries where dividing lines don't lend themselves to neat racial divisions, you get hippies against teddy boys, Hindus against Moslems or any other available in-groups. However, in our country, where we have the most advanced technology, we would appear to have the most advanced dehumanization. We have gone so far that we can even organize across age lines.

What we seem to have is a continuing value crisis, a crisis in shared tradition both secular and religious. It would not seem that any society so enamored with technological innovation and consensus values could possibly find a place for yesterday's ideas, experiences or even people. With our paradoxical mass culture and constant cross cultural contact, strongly internalized social norms and values fostered by cultural isolation seems unlikely. Social cohesion seems likely to require the imposition of external controls.[11] These will no doubt become increasingly sophisticated. A society which cannot effectively convey its culture to subsequent generations must look forward to continued unrest or the kind of monitoring portrayed by Orwell. The essential difference between the impending controls and fictional portraits of future society is that most novelists fail to acknowledge that what seems to be coming need not result from a sinister plot by a tyrannical dictator but could arise simply from citizen demand for some administrative system which will enable us to cope with the size and complexity of our condition. After all, the alternative to greater common understanding and larger population units sharing expectations is the unacceptable retribalization of society. It is hard to visualize such an occurrence unless it is a reaction to some catastrophe such as nuclear destruction.[12]

It should be clear that we are caught up in the midst of revolutionary changes, political, social and economic, much of them technologically generated. The pace of these changes is so rapid that it challenges our adaptive capacity. Whereas previously we had an opportunity to digest changes occurring in society and to absorb them into the base of our experience today we have little such opportunity.[13] Many are so overwhelmed by it all that they cop out by withdrawing into their own immediate little world or perhaps even into the escape offered by a wide variety of drugs. Many observers see in our situation an analogy to that of the sorcerer's apprentice: having started the process we can no longer stop it or even control its direction. Others are troubled by the uneven pace of change. They see a need to change our society and its faults yet they are often frustrated by their inability to move it forward. For some the frustration gives rise to the blind hostility and rage of the anarchist who would rather have nothing than an imperfect society.

THEORIES OF SOCIAL CHANGE

A theory of change is in itself troubling and unclear. For some years now, perhaps going back to the age of reason, Western man has popularly believed in the perfectability of man. Our technological advances imply daily that this view is accurate. Therefore it should surprise no one that most of us hold a cumulative or progressive view of change. Change is good, in and of itself, because we have come to believe that change is for the better. In fact, of course, it may not be. Modern man inclines toward linear view with endless improvement ahead.

Most traditional societies also view change as linear. However, they are much more likely to see the "good old days" with romantic nostalgia while seeing all subsequent events as a decline from earlier, heroic days.[14] Another quite different view of change as cyclical is seen in the work of such theorists as Spengler Toynbee and Sorokin.[15] Essentially, these views see society as the individual experiencing birth, growth, maturity and decline. Regardless of the particular system, it is interesting that advocates of the cyclical view tend to see their own society at the stage of decline.

Modern revolutionary thinking usually returns in one way or another to the Hegelian concept of thesis, antithesis and synthesis. Quite irrationally, Marx believed that his revolution of the proletariat would lead to the millennium and be the final revolution. We are now in the historic position to realize that this view, too, has failed to withstand the test of reality.

Most current social scientists are convinced of the inter related nature of social institutions. This, of course, reflects the contemporary structural-functional emphasis in social theory. Such a view has many practical implications for understanding social change and promotion of change.

Most current social scientists are convinced of the interrelated na- ing a complex society incline toward Maoist type revolution. The idea is that only by first destroying the entrenched society and its establishment, can real change be undertaken. However, in light of the interrelatedness of social institutions such an approach seems like another example of overkill. It should be possible to make just a few changes and touch off a chain reaction of change, a kind of domino theory of social change. Indeed this is exactly what we have been experiencing as a result of our technological advances.

INITIATING CHANGE

In many countries of the world change has been initiated by intent through the introduction of change agents.[16] It's true that the immediacy of the reward and the relatedness of the change to the existent culture are overriding considerations. However, not only is there ample evidence that it works but we know, after a quarter century, a great deal about the dynamics which operate and the mental health problems change generates.[17]

Social change desired by the people can usually be absorbed with relatively little disruption. Those against the desires of the population are not easily rooted. Change is most likely to occur in a heterogeneous, urban society where alternative models are readily available and behavior less deeply rooted in tradition. Material culture, as has been pointed out, changes more readily than non material elements like values just as learning which is late in life is unlearned more readily than that which was part of childhood socialization. We also know that the form of behavior is more easily changed than the meaning and that resistance is greatest in areas of greatest emotional investment. Most important, it has been repeatedly demonstrated that gradual changes are more readily accepted than sudden, shocking ones and once a start is made other changes follow.[18]

THE SOCIAL WORKER AS CHANGE AGENT

Even this brief enumeration indicates how close many traditional social work views actually are to the more recent concept of planned change and the function of change agents. It should be noted that many who reject the possibility of any but radical changes in a society do so because it tends to undermine their particular political philosophy and not because of lack of evidence that it works.

Social work has been influenced by these experiences with social change. Professionals are increasingly concerned lest they spend their time patching up instead of attacking the root causes of social ills.[19] Social workers are seeing themselves more and more as change agents.[20] Larger numbers express interest in group work and especially in community organization which is now seen in a whole new light. Along with this new self image is a change to more dynamic, outspoken approach to social issues. Here again we come full cycle. For it becomes all the more necessary, with this stance, to be armed with the full weight of knowledge as it is developed by the behavioral sciences and not to go off impulsively with tools inadequate to meet the new challenges of a changing society.

REFERENCES

1. Ewan Clague, "Democratic Trends and Their Significance," Hoke Simpson, ed. *The Changing American Population,* N. Y.: Institute of Life Insurance, 1962, 12-13.

2. See Kingsley Davis, "Urbanization — Changing Patterns of Living," in Simpson, *op. cit.,* 59-68.

3. Jean Gottman, *Megalopolis,* N. Y.: Twentieth Century Fund, 1961.

4. "The Troubled American," *Newsweek,* Oct. 6, 1969, 29-73.

5. Walter Lippman, *Public Opinion,* N. Y.: Harcourt, Brace and Co., 1922.

6. See Harry Specht, "Disruptive Tactics," *Social Work,* Vol. 14, No. 2, April 1969, 5-15.

7. For example, automobile advertisements are forever appealing to our sexual or status needs in marketing their products.

8. Donald N. Michael, *Cybernation: The Silent Conquest,* Santa Barbara, California: Center for the Study of Democratic Institutions, 1962.

9. For a good overview of anomie, see Robert K. Merton, *Social Theory and Social Structure,* N.Y.: Free Press of Glencoe, 1957, 131-194.

10. For example, see Jane Jacobs, *The Death and Life of Great American Cities,* N. Y.: Random House, 1961; and Edward Gross, "Centers of Identity In the Modern City," *Social Work,* Vol. 10, No. 3, July 1965, 22-31.

11. When Montreal Police struck in October 1969, we witnessed a good example of a modern metropolis momentarily without external compulsion.

12. One might compare the future portrayed in Orwell's *1984* with such depressing views as depicted in *The Futurist* Vol. II, No. 5, Oct. 1968. Even the shorter range view of the American Academy of Arts and Sciences' Committee on the Year 2000 portrays a dehumanized future which challenges our basic assumptions about individual worth.

13. The explosion of knowledge is currently estimated to double knowledge every 10 years.

14. One useful conceptualization of the time orientation of different societies may be found in Florence R. Kluckhohn's, "Family Diagnosis: Variations in the Basic Values of Family Systems," *Social Casework,* Vol. 39, Feb.-Mar., 1958, 63-72.

15. Oswald Spengler, *The Decline of the West,* 2 vol. Trans. by C. F. Atkinson, N. Y.: Knopf, 1926-28; Arnold Toynbee, *A Study of History,* 12 vols., London: Oxford University Press, 1934-1961; Pitrim Sorokin, *Sociological Theory Today,* Harper and Row, 1966.

16. These have been, public health nurses, agricultural or industrial experts, teachers, technical assistants, etc., under many national and international auspices.

17. Margaret Mead, ed., *Cultural Patterns and Technological Change,* N. Y.: Mentor, 262-303.

18. Bernard Berelson and Gary Steiner, *Human Behavior*, N. Y.: Harcourt, Brace and World, 613-619.

19. The profession, which has always seen itself as among the progressive elements of the society, has been hurt by the implications of the "Welfare Colonialism" charge.

20. A good example of this issue is the inclusion of two articles on social workers as advocates in *Social Work*, Vol. 14, 2, April 1969.

SOME SPECULATIONS ON THE SOCIAL IMPACT OF TECHNOLOGY

DAVID N. MICHAEL

I want to draw your attention to what I think are the important aspects of the social impact of technology that we have so far ignored or attended to only in passing. I do not intend to convince anyone of anything: I am not sure what the questions are in this area — much less what the answers might be. Rather, I want to sketch a variety of perspectives and circumstances that I think merit attention, so that you may determine whether or not these are significant issues for scholars and actionists concerned with the impact of technology on society on more than an occasional basis. These are issues that we ought to be concerned with at least as much as we have been with productivity, investment policies, employment, and so on.

Let me begin by making clear that I am not asserting that technology is a villain, or that technology is a saviour. The problem is not that simple. The positive and negative interplay between technology and social processes is much too complicated to comprehend if only one aspect, technology, rather than technology in the context of society as a whole is dealt with. In no sense am I insensitive to or unappreciative of the great opportunities implicit in technology, particularly in the new technologies. Nor may the odds on adverse consequences from these technologies be any higher than on favorable ones. But I believe that the consequences themselves, favorable or unfavorable, are of such magnitude that if they are negative, they will bring upon us much more serious trouble than we would have had in the past, in simpler days, when technologies had fewer derivative implications, and affected fewer people in a smaller area over a longer period of time.

Let me also make clear that I do not believe that the solutions to the problems we will discuss are to be found, by and large, in a moratorium on technological development. Such is the social environ-

Reprinted by permission of the publisher from D. Morse and A. Warner (eds.), *Technical Innovations in Society* (Columbia University Press, 1966) pp. 118-154.

ment technology has already produced that, unless we are to change our value system and way of life totally, we must use more technology to make an adequate environment out of the circumstances technology has already brought about. I fully expect the technologies to help deal with the problems the technologies produce. I also fully expect that unless we take a larger and deeper view of the social implications of technology than we have so far, we will not use our technologies or other resources sufficiently to protect us from the enormous potential for social disruption and disaster implicit in these technologies. Hence, I am going to emphasize aspects of the social impact of technology that I believe present problems which must be solved if we are to enjoy the advantages the technologies can provide. I think we can expect in our type of society, and in a society as rich as ours, that the opportunities will take care of themselves. Put another way, the opportunities do not need to be optimized, but the dangers, I think, must be minimized.

Sketchy and impressionistic as these observations will be, I have tried to organize them into three general categories. First I shall make some observations on the general considerations that should be applied to any estimate of the present and contemplated social impact of technology. Then, I want to mention three technologies which I expect will have a wide social impact in the next two decades or so, and which by their characteristics imply a far broader range of social impact than we have felt so far, certainly than we have studied so far. And finally, I will set out some examples of aspects of social impact that should be studied intensively now, if we are to be prepared to use the results of such studies for guiding the felicitous integration of technology and society in the years ahead.

Let me say something else by way of introduction. In many ways I will be implying that the methods and knowledge of our various disciplines are inadequate or nonexistent and, therefore, cannot help us understand what is happening to society vis-à-vis technology. I hope I will be able to imply convincingly that many, probably most, of what may be the significant issues are *not* being explored effectively and on a scale and with the attention they deserve. If I "get to you" I will thereby, inevitably, threaten our various senses of self and status and purpose; I will question who we are, what we do, why we are what we are, and how important we are to ourselves and to others.

There are typical ways to defend oneself against such threats: by "not hearing" or misunderstanding the speaker's choice of points of emphasis and context of qualifying remarks; by translating and transforming what he emphasizes into a problem or a syntax with which the auditor is comfortable and familiar, thereby shifting the plane of discourse; by attending to the speaker's mood rather than to what he says, and so on. Inevitably, these defenses will operate here just as they do throughout the community of persons and institutions whose favored perspectives and, thereby, senses of self, are challenged by the interplay of technology and society which makes obsolete or inadequate the conventional techniques for perceiving the society and dealing with it. Indeed, this type of threat to self and these responses to it, produced by a changed and changing world, conveyed from one person to another through the different perspectives of those involved, are in themselves important social impacts of technology about which we know too little, and which we need to understand much better.

With this forewarning, let me now turn to some general considerations on understanding the relationship between technology and society, which I think are too seldom appreciated or made central to the context when specific issues are explored.

1. It is important to remember that some of the significant impacts of technology derive from the accumulated effects of technological changes that have been under way for some time. Let me remind you of three examples: the population explosion, a direct product of medical technology initiated some years ago; the urban chaos that has been fundamentally exacerbated by transportation technology in the form of the private car; and the distortion and disruption of ecology in local areas and, probably, in much larger areas by the wholesale application of pesticides and fungicides, to say nothing of the continental pollution of the ecology by the waste products of many technologies. In the future some of these accumulated consequences will become more emphatic and complex, while the new technologies contribute their consequences too. The technologies we have to be concerned with thus include some older ones as well as the new ones. This is important: we do not have to wait for the new technologies contribute their consequences, too. The technologies we standing their impact. All we have to do is recognize our ignorance and indifference regarding the present social impact—and do something about it.

2. A major purpose of our preoccupation with technology and social change is to prepare for the future. But doing so is going to be very difficult. There are some social consequences of technology for

which we should have begun to prepare yesterday. For example, the type of education appropriate for a rapidly changing work force and for substantial increases in leisure probably requires fundamentally different attitudes and approaches by the teachers in primary and secondary schools than the present ones. But recruiting the teachers and teaching the teachers requires changes at least in the schools of education and in teachers colleges, and all such sequential changes take time to introduce. The upshot is that most of those teaching today's youngsters and imbuing them with the values and attitudes they will carry into their lives tomorrow are probably conveying the wrong things, because the teachers' were wrongly trained and perhaps, in part, wrongly selected. Similarly, problem-solving investigations in the area of urban affairs must be undertaken long in advance of the actual reconstruction and reorganization of our cities. The riots in Los Angeles and the water shortage in New York may, be mild precursors of the potential disasters that may otherwise overtake us.

In general, we do not understand and appreciate, and thereby tend to overlook, the nature of the time lag between recognition of a problem and the development of techniques for dealing with it.

We do not allow for—often we do not know how to allow for—the needed intervening period to accumulate knowledge and understanding. I suspect that over the next couple of decades or so, this gap between problem recognition and the development of solutions, or approximate solutions, is going to become increasingly serious: problems will confront us before we are able to deal with them knowledgeably. The integration of technology with other social processes and the felicitous sequencing of contingent social actions to accomplish the integration is going to be much more difficult than it has been in the past.

3. Value conflicts, and tensions between generations will very likely increase, especially between the new generation that is moving into political and professional power and is using new types of operational and substantive expertise, and the older generations already occupying the field. These conflicts and their various expressions in differing values and operating techniques will mean that both the pressures and the inhibitions to make the kind of social and technological changes that we are going to need are certain to be very great. As the distinguished public servant, systems theorist, and student of decision processes, Sir Geoffrey Vickers, puts it:

> In the transitional period from the conditions of free fall to those of regulation (at whatsoever level), political and social life is bound, I think,

to become much more collectivist or much more anarchic or—almost certainly—both. Communities national, subnational and even supranational will become more closely knit insofar as they can handle the political, social and psychological problems involved and more violent in their mutual rejections insofar as they cannot. The loyalties we accept will impose wider obligations and more comprehensive acceptance. The loyalties we reject will separate us by wider gulfs from those who accept them and will involve us in fiercer and more unqualified struggles.[1]

What the resolution or stalemate will be between the old and new approaches to the uses of knowledge and power via technology remains to be seen, but an understanding of this conflict in approaches will be prerequisite to an understanding of the social impact of technology.

4. Under what circumstances does an issue become significant or critical? What determines when small percents, such as the unemployment rate for example, become sufficiently large in absolute numbers to become a major issue? When does indifference become transformed into action, as for example, in the poverty program? When does the ability to extrapolate trends begin to carry real significance in terms of program implementation, as, for example, in the moon program, where the ability to use computer technology to predict whether we could succeed was an important factor in the decision to go ahead?

Understanding the general principles of when, or how, or why issues become important and become recognized as issues, would be essential for estimating the seriousness of or for coping with, among other things, the gap between posing a problem about and finding a solution to an impact of technology on society.

5. Often interpretations of the past are called upon to help interpret the present and to suggest solutions to expected problems in the future. By and large I think these interpretations have been inadequate. First of all, there is often only a surface similarity; the presumed analogy is based on a partial or on a misunderstood picture of the past. A prime example of this is the frequent submission of the Periclean age of Greece as evidence of what our future leisure patterns should or could be. That the "leisured" society of Greece numbered only in the tens of thousands, that it spent much of its time warring or doing those political tasks we have professionalized, that no women were involved, that the system lasted only a couple of generations and then decayed, all such considerations are left out of the supposed apt and happy analogy.

Or consider the argument that since we mastered the first Industrial Revolution, we will not have any enduring trouble with the second industrial revolution that the new technologies represent. But we have not mastered the first Industrial Revolution. Let us mention three social consequences of the first Industrial Revolution that are increasingly acute. While other factors have contributed to them and while in some form or another they may have existed previous to the first Industrial Revolution, undoubtedly our inability to deal with the consequences of that revolution have enormously exacerbated these conditions. The first is the increasing gap between the developed nations and the have-not nations that was widened by the technological prowess of the developed nations, and by their inability to share their technology with the underdeveloped nations. The second example is the persistence—the growth, in some cases—of slums and poverty. This peculiar type of degrading, enclaved existence was the direct result of the first Industrial Revolution's concentration of factory technology, and the resulting transfer of manpower from the farms to the factories. The third example is the alienation from and breakdown of earlier, more stable, systems of value and faith. There are very few students of this problem who feel that the Industrial Revolution has not contributed enormously to the complexity and persistence of the problem.

Another inadequacy in appealing to the past is that even if there is more than a surface similarity in the particular social processes involved, there usually are differences in the surrounding social or physical circumstances, which imply very different consequences than those occurring in the past. Two very important examples of such differences are worth mentioning.

First, never before in history has any nation had such a complex technology combined with a population as large as that of the U.S., now and as it will be—230 million around 1975, 250 million around 1980. Those who assert that because thus and such a technological consequence was coped with in the past, or that a specific social consequence is not new and neither, by implication, are its future consequences, have to consider whether the multiple social and physical consequences of a population of such huge size carry significantly different implications for the future.

The second difference, which we tend to overlook, is that today there very probably are different expectations than there were in the past of what the implications of technology on society will be. Because people are different today, they expect different things to happen to them as a result of technology than people did in the past. It does not help to say, "Their beliefs do not really jibe with the facts." (Especially since we probably do not know the facts). If they think, for example, that technological change is galloping along at a rate never before equalled, then this results in various reactions by business executives, scientists, pundits, and government officials—to say nothing of the man in the street. These reactions, very likely, are significantly different from those in the past, when this kind of issue did not cross most people's minds. For example, I strongly suspect (but we have not bothered to find out) that a recent major social consequence of the interaction of several technologies is that more types of people are concerned about the future social impact of technology, and more different viewpoints have arisen regarding it, and that these in turn are initiating other social consequences.

Let me now turn to three technologies, biological technology, cybernation, and social engineering. I expect these will, over the next two decades, have very great implications for the nature of society and for the place of the individual in it. I want to emphasize those implications that go beyond those we have tended to preoccupy ourselves with, not because I think they have been unimportant, but because I believe the ones I want to mention are equally important, perhaps more so. Let me again make clear that I recognize that many of the impacts will not be new in kind. However, I do believe that it is likely that the scale and scope, the potency, of their impact, as they interact with an already huge and enormously complex society will be of an unprecedented order of magnitude. In that potency of impact lie many exciting opportunities, and some very profound problems having to do with the place the individual has in a democratic society, and the way we conduct our lives. Again, I will emphasize problems not because I am certain that they will outrun the opportunities, but rather because I feel that if the problems are not dealt with effectively, the consequences may be so disastrous that we shall never enjoy the opportunities—at least not within the format of presently preferred values. (Of course, a different set of values may be all right or even better than the present ones. But what I want to emphasize is the kind of confrontations these technologies are to our present values, if only to indicate the necessity for understanding the social impact of technology better, so that we may invent or respond to a more appropriate set of values).

Perhaps the fundamental question that the potency of these technologies raises is how do we deliberately decide how we are going to balance the social costs and social benefits; obviously I mean infinitely more here than the dollar costs and benefits. I think we must do much more than hope for the best or retreat behind some inhuman "averaging out" philosophy. But what do we do if, as I believe they will, the consequences of these technologies will be upon us before we accumulate the understanding needed to establish such a balance—if we ever can accumulate such understanding?

In the application of biological technology—the engineering of man's biological self and his biological environment—we will face moral, ethical, psychological, and political issues, which will make those faced by the atomic scientists look like child's play. Biological and chemical warfare will very likely be used much more in local wars, even perhaps in the pacification activities of international police forces. But whether it is used to kill, hurt, nauseate, paralyze, cause hallucination, or to terrify military personnel and civilians, the systematic use of biological and chemical warfare will require the resolution of major moral and ethical problems—especially since the most likely victims will be nonwhites in Asia and Africa.

Psychopharmacology is another aspect of biological technology already beginning to confront us with interesting issues. What is to be the role of hallucinogenic chemicals in society? There are two schools of thought on this—even the theologians seem to have taken sides. One is that these chemicals represent sin and corruption; the other, that they are exciting means for enlarging emotional or aesthetic or religious experience. Moreover, new drugs will permit many people, who otherwise would be in mental institutions, to walk the streets and to engage in regular social activities. Questions arise about the "nature" of the individual. How do we judge the extent to which a person is "responsible" for himself in such circumstances? For, while the chemical affects the individual, the person is significant to himself and to society in his *social* context—at work, at home, at play. The consequences are social consequences. In deciding how to deal with such alterers of the ego and of experience (and consequently alterers of the personality after the experience), and in deciding how to deal with the "changed" human beings, we will have to face new questions such as, "Who am I?" "When am I who?" "Who are *they* in relation to me?"

As far as the hallucinogenic agents are concerned, how will we judge whether people, just because they want it, are entitled to a risky if richer emotional experience than that provided by their everyday life? Are these decisions to be left to the individual, like skiing or surfboarding, or will they need legal restrictions like homosexual liaisons or the present use of non-habitforming marijuana? In general, will "multiple" personalities and increasing amounts of idiosyncratic behavior simply be absorbed into the already proliferating scale of novelties, sensations, and leisure-time pursuits, or will they have to be controlled to facilitate the functioning of a stable society? Whatever way is chosen, what are the ethical, legal, political, and psychological considerations needed to help us understand the implications of such altered egos and their control?

A related aspect of biological technology merits mention here: with the increasing dissemination of birth control information and technology, we can expect the pressures on the poor to limit family size to become greater. Though such pressure already exists, in the form of inadequate housing for large, poor families, the pressure may well become more explicit as the "excuses" for having large families inadvertently are eliminated by the pervasive availability of birth control methods. If our laws and ways of operating come to condone this invasion of the right of couples to choose the number of children they want, then a new ethical issue will arise and it will reverberate into other areas of private affairs, conduct, and choice.

A third area in biological technology has to do with organ transplants. Some top research people in this area are convinced that in a few years techniques will have improved substantially. The problem then arises: Who is entitled to what transplant under what criteria of priority? We will have to do better than "women and children first." This situation already exists on a tiny scale with regard to the use of scarce kidney-substitute machines. Difficult as the decisions are now, they will become more difficult and more socially consequential when more people compete for more organs.

Though it is unlikely that organ transplantation will be available to such an extent as to increase substantially the number of people who will live longer, it is likely that developments in the technology of preventing and treating malignant diseases will mean that there will be still more older people in this society, which has not yet learned to deal humanely with the older population it now has. Thus, developments in biological technology, combined with those from cybernation, in particular, will add to the numbers and to the social problems of older people. The accumulated social impact on our political system, and thereby on our social priorities, will undoubtedly be substantial as the old become a larger proportion of the voting public. Here, too, our understanding of the situation is much too slight at present to give us the knowledge we need to plan effectively for this growing population.

Finally, there is the question of genetic engineering: the deliberate controlled alteration of human inheritance. Late in the next couple of decades, either the capability to do so will exist or almost certainly it will become clear that soon thereafter the capability will exist. Indeed, there are already expressions of exuberant optimism, as well as sober concern, about the possibilities this presents. The optimists, typically, are concerned with technological manipulation, pointing out that maybe we could give everybody an IQ of 140 and eliminate all inherited human "inadequacies." The concerned, typically, look at the looming social and ethical issues that arise from such actions. For example, what are the psychological and, therefore, social consequences of producing a generation of adults who, as youngsters, shared little with their parents because their IQs were so much higher? And who is to decide when an inherited "inadequacy" is one that should be eliminated by genetic engineering? Who will decide where the line is to be drawn on the definition of "inadequacy"? Fundamentally, who will make what decisions about which human beings are to be changed before they are born, and in what way? Or, for that matter, who will determine that we will not use the technology with its implicit potentialities for improving the race?

Cybernation—the application of automation to material processes and the application of computers to symbols—is the second technology I want to mention. I shall not dwell on the usual questions about cybernation's impact on employment; they have been discussed amply enough to demonstrate our awareness of the matter as a social impact —even if we are unclear on what the impact is, much less what it will be. (Indeed, I suspect we put so much of our emphasis on the employment effects of cybernation simply because, having some figures and concepts available, it is psychologically more comfortable to emphasize this narrow aspect of the issue than to struggle with the clear evidence of our wider ignorance.) However, two aspects of cybernation's effects on employment should be mentioned here to broaden the picture.

Substantial numbers of the relatively skilled, including the middle-level manager and the middle-level engineer, are going to be displaced; *Business Week, Newsweek,* and *Time,* a little late, acknowledge this.[2] The competences that have made these people economically valuable in the past will increasingly be made obsolete, either because cybernation, particularly computers, can do the job better, or because the process of rationalizing the overall activity in which they were involved will eliminate, or substantially reduce, the need for humans to do the tasks. Here we have members of a career-oriented, affluent segment of society, who were brought up to believe they possessed all the credentials for a lifetime of advancement, now forced to find another job, or to go back to school and learn something new. They are now perpetually under the threat of being displaced by younger men and by more sophisticated machines. Many of these people are already anxious and insecure personalities—as well as substantially in debt. It is likely, then, that they and their families will suffer considerable disruption as they revise their images of themselves: who they are, what they might become, and how others see them. What will happen to these ex-cynosures, to their aspirations, and to their way of living? And what political action will they take in response to the threats to their status and security?

There is another economic and emotional problem that cybernation's impact on employment level and employment changes will pose: What is to be the future of unskilled women in the work force? In the work force, of which one-third are women, about eighty percent are no more than semiskilled; many of them do the clerical and routine service jobs, which cybernation will replace as its application is accelerated by the increasing size of organizations responding to the increasing population. Now, about sixty percent of the $9,000 to $15,000 a year incomes in this country are those of families in which both spouses work. If the unskilled women lose their jobs, there will be less family income, less consumption. And there is also the question of psychic income; many women work for other reasons than to earn money. What will provide this psychic income?

Doubtless, many jobs could be invented, particularly in the human services area, which trained women could fill and which, because of the interpersonal nature of the task, no machine could do. As it now stands, however, and the poverty program demonstrates this, we are neither seriously inventing these jobs nor making the elaborate effort needed to motivate young women so that we can retrain them, and older women, for such jobs. It is likely that this problem will be upon us before techniques for job-producing, motivating, recruiting, and training are sufficiently developed, in which case there will be serious social consequences. But if we do develop such techniques, society will become significantly different from today's, because the roles of so many women will be so different from what they traditionally have been.

This leads me to the third technology: social engineering. I yield to no one in my reservations about the ability of the behavioral sciences to deal with complex issues at the present time, but the evidence to date indicates that this situation will very likely change dramatically in the next two decades. The combination of large research funds and the computer provides the social scientist with both the incentive and the technique to do two things he has always needed to do and never been able to do in order to develop a deep understanding of and technology for the manipulation of social processes.

On the one hand, the computer provides the means for combining in complex models as many variables as the social scientist wants in order to simulate the behavior of men and institutions. In the past, the behavioral scientist simply could not deal with all the many important variables that would help him understand and predict human behavior. Now he can. (This is not to say that everything that is important about the human condition can be so formulated, but much that is important can be put in these terms—almost certainly enough to bring about substantial improvements in our ability to understand and predict behavior). And then the social scientist can test these models against conditions representing "real life." For, on the other hand, the computer has a unique capacity for collecting and processing enormous amounts of data about the state of individuals and of society today—not that of ten years ago. Thus, the behavioral scientist not only can know the state of society *now* as represented by these data, but he can use them to test and refine his theoretical models. The convergence of government programs and the computer is of critical importance; it will result in an efflorescence of longitudinal studies of individual and institutional change as functions of the changes in the social and physical environment. Such knowledge, now essentially nonexistent, will inevitably increase our ability to effect social change. And given the convergence of the powerful technologies and our already enormously complex and huge society, it would seem that social manipulation will be necessary if we are to introduce appropriate changes in society at the appropriate times. The problem, of course, is: Who is to decide who is to be manipulated and for what ends?

Let me now turn to some general questions regarding the social impact of technology—questions that to some extent refer to circumstances already with us, and which seem to me to be greatly in need of serious and extensive study. Let me hasten to add that I am certain that in many cases we do not at present know how to study these problems, but if we do not start now to try to invent means for doing so, we shall be in a far worse position when the time comes for us to understand these issues better. Again, the time-lag problem bedevils us.

What happens to the sense of self in a world of giant and pervasive man-made events, especially when, at the same time, we insist on emphasizing the autonomy of the individual? We talk about the importance of the individual and of the wealth of options this world offers him. Yet we have surrounded him with pollution, radiation, megalopolis, etc., which, though man-made, may appear to many people to be of such power and scale as to dominate them like "acts of God." How does a man see himself in relation to his espoused ideal of individual autonomy when he also sees other *men* and man-made circumstances, as awesome and implacable and often as impersonal as "acts of God," framing his destiny?

What kind of personalities live most fully in the midst of multiple and simultaneous change? Daniel Bell has pointed out that we are experiencing the end of the rational vision, that events today (and more so tomorrow) do not have simple cause-and-effect sequences, that, instead, events all happen at once and in circular and probabilistic ways.[3] What kind of person can live meaningfully in that type of world, and can keep in touch with it?

I suspect three kinds of responses will have increasing social implications as technology alters the scale of events that define the individual to himself—and thereby the ways in which he responds to the world.

One response is that of "selective involvement." People pick the issues and things they are going to respond to and be responsible about, and ignore the rest. We know people do this now, deliberately or, more often, unconsciously: there are limits to the amount of information humans can process in a given amount of time.

Therefore, it behooves us to examine carefully the degree of validity, as measured by actual behavior, of the statement that a benefit of technology will be to increase the number of options and alternatives the individual can choose from. In principle, it could; in fact, the individual may use any number of psychological devices to avoid the discomfort of information overload, and thereby keep the range of alternatives to which he responds much narrower than that which technology in principle makes available to him.

Another type of response, now evident among returned Peace Corps volunteers, college students, and some executives, is withdrawal — pulling out of the big system, looking for environments in which one can have face-to-face relationships in a simple, less technologized more direct world.

A third response, protest, is exemplified by such things as the urban race riots and the Berkeley demonstrations. Here, the individual responds to overwhelming complexity by sidestepping the legal or ethical constraints that sustain or are at least associated with the complexity. (It is worth noting that a battle cry in the Berkeley protests was "Put your body where your punch card is!" It was one of the chief reasons for the sit-in in Sproul Hall). I suspect that these attempts, these experiments, to simplify an increasingly complex world will have very important social consequences, produced, in part, by a proliferating technology. If these responses are important in the future, we need to know much more about them, at least as responses to technology, than we do now.

Another way to look at the implications of technology for the individual is to consider the roles he plays. Two examples typify the unanswered and, for the most part, unstudied, questions in this area. The psychiatrist Robert Rieff has suggested that to the extent that tomorrow's society is service-oriented (material productivity becoming increasingly cybernated), many men will play roles which traditionally, in our society, have been women's roles, i.e., person-to-person helping roles. What, then, happens to the image and conduct of men? What happens to the relation between the sexes, as the hard-won pattern of women competing with men for "male" jobs is reversed and men begin to compete with women for "female" jobs?

A second role implication: as society puts more and more emphasis on rationalization, logic, science, and technology, and as our educational system reflects this emphasis from the lower grades on, what will be the role of the mother—the female—in preserving the ineffable, the intuitive, and the aesthetic in the basic learning experiences of the young? This, traditionally, has been what we expect of women, but traditionally we have deprecated those contributions, at least out of one side of our mouth. Will we come to appreciate this contribution more? Will we insist that women fulfill this role more effectively, or will we further deprecate its utility in a society oriented toward technology? And what effect will our choice have on our way of life and on societal goals?

The opportunities and problems that increased leisure—resulting from the increased productivity of the new technologies—provides, to help individuals find themselves or to extend the means by which they lose themselves, have been commented on extensively and, to my mind, unimaginatively and unperceptively. I will not explore the issue here. A couple of observations, however, are in order.

An increasing number of theologians and religious denominations are becoming concerned with this problem. Their theologies assert that it is through work that man gains his salvation and fulfills himself. If work is to be a much less significant part of life for more people, what are the revisions in theology and the revisions in religious bureaucracies required to cope with this? On the other hand, the Protestant ethic, in its original form, may not be as pervasive as we have surmised, or at least its modes of implementation may be changing. Instead of leisure being a reward for hard work, we "travel first and pay later"—which may mean, of course, that work is now a "punishment" for taking the leisure first. Or, of course, it may mean that many people no longer need the justification of work in order to comfortably enjoy a vacation.

We can assume that leisure should have meaning in addition to that associated with recreation and hobbies, as is now taught. But it is hard to see how the state of mind required for this is to be conveyed to young people in an educational system stressing efficiency, and by adults who themselves are products of the Protestant ethic. Tranquility, contemplation, loafing, the cultivation of self, require a different school and different teachers. Just how real or serious would be the variety of social consequences implicit in these observations remains to be seen. Again we have not studied and again we have not tried to lay out the implications in a sufficiently elaborate social and technological context.

What *is* to be the relationship between the churches and an increasingly rationalized and technologized society? In a society preoccupied with dealing with the average, with the mass of the population, with grandiose schemes for remaking man and his environment (often accompanied by an arrogance indistinguishable from *hubris*), will it be the role of the churches to insist on another set of values for judging the direction and purpose of man, in order to protect the ideal of the individual and the validity of extralogical and transcendent motives and experiences? Here, indeed, a profound confrontation between two cultures *may* occur or, perhaps, one may absorb the other. Whatever the case may be, the consequences of the new technologies for the churches are bound to be great.

Consider the changing role of the scientist and the scientist-engineer. The symbiosis between science and technology has, as we all know, evolved into big science and big technology, and these two, in turn, are dependent on big money, which inevitably means big politics. The result, as a Report of the Committee on Science in the Promotion of Human Welfare of the American Association for the Advancement of Science argues, is that the integrity of science has been eroded and that in the absence of procedures (which have not been invented, much less implemented) the erosion of the integrity of science will very likely increase in the future.[4] In part, this is because in the future still bigger technological investments in science and engineering will be needed. Hence, still more funds will have to be raised, and political methods will have to be used still more often to mediate between the needs of technology, the other needs of society, and the needs of competing groups within the science and engineering communities. Inevitably, there will be persistent, very likely increasing, confusion between the political and rhetorical validity and utility of scientific knowledge and its inherent scientific validity and utility. For not only will scientists and engineers turn to politics to get the technology they want in the first place, but they will use politics to praise, apologize for, or criticize the social consequences of that technology when they happen.

[The] combination of esoteric knowledge and political power alters the function and character of the scientific elites. They no longer merely advise on the basis of expert knowledge, but they are also the champions of policies promoted with unrivaled authority and frequently determined by virtue of it. In the eyes of both of the political authorites and the public at large, the scientific elites appear as the guardians of the *arcana imperii*, the secret remedies for public ills.

As the nature and importance of scientific knowledge transform the nature and functions of the scientific elites, the availability of democratic control becomes extinguished. Scientific knowledge is by its very nature esoteric knowledge; since it is inaccessible to the public at large, it is bound to be secret. The public finds itself in the same position vis-à-vis scientific advice as do the political authorities: unable to retrace the arguments underlying the scientific advice, it must take that advice on faith.[5]

The growing potency of social engineering will become a crucial ethical issue for the behavioral scientist. Whether he is working for the government, for business, for Madison Avenue, for the CIA, for the Poverty Program, or is doing basic research, the results of his work are going to be used to "guide," "stimulate," "motivate," and "manipulate" society. Again, it is the potency of the technology, its capacity to do wonderful good or monstrous evil, that will make the situation in the future different from the past.

This ethical problem: whether to assist in the growth of social engineering, is going to become ever more serious as the potency of social engineering increases. And right now we have no ethical or scientific models for dealing with this problem. One example of this dilemma: The Job Corps trainees will have very elaborate computerized reports prepared about them, to cover their whole social and psychological background, their experience in the Job Corps, and what happens to them for several years after they have left the Job Corps. The reason for these records is a very good one—they will improve the selection and training techniques. However, such a record also means that the Job Corps trainee will no longer have a private life: once recorded, his life history will always be available in this form. The dilemma that faces the social scientist is that on the one hand he needs this kind of information to improve the Job Corps, and that, on the other hand, so much personal information made available to as yet unspecified people, may completely undermine the conventional privilege and social advantages of privacy.

Underlying these issues is the profoundly important one: What are the implications, for the form and conduct of democratic political processes, of the complex social issues that technology generates and of the esoteric methods technology provides, for dealing with these complex issues? The increasing complexity of social problems and of the techniques for dealing with them will mean that the average well-educated person—to say nothing of the man in the street—will no longer be able to understand what the issues and the alternatives are.

This will be partly a matter of the complexity of the issues and of the technologies for defining, interpreting, planning for, and then dealing with, them. It will be partly a matter of the partial availability of knowledge. Often the issues will be politically sensitive and, as now, the interested parties will release only what they wish to release. Moreover, laymen able to use the knowledge, if they did have it, would need reasoning abilities which most people now lack. They would have to understand that the world picture is in most critical cases a statistical one, not black or white. These laymen would have to be comfortable dealing with multivariable problems operating in multiple feedback processes, where cause and effect are inextricably intermixed, and where it is often meaningless to try to differentiate one from the other. And they would have to be comfortable with making judgments based on a much longer time perspective than most people are used to now. They would have to be able to think ahead ten and twenty years, and make their judgments accordingly. These are not characteristics we are going to find in large numbers in our population: our educational system simply does not mass-produce such people—and evidently will not do so for some years to come. But if we are to operate a democracy, the need for such reasoning abilities will be upon us sooner than that. Indeed, it is already upon us. The political scientist and pundit, Joseph Kraft, recently observed:

> To apply common sense to what is visible on the surface is to be almost always wrong; it produces about as good an idea of how the world goes around as that afforded by the Ptolemaic system. A true grasp of even the slightest transaction requires special knowledge and the ability to use abstractions which, like the Copernican system, are at odds with common-sense impressions. Without this kind of knowledge, it is difficult to know what to think about even such prominent matters as the United Nations financing problem, or the bombing of North Vietnam, or the farm program, or the federal budget—which is one reason that most people don't know what they think about these questions. The simple fact is that the stuff of public life eludes the grasp of the ordinary man. Events have become professionalized.[6]

Moreover, the problems, whether they be urban renewal, air pollution, education for the new age, Medicare, international development programs, the exploitation of the oceans, assigning technology development priorities, etc., will be too complicated to be dealt with effectively by the techniques that have characterized our society to date. And the issues will be too critical, the potentials for and scale of disaster too great to stake our social survival upon conventional approaches—even when they are undertaken (as they rarely are) with the best of disinterested goodwill. All we have to do is to look at the looming disaster our cities represent, to recognize that we are going to have to do much better.

The tasks we face, then, will require the full use of whatever rationalized techniques we have, and these techniques will proliferate in the years ahead with advances in the social sciences, with increasing use of computers, data banks, simulation, system analyses, operations research, and so on.

In consequence, planners and decision makers will be confronted with a set of circumstances that will also suggest important changes in the democratic process. The competing demands for human and physical resources, necessarily expended over long periods of time, will require the development of ways to assign priorities and to revise costly efforts, even if it is politically uncomfortable and institutionally disruptive. At present we have neither the priority scheme nor the means for efficiently and reliably transcending conventional and institutional restraints. Yet, obviously, we will have to be able to choose between major technological and social developments, and we will have to be able to maintain or alter these decisions more in the light of their real accomplishments, rather than in the light of political commitments. Furthermore, because of the massive needs of the society, there will be a tendency to respond to average human and social requirements, rather than to the needs of the individual qua individual. This tendency will be exacerbated by the inherent characteristics of technologies, of systems analysis, and of operations research and computer simulation. The pressures to value those things most about the society that can be described and dealt with in terms of the techniques available, and the pressures to deal with the massive needs of the society will make it especially difficult for the policy maker and decision maker to preserve a sensitivity for and responsibility toward the idea of the idiosyncratic and extrarational needs of the individual.

If, then, we are to preserve the ideal of the cherished individual, we will need wise men more than we will need technically skilled men, though obviously we will need the technically skilled men too. As it is, we do not know how to produce wise men, and we do not know how to provide them with an environment that will encourage their wisdom to blossom and act. Yet without wise men, the chances are that the democratic concept and the Judeo-Christian tradition built around the obligations and rights of the individual will be lost under the crush of the vast needs of the society and the enormous potency of the technologies put into operation in a massive society to meet those needs. How shall we prepare for and invent the new forms of democracy and the new roles to be played by citizen and leader in such a system?

Above, I implied the need for the ability to change institutions rapidly. This, too, is a consequence of the impact of technologies on society, for through their efforts technologies make the mandates of institutions, and the validity of the operating styles within the mandates obsolete. Yet institutions persist and change only slowly and usually reluctantly—barring some kind of disaster. Some observers have pointed out the potentialities for society if we apply our technologies. They then bemoan the apathy of the public and the ineffectualness of institutions because they do not take advantage of the technologies. The usual interpretation of this state of affairs is that we lack "leadership." But this is a naive solution and a premature definition of the problem. The question really is how to change institutions so that leadership arises in a given situation and then acts. Here our formal knowledge, limited as it is, makes it clear that this is an extremely difficult condition to deal with expeditiously.

As institutions produce and use the new technologies, they inevitably will have to change at a rate concomitant with the changes produced in the society by the very technologies they have encouraged and applied. But getting institutions or, rather, the people in them, to shift their perspectives radically as technology radically alters reality; getting the members of institutions to risk statuses, self-images, empires, in order to prepare for future needs, is an enormously difficult task, usually only successfully accomplished after a major institutional disaster has occurred. Over the years we can expect that the social sciences will provide us with more knowledge about how to make these changes quickly (or perhaps provide us with an understanding of why, if we want to preserve a humanitarian set of values, institutions cannot be changed quickly). But even if we assume the former, there are still many years ahead in which institutions will lag behind in their ability to respond to the real environment as it is altered by technologies, and this lag will become increasingly dangerous. What we do now and in the long run about this impact of technology is a matter that I believe deserves intensive attention.

Perhaps we might do well to spend some significant portion of our professional time stockpiling solutions to social problems, which we cannot hope to get into our social system now, but which we can reasonably expect to apply if some of these problems back up on us to the point where we cannot cope with them within the present social format. It is after disasters that institutions can most easily be changed.

Let me close with some comments on the special social impact on scholars or action-oriented professionals of the very *question* of the social impact of technology. One direct effect of the new technologies is to challenge deeply the adequacy of our academic disciplines for dealing with the kind of world they are producing. We sit here and talk learnedly about economic and social processes—rates of change, institutional process, etc., — but my impression is that few of our disciplines or techniques are now really adequate. Even in the well-studied area of productivity and technological change we cannot be sanguine about our methods. As Solomon Fabricant recently said,

> The problem of measurement has not yet been solved . . . There are competing and widely differing measurements of technological change . . . I'm afraid that people talk about both the past and the future . . . with more confidence than is warranted by the available knowledge about technological change.[7]

In the few cases where our techniques are adequate, they are not being used broadly or intensively enough to deal with the multiple issues that must be understood if we are going to secure the advantages these new technologies possess.

If my impression is accurate, we face some very uncomfortable questions, which, as scholars and professionals, we are morally bound to wrestle with far more than we have until now. What about our research techniques? What must we do—and what must we abandon of what we now take status and comfort in — to get methods that adequately tackle the issues? We must find out what we should really be studying, even if it means breaking down cherished disciplinary barriers and repudiating the importance of the issues we have studied up to now. Over the next few decades many of our techniques are likely to become much more adequate, but what is our role until then? It seems to me that we belong to one of the institutions of society whose members and operating styles need to be shaken up quickly—we need to have our awareness of reality enlarged and refined and revised if we are to make our contribution in good conscience and with significant effect.

One might decide, of course, that even with all these conflicts and changes and even without the participation of the scholars, some kind

of accommodation will be worked out. Probably so, but there is the
possibility that the accommodation will be one we will not like. And
there is also the possibility that there will be no accommodation.
Certainly ours would not be the first society that disappeared because
it could not find a way to accommodate in time to changes generated
within it by its own momentum and style.

FOOTNOTES

1 "The End of Free Fall," p. 21. Mimeographed article (Fall, 1964).

2 "Computers: How They're Remaking Companies," *Business Week* (Feb.
29, 1964); "The Challenge of Automation," *Newsweek* (Jan. 25, 1965);
"The Cybernated Generation," *Time* (April 2, 1965).

3 Daniel Bell, "The Post-Industrial Society," in *Technology and Social
Change,* ed. by Eli Ginzberg (New York: Columbia University Press, 1964),
pp. 58-59.

4 *The Integrity of Science* (Washington, D.C., American Association for
the Advancement of Science, 1964).

5 Hans J. Morgenthau, "Modern Science and Political Power," *Columbia
Law Review,* CLIV (1964), 1402.

6 "The Politics of the Washington Press Corps," *Harper's Magazine* (June,
1965), pp. 101-2.

7 *Measurement of Technological Change* (Washington, D.C., Manpower
Administration, U.S. Department of Labor, 1965), p. 3.

DEHUMANIZATION: A COMPOSITE PSYCHOLOGICAL DEFENSE IN RELATION TO MODERN WAR

VIOLA W. BERNARD
PERRY OTTENBERG
FRITZ REDL

We conceive of dehumanization as a particular type of psychic defense mechanism and consider its increasing prevalence to be a social consequence of the nuclear age. By this growth it contributes, we believe, to heightening the risks of nuclear extermination.

Dehumanization as a defense against painful or overwhelming emotions entails a decrease in a person's sense of his own individuality and in his perception of the humaneness of other people. The misperceiving of others ranges from viewing them *en bloc* as "subhuman" or "bad human" (a long-familiar component of group prejudice) to viewing them as "nonhuman," as though they were inanimate items or "dispensable supplies." As such, their maltreatment or even their destruction may be carried out or acquiesced in with relative freedom from the restraints of conscience or feelings of brotherhood.

In our view, dehumanization is not a wholly new mental mechanism, but rather a composite psychological defense which draws selectively on other well-known defenses, including unconscious denial, repression, depersonalization, isolation of affect, and compartmentalization (the elimination of meaning by disconnecting related mental elements and walling them off from each other). Recourse to dehumanization as a defense against stresses of inner conflict and external threat is especially favored by impersonal aspects of modern social organization, along with such special technological features of nuclear weapons as their unprecedented destructive power and the distance between push button and victim.

We recognize that many adaptive, as well as maladaptive,[1] uses of self-protective dehumanization are requisite in multiple areas of con-

Reprinted by permission of the editor and the publisher from V. Bernard, P. Ottenberg, and F. Redl, in *Behavioral Science and Human Survival*, M. Schwebel (Ed.) Science and Behavior Books, Inc., Palo Alto, California, 1965.

temporary life. As a maladaptive defense in relation to war, however, the freedom from fear which it achieves by apathy or blindness to implications of the threat of nuclear warfare itself increases the actuality of that threat: the masking of its true urgency inactivates motive power for an all-out effort to devise creative alternatives for resolving international conflict. Dehumanization also facilitates the tolerating of mass destruction through bypassing those psychic inhibitions against the taking of human life that have become part of civilized man. Such inhibitions cannot be called into play when those who are to be destroyed have been divested of their humanness. The magnitudes of annihilation that may be perpetrated with indifference would seem to transcend those carried out in hatred and anger. This was demonstrated by the impersonal, mechanized efficiency of extermination at the Nazi death camps.

The complex psychological phenomenon which we call dehumanization includes two distinct but interrelated series of processes: *self-directed dehumanization* relates to self-image, and denotes the diminution of an individual's sense of his own humanness; *object-directed dehumanization* refers to his perceiving others as lacking in those attributes that are considered to be most human. Despite the differences between these two in their origins and intrapsychic relationships within over-all personality development and psychodynamic functioning, both forms of dehumanization, compounded from parts of other defenses, become usable by the individual for emotional self-protection. These two forms of dehumanization are mutually reinforcing: reduction in the fullness of one's feelings for other human beings, whatever the reason for this, impoverishes one's sense of self; any lessening of the humanness of one's self-image limits one's capacity for relating to others.

It seems to us that the extensive increase of dehumanization today is causally linked to aspects of institutional changes in contemporary society and to the transformed nature of modern war. The mushrooming importance in today's world of technology, automation, urbanization, specialization, various forms of bureaucracy, mass media, and the increased influences of nationalistic, totalitarian, and other ideologies have all been widely discussed by many scholars. The net long-term implications of these processes, whether constructive or destructive, are beyond the scope of this paper, and we do not regard ourselves qualified to evaluate them.

We are concerned here, however, with certain of their more immediate effects on people. It would seem that, for a vast portion of the world's population, elements of these broad social changes contribute to feelings of anonymity, impersonality, separation from the decision-making processes, and a fragmented sense of one's integrated social roles, and also to pressure on the individual to constrict his affective range to some machine-like task at hand. Similarly, the average citizen feels powerless indeed with respect to control over fateful decisions about nuclear attack or its aftermath.

The consequent sense of personal unimportance and relative help-lessness, socially and politically, on the part of so many people specifically inclines them to adopt dehumanization as a preferred defense against many kinds of painful, unacceptable, and unbearable feelings referable to their experiences, inclinations, and behavior. *Self-directed dehumanization* empties the individual of human emotions and passions. It is paradoxical that one of its major dynamic purposes is protection against feeling the anxieties, frustrations and conflicts associated with the "cog-in-a-big-machine" self-image into which people feel themselves pushed by socially induced pressures. Thus, it tends to fulfill the very threat that it seeks to prevent.

These pervasive reactions predispose one even more to regard other people or groups as less than human, or even nonhuman. We distinguish among several different types and gradations of *object-directed dehumanization*. Thus, the failure to recognize in others their full complement of human qualities may be either partial or relatively complete. Partial dehumanization includes the misperceiving of members of "out-groups," *en masse*, as subhuman, bad human, or superhuman; as such, it is related to the psychodynamics of group prejudice. It protects the individual from the guilt and shame he would otherwise feel from primitive or antisocial attitudes, impulses, and actions that he directs—or allows others to direct—toward those he manages to perceive in these categories: if they are sub-humans they have not yet reached full human status on the evolutionary ladder and, therefore, do not merit being treated as human: if they are bad humans, their maltreatment is justified, since their defects in human qualities are their own fault. The latter is especially true if they are seen as having superhuman qualities as well, for it is one of the curious paradoxes of prejudice that both superhuman and debased characteristics are ascribed simultaneously to certain groups in order to justify discrimination or aggression against them. The foreigner, for instance, is seen at once as "wicked, untrustworthy, dirty," and "uncanny, powerful, and cunning." Similarly, according to the canons of race prejudice, contradictory qualities of exceptional prowess and extraordinary defect—ascribed to Orientals, Negroes, Jews, or any other group—together make them a menace toward whom customary restraints on behavior do not obtain. The main conscious emotional concomitants of partial dehumanization, as with prejudice, are hostility and fear.

In its more complete form, however, object-directed dehumanization entails a perception of other people as non humans—as statistics, commodities, or interchangeable pieces in a vast "numbers game." Its predominant emotional tone is that of indifference, in contrast to the (sometimes strong) feelings of partial dehumanization, together with a sense of *non-involvement in the actual or foreseeable vicissitudes* of others. Such apathy has crucial psychosocial implications. Among these — perhaps the most important today — is its bearing on how people tolerate the risks of mass destruction by nuclear war.

Although this communication is primarily concerned with the negative and maladaptive aspects of dehumanization, we recognize that it also serves important adaptive purposes in many life situations. In this respect, it resembles other mental mechanisms of defense. Some of the ingredients of dehumanization are required for the effective mastery of many tasks in contemporary society. Thus, in crises such as natural disasters, accidents, or epidemics in which people are injured, sick, or killed, psychic mechanisms are called into play which divest the victims of their human identities, so that feelings of pity, terror, or revulsion can be overcome. Without such selective and transient dehumanization, these emotional reactions would interfere with the efficient and responsible performance of what has to be done, whether it be first aid, surgery, rescue operation, or burial.

Certain occupations in particular require such selectively dehumanized behavior.[2] Examples of these include law enforcement (police, judges, lawyers, prison officials); medicine (physicians, nurses, and ancillary personnel); and, of course, national defense (military leaders, strategists, fighting personnel). Indeed, some degree of adaptive dehumanization seems to be a basic requirement for effective participation in any institutional process. Almost every professional activity has some specific aspect that requires the capacity for appropriate detachment from full emotional responsiveness and the curtailment, at least temporarily, of those everyday human emotional exchanges that are not central to the task at hand, or which might, if present, impede it. The official at the window who stamps the passport may be by nature a warm and friendly man, but in the context of his job the emigrant's hopes or fears lie outside his emotional vision.

Margaret Bourke-White, the noted photographer, was at Buchenwald at the end of World War II as a correspondent. Her account of herself at that time aptly describes the adaptive use of dehumanization, both self-directed and object-directed: "People often ask me how it is possible to photograph such atrocities. . . . I have to work with a veil over my mind. In photographing the murder camps, the protective veil was so tightly drawn that I hardly knew what I had taken until I saw prints of my own photographs. I believe many correspondents worked in the same self-imposed stupor. One has to or it is impossible to stand it." (1)

The only occasions to date on which nuclear bombs have been used in warfare took place when the "baby bombs" were dropped on the civilian populations of Hiroshima and Nagasaki. Lifton (2) has reported on reactions among the Hiroshima survivors, as well as his own, as investigator. His observations are particularly valuable to us since, as a research psychiatrist, he was especially qualified both to elicit and to evaluate psychodynamic data. According to the survivors whom he interviewed, at first one experienced utter horror at the sudden, strange scene of mass deaths, devastation, dreadful burns, and skin stripped from bodies. They could find no words to convey fully these initial feelings. But then each described how, before long, the horror would almost disappear. One would see terrible sights of human beings in extreme agony and yet feel nothing. The load of feeling from empathic responsiveness had become too much to endure; all one could do was to try to survive.

Lifton reports that during the first few such accounts he felt profoundly shocked, shaken, and emotionally spent. These effects gradually lessened, however, so that he became able to experience the interviews as scientific work rather than as repeated occasions of vicarious agony. For both the survivors and the investigator, the "task" provided a focus of concentration and of circumscribed activity as a means of quelling disturbing emotions.

In these instances, the immediate adaptive value of dehumanization as a defense is obvious. It remains open to question, however, whether a further, somewhat related, finding of Lifton's will in the long run prove to be adaptive or maladaptive. He learned that many people in Japan and elsewhere cannot bear to look at pictures of Hiroshima, and even avoid the museum in which they are displayed. There is avoidance and denial of the whole issue which not infrequently leads to hostility toward the A-bomb victims themselves, or toward anyone who expresses concern for these or future victims. May not *this* kind of defense reaction deflect the determination to seek ways of preventing nuclear war?

We believe that the complex mechanism of dehumanization urgently needs to be recognized and studied because its use as a defense has been stepped up so tremendously in recent times, and because of the grave risks it entails as the price for short-term relief. This paper represents only a preliminary delineation, with main attention to its bearing on the nuclear threat.[3]

Many people, by mobilizing this form of ego defense, manage to avoid or to lessen the emotional significance for themselves of today's kind of war. Only a very widespread and deeply rooted defense could ward off the full import of the new reality with which we live: that warfare has been transformed by modern weaponry into something mankind has never experienced before, and that in all-out nuclear war there can be no "victory" for anyone.

The extraordinary complacency with which people manage to shield themselves against fully realizing the threat of nuclear annihilation cannot be adequately explained, we think, by denial and the other well-studied psychological defense mechanisms. This is what has led us to trace out dehumanization as a composite defense, which draws upon a cluster of familiar defenses, magnifying that fraction of each which is most specifically involved with the humanness of one's self-image and the perception of others. It operates against such painful feelings as fear, inadequacy, compassion, revulsion, guilt and shame. As with other mental mechanisms of defense, its self-protective distortions of realistic perceptions occur, for the most part, outside of awareness.

The extent to which dehumanization takes place consciously or unconsciously, although of considerable interest to us, is not relevant enough to this discussion to warrant elaboration. This also holds true for questions about why dehumanization as such has not hitherto received more attention and study in clinical psychiatry.[4] At least one possible reason might be mentioned, however. Most defense mechanisms were not studied originally in relation to such issues as war and peace, national destiny or group survival. Instead, they came under scrutiny, during the course of psychotherapy, as part of the idiosyncratic pathology of individual patients. This could have obscured the recognition of their roles in widespread collective reactions.

In order to avoid confusion we should also mention that the term "dehumanization" as we are using it, refers to a concept that is different from and not connected in meaning with the words "humane" and "humanitarian." "Inhumane" cruelty causes suffering; maladaptive dehumanization, as we point out, may also lead to suffering. Yet even these seemingly similar results are reached by very different routes; to equate them would be a mistake. A surgeon, for example, is treating his patient humanely when, by his dehumanization, he blots out feelings of either sympathy or hostility that might otherwise interfere with his surgical skill during an operation.

No one, of course, could possibly retain his mental health and carry on the business of life if he remained constantly aware of, and emphatically sensitive to, all the misery and injustice that there is in the world. But this very essential of dehumanization, as with other defenses, makes for its greatest danger: that the constructive self-protection it achieves will cross the ever-shifting boundaries of adaptiveness and become destructive, to others as well as to the self. In combination with other social factors already mentioned, the perfection of modern techniques for automated killing on a global scale engenders a marked increase in the incidence of dehumanization. Correspondingly, there is intensified risk that this collective reaction will break through the fragile and elusive dividing line that separates healthy ego-supportive dehumanization from the maladaptive callousness and apathy that prevent people from taking those realistic actions which are within their powers to protect human rights and human lives.

A "vicious cycle" relationship would thus seem to obtain between dehumanization as a subjective phenomenon and its objective consequences. Conscience and empathy, as sources of guilt and compassion, pertain to human beings; they can be evaded if the human element in the victims of aggression is first sufficiently obscured. The aggressor is thereby freed from conscience-linked restraints, with injurious objective effects on other individuals, groups, or nations. The victims in turn respond, subjectively, by resorting even more to self-protective dehumanization, as did the Hiroshima survivors whom Lifton interviewed.

One might argue, and with some cogency, that similar conversion of enemies into pins on a military map has been part of war psychology throughout history, so are we not therefore belaboring the obvious? The answer lies in the fundamental changes, both quantitative and qualitative, that nuclear weapons have made in the meaning of war. In fact, the very term "war," with its pre-atomic connotations, has become something of an outmoded misnomer for the nuclear threat which now confronts us. "Modern war"—before Hiroshima—reflected, as a social institution, many of the social and technological developments which we have already noted as conducive to increased dehumanization. But with the possibility of instantaneously wiping out the world's population—or a very large section of it—the extent of dehumanization as well as its significance for human survival have both been abruptly and tremendously accelerated.

In part, this seems to be due to the overtaxing of our capacity really to comprehend the sudden changes in amplitudes that have become so salient. In addition to the changed factors of *distance, time,* and *magnitude* in modern technology, there is the push-button nature of today's weaponry and the *indirectness* of releasing a rocket barrage upon sites halfway around the world, all of which lie far outside our range of previous experience. When we look out of an airplane window, the earth below becomes a toy, the hills and valleys reduced to abstractions in our mental canvas; but we do not conceive of ourselves as a minute part of some moving speck in the sky—which is how we appear to people on the ground. Yet it is precisely such reciprocal awareness that is required if we are to maintain a balanced view of our actual size and vulnerability. Otherwise, perceptual confusion introduces a mechanistic and impersonal quality into our reactions.

The thinking and feeling of most people have been unable as yet to come to grips with the sheer expansion of numbers and the frightening shrinkage of space which present means of transportation and communication entail. The news of an animal run over by a car, a child stuck in a well, or the preventable death of one individual evokes an outpouring of sympathetic response and upsets the emotional equanimity of many; yet reports of six million Jews killed in Nazi death camps, or of a hundred thousand Japanese killed in Hiroshima and Nagasaki, may cause but moderate uneasiness. Arthur Koestler has put it poignantly, "Statistics don't bleed; it is the detail which counts. We are unable to embrace the total process with our awareness; we can only focus on little lumps of reality." (3)

It is this unique combination of psychosocial and situational factors that seems particularly to favor the adoption of the composite defense we have called "dehumanization"—and this in turn acts to generate more and more of the same. The new aspects of time, space magnitude, speed, automation, distance, and irreversibility are not yet "hooked up" in the psychology of man's relationships to his fellow man or to the world he inhabits. Most people feel poorly equipped, conceptually, to restructure their accustomed picture of the world, all of a sudden, in order to make it fit dimensions so alien to their life-long learning. Anxiety aroused by this threat to one's orientation adds to the inner stress that seeks relief through the defense.

We are confronted with a *lag in our perceptual and intellectual development* so that the enormity of the new reality, with its potential for both destructive and constructive human consequences, becomes blurred in our thinking and feeling. The less elastic our capacity to comprehend meaningfully new significances, the more we cling to dehumanization, unable to challenge its fallacies through knowledge and reason. Correspondingly, the greater our reliance on dehumanization as a mechanism for coping with life, the less readily can the new facts of our existence be integrated into our full psychic functioning, since so many of its vital components, such as empathy, have been shunted aside, stifled, or obscured.

Together, in the writer's opinion, these differently caused but mutually reinforcing cognitive and emotional deficiencies seriously intensify the nuclear risk; latent psychological barriers against the destruction of millions of people remain unmobilized, and hence ineffective, for those who feel detached from the flesh and blood implications of nuclear war. No other mechanism seems to fit so well the requirements of this unprecedented internal and external stress. Dehumanization, with its impairment of our personal involvement, allows us to "play chess with the planets."

Whether it be adaptive or maladaptive, dehumanization brings with it, as we have noted, a temporary feeling of relief, an illusion of problems solved, or at least postponed or evaded. Whatever the ultimate effects of this psychic maneuver on our destiny, however, it would seem to be a wise precaution to try to assess some of its dangerous possibilities.

Several overlapping aspects of maladaptive dehumanization may be outlined briefly and in oversimplified form, as follows:

1. *Increased emotional distance from other human beings.* Under the impact of this defense, one stops identifying with others or seeing them as essentially similar to oneself in basic human qualities. Rela-

tionships to others become stereotyped, rigid, and above all, inexpressive of mutuality. People in "out-groups" are apt to be reacted to *en bloc*; feelings of concern for them have become anesthetized.

George Orwell illustrates this aspect of dehumanization in writing of his experience as a patient (4). His account also serves as an example of the very significant hazard, already mentioned, whereby professionally adaptive uses of this defense (as in medical education and patient care) are in danger of passing that transition point beyond which they become maladaptive and so defeat their original purpose.

> Later in the day the tall, solemn, black-bearded doctor made his rounds, with an intern and a troop of students following at his heels, but there were about sixty of us in the ward and it was evident that he had other wards to attend to as well. There were many beds past which he walked day after day, sometimes followed by imploring cries. On the other hand, if you had some disease with which the students wanted to familiarize themselves you got plenty of attention of a kind. I myself, with an exceptionally fine specimen of a bronchial rattle, sometimes had as many as a dozen students queuing up to listen to my chest. It was a very queer feeling—queer, I mean, because of their intense interest in learning their job, together with a seeming lack of any perception that the patients were human beings. It is strange to relate, but sometimes as some young student stepped forward to take his turn at manipulating you, he would be actually tremulous with excitement, like a boy who has at last got his hands on some expensive piece of machinery. And then ear after ear ... pressed against your back, relays of fingers solemnly but clumsily tapping, and not from any one of them did you get a word of conversation or a look direct in your face. As a non-paying patient, in the uniform nightshirt, you were primarily a *specimen*, a thing I did not resent but could never quite get used to.

2. *Diminished sense of personal responsibility for the consequences of one's actions.* Ordinarily, for most people, the advocacy of or participation in the wholesale slaughter and maiming of their fellow human beings is checked by opposing feelings of guilt, shame, or horror. Immunity from these feelings may be gained, however, by a self-automatizing detachment from a sense of *personal* responsibility for the outcome of such actions, thereby making them easier to carry out. (A dramatic version of the excuse, "I was only carrying out orders," was offered by Eichmann at his trial.)

One "safe" way of dealing with such painful feelings is to focus only on one's fragmented job and ignore its many ramifications. By blocking out the ultimately destructive purpose of a military bombing action, for instance, one's component task therein may become a source of ego-acceptable gratification, as from any successful fulfillment of duty, mastery of a hard problem, or achievement of a dangerous feat. The B-29 airplane that dropped the atomic bomb on Hiroshima was named Enola Gay, after the mother of one of its crew members. This could represent the psychological defense of displacing human qualities from the population to be bombed to the machine.

One of the crew members is reported to have exclaimed: "If people knew what we were doing we could have sold tickets for $100,000!" and another is said to have commented, "Colonel, that was worth the 25¢ ride on the 'Cyclone' at Coney Island." (5) Such reactions, which may on the surface appear to be shockingly cynical, not only illustrate how cynicism may be used to conceal strong emotions (as seems quite likely in this instance); they also suggest how one may try to use cynicism to bolster one's dehumanization when that defense is not itself strong enough, even with its displacement of responsibility and its focusing on one's fragmented job, to overcome the intensity of one's inner "humanized" emotional protest against carrying out an act of such vast destructiveness.

3. *Increasing involvement with procedural problems to the detriment of human needs.* There is an overconcern with details of procedure, with impersonal de-individualized regulations, and with the formal structure of a practice, all of which result in shrinking the ability or willingness to personalize one's actions in the interests of individual human needs or special differences. This is, of course, the particular danger implicit in the trend toward bureaucracy that accompanies organizational units when they grow larger and larger. The task at hand is then apt to take precedence over the human cost: the individual is seen more as a means to an end than as an end in himself. Society, the Corporation, the Five-Year-Plan—these become overriding goals in themselves, and the dehumanized man is turned into a cost item, tool, or energy-factor serving the mass-machine.

Even "scientific" studies of human behavior and development, as well as professional practices based on them, sometimes become dehumanized to a maladaptive extent (6). Such words as "communicate," "adjust," "identify," "relate," "feel," and even "love" can lose their personal meaningfulness when they are used as mere technical devices instead of being applied to specific human beings in specific life situations.[5] In response to the new hugeness of global problems,

patterns of speech have emerged that additionally reflect dehumanized thinking. Segmented-fragmented concepts, such as "fallout problem," "shelter problem," "civil defense," "deterrence," "first strike,"
"pre-emptive attack," "overkill," and some aspects of game theory,
represent a "move-countermove" type of thinking which tends to treat
the potential human victim as a statistic, and to screen out the total
catastrophic effect of the contemplated actions upon human lives. The
content of strategy takes on an importance that is without any relation to its inevitable *results,* the defense of dehumanization having
operated to block out recognition of those awesome consequences that,
if they could be seen, would make the strategy unacceptable. The defense, when successful, narcotizes deeper feelings so that nuclear war,
as "inevitable," may be more dispassionately contemplated and its
tactical permutations assayed. In the course of this, however, almost
automatic counteractions of anxiety are frequently expressed through,
such remarks as: "People have always lived on the brink of disaster,"
"You can't change human nature; there will have to be wars," and
"We all have to die some day."

4. *Inability to oppose dominant group attitudes or pressures.* As the
individual comes to feel more and more alienated and lonely in mass
society, he finds it more and more difficult to place himself in opposition to the huge pressures of the "Organization." Fears of losing occupational security or of attacks on one's integrity, loyalty, or family
are more than most people can bear. Self-directed dehumanization is
resorted to as a defense against such fears and conflicts: by joining the
party, organization, or club, and thus feeling himself to be an inconspicuous particle in some large structure, he may find relief from the
difficult decisions, uncertainties, and pressures of nonconformity. He
may also thereby ward off those feelings of guilt that would arise out
of participating in, or failing to protest against, the injustices and
cruelties perpetrated by those in power. Thus, during the Nazi regime,
many usually kindhearted Germans appear to have silenced their consciences by emphasizing their own insignificance and identifying with
the dehumanized values of the dictatorship. This stance permitted the
detached, even dutiful, disregard of their fellow citizens, which in
turn gave even freer rein to the systematic official conducting of
genocide.

5. *Feelings of personal helplessness and estrangement.* The realization of one's relatively impotent position in a large organization engenders anxiety[6] which dehumanization helps to cover over. The in-

ternalized perception of the self as small, helpless, and insignificant, coupled with an externalized view of "Society" as huge, powerful, and unopposable, is expressed in such frequently heard comments as: "The government has secret information that we don't have"; or, "They know what's right, who am I to question what they are doing?"; or "What's the use? No one will listen to me. . . ."

The belief that the government or the military is either infallible or impregnable provides a tempting refuge because of its renunciation of one's own critical faculties in the name of those of the powerful and all-knowing leader. Such self-directed dehumanization has a strong appeal to the isolated and alienated citizen as a protective cloak to hide from himself his feelings of weakness, ignorance and estrangement. This is particularly relevant to the psychological attraction of certain dangerous social movements. The more inwardly frightened, lonely, helpless, and humiliated people become, the greater the susceptibility of many of them to the seductive, prejudiced promises of demagoguery: the award of spurious superiority and privilege achieved by devaluating the full humanness of some other group— racial, religious, ethnic, or political. Furthermore, as an added advantage of the dehumanization "package," self-enhancing acts of discrimination and persecution against such victim groups can be carried out without tormenting or deterrent feelings of guilt, since these are absorbed by the "rightness" of the demagogic leader.

In recent decades and in many countries, including our own, we have seen what human toll can be taken by this psychosocial configuration. It has entered into Hitlerism, Stalinism, U.S.A. "lynch-mobism." If it is extended to the international arena, against a "dehumanized" enemy instead of an oppressed national minority, atomic weapons will now empower it to inflict immeasurably more human destruction and suffering.

The indifference resulting from that form of dehumanization which causes one to view others as inanimate objects enables one, without conscious malice or selfishness, to write off their misery, injustices, and death as something that "just couldn't be helped." As non-humans, they are not identified with as beings essentially similar to oneself; "their" annihilation by nuclear warfare is thus not "our" concern, despite the reality that distinctions between "they" and "we" have been rendered all the more meaningless by the mutually suicidal nature of total war.

Although this type of dehumanization is relatively complete, in the sense of perceiving others as not at all human, it may occur in an individual with selective incompleteness under certain special conditions only, while his capacity for other emotional ties is preserved. This may prove socially constructive or destructive, depending on the purposes to which it is put. Thus, we have already noted how "pulling a veil" over her mind helped Bourke-White adaptively in her socially positive job of reporting atrocities. But it was compartmentalized dehumanization that also helped many to commit those very atrocities; they were able to exterminate Jews with assembly-line efficiency as the Nazi "final solution" while still retaining access to their genuine feelings of warmth for family members, friends and associates.

These contradictory emotional qualities, often appearing side by side in the same person, are also evidenced—in the opposite direction —by outstanding deeds of heroic rescue by those who, under different circumstances, might well exhibit dehumanized behavior. Almost daily, the newspapers carry stories of exceptional altruism; individuals or whole communities devote their entire energies to the rescue of a single child, an animal, or perhaps (in wartime), a wounded enemy soldier. What accounts for the difference between this kind of response to the plight of others, and that of dehumanized callousness? How are the adaptive humanized processes released?

One research approach might consist of the detailed description and comparative analysis of sample situations of both kinds of these collective reactions, which have such opposite social effects. A case history of community apathy which could be compared in such a study with instances of group altruism already on record, was recently provided by A. M. Rosenthal, an editor of *The New York Times* (7). At first glance, perhaps, his account of dehumanization, involving but one individual and in peacetime, may not seem germane to our discussion about nuclear war. But the macrocosm is reflected in the microcosm. We agree with Mr. Rosenthal that the implications of this episode are linked with certain psychological factors that have helped pave the way for such broad social calamities as Fascism abroad and racial crises in this country, both in the North and South. It does not seem too far-fetched, therefore, to relate them to the nuclear threat as well.

For more than half an hour, one night in March, 1964, thirty-eight respectable, law-abiding citizens in a quiet middle-class neighborhood in New York City watched a killer stalk and stab a young woman in three separate attacks, close to her home. She was no stranger to these onlookers, her neighbors, who knew her as "Kitty." According to Rosenthal, "Twice the sound of their voices and the sudden glow of their bedroom lights interrupted him and frightened him off. Each time he returned, sought her out and stabbed her again. Not one person telephoned the police during the assault; one witness called after the woman was dead." Later, when these thirty-eight neighbors were asked about their baffling failure to phone for help, even though they were safe in their own homes, "the underlying attitude or explanation seemed to be fear of involvement—any kind of involvement." Their fatal apathy gains in significance precisely because, by ordinary standards, these were decent, moral people—husbands and wives attached to each other and good to their children. This is one of the forms of dehumanization that we have described, in which a reaction of massive indifference—not hostility—leads to grievous cruelty, yet all the while, in another compartment of the self, the same individual's capacity for active caring continues, at least for those within his immediate orbit.

Rosenthal describes his own reaction to this episode as a "peculiar paradoxical feeling that there is in the tale of Catherine Genovese a revelation about the human condition so appalling to contemplate that only good can come from forcing oneself to confront the truth. . . . the terrible reality that only under certain situations, and only in response to certain reflexes or certain beliefs, will a man step out of his shell toward his brother. In the back of my mind . . . was the feeling that there was, that there must be some connection between [this story and] the story of the witnesses silent in the face of greater crimes —the degradation of a race, children hungering. . . . It happens from time to time in New York that the life of the city is frozen by an instant of shock. In that instant the people of the city are seized by the paralyzing realization that they are one, that each man is in some way a mirror of every other man. . . . In that instant of shock, the mirror showed quite clearly what was wrong, that the face of mankind was spotted with the disease of apathy—all mankind. But this was too frightening a thought to live with, and soon the beholders began to set boundaries for the illness, to search frantically for causes that were external and to look for the carrier."

As we strive to distinguish more clearly among the complex determinants of adaptive-maladaptive, humanized-dehumanized polarities of behavior, we recognize that stubborn impulses toward individualization are intertwined with the dehumanizing trends on which we have focused. Both humanization and dehumanization are heightened by interpenetrating social and psychological effects of current technological and institutional changes. The progress of the past hundred years has markedly furthered humanization: it has relieved much of human drudgery and strain, and helped to bring about increased leisure and a richer life for a larger part of the world's population. Despite the blurring of personal distinctiveness by excessive bureaucracy, there are now exceptional opportunities, made possible by the same technology that fosters uniformity, for the individual to make rapid contact with, and meaningful contribution to, an almost limitless number of the earth's inhabitants. The same budgets, communication networks, transportation delivery systems, and human organizations that can be used to destroy can also be turned toward the creative fulfillment of great world purposes.

Our situation today favors contradictory attitudes toward how much any individual matters in the scheme of things, both subjectively and from the standpoint of social reality. At one extreme a few individuals in key positions feel—and are generally felt to have—a hugely expanded potential for social impact. Among the vast majority there is, by contrast, an intensified sense of voiceless insignificance in the shaping of events. Objectively, too, there is now among individuals a far greater disparity in their actual power to influence crucial outcomes. More than ever before, the fate of the world depends on the judgment of a handful of heads of state and their advisers, who must make rapid decisions about actions for which there are no precedents. Ideas and events, for better or worse, can have immediate global impact.[7] A push-button can set a holocaust in motion; a transatlantic phone call can prevent one.

In spite of humanizing ingredients in modern life, and the fact that men of good will everywhere are striving ceaselessly toward goals of peace, freedom and human dignity, we nevertheless place primary emphasis, in this paper, on dehumanization because we feel that the dangers inherent in this phenomenon are particularly pervasive, insidious, and relevant to the risk of nuclear war.

From a broad biological perspective, war may be viewed as a form of aggression between members of the same species, Homo sapiens. The distinguished naturalist, Lorenz, has recently pointed out a difference, of great relevance to the relationship between dehumanization and nuclear warfare, in the intraspecies behavior of animals who live in two kinds of groups (8). In the one, the members live together as a crowd of strangers: there are no expressions of mutual aggression, but neither is there any evidence of mutual ties, of relationships of affection, between individuals in the group. On the other hand, some of the fiercest beasts of prey—animals whose bodily weapons are capable of killing their own kind—live in groups in which intense relationships, both *aggressive and affectionate,* exist. Among such animals, says Lorenz, the greater the intraspecies aggression, the stronger the positive mutual attachments as well. These latter develop, through evolution, out of those occasions, such as breeding, when cooperation among these aggressive animals becomes essential to their survival as a species.

Furthermore—and this is of the utmost importance for survival— the greater the capacity for mutual relationships, the stronger and more reliable are the *innate inhibitions* which prevent them from using the species-specific weapons of predatory aggression, fangs, claws or whatever, to maim or kill a member of their own species, no matter how strong the hostile urge of one against another. For example, when two wolves fight, according to Lorenz, the potential victor's fangs are powerfully inhibited at what would be the moment to kill, in response to the other's ritualized signal of immobile exposure to his opponent of his vulnerable jugular.

Man's weapons, by contrast, are not part of his body. They are thus not controllable by reflexes fused into his nervous system; control must depend, instead, on psychological inhibitions (which may also function through social controls of his own devising). These psychic barriers to intraspecies aggression—which can lead to our becoming extinct—are rooted in our affiliative tendencies for cooperation and personal attachment. But these are the very tendencies that, as this paper has stressed, dehumanization can so seriously undermine.

Lorenz speaks of a natural balance within a species—essential to its preservation—between the capacity for killing and inhibition. In that sense, perhaps, man jeopardizes his survival by disturbing, with his invention of nuclear bombs, such a balance as has been maintained throughout his long history of periodic "old-style" wars. Such a dire imbalance would be increased by any shift on the part of the "human animal" toward a society essentially devoid of mutual relationships. For this would vitiate the very tendencies toward emotional involvement and cooperation which are the source of our most reliable inhibitions against "over-killing." Therefore, in terms of the parallels suggested by Lorenz, in order to protect ourselves against the doom of extinction as a species, we must encourage and devise every possible means of safeguarding the "family of man" from becoming an uncaring crowd. Not merely the limiting or halting, but the reversing of maladaptive dehumanization emerges as a key to survival.

What can be done to counteract these dangers? Assuredly, there is no single or ready answer. The development of psychic antidotes of *re*humanization must involve a multiplicity of variables, levels of discourse and sectors of human activity, commensurate in complexity with the factors that make for *de*humanization. Our attempt in this paper to identify this mental mechanism, and to alert others to its significance, its frequency and its inter-relatedness to nuclear risk, represents in itself a preliminary phase of remedial endeavor. For the very process of recognizing a psychosocial problem such as this, by marshaling, reordering and interpreting diverse sets of facts to find new significances in them, is a form of social action, and one that is especially appropriate to behavioral scientists. Beyond this initial posing of the problem, however, any chance of effectively grappling with it will require the converging efforts of those in many different professions and walks of life.

Rehumanization as a mode of neutralizing the dangerous effects that we have stressed should not be misconstrued as aiming at the reestablishment of pre-nuclear age psychology—which would be impossible in any case. We cannot set history back nostalgically to "the good old days" prior to automation and the other changes in contemporary society (nor were the conditions of those earlier days really so "good" for the self-realization of a large portion of the population.) On the contrary, the process of rehumanization means to us a way of assimilating and re-integrating, emotionally and intellectually, the profound new meanings that have been brought into our lives by our own advances, so that a much fuller conviction than ever before of our own humanity and interdependence with all mankind becomes intrinsic to our basic frame of reference.

The imperative for speeding up such a universal process of psychological change is rooted in the new and *specific* necessity to insure survival in the face of the awesome irreversibility of nuclear annihilation. The most essential approaches toward achieving this goal, however, lead us into such *general* and only seemingly unrelated issues as the degree of political freedom and social justice; our patterns of child care and child-rearing; and our philosophy of education, as well as the quality of its implementation. For the process of dehumanization, which eventuates in indifference to the suffering implicit in nuclear warfare, has its beginnings in earlier periods and other areas of the individual's life. It is through these areas that influences conducive to rehumanization must be channeled.

We need to learn more, and to make more effective use of what is already known about how to strengthen people's capacity to tolerate irreducible uncertainty, fear, and frustration without having to take refuge in illusions that cripple their potential for realistic behavior. And we urgently need to find ways of galvanizing our powers of imagination (including ways of weakening the hold of the emotionally-based mechanisms that imprison it).

Imagination and foresight are among the highest functions of the human brain, from the evolutionary standpoint, and also among the most valuable. They enable us to select and extrapolate from previously accumulated experience and knowledge, in order to create guidelines for coping with situations never before experienced, whose nature is so far unknown.

Other kinds of learning ordinarily serve us well in the complicated process of establishing behavior patterns for meeting new life situations. We are able to learn by trial and error, for example, from our firsthand experiences and from successively testing the value of alternative approaches as similar situations arise. Also, we learn much by vicariously living through the reported experiences of others.

Through imagination, however, a completely new situation can be projected in the mind in its sensate and vivid entirety, so that the lessons it contains for us can be learned without the necessity of going through it in real life. This form of "future-directed" learning, which creative imagination makes possible, is therefore uniquely advantageous in dealing with the problematic issues of thermonuclear war; it permits us to arrive at more rational decisions for preventing it without having to pay the gruesome price of undergoing its actuality.

The fact is that the "once-and-for-all" character of full-scale nuclear war renders the methods of "learning through experience"—our own or others'—not only indefensible (in terms of the human cost) but also utterly unfeasible. The empirical privilege of "profiting" from an experience of that nature would have been denied to most if not all of humanity by the finality of the experience itself.

Accordingly, it would seem that whatever can quicken and extend our capacity for imagination, in both the empathic and conceptual spheres, is a vital form of "civil defense." It requires, to begin with, all the pedagogic ingenuity that we can muster to overcome the lag in our intellectual development that keeps us from fully comprehending the new dimensions of our existence. Yet, our endeavors to develop new modes of thinking can be cancelled out by the constricting and impeding effects of dehumanization. The terrible potential of this subtle mechanism to facilitate the depopulating of the earth lies in its circumventing human restraints against fratricide. We are faced, therefore, with the inescapable necessity of devising ways to increase opportunities for meaningful personal relationships and maximum social participation throughout the entire fabric of our society.

NOTES

1 Adaptive and maladaptive refer to a person's modes of coping with internal and external stress. The distinction hinges on the extent to which such coping is successful with respect to the optimal overall balance of the individual's realistic interests and goals.

2 These occupations, therefore, carry the extra risk of their requisite dehumanization becoming maladaptive if it is carried to an extreme or used inappropriately.

3 Because of this primary emphasis, we shall refrain from exploring many important facets of dehumanization which seem less directly relevant to the threat of nuclear warfare. Yet, it permeates so many aspects of modern life that, for clarity in describing it, our discussion must ramify, to some extent, beyond its war-connected context. Still we have purposely neglected areas of great interest to us, especially with regard to psychopathology, psychotherapy, and community psychiatry, which we think warrant fuller discussion elsewhere.

4 No doubt, when the phenomenon is part of a mental disorder, it has been dealt with therapeutically, to some degree, under the names of other defense mechanisms.

5 Within our own discipline this is all too likely to occur when thousands of sick individuals are converted into "cases" in some of our understaffed and oversized mental hospitals. Bureaucratic hospital structure favors impersonal experience. In an enlightening study (6), Merton J. Kahne points up how this accentuation of automatic and formalized milieu propensities thwarts the specific therapeutic need of psychiatric patients for opportunities to improve their sense of involvement with people.

On another occasion we hope to enlarge on how and why maladaptive uses of dehumanization on the part of professionals, officials, and the general public hamper our collective effort as a community to instill more sensitivity to individual need into patterns of congregate care, not only in mental hospitals but also in general hospitals, children's institutions, welfare and correctional facilities, etc.

⁶ This has been particularly well described in novels by Kafka and Camus.

⁷ The news of President Kennedy's assassination circled the earth with unparalleled speed, and evoked a profound worldwide emotional response.

REFERENCES

1. Bourke-White, M., *Portrait of Myself*, New York, Simon and Schuster, 1963.

2. Lifton, R., "Psychological effects of the atomic bomb in Hiroshima; the theme of death," *Daedalus, Journal of the Amer. Acad. of Arts and Sciences*, 462-497, Summer, 1963.

3. Koestler, A. "On disbelieving atrocities," in *The Yogi and the Commissar*, New York, Macmillan, 1945.

4. Orwell, G. "How the poor die," in *Shooting an Elephant*, New York, Harcourt, Brace, 1945.

5. *Yank, the Army Weekly*, New York, Duell, Sloane and Pearce, 1947, p. 282.

6. Kahne, M. J., "Bureaucratic Structure and Impersonal Experience in Mental Hospitals," *Psychiatry*, 22, 4, 363-375, 1959.

7. Rosenthal, A. M., *Thirty-Eight Witnesses*, New York, McGraw-Hill, 1964.

8. Lorenz, K., *Das Sogenannte Böse—Zur Naturgeschichte der Aggression*, Vienna, Dr. G. Borotha-Schoeler Verlag. 1963.

THE SOCIAL WORKER IN THE NUCLEAR AGE

ESTHER W. FIBUSH

For some time the reading public has been confronted by material from various professions and disciplines concerning the meaning of the new world in which we are living today, a world in which our perception and understanding of reality must be adjusted to the revolutionary impact of man's discovery and use of atomic energy. As James R. Newman wrote in his review of *The New World,* the process of "scientific digestion" has far outstripped that of "social digestion."[1] The implications of this new world are vast and as yet relatively undefined, but we are already threatened by the possibility that man's newly acquired power to destroy all of mankind will overtake us before we have learned to use this same power to benefit mankind.

That social workers are aware of this problem is affirmed by the resolutions passed by the 1958 Delegate Assembly of the National Association of Social Workers on disarmament and the peaceful uses of atomic energy, and by the Assembly's 1960 statement recommending a study of issues and appropriate action.[2] The question of survival is thus recognized by social workers as a subject suitable for consideration, but it has not yet been taken out of the pigeonhole of social action and brought into the entire professional arena of social work. It remains a matter vulnerable to the label of "controversial issue" rather than a matter for professional scientific exploration by social workers. It is seen as a question to be studied by experts in many other fields, however—by authorities on theories of deterrence, problems of disarmament, political and economic issues, diplomacy and world affairs, or by experts in social psychology, mass communication media, and education.

Judging from the social work literature over the last few years, the professional significance of the problem to the field of social work as a whole is not sufficiently appreciated. A notable exception is Brock Chisholm's paper on the deliberations on the future of Hull House.[3] Dr. Chisholm not only defined the problem—that for the first time

Reprinted from *Social Work,* Vol. 8, No. 1 (January, 1963), pp. 3-8, by permission of the National Association of Social Workers, Inc. and the author.

in history the survival of the human race itself is at stake—but placed it squarely within the field of social work as a professional question relevant to all other professional questions. The issue of human survival was seen as relevant to considerations of community organization, programs for individual and group welfare, and research studies and demonstration projects, and these professional activities were viewed as having their own contribution to make to the issue of human survival.

Increasing public recognition of the need for research on and study of this question is indicated not only by formation of the Arms Control and Disarmament Agency by the government, but also by the growing number of seminars, study groups, and working conferences, and by the establishment of organizations for the purpose of conducting research on peace and related matters—the Center for the Study of Conflict Resolution at the University of Michigan, the Committee on Research in International Conflict at Washington University in St. Louis, the Peace Research Institute in Washington, D.C., the Carnegie Endowment for International Peace and the Institute for International Order in New York, and a number of other groups and organizations, large and small.[4]

Since many of these organizations study psychological and social factors as well as political and economic, and as they are undoubtedly aware of the value of a multi-disciplinary approach, it seems likely that the services of professional social workers are, or certainly should be, involved. Needless to say, so great and overriding a problem will inevitably demand a more multi-dimensional approach, but this does not rule out the possibility and the obligation of individual contribution by social workers and their agencies or by the social work profession as such.

INTEGRATING CONCEPTS

It seems imperative, in any case, that social workers become cognizant of the relevance of the issue of survival to the personal problems of their clients, the relevance of the individual problems of clients to the larger, total issue of human survival, and the two-way relevance of many other public issues as well. Social workers, whatever their special area of practice, are constantly and necessarily engaged in enabling clients to perceive and to cope with reality. In order to do so appropriately in a nuclear age in which once realistic attitudes and actions are now useless or dangerous, it is necessary for the social worker to face the prospect of modifying his own conception of reality.

With regard to a question as universal as that of the survival of the human race, an effort must be made to think in terms of many frames of reference—not only the psychological and the sociological, the anthropological and the biological, the political and the economic, but in terms also of historical events and of the current events of the day. It is obvious that the social worker cannot be equally expert in all these fields, but he must be cognizant of their significance to his client's world and to his own if he is to make a contribution to the solution of the problem of human survival. A scientific approach to any significant social problem of our time requires, not complete mastery of every field, but the ability to select and use appropriately materials, concepts, and methods from more than one discipline.[5]

Such an approach does not imply a replacement of old concepts by new, or of concepts from one frame of reference by those from another, but rather an integration of compatible and complementary concepts.[6] Too often the trend in social work seems to be toward replacement of one set of concepts by another, with social workers "following the leader" this way and that, without a sufficiently selective and comprehensive approach. What the social worker needs is a "multi-dimensional understanding of man-in-society"[7] and the ability to incorporate this into his professional perspective on current reality.

It is not necessary for the profession to change its nature in order to cope with the problems of a nuclear world. On the contrary, what is needed is an application of the traditional role of social work to present questions. This role has always represented an effort to promote understanding of and dealing with problems that arise from a multitude of factors, from inner psychobiological dynamics and outer sociopolitical-economic forces, from individual pathology and group pathology. In the absence of an adequate theoretical structure for incorporating all the various frames of reference and the various sources of data into one organic whole, it is the professional awareness of the social worker that operates as the evaluating and integrating instrument.[8] "What the instrumentation technique is to the physicist, the cultivation of favorable human points of vantage is for most social scientists."[9]

A Scientific and Humanitarian Endeavor

Traditionally, the social worker has been in an unusually favorable point of vantage with regard to human problems, and needs only to continue to capitalize on this position. One of the advantages of the social work profession is that it is both a scientific endeavor and a humanitarian one. The scientific base for social work has been spelled out many times, and though there may be differences within the profession on aspects of theory and practice, there can no longer be any question of the professional commitment to a scientific approach.

Scientific thinking is an elaborated manifestation of the secondary process, and in its most extreme instances, when it moves from abstractions to equations, scientific thinking becomes remote from the reality of the living human being.[10] In part, the fact that nuclear energy has become more a threat than a boon to mankind is due to this alienation of science from the individual human life. But while science may be alien from the reality of human beings in some of its manifestations, the scientist need not be. Lasswell suggests that Freud's use of the noncommittal role was not only a conscious therapeutic strategy (and, it should be added, a deliberately chosen method of scientific inquiry) but also an expression of the high value he placed on human dignity.[11]

Social work, with its humanitarian tradition, is advantageously placed to demonstrate that scientific procedure does not have to produce alienation from human reality—that within the person of the scientific practitioner it is possible to maintain an attitude of scientific objectivity in gathering and evaluation of data without sacrificing a concern for human needs. An objective pursuit of facts in a nonjudgmental fashion, as practiced in social casework, is itself a scientific approach to the solution of human problems and the meeting of human needs.

Recognizing Bias

In the social sciences (and indeed in all science) it would seem desirable that the practitioner be explicitly aware of the assumptions and implications of his work and its "moral and political meaning for the society in which he works and for his role within that society."[12] That one cannot assume that such awareness is always achieved is indicated by the attention given to the problem of bias and the effort to designate its existence, if it cannot be eliminated, in all social science projects of professional stature. The social worker must also give attention to the problem of bias if he is to qualify as the scientific practitioner he professes to be.

The self-awareness that social work has painstakingly developed out of its close association with psychoanalytic concepts has made it possible for the practitioner to promote in his own way the goal of neutrality set up by Freud. By careful attention to transference and countertransference factors, by constantly searching for and working to eliminate emotional blindspots within himself, and by subjecting his practice to the critical review of colleagues and experts from related disciplines, the social worker has not arrived at absolute objectivity but has provided himself with a device whereby subjectivity can be brought to consciousness and thus made amenable to control.

This self-corrective mechanism needs to be extended beyond the realm of psychodynamics, however, and applied to the many other frames of reference with which the social worker must deal. In an age when the survival of the human race is at stake, the social worker cannot afford to act unthinkingly on a socioeconomic bias, for instance, as the standard bearer for "middle-class values." Such procedure need not be criticized only for its denial of client self-determination (though certainly it should be criticized on that score) but also for the unscientific nature of the practice involved.[13]

Even when practice is not itself dominated by a promotion of some value system other than that which the client himself chooses (when treatment has restored to him the capacity for making a rational choice), it needs to be scrutinized from the standpoint of focus. Bias can be acted out as much by the selection of problems to explore and treat as by the effort to impose cultural or psychological "norms" on clients. When practice is limited to therapy of individual psychopathology without sufficient regard for the multitude of environmental factors involved, this is a bias that may be readily recognized. When practice devotes itself to some of the important environmental factors (for instance, the family constellation and interaction) without sufficient regard for others (such as the socioeconomic or political reality within which the family lives), bias may not be recognized so automatically.

When the practitioner's identification with one set of sociological or cultural values, with one or another of the multiplicity of institutions within our social structure, goes unrecognized, the social worker may well fall into the error of acting out bias of which he is unaware. Such errors may eventually be corrected as the profession grows toward a more comprehensive professional insight, but they are a luxury that social work can ill afford to perpetuate at the present time. Mankind's continuing dialogue concerning conflicting goals and relative values and the ways and means of achieving them can only continue if the human race continues. It would seem, therefore, that the value of human survival becomes the "bias" on which consideration of other values depends; it is from this bias that all prior and subsequent questions herein are being raised.

RE-EVALUATING REALITY

From this standpoint, the social worker has the obligation of examining his current conception of reality and determining where it requires revision in light of current facts. This needs to be done on the levels of local, national, and international affairs and with some knowledge of facts from all the social sciences, demanding especially a contact with modern formulations of economic and political problems and some understanding of the implications of historical and current events. For instance, instead of resting comfortably in a conventional, ambiguous concept of "the free society," leading thinkers of our day are grappling with the question of how to define a free society and how to achieve it in the face of a corporate economy such as that of the United States today.[14]

Having found that a free society is not an accomplished fact requiring only further reforms and extension of existing benefits, but something to be redefined in modern terms and worked toward in new ways, political scientists are re-evaluating past policies and theories in the light of current world realities. Such explorations into the nuclear age are not reassuring. "The spectacle of the contemporary world—genuinely apprehended—is enough to reduce the mind to black terror; the reason of man seems a poor counterpoise."[15]

It would be pleasant to dismiss the task of re-evaluating reality in terms of a nuclear age and to confine oneself to local problems and to the psychopathology of individual clients. Even here, however, the social worker is insufficiently informed without some knowledge of developments beyond the boundaries of his own nation. Perhaps he can still hope to understand the problems of Negro clients simply from the standpoint of local or national conditions, and from their own individual psychodynamics, but he will not for long be able to ignore the growing impact of the emerging African nations on Negroes who are still struggling to emerge here.

CLINICAL DATA AS AN INFORMATION SOURCE

These are but a few examples of the ways in which the social worker may need to broaden his horizon and correct his perspective on reality. Great as the task may be, it is relatively simple and well defined, and requires only as much effort as the social worker already devotes to keeping up with the literature in his own field. The more difficult task, but the one whereby social work may hope to make its best contribution, is the task of bringing to bear on the problems of the modern world that which can be learned from the problems of individual clients. This is not only a task for researchers and theoreticians, but also for practitioners. As Hartmann has pointed out, theoretical concepts from both sociology and psychology must be checked by actual clinical data, being as specific as possible as to both aspects.[16] Clinical data from case records have long been recognized as potentially a rich source of information, but thus far insufficient use has been made of this material.[17]

One can only speculate at this point as to what can be learned from clinical data that might be of value to an understanding of the problem of human survival. One occasionally encounters clients with neurotic of even psychotic expressions of "cold war anxiety." Conceivably, the sorting out of the reality from the pathology in such cases might be not only a therapeutic procedure but also one that would suggest some hypotheses as to the etiology and dynamics of reactions experienced in less gross a form by members of the general population. Instances of superficial "pseudo-concern" might be discovered to be related to concepts of status, role, or self-image—and/or to an hysterical or compulsive character structure. Rational concern might prove to be but one aspect of an ego structure capable of accurate appraisal of other aspects of reality—and/or may equate with educational or socioeconomic factors.

Competent observers have commented on the prevalence of "atomic incredulity," the inability of individuals in all walks of life to incorporate into their view of things the revolutionary impact of the nuclear threat.[18] Unconcern or apathy may be found associated in some clients with submissiveness and passivity, or with defense mechanisms of intellectualization, rationalization, and isolation, and/or an overexposure to mass communication media. Brock Chisholm's speculations might be confirmed clinically by evidence of individual manifestations of regression in the face of the nuclear threat. Or the use of inhibition and denial of the threat might be found to be part of a massive use of repression within the personality as a whole. Perhaps evidence will indicate that "cold war" anxiety, repressed from direct awareness, is invading other areas of a personality. Such a diverting of anxiety into other channels might be discoverable among the "acting out" adolescents who are brought to social agencies for treatment.

The effect of economic pressures or of politically frustrating circumstances would need to be considered. A study of case material in this regard might provide a valuable body of information related to socioeconomic-political concepts. Lasswell's theory of political activity as a tension-reducing mechanism, Hutchins' faith in man as a political animal, and Grotjahn's feeling that the clue to the future will be found within the dynamics of the family might all be evaluated further in the light of actual clinical data. Erikson's study of Martin Luther demonstrates the possibility of integrating psychodynamic and historical material, suggesting that the practitioner might similarly be able to find connections between the emotional trends of individual clients and public trends of the day.[19]

This is not to suggest that social workers set up practice deliberately to pursue such theoretical considerations, but rather to alert them to the possible significance of clinical data encountered in daily practice. Planned research might then be designed to explore further the various hypotheses supported by such material.

It seems clear, at any rate, that there is hope that social workers can derive from their experience with their clients something to contribute toward an understanding of the problems of the new world in which they live, and thus, perhaps, to the continued existence of mankind in a nuclear age. "Since war has outlived its time, we must find a way to live together; if we don't, the time for study and for worry is over with fatal definiteness."[20] There is both consolation and challenge in the thought that there may yet be time for social workers to study, and if they have not thus far embarked on the process of study, it is perhaps high time that they begin at least to worry.

NOTES

1 James R. Newman, review of Richard G. Hewleu and Oscar E. Anderson, Jr., *The New World, 1939/1946* (University Park: Pennsylvania State University Press) in *Scientific American*, Vol. 207, No. 2 (August 1962), pp. 141-142.

2 "Goals of Public Social Policy: Recommended Changes," *NASW News*, Vol. 7, No. 4 (August 1962), p. 34.

3 "What Private Effort Can Do in the Field of Mental Health," *Social Service Review*, Vol. 36, No. 2 (June 1962), pp. 175-184.

4 Donald N. Michael, "Basic Research For Peace," *The Nation*, Vol. 195, No. 5 (September 1, 1962), p. 84.

5 C. Wright Mills, *The Sociological Imagination* (New York: Oxford University Press, 1959), p. 142.

6 Ernest Van Den Haag, "Psychoanalysis and the Social Sciences: Genuine and Spurious Integration," in *Psychoanalysis and Social Science*, Hendrik M. Ruitenbeek, ed. (New York: E. P. Dutton & Co., 1962), p. 168.

7 Morton I. Teicher, "Man in Society," *Social Casework*, Vol. 40, No. 8 (October 1959), p. 444.

8 *See* Talcott Parsons, "Psychoanalysis and the Social Structure," and Heinz Hartmann, "The Application of Psychoanalytic Concepts to Social Science," both reprinted from *Psychoanalytic Quarterly*, Vol. 19, No. 3 (1950), in Ruitenbeek, *op. cit.*, pp. 46-72.

9 Harold D. Lasswell, *Psychopathology and Politics* (New York: The Viking Press, 1960), p. 202.

10 John R. Seeley, "Psychoanalysis: Model for Social Science," in Ruitenbeek, *op. cit.*, p. 105.

11 "Impact of Psychoanalytic Thinking on the Social Sciences," in Ruitenbeek, *op. cit.*, p. 23.

12 Mills, *op. cit.*, p. 77.

13 Alvin L. Schorr, "The Trend to Rx," *Social Work*, Vol. 7, No. 1 (January 1962), pp. 59-66.

14 *See* A. A. Berle, Jr., *Economic Power and the Free Society;* W. H. Ferry, *The Corporation and the Economy;* and Robert M. Hutchins and Joseph P. Lyford, *The Political Animal* (all published by the Center for the Study of Democratic Institutions, Santa Barbara, Calif., 1957, 1959, 1962, respectively).

15 Edmund Stillman and William Pfaff, *The New Politics: America and the End of the Postwar World* (New York: Coward McCann, 1961), p. 142.

16 In Ruitenbeek, *op. cit.*, p. 72.

17 In large measure, case records have not been used because they have not been set up in ways that make them easily available and readily usable

for research purposes. Here in itself is a task especially appropriate for the practicing social worker and his agency.

[18] Stillman and Pfaff, *op. cit.*, p. 132.

[19] Erik H. Erikson, *Young Man Luther: A Study in Psychoanalysis and History* (New York: W. W. Norton & Co., 1958).

[20] Martin Grotjahn, *Psychoanalysis and the Family Neurosis* (New York: W. W. Norton & Co., 1960), p. 135.

SOME ISSUES CONCERNING THE CONTROL OF HUMAN BEHAVIOR: A SYMPOSIUM

CARL R. ROGERS
B. F. SKINNER

I—Skinner

Science is steadily increasing our power to influence, change, mold—in a word, control—human behavior. It has extended our "understanding" (whatever that may be) so that we deal more successfully with people in nonscientific ways, but it has also identified conditions or variables which can be used to predict and control behavior in a new, and increasingly rigorous, technology. The broad disciplines of government and economics offer examples of this, but there is special cogency in those contributions of anthropology, sociology, and psychology which deal with individual behavior. Carl Rogers has listed some of the achievements to date in a recent paper (1956). Those of his examples which show or imply the control of the single organism are primarily due, as we should expect, to psychology. It is the experimental study of behavior which carries us beyond awkward or inaccessible "principles," "factors," and so on, to variables which can be directly manipulated.

It is also, and for more or less the same reasons, the conception of human behavior emerging from an experimental analysis which most directly challenges traditional views. Psychologists themselves often do not seem to be aware of how far they have moved in this direction. But the change is not passing unnoticed by others. Until only recently it was customary to deny the possibility of a rigorous science of human behavior by arguing, either that a lawful science was impossible because man was a free agent, or that merely statistical predictions would always leave room for personal freedom. But those who used to take this line have become most vociferous in expressing their alarm at the way these obstacles are being surmounted.

Reprinted by permission of the authors and publisher from *Science*, Vol. 124, (November 30, 1956), pp. 1057-1066.

Now, the control of human behavior has always been unpopular. Any undisguised effort to control usually arouses emotional reactions. We hesitate to admit, even to ourselves, that we are engaged in control, and we may refuse to control, even when this would be helpful, for fear of criticism. Those who have explicitly avowed an interest in control have been roughly treated by history. Machiavelli is the great prototype. As Macaulay said of him, "Out of his surname they coined an epithet for a knave and out of his Christian name a synonym for the devil." There were obvious reasons. The control that Machiavelli analyzed and recommended, like most political control, used techniques that were aversive to the controllee. The threats and punishments of the bully, like those of the government operating on the same plan, are not designed—whatever their success—to endear themselves to those who are controlled. Even when the techniques themselves are not aversive, control is usually exercised for the selfish purposes of the controller and, hence, has indirectly punishing effects upon others.

Man's natural inclination to revolt against selfish control has been exploited to good purpose in what we call the philosophy and literature of democracy. The doctrine of the rights of man has been effective in arousing individuals to concerted action against governmental and religious tyranny. The literature which has had this effect has greatly extended the number of terms in our language which express reactions to the control of men. But the ubiquity and ease of expression of this attitude spells trouble for any science which may give birth to a powerful technology of behavior. Intelligent men and women, dominated by the humanistic philosophy of the past two centuries, cannot view with equanimity what Andrew Hacker has called "the specter of predictable man" (1954). Even the statistical or actuarial prediction of human events, such as the number of fatalities to be expected on a holiday weekend, strikes many people as uncanny and evil, while the prediction and control of individual behavior is regarded as little less than the work of the devil. I am not so much concerned here with the political or economic consequences for psychology, although research following certain channels may well suffer harmful effects. We ourselves, as intelligent men and women, and as exponents of Western thought, share these attitudes. They have already interfered with the free exercise of a scientific analysis, and their influence threatens to assume more serious proportions.

Three broad areas of human behavior supply good examples. The first of these—*personal control*—may be taken to include person-to-person relationships in the family, among friends, in social and work groups, and in counseling and psychotherapy. Other fields are *education* and *government*. A few examples from each will show how nonscientific preconceptions are affecting our current thinking about human behavior.

Personal Control. People living together in groups come to control one another with a technique which is not inappropriately called "ethical." When an individual behaves in a fashion acceptable to the group, he receives admiration, approval, affection, and many other reinforcements which increase the likelihood that he will continue to behave in that fashion. When his behavior is not acceptable, he is criticized, censured, blamed, or otherwise punished. In the first case the group calls him "good"; in the second, "bad." This practice is so thoroughly ingrained in our culture that we often fail to see that it is a technique of control. Yet we are almost always engaged in such control, even though the reinforcements and punishments are often subtle.

The practice of admiration is an important part of a culture, because behavior which is otherwise inclined to be weak can be set up and maintained with its help. The individual is especially likely to be praised, admired, or loved when he acts for the group in the face of great danger, for example, or sacrifices himself or his possessions, or submits to prolonged hardship, or suffers martyrdom. These actions are not admirable in any absolute sense, but they require admiration if they are to be strong. Similarly, we admire people who behave in original or exceptional ways, not because such behavior is itself admirable, but because we do not know how to encourage original or exceptional behavior in any other way. The group acclaims independent, unaided behavior in part because it is easier to reinforce than to help.

As long as this technique of control is misunderstood, we cannot judge correctly an environment in which there is less need for heroism, hardship, or independent action. We are likely to argue that such an environment is itself less admirable or produces less admirable people. In the old days, for example, young scholars often lived in undesirable quarters, ate unappetizing or inadequate food, performed unprofitable tasks for a living or to pay for necessary books and materials or publication. Older scholars and other members of the group offered compensating reinforcement in the form of approval and admiration for these sacrifices. When the modern graduate student receives a generous scholarship, enjoys good living conditions, and has his research and publication subsidized, the grounds for evaluation seem to be pulled from under us. Such a student no longer *needs* admiration to carry him over a series of obstacles (no matter how much he may need it for other reasons), and, in missing certain familiar objects of admiration, we are likely to conclude that such *conditions* are less admirable. Obstacles to scholarly work may serve as a useful measure of motivation—and we may go wrong unless some substitute is found —but we can scarcely defend a deliberate harassment of the student for this purpose. The productivity of any set of conditions can be evaluated only when we have freed ourselves of the attitudes which have been generated in us as members of an ethical group.

A similar difficulty arises from our use of punishment in the form of censure or blame. The concept of responsibility and the related control using punishment. Was so-and-so aware of the probable con- control using punishment. Was So-and-So aware of the probable consequences of his action, and was the action deliberate? If so, we are justified in punishing him. But what does this mean? It appears to be a question concerning the efficacy of the contingent relations between behavior and punishing consequences. We punish behavior because it is objectionable to us or the group, but in a minor refinement of rather recent origin we have come to withhold punishment when it cannot be expected to have any effect. If the objectionable consequences of an act were accidental and not likely to occur again, there is no point in punishing. We say that the individual was not "aware of the consequences of his action" or that the consequences were not "intentional." If the action could not have been avoided—if the individual "had no choice"—punishment is also withheld, as it is if the individual is incapable of being changed by punishment because he is of "unsound mind." In all these cases—different as they are—the individual is held "not responsible" and goes unpunished.

Just as we say that it is "not fair" to punish a man for something he could not help doing, so we call it "unfair" when one is rewarded beyond his due or for something he could not help doing. In other words, we also object to wasting *reinforcers* where they are not needed or will do no good. We make the same point with the words *just* and *right*. Thus we have no right to punish the irresponsible, and a man has no right to reinforcers he does not earn or deserve. But concepts of choice, responsibility, justice, and so on, provide a most inadequate analysis of efficient reinforcing and punishing contingencies because they carry a heavy semantic cargo of a quite different sort, which obscures any attempt to clarify controlling practices or to improve techniques. In particular, they fail to prepare us for techniques based on other than aversive techniques of control. Most people would object to forcing prisoners to serve as subjects of dangerous medical experiments, but few object when they are induced to serve by the offer of return privileges—even when the reinforcing effect of these privileges has been created by forcible deprivation. In the traditional scheme the right to refuse guarantees the individual against coercion or an unfair bargain. But to what extent *can* a prisoner refuse under such circumstances?

We need not go so far afield to make the point. We can observe our own attitude toward personal freedom in the way we resent any interference with what we want to do. Suppose we want to buy a car of a particular sort. Then we may object, for example, if our wife urges us to buy a less expensive model and to put the difference into a new refrigerator. Or we may resent it if our neighbor questions our need for such a car or our ability to pay for it. We would certainly resent it if it were illegal to buy such a car (remember Prohibition); and if we find we cannot actually afford it, we may resent governmental control of the price through tariffs and taxes. We resent it if we discover that we cannot get the car because the manufacturer is holding the model in deliberately short supply in order to push a model we do not want. In all this we assert our democratic right to buy the car of our choice. We are well prepared to do so and to resent any restriction on our freedom.

But why do we not ask *why* it is the car of our choice and resent the forces which made it so? Perhaps our favorite toy as a child was a car, of a very different model, but nevertheless bearing the name of the car we now want. Perhaps our favorite TV program is sponsored by the manufacturer of that car. Perhaps we have seen pictures of many beautiful or prestigeful persons driving it—in pleasant or glamorous places. Perhaps the car has been designed with respect to our motivational patterns: the device on the hood is a phallic symbol; or the horsepower has been stepped up to please our competitive spirit in enabling us to pass other cars swiftly (or, as the advertisements say, "safely"). The concept of freedom that has emerged as part of the cultural practice of our group makes little or no provision for recognizing or dealing with these kinds of control. Concepts like "responsibility" and "rights" are scarcely applicable. We are prepared to deal with coercive measures, but we have no traditional recourse with respect to other measures which in the long run (and especially with the help of science) may be much more powerful and dangerous.

Education. The techniques of education were once frankly aversive. The teacher was usually older and stronger than his pupils and was able to "make them learn." This meant that they were not actually taught but were surrounded by a threatening world from which they could escape only by learning. Usually they were left to their own resources in discovering how to do so. Claude Coleman has published a grimly amusing reminder of these older practices (1953). He tells of a schoolteacher who published a careful account of his services during 51 years of teaching, during which he administered: ". . . 911,527 blows with a cane; 124,010 with a rod; 20,989 with a ruler; 136,715 with the hand; 10,295 over the mouth; 7,905 boxes on the ear; [and] 1,115,800 slaps on the head. . . ."

Progressive education was a humanitarian effort to substitute positive reinforcement for such aversive measures, but in the search for useful human values in the classroom it has never fully replaced the variables it abandoned. Viewed as a branch of behavioral technology, education remains relatively inefficient. We supplement it, and rationalize it, by admiring the pupil who learns *for himself;* and we often attribute the learning process, or knowledge itself, to something *inside* the individual. We admire behavior which seems to have inner sources. Thus we admire one who *recites* a poem more than one who simply *reads* it. We admire one who *knows* the answer more than one who *knows where to look it up.* We admire the *writer* rather than the *reader.* We admire the arithmetician who can do a problem in his head rather than with a slide rule or calculating machine, or in "original" ways rather than by a strict application of rules. In general we feel that any aid or "crutch"—except those aids to which we are now thoroughly accustomed — reduces the credit due. In Plato's *Phaedrus,* Thamus, the king, attacks the invention of the alphabet on similar grounds! He is afraid "it will produce forgetfulness in the minds of those who learn to use it, because they will not practice their memories. . . ." In other words, he holds it more admirable to remember than to use a memorandum. He also objects that pupils "will read many things without instruction . . . [and] will therefore seem to know many things when they are for the most part ignorant." In the same vein we are today sometimes contemptuous of book learning, but, as educators, we can scarcely afford to adopt this view without reservation.

By admiring the student for knowledge and blaming him for ignorance, we escape some of the responsibility of teaching him. We resist any analysis of the educational process which threatens the notion of inner wisdom or questions the contention that the fault of ignorance lies with the student. More powerful techniques which bring about the same changes in behavior by manipulating *external* variables are decried as brainwashing or thought control. We are quite unprepared to judge *effective* educational measures. As long as only a few pupils learn much of what is taught, we do not worry about uniformity or regimentation. We do not fear the feeble technique; but we should view with dismay a system under which every student learned everything listed in a syllabus—although such a condition is far from unthinkable. Similarly, we do not fear a system which is so defective that the student must *work* for an education; but we are loath to give credit for anything learned without effort— although this could well be taken as an ideal result—and we flatly refuse to give credit if the student already knows what a school teaches.

A world in which people are wise and good without trying, without "having to be," without "choosing to be," could conceivably be a far better world for everyone. In such a world we should not have to "give anyone credit"—we should not need to admire anyone—for being wise and good. From our present point of view we cannot believe that such a world would be admirable. We do not even permit ourselves to imagine what it would be like.

Government. Government has always been the special field of aversive control. The state is frequently defined in terms of the power to punish, and jurisprudence leans heavily upon the associated notion of personal responsibility. Yet it is becoming increasingly difficult to reconcile current practice and theory with these earlier views. In criminology, for example, there is a strong tendency to drop the notion of responsibility in favor of some such alternative as capacity or controllability. But no matter how strongly the facts, or even practical expedience, support such a change, it is difficult to make the change in a legal system designed on a different plan. When governments resort to other techniques (for example, positive reinforcement), the concept of responsibility is no longer relevant and the theory of government is no longer applicable.

The conflict is illustrated by two decisions of the Supreme Court in the 1930's which dealt with, and disagreed on, the definition of control or coercion (Freund, *et al.*, 1954, p. 233). The Agricultural Adjustment Act proposed that the Secretary of Agriculture make "rental or benefit payments" to those farmers who agreed to reduce production. The government agreed that the Act would be unconstitutional if the farmer had been *compelled* to reduce production but was not, since he was merely *invited* to do so. Justice Roberts expressed the contrary majority view of the court that "The power to confer or withhold unlimited benefits is the power to coerce or destroy." This recognition of positive reinforcement was withdrawn a few years later in another case in which Justice Cardozo (Freund, *et al.*, 1954, p. 244) wrote "To hold that motive or temptation is equivalent to coercion is to plunge the law in endless difficulties." We may agree with him, without implying that the proposition is therefore wrong. Sooner or later the law must be prepared to deal with all possible techniques of governmental control.

The uneasiness with which we view government (in the broadest possible sense) when it does not use punishment is shown by the reception of my utopian novel, *Walden Two* (Skinner, 1948b). This was essentially a proposal to apply a behavioral technology to the construction of a workable, effective, and productive pattern of government. It was greeted with wrathful violence. *Life* magazine called it "a travesty on the good life," and "a menace . . . a triumph of mortmain or the dead hand not envisaged since the days of Sparta . . . a slur upon the name, a corruption of an impulse." Joseph Wood Krutch devoted a substantial part of his book, *The Measure of Man* (1954), to attacking my views and those of the protagonist, Frazier, in the same vein, and Morris Viteles has recently criticized the book in a similar manner in *Science* (1955). Perhaps the reaction is best expressed in a quotation from *The Quest for Utopia* by Negley and Patrick (1952):

> "Halfway through this contemporary utopia, the reader may feel sure, as we did, that this is a beautifully ironic satire on what has been called 'behavioral engineering.' The longer one stays in this better world of the psychologist, however, the plainer it becomes that the inspiration is not satiric, but messianic. This is indeed the behaviorally engineered society,

and while it was to be expected that sooner or later the principle of psychological conditioning would be made the basis of a serious construc-tion of utopia—Brown anticipated it in *Limanora*—yet not even the effective satire of Huxley is adequate preparation for the shocking horror of the idea when positively presented. Of all the dictatorships espoused by utopists, this is the most profound, and incipient dictators might well find in this utopia a guidebook of political practice."

One would scarcely guess that the authors are talking about a world in which there is food, clothing, and shelter for all, where everyone chooses his own work and works on the average only 4 hours a day, where music and the arts flourish, where personal relationships de-velop under the most favorable circumstances, where education pre-pares every child for the social and intellectual life which lies before him, where—in short—people are truly happy, secure, productive, creative, and forward-looking. What is wrong with it? Only one thing: someone "planned it that way." If these critics had come upon a society in some remote corner of the world which boasted similar advantages, they would undoubtedly have hailed it as providing a pattern we all might well follow—provided that it was clearly the result of a natural process of cultural evolution. Any evidence that intelligence had been used in arriving at this version of the good life would, in their eyes, be a serious flaw. No matter if the planner of *Walden Two* diverts none of the proceeds of the community to his own use, no matter if he has no current control or is, indeed, unknown to most of the other members of the community (he planned that, too), somewhere back of it all he occupies the position of prime mover. And this, to the child of the democratic tradition, spoils it all.

The dangers inherent in the control of human behavior are very real. The possibility of the misuse of scientific knowledge must always be faced. We cannot escape by denying the power of a science of behavior or arresting its development. It is no help to cling to familiar philosophies of human behavior simply because they are more reas-suring. As I have pointed out elsewhere (Skinner, 1955), the new techniques emerging from a science of behavior must be subject to the explicit countercontrol which has already been applied to earlier and cruder forms. Brute force and deception, for example, are now fairly generally suppressed by ethical practices and by explicit gov-ernmental and religious agencies. A similar countercontrol of scien-tific knowledge in the interests of the group is a feasible and promising possibility. Although we cannot say how devious the course of its evolution may be, a cultural pattern of control and countercontrol will presumably emerge which will be most widely supported because it is most widely reinforcing.

If we cannot foresee all the details of this (as we obviously cannot), it is important to remember that this is true of the critics of science as well. The dire consequences of new techniques of control, the hidden menace in original cultural designs—these need some proof. It is only another example of my present point that the need for proof is so often overlooked. Man has got himself into some pretty fixes, and it is easy to believe that he will do so again. But there is a more optimistic possibility. The slow growth of the method of science, now for the first time being applied to human affairs, *may* mean a new and exciting phase of human life to which historical analogies will not apply and in which earlier political slogans will not be appropriate. If we are to use the knowledge that a science of behavior is now making available with any hope of success, we must look at human nature as it is brought into focus through the methods of science rather than as it has been presented to us in a series of historical accidents.

If the advent of a powerful science of behavior causes trouble, it will not be because science itself is inimical to human welfare but because older conceptions have not yielded easily or gracefully. We expect resistance to new techniques of control from those who have heavy investments in the old, but we have no reason to help them preserve a series of principles that are not ends in themselves but rather outmoded means to an end. What is needed is a new conception of human behavior which is compatible with the implications of a scientific analysis. All men control and are controlled. The question of government in the broadest possible sense is not how freedom is to be preserved but what kinds of control are to be used and to what ends. Control must be analyzed and considered in its proper proportions. No one, I am sure, wishes to develop new master-slave relationships or bend the will of the people to despotic rulers in new ways. These are patterns of control appropriate to a world without science. They may well be the first to go when the experimental analysis of behavior comes into its own in the design of cultural practices.

II—ROGERS

There are, I believe, a number of matters in connection with this important topic on which the authors of this article, and probably a large majority of psychologists, are in agreement. These matters then are not issues as far as we are concerned, and I should like to mention them briefly in order to put them to one side.

Points of Agreement. I am sure we agree that men—as individuals and as societies—have always endeavored to understand, predict, influence, and control human behavior—their own behavior and that of others.

I believe we agree that the behavioral sciences are making and will continue to make increasingly rapid progress in the understanding of behavior, and that as a consequence the capacity to predict and to control behavior is developing with equal rapidity.

I believe we agree that to deny these advances, or to claim that man's behavior cannot be a field of science, is unrealistic. Even though this is not an issue for us, we should recognize that many intelligent men still hold strongly to the view that the actions of men are free in some sense such that scientific knowledge of man's behavior is impossible. Thus Reinhold Niebuhr, the noted theologian, heaps scorn on the concept of psychology as a science of man's behavior and even says, "In any event, no scientific investigation of past behavior can become the basis of predictions of future behavior." (1955, p. 47). So, while this is not an issue for psychologists, we should at least notice in passing that it is an issue for many people.

I believe we are in agreement that the tremendous potential power of a science which permits the prediction and control of behavior may be misused, and that the possibility of such misuse constitutes a serious threat.

Consequently Skinner and I are in agreement that the whole question of the scientific control of human behavior is a matter with which psychologists and the general public should concern themselves. As Robert Oppenheimer told the American Psychological Association last year (1956a) the problems that psychologists will pose for society by their growing ability to control behavior will be much more grave than the problems posed by the ability of physicists to control the reactions of matter. I am not sure whether psychologists generally recognize this. My impression is that by and large they hold a laissez-faire attitude. Obviously Skinner and I do not hold this laissez-faire view, or we would not have written this article.

Points of Issue. With these several points of basic and important agreement, are there then any issues that remain on which there are differences? I believe there are. They can be stated very briefly: Who will be controlled? Who will exercise control? What type of control will be exercised? Most important of all, toward what end or what purpose, or in the pursuit of what value, will control be exercised?

It is on questions of this sort that there exist ambiguities, misunderstandings, and probably deep differences. These differences exist among psychologists, among members of the general public in this country, and among various world cultures. Without any hope of achieving a final resolution of these questions, we can, I believe, put these issues in clearer form.

Some Meanings. To avoid ambiguity and faulty communication, I would like to clarify the meanings of some of the terms we are using.

Behavioral science is a term that might be defined from several angles but in the context of this discussion it refers primarily to knowledge that the existence of certain describable conditions in the human being and/or in his environment is followed by certain describable consequences in his actions.

Prediction means the prior identification of behaviors which then occur. Because it is important in some things I wish to say later, I would point out that one may predict a highly specific behavior, such as an eye blink, or one may predict a class of behaviors. One might correctly predict "avoidant behavior," for example, without being able to specify whether the individual will run away or simply close his eyes.

The word *control* is a very slippery one, which can be used with any one of several meanings. I would like to specify three that seem most important for our present purposes. *Control* may mean: (i) The setting of conditions by B for A, A having no voice in the matter, such that certain predictable behaviors then occur in A. I refer to this as external control. (ii) The setting of conditions by B for A, A giving some degree of consent to these conditions, such that certain predictable behaviors then occur in A. I refer to this as the influence of B on A. (iii) The setting of conditions by A such that certain predictable behaviors then occur in himself. I refer to this as internal control. It will be noted that Skinner lumps together the first two meanings, external control and influence, under the concept of control. I find this confusing.

Usual Concept of Control of Human Behavior. With the underbrush thus cleared away (I hope), let us review very briefly the various elements that are involved in the usual concept of the control of human behavior as mediated by the behavioral sciences. I am drawing here on the previous writings of Skinner, on his present statements, on the writings of others who have considered in either friendly or antagonistic fashion the meanings that would be involved in such control. I have not excluded the science fiction writers, as reported recently by Vandenberg (1956), since they often show an awareness of the issues involved, even though the methods described are as yet fictional. These then are the elements that seem common to these different concepts of the application of science to human behavior.

(1) There must first be some sort of decision about goals. Usually desirable goals are assumed, but sometimes, as in George Orwell's book *1984,* the goal that is selected is an aggrandizement of individual power with which most of us would disagree. In a recent paper Skinner suggests that one possible set of goals to be assigned to the behavioral technology is this: "Let men be happy, informed, skillful, well-behaved and productive." (1955-1956) In the first draft of his part of this article, which he was kind enough to show me, he did not mention such definite goals as these, but desired "improved" educational practices, "wiser" use of knowledge in government, and the like. In the final version of his article he avoids even these value-laden terms, and his implicit goal is the very general one that scientific control of behavior is desirable, because it would perhaps bring "a far better world for everyone."

Thus the first step in thinking about the control of human behavior is the choice of goals, whether specific or general. It is necessary to come to terms in some way with the issue, "For what purpose?"

(2) A second element is that, whether the end selected is highly specific or is a very general one such as wanting "a better world," we proceed by the methods of science to discover the means to these ends. We continue through further experimentation and investigation to discover more effective means. The method of science is self-correcting in thus arriving at increasingly effective ways of achieving the purpose we have in mind.

(3) The third aspect of such control is that as the conditions or methods are discovered by which to reach the goal, some person or some group establishes these conditions and uses these methods, having in one way or another obtained the power to do so.

(4) The fourth element is the exposure of individuals to the prescribed conditions, and this leads, with a high degree of probability, to behavior which is in line with the goals desired. Individuals are now happy, if that has been the goal, or well-behaved, or submissive, or whatever it has been decided to make them.

(5) The fifth element is that if the process I have described is put in motion then there is a continuing social organization which will continue to produce the types of behavior that have been valued.

Some Flaws. Are there any flaws in this way of viewing the control of human behavior? I believe there are. In fact the only element in this description with which I find myself in agreement is the second. It seems to me quite incontrovertibly true that the scientific method is an excellent way to discover the means by which to achieve our goals. Beyond that, I feel many sharp differences, which I will try to spell out.

I believe that in Skinner's presentation here and in his previous writings, there is a serious underestimation of the problem of power. To hope that the power which is being made available by the behavioral sciences will be exercised by the scientists, or by a benevolent group, seems to me a hope little supported by either recent or distant history. It seems far more likely that behavioral scientists, holding their present attitudes, will be in the position of the German rocket scientists specializing in guided missiles. First they worked devotedly for Hitler to destroy the U.S.S.R. and the United States. Now, depending on who captured them, they work devotedly for the U.S.S.R. in the interest of destroying the United States, or devotedly for the United States in the interest of destroying the U.S.S.R. If behavioral scientists are concerned solely with advancing their science, it seems most probable that they will serve the purposes of whatever individual or group has the power.

But the major flaw I see in this review of what is involved in the scientific control of human behavior is the denial, misunderstanding, or gross underestimation of the place of ends, goals or values in their relationship to science. This error (as it seems to me) has so many implications that I would like to devote some space to it.

Ends and Values in Relation to Science. In sharp contradiction to some views that have been advanced, I would like to propose a two-pronged thesis: (i) In any scientific endeavor—whether "pure" or applied science—there is a prior subjective choice of the purpose or value which that scientific work is perceived as serving. (ii) This subjective value choice which brings that scientific endeavor into being must always lie outside of that endeavor and can never become a part of the science involved in that endeavor.

Let me illustrate the first point from Skinner himself. It is clear that in his earlier writing (1955-1956) it is recognized that a prior value choice is necessary, and it is specified as the goal that men are to become happy, well-behaved, productive, and so on. I am pleased that Skinner has retreated from the goals he then chose, because to me they seem to be stultifying values. I can only feel that he was choosing these goals for others, not for himself. I would hate to see Skinner become "well-behaved," as that term would be defined for him by behavioral scientists. His recent article in the *American Psychologist* (1956) shows that he certainly does not want to be "productive" as that value is defined by most psychologists. And the most awful fate I can imagine for him would be to have him constantly "happy." It is the fact that he is very unhappy about many things which makes me prize him.

In the first draft of his part of this article, he also included such prior value choices, saying for example, "We must decide how we are to use the knowledge which a science of human behavior is now making available." Now he has dropped all mention of such choices, and if I understand him correctly, he believes that science can proceed without them. He has suggested this view in another recent paper, stating that "We must continue to experiment in cultural design . . . testing the consequences as we go. Eventually the practices which make for the greatest biological and psychological strength of the group will presumably survive" (Skinner, 1955, p. 549).

I would point out, however, that to choose to experiment is a value choice. Even to move in the direction of perfectly random experimentation is a value choice. To test the consequences of an experiment is possible only if we have first made a subjective choice of a criterion value. And implicit in his statement is a valuing of biological and psychological strength. So even when trying to avoid such choice, it seems inescapable that a prior subjective value choice is necessary for any scientific endeavor, or for any application of scientific knowledge.

I wish to make clear that I am not saying that values cannot be included as a subject of science. It is not true that science deals only with certain classes of "facts" and that these classes do not include values. It is a bit more complex than that, as a simple illustration or two may make clear.

If I value knowledge of the "three R's" as a goal of education, the methods of science can give me increasingly accurate information on how this goal may be achieved. If I value problem-solving ability as a goal of education, the scientific method can give me the same kind of help.

Now, if I wish to determine whether problem-solving ability is "better" than knowledge of the three R's, then scientific method can also study those two values but *only*—and this is very important—in terms of some other value which I have subjectively chosen. I may value college success. Then I can determine whether problem-solving ability or knowledge of the three R's is most closely associated with that value. I may value personal integration or vocational success or responsible citizenship. I can determine whether problem-solving ability or knowledge of the three R's is most closely associated with one of these values. But the value or purpose that gives meaning to a particular scientific endeavor must always lie outside of that endeavor.

Although our concern in this symposium is largely with applied science, what I have been saying seems equally true of so-called "pure" science. In pure science the usual prior subjective value choice is the discovery of truth. But this is a subjective choice, and science can never say whether it is the best choice, save in the light of some other value. Geneticists in the U.S.S.R., for example, had to make a subjective choice of whether it was better to pursue truth or to discover facts which upheld a governmental dogma. Which choice is "better"? We could make a scientific investigation of those alternatives but only in the light of some other subjectively chosen value. If, for example, we value the survival of a culture, then we could begin to investigate with the methods of science the question of whether pursuit of truth or support of governmental dogma is most closely associated with cultural survival.

My point then is that any endeavor in science, pure or applied, is carried on in the pursuit of a purpose or value that is subjectively chosen by persons. It is important that this choice be made explicit, since the particular value which is being sought can never be tested or evaluated, confirmed or denied, by the scientific endeavor to which it gives birth. The initial purpose or value always and necessarily lies outside the scope of the scientific effort which it sets in motion.

Among other things this means that if we choose some particular goal or series of goals for human beings and then set out on a large scale to control human behavior to the end of achieving those goals, we are locked in the rigidity of our initial choice, because such a scientific endeavor can never transcend itself to select new goals. Only subjective human persons can do that. Thus if we chose as our goal the state of happiness for human beings (a goal deservedly ridiculed by Aldous Huxley in *Brave New World*), and if we involved all of society in a successful scientific program by which people became happy, we would be locked in a colossal rigidity in which no one would be free to question this goal, because our scientific operations could not transcend themselves to question their guiding purposes. And without laboring this point, I would remark that colossal rigidity, whether in dinosaurs, or dictatorships, has a very poor record of evolutionary survival.

If, however, a part of our scheme is to set free some "planners" who do not have to be happy, who are not controlled, and who are therefore free to choose other values, this has several meanings. It means that the purpose we have chosen as our goal is not a sufficient and a satisfying one for human beings but must be supplemented. It also means that if it is necessary to set up an elite group which is free, then this shows all too clearly that the great majority are only the slaves—no matter by what high-sounding name we call them—of those who select the goals.

Perhaps, however, the thought is that a continuing scientific endeavor will evolve its own goals; that the initial findings will alter the directions, and subsequent findings will alter them still further, and that science somehow develops its own purpose. Although he does not clearly say so, this appears to be the pattern Skinner has in mind. It is surely a reasonable description, but it overlooks one element in this continuing development, which is that subjective personal choice enters in at every point at which the direction changes. The findings of a science, the results of an experiment, do not and never can tell us what next scientific purpose to pursue. Even in the purest of science, the scientist must decide what the findings mean and must subjectively choose what next step will be most profitable in the pursuit of his purpose. And if we are speaking of the application of scientific knowledge, then it is distressingly clear that the increasing scientific knowledge of the structure of the atom carries with it no necessary choice as to the purpose to which this knowledge will be put. This is a subjective personal choice which must be made by many individuals.

Thus I return to the proposition with which I began this section of my remarks—and which I now repeat in different words. Science has its meaning as the objective pursuit of a purpose which has been subjectively chosen by a person or persons. This purpose or value can never be investigated by the particular scientific experiment or investigation to which it has given birth and meaning. Consequently, any discussion of the control of human beings by the behavioral sciences must first and most deeply concern itself with the subjectively chosen purposes which such an application of science is intended to implement.

Is the Situation Hopeless? The thoughtful reader may recognize that, although my remarks up to this point have introduced some modifications in the conception of the processes by which human behavior will be controlled, these remarks may have made such control seem, if anything, even more inevitable. We might sum it up this way: Behavioral science is clearly moving forward; the increasing power for control which it gives will be held by someone or some group; such an individual or group will surely choose the values or goals to be achieved; and most of us will then be increasingly controlled by means so subtle that we will not even be aware of them as controls. Thus, whether a council of wise psychologists (if this is not a contradiction in terms), or a Stalin, or a Big Brother has the power, and whether the goal is happiness, or productivity, or resolution of the Oedipus complex, or submission, or love of Big Brother, we will inevitably find ourselves moving toward the chosen goal and probably thinking that we ourselves desire it. Thus, if this line of reasoning is correct, it appears that some form of *Walden Two* or of *1984* (and at a deep philosophic level they seem indistinguishable) is coming. The fact that it would surely arrive piecemeal, rather than all at once, does not greatly change the fundamental issues. In any event, as Skinner has indicated in his writings, we would then look back upon the concepts of human freedom, the capacity for choice, the responsibility for choice, and the worth of the human individual as historical curiosities which once existed by cultural accident as values in a prescientific civilization.

I believe that any person observant of trends must regard something like the foregoing sequence as a real possibility. It is not simply a fantasy. Something of that sort may even be the most likely future. But is it an inevitable future? I want to devote the remainder of my remarks to an alternative possibility.

Alternative Set of Values. Suppose we start with a set of ends, values, purposes, quite different from the type of goals we have been considering. Suppose we do this quite openly, setting them forth as a possible value choice to be accepted or rejected. Suppose we select a set of values that focuses on fluid elements of process rather than static attributes. We might then value: man as a process of becoming, as a process of achieving worth and dignity through the development of his potentialities; the individual human being as a self-actualizing process, moving on to more challenging and enriching experiences; the process by which the individual creatively adapts to an ever-new and changing world; the process by which knowledge transcends itself, as, for example, the theory of relativity transcended Newtonian physics, itself to be transcended in some future day by a new perception.

If we select values such as these we turn to our science and technology of behavior with a very different set of questions. We will want to know such things as these: Can science aid in the discovery of new modes of richly rewarding living? more meaningful and satisfying modes of interpersonal relationships? Can science inform us on how the human race can become a more intelligent participant in its own evolution—its physical, psychological and social evolution? Can science inform us on ways of releasing the creative capacity of individuals, which seems so necessary if we are to survive in this fantastically expanding atomic age? Oppenheimer has pointed out (1956b) that knowledge, which used to double in millennia or centuries, now doubles in a generation or a decade. It appears that we must discover the utmost in release of creativity if we are to be able to adapt effectively. In short, can science discover the methods by which man can most readily become a continually developing and self-transcending process, in his behavior, his thinking, his knowledge? Can science predict and release an essentially "unpredictable" freedom?

It is one of the virtues of science as a method that it is as able to advance and implement goals and purposes of this sort as it is to serve static values, such as states of being well-informed, happy, obedient. Indeed we have some evidence of this.

Small Example. I will perhaps be forgiven if I document some of the possibilities along this line by turning to psychotherapy, the field I know best.

Psychotherapy, as Meerloo (1955) and others have pointed out, can be one of the most subtle tools for the control of *A* by *B*. The therapist can subtly mold individuals in imitation of himself. He can cause an individual to become a submissive and conforming being. When certain therapeutic principles are used in extreme fashion, we call it brainwashing, an instance of the disintegration of the personality and a reformulation of the person along lines desired by the controlling individual. So the principles of therapy can be used as an effective means of external control of human personality and behavior. Can psychotherapy be anything else?

Here I find the developments going on in client-centered psychotherapy (Rogers, 1951) an exciting hint of what a behavioral science can do in achieving the kinds of values I have stated. Quite aside from being a somewhat new orientation in psychotherapy, this development has important implications regarding the relation of a behavioral science to the control of human behavior. Let me describe our experience as it relates to the issues of this discussion.

In client-centered therapy, we are deeply engaged in the prediction and influencing of behavior, or even the control of behavior. As therapists we institute certain attitudinal conditions, and the client has relatively little voice in the establishment of these conditions. We predict that if these conditions are instituted, certain behavioral consequences will ensue in the client. Up to this point this is largely external control, no different from what Skinner has described, and no different from what I have discussed in the preceding sections of this article. But here the similarity ceases.

The conditions we have chosen to establish predict such behavioral consequences as these: that the client will become self-directing, less rigid, more open to the evidence of his senses, better organized and integrated, more similar to the ideal which he has chosen for himself. In other words, we have established by external control conditions which we predict will be followed by internal control by the individual, in pursuit of internally chosen goals. We have set the conditions which predict various classes of behaviors—self-directing behaviors, sensitivity to realities within and without, flexible adaptiveness—which are by their very nature unpredictable in their specifics. Our recent research (Rogers and Dymond, 1954) indicates that our predictions are to a significant degree corroborated, and our commitment to the scientific method causes us to believe that more effective means of achieving these goals may be realized.

Research exists in other fields—industry, education, group dynamics—which seems to support our own findings. I believe it may be conservatively stated that scientific progress has been made in identifying those conditions in an interpersonal relationship which, if they exist in *B*, are followed in *A* by greater maturity in behavior, less dependence on others, an increase in expressiveness as a person, an increase in variability, flexibility and effectiveness of adaptation, an increase in self-responsibility and self-direction. And, quite in contrast to the concern expressed by some, we do not find that the creatively adaptive behavior which results from such self-directed variability of expression is a "happy accident" which occurs in "chaos." Rather, the individual who is open to his experience, and self-directing, is harmonious not chaotic, ingenious rather than random, as he orders his responses imaginatively toward the achievement of his own purposes. His creative actions are no more a "happy accident" than was Einstein's development of the theory of relativity.

Thus we find ourselves in fundamental agreement with John Dewey's statement: "Science has made its way by releasing, not by suppressing, the elements of variation, of invention and innovation, of novel creation in individuals." (Ratner, 1939, p. 359). Progress in personal life and in group living is, we believe, made in the same way.

Possible Concept of the Control of Human Behavior. It is quite clear that the point of view I am expressing is in sharp contrast to the usual conception of the relationship of the behavioral sciences to the control of human behavior. In order to make this contrast even more blunt, I will state this possibility in paragraphs parallel to those used before.

(1) It is possible for us to choose to value man as a self-actualizing process of becoming; to value creativity, and the process by which knowledge becomes self-transcending.

(2) We can proceed, by the methods of science, to discover the

conditions which necessarily precede these processes and, through continuing experimentation, to discover better means of achieving these purposes.

(3) It is possible for individuals or groups to set these conditions, with a minimum of power or control. According to present knowledge, the only authority necessary is the authority to establish certain qualities of interpersonal relationship.

(4) Exposed to these conditions, present knowledge suggests that individuals become more self-responsible, make progress in self-actualization, become more flexible, and become more creatively adaptive.

(5) Thus such an initial choice would inaugurate the beginnings of a social system or subsystem in which values, knowledge, adaptive skills, and even the concept of science would be continually changing and self-transcending. The emphasis would be upon man as a process of becoming.

I believe it is clear that such a view as I have been describing does not lead to any definable utopia. It would be impossible to predict its final outcome. It involves a step-by-step development, based on a continuing subjective choice of purposes, which are implemented by the behavioral sciences. It is the direction of the "open society," as that term has been defined by Popper (1945), where individuals carry responsibility for personal decisions. It is at the opposite pole from his concept of the closed society, of which *Walden Two* would be an example.

I trust it is also evident that the whole emphasis is on process, not on end-states of being. I am suggesting that it is by choosing to value certain qualitative elements of the process of becoming that we can find a pathway toward the open society.

The Choice. It is my hope that we have helped to clarify the range of choice which will lie before us and our children in regard to the behavioral sciences. We can choose to use our growing knowledge to enslave people in ways never dreamed of before, depersonalizing them, controlling them by means so carefully selected that they will perhaps never be aware of their loss of personhood. We can choose to utilize our scientific knowledge to make men happy, well-behaved, and productive, as Skinner earlier suggested. Or we can insure that each person learns all the syllabus which we select and set before him, as Skinner now suggests. Or at the other end of the spectrum of choice we can choose to use the behavioral sciences in ways which will free, not control; which will bring about constructive variability, not conformity; which will develop creativity, not contentment; which will facilitate each person in his self-directed process of becoming; which will aid individuals, groups, and even the concept of science to become self-transcending in freshly adaptive ways of meeting life and its problems. The choice is up to us, and, the human race being what it is, we are likely to stumble about, making at times some nearly disastrous value choices and at other times highly constructive ones.

I am aware that to some, this setting forth of a choice is unrealistic, because a choice of values is regarded as not possible. Skinner has stated:

> "Man's vaunted creative powers . . . his capacity to choose and our right to hold him responsible for his choice—none of these is conspicuous in this new self-portrait (provided by science). Man, we once believed, was free to express himself in art, music, and literature, to inquire into nature, to seek salvation in his own way. He could initiate action and make spontaneous and capricious changes of course. . . . But science insists that action is initiated by forces impinging upon the individual, and that caprice is only another name for behavior for which we have not yet found a cause." (1955-1956, pp. 52-53).

I can understand this point of view, but I believe that it avoids looking at the great paradox of behavioral science. Behavior, when it is examined scientifically, is surely best understood as determined by prior causation. This is one great fact of science. But responsible personal choice, which is the most essential element in being a person, which is the core experience in psychotherapy, which exists prior to any scientific endeavor, is an equally prominent fact in our lives. To deny the experience of responsible choice is, to me, as restricted a view as to deny the possibility of a behavioral science. That these two important elements of our experience appear to be in contradiction has perhaps the same significance as the contradiction between the wave theory and the corpuscular theory of light, both of which can be shown to be true, even though incompatible. We cannot profitably deny our subjective life, any more than we can deny the objective description of that life.

In conclusion then, it is my contention that science cannot come into being without a personal choice of the values we wish to achieve. And these values we choose to implement will forever lie outside of the science which implements them; the goals we select, the purposes we wish to follow, must always be outside of the science which achieves them. To me this has the encouraging meaning that the human person, with his capacity of subjective choice, can and will always exist, separate from and prior to any of his scientific undertakings. Unless as individuals and groups we choose to relinquish our capacity of subjective choice, we will always remain persons, not simply pawns of a self-created science.

III—SKINNER

I cannot quite agree that the practice of science *requires* a prior decision about goals or a prior choice of values. The metallurgist can study the properties of steel and the engineer can design a bridge without raising the question of whether a bridge is to be built. But such questions are certainly frequently raised and tentatively answered. Rogers wants to call the answers "subjective choices of values." To me, such an expression suggests that we have had to abandon more rigorous scientific practices in order to talk about our own behavior. In the experimental analysis of other organisms I would use other terms, and I shall try to do so here. Any list of values is a list of reinforcers—conditioned or otherwise. We are so constituted that under certain circumstances food, water, sexual contact, and so on, will make any behavior which produces them more likely to occur again. Other things may acquire this power. We do not need to say that an organism chooses to eat rather than to starve. If you answer that it is a very different thing when a man chooses to starve, I am only too happy to agree. If it were not so, we should have cleared up the question of choice long ago. An organism can be reinforced by—can be made to "choose"—almost any given state of affairs.

Rogers is concerned with choices that involve multiple and usually conflicting consequences. I have dealt with some of these elsewhere (Skinner, 1953) in an analysis of self-control. Shall I eat these delicious strawberries today if I will then suffer an annoying rash tomorrow? The decision I am to make used to be assigned to the province of ethics. But we are now studying similar combinations of positive and negative consequences, as well as collateral conditions which affect the result in a laboratory. Even a pigeon can be taught some measure of self-control! And this work helps us to understand the operation of certain formulas—among them value judgments—which folk-wisdom, religion, and psychotherapy have advanced in the interests of self-discipline. The observable effect of any statement of value is to alter the relative effectiveness of reinforcers. We may no longer enjoy the strawberries for thinking about the rash. If rashes are made sufficiently shameful, illegal, sinful, maladjusted, or unwise, we may glow with satisfaction as we push the strawberries aside in a grandiose avoidance response which would bring a smile to the lips of Murray Sidman.

People behave in ways which as we say, conform to ethical, governmental, or religious patterns because they are reinforced for doing so. The resulting behavior may have far-reaching consequences for the survival of the pattern to which it conforms. And whether we like it or not, survival is the ultimate criterion. This is where, it seems to me, science can help—not in choosing a goal, but in enabling us to predict the survival value of cultural practices. Man has too long tried to get the kind of world he wants by glorifying some brand of immediate reinforcement. As science points up more and more of the remoter consequences, he may begin to work to strengthen behavior, not in slavish devotion to a chosen value, but with respect to the ultimate survival of mankind. Do not ask me why I want mankind to survive. I can tell you why only in the sense in which the physiologist can tell you why I want to breathe. Once the relation between a given step and the survival of my group has been pointed out, I will take that step. And it is the business of science to point out just such relations.

The values I have occasionally recommended (and Rogers has not led me to recant) are transitional. Other things being equal, I am betting on the group whose practices make for healthy, happy, secure, productive, and creative people. And I insist that the values recommended by Rogers are transitional, too, for I can ask him the same kind of question. Man as a process of becoming—*what?* Self-actualization—for what? Inner control is no more a goal than external.

What Rogers seems to me to be proposing both here and elsewhere (Rogers, 1956), is this: Let us use our increasing power of control to create individuals who will not need and perhaps will no longer respond to control. Let us solve the problem of our power by renouncing it. At first blush this seems as implausible as a benevolent despot. Yet power has occasionally been foresworn. A nation has burned its Reichstag, rich men have given away their wealth, beautiful women have become ugly hermits in the desert, and psychotherapists have become nondirective. When this happens, I look to other possible reinforcements for a plausible explanation. A people relinquish democratic power when a tyrant promises them the earth. Rich men give away wealth to escape the accusing finger of their fellowmen. A woman destroys her beauty in the hope of salvation. And a psychotherapist relinquishes control because he can thus help his client more effectively.

The solution that Rogers is suggesting is thus understandable. But is he correctly interpreting the result? What evidence is there that a client ever becomes truly *self*-directing? What evidence is there that he ever makes a truly *inner* choice of ideal or goal? Even though the therapist does not do the choosing, even though he encourages "self-actualization"—he is not out of control as long as he holds himself ready to step in when occasion demands—when, for example, the client chooses the goal of becoming a more accomplished liar or murdering his boss. But supposing the therapist does withdraw completely or is no longer necessary—what about all the other forces acting upon the client? Is the self-chosen goal independent of his early ethical and religious training, of the folk-wisdom of his group, of the opinions and attitudes of others who are important to him? Surely not. The therapeutic situation is only a small part of the world of the client. From the therapist's point of view it may appear to be possible to relinquish control. But the control passes not to a "self," but to forces in other parts of the client's world. The solution of the therapist's problem of power cannot be *our* solution, for we must consider *all* the forces acting upon the individual.

The child who must be prodded and nagged is something less than a fully developed human being. We want to see him hurrying to his appointment, not because each step is taken in response to verbal reminders from his mother, but because certain temporal contingencies, in which dawdling has been punished and hurrying reinforced, have worked a change in his behavior. Call this a state of better organization, a greater sensitivity to reality, or what you will. The plain fact is that the child passes from a temporary verbal control exercised by his parents to control by certain inexorable features of the environment. I should suppose that something of the same sort happens in successful psychotherapy. Rogers seems to me to be saying this: Let us put an end, as quickly as possible, to any pattern of master-and-slave, to any direct obedience to command, to the submissive following of suggestions. Let the individual be free to adjust himself to more rewarding features of the world about him. In the end, let his teachers and counselors "wither away," like the Marxist state. I not only agree with this as a useful ideal, I have constructed a fanciful world to demonstrate its advantages. It saddens me to hear Rogers say that "at a deep philosophic level" *Walden Two* and George Orwell's *1984* "seem indistinguishable." They could scarcely be more unlike—at any level. The book *1984* is a picture of immediate aversive control for vicious selfish purposes. The founder of *Walden Two*, on the other hand, has built a community in which neither he nor any other person exerts any *current* control. His achievement lay in his original *plan,* and when he boasts of this ("It is enough to satisfy the thirstiest tyrant") we do not fear him but only pity him for his weakness.

Another critic of *Walden Two*, Andrew Hacker (1955), has discussed this point in considering the bearing of mass conditioning upon the liberal notion of autonomous man. In drawing certain parallels between the Grand Inquisition passage in Dostoevsky's *Brothers Karamazov,* Huxley's *Brave New World,* and *Walden Two,* he attempts to set up a distinction to be drawn in any society between conditioners and conditioned. He assumes that "the conditioner can be said to be autonomous in the traditional liberal sense." But then he notes: "Of course the conditioner has been conditioned. But he has not been conditioned by the conscious manipulation of another *person."* But how does this affect the resulting behavior? Can we not soon forget the origins of the "artificial" diamond which is identical with the real thing? Whether it is an "accidental" cultural pattern, such as is said to have produced the founder of *Walden Two,* or the engineered environment which is about to produce his successors, we are dealing with sets of conditions generating human behavior which will ultimately be measured by their contribution to the strength of the group. We look to the future, not the past, for the test of "goodness" or acceptability.

If we are worthy of our democratic heritage we shall, of course, be ready to resist any tyrannical use of science for immediate or selfish purposes. But if we value the achievements and goals of democracy we must not refuse to apply science to the design and construction of cultural patterns, even though we may then find ourselves in some sense in the position of controllers. Fear of control, generalized beyond any warrant, has led to a misinterpretation of valid practices and the blind rejection of intelligent planning for a better way of life. In terms which I trust Rogers will approve, in conquering this fear we shall become more mature and better organized and shall, thus, more fully actualize ourselves as human beings.

REFERENCES

Coleman, C. The hickory stick. *Bull. Amer. Assoc. Univ. Professors,* 1953, 39, 457-473.

Freund, P. A., *et al. Constitutional law: Cases and other problems.* Vol. 1. Boston: Little, Brown, 1954.

Hacker, A. The specter of predictable man. *Antioch Rev.,* 1954, 14, 195-207.

Hacker, A. Dostoevsky's disciples: Man and sheep in political theory. *J. Politics,* 1955, 17, 590-613.

Krutch, J. W. *The measure of man.* New York: Bobbs-Merrill, 1954.

Meerloo, J. A. M. Medication into submission: danger of therapeutic coercion, *J. Nerv. Ment. Dis.,* 1955, 122, 353-360.

Negley, G., and Patrick, J. M. *The quest for utopia.* New York: Schuman, 1952.

Niebuhr, R. *The self and the dramas of history.* New York: Scribners, 1955.

Oppenheimer, J. R. Science and our times. *Roosevelt U. Occasional* 127-135.

Oppenheimer, J. R. Science and our times. *Roosevelt U. occasional Papers,* 1965b, No. 2.

Popper, K. R. *The open society and its enemies.* London: Routledge & Kegan Paul, 1945.

Ratner, J. (Ed.) *Intelligence in the modern world: John Dewey's philosophy.* New York: Modern Library, 1939.

Rogers, C. R. Implications of recent advances in prediction and control of behavior. *Teachers Coll. Rec.,* 1951, 57, 316-322.

Rogers, C. R., and Dymond, R. (Eds.) *Psychotherapy and personality Change.* Chicago: U. of Chicago Press, 1954.

Skinner, B. F. *Walden Two.* New York: Macmillan, 1948.

Skinner, B. F., *Science and human behavior.* New York: Macmillan, 1953.

Skinner, B. F. The control of human behavior. *Trans. N. Y. Acad. Sci.,* 1955, 17, 547-551.

Skinner, B. F. Freedom and the control of men. *Amer. Scholar,* Winter, 1955-1956, 25, special issue, 47-65.

Skinner, B. F. A case history in scientific method. *Amer. Psychologist,* 1956, 11, 221-233.

Vandenberg, S. G. Great expectations or the future of psychology (as seen in science fiction). *Amer. Psychologist,* 1956, 11, 339-342.

Viteles, M. S. The new utopia. *Science,* 1955, 122, 1167-1171.

TOWARD THE THERAPEUTIC STATE

THOMAS S. SZASZ

Valeriy Tarsis is a literary critic, translator, and writer. In 1960 he sent an English publisher a manuscript which was highly critical of life in Khrushchev's Russia. This work, *The Blue-bottle*, appeared in England in October, 1962, under the pseudonym Ivan Valeriy. Actually, Tarsis had opposed the use of a pseudonym and made no secret in Russia of having sent his book abroad. In August, 1962, two months before the appearance of *The Blue-bottle* in London, Tarsis was arrested and committed to the Koshchenko psychiatric hospital in Moscow. News of his fate soon reached the West and an article about it by the British journalist Edward Crankshaw appeared in *The Observer* for February, 1963. In March, Tarsis was released.

Ward 7[1] is Tarsis' account of what happened to him in the "mental hospital." It was written shortly after his release and smuggled to England in the summer of 1964. In this autobiographical novel, Valentine Alamazov, a Russian writer, is arrested and incarcerated in a psychiatric institution for the same offense as Tarsis had been; he is held in the notorious Russian insane asylum, the "Villat Kanatchikov," the nickname in Moscow for the Koshchenko Hospital; and he is released after protests from the West.

This, in bare outline, is the plot of *Ward 7* and the story of the events behind it. The question is: What shall we make of it?

I have seen many English and American comments on this book; all deal with it as political criticism. Nearly a year before the book's American publication, such an interpretation was offered by Mr. C. L. Sulzberger, in *The New York Times* for October 28, 1964:

> Khrushchev . . . conducted a running battle with writers who felt sufficiently revitalized by his reforms to fight for total freedom. Khrushchev struck back by restraining some of the boldest of these spirits—not in prisons or concentration camps, but in mental homes and sanatoriums.

After briefly reviewing the book, and noting that "The material condi-

Reprinted by permission of the author and *The New Republic* from *The New Republic,* December 11, 1965. © 1965, Harrison-Blaine of New Jersey, Inc.

tions of Ward 7 are not too bad. . . . All they (the 'patients') lack is freedom," Mr. Sulzberger concluded:

> When contemplating this strange book one cannot but wonder if in any way the system that invented *Ward 7* under Khrushchev as a halfway house to prison might now be affecting Khrushchev himself. In Stalin's day, political disgrace terminated in torture cells, execution cellars or Siberian barbed wire enclaves. Khrushchev, to his enduring credit, virtually did away with all that. . . .

The supposition that *Ward 7* should be read as political commentary on contemporary Soviet society is further borne out by Mr. Elliot Graham of E. P. Dutton & Co. Tarsis was eager to have *Ward 7* published in the West, writes Mr. Graham, "because although the Soviet government claims that there are no political prisoners in the Soviet Union, the practice of putting inconvenient citizens into lunatic asylums seems to have become fairly widespread and is all the more shocking because this can be done without putting them on trial and because the term of their detention is indefinite."

These comments do not, in my opinion, penetrate to the significant lessons in this book. Approached as a piece on psychiatric hospitalization—as an exposé, as it were, of the Soviet mental hospital system—what do we find? The same claim—that they have been incarcerated improperly and unjustly—is made by people in mental hospitals all over the world. How do we judge whether such a claim is valid or not?

The irony of *Ward 7* will elude those who do not mentally substitute a German, a Frenchman, or an American for Valeriy Tarsis. Suppose an American poet were committed to a mental hospital and were to claim that he is sane; who would believe him? Valeriy Tarsis was confined for 6 months; Ezra Pound, for 13 years.

Our logic concerning involuntary mental hospitalization is evidently this: If a Russian is committed as insane, it is because he is sane but loves liberty too much; if an American is committed as insane, it is because he is insane but loves liberty so little that by depriving him of it we provide him with a "therapeutic milieu." "This is the only court," said a judge in Chicago, "where the defendant always wins. If he is released, it means he is well. If he is committed, it is for his own good." Pity the poor Russians, deprived of such guarantees of the "civil rights of mentally ill."

Actually, Tarsis' comments about psychiatry and psychiatrists are far more detailed and damaging than his observations about Soviet society or the Soviet political system. Here are a few examples:

The hero, Alamazov, has been taken to the hospital by force: "In the morning Alamazov was examined by the head city psychiatrist, exactly as a prisoner is examined by a magistrate. He was brought to Dr. Yanushkevich's consulting room under guard. The doctor made no attempt to treat him as a patient; illness was never mentioned. Pink and smug, he seemed to take his role as prosecutor for granted."

Alamazov's view of the situation is this: "I don't regard you as a doctor. You call this a hospital, I call it a prison to which, in a typically fascist way, I have been sent without trial. So now, let's get everything straight. I am your prisoner, you are my jailer, and there isn't going to be any nonsense about my health or relations, or about examination and treatment. . . ." Clearly, Alamazov has no insight into his condition: the poor fellow does not even realize he is sick!

Then there is this revealing exchange between Alamazov and Professor Stein, one of the nastier psychiatric types in the hospital:

[Stein] "We shall get acquainted. Valentine Ivanovich. . . . Tell us why you are here—what are your symptoms?"—Alamazov glared at him with such contempt that Stein looked uncomfortable. "I have not the slightest wish to get acquainted with you, but evidently I must. The reason I am here is that I was brought in by the police. My health is excellent. It's your job to make me ill. But I warn you, you won't succeed."—"How you actually got here is irrelevant. The point you should keep in mind is that healthy people are not in hospitals."—"That's exactly what the Cheka interrogators used to say to their victims: 'Innocent people are not in prison. You say you are innocent, that means you are anti-Soviet, so prison is the place for you.' The only difference is that now it's the madhouse."—"I see. . . . You don't sound exactly sane!"

It would be a grave mistake to believe that *Ward 7* is populated only by political dissenters. Many of the inmates are ordinary people, like the elderly husband who stood in the way of his wife's fuller sexual life. This is Tatyana speaking to her friend Anna:

"It's quite simple. You write to the clinic. You tell them that your husband, who is much older than you are and beginning to be impotent, is insanely jealous and has been threatening your life."—"It's true. He said 'I'll kill you'."

I was intrigued, and pleased, by the views Tarsis put in the mouth of Professor Nezhevsky. Nezhevsky is an elderly psychiatrist, at odds with the police methods of his Soviet colleagues. In a conversation with a

French psychiatrist, René Gillard, Nezhevsky says, "I told them at the Ministry that you avoid drugs, . . . your staff are forbidden to talk about 'illness,' the patients . . . are free to come and go. . . ." Replies Gillard: "So you stick to happiness pills?" "Yes, exactly," says Nezhevsky. "Happiness pills. Andaxin, aminodin, and the rest of the muck—our doctors think the world of it." And so on, until at the end, Gillard says: "I must say, the idea of compulsory treatment really revolts me. We'd never stand for it."

On the day I write this—responding partly to CORE demonstrations and draft-card burning by a Syracuse youth—Mayor William F. Walsh of Syracuse offered a "six-point legislative program beamed at reducing youthful crime and *civil disobedience.* . . ." Walsh asked that "a treatment and research center for juvenile delinquents be included in the new multi-million-dollar *mental health center* to be built here."

No, *Ward 7* is not only in Moscow. Nor is *Ward 7* a recent phenomenon. Psychiatric sanctions have been with us for centuries. Successors to the witch hunts, they are one of the manifestations of a passage, in Western societies, from theological to secular, and from magical to "scientific," methods of *social control.* However, only through the creation of vast psychiatric bureaucracies in modern mass societies has involuntary mental hospitalization become a major force in the police powers of the state. To attribute this evil to Communism, or to Capitalism, would thus be both an oversimplification and an evasion.

Indeed, by alluding to Chekhov's *Ward No. 6,* Tarsis admits that he knows this. Chekhov, himself a physician, had as his protagonist not a patient, but a psychiatrist—Dr. Andrei Yefimich. The psychiatrist is honest and soon cannot tolerate the task he has unwittingly assumed. He then commits the fatal mistake of actually engaging a patient in *conversation*—as if such a thing were possible with one who is insane! The dramatic end follows swiftly: the psychiatrist is declared insane, is committed to the hospital, and following a near-fatal beating by an attendant, dies of a stroke. Before he is declared insane, Chekhov's psychiatrist has this to say:

> I am serving an evil cause, and receive my salary from people whom I dupe; I am not honest. But then I, by myself, am nothing; I am but a particle of a necessary social evil: all the district bureaucrats are harmful and receive their salaries for nothing. Therefore it is not I who am to blame for my dishonesty but the times.

It is necessary to be absolutely clear about two points, lest *Ward 7* be misread: 1. Neither involuntary mental hospitalization as such, nor its political uses and abuses, was discovered by the Soviets. 2. The fundamental logic behind commitment has been accepted throughout the world for several centuries, and is still widely accepted today: according to it, it is "humane" and "helpful" to deprive a person of his *liberty*—a right second only to his right to his life—on the ground of "mental illness" (or because such "illness" renders him "dangerous to himself and others") ; if so, the only question is to define and determine what mental illness is or who is mentally ill.

Thus, Tarsis explains, it is "assumed, by doctors and politicians, writers and ideologists, that anyone dissatisfied with the socialist paradise must be a lunatic. . . ." Every one of the modern nation-states has, in the course of the last century-and-a-half, produced its own definitions and theories of lunacy. It is in this way that both a political and a psychiatric analysis of *Ward 7* must come to the same thing: a better understanding of secular society, its bureaucracies, and its methods of social control—among them, institutional psychiatry.

The list of famous persons deprived of liberty by means of psychiatric incarceration would run to several pages; for example, Secretary of State Forrestal, Governor Earl Long, General Edwin Walker, Ezra Pound, Norman Mailer, and Mary Todd Lincoln in the United States; in Germany—Marga Krupp, the wife of Fritz Krupp, committed by the Kaiser for making a nuisance of herself with complaints about her husband's homosexual orgies; and, in Austria-Hungary, Ignaz Semmelweiss, discoverer of childbed fever, for upsetting his colleagues and the public with the view that the disease was caused by the doctors' dirty hands.

Only a short time ago, men believed that slavery was a good institution, so long as only the proper people were enslaved: in historical order, the proper persons were the enemy vanquished in battle, the heathen, and the Negro. At long last, mankind concluded that slavery was a basic human wrong, regardless of who was placed in the class of slaves or why. I consider involuntary mental hospitalization also a basic human wrong. No adult should ever be cast in the sick role through the power of the state. The only deviance of which a person should be accused by the government is law-breaking; and once so charged, he should, of course, enjoy all the protection of the Constitution.

Many years ago, Lord Russell predicted that the Communist East and the Free West will, under the pressure of the forces of collectivism, drift even closer together until the differences between the two will be indistinguishable. Years later, Orwell warned of the same dismal future in *Animal Farm*. The concluding paragraph reads thus· "Twelve voices were shouting . . . and they were all alike. No question, now, what had happened to the faces of the pigs. The creatures outside looked from pig to man, and from man to pig, and pig to man again; but already it was impossible to say which was which."

The nature of the "machine" that homogenizes man and pig now seems clear: it is the modern state, regardless of whether it is the police state of the East or the bureaucratic state of the West. By substituting "private happiness" for "public happiness," all modern societies tend to wean the individual from the *polis,* and thus deprive him of a voice in the decision of all but his most trivial interests. The result is depoliticized man. It is small wonder, then, that the "Psychological Man" of today is more interested in mental health than in liberty. Thus it is inevitable that the individual seems less a citizen and more a patient.

But not only is the nature of modern bureaucratic mass society as a depoliticizing apparatus clear. It is also clear that institutional psychiatry is an important cog in it: the Russians call it Ward 7 and Villat Kanatchikov; we call it the state hospital and the community mental health center. Totalitarian tyranny and popular (non-constitutional) democracy thus rush to meet each other in the Therapeutic State.

NOTES

[1] *Ward 7, An Autobiographical Novel,* by Valeriy Tarsis, translated by Katya Brown (Dutton).